FAMILY MEDIATION, ARBITRATION AND COLLABORATIVE PRACTICE HANDBOOK

FIFTH EDITION

Barbara Landau
Ph.D., LL.B., LL.M.
Psychologist, Mediator and Member of the Ontario Bar

Lorne Wolfson
LL.B., LL.M.
Member of the Ontario Bar

Niki Landau
B.F.A., M.A.
Conflict Resolution Trainer and Mediator

Family Mediation, Arbitration and Collaborative Practice Handbook, Fifth Edition

October 2009

Members of the LexisNexis Group worldwide

Canada	LexisNexis Canada Inc, 123 Commerce Valley Dr. E. Suite 700, MARKHAM, Ontario
Australia	Butterworths, a Division of Reed International Books Australia Pty Ltd, CHATSWOOD, New South Wales
Austria	ARD Betriebsdienst and Verlag Orac, VIENNA
Czech Republic	Orac, sro, PRAGUE
France	Éditions du Juris-Classeur SA, PARIS
Hong Kong	Butterworths Asia (Hong Kong), HONG KONG
Hungary	Hvg Orac, BUDAPEST
India	Butterworths India, NEW DELHI
Ireland	Butterworths (Ireland) Ltd, DUBLIN
Italy	Giuffré, MILAN
Malaysia	Malayan Law Journal Sdn Bhd, KUALA LUMPUR
New Zealand	Butterworths of New Zealand, WELLINGTON
Poland	Wydawnictwa Prawnicze PWN, Warsaw
Singapore	Butterworths Asia, Singapore
South Africa	Butterworth Publishers (Pty) Ltd, Durban
Switzerland	Stämpfli Verlag AG, Berne
United Kingdom	Butterworths Tolley, a Division of Reed Elsevier (UK), London, WC2A
USA	LexisNexis, Dayton, Ohio

Library and Archives Canada Cataloguing in Publication

Landau, Barbara

Family mediation, arbitration and collaborative practice handbook / Barbara Landau, Lorne Wolfson, Niki Landau — 5th ed.

Fourth ed. published under title: Family mediation and collaborative practice handbook.
1st-3rd eds. published under title: Family mediation handbook.
Accompanied by a CD-ROM.
Includes bibliographical references and index.
ISBN 978-0-433-46079-4

1. Family mediation — Canada. 2. Family mediation — Ontario. 3. Divorce mediation — Canada. 4. Divorce mediation — Ontario. 5. Dispute resolution (Law) — Canada. 6. Dispute resolution (Law) — Ontario. I. Wolfson, Lorne Howard, 1950- II. Landau, Niki III. Landau, Barbara. Family mediation and collaborative practice handbook. IV. Title.

KE569.L35 2009 346.7101'5 C2009-905634-8
KF535.L35 2009

Printed and bound in Canada.

Preface

We are honoured to be invited to offer a fifth edition of what has been recognized as the leading Canadian text on Family Mediation and non-adversarial dispute resolution. When this text was first produced in 1987 the menu of choices for separating couples was limited — an adversarial court battle on one end, negotiation with lawyers in the middle and mediation and kitchen table "do-it-yourself" agreements at the other end. Each subsequent edition added more choices to what is now a fairly wide continuum. This edition adds still more options as we search for constructive family processes that are tailored to individual needs and circumstances.

Sadly, the number of families needing assistance in navigating this difficult life passage has not diminished. The family courts continue to be overwhelmed and couples face long delays in resolving issues affecting their children. Many parents are seeking options for resolving disputes cooperatively so they can co-parent as colleagues and parenting partners — without the collateral damage of high conflict to their children. This edition continues to encourage out-of-court, cooperative options for all appropriate participants.

However, cooperative approaches do not work for everyone. While most people resolve most issues out of court, some people and some issues require additional support or more definitive intervention by a neutral third party. Legal costs continue to be out of reach to many, lengthy delays in reaching a resolution are frustrating and court is seen as a last resort. To bridge the gap for those with more intractable disputes, this edition adds mediation-arbitration, arbitration and parenting coordination to the continuum of choices. These options share many of the benefits of mediation and collaborative practice in that couples can assist in designing the process — to achieve more or less formality, they can choose the facilitator or decision-maker, and they can achieve a timely result. These choices have an additional benefit for high-conflict couples in that there is finality if couples reach an impasse on one or more issues. Also, if conflicts continue after an agreement or court order, couples can retain a parenting coordinator to assist in managing and resolving ongoing disputes.

Since the last edition, domestic violence has continued to be the subject of considerable research and discussion. This issue is relevant to all of the processes discussed in this book and we have summarized the new insights, addressed the implications for each process, including new legal requirements, and provided new tools for practitioners.

We have also updated the chapters on family law, custody, property and child and spousal support. The Spousal Support Guidelines have proven to be very useful for reducing litigation and the latest case law is included on this and other relevant issues.

Again, we have supplemented the book with extensive practical Appendices and a CD-ROM so that those in the field have an enriched set of resources to refer to.

Finally, we offer our thanks to the many thousands of practitioners who share our commitment to help separating families. Our hope is that this edition will continue to benefit professionals who are seeking a more supportive outcome for those entering this difficult life passage.

About the Authors

Barbara Landau, Ph.D., LL.M. President, Cooperative Solutions: psychologist, lawyer, mediator, arbitrator and trainer. She is a Certified Comprehensive Family Mediator, a Certified Family Arbitrator and trainer in Collaborative Practice. Barbara received the *Long Term Achievement Award (FAMMA)* from Family Mediation Canada, 2004, the *Distinguished Mediator Award* from the Association for Conflict Resolution, 2003; and the *Award for Excellence in Dispute Resolution* from the Ontario Bar Association, ADR Section, 2002. Her family mediation and arbitration training programs are offered through Conrad Grebel University College, University of Waterloo, and her Collaborative Practice programs through Cooperative Solutions.

Lorne H. Wolfson, LL.B., LL.M., is a certified specialist in family law at the Toronto law firm Torkin Manes. He is a Dispute Resolution Officer of the Ontario Superior Court of Justice and a member of the Family Law Rules Committee. He is the Chair of the Family Law Specialty Committee of The Law Society of Upper Canada, Fellow of the International Academy of Matrimonial Lawyers, and selected for Best Lawyers in Canada (2006-2009). Lorne teaches Family Arbitration through Conrad Grebel College, University of Waterloo.

Niki Landau, B.F.A., M.F.A., is a mediator and conflict resolution trainer. She is trained in Alternative Dispute Resolution, Community Mediation, and Basic and Advanced Family Mediation, and specializes in Conflict Resolution, Mediation and Communication Skills training. Ms. Landau is a Roster Trainer at St. Stephen's Conflict Resolution Service, was the Training Coordinator there from 1998–2001, and founded the Co-Parenting Project in 2007. She has been a coach and trainer for Cooperative Solutions and Organizational Strategies Group since 1995.

CD-ROM Information

Introduction

The enclosed CD-ROM contains supplementary Appendices to the *Family Mediation, Arbitration and Collaborative Practice Handbook*, Fifth Edition, and is designed to be used in conjunction with that text. The text is in Word 2003, Excel 2003 or Adobe Acrobat PDF format.

System Requirements

The files on the enclosed CD-ROM have been designed for use on a personal computer with the following capabilities and configuration:

IBM or IBM-compatible with a hard drive and CD-ROM drive

Windows 95 or higher operating system

Microsoft Word for Windows 97 or higher software

At least 4.5 MB of hard disk space

Copying Files to Hard Drive

Before they can be used, files must be copied from the CD-ROM to a local hard drive or network drive. Create a folder (*e.g.*, "Family Mediation, Arbitration and Collaborative Practice Handbook") on the drive into which you wish to copy the files. Open My Computer for a list of drives and folders to which you have access. Click on your CD-ROM drive. Select the files and copy to the Family Mediation, Arbitration and Collaborative Practice Handbook folder.

Retrieving, Saving and Printing a File

Files are accessed in the same way as any other Word, Excel or PDF file. Within Microsoft Word, Excel or Acrobat, select Open from the File menu, choose the drive and folder into which the files were copied, and then select the file you wish to open. If you make changes to the file, save the file under a new file name to preserve the text of the original file.

Depending on the application you are using, you may have different print options available to you. The type of printer you use will also have an effect on the final appearance of the text. Any style changes you elect to use may require adjustment or realignment to achieve desired page lengths or page layout.

Table of Contents

Summary of Chapters

Chapter One — Overview of Dispute Resolution Options

This chapter provides a historical background to the ever-expanding choices for couples wishing to resolve their family disputes out of court. It summarizes a wide variety of non-adversarial choices, such as Counselling, Mediation, Collaborative Practice, and Collaborative Mediation, as well as increasingly adversarial approaches, such as Assessments, Arbitration, Litigation, Special Masters, and Parenting Coordinators for resolving family law issues. The increasing use of a multi-disciplinary team approach, including mental health professionals, financial specialists, and lawyers, is described.

On a systemic level, some jurisdictions require that couples attend one or two Family Information Sessions at an early stage so that couples are better informed about the impact of separation on them and their children and are educated about the choice of options at an early stage.

Also canvassed are concerns about domestic violence as this affects the choice of an appropriate process for high- and low-risk couples.

Chapter Two — Screening for Appropriateness

This chapter sets the stage for Mediation, Collaborative Law, and Arbitration by describing the roles and expectations of referral sources, lawyers, clients, and the mediator.

An important consideration is determining which processes are best suited to particular couples. A significant factor is whether there are concerns about domestic violence, power and control issues, or substance abuse. Recent research on the various patterns of domestic violence in families is summarized to assist in making this assessment. The Landau Screening Tool is described as an instrument for determining who are appropriate candidates for Mediation, Collaborative Law, and Arbitration. For those who are or may be appropriate, practice tips are included for altering the process, setting ground rules or pre-requisites to increase safety and to ensure a good-faith process. Important considerations for Parenting Plans are described for low- and high-conflict couples. For those who are not appropriate, suggestions are made for safe termination and referral to other resources. The importance of using interim agreements is discussed. The emphasis in this chapter is on ethical and practice issues that might arise at various points in the process, particularly during the initial screening.

Chapter Three — Managing the Process

This chapter addresses the reasons that couples have difficulty communicating, and offers practical suggestions for improving this communication. It also discusses how to deal with serious power imbalances, including the involvement of interdisciplinary resources. This chapter contains helpful hints for encouraging collaboration among an interdisciplinary team of professionals to maximize the opportunities for a successful outcome.

Chapter Four — Mediation in Practice

This chapter focuses on the theory and principles underlying an interest-based bargaining model and explains how these principles are applied to family disputes in both Mediation and Collaborative Law. While there are differences in procedure between Mediation and Collaborative Law, the underlying theory, facilitation skills, and goals of each process are similar.

In this chapter, the Mediation procedure is set out in detail, including the objectives for meetings with counsel, the parties, children, and other significant individuals during the course of Mediation. Particular emphasis is given to the development of a "Parenting Plan", which is central to custody and access issues.

Chapter Five — Collaborative Practice

This chapter looks at the expanded menu of choices available to clients. Specifically, the Collaborative Law, Collaborative Divorce, and Collaborative Mediation models are described in detail. The steps in each model are explained and the advantages to clients, lawyers, and mediators from these options are included. The roles of other professionals, such as divorce coaches, child specialists, financial advisors, and valuators, who assist in this interdisciplinary approach, are described. Also discussed is the role of children in the collaborative models; that is, how can their views and preferences be heard without putting children in the middle of their parents' dispute?

Chapter Six — Custody Assessments

This chapter compares the procedure in Custody Assessments with that of Mediation of custody and access disputes. It explores the purpose of a Custody Assessment, the differences between Mediation and Assessments, and the procedure to be followed. In addition, specific information is given as to the contents of an acceptable Custody Assessment report.

Chapter Seven — Family Law Arbitration

This new chapter describes in detail the provisions of the revised *Arbitration Act, 1991* as it pertains to family matters. The role and powers of arbitrators and the courts, and the method for conducting a family law arbitration, are covered in this chapter.

Chapter Eight — Dispute Resolution Outcomes

This chapter contains practical information with respect to preparing memoranda of understanding, minutes of settlement, arbitral awards, or reports in cases where the parties have arrived at a full agreement, a partial agreement, or in some cases no agreement at all. In addition this chapter clarifies the differences in reporting requirements for mediators depending on whether the Mediation is a closed or open process.

Chapter Nine — Protecting the Best Interests of Children

This chapter offers extensive information about the responses of children to separation and divorce. Included is recent research about the key factors affecting children's post-separation adjustment, as well as the criteria to consider in developing residential schedules for children. The focus is on how to encourage resiliency in children and minimize the negative consequences associated with separation and divorce. This information is essential for mediators, child specialists, and divorce coaches who help parents work out Parenting Plans. It is also important for the collaborative lawyer to understand and appreciate while working as part of an interdisciplinary team. This chapter also outlines in detail the type of background information a mediator or a collaborative lawyer might collect in order to have a context for understanding each client's unique perspective, special concerns, priorities, needs, and objectives. This is helpful both with respect to a Parenting Plan, and in creating an agreement dealing with financial and property issues.

Chapter Ten — Legal Issues: Custody and Access

This chapter summarizes the law with respect to custody and access, and includes new developments and difficult issues that affect the creation of Parenting Plans. For example, recent court decisions with respect to mobility, who is appropriate for joint custody and whether marriage contracts and separation agreements can be relied on, are covered. In addition, the use of language to describe parenting responsibilities, and how to deal with access or "contact" difficulties, are discussed. This chapter will be of particular interest to non-lawyers who are looking for a clear, concise, and readable outline of the most important features of family law for the purpose of protecting children.

Chapter Eleven — Legal Issues: Support and Property

This chapter has been expanded to include a detailed analysis of the *Federal Child Support Guidelines*, as well as a more extensive discussion of property rights under provincial property legislation. The section on spousal support has been updated to include a section on variation as well as the *Spousal Support Advisory Guidelines*. The section dealing with the rights of common-law and same-sex spouses has been revised to reflect recent case law. Finally, the section dealing with the income tax implications of support and property transactions has been substantially expanded.

Although non-lawyers cannot give legal advice, it is important for the mental health professional who is acting as a mediator or assisting in a collaborative process to understand the legal context relevant to the issues in dispute.

Chapter Twelve — The Mediator as Expert Witness

This chapter sets out specific, detailed information with respect to the role of the mediator/assessor as expert witness in those cases that do go to litigation. The difference between privilege and confidentiality is discussed, and the guidelines for giving testimony in court, including the qualifications of an expert witness, are explored in some detail. Practical suggestions are given for those mental health professionals who are to appear as expert witnesses and for the lawyer who requires the services of an expert witness in a family law trial.

Chapter Thirteen — Professional Conduct Issues

The final chapter discusses in some detail the rules of professional conduct for mediators, collaborative lawyers, and arbitrators. In addition, it explores the areas of conflict between mental health professionals and lawyers, as well as within the legal profession, with respect to lawyers acting as mediators. All mediators and arbitrators and those referring to these professionals need to be aware of the ethical code of conduct expected from those who practise. This chapter also outlines the standards for training for those wishing to become Certified Family Mediators or Certified Family Arbitrators in the ADR Institute and Accredited Family Mediators in the Ontario Association for Family Mediation.

The *Family Mediation, Arbitration and Collaborative Practice Handbook* clearly describes the goals, theory and the procedures followed in all of these and other process options. It covers all of the material necessary to inform clients about these services, and the up-to-date research, communication skills, and documents needed to set up a professional practice.

Each chapter contains an annotated bibliography, a handy reference for the reader who may wish to explore particular subjects in more detail.

In addition, practical precedent material is provided for all steps in the Mediation, Collaborative Law, and Arbitration processes, and will be particularly helpful for those who are new to the field. The appendices are organized into eight categories:

- Appendix I — Screening for Domestic Violence
- Appendix II — Mediation
- Appendix III — Collaborative Practice
- Appendix IV — Custody Assessments
- Appendix V — Family Arbitration
- Appendix VI — Dispute Resolution Outcomes
- Appendix VII — Legal Documents
- Appendix VIII — Professional Conduct and Qualifications

Additional precedents in many of these categories are available on the accompanying CD-ROM.

The book's format can easily be used for lectures, quick reference, or as a practical guide. It covers the law related to custody and access, as well as property division, child and spousal support, and ethical issues relevant to mediators, arbitrators, and collaborative practitioners. This handbook will be of interest to mental health professionals, lawyers, financial specialists, divorce coaches, clergy, and others who offer assistance to separating and divorcing families.

Chapter One

Overview of Dispute Resolution Options

The past 40 years have seen enormous changes in the practice of Family Law, both in substantive law, and, as important, in the processes available to clients going through separation and divorce. When the authors entered the field, the choices were: "kitchen table" negotiations between clients, negotiation between lawyers, an assessment with each side retaining his/her own hired gun, and litigation. Today we have an ever-expanding menu of dispute resolution choices.

What is exciting is the opportunity to offer clients a wide range of options that can be personally tailored to address their needs. As this edition will reveal, these constructive choices can be selected individually or creatively combined (within ethical constraints). There has also been an unprecedented increase in the cooperation between different professionals involved in the divorce process. This cooperation is possible because of a shift from providing expertise in order to defeat the opposing client, to the far more constructive objective of supporting both clients in making their own informed decisions, taking into account the needs of all family members, and, in particular, protecting the children.

Mediation and Collaborative Practice are logical choices for cooperative families. A blend of these options, known as Collaborative Mediation, applies the best of both approaches and offers a cost-effective, flexible and cooperative choice.

In the past there were few options for high conflict or distrustful clients. That is the major change since the last edition. Today clients with more intractable or complex disputes have choices outside of court. Family arbitration, mediation-arbitration, and parenting coordination allow these couples to resolve their issues more efficiently and with greater control over the process.

A. THE DEVELOPMENT OF DISPUTE RESOLUTION OPTIONS

Today, family laws reflect significant changes in social attitudes to marriage breakdown. Fault is no longer a necessary ingredient for being granted a divorce, couples are encouraged to reach non-adversarial resolutions that they believe are fair and will encourage ongoing cooperation between parents that ensure better long term outcomes for children.

Legislation clarifies the responsibilities of parents through specific criteria for protecting the best interests of children, with fault and parental conduct only a factor if the conduct is directly relevant to safety, abuse or the capacity to parent. *Child Support Guidelines* and *Spousal Support Advisory Guidelines* have as their goal reducing litigation by providing greater certainty as to each parent's obligation or entitlement.

In the past few years there have been shifts in the definition of marriage to include same-sex couples, more than two parents, and the rights of common-law partners. The reality of separation and divorce has become a sad, but accepted, part of our culture and divorce is no longer seen as a moral failure. We have become more sophisticated in our assessment of the impact of divorce, less anxious about its consequences for children, and more supportive of both parents taking a significant and active role, unless issues of abuse, neglect or lack of capacity are raised.

All of these changes have resulted in important shifts in the way our legal system approaches separation and divorce. Increasingly the emphasis has been on cooperative approaches, such as negotiation, mediation, and collaborative practice to assist couples in reaching an early resolution of the issues in dispute, particularly where children are involved. When those efforts fail to produce consensual parenting arrangements, there are several options for achieving a result. A custody/access evaluation performed by an impartial professional with a report that can be submitted to a judge may be helpful, or the parties may choose mediation-arbitration or family arbitration to obtain a binding award to resolve any outstanding parenting or financial issues. In high conflict cases, a parenting coordinator can, on consent, be appointed to implement parenting arrangements and resolve disputes that arise following an agreement or court order. This process reduces the need for revolving-door applications to court to clarify or address ongoing disputes.

These options reflect the increasing awareness by legislators and judges that, while the spousal relationship has ended, there is a need to encourage a cooperative environment for the sake of children. While adversarial procedures lead to bitterness and hostility between the parents, research consistently demonstrates that the ones who suffer the most as a result of an adversarial divorce are those who are least at fault — namely the children.

Set out below are some examples of legislation related to out-of-court dispute resolution options.

1. Family Law: The Evolution of Mediation and Family Arbitration in Family Law

(A) FEDERAL LEGISLATION — THE *DIVORCE ACT*

The present *Divorce Act*[1] encourages a no-fault approach to divorce by stating that the sole ground for a divorce is "marriage breakdown". A divorce can now be obtained after a one-year separation or more quickly if one spouse alleges adultery or cruelty as the basis for the marriage breakdown.

---

[1] R.S.C. 1985, c. 3 (2nd Supp.), s. 8.

This Act requires lawyers to advise their clients to consider mediating any issues in dispute (including custody and child and spousal support) prior to litigating these issues. Section 9(1)(*b*) also requires lawyers to inform their clients about mediation services that are available in the community. In addition, lawyers are obligated to try to resolve matrimonial issues through negotiation rather than litigation.

The "best interests of children" is the sole criterion for determining custody of and access to children. Any person can apply for custody of or access to children; that is, persons other than biological parents or relatives can apply if they have a meaningful relationship with the child.

Joint custody is an option for judges to consider in custody awards in appropriate cases. The principle of encouraging maximum contact between the child and both parents, consistent with the child's best interests, is set out in the legislation. The judge must consider which parent will facilitate maximum contact with the other parent when determining who will be awarded custody. Conduct, except ability to parent, is not considered when determining custody and access.

Need, ability to pay, and compensation for roles in the marriage are the criteria for determining awards for spousal maintenance. Fault and matrimonial misconduct are expressly excluded in determining entitlement to and quantum of support. *Spousal Support Advisory Guidelines* created several years ago are increasingly relied on by lawyers and judges in arriving at both the quantum and duration of spousal support.

Child Support Guidelines, incorporated in 1997, have created a minimum standard for determining child support and over the past several years these Guidelines have improved the financial status of children. The Guidelines have created greater certainty about the obligation to pay, but despite this there may still be disputes about the calculation of income, whether there should be a reduction in payments based on the percentage of time the children spend in each parent's care or the sharing of certain expenses.

(B) PROVINCIAL LEGISLATION

The Ontario Children's Law Reform Act and the Ontario Family Law Act, 1990

In Ontario, on consent of the parties, the court can order mediation with respect to custody and access under s. 31 of the *Children's Law Reform Act*,[2] as well as for child and spousal support and the division of assets under s. 3 of the *Family Law Act*.[3]

---

[2] R.S.O. 1990, c. C.12.

[3] R.S.O. 1990, c. F.3.

The Ontario Family Law Statute Amendment Act, 2007

Several years ago, the Ontario government had an extended debate about whether family arbitration should be permitted, based on concerns raised about binding decisions being made under foreign or religious based law without any safeguards for parties who might be under duress or not familiar with their rights under Canadian law. The outcome was to preserve the parties' right to select this helpful option, but within clear parameters as set out in the the Ontario *Family Law Statute Amendment Act, 2006*,[4] namely, to be enforceable, decisions must be made under Canadian or provincial law, all clients must have independent legal advice and be screened separately for domestic violence and power imbalances, and some appeal rights are protected. See Chapter 7 for an in-depth discussion.

The Manitoba Court of Queen's Bench Act

In Manitoba, under the *Court of Queen's Bench Act*,[5] the court can make a referral to a conciliation officer to resolve any matter without a formal trial. The judge or Master can make this order at any stage of the proceedings and can appoint either a conciliation officer or any other person on the consent of the parties. In practice, the Provincial Court of Manitoba (Family Division) in Winnipeg requires that every couple attend at least one mediation session in cases where there is an application for custody of or access to children. That is, the couple must attend at least one mandatory mediation session before they will be permitted to litigate custody and access issues.

The British Columbia Family Relations Act

The *Family Relations Act*[6] of British Columbia permits the court to appoint a family court counsellor to assist in the resolution of family law matters. This is not restricted to custody and access issues.

In addition, in most provinces:

- The "best interests of children" is the sole criterion for determining custody of and access to children.
- Need and ability to pay are the criteria for determining child and spousal support.
- Matrimonial misconduct is specifically excluded from determinations of custody, access, and support.
- Domestic violence directed at a spouse or child, or witnessed by a child, is a factor in determining a parenting plan.
- The value of all assets acquired during the course of the marriage (with certain exceptions, such as gifts or inheritances from third parties) is

---

4 S.O. 2006, c. 1.

5 S.M. 1988-89, c. 4 [also C.C.S.M., c. C280].

6 R.S.B.C. 1996, c. 128.

divided equally at the end of the marriage, based on the philosophy of marriage as an economic and social partnership. The trend is toward sharing all assets with very limited judicial discretion to vary the 50-50 split. Limiting judicial discretion reduces the likelihood of an adversarial battle, because the more accurately the parties can predict the outcome in court, the easier it is to arrange a settlement.

Quebec Code of Civil Procedure

According to a provision of the *Code of Civil Procedure*[7] passed in 1997, couples who file a dispute are required to attend an "information session" with a mediator to consider the use of mediation for such issues as custody, spousal support, child support, and division of property. In order to encourage the use of mediation, the government funds up to six mediation sessions for couples who have not yet had a court judgment and three sessions for those wishing to vary an existing order. The mediators may come from a variety of backgrounds, including social work, psychologists, counsellors, lawyers, and notaries.

New Brunswick Domestic Legal Aid[8]

From 1993, New Brunswick's Domestic Legal Aid Plan has offered a unique program to encourage the non-adversarial resolution of family disputes. Separating or divorcing couples can receive free mediation services and legal advice to resolve custody and access issues as well as disputes over spousal and child support and routine property claims. A Court Social Worker acts as mediator and drafts a tentative agreement which is finalized with the assistance of the Family Solicitor. These services are provided free of charge. There is an initial screening for domestic violence and mediation services are not offered to couples whose relationship involves abuse or family violence.

B. NON-ADVERSARIAL METHODS OF DISPUTE RESOLUTION

Clinical research has underlined the importance of cooperation by parents in the interests of their children, and demonstrated that divorce is a complex experience, with many individuals going through stages that are somewhat similar to a grieving process. The ground-breaking research of Drs. Wallerstein and Kelly that followed 60 families over a 25-year period documents the long-term negative emotional repercussions for both parents and children. Litigation exacerbates and prolongs the emotional strain on all parties and in particular is most associated with harmful consequences for children. Their work gave considerable impetus to non-adversarial options. More recent longitudinal studies, by researchers such as Mavis Hetherington, Robert Emery, Constance

---

7 R.S.Q. 1997, c. 42.

8 New Brunswick Domestic Legal Aid, 1993.

Ahrons, and Rhonda Freeman demonstrate that by encouraging cooperation between parents, children can be largely insulated from such negative outcomes.

Further impetus for changing the procedure in family law cases comes from the tremendous backlog of cases in the courts, the great expense of family law litigation, and the tremendous increase in the number of children affected by marriage breakdown. Although statistics show a slight leveling off in the rate of marital breakdowns, it is still estimated that each year approximately 1.5 million children in the United States and an additional 150,000 children in Canada experience separation. To deal with the problem of long trial lists, a number of jurisdictions in the United States now require couples to attend at least one mandatory meeting with a mediator prior to litigating custody and access issues. In Canada, mediation can only be ordered or arranged on consent in many provinces. However, in parts of Quebec, Manitoba, Saskatchewan, Alberta, and New Brunswick, couples can be ordered to attend at least one meeting with a mediator, but only after they have been screened for domestic violence. In several provinces parents are required to attend a Family Information Session prior to proceeding with litigation. In other provinces or parts of provinces, the sessions are voluntary, but attendance is strongly encouraged. These programs encourage non-adversarial alternatives and have been effective in reducing court appearances.

Clients can choose from a number of options for resolving conflict and may be involved with more than one method. Therefore, it is important to understand the range of options available for both non-adversarial and adversarial dispute resolution. This information is helpful in advising clients about the most appropriate method(s) for their particular situation. Section 9 of the *Divorce Act* requires that lawyers advise clients who are planning to separate about counselling and/or mediation services before initiating a more adversarial approach.

1. Counselling

Counselling is a process whereby clients and/or their children are assisted in dealing with their personal and interpersonal conflicts that are associated with the separation or that pre-date the separation. The counselling may be brief or long-term, depending upon the severity of the problem and the commitment of the client. Counselling is intended to assist clients in self awareness, self esteem and improved communication and problem-solving techniques. The counselling can be offered to one or both spouses, the entire family or to any combination of parents and child(ren). Counselling may take place before, during or following the separation and can be combined with other options.

2. Mandatory Family Information Session

In some jurisdictions in North America, for example in parts of Ontario, Alberta, Saskatchewan, British Columbia, Nova Scotia, Quebec, and the Yukon, any parent who commences a family law matter and his/her partner must attend at least one family information session prior to proceeding to court. This educational session is designed to help the parties to better understand the options for resolving their legal dispute, including the option of mediation. It is designed to assist them to understand the emotional impact of separation on the adults and the children and to encourage more appropriate communication between separating parents so as to protect the children from ongoing conflict.

During these sessions, couples who have experienced violence are cautioned about the risks that various options may pose. They are encouraged to speak to a professional about the violence and ensure that a safe and appropriate choice of service is made.

3. Mediation

Family Mediation involves an impartial professional, selected by the parties, who helps them reach a voluntary settlement that has been designed by them. Ideally the settlement is a fair and reasonable resolution of their competing needs and interests, such that neither party is a complete winner and neither party suffers a humiliating loss. Because the settlement is reached voluntarily by the parties themselves, it is more likely to be carried out without the need for external enforcement or further litigation. The non-adversarial nature of the process and the emphasis on cooperation are likely to reduce tension and encourage future cooperative behaviour. This is an important policy objective where children are involved.

To ensure that the agreement is reached voluntarily by informed parties, the mediator encourages the parties to obtain independent legal advice before mediation begins and certainly before any agreement is finalized.

Note: It is inappropriate for the mediator to provide personal counselling to either partner individually during or after mediation as this would compromise the mediator's neutrality.

(A) "CLOSED" AND "OPEN" MEDIATION

There are two basic forms of family mediation that separating partners may choose, *closed* or *open*. There are some essential differences between the two:

In *Closed Mediation*:

- The mediator's report includes only the issues that the parties themselves have resolved.
- If the parties fail to obtain a resolution on one or more issues, the mediator's report will contain a description of any agreement reached, as well as a statement specifying which issues remain unresolved.
- All other information disclosed to the mediator remains confidential and unreported (with the exception of child abuse data).
- The mediator may not give evidence in subsequent litigation.

In *Open Mediation*:

- The mediator's report may include any information that is considered relevant to the issues being mediated.

- If there is a resolution of the issues, the report will usually be restricted to a description of the agreement reached.
- The mediator may not give evidence in subsequent litigation.

Note: Parties can choose a hybrid, namely they can agree that any report will only be used *by the parties and their lawyers* for the purpose of achieving a settlement and *will not* be used in a court proceeding. This is the preferred option for collaborative processes as the professionals and clients are committed to resolving matters out of court.

Also, they can agree to have "open" mediation for some issues, *e.g.*, parenting, and "closed mediation" for other issues, *e.g.*, valuation of a home or business, depending on the needs of the clients and the mediator's areas of expertise. This is often called "*partially open mediation*".

In choosing between open and closed mediation, the parties will want to consider the following factors:

- Some mediators restrict their practice to either open or closed mediation.
- With closed mediation, there is an assumption that the total confidentiality of the process may make the parties less apprehensive about disclosing personal information. (That impression is not supported by research or experience.)
- With open mediation, if the process breaks down the mediator may prepare a report outlining the differences in the parties' positions.
- In open mediation, any information acquired during the mediation can be used in the report.
- In open mediation, if requested by one or both parties, the mediator may make recommendations as to how the unresolved issues might be resolved.
- For this reason, if open mediation is selected, it is important to choose a mediator with sufficient expertise to make a recommendation about the issues in dispute.
- Open mediation may eliminate the need to commence a new process, such as an assessment, thereby saving time, money, and further intrusions by another professional.

4. Collaborative Family Law, Collaborative Divorce, and Collaborative Mediation

Collaborative Family Law emerged in the early 1990's, as a model for encouraging lawyers to use their skills as problem solvers, rather than litigators with couples going through separation. A key feature is that the lawyers must be specially trained in many of the skills used by mediators and both lawyers and their clients must agree in writing at the outset to resolve their issues without litigation. The clients are encouraged to take the primary role in negotiating agreements that they believe will meet their own and their children's needs. The lawyers' knowledge and creative problem-solving skills are directed at reaching an integrative solution that everyone can say "yes" to and that the parties feel committed to uphold.

Since 2000, Collaborative Family Law has increasingly been referred to as *Collaborative Practice* or *Collaborative Divorce*, to reflect a shift toward an integrated, cross-disciplinary, team model for delivering professional services to divorcing clients. It is the legal equivalent of a multi-disciplinary team in the mental health field. In cases that require a range of expertise, for example, to assist parents as a communication coach, or with developmentally appropriate parenting plans, or to value a business, or to offer sophisticated tax advice, the family can benefit from the coordinated efforts of several professionals, all acting in an impartial capacity, to resolve their outstanding issues in a cost-effective and non-adversarial manner.

While other professionals may be added to a Collaborative Law case, the Collaborative Divorce tends to be more of an ongoing working relationship between team members rather than an ad hoc arrangement. As with a Collaborative Law case, those professionals who are assisting the couple must agree to withdraw if the matter goes to court.

In this text the emphasis will be on *Collaborative Mediation*, that is, a process that begins with clients selecting mediation as their preferred method of dispute resolution. These clients frequently have not yet seen a lawyer or have had minimal contact and not yet retained counsel. They are usually anxious about involvement with lawyers, fearing that their hopes for a non-adversarial resolution will be disappointed. They may also be worried about losing control of their decision-making and prefer a process that encourages them to design their own terms for separation.

Collaborative Mediation offers this opportunity. As mediators we are obliged to send people for independent legal advice. Now we can include the lawyers, who have been specially trained as collaborative lawyers, under the umbrella of a Collaborative Mediation Participation Agreement and have the mediator, both clients, and both counsel committed to the same non-adversarial process.

In some cases the mediator will assist the parties to mediate all issues (comprehensive mediation) and the collaborative lawyers will attend a five-way meeting, at an appropriate time, to clarify roles and time lines and will not meet again unless a difficult issue arises, an impasse is reached, or the memorandum of understanding is ready for review by the lawyers. In other cases, the mediator may be assisting with the parenting plan and then transferring primary responsibility for financial issues to the collaborative lawyers. In any case all will have signed a Collaborative Mediation Participation Agreement at a five-way meeting.

5. Divorce Coaching

Divorce Coaching involves a trained professional working with one, or possibly both parents, to improve their communication skills, or to improve specific skills, such as caring for an infant. The coach acts in a neutral manner with respect to issues in dispute, even when assisting one party. The goal is to reduce conflict during negotiation about separation and to help the client articulate future goals and needs in a constructive manner. These professionals are often included in a Collaborative Team.

6. Divorce Financial Analyst

A Divorce Financial Analyst is a specialist in offering financial planning advice to separating and divorcing clients. These professionals may be hired by one or by both parties to assist in a neutral capacity with negotiations related to property division and support. The goal is to ensure that both parties make informed and fair decisions about their financial future and provide for the well being and security of all family members. These professionals are often included in Collaborative Mediation or a Collaborative Team.

7. Child Specialist

A Child Specialist can also be retained to assist one or more children to adjust to the separation and to articulate their needs and preferences. They can help parents to "hear" the children's voices when they are creating a parenting plan.

C. ADVERSARIAL METHODS OF DISPUTE RESOLUTION

There are also adversarial methods for resolving conflict. That is, in the event of an impasse, a third party can make decisions, potentially binding decisions, to resolve outstanding disputes.

1. Negotiation

Negotiation is a bargaining process that can be utilized in any of the non-adversarial or adversarial methods of conflict resolution. It basically involves the exchange of something by one of the parties in return for something else by the other party, which both perceive to be fair and equitable. Negotiation can occur between the parties or between their counsel, with or without the assistance of an intermediary. It may occur face to face, by letter, or by telephone, and is frequently applied to resolve a broad range of deadlocks.

2. Custody-access Assessment

Custody-access assessment is a process whereby a trained mental health professional prepares a report about the parenting arrangements that may best meet the child's needs, given the capabilities of the parents. Information is obtained through a variety of sources, and recommendations are then made for a parenting plan that is seen to be in the best interests of the child. If the parties and both counsel agree, the assessor should review the recommendations with the parents and encourage them to cooperate in implementing a parenting plan. Whatever the parents agree on is more likely to be followed by the parents in the future.

3. Litigation

Litigation is a process whereby a judge arrives at a legal resolution of the differences between the opposing parties (or litigants). In Family Law, litigation is used as a last resort, especially for resolving custody and access disputes. Recent legislation and court procedure encourages the use of alternative dispute resolution, including mediation, for family matters.

4. Family Arbitration

Family arbitration is a process whereby a neutral third party who is chosen by both sides functions in a quasi-judicial capacity. It differs from mediation in that binding decisions will be made by the neutral party on behalf of the disputants. In arbitration, the decisions and recommendations of the arbitrator may be appealed on more limited grounds.

This process is a more recent addition for couples who are concerned about the long delays in achieving a litigated result, do not believe they can reach a negotiated or mediated result, and want the opportunity to select their own expert to make an award. This is essentially a "rent-a-judge" process in which a highly competent Family Law professional, usually a lawyer, is hired by both parties and their counsel to hold a hearing or a less formal process and render a timely, binding decision on specific contentious issues.

5. Mediation/Arbitration (or Med/Arb)

Med/Arb is a process that commences as mediation and under pre-determined conditions, when an impasse is reached, the mediator is authorized by the parties to arbitrate, that is to make binding judgments with respect to specific unresolved issues. Usually the individual chosen to fulfill this role has substantive expertise in these issues.

This option is available to couples who wish to resolve matters in mediation if possible, but either they have doubts that they will succeed to resolve all issues, or have some important timelines for resolution that cannot be met in litigation. They do need a definitive result, but to the extent possible, they want to preserve goodwill.

Another option available to the parties at the outset is that two different professionals could be involved, one as mediator, with the other person stepping in as arbitrator in the event that mediation of one or more issues reaches an impasse.

6. Parenting Coordinator or Special Master

This approach is often used with high-conflict couples once a Separation Agreement, award, or court order is in place. A Parenting Coordinator or Special Master is an individual who is selected by the parties to educate, mediate and if necessary arbitrate disputes between parents over the implementation of a Parenting Plan or other issues related to the children. A Parenting Coordinator or Special Master can assist when there is a concern that one or both parties may violate the agreement or be unable to negotiate with each other if circumstances change. The Parenting Coordinator or Special Master acts in an impartial manner, with respect to the parties, to protect the best interests of the child.

This is an option for couples who are concerned about possible future disagreements or breaches of agreements reached in negotiation or mediation, or of orders made in arbitration or litigation. These couples usually have great difficulty disengaging, low levels of trust, and are "stuck on anger". Contracts are usually for a fixed time period or until the happening of some event, *e.g.*, a child entering full-time attendance at school. This is a relatively efficient and less adversarial approach than multiple returns to court.

D. OPEN MEDIATION, CLOSED MEDIATION, AND CUSTODY ASSESSMENTS

There has been considerable confusion about the essential differences between open and closed mediation and custody assessments. The following chart sets out the similarities and differences between the three procedures.

Closed Mediation	***Open Mediation***	***Assessment***
This is a *non-adversarial* method of dispute resolution that parties participate in voluntarily in the hope of avoiding an adversarial court proceeding. The parties in dispute meet with the *mediator*.	This is a *non-adversarial* method of dispute resolution that parties participate in voluntarily in the hope of avoiding an adversarial court proceeding. The parties in dispute meet with the *mediator*.	This is an *adversarial process*, in that it contemplates adversarial court proceedings and may be entered into voluntarily or by court order. The parties in dispute usually meet with the *assessor*.*
Discussions are *confidential* and it is agreed that the parties will *not* subpoena the mediator to court. Usually *no* conclusions or recommendations are made by the mediator to the court. All *agreements* arise from the parties themselves on a voluntary basis.	Discussions are *not* confidential, and it is agreed that the mediator can be *subpoenaed* by the parties to court. Usually *no* conclusions or recommendations are made by the mediator to the court. All *agreements* arise from the parties themselves on a voluntary basis.	Discussions are *not* confidential, and it is agreed that the assessor can be *subpoenaed* by the parties to court. The assessor makes *recommendations* and arrives at a *conclusion* that may be communicated to the court. There is *no* requirement that the parties reach an agreement.

Closed Mediation	***Open Mediation***	***Assessment***
Only the terms of an agreement or the fact that there is no agreement is disclosed.	The terms of the agreement, or the fact that there is no agreement, is disclosed, and the mediator may report on the mediation process and, if requested, may make recommendations about issues in dispute. This presumes that the mediator has sufficient expertise to make a recommendation.	The assessor puts forward recommendations for a court-ordered agreement.
The parties, and usually the children, are seen by the mediator in a combination of individual and group sessions for the purpose of assisting the parties to arrive at a mediated agreement on the parenting arrangement that is in the best interests of the children.	The parties, and usually the children, are seen by the mediator in a combination of individual and group sessions for the purpose of assisting the parties to arrive at a mediated agreement on the parenting arrangement that is in the best interests of the children.	The parties and the children are seen by the assessor in a combination of individual and group sessions. In addition, extensive investigations are carried out and information is collected from collateral sources, *e.g.*, visits and discussions with teachers, family doctors, other relevant professionals, *etc*. This information is used for the purpose of evaluating parenting capacity and helping the assessor to arrive at a recommendation.

* Some mediators prefer to begin the mediation process by meeting with each party individually prior to a joint meeting. This is particularly likely in cases of alleged abuse or intimidation.

The success of non-adversarial techniques and out-of-court approaches, such as mediation, collaborative practice, family arbitration, and parenting coordination, has stimulated reforms of Family Law and court processes. The trend in Family Law across North America and internationally is toward less adversarial methods that encourage early settlement on a cooperative basis, with the assistance of impartial professionals, as well as independent legal advice. By moving away from fault and toward more consistent, predictable, and objective criteria, the legislation is highly compatible with a more cooperative approach to dispute resolution in family law cases.

E. CONCERNS ABOUT NON-ADVERSARIAL OPTIONS

From the time that non-adversarial options entered the menu of choices, women's advocates and lawyers representing abused women have raised serious concerns. The concerns are important to acknowledge and to address, as the viability of cooperative approaches depends on being able to determine who are appropriate and who are not appropriate candidates for each type of option. In cases of domestic violence (that is, violence that includes physical, emotional, psychological, and sexual harm, as well as other forms of power and control over finances, freedom to make decisions and socialize, *etc.*), the concerns are that:

1. Abused women may not be able to safely and effectively represent their own and their children's interests;
2. Non-adversarial options, in particular mediation, take place in private, without the safeguards of a legal system and usually without counsel being present. Therefore, women may not be aware of or may not feel safe enough to assert their entitlements;
3. Abused women may give up financial security as a trade-off for care and control of the children;
4. Abused women may be bullied into decisions that are unfair, unwise, or unsustainable out of fear or to escape a threatening or abusive relationship — and the pattern of abuse may not be detected or taken seriously by the mediator or the collaborative lawyers;
5. Women may have experienced systemic discrimination such that they cannot negotiate as equals, especially when addressing financial issues and therefore require the support of the legal system;
6. The outcome of a mediation, assessment, or collaborative process may create an ongoing risk for abused women and their children. Specifically, decisions that encourage ongoing cooperation and that result in frequent transfers of children between homes, shared decision-making, ongoing communication between ex-spouses, *etc.*, may put women and children at risk of further control and abuse; and
7. Abusers may not be held accountable for their abusive and controlling behaviour and in fact may be rewarded in a non-adversarial process with greater involvement in the family than would happen in court. This may pose a safety risk for women and children.

Increasingly, women's advocates, mediators, assessors, parenting coordinators, and collaborative professionals are working together to ensure that the common goals of a safe, affordable, and effective approach to resolving issues at the time of separation are achieved. This edition will highlight the latest research and experience in trying to assess which couples are appropriate for which services. The complex question of which outcomes are likely to be most appropriate for children and for the safety of an abused spouse will be addressed. Finally, recent research makes it clear that the issue of domestic violence is much more complex than has been acknowledged in the past.

Domestic violence appears in several different patterns, with both women and men acting in the role of perpetrator and victim. We will describe the key patterns and clarify which patterns are most likely to be of concern in cases of marriage breakdown. It is important for practitioners to be aware of the differences and in particular to understand how to screen couples for appropriateness for different options and for different outcomes.

SUMMARY

The shift from an adversarial approach to Family Law to the increasing use of cooperative models, such as mediation and Collaborative Law, as well as options such as family arbitration, mediation-arbitration, and parenting coordination for higher conflict couples, have made it possible for many more families to avoid courts, to resolve their issues more quickly, and to maintain a more constructive relationship. This shift requires that the practitioner carefully screen each participant to determine who is likely to benefit from each of the various choices.

ANNOTATED BIBLIOGRAPHY

Abella, Judge R. "Procedural Aspects of Arrangements for Children Upon Divorce". (1983), 61 *Canadian Bar Review* 443. This article examines the present adversarial system and recommends non-adversarial refinements to the present process, such as pre-trials, mediation, expert assessments, and independent legal representation for children for the adjudication of custody and access disputes.

Ahrons, C. *We Are Still Family: What Grown Children Have to Say About Their Parents' Divorce.* New York: HarperCollins, 2004. This book reflects the experiences and wisdom of 173 children of divorce. It dispels some of the current, negative myths about the impact of divorce, contains helpful guidance for parents currently struggling with the challenges of separation, highlights individual differences in resilience, and optimistically states that it is never too late to improve the lives of your children.

Baris, M., Coates, C., Duvall, B., Garrity, C., Johnson, E. and LaCrosse, E. *Working with High Conflict Families of Divorce: A Guide for Professionals.* New Jersey: Jason Aronson Inc., 2001. This is a valuable guide to several options for assisting "revolving door" clients; that is, those who continually return to court. It contains very helpful descriptions of each role along with potential ethical pitfalls. It also includes practical precedents for contracting with high conflict couples.

Boulle, L., and Kelly, K.J. *Mediation Principles, Process, Practice, Canadian Edition.* Toronto: Butterworths Canada, 1998. An excellent resource for mediating civil disputes.

Brownstone, Judge H. *Tug of War: A Judge's Verdict on Separation, Custody Battles, and the Bitter Realities of Family Court.* Toronto: ECW Press, 2009. This is a delightfully candid plea for parents to avoid adversarial battles. It paints a realistic picture of what litigants can expect should they embark on a court process to resolve their disputes.

Cameron, N. *Collaborative Practice: Deepening the Dialogue.* Vancouver: The Continuing Legal Education Society of B.C., 2004. This book outlines the thinking that led to an experienced Family Law lawyer adopting an interdisciplinary Collaborative model.

Chornenki, G.A., and Hart, C.E. *Bypass Court — A Dispute Resolution Handbook, Third Edition.* Markham: LexisNexis Canada, 2005. An easy-to-read guide to ADR for non-Family Law cases by two excellent mediators.

Cochrane, M. *Surviving Your Divorce: A Guide to Canadian Family Law, Fourth Edition.* Toronto: Wiley, 2007. This is a helpful book for parents and common law spouses going through a separation. It gives an overview of Canadian Family Law on a wide range of topics including the emotional stages of marriage breakdown, domestic violence, and alternatives to going to court (mediation and arbitration).

Emery, R. *The Truth About Children and Divorce.* New York: Penguin Books, 2004. This is an excellent, easy-to-read resource for all professionals involved with separating couples and should be recommended reading for their clients. This book deals with all the practical questions that clients ask and practitioners need to be able to answer, including how to tell children about a separation, developmentally appropriate Parenting Plans, and how these plans need to be modified for high conflict couples.

Fisher, R., Ury, W., and Patton, B. *Getting to Yes: Negotiating Agreement Without Giving In, Second Edition.* New York: Penguin Books, 1991. This was the seminal book that began the interest-based or principled approach to negotiation and sets out the theoretical framework for interest-based mediation.

Folberg, J., Taylor, A., and Salem, P. *Divorce and Family Mediation: Models, Techniques, and Applications*. Guilford Press, 2004. This thorough text covers the theory and practice of mediation with articles by many leaders in the family mediation field.

Hetherington, M., and Kelly, J. *For Better or Worse: Divorce Reconsidered.* New York: W.W. Norton and Co., 2002. This book is a review of the recent literature on divorce and debunks some of the traditional stereotypes about the negative impact of divorce on children.

Landau, B., and Landau, S. *Collaborative, Family Law, Collaborative Divorce & Collaborative Mediation.* ADR Manual, CCH, Canada, 2002. This extensive article describes these non-adversarial models in detail, setting out the steps in each and includes precedents for those setting up a Collaborative Practice.

Lang, M., and Taylor, A. *The Making of a Mediator — Developing Artistry in Practice.* San Francisco, California: Jossey-Bass, 2000. An excellent resource for the more advanced family mediator. This sets out a model for self-reflection on mediator skills, written by two excellent practitioners.

Macfarlane, J. *Rethinking Disputes.* Toronto: Emond Montgomery Publications Limited, 1997. An excellent overview of ADR processes and the shift from rights-based to interest-based options.

Macfarlane, J. *The New Lawyer: How Settlement is Transforming The Practice of Law.* Vancouver: UBC Press, 2008. An important text that reflects on the shift in the role of lawyers and the skills needed to be effective. Interviews with both clients and lawyers highlight how lawyers need to adapt to the client's desire for a less adversarial approach to dispute resolution.

Mayer, B. *The Dynamics of Conflict Resolution — A Practitioner's Guide.* San Francisco, California: Jossey-Bass Inc., 2000. The author, a gifted mediator, describes how successful mediators, facilitators, and negotiators draw on their own creative internal processes to resolve conflicts. The book presents powerful concepts for becoming a more effective negotiator, facilitator, and mediator.

Noble, C., Dizgun, L., and Emond, P. *Mediation Advocacy — Effective Client Representation in Mediation Proceedings.* Toronto: Emond Montgomery Publications Ltd., 1998.

Picard, C., Bishop, P., Ramkay, R., and Sargent, N. *The Art and Science of Mediation.* Toronto: Emond Montgomery Publications Ltd., 2004.

Saposnek, D. *Mediating Child Custody Disputes.* San Francisco: Jossey-Bass Publishers, 1998. This book is a practical and comprehensive approach to the resolution of child custody disputes by a highly respected child psychologist.

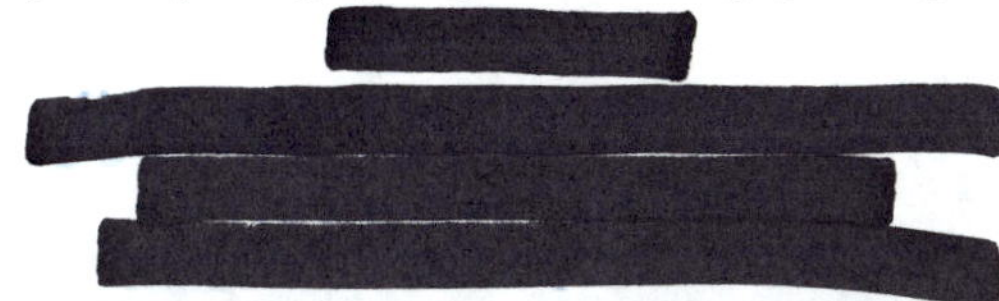

Schepard, Andrew. *Special Issue: Domestic Violence*, Family Court Review: An Interdisciplinary Journal, Vol. 46, no. 3, July 2008. Wiley-Blackwell. This important special issue summarizes the latest research and thinking about domestic violence and provides a more sophisticated understanding of this difficult topic.

Stitt, A., ed. *Alternative Dispute Resolution Practice Manual.* Toronto: CCH Canadian Ltd., 1996. This manual discusses ADR applications in a wide range of subject areas including family, school, environmental, commercial, landlord and tenant, public policy disputes, *etc.* It includes descriptions of a wide range of dispute resolution strategies including mediation, arbitration, negotiation, judicial mini-trials, pre-trial conferences, and others, in both the private and public sector. This valuable practice manual is updated quarterly.

Taylor, A. *The Handbook of Family Dispute Resolution Mediation Theory and Practice.* San Francisco, California: Jossey-Bass, 2002. This is an excellent text for mediators helping to create Parenting Plans. There is a very helpful developmental guide to parenting arrangements by age of child and nature of the parent-child relationship.

Taylor, A., and Bing, H. "Settlement by Evaluation and Arbitration: A New Approach for Custody and Visitation Disputes". (1994), 32 *Family and Conciliation Courts Review* 4, 432-44.

Tesler, P. *Collaborative Law: Achieving Effective Resolution in Divorce without Litigation.* Section of Family Law, American Bar Association, 2001. Tesler's book is the first major book describing in detail the Collaborative Family Law process and how it differs from an adversarial process. It has practical checklists and precedents, especially directed at an American audience, but easily adapted in other jurisdictions.

Tesler, P., and Thompson, P. *Collaborative Divorce: The Revolutionary New Way to Restructure Your Family, Resolve Legal Issues, and Move on with Your Life.* Collins: 2006.

Webb, S., and Ousky, R. *The Collaborative Way to Divorce: The Revolutionary Method that Results in Less Stress, Lower Costs, and Happier Kids — Without Going to Court.* New York: Hudson Street Press, 2006. This book is directed at clients as well as divorce professionals and is an enthusiastic and clear outline of the Collaborative model and its benefits.

Wiseman, J.M. *Mediation Therapy: Short Term Decision-Making For Couples and Families in Crisis.* Massachusetts/Toronto: Lexington Books, 1990.

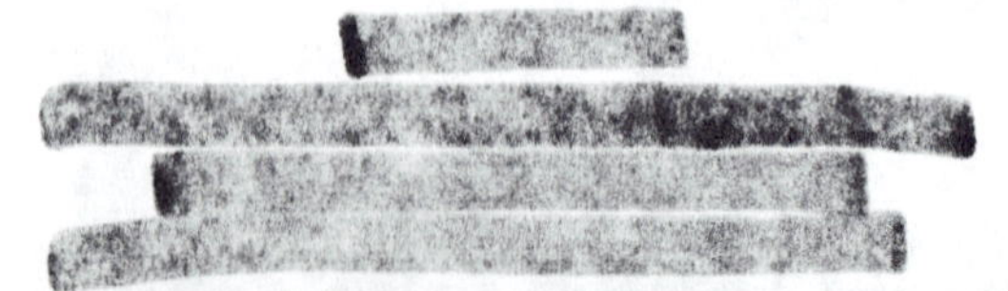

Chapter Two

Screening for Appropriateness

A. EXPECTATIONS OF REFERRAL SOURCES

Referrals for mediation, collaborative law and family arbitration come from a variety of sources. At present most referrals for mediation come from counsellors, the clients directly, or from family lawyers. If clients begin by seeing a mediator first, most mediators will refer the clients to collaboratively trained lawyers as this approach is consistent with the clients' wish to participate in a non-adversarial process. If clients begin by seeing collaborative lawyers, and there are young children, the collaborative lawyers will usually refer the couple to mediation to create a Parenting Plan.

Referrals to collaborative practice or family arbitration usually come from lawyers themselves. A Family Law lawyer may advise the client as to the various process options, including mediation, collaborative law, med-arb or family arbitration, as well as traditional negotiation and litigation. It is essential to assess both parties for their willingness and appropriateness for each option.

Depending on the process selected, the expectations will likely be somewhat different. The following expectations will assist the mediator, collaborative lawyers, or arbitrator in establishing a relationship with the clients and with each other:

- Agreement by both parties to enter into mediation and to retain collaboratively trained counsel. (If only one client selects mediation or collaborative law, it cannot proceed.)
- Description of each participant's role so that each person is clear about expectations and timelines and the team works cooperatively.
- Clarification as to whether the mediator will be signing a Collaborative Mediation Participation Agreement with the clients and both collaborative lawyers, which will include everyone in the commitment to avoid court.
- If the clients select med-arb or family arbitration, agreement as to the specific issues to be addressed, the process to be followed in the arbitration phase, and the type of appeal rights.

B. EXPECTATIONS OF CLIENTS

Expectations of the clients coming for mediation can vary greatly. There may be an expectation that:

- mediation has as its objective reconciliation or counselling;

- the mediator will support the position of one partner by assigning blame against the other; or
- the mediator will decide the issues in dispute (particularly if the mediator is a solicitor).

It is important that the mediator correct such misconceptions, by clarifying with clients that:

- Mediation is not counselling; that is, discussions are focused on negotiating a settlement of the issues in dispute.
- The mediator is an impartial professional who will not take sides. (Parties often want to convert the mediator into an ally.)
- Mediation is not a process for personal attack or blame. Such behaviour is discouraged by the mediator setting ground rules for constructive communication.
- Mediation is not arbitration; that is, the parties, not the mediator, make the decisions.

Clarifying expectations may reveal that the parties are looking for a different process, for example, an arbitrator who will make binding decisions or someone who will explore reconciliation.

C. EXPECTATIONS OF MEDIATOR OR ARBITRATOR

The mediator or arbitrator will want assurances on the following matters prior to commencing:

- Both parties and their lawyers are willing to proceed with family mediation or arbitration, have agreed on the issues to be addressed, and are satisfied with the professional selected.
- The parties are appropriate candidates for mediation or arbitration; that is, they are capable of negotiating or speaking on their own behalf without fear of retaliation, intimidation, or duress.
- A decision has been made as to whether the mediation phase will be open or closed, and the implications of both types of mediation are fully understood by the parties and their lawyers. The mediator or arbitrator will be provided with full disclosure of all information pertinent to the issues in dispute. For example, if financial or property issues are to be addressed, the parties and their counsel agree to provide full and frank disclosure.
- The parties will consider involving any persons relevant to the issues addressed (*e.g.* the child's teacher, family doctor or therapist, new partner or alternate care-giver, *etc.*).
- Responsibility for payment of the professional's fee is agreed upon.
- A mediation or arbitration contract integrating the information set out above will be signed by both parties (and their counsel) prior to commencing.

D. EXPECTATIONS OF COUNSEL

Before accepting a client for collaborative law or referring a client to mediation or family arbitration, it is important for the lawyer to conduct his or her own screening interview. That is, the lawyer should determine whether:

- there has been a history of physical, psychological, economic, substance, or other abuse in the relationship;
- the client would feel endangered either before, during, or after a mediation, collaborative law, or family arbitration session;
- the client would be intimidated when negotiating face to face with the other party;
- the clients are relatively equal in power (that is, the client would be able to assert his or her own point of view); and
- the client is able to articulate his/her own needs, without fear of reprisal, separate and apart from those of the children and the other spouse.

If both clients believe they could participate with the support of the lawyer or other professionals, and with clear communication ground rules, then any of these options may be suitable, and a referral should be made to the option that both clients select.

E. SCREENING FOR APPROPRIATENESS

Before formally accepting the clients for mediation, collaborative law, or family arbitration, the mediator, or a screener selected by the lawyers, must screen the clients to be sure that they are appropriate candidates.

Note: In mediation or med-arb, the mediator usually conducts the screening. In family arbitration, the arbitrator is not permitted to screen the clients (as this might create a bias toward one client); however, both clients must be screened in advance, individually by a trained screener (preferably by the same screener).

In order to qualify, the parties must be able to negotiate or represent themselves safely, voluntarily, and competently in order to reach a fair agreement or award. That means the parties should enter mediation, collaborative law, or family arbitration voluntarily (although some jurisdictions do mandate a minimum of one meeting with a mediator, especially if issues related to children are involved). Clients in all processes should be informed about their legal rights and responsibilities and they should feel safe while meeting face to face with the other party — that is, they should not be concerned about physical, psychological, or economic reprisals as a result of something they might say — and they should reach an agreement voluntarily or receive an award that they believe to be fair.

There are a number of factors that should be evaluated by both the mediator or screener and the lawyer in order to decide whether to accept the clients as candidates for mediation, collaborative law or family arbitration.

F. PATTERNS OF INTIMATE PARTNER VIOLENCE

Recent research has led to a more sophisticated understanding of domestic violence. There are several patterns of abusive relationships that are relevant to the concerns about power imbalance, safety, and protection of children. These considerations impact the choice of options for dispute resolution as well as how to structure a safe parenting plan.

1. Definitions

a. Coercive Controlling Violence: Coercive Controlling Violence is a misuse of power and a violation of trust. This is classic battering in which an abuser (usually male) uses force or a variety of tactics in an escalating pattern aimed at intimidating and controlling the victim. Physical and sexual abuse are often accompanied by such tactics as threats, psychological and emotional abuse, isolation, manipulation of children, and economic control.

b. Separation Instigated Violence: The first violent incident occurs at the time of separation with no prior history of coercive controlling behaviour.

c. Violent Resistance or Self Defence: This is usually the female victim's response to a coercive control pattern by her partner.

d. Situational Couple Violence: Unresolved disagreements spiral out of control, but this is not part of a pattern of coercive control. There can be a female or male perpetrator, but women are more likely to sustain serious injury.

e. Mental Illness and Substance Abuse: Violence may stem from severe mental illness and abuse of alcohol and drugs. This may exacerbate any of the other categories.

We need to be concerned primarily about the first two categories because they are far more prevalent in cases of separation and divorce. These are the statistics that police, hospitals, and women's shelters report and they deal with the greatest risk of future harm. For example, 79 per cent of women contacting shelters experienced Coercive Controlling Violence, 29 per cent was Situational Couple Violence.[1] In heterosexual relationships, one U.S. study found that 97 per cent of Coercive Controlling Violence was male perpetrated[2] and a British

---

[1] I.H Frieze and A. Brown, "Violence in Marriage" in L. Ohlin and M. Tonry, eds., *Family Violence* (Chicago: The University of Chicago Press, 1989), 163-218; J.R. Johnson, "A child-centered approach to high conflict and domestic violence families: Differential assessment and interventions" (2006), 12 *Journal of Family Studies* 15-36.

[2] J.R. Johnson, *ibid.*

study found 87 per cent.[3] In the U.S. study, 76 per cent of cases the violence had escalated over time[4] and 88 per cent of female victims had been injured with 67 per cent being severely injured[5]. In such cases, it is unlikely that the victim can negotiate safely, freely, and without coercion with the batterer.

2. The Responsibility of the Mediator or Other Screener

(A) Screening for Power Imbalances, Control, and Domestic Violence

Mediators, mediator-arbitrators, and parenting coordinators usually conduct their own separate screening of both clients. Note that arbitrators are not permitted to screen the participants but are required by law to have someone else, either the lawyer for each client or a trained professional, conduct the screening and prepare a brief report that indicates whether or not the clients are appropriate candidates. The mediator or other screener (both will be referred to as "the screener") can carry out the screening in a number of different ways:

- *Intake telephone calls* — This is a brief screening interview conducted by the screener or an intake worker or administrative staff.
- *Client questionnaire* — The clients can be asked to respond in writing to a questionnaire that is sent to each of them separately.
- *Individual meeting* — The screener screens each client separately before the mediation commences.

For a variety of reasons, individuals may be reluctant to admit to a history of abuse or control. For example, they may be ashamed of the abuse, blame themselves for what has occurred, be afraid of the consequences of divulging "family secrets", or not want to appear disloyal. Individuals from particular cultural or religious groups may find it even less acceptable to share this information, especially with someone with a different background. Also, the presence or absence of a family support system may make it easier or more difficult to report abuse. Therefore, it is helpful to use more than one method to screen clients, and to be alert to signs of abuse throughout the mediation collaborative law or arbitration process. See Appendix I.2 and Appendix I.3 for

---

[3] N. Graham-Kevan and J. Archer, "Intimate terrorism and common couple violence: A test of Johnson's predictions in four British samples" (2003), 18 *Journal of Interpersonal Violence* 1247-1270.

[4] J.R. Johnson, "A child-centered approach to high conflict and domestic violence families: Differential assessment and interventions" (2006), 12 *Journal of Family Studies* 15-36.

[5] M.P. Johnson, *A Typology of Family Violence: Intimate Terrorism, Violent Resistance, and Situational Couple Violence* (Boston: Northeastern University Press, 2008); J.M. Leone, M.P. Johnson, C.L. Cohan, and S.E. Lloyd, "Consequences of male partner violence for low income minority women" (2004), 66 *Journal of Marriage and Family* 472-490; M.P. Johnson and J.M. Leone, "The differential effects of patriarchal terrorism and common couple violence: Findings from the National Violence Against Women survey" (2000), 26 *Journal of Family Issues* 322-349.

suggested questions that can be asked in a Client Questionnaire or a telephone intake.

3. Objectives of Screening

The purpose of screening is to determine whether each party has the ability to negotiate on his or her own behalf or participate freely and competently, so that any agreement reached meets the prerequisites of a valid contract. It is also important to determine that the clients are entering the process voluntarily. In all cases it is important to determine whether there are any concerns about the safety of the participants or their children at the time they are addressing their separation issues. Separation is a time when the risk of violence escalates and the mediator, arbitrator or other professional needs to assess and minimize any risks. That is, during screening it is important to determine that:

- both parties are participating voluntarily;
- both parties and their children are not at risk of imminent physical or psychological harm;
- both parties are informed as to their rights and obligations under the law;
- each believes that the other is negotiating or participating in good faith; and
- any agreement or outcome is reached without duress or intimidation.

4. Type of Information Sought

During the screening, it is important to determine whether there are control issues, a serious imbalance in power, or domestic violence by asking questions about the following:

- why the marriage ended;
- how decisions were made in the marriage;
- how anger was expressed;
- any instances of physical, verbal, or sexual abuse;
- any concerns with respect to drug or alcohol abuse;
- whether each party is comfortable negotiating or arbitrating in the same room as the other party; and
- any concerns about the safety of either party before, during, or after a joint session.

If these questions are asked in person, then the intake person must listen for both what is said and what is not said. Silences or hesitations may indicate that there is a problem requiring further investigation. There may be an increased risk if the parties are still living under one roof, especially if one party has not accepted the reality of the separation.

5. The Landau Domestic Violence Screening Interview (see Appendix I.3)

The following are areas to explore when screening for domestic violence and control issues in the first individual meetings with the parties. The same format can be followed for any initial individual meetings, with a mediator, screener, or lawyer, whether or not there is a concern about violence, as the information gathered will be useful in helping to understand the issues and history that may impact the mediation, arbitration, or collaborative law.

(A) Mediation Screening Process

- Some mediators choose to meet the parties together before holding an individual screening meeting. However, if any concerns about domestic violence or control issues have surfaced in the phone screenings and/or the client questionnaire, it is important to meet individually with each party before the joint meeting in which the Retainer Contract is signed.
- Meet first with the abused party, or the party who is most at risk, and second with the alleged abusive party, preferably on different days, in order to gather the information necessary to either proceed with mediation or to safely terminate.
- At the beginning of the individual meetings, it is important to make it clear to each party that the purpose of the meeting is not to begin the mediation process, but to determine whether or not mediation is the best process for them. If domestic violence is discovered in the individual meeting with Party A, and mediation is deemed inappropriate, then the mediator should create a safety plan with Party A and safely terminate in the meeting with Party B.

(B) Arbitration Screening Process

- Since the arbitrator is not permitted to do the screening, it is strongly recommended that the same person screen both parties. This person should be trained and competent to do screening in cases of domestic violence. The arbitrator can have a roster of people who he or she trusts or can rely on a person agreed upon by the lawyers. This person must screen prior to commencing the arbitration and a confidential Screening Report must be sent to the arbitrator prior to commencing the arbitration.
- The screener must meet with the parties individually to determine whether they understand the arbitration process, are entering voluntarily, are able to present their issues or instruct counsel without duress, and do not have concerns about the safety of their children or themselves during or following arbitration sessions.

The following are areas to canvass in the individual screening meetings in both mediation and arbitration:

1. DECISION TO SEPARATE
   - The question about how the decision to separate was reached is intended to give a context to the current situation, as well as to determine the level of escalation, any power imbalances, and the readiness of each party to separate. If there has been domestic violence in the relationship, there is a good chance that the separation was linked to the violence in some way.

2. FAMILY HISTORY
   - This question is intended to establish some context for the important role models and significant influences on each party, to determine the impact of their family history on their experience growing up and on their current situation.
   - Questions about their family of origin establish what support systems the individual currently has (both psychological and financial), how their family is responding to the separation, and whether or not the family may be a constructive or destructive influence on the parties.
   - Family history establishes what values the individual may be responding to in terms of parenting, the attitude to the couple's relationship (were they supportive or critical), and the acceptability of separation or divorce.
   - Family history is especially helpful in revealing issues of abuse. Since children of abuse often end up in abusive relationships themselves, it is important to include a family history when screening for abuse. Other important issues are the presence of mental illness, drug or alcohol dependence, or hereditary physical illnesses.

3. HISTORY OF THE RELATIONSHIP
   - This question is intended to give a context to the relationship, in order to better understand some of the issues surrounding the separation.
   - The mediator should screen for physical, verbal, psychological, sexual, and alcohol/drug abuse in the couple's relationship.
   - It is important to discuss a "timeline" for the relationship, or the major events that contributed to the marriage breakdown. Particular attention should be paid to the triggering events in deciding to separate, including any current safety concerns for the children or either parent. Often a couple has experienced a number of traumatic events and not been able to support or grieve with each other at key times. Understanding such patterns can reduce anger and blame and promote acceptance and healing.

4. DECISION-MAKING
   - It is important to establish how decisions were made in the relationship, including decisions about finances, children, personal growth, and moral or religious values. Whether these decisions were made jointly or by one

individual without consultation can be a predictor of the decision-making process in mediation and arbitration.

See Appendix I.6, Linda Girdner's Conflict Assessment Protocol, with respect to specific questions about how decision-making was handled in the relationship, in order to assess issues of domestic violence, control, or power imbalances.

5. DEALING WITH ANGER
   - In order to establish whether the parties are able to negotiate freely without fear or intimidation, it is important to ask questions about how each party expresses and is impacted by expressions of anger. For some couples a relatively high level of conflict may not feel intimidating; whereas with others, one or both may be unable to negotiate with more subtle expressions of anger or displeasure.

See Appendix I.6, Linda Girdner's Conflict Assessment Protocol, with respect to questions about how anger was handled in the relationship, to determine each person's response to possible examples of domestic violence, control, or power imbalances.

6. GOALS FOR THE PROCESS AND THE FUTURE
   - This question establishes the individual's hopes and goals for mediation, collaborative law, or arbitration and beyond. Is the person able to describe a viable plan that includes the safety of the children and themselves, some reasonable financial plan, a place to live, and other basic necessities? The individual must have an understanding of his or her legal entitlements, responsibilities, and the ability to negotiate for what they need — or a willingness to obtain this information before entering an agreement.
   - If there have been incidences of violence and/or control, this question can help to determine which processes are reasonable choices and if the party has the capacity to negotiate in his or her own interest.
   - If mediation or arbitration are not appropriate, this question will help to establish what process to suggest, and how to safety plan *with the individual.*

Also see Desmond Ellis's DOVE Screening Tool in Appendix I.7.

6. Screening Categories (see Appendix I.4)

Mediators, collaborative lawyers, and screeners for arbitration may find it helpful to place clients into three categories depending on whether their relationships involve:

CATEGORY A. APPROPRIATE: Both parties are entering mediation, arbitration, or collaborative law VOLUNTARILY, both have CAPACITY, and SAFETY is not a concern.

[No Violence or Fear of Violence and No Abusive or Controlling Behaviours]

OUTCOME A: Mediation/Arbitration/Collaborative Law can proceed without specialized conditions. Screening for violence, controlling and coercive tactics continues throughout the process.

CATEGORY B. POSSIBLY APPROPRIATE: Both parties are entering mediation, arbitration or collaborative law VOLUNTARILY and both would have capacity and safety would not be a concern IF certain CONDITIONS were met and/or there was a SPECIALIZED PROCESS. In order for mediation or arbitration to go ahead, both parties have to agree to the conditions/changes.

[No Violence or Fear of Violence, but other Abusive or Controlling Behaviours]

OUTCOME B: Victim DOES want to mediate, arbitrate, or selects collaborative law. Both parties may have capacity if SPECIALIZED PROCESS and under certain CONDITIONS. If both agree to conditions as prerequisite, then mediation or collaborative law continue with ongoing screening and enforcement of conditions. If one or both do not agree to conditions, NO MEDIATION, ARBITRATION, OR COLLABORATIVE LAW and, if necessary, safety planning and referral.

CATEGORY C. NOT APPROPRIATE: The victim does NOT want to mediate, arbitrate or participate in collaborative law and/or or both parties LACK CAPACITY, and/or SAFETY IS A CONCERN, and a specialized process would not satisfy these issues.

[Violence or Fear of Violence]

OUTCOME C: No Mediation/Arbitration/Collaborative Law. Safety planning and referral.

What is most important is to determine the impact of the behaviour on the clients' ability to participate in negotiations on their own behalf. Under specialized conditions, some clients may be able to proceed even in the presence of violence or control, but others would lack the capacity to negotiate. It is very important to screen both the alleged victim and perpetrator when determining appropriateness.

7. Options Following Screening

At the end of the screening process, the screener should decide, taking into account the views of the clients, whether the clients are:

- appropriate for mediation, collaborative law, or arbitration conducted in the usual way;
- possibly appropriate for mediation, collaborative law, or arbitration under specific circumstances; or
- not appropriate for mediation, collaborative law, or arbitration.

Depending on the category that the clients are placed into, the following can act as a guideline:

A. *Where the parties are appropriate for mediation, collaborative law, or arbitration conducted in the usual way* — These are cases where the couple has a history of consultation or joint decision-making, they respect each other's point of view, including the right to hold different points of view, neither party feels afraid or intimidated, and both believe the other is acting in good faith. Therefore, mediation, collaborative law, or arbitration can proceed with primarily joint meetings.

B. *Where the parties are possibly appropriate for mediation, collaborative law, or arbitration under specific circumstances* — In these cases, there may have been a history of some abuse, primarily verbal or psychological, or an isolated incident of physical abuse in the past, which the abuser has acknowledged, and the abuser has demonstrated a change in behaviour. The abuser may have participated in anger management counselling or be prepared to do that at the present time, and the abusive incidents can be discussed in the mediation or collaborative law four-way meetings and possibly shared jointly in arbitration (they are not a family secret). In these cases, the mediator or lawyers should make it clear that violence and intimidation are unacceptable and will result in the mediation or collaborative law process being terminated, should there be any further incidents. The arbitrator can make a general statement about the fact that screening for domestic violence is required and he needs to ensure on an ongoing basis that the participants are safe and participating freely and without duress.

Also, if the victim has had counselling, is removed from the situation without recent incidents, and feels confident about proceeding, the mediator, collaborative lawyer, or arbitrator should consider the victim's wishes carefully. It would be particularly important to ensure that both parties are in fact participating voluntarily and feel they can express their own point of view. There would need to be ground rules for communication and implementation of a safety plan, such as having the abuser arrive early for appointments and stay later, so that the victim of abuse can enter and leave the process without the fear of being followed.

In these cases, it is essential that the parties have independent legal advice. These cases may be assisted by highly trained lawyers, who are aware of the circumstances, and able to ensure that their client participates in good faith, provides the required financial disclosure, and avoids behaviour that could be seen as intimidating.

The advantage of collaboratively trained lawyers is that the parties must agree to conduct their negotiations without threats of court or other forms of duress. One requirement might be that the violence is disclosed so that appropriate ground rules can be established, additional resources arranged, and monitoring of behaviour and other commitments is possible. Examples of special provisions that might enhance safety in collaborative law are:

- respectful communication during and between sessions
- no threats, withholding of financial support or refusal to return children
- agreement not to discuss issues that contribute to escalating tension between sessions; especially no pressure to give up entitlements or accept unreasonable concessions
- prompt and complete financial disclosure without resistance.

If clients do not agree or adhere to ground rules, then traditional legal representation would be appropriate.

Arbitration is usually a more formal process with somewhat less flexibility, except with the consent of all parties. Mediation and Collaborative Law may offer more choices for adapting the process. For example, in these cases, most if not all of the mediation or collaborative law sessions could be conducted individually. This is sometimes referred to as a "shuttle" process, that is, the mediator or collaborative lawyers would relay proposals between the parties who would be in separate rooms.

In arbitration, based on the Screening Report, the arbitrator could modify the process or set ground rules or conditions to ensure safety and prevent coercion. If the parties agree, the arbitration could proceed. For example, if one party does not feel safe in the same room as the other, it might be possible to use a modified shuttle process in which the clients are in separate rooms but the arbitrator and both counsel move back and forth between them.

If the parties are willing to meet in the same room but are uncomfortable, each could be offered the option of bringing a support person, such as their lawyer, if this would ease the tension. In any case, the mediator, collaborative lawyers, or counsel in an arbitration would need to be alert to the use of duress or intimidation in the process, and would want to monitor the clients to make sure there were no reprisals after a session. These changes have increased the range of participants who can benefit from these process options.

C. *Where the parties are not appropriate for mediation, collaborative law, or arbitration* — These are clients who are unable to negotiate safely, are not participating voluntarily, and are unable to reach an agreement without threats to their physical safety, economic security, or psychological health. The task of the screener in this case is to safely terminate the screening process so that the parties are directed to alternative options of resolving their family law problems and, to the extent possible, protected from further abuse. While these cases may be able to be handled in a specially designed process that uses a "shuttle" approach, it is unlikely that either party would have the capacity to negotiate reasonably and in good faith with the other. These cases often require judicial safeguards, such as criminal charges, probation conditions (including attendance at an anger management program), restrictions on communication, and a court order to attend (separately) at a Parenting Coordinator for the resolution of new disputes.

For additional information about Family Arbitration, see Chapter 7.

Interview with Victim	Interview with Abuser
Suspicion of abuse	Decision not to use mediation, collaborative law, or arbitration
1. Confirm the suspicion & assess capacity & voluntariness *if **yes** go to step 2, If **no** go to 4*	1. Assess capacity to use mediation, collaborative law, or arbitration *if **yes** go to step 2, if **no** go to 4*
2. Safety planning & referral to alternatives	2. Decision not to use mediation, collaborative law or arbitration
3. Safe termination strategy	3. Safe termination & referral to alternatives
4. *Proceed with mediation &/or collaborative law or arbitration*	4. *Proceed with mediation &/or collaborative law or arbitration*
Note: If the victim alleges abuse or does NOT want to mediate or participate in collaborative law or arbitration, the process does NOT proceed. The screener does not try to determine whether in fact the alleged abuse occurred, although this may be an important question for the lawyers.	

8. Safe Termination Following Screening*

The following are some "do's" and "do not's" for the screener with respect to safe termination of the screening process:

(a) *Do's — Meeting with the victim individually* — The screener should:

- discuss with the victim concerns about the process option and alternatives that might better protect her and the children;
- ask the victim what would be a helpful approach for terminating safely; and
- tell the victim what the screener will tell the abuser, and make a safety plan with respect to her and the children in case the abuser blames the victim.

(b) *Do's — Meeting with the abuser individually* — The screener should:

- assist the abuser to see that the process option is unlikely to be suitable or productive or meet his needs (that is, it is not likely to succeed and therefore there will be added delay and cost);
- utilize the abuser's language, information, and rationale, if appropriate;
- state that the screener has a "gut feeling", based on his or her experience that the particular process option is unlikely to succeed in this case, that is, take personal responsibility for termination;

- if guidelines are set and not adhered to where the couple is possibly appropriate, focus on this as the basis for termination; and
- tell the abuser that he is not ready for the process option, and suggest what needs to happen first (for example, counselling with respect to the effects of separation). They may be ready in the future.

(c) *Do Not's*

- If the abuse has not already been disclosed, the screener should not reveal abuse to the abuser's solicitor or to court because this could endanger the victim.
- An exception might be made with the permission of the victim, if she wishes to proceed in a specially designed process. Such a process could only go forward if the abuse was acknowledged by the abuser and safeguards were agreed upon and monitored.
- The screener should not blame or put down the victim.

* **Note:** As statistics reveal that most victims of domestic violence are women, the feminine pronoun is used here to denote the victim. Where this is not the case, the appropriate gender should be substituted.

9. Safety Planning

(a) *Questions to ask the victim* — It is important for the screener to determine whether the victim is in danger, or will be in danger, once the abuser learns the process option is not proceeding. Therefore, it is important to assist the victim to consider a safety plan. The following questions would be helpful:

- Are you worried about your safety now? How will he react to not proceeding with whichever option had been selected?
- Do you feel safe in your present living arrangement (especially if they are still living together)? *If not*, have you talked to a woman's advocate or lawyer? (She should be encouraged to do this — give her names, addresses, and phone numbers, and help her to make contact.)
- Do you know of any emergency shelters in case you need to find a place of safety for you and the children? (Give names and phone numbers.)
- Do you have any other safe place to go? Do you have any money? Have you ever contacted the police?

(b) *Questions to ask the abuser* — The screener has a responsibility to assist both parties, including the abuser, to find resources that are appropriate in their case. The following questions would be helpful:

- Do you have a lawyer? (He should be encouraged to get one. Give names, addresses, and phone numbers.)
- Do you have a counsellor? (He should be encouraged to get one and to enter an Anger Management or a Batterer's Treatment Program if appropriate.)

Even though a particular option may not be appropriate at the present time for clients, if they take appropriate steps, and if the abuser changes his behaviour and the victim feels safer and more empowered, it may be possible for them to enter that process at a later date. One important reason has already been discussed, that is, concerns about domestic violence, which may make it impossible for clients to negotiate safely or to reach agreements voluntarily.

10. Referral to Alternatives

If mediation is not appropriate in a particular case, there is a professional responsibility to assist the clients to find constructive alternatives that may be helpful. Often the parties need more than one of the following options:

(a) Counselling — individual or group.

(b) Attendance at an Anger Management Program — possibly as a precondition following which other options might be available.

(c) A Custody Assessment — instead of mediation or arbitration. This may be particularly appropriate if there are concerns about the capacity to parent, child abuse, or if the children have special needs.

(d) A Parenting Coordinator or Special Master — if the issues have arisen following an agreement or court order.

(e) A Restraining Order or Peace Bond — if there are safety concerns.

(f) A Shelter or Domestic Violence Clinic — if there is an imminent risk of harm to the parent or child.

G. ESTABLISHING IMPARTIALITY: MEDIATOR OR ARBITRATOR

It is essential that clients see the mediator or arbitrator as impartial. Impartiality means that the parties do not feel that one party was treated more favourably than the other. That is, the process was fair, each party had an opportunity to explain his or her views, the outcome reflected the best interests of the children, and was a reasonable settlement of the issues. For an agreement to last, and be carried out in a spirit of cooperation, both parties must feel that they were treated respectfully and fairly and that they were participating voluntarily, and without coercion.

These values are also important for collaborative law; however, the lawyers walk a tight rope between being seen as advocates for their client, and advocates for the process and the best interests of children.

For these reasons, it is essential that the mediator and arbitrator establish his or her impartiality with both clients and solicitors from the outset. For additional information about arbitration see Chapter 7.

Note: It is important for the mediator to clarify that where there are concerns about the safety of either client, the children, the mediator, arbitrator, or his or her staff, steps must be taken to address the safety concerns. **That is, the need to protect an individual's safety supersedes the duty to be impartial.**

H. IMPACT ON PARENTING PLANS AND OTHER RECOMMENDATIONS

1. Concerns re Parenting Plans in High-conflict/Abusive Relationships:

- safety of children and other spouse;
- if one or both parents fall below the standard of care set out in the *Child and Family Services Act*,[6] there is an obligation to report to the CAS;
- the competence of both parents to parent and to protect the child must be assessed;
- if there are threats to the future safety of the other parent, there is an obligation to warn the other parent and to report to the police;
- recommendations to support services should be considered such as parenting programs, anger management, addiction treatment, communication coaching, mental health services, as well as parenting coordination.

---

[6] R.S.O. 1990, c. C.11.

ISSUE	NON-ABUSIVE RELATIONSHIPS	ABUSIVE RELATIONSHIPS
PARENTING SCHEDULE	• Flexibility is possible • Schedule can be adapted by mutual consent based on child's stage of development, parent's work schedule, special occasions, *etc.*	• Specific pick-up and return times • Clear consequences if late/no show • Flexibility not advised (except for child-related emergencies) • Exchanges through third party and/or in neutral (public) setting • Minimize need for ongoing negotiations, communication, or disputes re scheduling • Short day visits (increase if child is comfortable and no further abuse) • No alcohol or drugs before or during visits. Cancel visit and call police if breach • Consider supervised visits or supervised access centre • Require addiction counselling, anger management, or therapy as prerequisite for unsupervised visits • Start with short-term interim agreement to monitor compliance

ISSUE	NON-ABUSIVE RELATIONSHIPS	ABUSIVE RELATIONSHIPS
DECISION-MAKING	• Consult in advance and likely make joint decisions in the best interests of child	• Not likely to agree • Joint decision making likely creates an opportunity for intimidation and coercion • Primary/custodial parent makes decisions. On significant issues (*e.g.*, a change of the type of school), allow a specific time for input from other parent. If ongoing harassment or risk, custodial parent can decide and inform other parent after
CHILDCARE RESPONSIBILITIES	• Likely share responsibilities according to competence, availability and willingness	• Custodial parent likely to carry most of the responsibilities • Need consistent health care (*i.e.*, same doctor if possible)
COMMUNICATION	• Encourage regular sharing of parental information, *e.g.,* weekly telephone meetings when children not present or able to overhear, monthly meetings in a public place with agenda in advance, exchange a parenting notebook, *etc.* • Information exchanged is re children, *e.g.*, health care, scheduling, school performance, behaviour, *etc.*	• Limit communication, *i.e.*, avoid direct contact • Use third parties, *e.g.*, teacher, family doctor • Encourage independent access to information, *e.g.*, both parents get report card, medical reports, *etc.* (subject to the child's right of confidentiality) • Avoid sharing information that could endanger the child, *i.e.*, that could make a parent angry

I. TERMINATION

The different process options have different ways they can be terminated.

Mediation can be terminated by the clients (parties) or the mediator, but not by the lawyers. The lawyer may advise his or her client to terminate mediation or may raise concerns with the mediator. However, the actual decision to terminate rests with the client(s) or the mediator.

With court-ordered mediation, it would be necessary to return to court to have the original order withdrawn or terminated by the judge. (When mediation is terminated, the judge may decide to order an assessment or family investigation.)

There are a number of reasons why the clients or the mediator may wish to terminate mediation, or the lawyer(s) may advise such termination. Refer to Chapter 8 for a complete discussion of the termination process.

Collaborative Law can be terminated by either client or either lawyer. In *Collaborative Mediation*, if the mediator has concerns, he or she can raise these with the clients and/or the lawyers (unless notifying others would create a danger). The mediator could decide to terminate the mediation process. However, the decision about whether to continue the collaborative process rests with the clients and the lawyers. If either client or lawyer believes the other party is not acting in good faith, is refusing to make reasonable financial disclosure, or is using threats or intimidation, then the collaborative process will likely end and both lawyers will withdraw. In this case the clients will need assistance to find other options (*e.g.*, litigation counsel).

Mediation-arbitration can be terminated by a joint notice in writing delivered during the mediation phase. It is essential that the parties be given an opportunity to mediate prior to the arbitration. If the mediation is not successful, the arbitrator can proceed to hold an arbitration in keeping with the powers set out in the *Arbitration Act, 1991*.[7] It is important that these terms be clearly set out in the Med-Arb Agreement to avoid future misunderstanding.

Arbitration cannot be terminated by one party only once they have entered into the arbitration, except if the arbitrator is removed by a court order or resigns. An arbitration ends when the arbitrator delivers his or her Award and any period of time for making corrections has passed.

SUMMARY

This chapter has highlighted a number of practical issues that impact both mediation and collaborative law. Of particular importance is screening clients to determine their appropriateness for a non-adversarial process. Both mediation and collaborative law require a commitment to good faith bargaining and a voluntary resolution of the issues in dispute. In the event these non-adversarial

---

[7] S.O. 1991, c. 17.

processes are not appropriate, the professional should assist the couple to find appropriate alternative resources.

ANNOTATED BIBLIOGRAPHY

Baris, M., Coates, C., Duvall, B., Garrity, C., Johnson, E., and LaCrosse, E. *Working with High Conflict Families of Divorce: A Guide for Professionals.* New Jersey: Jason Aronson Inc., 2001. This is a valuable guide to several options for assisting "revolving door" clients; that is, those who continually return to court. It contains very helpful descriptions of each role along with potential ethical pitfalls. It also includes practical precedents for contracting with high conflict couples.

Barsky, A. "Issues in the Termination of Mediation Due to Abuse". (1995), 13 *Mediation Quarterly* 1. Barsky describes a strategic framework for analyzing ethical dilemmas when abuse is present.

Boyan, S.M., and Termini, A.M. *The Psychotherapist as Parenting Coordinator in High Conflict Divorce: Strategies and Techniques*. New York: The Haworth Clinical Practice Press, 2005.

Benjamin, M., and Irving, H. "Towards a Feminist-Informed Model of Therapeutic Family Mediation". (1992), 10(2) *Mediation Quarterly* 129-53.

Eddy, B. *High Conflict People in Legal Disputes*. Canada: Janis Publications Ltd., 2006. This is an excellent reference to understand the dynamics of borderline and personality disordered clients and strategies for managing these difficult clients.

Ellis, D. *Family Mediation Pilot Project: Final Report*. Oakville, Ont., 1994. This research examined the cost effectiveness, client satisfaction, and incidence of domestic violence in mediation versus litigation clients.

Family Court Review, An Interdisciplinary Journal, Special Issue: Domestic Violence, 46, 3, July 2008.

Folberg, J., Taylor, A., and Salem, P. *Divorce and Family Mediation: Models, Techniques, and Applications*. Guilford Press, 2004. This thorough text covers the theory and practice of mediation with articles by many leaders in the family mediation field.

Freeman, R., Lambert, K., and Nosko, A. *Working Towards Eliminating Male Violence Against Women: A Group Intervention for Abusive Men: Pilot Project Outcome Report*. Toronto: Family Service Association of Metro Toronto, 1994.

Frieze, I.H., and Browne, A. "Violence in Marriage". In L. Ohlin and M. Tonry, eds., *Family Violence* (pp. 163-218). Chicago: The University of Chicago Press, 1989.

Girdner, L. "Mediation Triage: Screening for Spouse Abuse in Divorce Mediation". (1990), 6 *Mediation Quarterly*, 365-76. This article provides a very useful guide for screening clients for domestic violence concerns. This screening is conducted with the clients separately and helps both the clients and the mediator decide whether mediation would be safe and appropriate in a particular case.

Girdner, L., ed. "Special Issue: Domestic Violence". (1990), 7 *Mediation Quarterly.*

Graham-Kevan, N., and Archer, J. "Intimate terrorism and common couple violence: A test of Johnson's predictions in four British samples." *Journal of Interpersonal Violence*, 18, 1247-1270, 2003.

Grillo, T. "The Mediation Alternative: Process Dangers for Women". (1991), 100 *Yale Law Review*, 1545-610.

Hart, B. *Mediation for Battered Women: Same Song, Second Verse, Little Bit Louder, Little Bit Worse*. New York: National Center on Women and Family Law, 1984.

Jaffe, P., Wolfe, D., and Wilson, S. *Children of Battered Women, Volume 21.* Newbury Park, California: Sage Publications, 1990. This book summarizes the impact on children of witnessing violence directed at their mothers. It also reviews the literature on the number of children who are battered when their mothers are battered. Information is provided about the long-range consequence for these children and the likelihood that these children will become either batterers or victims of abuse.

Johnson, J.R. "A child-centered approach to high conflict and domestic violence families: Differential assessment and interventions" (2006), *Journal of Family Studies*, 12,15-36.

Johnson, M.P., *A Typology of Family Violence: Intimate Terrorism, Violent Resistance, and Situational Couple Violence*. Boston: Northeastern University Press, 2008.

Johnson, M.P., and Leone, J.M. "The differential effects of patriarchal terrorism and common couple violence: Findings from the National Violence Against Women survey." (2000), *Journal of Family Issues*, 26, 322-349.

Johnston, J., and Campbell, L. "A Clinical Typology of Interparental Violence in Disputed-Custody Divorces". (1993), 63 *American Journal of Orthopsychiatry* 1. Based on two studies of high-conflict divorcing families, four characteristic profiles of interparental violence were identified: ongoing or episodic battering by males, female-initiated violence, interactive violence controlled by males, and violence engendered by separation or post-divorce trauma. A fifth profile consisted of psychotic and paranoid reactions. These different profiles generate different issues to consider in mediation.

Johnston, J., and Roseby, V. *In the Name of the Child — A Developmental Approach to Understanding and Helping Children of Conflicted and Violent Divorce*. New York, New York: The Free Press, 1997. This book is an important resource on the impact of high-conflict divorce on children.

Kelly, J. "Power Imbalance in Divorce and Interpersonal Mediation: Assessment and Intervention". (1995), 13 *Mediation Quarterly* 2, 85-98. This article presents a framework for understanding the conditions that create unequal power in mediation. A variety of mediator interventions are discussed which may empower disputants when differences in power threaten the integrity of the mediation process and its outcome.

Kelly, J., and Duryee, M. "Women's and Men's Views of Mediation in Voluntary and Mandatory Mediation Settings". (1992), 30 *Family and Conciliation Courts Review*, 34-49. This article reports findings regarding women and mediation from a combined group of 184 persons who received mediation services from the Alameda County Superior Court Family Court Services or the Northern California Mediation Center. This empirical study refutes many of the feminist criticisms of mediation and demonstrates that women do feel empowered by the mediation process.

Landau, B. "Qualifications of Family Mediators: Listening to the Feminist Critique". In C. Morris and A. Pirie, eds. *Qualifications for Dispute Resolution: Perspectives on the Debate*. Victoria, B.C.: U. Vic. Institute for Dispute Resolution, 1994. This chapter summarizes the feminist critique of family mediation and makes suggestions for changes in family mediation practice and the training of mediators.

Landau, B. "Family Mediation: An Alternative Dispute Resolution Manual". In A. Stitt, ed. *Alternative Dispute Resolution Practice Manual.* Toronto: CCH Canadian Limited, 1996. This chapter contains an introduction to family mediation practice and highlights important policy issues.

Leone, J.M., Johnson, M.P., Cohan, C.L., and Lloyd, S.E. "Consequences of male partner violence for low-income minority women." (2004), *Journal of Marriage and Family*, 66, 472-490.

McIsaac, H., ed. "Special Issue: Domestic Violence". (1995), 33 *Family and Conciliation Courts Review*. This entire issue is devoted to articles on domestic violence.

MacLeod, L., and Shin, M. *Isolated, Afraid and Forgotten: The Service Delivery Needs and Realities of Immigrant and Refugee Women Who Are Battered.* Ottawa: National Clearinghouse on Family Violence, Health and Welfare Canada, 1990.

Mediation in Cases of Domestic Abuse: Helpful Option or Unacceptable Risk? The Final Report of the Domestic Abuse and Mediation Project. Coordinated by the Maine Court Mediation Service, 1992.

Pearson, J. *Divorce Mediation and Domestic Violence.* Denver: Center for Policy Research, 1996.

Perry, L. "Mediation and Wife Abuse: A Review of the Literature". (1994), 11(4) *Mediation Quarterly*, 313-27. This article reviews the concerns of those opposed to the use of mediation in such cases and outlines models of mediation, including screening procedures and special techniques, used by mediators to address the dynamics of violence.

Report from the Toronto Forum on Women Abuse and Mediation. Toronto: 1993. This important report was prepared by leading mediators and women's advocates working together to suggest standards of practice, policies, and protocols for the safe, fair, and specialized practice of mediation in cases involving abuse against women. Central to this report is the rebuttable presumption against the use of mediation in cases of domestic abuse. This report makes suggestions as to the education and training of family mediators with respect to abuse, techniques for pre-mediation screening, safety measures, and specialized mediation processes that should be considered, including techniques for safe termination and alternatives to mediation in those cases where mediation is inappropriate.

Saposnek, D. *Mediating Child Custody Disputes.* San Francisco: Jossey-Bass Publishers Inc., 1998. See particularly Part Two, "Structuring the Mediation Process", p. 85. This early text contains a number of concrete suggestions and case examples of mediation in practice.

Schaeffer, M. "Divorce Mediation: A Feminist Perspective". (1988), 46 *University of Toronto Faculty of Law Review* 62-200.

Schepard, Andrew. *Special Issue: Domestic Violence, Family Court Review: An Interdisciplinary Journal*, Vol. 46, no. 3, July 2008. Wiley-Blackwell. This important special issue summarizes the latest research and thinking about domestic violence and provides a more sophisticated understanding of this difficult topic.

Vallee, B. *The War on Women.* Toronto: Key Porter Books Ltd., 2007. This book documents several cases of women who murdered their abusive spouses. It offers an insight into the terror these women experienced and illustrates the type of cases that would be clearly inappropriate for ADR.

Chapter Three

Managing the Process

A. PROCESS SKILLS FOR MEDIATION AND COLLABORATIVE PRACTICE

This chapter focuses on the skills needed to manage either a mediation (including the mediation portion of med-arb and parenting coordination) or a collaborative law process. Chapter 7 examines the skills needed for arbitration.

Successful collaboration means that the mediator and lawyers must manage a process that:

- Separates the people from the problem to address emotional distress, personality differences, value differences, and historic grievances so that these do not contaminate problem solving;
- Focuses on interests as a way to address the clients' genuine concerns and needs;
- Ensures that the full range of psychological and process interests are identified and acknowledged, in addition to substantive needs, so that agreements are reached respectfully and more likely to last;
- Encourages the generation of creative options that are tailored to meet the client's unique circumstances and reflects their values — and goes beyond the one size fits all approach of the law;
- Identifies and articulates the criteria for evaluating options; and
- Clearly expresses the areas of agreement, including who has what responsibility, by when, and at what cost.

There are several challenges in managing such a process:

1. The parties are often unable to communicate effectively with one another.
2. One or both of the parties may be unwilling or unable to participate in a collaborative process because of psychological, emotional, or strategic reasons.
3. There may be serious power imbalances between the parties that preclude fair negotiations.
4. Inevitable impasses may derail otherwise promising negotiations.
5. A satisfactory solution might require professional expertise beyond that of the mediator or lawyers.
6. The lawyers may still be behaving in a more traditional adversarial manner.

1. Helping Parties Communicate More Effectively

The mediator and collaborative lawyer have the difficult task of assisting the couple to communicate more effectively about the very issues that caused the separation, and then make a plan for the future, at a time when self-esteem and goodwill are at their lowest point. One of the primary reasons given for marriage failure is difficulty in communication between the parties. Spouses will often state that one or both of them are unable to understand:

- each other's feelings — often spouses give ambivalent messages to each other about their satisfaction with the marriage;
- each other's motives for leaving the marriage or for wanting it to continue;
- why one or both were unhappy during the marriage; and/or
- what was expected of them by the other spouse to save the marriage.

The spouses often report that they never clarified or discussed feelings of anger, disappointment, or resentment, and as a result, important issues in the marriage were unresolved. Such couples generally have a long history of distrust and suspicion about the other partner's motives and behaviour.

Mediation and collaborative law are approaches that depend on effective communication in order to reach an agreement. The task is made difficult because the mediator or collaborative lawyers are faced with two people who by this time usually dislike each other, are very poor communicators, are highly distrustful, and are fearful of being hurt again. It is essential that the mediator and/or the collaborative lawyers help the parties to develop more effective communication techniques from the very beginning or the mediation and collaborative approach will likely fail. Because the sessions, particularly the initial sessions, are likely to be highly emotionally charged, it is important for the mediator and collaborative lawyers to explain certain basic communication skills or ground rules prior to beginning the content of the discussion. There are several reasons for establishing basic communication skills in the initial meeting, namely:

- The parties can begin to communicate more effectively right from the beginning.
- The parties are more likely to absorb information about communication techniques when they are not in the midst of discussing emotionally charged information.
- The parties are likely to present their information more effectively and more constructively, that is, with less conflict and assignment of blame, if they have discussed appropriate methods of communication.
- By developing more effective communication skills from the beginning, the mediator and collaborative lawyers are improving the chances of the parties listening to each other, reducing their tension, and beginning the process of talking constructively about the issues in dispute.
- In the initial meeting, some basic ground rules should be set, and the parties asked for their commitment to follow the guidelines. These

guidelines are often helpful, later in the process, to remind the parties to continue to communicate respectfully.

- These guidelines could include: speaking one at a time, not interrupting the other person, and speaking in the first person about how a situation impacts that speaker — an "I message", rather than making blaming statements, a "you message". The mediator and collaborative lawyers could also ask the parties if there are any guidelines that would help them to communicate effectively with each other.

The following examples of listening and communication techniques should be taught to the parties throughout the process:

- *Speaking in the first person.* That is, if a party has a concern, the party should state that concern as his or her own concern, not as a general concern or as a concern of some other person. For example, "I am concerned about the fact that you make hostile comments about me in front of the children," rather than, "It is not a good idea for children to hear parents badmouthing each other."
- *Making eye contact with each other* when they are speaking.
- *Directing comments about the other spouse to that spouse* rather than to the mediator or the lawyers.
- *Speaking one at a time* and not interrupting the other.
- *Making direct statements about how they feel* rather than trying to elicit the mediator's or lawyers' disapproval of the other spouse (and approval of themselves). For example, "I think that you should pick up the children for an access visit at the time that you agreed. It is very disappointing to the children when you are late," rather than a question addressed to the mediator or lawyers, "Don't you think that it is psychologically damaging to children when parents are late for access visits?"
- *Stating specifically the behaviour that is upsetting* rather than attacking the other spouse in more general terms. In addition, each spouse should state the behaviour that he or she would prefer, so that the discussion can become focused on what behaviour is upsetting and what changes are needed, rather than defending against personal attacks. For example, "It is upsetting to me when you change access arrangements at the last minute. I would appreciate it if you would notify me of changes at least two days in advance" (statement of the problem); "I would be much more willing to cooperate if you would ask me if it was convenient to change the access arrangements rather than just telling me that you are changing them, without any concern for alternative plans that I may have made" (specifying the preferred behaviour).
- *Paraphrasing what he or she heard the other spouse saying.* This ensures that both spouses are listening to each other, and it also helps to clarify any confusion or misinterpretation.
- *Asking for clarification* rather than attacking the other spouse. That is, they should be sure that they have correctly understood any

communication, before they become upset. Too often, couples who are already upset and distrustful of each other misinterpret both the intent and the actual content of the communication. A great deal of hostility can be eliminated if they learn to ask for clarification. For example, "I am not sure that I understand why the cottage is so important to you, could you explain that again please," or, "Could you give me some more information about why your child support cheque will be late this month?" rather than, "You are a liar and a deadbeat — there you are doing it again — I knew I could not trust you!"

- *Using direct versus indirect statements.* For example, "I was upset when you telephoned last night and did not tell me that the parent-teacher interviews will be held next week," rather than, "You never communicate with me about how the children are doing in school."
- *Identifying feelings*, that is, the person's own feelings and his or her perception of the feelings expressed by the other person. For example, "It made me feel hurt when you said that I was not a good mother," or, "I guess it must have made you feel angry when I refused to invite your parents to the children's birthday party."
- *Talking about feelings* rather than acting them out through aggressive retaliatory behaviour. For example, one spouse might say, "It makes me feel that you do not really care about your children when you refuse to pay child support," rather than cutting off access to the non-paying spouse. An even better approach would be for the spouse to *ask for clarification.* For example, "Is there some reason why you are not contributing to the extra-curricular activities?" This permits the other spouse to give some explanation for his or her behaviour, such as, "I am now unemployed," or, "I feel that you are interfering with my relationship with the children so that I did not feel like paying additional amounts for the activities, especially when you did not consult me in advance." By asking for clarification, important issues that need to be dealt with in mediation or collaborative law can be identified. These issues would not be resolved if the parties resorted to acting-out behaviour.
- *Accepting the fact that each person is entitled to his or her own perception of a situation.* That is, rather than putting the mediator or collaborative lawyers in the position of judging who is right or wrong, or who is lying or truthful, both parties need to accept that they may perceive situations differently and therefore may feel and act differently.

It is very important that the mediator and collaborative lawyers not only teach these communication skills, but also model the skills by using them in their own communication with the parties, and, in the case of the lawyers, with each other. This will help to create an atmosphere of respect in the process, allowing the conflict to be defused and encouraging some mutual understanding. At the same time there should be sensitivity to cultural differences, ensuring that specific communication skills are appropriate to the cultural background of the parties.

B. CONSTRUCTIVE PROBLEM SOLVING

Once the mediator or collaborative lawyers have taught the parties basic communication techniques, the next step is to help the parties orient toward their future relationship rather than dwelling on events and feelings of the past. The following should be emphasized:

- What has happened in the past cannot be changed. While these events will certainly colour the parties' perceptions, nevertheless it is important for them to make a commitment to be different today. The focus of mediation or collaborative law should be on determining what type of relationship the parties would like to have in the future.
- The parties should not expect that the relationship will change overnight or that there will be no setbacks. The important thing is to recognize and encourage each other when positive steps are made and not to become overly upset or discouraged when difficulties arise. The parties should use the communication techniques explained above in order to avoid undue hostility.
- Each spouse should tell the other spouse when he or she has done something right. For example, "I really appreciated it when you called to ask whether it would be convenient for me to change the access arrangements this weekend. I felt that you were giving me a choice and that you were concerned about disrupting my plans. It felt good to cooperate." Or, "When you agreed to let me remain in the matrimonial home with the children for the next three years, I was really relieved. It will offer me and the children some time to adjust to our new circumstances without an immediate upheaval. I really appreciate it and know that this means a considerable financial sacrifice for you." So often in cases of marriage breakdown, the parties get no positive reinforcement, but only hear about the things that they did wrong. This is particularly true of cases that go to litigation. In order to encourage more cooperative behaviour in the future, the parties must learn to give each other positive reinforcement for improved behaviour in the present.
- The focus should be on establishing any positive aspects that did or may still exist in the relationship. This may be helpful in encouraging the parties to cooperate in the future. For example, was there a period when they communicated well, were supportive of each others goals, shared values, and trusted and respected each other? It is helpful to remind separating couples of what they admired — and may still admire in each other. While clients usually begin mediation at a stage of anger and hurt, this conversation often gets people in touch with shared feelings of sadness and loss. This constructive reflection can rebuild trust and create some optimism for continuing as parenting partners in the future.
- Where there have been major life stresses, such as the death of a child or a prolonged illness in a sibling or parent, or the failure of a business, couples can reframe these events in terms of not finding ways of

responding that met the other parent's needs. This can shift each person's narrative from blaming the other parent for everything that has gone wrong, to seeing the situation as one of personality differences, a failure to communicate needs clearly, or an inability to respond authentically in a way that comforted the other person. Such a reframe or shift in the narrative is helpful in reducing blame, and may help the couple reach some sense of respectful closure and begin to move on.

In addition to improving the parties' ability to communicate, the mediator and collaborative lawyers need to focus the discussion on the particular issues in dispute. If an increase in the level of trust, a willingness to cooperate, and an improvement in communication skills has been successfully established, then the next step is to help the parties identify some objective criteria or governing principles for resolving those issues that are in dispute. For example, if one issue is custody of or access to children, then the mediator might determine whether the parents agree that the best interests of the children ought to be the primary criterion for evaluating a solution, as opposed to whether one parent wins or loses. The mediator could spend some time with the parents identifying what is meant by "best interests of the children". For example, the parties might agree on the following:

- It is desirable for children to have a close, loving relationship with both parents.
- Children should feel comfortable expressing feelings of love and respect for one parent in the other parent's presence.
- Parents (and their new partners and extended family members) should not criticize or demean the other parent in the children's presence.
- Children should spend considerable time with both parents, in keeping with the children's needs, stage of development, and wishes, and with the ability and willingness of the parents to spend time with the children.

It is important that these general principles or criteria be established before dealing with the specific questions of where the children will live and at what specific times the children will see each parent. The aim is to help the parents deal with these issues in terms of the children's needs rather than their own bargaining position.

As a further example, if the issue to be resolved is with respect to spousal or child support, the parties could be asked to come to an agreement on some basic principles to apply in resolving this dispute. The parties should be advised by their collaborative lawyers of the criteria set out in the family law legislation, such as the *Child Support Guidelines* and the advisory *Spousal Support Guidelines* as one approach to the issue. In addition, they should be encouraged to generate criteria that fit their own values and concepts of fairness. For example, with respect to spousal support, the criteria might be that the level of spousal support should be fair and reasonable given each spouse's ability to earn income and each spouse's financial needs. Or the parties might decide that the children should enjoy approximately the same standard of living in each home. The parties could then be asked to determine:

- what amount of spousal support should be paid; and
- for how long, or until what conditions occur, should support be paid.

The parties might agree that the following criteria would be important, for example:

- the present level of income of both spouses;
- their educational history;
- work experience;
- the length of the marriage;
- their length of time out of the workforce;
- their need for retraining;
- the financial responsibilities of both spouses;
- the age and health of the spouses;
- the age and health of the children;
- the standard of living enjoyed by the spouses prior to separation;
- the level of income required for both spouses to be self-sufficient; and
- a realistic time frame for achieving financial independence. For some spouses it may be unrealistic ever to achieve full financial independence, but perhaps some partial goal could be reached.

It is important to focus the parties on realistic, objective criteria, rather than each party's position, which may be based on emotional factors, such as a desire for revenge for a matrimonial fault.

The previous discussion centred on improving communication techniques and changing behaviour patterns, which should, in turn, increase the chances of reaching a settlement. While many couples will successfully resolve all of the issues in dispute, some couples will not settle some or all of the issues because:

- One or both do not wish to end the spousal relationship.
- One spouse wants to punish the other spouse for feelings of hurt or humiliation suffered in the marriage breakdown.
- Delaying a settlement is to the spouse's advantage in the courts.
- There is not sufficient trust by one or both spouses to reach a full settlement.
- One spouse has strong feelings of guilt about settling. That is, a spouse may not be able to settle the issue of custody because of a concern that the children will later blame him or her for abandoning them. This type of parent often needs a court order or at least a professional's recommendation before he or she can agree to the other spouse having the primary residence or sole custody of the children.

These are important factors for the mediator and collaborative lawyers to recognize when they arise. They need to be prepared with some special techniques for dealing with each of these potential obstacles to a settlement.

In addition, there are circumstances in which the parties reach agreement that should cause the mediator or collaborative lawyers some concern. For example, situations where one party is too eager to settle, particularly where the settlement may not be in the best interests of the children or may be an unfair or unreasonable financial settlement. This often occurs when:

- one spouse feels completely dominated by the other spouse, or is under physical or emotional duress to reach a settlement (whether the duress is real or perceived). In this situation a spouse may submit to the other spouse's demands to avoid conflict or prevent some feared retaliation;
- the spouses are of such unequal bargaining power, for example, in verbal skills, self-confidence, or control of important resources, that one spouse gives up immediately in defeat;
- one spouse may be prepared to accept an unreasonable settlement on one issue in order to win on the issue that is most important to him or her. For example, in a custody battle, a spouse may forgo reasonable support or a reasonable division of property in order to gain custody.
- one spouse feels totally responsible for the marriage breakdown and wants to atone for his or her guilt by giving up everything to the other spouse; or
- one spouse is so anxious to end the marriage and not have to deal face to face with the other spouse that he or she is prepared to concede everything in the mediation. A variation of this type of individual is a spouse who is so angry at the other spouse that he or she cannot accept anything from that spouse, even if it would be reasonable for the spouse or the children to do so.

Both the failure to settle and an unreasonable settlement should be of concern, particularly when it affects the welfare of children. Several examples will be given of situations described above in order to give the mediator and collaborative lawyer a better appreciation of the problem and of the techniques for resolving or dealing with these situations.

1. Encouraging Parents to Collaborate

Couples who are separating go through a series of stages in a grieving process that is very similar to grieving following the death of a spouse. It is important to understand these patterns and how to intervene so as to move the individuals from a response of denial, anger, hurt, guilt, to one of acceptance. Individuals vary in the time it takes to reach acceptance and many move forward and backward many times before achieving a sense of renewed stability. Therefore, it is essential for the mediator and collaborative lawyer to have the necessary skills to encourage collaborative behaviour, even while the individuals are still grieving their losses.

(A) The Stonewalling Parent

It may be in one party's interest to delay a settlement. This can arise in cases involving custody and access, and in financial disputes. For example, in custody cases, the party who has *de facto* custody of the children is at a considerable advantage in that a court usually awards custody to the parent who has had the primary care and control of the children from the date of the separation. The reason for this is that the court considers the stability of the children to be a very significant factor in determining custody. As a result, the parent who has the care and control of the children at the time of mediation will have less motivation to settle than the party who does not have *de facto* custody. If the mediation is delayed or prolonged and no resolution is reached, the party with *de facto* custody will have gained a considerable advantage over the other party by the time the matter reaches trial.

A stonewalling or delaying tactic can also be used to the advantage of one party over the other. For example, in determining the level of spousal support to award, the court will take into consideration the level of support and the length of time an interim arrangement has been in effect. If one party has managed to survive financially for some period of time on a low level of support, the court will take this level of support into account. It is therefore to the advantage of the payor spouse to delay matters and to agree to a low level of support in any interim agreement.

The reasons for stonewalling set out above are related to improving a spouse's position in court. In some cases a spouse may stonewall for very different reasons, such as:

- not wanting to end the spousal relationship;
- not wanting to lose face by making concessions to the other spouse; or
- not wanting to lose face in the eyes of a third party (for example, a new partner or the spouse's lawyer).

When a mediator or collaborative lawyer suspects that one party is not negotiating in good faith, they should take the following steps:

- *Discuss with the parties the concerns about possible stonewalling.* Perhaps a better way of dealing with this issue is to discuss the significance of a time delay in the first meeting, that is, before either party has shown any evidence of stonewalling. By raising the issue the mediator or collaborative lawyer may prevent this problem from arising;
- *Encourage the parties to come to an interim agreement* that would be the least prejudicial to both parties during the course of mediation or collaborative law;
- *Help the parties to agree on an early termination date*, or at least a date by which progress will be reviewed, at the outset of the mediation or collaborative law in order to prevent one side from prolonging matters unnecessarily.

These are preventive steps that it is hoped will avoid or minimize the effects of stonewalling. If the problem continues, then some of the following techniques could be used to resolve the impasse:

- *Breaking the issues in dispute into sub-parts,* so that the parties can deal with each issue in smaller pieces, rather than an all-or-nothing approach. For example, if access is in dispute, rather than dealing with each spouse's entire access plan, the discussions could focus on whether access should be supervised or unsupervised; whether access should be daytime only or should include overnight visits; whether access should include midweek visits; and whether telephone access should be specified or left open to the parents' discretion. Once agreement has been reached on these types of parameters, then the discussion can focus on such things as how many weekends and for what length of time on a weekend, or on what special days during the year, such as Mother's Day, Father's Day, Christmas Day, or the child's birthday. In the event that the parties reach agreement on some of the sub-issues, they should be praised and encouraged by the mediator for making progress toward a settlement. It is often easier to reach agreement on smaller issues and gradually build toward resolving the entire issue.

- *Meeting individually with each spouse.* This is often called an individual caucus. The individual caucus can be held on a separate day or can be part of a joint session. That is, the mediator or collaborative lawyer can ask one spouse to leave the room so that the mediator or each lawyer can spend some time with each spouse individually before returning to a joint session. During the individual sessions, the mediator or collaborative lawyer can determine what the road blocks are to agreement and can encourage each of the parties to generate some realistic alternatives that may lead to a settlement. It may be easier to arrive at more reasonable proposals in an individual session rather than in a joint meeting, because the parties may be concerned about losing face in each other's presence.
- *Helping the parties refocus their attention on the principles they have agreed upon as the basis for a settlement.* For example, the best interests of the children or a fair and reasonable financial settlement could be discussed in the context of a time delay. The parties could be asked whether it is in the best interests of the children to have a long period of uncertainty with respect to a parenting plan, or whether it is fair and reasonable for the children to suffer unnecessary hardship as a result of a delay in determining support.

If the parties fail to respond to these techniques and if the delay is significantly prejudicing one spouse, then the mediator or collaborative lawyer should state his or her concerns to the parties and the counsel and should terminate or suspend the mediation or collaborative process. This would allow the disadvantaged spouse to make an immediate application to court for resolution of the dispute. In the case of collaborative law, the original lawyers would have to withdraw and new lawyers retained.

(B) THE REJECTED PARENT

A parent who is rejected will respond in one of several ways, namely:

- *intense anger* at the other partner, often in proportion to the feelings of lowered self-esteem, humiliation, or rejection;

- *depression* — the parent may be immobilized from taking any constructive action because of strong feelings of inadequacy resulting from the rejection; or
- *cautious hope* — the parent may believe that the rejection is temporary, or that if he or she makes a change in behaviour a reconciliation will be possible.

It is extremely important to deal with each of these feelings at an early stage. The spouses will not be able to deal with the practical issues in dispute until their feelings have been addressed. Therefore, dealing with feelings actually facilitates mediation and removes a primary obstacle to settlement, namely, the client's self-esteem and feelings about the other partner. It is also important for the parties to stop blaming each other so that they can be mobilized to take more constructive action. This is in their own interest as well as in the interests of their children.

The Angry Parent

There are a number of techniques that can be used to deal with an intensely angry parent:

- *Arrange individual sessions* in the early stages. The client needs an opportunity to ventilate in a supportive atmosphere; however, it could be extremely destructive to the mediation or collaborative law process if the client was permitted to ventilate in the other partner's presence.
- *Help the spouse to identify the source of the anger.* For example, "I am angry because my partner humiliated me by leaving me for someone else." Encourage the spouse to talk through what it is that he or she is specifically concerned about and to share the fears and frustrations that are behind the anger.
- *Determine whether the reasons for the anger are grounded in the past or are continuing in the present.* Ask the spouse to determine in what way the anger will affect the spouses' future relationship.
- *Ask the spouse to consider ways in which the anger could be reduced.* For example, is it important that the partner recognize the cause of the anger and apologize for the humiliation? Does the spouse need to rebuild his or her self-confidence independent of the previous relationship (for example, through a new, more satisfying relationship or through psychotherapy)?
- *Help the spouse to develop techniques* for controlling the anger or expressing it more constructively.
- *Help the spouse to appreciate the effects* on the other partner and in particular on the children, of hanging on to the anger, rather than learning more constructive techniques for dissipating or controlling the anger.

Parents are often motivated to change their behaviour when they recognize the destructive impact on them and in particular on their children. These spouses often need some concrete suggestions for changing their behaviour and some positive feedback to rebuild their self-confidence.

The Depressed Parent

If the mediator or collaborative lawyer believes that a parent is very depressed and overcome by feelings of inadequacy as a result of the marriage breakdown, they should recommend that the individual obtain appropriate professional assistance such as:

- individual psychotherapy or counselling;
- group therapy, that is, a support group of individuals with similar problems;
- vocational counselling; or
- assistance with budgeting or financial management.

The mediator and collaborative lawyer should discuss the client's emotional state with him or her in an individual session before making a recommendation for additional assistance. In the event that the client is too depressed to reasonably negotiate the issues in dispute, the following should be considered:

- *delaying for some period of time* until the individual has the appropriate counselling. This should not be done without discussions with both clients and both counsel. It would be important to discuss the implications of a time delay as opposed to the implications of attempting to proceed when one party is not emotionally able to negotiate on equal terms;
- *continuing once the supportive assistance has been initiated.* In cases where the individual is still functioning at a fairly reasonable level, this might be a desirable alternative; or
- *terminating.* Mediation and collaborative law are not appropriate techniques when the client is extremely depressed.

The Hopeful Parent

It is important to clarify whether the parties intend to separate or reconcile at an early stage. If one party is hoping for a reconciliation and the other is determined to separate, then this information must be clarified so that the parties are not bargaining under a false impression.

It is often the case that one party is unrealistic in his or her hopes for reconciliation. This party may offer to give up virtually everything in order to please the other party, in the hope that the party will return to the marriage. Once the party is disillusioned, he or she is often angry at the mediator or his or her lawyer, as well as himself or herself for permitting an unfair bargain. It is important to clarify each party's position on reconciliation versus separation as early as possible. The mediator or lawyer could discuss this issue further in an individual session.

If one or both clients are depressed persons or need counselling, an early referral should be made for appropriate assistance. For example, if the spouse is anxious about managing financially on his or her own, he or she should be referred for career counselling and budgeting assistance. Such specific information may increase self-confidence and help the spouse to accept being single again.

If one party is making an unreasonable settlement because of unrealistic hopes, the parties should be encouraged to reach an interim, time-limited agreement that can be reviewed at some point in the future when the party may be more realistic.

(C) THE GUILTY PARENT

In this case, the parent who feels responsible for the marriage breakdown may make concessions to the other parent out of guilt, rather than out of a firm belief that a particular plan is fair, reasonable, or in the children's best interests. For example, a parent who has committed adultery may agree to give up all of his or her assets, pay an unreasonably high level of support, or give custody of the children to the other parent in order to atone for his or her behaviour. For this reason the mediator and collaborative lawyer should:

- *be sensitive to non-verbal as well as verbal cues* to indicate that a parent is feeling extremely guilty (for example, excessive crying or little eye contact);
- *determine whether one parent is behaving out of guilt and the other parent is behaving out of a need for revenge.* Once this issue has been identified the parties should be encouraged to talk about it both together and separately;
- *help both of the spouses refocus* away from the assignment of blame and onto the particular issues in dispute. That is, even though a party may have caused the marriage breakdown, that does not necessarily mean that that person is not needed by the children and does not have good parenting skills. Both spouses should be made aware of the fact that in many provinces the legislation specifically states that marital misconduct is not a factor in determining custody of or access to children unless that conduct is relevant to parenting. The federal *Divorce Act*,[1] which applies to all provinces and territories, also takes this position. In such cases, a spouse often needs an acknowledgement or an apology for the impact of this behaviour on their self-esteem before they can move forward with the negotiations. If this can be encouraged and if the spouses understand that a court will not use matrimonial fault as a factor in determining custody, this should help to refocus the process onto the best interests of the children;
- *explain to spouses who are mediating or negotiating financial issues* that most provinces specifically exclude marital misconduct as a factor to be considered in determining eligibility for support or the quantum of

---

[1] R.S.C. 1985, c. 3 (2nd Supp.), s. 16(9).

support. This is the same type of approach as with custody, and should be discussed because spouses often believe that they will be entitled to a higher level of support if they are the innocent party in the marriage breakdown. It is particularly important to clarify this matter, because previous legislation in most provinces did award support on the basis of matrimonial fault. Matrimonial fault is specifically eliminated as a criterion in the *Divorce Act*,[2] which applies across all provinces and territories.

If the mediator or collaborative lawyer is unable to resolve successfully the issue of guilt, and if this guilt is interfering with the ability to reach a reasonable solution, then this should be discussed with the spouse individually with a view to delaying the mediation or negotiation until that spouse receives individual counselling. If the spouse agrees to a delay, this should be discussed with both spouses and both counsel. Following this discussion, if the parent who is feeling guilty wishes to continue the mediation, the spouses should be encouraged to reach a time-limited interim settlement, so that the spouse can reconsider his or her decision at a later date.

If the guilty spouse wishes to proceed to a final settlement, the advice given to the client should be documented and the client should be given a copy of the note outlining the mediator's or lawyer's concerns.

If the client is in mediation, he or she should be strongly encouraged to get independent legal advice before finalizing any agreement. If despite these efforts the client wants to proceed, as long as the settlement reached does not jeopardize the health or safety of the children and the client has legal representation, the mediator should exercise his or her discretion as to whether or not to terminate the mediation.

2. Overcoming Impasses

The mediator or collaborative lawyer may find that the parties get stuck or reach an impasse at several points during the process. Often the reason for the impasse has to do with how the parties are feeling about each other rather than with the substance of the issues in dispute. In order to resolve impasses successfully, the mediator and lawyers have to avoid being caught up in the conflict between the spouses, and have to skillfully redirect the spouses to the practical task of arriving at a negotiated settlement. There are a number of techniques for dealing with impasses, some of which were mentioned previously under the discussion of communication techniques. Examples of approaches that could be used are:

- *Reframing the issue.* For example, "I wonder whether the issue is that the children must be returned home by 5:00 p.m. on Sunday, or whether the issue is really that you feel it is important for the children to have time to unwind and readjust before going to bed following an access visit. If it is

[2] *Ibid.*

the latter, let's discuss how long it takes your children to readjust before their bedtime."

- *Identifying the underlying feelings or problem.* For example, "I get the feeling that you are very angry about having to do all the transporting of the children for access visits. Is that a factor in your refusal to agree to more frequent visits?"
- *Recognizing the impasse.* For example, "We seem to be stuck on this point."
- *Identifying the criteria that can be used to evaluate different alternatives.* For example, if the issue is the choice of a doctor for the children, the parents might suggest such criteria as location of the office, hours of business, specialization (pediatrician versus general practitioner), and access to a particular hospital. Or, if the issue is division of particular assets, the criteria might include the appraised value of the property or a particular mechanism for selection, such as one spouse drawing up two lists of items and the other spouse selecting the list he or she wants.
- *Having each of the clients take responsibility for the impasse.* That is, "We seem to be stuck, what can you do about this?"
- *Providing information to the clients to break the impasse.* For example, information about the effects of parental conflict upon the children.
- *Suggesting several substantive or procedural alternatives,* particularly face-saving options. For example, if one party wants to spend every weekend with the children and the other party wants to offer every other weekend, the mediator might consider alternatives for a compromise. One possibility is that, in those months where there are five weekends, one party could have three of the weekends and the other party two weekends. Another option would be to offer a greater number of long weekends that occur on statutory holidays or professional development days.
- *Holding an individual caucus with each spouse* and then bringing them together after considering the options separately.
- *Letting the parties think about the session and come back with a proposal the next time.* The mediator could give the spouses homework to complete, such as listing the advantages and disadvantages of each of the options that have been considered.
- *Asking the spouses to write out the advantages and disadvantages of the proposals from the other spouse's point of view.* This technique attempts to get each spouse to stand in the other spouse's shoes; that is, it encourages both spouses to consider the others' point of view.
- *Having the spouses submit a written final offer.* The mediator or an impartial financial expert selected by both parties picks the best proposal and uses it as the basis for discussion. This technique is moving somewhat closer to arbitration, although the mediator or expert may not make the final decision.

- *Having a specific issue referred to arbitration.* The parties can select the arbitrator and define the narrow issue in dispute and agree in advance to follow the arbitrator's decision.

3. Reducing Power Imbalances

The mediation process presumes that the parties are able to negotiate with each other on relatively equal terms. If there is a significant imbalance in power between the two spouses, this may undermine the mediation process. While this is also true for collaborative law, the lawyers may be able to offset some of the imbalance. They should still screen for such imbalances and discuss how they will be dealt with.

The following are some reasons for an imbalance of power between the parties:

- domestic violence, including physical, verbal, and psychological abuse;
- lack of information;
- difference in education;
- difference in intellectual ability;
- difference in verbal ability;
- difference in culture or language;
- difference in age;
- difference in socio-economic status;
- difference in personality (for example, dominant versus submissive);
- difference in the availability of a support system for each spouse (for example, extended family, close friends, or organizations such as the church); or
- difference in attitude to the marriage breakdown; that is, one spouse may feel responsible for the marriage breakdown and very guilty about its effects on the family.

The following are methods that might be used for dealing with the various types of power imbalance:

- Referring both the victims of abuse and abusers to appropriate resources, such as shelters, women's advocates, anger management groups, and counselling. In these cases, mediation would usually be terminated.
- Ensuring that the spouses make full disclosure to each other of all relevant information.
- Ensuring that the spouses obtain independent legal advice before signing any agreement.
- Referring the spouses for appropriate outside assistance, such as to an accountant, mental health professional, or vocational counsellor.
- Ensuring that only one individual speaks at a time.
- Preventing the spouses from interrupting each other.
- Preventing one spouse from attacking the other personally.

- Restating the position of the weaker spouse. That is, if the weaker spouse is not as articulate as the stronger spouse, the mediator or collaborative lawyer can help to state the spouse's position more clearly.
- Helping the clients to make more direct statements about their wishes. The mediator or collaborative lawyer can assist the weaker spouse to voice his or her demands, rather than continuing to carry all the responsibility and resenting the more dominant spouse. For example, "I want you to assist with the transportation of children to and from access visits."
- Pointing out certain process aspects of the communication that the spouses may not be conscious of. For example, one spouse may always look at the mediator or lawyers when he or she wants assistance rather than make demands directly to the other spouse, or one spouse may always precede a request for cooperation with a criticism. In a private caucus, this behaviour pattern and the response of the other spouse to this behaviour should be discussed.
- Requesting an individual session with one spouse or recommending an individual caucus during a joint session in order to assist a weaker spouse.
- Giving positive reinforcement and support during the session whenever the weaker spouse demonstrates more assertive behaviour.
- Giving positive reinforcement to the more dominant spouse whenever he or she demonstrates cooperative behaviour.

If the imbalance of power is so great that one or both spouses is unable to assert his or her own position without fear or duress or if the possibility of a fair outcome is in doubt, then this should be discussed directly with both clients and the mediation or collaborative process should be terminated.

4. Involving Other Professionals

There are some problems that arise during mediation or collaborative law that require the expertise of another professional. In some situations, mediation can continue concurrently with the involvement of the other professional. In other instances, mediation may have to be suspended or even terminated. This would depend on the reason for referral. The mediator should discuss both the reason for referral and its effect on the mediation process with both clients before the referral is made.

The following list includes examples of professionals who may have special skills to offer, in addition to mediators or collaborative lawyers:

- *certified financial planners or certified divorce specialists* — for assistance in completing financial disclosure, calculating net family property values, thinking creatively about settlements in order to meet the client's objectives, financial planning;
- *child specialists* — for expertise in meeting with children and assisting in creating parenting plans that meet the needs of the children;

- *accountants* — for information about tax implications, help in understanding corporate financial statements, business valuations, *etc.*;
- *property appraisers* — for appraisals of commercial, residential, and personal property;
- *investment analysts and pension experts* — to determine the present value of pensions, RRSPs, and annuities, and to obtain information regarding returns on investments;
- *mental health professionals* (for example, psychologists, psychiatrists, and social workers) — for emotional support and counselling;
- *vocational counsellors* — for information on career alternatives and retraining; and
- *budget counsellors* — for assistance in money management, particularly with respect to managing household expenses.

C. COLLABORATIVE COMMUNICATION AMONG PROFESSIONALS

While collaborative lawyers and mediators need to hone their skills to encourage their clients to collaborate, as important are skills for collaborative communication with each other. In traditional legal practice lawyers refer to the other counsel as "my friend", but often behave in distinctly unfriendly ways. The tone set and the way collaborative lawyers relate to each other and to other members of the team will have a very significant impact on the way the clients relate to each other.

If lawyers can make the shift from adversarial and battle metaphors of "winning over" or "defeating" the other side, and instead can use their strategic thinking and skill set to "work with" for the benefit of the team as a whole, the collaborative process will almost always succeed. Lawyers have been trained, and their *Rules of Professional Conduct* require, that they behave as advocates for their clients. This creates tension because it seems to contradict the expectations of a collaborative process.[3] What may be helpful for collaborative lawyers is to take a longer term view, which is shared by most clients. That is, for most clients, a successful outcome is not getting the newer car or no financial responsibilities or a piece of property — although they may direct their hurt and anger at these items early in the negotiations; it is

- having a good relationship with their children;
- not causing their children harm through ongoing conflict;

---

[3] 4.01 The Lawyer as Advocate

(1) When acting as an advocate, a lawyer shall represent the client resolutely.

.... Commentary

"The lawyer has a duty to the client to raise fearlessly every issue, advance every argument, and ask every question, however distasteful, which the lawyer thinks will help the client's case and to endeavour to obtain for the client the benefit of every remedy and defence authorized by law. ..." Feb. 2005 at p. 58.

- having the other parent willing to cooperate with them and be flexible if needed;
- having the other parent want to share relevant information and include them in life cycle events;
- maintaining a good relationship with extended family members on the "other side" with whom they previously had a close relationship;
- using their money to provide for their family, rather than fuel unnecessary litigation;
- maintaining their dignity and self-respect — they made a deal they can live with and that provides reasonably for their children;
- arriving at a deal they believe is fair to them and to others;
- achieving some closure and being able to move on to a new life with a new relationship that is not burdened with the past.

In this context, advocacy takes on a different and broader context that reflects the underlying values and interest of clients. While collaborative lawyers do need to maintain their role as advocates, they can assist their client by holding up a mirror to the client's best intentions and ask the client whether they would like to be assisted to achieve this broader and usually more durable set of objectives. This is particularly true of clients entering mediation or a collaborative process.

Collaborative lawyers need to shift their skills from traditional advocacy *against* the other side to advocating on behalf of outcomes that will benefit and be accepted by everyone. In this way the clients will achieve the goals set out above — and will avoid a litigated battle. This requires a thoughtful approach to communication that has as its core — we are part of a team effort to reach an outcome that will be satisfactory to all concerned — the couple as well as children and significant others. The following are suggestions for enhancing communication skills among lawyers, clients, mediators, and other professionals who may be working together in an interdisciplinary team.

- Communicate *respectfully* — as you would with another member of the same team.
- *Do not* send demanding, threatening or disrespectful letters — the clients respond as if the other parent sent the letter. Change the language of "lawyer" letters, *i.e.*, do not use formal legal or adversarial language such as "Parties" or "Versus", or arbitrarily short time lines, *etc*.
- Listen actively to the other lawyer — A helpful rule is "*Listen before you can be listened to*."
- Identify issues of urgency to one or both clients and mention areas of common ground.
- Be responsive and concerned about *both* clients' concerns. If appropriate empathize with the other client (*e.g.*, death of a family member, loss of a job, *etc*.) or acknowledge something positive (*e.g.*, "Thank you for the prompt response to my request for financial information.").
- If concerns about domestic violence, child abuse or control are raised, take them seriously as a problem to be addressed together (unless this

would create a safety risk). Do not minimize or exaggerate the problem. Do not join the client in attacking the other client or defending your client. Try to stay focused on "What is the nature of the problem?" "How does the concern relate to the issues at hand or the ability to negotiate safely, voluntarily and without duress?" And, "What can we do to address the problem in a way that meets everyone's needs and is in keeping with the objectives of a collaborative process."

- Review alternative processes in light of client's wishes, capacity, and circumstances.
- If you and the other lawyer have "baggage" — deal with it separately from your clients. This is an excellent time to retain a mediator to resolve the differences between you.
- Set a positive, optimistic tone. Let the other lawyer know you appreciate the effort he or she is making.
- Meet in a comfortable environment — with refreshments.
- Encourage the clients to take the primary role. Have faith in the *wisdom* of your clients — they have to live with the results. Don't make the clients feel they have to please you with their agreement.
- The focus should be on resolving the clients' situation in the least damaging, most satisfactory way for all who are affected.
- Expand your time frame: Not everything may be comfortably accomplished at once. The clients may be at different stages in their grieving and able to proceed at different paces. Both lawyers need to understand and manage expectations regarding how fast the process will proceed.
- Keep in regular touch with the client and other lawyer to minimize surprises. Check out rumours, fears and assumptions as soon as possible to clarify misunderstandings and prevent matters from escalating. Help the clients anticipate changes in the future and decide the process for addressing these.
- Offer information if requested — do not take over and control either the discussion or the outcome. Stay calm and open to persuasion. Model constructive negotiating skills. Be helpful to the family unit, while respecting your client's interests. Be transparent and reliable.
- Intervene if conversations become destructive: remind clients of guidelines for constructive communication, actively listen to and reframe emotionally difficult topics, ask open-ended questions with an attitude of curiosity — rather than blame or fault finding, use cooling off. Humour sometimes helps to reduce tension. Don't take their lives personally!
- Draft agreements so that they are in language the clients can read to their children and family members. Write in language they will feel committed to carrying out. Don't use legalese. Don't use "husband and wife" — that is what they are NOT going to be — or "Parties", which suggests litigation. Use their names and the children's names to create a personalized document.

- End the process on a note of optimism, congratulating everyone for their efforts, and acknowledging the distance they have come. Build confidence for similar problem solving in the future.

SUMMARY

This chapter has offered a number of suggestions for assisting couples and the professionals to communicate more effectively. If mediators and collaborative lawyers adopt these suggestions, it will increase the likelihood that clients will reach a lasting settlement and be able to problem solve with each other more constructively in the future.

ANNOTATED BIBLIOGRAPHY

Ahrons, C. *We Are Still Family: What Grown Children Have to Say About Their Parent's Divorce.* New York: HarperCollins, 2004. This book reflects the experiences and wisdom of 173 children of divorce. It dispels some of the current, negative myths about the impact of divorce, contains helpful guidance for parents currently struggling with the challenges of separation, highlights individual differences in resilience, and optimistically states that it is never too late to improve the lives of your children.

Ahrons, C. *The Good Divorce: Keeping Your Family Together when Your Marriage Comes Apart.* New York: Harper-Collins Publishers, 1994. Ahrons defines the "good divorce" and challenges the myth that divorce inevitably turns adults into bitter enemies. Ahrons provides a number of specific suggestions to help families continue to meet the needs of their children.

Baris, M., Coates, C., Duvall, B., Garrity, C., Johnson, E., and LaCrosse, E. *Working with High Conflict Families of Divorce: A Guide for Professionals.* New Jersey: Jason Aronson Inc., 2001. This is a valuable guide to several options for assisting "revolving door" clients; that is, those who continually return to court. It contains very helpful descriptions of each role along with potential ethical pitfalls. It also includes practical precedents for contracting with high conflict couples.

Barrette, P. *Positive Parenting During Separation & Divorce.* Ancaster, Ontario: Reconcilable Differences, 1994. This booklet contains helpful information about the needs of children at different stages of development. It also highlights "games" parents play that triangulate their children and add considerable stress following separation.

Boyan, S.M., and Termini, A.M. *The Psychotherapist as Parenting Coordinator in High Conflict Divorce: Strategies and Techniques*. New York: The Haworth Clinical Practice Press, 2005.

Brown, E. *Patterns of Infidelity and Treatment*. New York: Brunner/ Mazel, Inc., 1991. This book explores why spouses are unfaithful and what the consequences are for the marriage.

Eddy, B. *High Conflict People in Legal Disputes*. Canada: Janis Publications Ltd., 2006. This is an excellent reference to understand the dynamics of borderline and personality disordered clients and strategies for managing these difficult clients.

Emery, R. *The Truth About Children and Divorce*. New York: Penguin Books, 2004. This is an excellent, easy to read resource for all professionals involved with separating couples and should be recommended reading for their clients. This book deals with all the practical questions that clients ask and practitioners need to be able to answer, including how to tell children about a separation, developmentally appropriate Parenting Plans, and how these plans need to be modified for high conflict couples.

Goldhar-Lerner, H. *The Dance of Anger: A Woman's Guide to Changing the Patterns of Intimate Relationships*. New York: Harper & Row, Publishers, 1985. This book is an excellent resource for both men and women who want to understand (and change) their repetitive patterns of couple conflict.

Gray, J. *Men Are from Mars, Women Are from Venus: A Practical Guide for Improving Communication and Getting What You Want in Your Relationships*. New York: Harper-Collins, 1990.

Gray, J. *Men, Women, and Relationships: Making Peace with the Opposite Sex*. Hillsboro, Oregon: Beyond Words Publishing, Inc., 1993.

Gray, J. *Mars and Venus Together Forever: Relationship Skills for Lasting Love (A New, Revised Edition of "What Your Mother Couldn't Tell You and Your Father Didn't Know")*. New York: Harper Perennial (a division of Harper-Collins Publishers), 1994. John Gray has written a valuable set of books about male-female communication, including techniques for improving relationships between men and women.

Hickey, E., and Dalton, E. *Healing Hearts: Helping Children and Adults Recover From Divorce*. Carson City, Nevada: Gold Leaf Press, 1994. This is an excellent book to help parents to heal emotionally so that they can in turn help their children deal constructively with the challenges and changes brought by divorce.

Jaffe, P., Wolfe, D., and Wilson, S. "Children of Battered Women." *Developmental Clinical Psychology and Psychiatry.* Newbury Park, California: Sage Publications, 1990. This publication summarizes the research on the impact of family violence on children, including gender differences.

Johnston, J., and Campbell, L. *Impasses of Divorce: The Dynamics and Resolution of Family Conflict.* New York: The Free Press, 1988. This book makes an important contribution toward understanding the dynamics of high conflict couples and offers innovative approaches to mediation.

Johnston, J., and Campbell, L. "A Clinical Typology of Interparental Violence in Disputed-Custody Divorces". (1993), 63 *American Journal of Orthopsychiatry* 1. Based on two studies of high-conflict divorcing families, four characteristic profiles of interparental violence were identified: ongoing or episodic battering by males, female-initiated violence, interactive violence controlled by males, and violence engendered by separation or post-divorce trauma. A fifth profile consisted of psychotic and paranoid reactions. These different profiles generate different issues to consider in mediation.

Kelly, J. "Power Imbalance in Divorce and Interpersonal Mediation: Assessment and Intervention". (1995), 13 *Mediation Quarterly* 2, 85-98. This article presents a framework for understanding the conditions that create unequal power in mediation. A variety of mediator interventions are discussed which may empower disputants when differences in power threaten the integrity of the mediation process and its outcome.

Kubler-Ross, E. *On Death and Dying.* New York: Macmillan, 1969. This is the seminal book on death and dying. Those who work with separated couples observe that adults, as well as children, go through stages of grieving that are parallel to the response of losing a loved one through death.

Lansky, V. *Divorce Book for Parents: Helping Your Children Cope with Divorce and its Aftermath.* New York: Signet (a division of Penguin Books U.S.A., Inc.), 1989. Lansky is a divorced parent with many practical tips for preparing both adults and children for the experience of separation.

Lund, M. "A Therapist's View of Parental Alienation Syndrome" (1995), 33 *Family and Conciliation Courts Review* 3, 308-323. This article explores many possible reasons for Parent Alienation Syndrome and suggests possible interventions.

Macfarlane, J. *Rethinking Disputes.* Toronto: Emond Montgomery Publications Limited, 1997. An excellent overview of ADR processes and the shift from rights-based to interest-based options.

Myers, S., and Filner, B. *Mediation Across Cultures: A Handbook about Conflict and Culture*. San Diego, 1993.

Ross, J., and Corcoran, J. *Joint Custody with a Jerk: Raising a Child with an Uncooperative Ex*. New York: St. Martin's Press, 1996. This is a helpful guide to constructive communication with an ex-spouse. Despite a provocative title, this book encourages self reflection about steps each parent could take to create a less conflicted environment for children.

Sheilds, R., Ryan, J., and Smith, V. *Collaborative Family Law: Another Way to Resolve Family Disputes.* Thomson Canada Ltd., 2003. This is a thorough, clear and reader-friendly book that can be offered to clients to assist them, as well as other professionals who are engaging in a Collaborative Law process. It has many helpful examples of communication skills for both mediators and collaborative lawyers.

Stone, D., Patton, B., and Heen, S. *Difficult Conversations: How to Discuss What Matters Most*. New York: Penguin Books, 1999. This is an excellent skill building book for mediators and collaborative lawyers in their personal and professional lives.

Tannen, D. *That's Not What I Meant*. New York: Ballantine Books, 1987. This readable book shows us why conversations and consequently friendships and marriages can break down even with the best intentions. Often it's not what you say, but how you say it, that counts. The success or failure of any relationship — at home, on the job, or on a date — depends on conversational signals like voice level, pitch and intonation, rhythm and timing, and simple turns of phrase.

Tannen, D. *You Just Don't Understand.* New York: Ballantine Books, 1991. An excellent resource in the field of interpersonal relations, and a readable account of the complexities of communication between men and women. This book helps to put gender differences in communication into a manageable perspective.

Tesler, P. *Collaborative Law: Achieving Effective Resolution in Divorce without Litigation.* Section of Family Law, American Bar Association, 2001. Tesler's book is the first major book in describing in detail the Collaborative Family Law process and how it differs from an adversarial process. It has clear and easy to follow practical examples of communication techniques and ways to prevent and overcome difficulties in collaborative processes.

Trafford, A. *Crazy Time: Surviving Divorce*. New York: Bantam Books, 1982. Trafford, a journalist who experienced divorce, interviewed several hundred separated people in order to better understand the experience of separation. This is a helpful book for parents who are recently separated.

Winslade, J., and Monk, G. *Narrative Mediation: A New Approach to Conflict Resolution.* San Francisco: Jossey-Bass, 2001. This book provides a helpful theoretical model for working with separating couples, particularly with those who have become stuck in their projection of blame and ascription of negative motives to the other. By shifting the "story" each has created about the other, there is often the possibility of reframing the conflict in more constructive ways that allows the parties to move forward and reach agreement.

Chapter Four

Mediation in Practice

A. OBJECTIVES OF MEDIATION, COLLABORATIVE LAW, AND ARBITRATION

This chapter highlights the mediation process, but the discussion of objectives and interest-based theory apply equally to med-arb (at least for the mediation part of the process) and to collaborative law. Each of these process options is the focus of a different chapter.

Mediators and collaborative lawyers tend to have similar objectives and can usually agree on basic ethical standards, although they may use somewhat different procedures or steps in their process. Despite differences in the procedure followed, each step should in some way further such overall objectives as:

- ensuring that both parties feel safe and comfortable expressing their needs and concerns and that any agreement is reached without duress or intimidation;
- fostering cooperation and trust between the parties, such that the parties will be able to share parenting tasks and significant information about their children and their financial needs;
- improving the parties' ability to communicate, such that they can understand each other's feelings about the marriage breakdown and share information and make necessary decisions together;
- providing an opportunity for parties to reassess their perceptions and assumptions about each other;
- ensuring that all relevant parties have an opportunity to have their views and needs heard, such that the parties gain an increasing sense of self-confidence, self-reliance and a feeling they have been dealt with fairly;
- reducing tension and conflict, particularly when children are involved, such that the children can continue to have a close relationship with both parents, free from intense conflicts of loyalty;
- obtaining full disclosure of all relevant facts, such that decisions are made on the basis of adequate information and after a consideration of alternative proposals for resolving the issues in dispute;
- encouraging private ordering and self-determination such that the parties arrive at their own, voluntary resolution of the issues in dispute;
- arriving at a fair and reasonable settlement, such that an adversarial court proceeding is avoided.

Before describing the steps in mediation or collaborative practice (see Chapter 5) or the med-arb and arbitration process (see Chapter 7), it is important to understand the principles underlying these approaches. These principles are based on the Harvard Negotiation Model and are adapted from the seminal book on the subject, *Getting to Yes,* by Roger Fisher and William Ury.[1] These principles are often referred to as *interest-based bargaining* and apply to negotiation as well as mediation, med-arb, and collaborative law. These principles can be contrasted with two other approaches: rights-based and power-based negotiation.

Rights-based negotiation focuses on who is RIGHT according to some external standard, such as the law, a contract, case precedent, or a majority vote. Often a third party decision-maker, for example, a judge or arbitrator, is involved to weigh competing claims and determine who is right. Arbitration and litigation are rights-based processes and result in winners and losers.

Power-based negotiation relies on might is right, whoever has superior power can impose their outcome on the other. The superiority can be in physical power, knowledge, resources, position in a hierarchy, *etc.* Examples of power-based approaches are strikes, lock-outs, threats and violence. In cases of domestic violence, a perpetrator may use intimidation, fear, withholding resources, or physical abuse to control the outcome of negotiations — and undermine any attempt at an interest-based approach.

B. INTEREST-BASED NEGOTIATION

Principled negotiation involves the following steps:

1. Separating the *people* from the problem.

The feelings the parties have about each other should be separated from the objective aspects of the problem. For example, in order to resolve a dispute about household contents, it is important to help the parties get past their anger at each other in order to divide the contents in a rational way, based on what each needs.

The parties should be helped to see themselves as working side by side in attacking the problem, rather than working in opposition and attacking each other. This can be accomplished using structural devices, such as having the parties actually sit side by side facing a flip chart, instead of glaring at each other across a table. Another powerful way to achieve this objective is to have the parties agree on a mutual problem statement. For example: "*How can we divide the household contents fairly so that we each get what we most need or what has the most meaning to each of us?*"

2. Focusing on *interests*, not positions.

A *position* is what a party wants or demands as his or her preferred outcome. A position, as opposed to an interest, is a specific solution put forward by a party

[1] R. Fisher, W. Ury and B. Patton, *Getting to Yes: Negotiating Agreements Without Giving In,* 2d ed. (New York: Penguin Books, 1991).

to settle the issues in dispute. This position is intended to meet the underlying needs or interests of one of the parties. A position represents the best outcome for that party and does not take into account the wants or needs of others. Often, that party cannot even visualize an alternative solution. For example: "*I want custody of the children.*" (As opposed to, "*I want to continue to play an important role in the lives of our children.*")

An *interest* is *why* a party has taken a particular position. Sometimes, interests are subconscious and even the party is not aware of them.

Interests may fall into three categories:

- *Substantive Interests* — These are quantifiable or objective needs such as the matrimonial home, spousal or child support, or custody of the children. A substantive interest might be described as follows:
  - — General: "*I want a home to live in.*"
  - — Specific: "*I want exclusive possession of the matrimonial home for at least five years.*"
- *Procedural Interests* — These are a party's expressed needs with respect to the dispute resolution process. For example: "*It is important that we use a non-adversarial approach for deciding on a parenting plan so that we minimize the conflict between us in the interests of our children.*" Or, "*It is important that I have a voice in the process and see that my views are taken into account.*"
- *Psychological Interests* — These are a party's emotional needs arising out of the behaviour of the other party. For example: "*It is important for me to know that I can trust the other person to keep a commitment both to me and to our children.*" Or, "*It is important that I feel respected and that the other person acknowledge my feelings about the separation.*"

3. Creating a *mutual problem statement.*

Each party has a position, which is the result of a set of interests. In a conflict, the parties proceed as if their interests are necessarily in opposition.

An important task for the mediator or collaborative lawyers is to assist the parties to reframe their conflict into a *mutual problem statement* that encompasses the important needs and interests of all parties. This is a key step in interest-based negotiation as it opens up the possibility that while interests may be different, they are often not in opposition.

A mutual problem statement is a statement of intention by the parties to achieve, to the extent possible, a *win/win* result based on meeting each of the parties' important interests. The format is often: "*How can we on the one hand ... while at the same time ...?*"

For example: "*How can we develop a parenting plan that gives the children the stability and predictability they need while at the same time ensuring that the children maintain a significant relationship with both parents and their extended family?*" Or, "*How can we ensure that there is adequate provision for Sally to live independently and in reasonable comfort when she retires, while at the same time ensuring that William will be able to retire at age 65 and maintain the family cottage for the benefit of the children and grandchildren?*"

4. Generating options for *mutual gain.*

This is a creative process of generating a number of options, beyond each party's initial position, to be sure that the most satisfactory resolution for both parties is achieved. In the case of family mediation and collaborative law, it is important to ensure that the needs and interests of children, extended family members, and new partners are considered.

Too often, each party can see only a small number of alternatives for resolving the dispute. Since these alternatives tend to meet only one party's needs, a resolution is impossible.

Parties should generate as many options as possible, *without comment*, before any evaluation takes place. It is a good idea to record all of the options on a flip chart and summarize them in a progress note, so that the parties can see both their own and the other parties' options. It is helpful to reassure parties that putting an option on the flip chart or in a progress note does not mean it has been accepted, it has just been put forward for consideration.

The parties should be encouraged to propose options that also meet the needs of the other party. This is especially important in order to build trust and goodwill in the process and to stimulate creative mutual problem solving.

It is often helpful to "fractionalize" the options, that is, propose options that address part of the problem, and build incrementally towards a whole solution. This is particularly helpful for complex or emotionally loaded issues.

In a win/win solution, the final agreement is usually constructed from a variety of options, without regard for who actually proposed them.

5. Using *objective criteria* for evaluating options.

Before evaluating the alternatives, the parties should agree on some fair and objective criteria or factors for discriminating between useful and non-useful options, for example, cost, convenience, age of the children, *etc.* Many of the criteria will derive from the *interests* of the parties. Rather than argue over options for personal reasons, it is helpful to use "objective" criteria.

It is important to avoid making decisions based on inadequate information, duress, or conflict avoidance. These decisions are often questioned later and may result in the agreement not being followed. The most durable agreements are those reached *voluntarily*, by *informed* participants, who are not under duress.

These principles form the basis for interest-based negotiation and the mediation model. This model is used for marriage breakdown and other family conflicts (including parent-child and multi-generational issues, child welfare concerns, adoption, small family business disputes, international disputes, work-place conflicts, victim-offender issues, as well as commercial, environmental, and other disputes). While the model is applied somewhat differently depending on the type of issue, the model itself consists of similar steps and objectives.

This chapter applies the interest-based approach to mediation, med-arb, and collaborative law. While there are some differences between the process of mediation and collaborative law, the goals, skills, and application of an interest-based approach make the similarities more significant than the differences. Often, mediation is used to create parenting plans and collaborative law is used to resolve financial and property issues. While the substantive expertise or training of the professionals differs, clients benefit most from a seamless level of cooperation between all professionals engaged in a non-adversarial outcome.

C. APPLYING THE INTEREST-BASED MODEL

1. Developing the Strategy — Prior to the First Session

The eventual success or failure of the conflict resolution process may depend on decisions made at this stage. Many of the issues may seem unimportant or obvious, but they are neither. It is important in mediation, med-arb, collaborative practice, and in arbitration (which is really a rights-based process) to think strategically about each step of the process. In all of these processes the following should be considered:

- contacting both solicitors and/or parties by phone and/or letter;
- clarifying initial expectations of clients and referral source;
- explaining all of the viable options, including the option of litigation;
- determining whether the parties are willing to participate voluntarily;
- assessing the readiness to mediate, negotiate, or arbitrate: Are the parties aware of their rights and responsibilities? Are they able to negotiate/ speak on their own behalf with the other party?
- assessing the emotional state of the clients and children and whether there are urgent issues that are a priority;
- determining whether domestic violence, intimidation, emotional disturbance, drug or alcohol abuse are an issue. A screener (either the mediator or someone selected as a screener for collaborative practice or arbitration) needs to assess safety and appropriateness for the various options;
- addressing who might be asked to participate in the process, including children, extended family members, new partners, divorce coaches, a mediator, valuators, other witnesses (for arbitration), *etc.*;
- exploring the options for designing the process, disclosure required, expected outcome (a memorandum of understanding, a Separation Agreement, or an Award, *etc.*);
- discussing payment of fees; and
- setting date, time, and place to meet.

The following description of the interest-based process is applicable to mediation (including the mediation portion of med-arb) and collaborative practice and is used to address issues where the parties disagree. The arbitration process will be described in detail in Chapter 7. What is special to separation and divorce is that frequently these cases are complex and involve a number of issues with substantive, procedural, and psychological components. Due to the emotional context of separation, the parties often are not clear at the outset as to where they are in agreement and where there are significant differences. Emotional responses may obscure their assumptions about each other. As couples work through the elements of a parenting plan or financial issues, it is helpful for the mediator or collaborative lawyers to expect that even in conflicted cases, there may be areas of agreement. Where there is clear agreement and no evidence of duress, there is no need to follow all the steps of an interest-based process. Instead, the professional acts as a facilitator and identifies and records the agreement.

The interest-based model described below is applied to each item where there are differences.

2. Implementing the Strategy

At the meetings, the parties should try to achieve the following goals:

- The mediator or collaborative lawyer should introduce the process.
- The parties should be assisted to achieve the following goals:
    - — exchange positions
    - — explore interests
    - — define a mutual problem
    - — generate options
    - — establish criteria
    - — reach agreement.

(A) Introducing the Process

The mediator or collaborative lawyer should attempt to:

- Set a constructive tone: Welcome people and put them at ease.
- Establish a joint problem-solving climate.
- Explain the purpose: Make it clear why a process has been initiated, and why this one.
- Describe the process: What steps will be followed in solving the problem?
- Clarify roles: The collaborative lawyers', the mediator's, and the parties'.
- Ask for the parties' explicit commitment to a *collaborative problem-solving process* with a goal of reaching a *mutually acceptable, win/win outcome.*
- Set guidelines for behaviour (respectful communication, no interruptions) and for the meeting process (time limits, opportunities to "caucus", breaks).

(B) EXCHANGING POSITIONS

- The participants exchange positions — Each participant makes an opening statement identifying the issue(s) and outlining what he/she hopes to accomplish in the process. This may include his/her preferred solution. The mediator or collaborative lawyer should ensure that each participant hears and understands the other participant's position.
- Agreements and disagreements are noted — Areas of agreement and disagreement should be noted.
- Issues are prioritized — The parties, with the assistance of the mediator or collaborative lawyers, determine an order of priority for dealing with issues. They should start with those that are least difficult to reach an agreement on, or those that are most urgent.
- The participants develop an agenda — The parties agree on the agenda, including the sequence of items.

(C) EXPLORING INTERESTS

For each issue:

- The participants exchange interests — Each participant's underlying interests, concerns and needs are explored. The mediator or collaborative lawyers should ensure that each participant hears and understands the other participant's interests, concerns, and needs.
- Mutual and non-competing interests are noted — Mutual interests are those that the parties share. Non-competing interests are those that are important to one party and do not interfere with the other party's interests.

Throughout the discussion:

- A collaborative atmosphere should be maintained — It is important to reinforce a constructive sharing of views, and discourage intimidation, threats, or "bottom-lining".

(D) DEFINING A MUTUAL PROBLEM

This encourages the parties to "sit on the same side of the table", solving a mutual problem collaboratively, instead of fighting for their own positions.

- The parties should use mutual and non-competing interests to state a joint problem. For example: "*How can we (meet A's needs) while at the same time (meeting B's needs)?*"

(E) GENERATING OPTIONS

- The problem should be "fractionalized" — The participants should break the problem into smaller pieces and generate options for each piece.
- The parties brainstorm in individual, small group, or joint sessions — They should avoid criticizing each other's options.

- The pie must be expanded (where possible) so that there are increased benefits for all if a solution is reached — This is an *integrative orientation* (as opposed to a *distributive orientation*, which presumes that the pie is fixed, so that if one person gets a share, the others get less).

(F) ESTABLISHING CRITERIA

The parties develop objective criteria for evaluating options, following these steps:

- Start with the mutual problem statement — Each interest becomes one of the criteria.
- Add other criteria — Any other important factors, such as cost, deadlines, *etc.*
- Agree on weightings for criteria — Which criteria are essential in any solution; which are particularly important to either party; which are desirable, if there are sufficient resources, etc.

(G) REACHING AGREEMENT

- The options should be ranked according to objective criteria — Win/win options first, versus win/lose options.
- Then trade-offs should be attempted — The parties should consider exchanging items that have a different level of priority for different participants. Where conflicts are over scarce resources and the pie cannot be expanded, the mediator or collaborative lawyers should ask the participants to consider what they would trade off (*e.g.*, something of lesser significance for something of greater significance to that individual).
- An agreement should be formulated (preferably in writing) — The agreement reached should be specified in as much detail as possible (including timelines and responsibilities). Each participant's role in carrying out the agreement should be clarified.
- Consideration should be given to what will happen if there are future impasses — The parties should consider a process for dealing with future disagreements (*e.g.*, would a Parenting Coordinator be helpful?). They should develop a plan preventatively to avoid unwanted situations in the future.
- There should be a process to evaluate and monitor the agreement — A review might be held, with specific objectives, at a future date (*e.g.*, when an infant enters full-time attendance at school).

The interest-based model described above is put into practice in a series of meetings that will vary with the needs of the particular case and the style of the mediator or collaborative lawyers. The following is an outline of some of the major meetings that might take place in a family mediation, including the objectives and the procedure followed.

The interest-based theoretical model is then applied to a series of steps or meetings in both Mediation and Collaborative Law. What follows is a detailed description of the steps that are followed in a family mediation. See Chapter 5 for a detailed description of the steps in a Collaborative Law model.

D. STEPS IN A MEDIATION

Note: Assume there has already been a screening for appropriateness using an individual telephone or face-to-face interview and/or a written questionnaire completed separately by each parent.

1. Meeting with Counsel

If both parties are represented, the mediator should first determine whether the lawyers are trained as Collaborative Family Law (CFL) lawyers, and if so, whether the clients have retained them to act collaboratively. If so, everyone will have agreed that neither the counsel nor the mediator will be called to court.

(A) OBJECTIVES

Where both parties are represented at the outset of mediation, it is desirable to hold a meeting with both counsel (without the parties) prior to beginning the mediation to accomplish the following objectives:

- To clarify that the mediator will act impartially as between the parties. One concern frequently raised is that the mediator may be biased in favour of the solicitor or client who recommended the mediator. One way of dealing with this spoken or unspoken concern is to have both solicitors meet with the mediator.
- To build trust between the mediator and counsel. Counsel may not have worked with a particular mediator previously and may have some questions and concerns about the mediator's experience and competence for dealing with a particular issue.
- To build confidence in the mediation process as a method for resolving the particular issues in dispute. Counsel need an opportunity to discuss the process their clients will follow, what will happen if one or more issues are not resolved, and how the mediation process will relate to other issues that are not referred to mediation.
- To clarify for counsel the contract with the clients. That is, what is expected of the mediator and what the mediator expects of the clients and counsel. For example, there should be clarification about whether the mediation is open or closed, what issues are to be addressed and whether the mediator is being asked for recommendations in the event that the parties fail to reach an agreement on one or more issues. If CFL lawyers are involved, any recommendations would only be made to the clients and counsel for the purpose of facilitating a settlement. In the

event one or both parents decided to go to court, the mediator and both counsel would withdraw from the case.

- To establish how the mediator's fees are to be paid. It is usual for the clients to share the mediator's fees either equally or, if this is not possible, in proportion to their income. It is desirable to have some splitting of fees so that both parties see the mediator as impartial.
- To obtain from counsel a summary of the history of the case. Counsel should provide the mediator with any relevant documents, reports, or correspondence. Both counsel should have copies of all materials given to the mediator. In collaborative law cases, there would be no court documents.
- To establish a cooperative atmosphere with counsel. This is necessary to encourage counsel to support a non-adversarial approach to resolving the issues in dispute.

(B) Procedure for Meeting with Counsel

The meeting with counsel should be held in the mediator's office if possible, or if not possible, in some other neutral setting (preferably not in the office of either lawyer, unless both lawyers and parties agree). A face-to-face meeting is preferred, but if this is not possible then a conference call could be used.

The clients are usually not invited to attend this initial meeting, because the lawyers are usually more relaxed, more willing to share information, and more direct in stating their concerns if the clients are not present.

During the course of the meeting, the mediator should:

- determine the issues to be resolved in the mediation process (for example, custody and access, child or spousal support, division of property, or exclusive possession of the matrimonial home);
- review with the lawyers the experience and qualifications of the mediator for dealing with the particular issues to be mediated;
- clarify what other issues are in dispute and how the lawyers intend to deal with them (for example, is this a collaborative file with the intention of avoiding litigation or is litigation pending on any other issue, such as support, at the same time as custody and access are to be mediated?);
- clarify whether the mediation is to be open or closed;
- establish whether the mediator is to make recommendations in the event that a settlement is not reached on one or more issues;
- determine whether there are any concerns or questions with respect to the mediator's qualifications, competence, or biases. Invite discussion openly on these matters, because if they are not dealt with at this point, they could act as a hidden agenda later and result in the lawyers losing confidence in any potential settlement reached in the mediation process;
- clarify the procedure to be followed, that is, whether the parties are to be seen together or separately for the initial interview;

- determine whether there are other significant individuals who should be seen during the mediation process. For example, if the mediation concerns custody of or access to children, the mediator is strongly encouraged to meet with the children and determine their views, concerns, and preferences at some point during the mediation process;
- determine whether secondary sources should be contacted (for example, other mental health professionals, such as psychologists, psychiatrists, or social workers for information in relation to parenting capacity or the needs of the children, or an accountant with respect to financial status);
- determine the time frame for the mediation (for example, are there court dates pending? Is there a concern about the status quo in relation to either children or financial matters?);
- explain the need for disclosure of all information that is relevant to the issues in dispute. The mediator should indicate that he or she will determine what is relevant and will need the assistance and cooperation of counsel in ensuring that the parties recognize the need for full disclosure. If financial issues are being mediated, the mediator may ask the lawyers to assist their clients in preparing financial disclosure forms. In order to minimize an adversarial approach and reduce costs, the mediator should assist the clients, with the support of their lawyers, to agree on a single valuator for each asset that requires valuation, such as pensions, the matrimonial home, a family business, *etc*. In cases where custody of or access to children is an issue, counsel should be informed that clients will be asked to sign releases of information for schools, family doctors, mental health professionals, and other sources that may have information relevant to the needs of the children or the parenting skills of the parties.

The mediator should show the lawyers the Mediation Retainer Agreement during this meeting. It is advisable for the mediator to obtain the signatures of the lawyers on the retainer as well as those of the clients, in order to avoid any confusion in the future as to the terms of the retainer and whether the mediation is open or closed. Particularly in closed mediation cases, the mediator is advised to obtain the written agreement of the solicitors not to subpoena the mediator to court in the event that mediation fails and the matter proceeds to court. Having both the lawyers and the clients sign a written retainer outlining their expectations of the mediator prevents future disputes about what the mediator is expected to do, what information the mediator will have available, and how the mediator will be paid.

The mediator should explain to counsel that he or she may contact the lawyers at various stages of the mediation process in order to give them feedback on progress and if necessary to seek assistance from the lawyers in resolving a conflict. It should be made clear that the mediator will not have a confidential relationship with one solicitor, but rather will have open communication with both solicitors, and if an issue of concern arises, both solicitors will be contacted and given full information.

Note that subsequent contacts can be by telephone, by letter, or by face-to-face meeting, if that is necessary. At times, it may be desirable to have a meeting of both counsel with the clients to resolve a particularly difficult issue. During such a meeting, the mediator may spend time with various combinations of persons, for example:

- with the parties alone;
- with the solicitors alone;
- with one solicitor and his or her client and then the other solicitor and his or her client; and/or,
- with all of the parties together.

That is, the mediator can use a form of shuttle diplomacy or hold caucuses with various subgroups in order to resolve a particularly difficult matter. It is advisable at the end of such a meeting to draw up a statement of those issues that have been resolved and the nature of the resolution reached. In addition, any issues not resolved should be noted and a statement made as to how those issues are to be dealt with in the future. Also, any agreement reached may be in the form of an interim agreement or may deal with only one of several issues that have been sent to mediation.

During the course of mediation, the parties may ask the mediator to discuss issues that were not part of the original mediation contract. For example, if the parties have been discussing custody of or access to children, the parties may also wish to discuss exclusive possession of the matrimonial home and possibly support. Usually this occurs in cases where the mediation has been successful in establishing a cooperative atmosphere and in building trust between the parties. The lawyers should be assured that the mediator will not deal with issues that have not been agreed upon without first contacting the lawyers and obtaining their approval. It would be advisable to confirm any changes to the original agreement in a letter or amended mediation contract sent to both counsel and both clients.

2. Meeting with Parties

(A) Objectives of Initial Meeting

The mediator tries to accomplish the following general objectives in the initial meeting with the parties:

- to establish that the mediator will act as an impartial person as between the parties;
- in the event that the clients have not yet retained counsel, to refer them to lawyers, especially collaboratively trained lawyers, to ensure they are informed as to their legal responsibilities and rights;
- to observe the nature of the communication between the parties and to ensure that both appear to be able to articulate their views without threats or intimidation; and

- to reduce tension and help the parties develop more constructive ways of dealing with conflict (this is particularly important if children are involved)

In the event that custody of or access to children is an issue, the mediator attempts to fulfill these additional objectives:

- to help the parties appreciate that their parenting role will continue, even though their spousal role may end;
- to help the parents appreciate the importance to the children of cooperating in their parenting role;
- to provide the parties with information about the effects of separation and divorce on children;
- to obtain a relevant marital history, family history, and a description of the extent to which parenting tasks were shared during the marriage;
- to educate the parents with respect to options available under the law for resolving custody and access issues (that is, for sharing parental responsibilities such as sole custody arrangements, shared parenting and joint custody arrangements); and
- to determine other relevant sources of information with respect to the children's needs and the parenting capacity of each parent (for example, other primary caretakers such as nannies, new partners, members of the extended family, schoolteachers, and family doctors). Preference should be given to individuals with direct, frequent, and fairly long-term contact, especially if they have been involved in an impartial capacity with the family.

If financial matters are at issue, the mediator tries to meet the following objectives:

- to obtain full and complete financial disclosure;
- to obtain the names of relevant sources to contact with respect to financial matters (for example, the family accountant or an experienced real estate appraiser);
- to assist the parties to reach agreement on a single valuator for each asset that requires valuation, *e.g.*, pension or matrimonial home or family business, so as to reduce unnecessary costs;
- if counsel are involved, to suggest that the clients discuss any valuators with their counsel before retaining them to avoid any conflict over the selection;
- to educate the parties about the general guidelines provided under the law with respect to support obligations, division of assets, debts, pensions, and other financial matters; and
- if the clients have not yet retained counsel, to refer them to independent counsel for legal information prior to commencing mediation and certainly before signing any agreement. Where reasonable, the clients should be referred to collaboratively trained lawyers so as to minimize any chance that they will end up in court;

- In any event, the mediator should be careful not to give any legal advice to either party regarding the position that he or she ought to take.

(B) MEETING WITH PARTIES

In order to achieve these objectives, the mediator will usually need to hold several meetings during which the parties are seen together and individually. For the first meeting, some mediators prefer to meet with both parties together and others prefer to meet with both parties individually. There are advantages and disadvantages to each approach and, of course, the mediator should take into account the particular circumstances and feelings of the parties before adopting a particular approach.

An initial meeting with both parties together has the following advantages:

- It encourages the parents to see the mediator as an impartial person.
- It decreases the suspicion and mistrust directed at both the mediator and the other party.
- It highlights the importance of communication between the parties.
- It allows the parties to hear each other's views on why the marriage broke down and to deal with unresolved emotional feelings between the parties.
- It sets the stage for dispute resolution directly between the parties.
- It sets the focus on improved communication, particularly with respect to parenting, rather than on individual positions in the conflict.

The advantages of an individual meeting are as follows:

- The parties may be more comfortable meeting the mediator alone, prior to a confrontation with the other party.
- It permits each spouse to tell his or her version of the marriage breakdown without interruption by the other spouse.
- It allows each spouse to develop rapport individually with the mediator in a less stressful environment.
- It offers an opportunity for venting emotional feelings and for obtaining individual support from the mediator prior to beginning negotiations.
- It allows the mediator to evaluate each spouse individually and determine the relative bargaining power, the attitude to reconciliation, and any significant concerns or allegations about the other spouse with respect to the children.

In cases where domestic violence is suspected, or where there is insufficient background information, the first meeting should be an individual meeting. For inexperienced mediators, it is probably best to start with an individual meeting.

Whether the initial meeting is held jointly or with the parties individually, the mediator should ensure that the parties feel relaxed and comfortable. Each party should be reassured that he or she will have an opportunity to be heard without interruption and will have an opportunity to respond to any concerns or allegations raised by the other party. If the parties are particularly anxious, it may be easier to deal with basic demographic information at the outset, rather than highly charged emotional issues.

At this meeting, the mediator should review the mediation contract for the following purposes:

- to ensure that there is agreement on the issues to be resolved in mediation;
- to determine whether the mediation is open or closed;
- to determine whether the mediator is expected to make recommendations;
- to ensure the clients are aware of the importance of independent legal advice and in particular are given information about Collaborative Family Law lawyers;
- to determine what should happen should one or both parties decide to go to court;
- to establish a basic procedure to be followed in the mediation;
- to determine who needs to be seen; and
- to determine how the fees will be paid.

Provided domestic violence is not a concern, the mediator should ask what has led to the decision to separate, then obtain a history of the marriage and a family and parenting history (this is particularly important if custody of and access to children are an issue). The mediator should also determine the present status of the parties with respect to each of the issues in dispute that are referred to mediation.

If the parties are meeting together, the mediator should ensure that each party has an opportunity to present his or her version of the marital and parenting history and his or her position on each issue, without being interrupted by the other party. It is advisable for the mediator to explain the communication process in advance, so that the parties do not feel personally attacked by the mediator if the mediator intervenes to discourage interruption. It is also advisable for the mediator to explain some basic ground rules, such as the following:

- Each party should make statements about how he or she personally feels, but not about how he or she believes the other person feels.
- Each party should not refute or criticize how the other person feels. That is, each person can only know how he or she feels and should not make disqualifying or denigrating statements about the other party.
- The parties should ask each other questions to determine how the other person felt or perceived an event, rather than presuming how the other person felt and then attacking that feeling or perception.
- If a party wishes to disagree with a factual statement or a perception of an event, the mediator should assure both parties that they will each have a turn to respond after the other party speaks. It is important for the mediator to encourage good listening skills from the initial meeting with the parties.

It is often important to clarify each person's position with respect to the marriage breakdown. Some individuals may still be hoping for a reconciliation, while others may be well along in the process of accepting a divorce. If there is a real imbalance between the parties in their attitude to the marriage breakdown, this could undermine the mediation process, whether the issues relate to children or to finances. If one partner is extremely angry, hurt, depressed, or unrealistically expecting a reconciliation, these feelings need to be discussed and clarified before the actual process of negotiation can begin.

The parties should then be asked their position on each of the issues to be mediated. It is helpful to put these on a flip chart to ensure clarity and to ensure that each party feels that his or her preferred outcome has been heard.

Beginning with the least contentious issue, the parties should be encouraged:

- to explain why they feel their positions are so important. That is, they should explain their interests so that each fully understands the needs and concerns of the other party.

Once the interests are understood, then the parties should be encouraged:

- to begin generating options or alternative solutions to each of the issues in dispute;
- to see that a successful settlement is usually one in which each party feels that he or she has made gains on some issues that are particularly important to that individual and has made concessions on other issues that may be more important to the other person; and
- to understand that negotiations are rarely successful if one party tries to be a total winner and to humiliate the other party by a total defeat.

The mediator should demonstrate good problem-solving techniques, such as helping the parties generate a range of alternatives and apply objective criteria to evaluate these alternatives.

In the first meeting it is important to obtain the parties' agreement to maintain the status quo with respect to the issues in dispute. It may be necessary to develop an interim plan for such matters as interim custody and access, interim support, or exclusive possession of the matrimonial home (if these issues are in dispute). To the extent possible, these interim plans should not unduly prejudice either party with respect to his or her legal position. However, both parties should recognize that interim arrangements may have long-term consequences if the parties do end up in court.

(C) PARENTING PLAN

The most important goal of the parenting meetings is the development of a Parenting Plan. This may take several meetings, depending on the level of cooperation between the parties, their ability to communicate with each other, and any special needs of the children or special concerns raised by the parents. While parents entering mediation are focused on who will have "custody" of the children and on a regular residential schedule, this is only a small part of a larger Parenting Plan. In fact, a well thought out Parenting Plan includes agreements as to how parenting responsibilities will be carried out, how decisions are made, how parents will communicate, how mobility and other significant (predictable and unforeseen) changes will be handled, and addresses many other issues that affect a particular family. An example of a Parenting Plan outline can be found at Appendix II.7. The mediator tries to achieve the following objectives in these meetings:

- to clarify how each parent will contribute to carrying out the tasks or responsibilities of parenting (such as, who will transport the children to and from school, sports activities, dance classes, swimming lessons, doctor and dentist appointments; who will stay home with the child when he or she is ill or make daycare arrangements during school breaks or on professional development days if both parents are working);
- to determine how significant decisions concerning the children will be made (for example, will decisions about the children's health care, choice of school, religious upbringing, or extracurricular activities be made by one parent, by one parent after consultation with the other, or by both parents jointly?);
- to discuss and agree on the involvement of extended family members and new partners (for example, will new partners be introduced to the children? When? Will grandparents or new partners be welcome at extracurricular activities? What if the other parent plans to attend? Who can care for the children if both parents are unavailable? How will the children feel about these decisions?);
- to clarify the residential schedule, that is, the times that the children will spend with each parent, during the school year (for example, will the children spend alternate weekends with each parent? If so, how is a weekend defined — that is, does it begin on Thursday or Friday after school or Saturday morning? Does it end Sunday night or Monday or Tuesday morning? Will the children spend time midweek with the other parent? If so, how often and will it be for dinner or for an overnight? Or, will the children spend alternate weeks in each parent's home? Or will the parents alternate homes on a weekly basis with the children remaining in the matrimonial home (a plan known as "nesting")? Will there be opportunities for each parent to have some "one-on-one" time with each child to adjust to the separate interests and stage of development of each child?);
- to clarify how the children will spend the school breaks, statutory holidays, professional development days, children's and parents' birthdays, Mother's Day/ Father's Day, religious events, *etc.*;
- to establish the process for dealing with a material change in either parent's or the child's circumstances (for example, a parent's proposal to move to a different jurisdiction with the children of the marriage, the birth of children from a new relationship, or the inability to care for the children as a result of disability, death, or changed economic circumstances); and
- to determine a dispute resolution mechanism for handling disagreements about significant parenting issues (for example, discussion between the parents themselves, a return to mediation, negotiation between solicitors,

parenting coordination (med-arb), or, if all previous steps fail, arbitration or litigation).

It is important to clarify with the parents that as long as both have access to the child, they are equally entitled to information about the child's school progress, medical and dental care, and other information relevant to the child's well-being. For example, both parents can ask to attend parent-teacher meetings, request copies of report cards, or ask to speak to the child's health-care providers, as long as there is no order to the contrary. This is often reassuring to the parent who spends less time with the child.

The usual mediation process involves a number of joint as well as individual meetings. Depending on the nature of any issues to be resolved, this may include meetings with children, new partners, grandparents, and other individuals, for example, if their consent is needed for certain decisions or if their cooperation is needed for parts of the Parenting Plan.

3. Meeting with Parents and Children

(A) Objectives

In the case of custody or access issues, it is generally recommended that the mediator, and possibly the arbitrator, meet with the children directly in order to determine their views, concerns, and preferences. This presumes that the mediator (or arbitrator) has the appropriate training and skill to interview children. If the mediator (or arbitrator) does not have such training, he or she should partner with a child specialist or contact another professional who already has an ongoing relationship with the child (*e.g.*, a teacher, play therapist, or counsellor).

If the mediator is expected to prepare a report with recommendations or if the arbitrator is expected to prepare a custody award, it is important for him or her to see the children alone, and to see the children in conjunction with each parent, in order to form an impression about the parenting arrangements that may best meet the children's needs.

Depending on the issues in dispute, the parents' expectations of the mediator or arbitrator, and the needs of the case, the following types of meeting may be held.

A Meeting of the Entire Family

This is a meeting of all of the children, with both parents present. It is recommended in cases where the parties have not as yet separated and in cases where the parties have separated but there is a history of ongoing conflict involving polarization of the children's feelings about the parents. The primary aim of such a meeting would be for the parents to explain to the children together that the purpose of mediation is to arrive at a cooperative settlement or that arbitration is to work out a plan with both parent's participation.

A Meeting with Each Parent and All of the Children

This permits the mediator or arbitrator:

- to observe the parenting style of each parent separately with all of the children;
- to note the capacity of each parent to offer affectionate, supportive behaviour;
- to determine similarities and differences in each parent's ability to set reasonable limits and apply discipline techniques; and
- to assess the parents' respective awareness of the children's needs and their willingness to participate in various aspects of parenting.

This information could be the basis of an important discussion with the parents about their perception of the children's needs and differences in their approach to parenting or could be used as evidence to establish the children's best interests.

A Meeting with Each Parent with the Children Individually

This is recommended where a child has a conflict with one parent. For example, children are often caught up in a tug of loyalties between the parents and may express a great deal of anger toward one parent. An individual meeting may allow the child and parent to begin resolving their difficulties. Often, the source of the difficulties is that the child feels abandoned or rejected by the parent and is expressing his or her own feelings through anger.

A Meeting with All of the Children

This is particularly useful when the children are very supportive of each other or in cases where the children have been polarized as a result of a loyalty conflict, with each child supporting a different parent.

A Meeting with Each Child Individually

This meeting permits the mediator (or arbitrator):

- to determine each child's individual concerns and preferences;
- to assess the emotional impact of the separation on each child; and
- to determine whether the child has experienced abuse or witnessed abuse.

This meeting is important when the child is old enough to express concerns or has a point of view, and the parents are unsure what type of plan will be most appropriate for a particular child. If older children are not offered an opportunity to express their views and concerns, they may resist the plan put forward by their parents.

A Meeting with Each Parent Individually

This is not possible in arbitration but is part of the mediation or med-arb process. It gives the mediator an opportunity:

- to obtain relevant family history;
- to determine the specific concerns and wishes of each spouse, including concerns about abuse or intimidation;
- to give each parent feedback about the needs, interests, and wishes of each child; and
- to explore alternatives in a less threatening, more supportive atmosphere.

A Meeting with All of the Children and Both Parents to Achieve Closure

In high-conflict families, it may be desirable for the mediator to have the children present immediately after the parents reach an agreement, in order to explain the terms of the agreement as they affect the children. The children may be helpful in encouraging the parents to take a more cooperative approach in their future dealings with each other as parents. For example, the children can tell the parents how upsetting it is when they fight and ask the parents to behave in a friendlier, less hostile manner, particularly when the children are present. It should be agreed that the children will not be used as message carriers between the parents and that the children can object if either parent makes negative statements about the other.

(B) MEETING WITH PARENTS AND CHILDREN

Where some combination of meetings is being held between the parents and the children, the following procedures are recommended.

In cases where the mediator is expected to prepare a report with recommendations or an arbitrator an award, it is preferable to observe the children and their parents in a natural setting, such as their home, rather than in the more formal, unfamiliar atmosphere of the mediator's or arbitrator's office. Children, particularly children under the age of 10, are usually far more comfortable and likely to respond more openly in their home setting. However, this is a matter of individual preference, and may involve considerations such as the cost and convenience of a home visit.

The parents should give the children a clear statement that each child can speak freely and openly with the mediator or arbitrator and not fear any recriminations or pressure to divulge to the parents what they have said. It is helpful if parents can explain to the children that they will not be hurt or upset by what the children say, and encourage the children to speak honestly so as to create a parenting plan that will be in the children's best interests.

Each child should be asked if there is anything that he or she does not want shared with the parents. The mediator or arbitrator should explain that the child's safety is most important and he or she may not be able to keep information confidential if the information suggests that the children are at risk of harm.

The mediator should make it clear at the outset that the parents will be making the decisions about the children. That is, neither the children nor the mediator will be making the decisions; however, input from the children is important in arriving at decisions. The mediator should reassure the children that the mediator will not ask the children to state which parent they love most or who they want to live with.

In the case of arbitration, the arbitrator will be deciding after gathering evidence presented by both parents and the children. In this case the arbitrator can reassure the children that they will not be asked to take sides and that their parents have selected the arbitrator to assist them in arriving at the best parenting plan.

In addition, the children need reassurance that each parent:

- will take care of the children's basic needs, despite the separation and divorce;
- will continue to love the children and that the children will be permitted to love both parents;
- will make an effort not to undermine the relationship between the children and the other parent (for example, by belittling, criticizing, or making negative comments about the other parent in the children's presence);
- will not pressure the children to reject the other parent or manipulate the children to choose him or her;
- will not use the child as a messenger, that is to carry messages between the parents; and
- will support the children's right to respect and love both of their parents and their extended family and to maintain a close and loving relationship with all of these important individuals.

The individual meeting with each child must be held in private, in a setting that is as comfortable as possible for the child, that is, preferably in their own home and in a room that the child chooses.

During the course of the meeting with each child, the following types of information should be gathered:

- feelings about the separation — depression, anger, feelings of rejection or abandonment, feelings of relief;
- reconciliation wishes — how realistic does the child feel these wishes are?
- the child's basic daily routine with each parent;
- the amount of time spent with each parent before and after the separation;
- if the parents are already living separately, how the child feels about the amount of time spent and the pattern — too little or too much time with each parent?

- is the pattern of time too frequent or too widely spaced, are the blocks of time too short or too long, are there too few or too many overnight visits?
- the importance to the child of remaining in the matrimonial home and the neighbourhood — close to friends, school, community activities;
- the parenting responsibilities of each parent during the marriage and subsequent to the marriage (for example, feeding, bathing, shopping, doctor appointments, after-school activities, wake-up and bedtime routines);
- the attitude of both parents to contact with and telephone calls from the other parent — is contact with the other parent encouraged or obstructed?
- whether the parents are prompt in picking up and delivering the children;
- whether the parents follow any interim schedule reliably;
- the attitude of the parents to each other and their behaviour at transfer times or whenever the child is present;
- the relationship of the child to each parent, especially the feeling of being valued and supported;
- the relationship of the child with siblings, step-siblings, and extended family and whether these relationships are encouraged or undermined by each parent;
- discipline techniques of each parent — is the child afraid of either parent or fearful of their conduct toward the other parent?
- loyalty conflicts — to what extent do these seem to be fostered by the parents?
- symptoms of stress or disabilities — school performance, difficulties with peers, nightmares, alcohol or drug abuse, emotional difficulties, physical symptoms;
- strengths and weaknesses of each parent in terms of parenting capacity, drug or alcohol abuse, life-threatening illness, emotional difficulties, *etc.*;
- the relationship between each parent and any new partner and between each child and that partner;
- the likelihood that the parents could act cooperatively in the best interests of the children in future parenting arrangements; and
- the child's wishes regarding changes in present arrangements or relationships.

4. Meeting with Significant Others and/or Collecting Information from External Sources

(A) Objectives

Depending on the type of issues being dealt with in mediation, and whether any individuals have relevant information or are having a significant effect on the process (either facilitating or obstructing the process), the mediator should consider the following meetings or data collection:

Note: In arbitration this information might better be presented as evidence in a hearing, as there is a concern about data collection when the parties do not have a chance to respond.

- Meeting individually with new partners and a joint meeting with both parties and any new partners. The purpose of this meeting would be to determine the new partner's role with respect to parenting responsibilities for children or with respect to financial matters such as contribution to household expenses and spousal support. If there is ongoing conflict between a parent and new partner, it is recommended that an additional meeting be held with the new partner(s) and the two parties after an agreement has been reached by the parties. The purpose is to ensure that the new partner(s) will support the settlement and to reduce tension.
- Meeting with nannies or other significant caretakers to obtain information with respect to parenting arrangements, children's care, special needs of children, and ability of each parent to meet these needs. This meeting is more appropriate in open mediation if the mediator is being asked for recommendations.
- Telephone call or meeting with school teachers to obtain information with respect to each child's school performance, special academic needs, and involvement of parents in meeting these needs.
- Telephone call to family doctor to obtain health care information about any special dietary needs, allergies or other health considerations.
- Telephone call to other mental health professionals who have been offering counselling assistance, to obtain information about their emotional needs, family relationships, and other matters relevant to parenting arrangements.
- Telephone call or meeting with property appraisers, business valuators, or pension valuators to obtain appraisals of all interests in property.
- Telephone call or meeting with the accountant to obtain information on the financial needs and means of each party and on each party's net family property.

5. Contacts upon Completion of Mediation

At the point of termination of the mediation, either because an agreement has been reached or because the mediation process has been unsuccessful, both counsel should be contacted by the mediator.

If the mediation process has reached an impasse on one or more issues, the mediator may suggest a meeting with both counsel to determine whether there is any possibility of breaking the impasse and resuming mediation or achieving a settlement on the outstanding issue(s) through negotiations between the lawyers. This is particularly helpful if collaboratively trained lawyers are involved.

In med-arb, if an impasse is reached, the arbitration will proceed following a discussion with counsel and the parties as to the level of formality desired. If either party requests a hearing, then a hearing will take place, in person or by conference call. Other options include written submissions, brief oral submissions, final-offer selection or other agreed-upon steps prior to the arbitrator releasing an award to the parties and their counsel.

Following the successful completion of the mediation process, the mediator prepares a draft memorandum of understanding with respect to the issues that have been resolved. The parties should be encouraged to obtain independent legal advice prior to signing any agreement. A copy of the memorandum should be sent to each party's solicitor to review with his or her client. If a collaborative process has been chosen, this is an ideal time to hold a final five-way meeting so that any proposed changes can be discussed, and any agreed-upon changes can be incorporated into the memorandum of understanding.

If the mediator is not a lawyer, then either one of the lawyers should redraft the memorandum to include the appropriate release clauses, and other necessary legal formalities. Another option is to append the memorandum of understanding with respect to a Parenting Plan to the rest of the Separation Agreement.

6. Reporting Differences Between "Open" and "Closed" Mediation

If the mediation was *closed mediation* and no issues were resolved:

- the mediator should send a letter to counsel indicating that no agreement was reached; and
- a copy of the letter should be forwarded to each party.

If the mediation was *closed mediation* and agreement was reached on some issues:

- the mediator should prepare a draft memorandum of understanding with respect to those issues that were resolved;
- the mediator should prepare a covering letter outlining which issues were not resolved;
- the mediator should not comment upon or make recommendations about the issues that were not resolved; and
- the mediator should send a copy of the memorandum of understanding and the covering letter to both counsel and both parties.

If the mediation was *open mediation* and one or more issues were not resolved:

- the mediator should prepare a draft memorandum of understanding with respect to those issues that were resolved;
- in a report or letter, the mediator should indicate those issues that were not resolved. If the mediator was asked to prepare recommendations, then the mediator should submit his or her recommendations for resolving the outstanding issues;
- the mediator could comment on the process followed and each party's position with respect to the unresolved issues; and
- the mediator could indicate that he or she would be willing to assist the parties should there be any difficulties in the implementation of the mediation settlement or should difficulties arise at a later date.

SUMMARY

This chapter contains a detailed description of the steps in the mediation model, with an emphasis on the development of a Parenting Plan. Suggestions are made as to how the mediator can work with the lawyers for the parties in the event that mediation reaches an impasse. If the mediation is successful, the mediator prepares a memorandum of understanding outlining the agreement reached. Similarities were noted between the steps in mediation, med-arb, and arbitration. See Chapter 7 for a more detailed description of the arbitration process.

ANNOTATED BIBLIOGRAPHY

Ahrons, C. *We Are Still Family: What Grown Children Have to Say About Their Parent's Divorce.* New York: HarperCollins, 2004. This book reflects the experiences and wisdom of 173 children of divorce. It dispels some of the current, negative myths about the impact of divorce, contains helpful guidance for parents currently struggling with the challenges of separation, highlights individual differences in resilience, and optimistically states that it is never too late to improve the lives of your children.

Bienenfeld, F. *My Mom and Dad Are Getting a Divorce*. EC. Corp., 1980. This is a book for young children to read to help them deal with their feelings with respect to separation and divorce.

Blau, M. *Families Apart: Ten Keys to Successful Co-Parenting*. New York: Berkeley Publishing Group, 1995. Blau draws on her experience and research as a divorced parent. She identifies and discusses the factors that promote successful co-parenting.

Baruch Bush, R., and Folger, J. *The Promise of Mediation: Responding to Conflict through Empowerment and Recognition*. San Francisco: Jossey-Bass Publishers, 1994. This is an important book dealing with the theoretical basis for or objectives of mediation. The authors describe four different theories or "stories" about the goals of mediation: namely, the "Satisfaction Story", the "Social Justice Story", the "Transformation Story", and the "Oppression Story", and recommend a transformative model in cases of ongoing relationships.

Coleman, Daniel, *Emotional Intelligence: Why It Can Matter More Than IQ*. New York: Bantam Books, 1997.

Coulter, L. *Two Homes: A Parent's Guide to Joint Custody in Canada*. Toronto: HarperCollins Publishers, 1990. Coulter, a divorced parent, writes this book as a guide for parents who are considering a shared Parenting Plan. She discusses different types of Parenting Plans, as well as the impact of divorce on children.

Emery, R. *The Truth About Children and Divorce.* New York: Penguin Books, 2004. This is an excellent, easy-to-read resource for all professionals involved with separating couples and should be recommended reading for their clients. This book deals with all the practical questions that clients ask and practitioners need to be able to answer, including how to tell children about a separation, developmentally appropriate Parenting Plans, and how these plans need to be modified for high conflict couples.

Erickson, S., and McKnight Erickson, M. *Family Mediation Casebook: Theory and Process*. New York: Brunner/Mazel, Inc., 1988. This book contains several case studies of families in mediation and is particularly helpful for new practitioners.

Fisher, R., Ury, W., and Patton, B. *Getting to Yes: Negotiating Agreement Without Giving In, Second Edition.* New York: Penguin Books, 1991. This was the seminal book that began the interest-based or principled approach to negotiation and sets out the theoretical framework for interest-based mediation.

Folberg, J., Taylor, A., and Salem, P. *Divorce and Family Mediation: Models, Techniques, and Applications*. Guilford Press, 2004. This thorough text covers the theory and practice of mediation with articles by many leaders in the family mediation field.

Gold, L. *Between Love and Hate: A Guide to Civilized Divorce*. New York: Plenum Press, 1992. This book looks at the impact of separation and divorce on parents and children. It has a number of practical tools for assisting parents in arriving at parenting arrangements post-separation. It is a very thorough and constructive guide that would be useful for mediators and parents to read.

Johnson, L., and Rosenfeld, G. *What You Need to Know to Help Kids Survive a Divorce: Divorced Kids, a Positive, Practical Guide to Help Children Cope With: The Loss of a Relationship, Feelings of Abandonment, Step-Families, Unspoken Fears, and Much More*. New York: a Fawcett-Crest Book, published by Ballantine Books, 1992.

Johnston, J., and Campbell, L. *Impasses of Divorce: The Dynamics and Resolution of Family Conflict*. New York: The Free Press, 1988. This book sets out a model and practical steps for dealing with high conflict couples.

Mayer, B. *The Dynamics of Conflict Resolution: A Practitioner's Guide.* San Francisco: Jossey-Bass, 2000. This is an excellent text for understanding the nature of conflict and strategies for dealing with it constructively.

Mayer, B. *Beyond Neutrality: Confronting the Crisis in Conflict Resolution.* San Francisco: Jossey-Bass, 2004. This is an advanced theoretical book that questions the role of the mediator and asks whether our task is the *resolution* of disputes OR the *management* of more intractable conflicts.

Ricci, I. *Mom's House, Dad's House: Making Two Homes for Your Child, Second Edition.* New York: A Fireside Book, published by Simon & Schuster, 1997. This is a practical and systematic guide for parents who are considering a shared parenting arrangement after divorce. Ricci describes how to shift from a spousal relationship, which is ending, to a parenting relationship, which is continuing. She has a number of practical tips, checklists, guidelines, sample agreements, *etc.*, which parents can adapt to their own situation.

Rofes, E. *The Kid's Book of Divorce: By, For, and About Kids.* New York: Vintage Books, a division of Random House, 1982.

Saposnek, D. *Mediating Child Custody Disputes, Revised Edition.* San Francisco: Jossey-Bass Publishers, 1998. This book is a useful guide for mediators and contains a number of concrete suggestions and case examples of mediation in practice.

Taylor, A. *The Handbook of Family Dispute Resolution Mediation Theory and Practice.* San Francisco, California: Jossey-Bass, 2002. This is an excellent text for mediators helping to create Parenting Plans. There is a very helpful developmental guide to parenting arrangements by age of child and nature of the parent-child relationship.

Visher, E., and Visher, J. *How to Win as a Step Family, Second Edition.* New York: Brunner/Mazel, Publishers, 1991. This is a very helpful book, with many practical suggestions, to guide parents in creating a successful step-family.

Chapter Five

Collaborative Practice

A. SEPARATION AND DIVORCE

Since the last edition, there have been some important additions to the menu of dispute resolution alternatives that supplement, work cooperatively with, or offer an alternative to mediation. One major change across North America is the recognition that collaborative practice involves a working team of lawyers and other professionals. The following objectives are shared by these processes, namely:

- they are non-adversarial and win-win, rather than win-lose;
- they are premised on interest-based negotiations;
- clients require independent legal advice, while maintaining control over decision-making;
- professionals act as advisors, respectful communication role models and coaches for the clients;
- the focus is on constructive problem solving with all participants seeking mutually beneficial solutions, rather than attacking each other and seeking solutions that benefit one side to the detriment of the other;
- an interdisciplinary approach is desirable in most cases. That is collaboratively trained lawyers work cooperatively with one or more of the following: mediators, divorce coaches, certified financial planners or certified divorce specialists, financial planners, pension valuators, business valuators, real estate appraisers, or others as required;
- the professionals model constructive communication skills, including active listening, reframing, and "I" messages to diffuse strong feelings and build trust;
- clients are encouraged to take the primary role in negotiating agreements that they believe will meet their own and their children's needs. The professionals offer their assistance, in actively seeking a win-win outcome as defined by the clients;
- the professionals' knowledge and creative problem-solving skills are directed at reaching an integrative solution that everyone can say "yes" to and that the parties feel committed to uphold;
- both parties and the professionals must sign a Collaborative Participation Agreement at the outset, agreeing *not to litigate* if an impasse is reached;
- both parties and the professionals agree to withdraw if a party chooses to litigate, except as otherwise agreed to by both parties in their Collaborative Participation Agreement;

- before substantive issues are addressed, all professionals and the participants agree on guidelines for respectful communication (both within and between sessions) and a process for resolving conflicts or addressing potential impasses;
- all participants agree to protect the children by not involving them as confidants or combatants in the disputes;
- clients do not engage partisan experts, they retain professionals jointly who act in an impartial manner;
- collaborative professionals are bound by special Rules of Conduct that encourage constructive problem solving and discourage hostile correspondence, angry affidavits, threats of litigation, take it or leave it offers or other intimidating or power-based tactics;
- the parties are required to act in good faith and to make full disclosure of all relevant information at the earliest opportunity to ensure a fair and expeditious settlement;
- compared to litigation, the process is likely to be more affordable and less emotionally stressful.

While these processes share many common objectives, there are significant differences, largely based on choices clients make as to their preferred primary process or their preferred primary professional. Clients now have a number of non-adversarial, interest-based options and need to reflect on their own situation and the special features of each option in order to select between them. The exciting new development is that a number of professional disciplines are being taught the same non-adversarial process skills so that clients are assured of a team of resource professionals all committed to the same goal — a client-centred, efficient, good faith process that minimizes destructive conflict.

Descriptions of each of the major process options and the roles of different professionals are set out below.

1. What Is Collaborative Family Law?

Collaborative Family Law ("CFL") is an exciting development in Family Law that has spread to Ontario via the United States and the Western provinces. Both clients select collaboratively trained lawyers who blend the communication skills of mediators with the problem-solving skills of lawyers.

CFL represents a paradigm shift from the traditional role of a lawyer. Fundamentally, a collaborative lawyer uses his or her skills to model and teach clients how to be more effective negotiators. Collaborative lawyers act as legal advisors and process facilitators, rather than decision-makers.

The key to CFL is that everyone agrees that they will not litigate and *if one client decides to litigate, contrary to this agreement, both lawyers must withdraw.*

(A) STEPS IN COLLABORATIVE FAMILY LAW*

CFL follows a specific set of steps, based largely on a series of four-way meetings, and interspersed with feedback or debriefing sessions involving each lawyer and his/her client and then lawyers with each other. These steps include:

- an initial meeting between a lawyer and his/her client in which a range of options are discussed for addressing the issues in a separation or divorce;
- if the clients select CFL, they sign a Collaborative Retainer with their own lawyer;
- the lawyers meet
  - — to develop a positive working relationship
  - — to share general observations about their clients (*e.g.*, how they are adjusting to the separation)
  - — to outline the issues to be addressed
  - — to identify client priorities and urgent issues
  - — to discuss whether other impartial professionals might be needed, *etc.*
  - — to agree on a date, location, and agenda for the first four-way meeting
  - — to discuss how the initial meeting will be conducted, including each of their roles
  - — to consider communication ground rules; and
  - — to discuss the wording of a Collaborative Participation Agreement;
- the lawyers each meet individually with their client to prepare for the first four-way meeting;
- the parties and their lawyers hold a four-way meeting, during which they sign a Collaborative Participation Agreement agreeing to make full disclosure of all relevant information and *not to litigate* if an impasse is reached. If a party decides to litigate, despite this agreement, the lawyers *must withdraw* and turn the matter over to counsel from a different firm;
- a series of four-way meetings are scheduled with agendas worked out in advance;
- in between meetings, the lawyers review the progress being made both with their clients and with each other, in terms of the impact on their relationship with each other, how effective they each were, and how they might be more supportive to ensure that everyone is clear as to future expectations and time lines;
- each lawyer may recommend that his/her client take advantage of other professionals, such as:
  - — one or two divorce coaches to assist with communication in relation to the separation
  - — supportive counselling for other mental health issues
  - — a mediator for parenting issues

* For a detailed description of the steps applied to a case example, see Appendix III.5 and Appendix III.6, as well as the CD-ROM for several helpful and practical tools.

— a business valuator, actuary to value pensions, a Certified Divorce Specialist, or a financial planner to advise on financial settlements or future budgeting, real estate appraiser, *etc;*

- each lawyer is still in the role of an advisor and advocate for his/her client: the goal is not "winning over" the other party, but "winning with" the other party, in a way that benefits all affected family members;
- lawyers need to explain to their clients that unlike an adversarial process, they will address questions and make supportive or validating comments to the "other side" in an effort to build a positive working relationship;
- tasks are assigned to each participant to complete prior to each four-way meeting. In each meeting, one of the lawyers takes notes of the agreements reached and prepares a summary, including the agenda, to distribute at the next meeting;
- four-way meetings are held until an agreement satisfactory to the participants is reached (even if it is different from what the law would provide) and then one of the lawyers draws up a draft Separation Agreement for the other to review and everyone to sign at a final four-way meeting.

Note: In the event the clients reach an impasse, do not act in good faith, or threaten to or commence litigation, the collaborative lawyers are required to withdraw. Therefore, the lawyers, as well as the clients, have a considerable investment in a successful resolution. This represents a major shift in the traditional adversarial approach to family law cases.

The CFL model was created by a Minnesota lawyer, Stu Webb, in the early 1990's and since then has sparked the development of other models that involve an interdisciplinary partnership.

(B) The Paradigm Shift for Collaborative Lawyers

Participation as a collaborative lawyer requires much more than a change in the type of meetings or steps in the process — that is really the surface change. The deeper change is in the entire mindset, important skill sets, attitude, and management of the process from beginning to end. For a discussion of the underlying interest-based theory and model as it applies to negotiation, mediation, and collaborative law, see Chapter 4.

To succeed, collaborative lawyers need to:

- Shift from a rights-based mindset to an interest-based approach. This means many things, including letting go of the current legal regimes' way of resolving cases in favour of seeing this as one option for achieving a settlement. It also means asking different questions to establish each client's priorities, goals, and preferred outcomes and then measuring success by these benchmarks, rather than the current family law regime.
- Recognize that Family Law regimes vary from jurisdiction to jurisdiction and are reformed or interpreted differently over time as a way of

adjusting to or catching up with broader social trends. Collaborative lawyers see each family unit as an opportunity to revisit the relevance and helpfulness of the current legal regime.

- Focus on the unique goals and objectives for both parties for the process, in terms of their future relationship with their partner post-separation, how they want to participate in their children's lives, what their needs, fears and concerns are for their financial future (given their employment status, health, age of the children, *etc.*), how important it is for them to remain in the matrimonial home and why, the extent to which they need security and predictability, what they need in order to rebuild their self-esteem or optimism for the future.
- Jointly consider the family unit as the client in addition to the client who retained you. Parents usually want an outcome that is best for their children that protects them from the harmful consequences of divorce. They want to achieve a fair financial result that reflects their unique circumstances, values and allows for some personal healing, security, and optimism for the future. Collaborative lawyers encourage the clients to retain this constructive focus, even during difficult discussions.
- Consider the client's current emotional state or stage of grieving, *e.g.*, is the client severely depressed, stuck on rage, unrealistically hoping for a reconciliation, guilt ridden — or have they achieved a healthy disengagement? Will this emotional state likely shift and how will this impact their ability to negotiate? How should this impact the pace of the negotiations? What resources would be helpful, such as referral to counselling or a divorce coach, to ensure that the client is able to negotiate from a position of enlightened self-interest and compassion for all those impacted by the end of the relationship?
- Consider the differences in personality and temperament of both clients and both lawyers. How will these differences impact the process and what strategies will be used to deal with these differences when they are an obstacle to progress?
- Discuss the relative comfort of the clients with risk. For example, one client may be very risk-averse and prefer outcomes that offer certainty over maximizing financial returns, while the other may be quite comfortable with uncertainty and prefer higher-risk choices that offer the possibility of a higher return.
- Understand both clients' values, especially regarding their attitude to separation and family roles. If one party had an affair during the marriage, this will inevitably skew the discussions and needs to be dealt with before progress can be made. For example, the "injured" party will probably need an acknowledgement or apology — at least for the impact of the affair on the other's self-esteem and the ability to trust the other person.
- Consider the dynamics created by the involvement of various "cheer-leaders", such as extended family members and new partners. These

individuals can assist in moving the process forward to a successful conclusion or they can create a major impediment to a resolution, depending on the timing of their involvement (*e.g.*, a new partner involved before the relationship ended or within the first year following the break-up, will almost always become the focus of displaced hurt and anger), their personalities and whether they see their alliance as with the client who was rejected or with the one who chose to separate — or whether they see the family as a whole as their connection.

- See the other lawyer (and other involved impartial professionals) as their partner in problem solving and assisting the family as a whole. While the lawyer remains the legal advisor and advocate for his or her own client, the role is more of an educator of the client as to his or her legal obligations and entitlements, a clarifier when the client needs assistance in articulating his or her point of view, an expert in preparing whatever documentation is needed for an uncontested process, and a resource for options and expertise when the client needs such assistance.
- Learn how to ask "open ended" questions so that clients are invited to "tell their story" and feel that their contributions are valued.
- Consider the adage, "We were given two ears and one mouth so that we could listen twice as much as we speak." Begin to practise this with the other lawyer so that when the clients are present the balance of time is spent with the lawyers listening to their clients.
- Work as a team member with the other lawyer and any other professional to co-facilitate meetings, arrange for the time, location, agenda, participants, and any advance preparation. Lawyers are more familiar with setting up one-on-one meetings with their clients or the other lawyer, or four-way meetings that are conducted in a rights-based exchange of demands, maximizing each side's individual outcome and mindset. Often lawyers would expect others to work at their convenience, set the agenda without consultation and not reflect on the impact of their demands on the children or other third parties. Lawyers are used to working as advocates without the need to consult with, take into account, or accommodate the views, preferences and time considerations of others.
- Write respectful letters and hold respectful conversation on the phone and in person with the other lawyer and the other client. The lawyer needs to fully understand that their success and the success of their client depend on the other side *wanting to cooperate*. Collaborative lawyers recognize that when a lawyer behaves in an intimidating or authoritarian manner, it invites the other side to retaliate or to withdraw, so it is contrary to their own client's interest.
- Know when their own personality, values, and preferred outcomes are getting in the way of really listening to their clients' views and goals, and seeking appropriate assistance to deal with the situation in a constructive professional manner.

(C) CO-FACILITATION IN THE COLLABORATIVE FAMILY LAW PROCESS

Lawyers using the CFL model require the same skills as a mediator with the additional challenge of needing to co-facilitate a case with another person, often an unknown partner. The special challenges of needing to coordinate with someone else who has a busy schedule and may be located miles away, in addition to coordinating with clients, whose locations and schedules need to be considered, is a daunting task that requires considerable patience. Perhaps the biggest hurdle to overcome is client expectations with respect to the conduct of the "other" lawyer. Clients will almost always project their fears and anxiety onto the imagined image of their partner's lawyer. Clients who are feeling distrustful and angry or insecure about their own situation, will most likely begin with beliefs that demonize the other lawyer, such as, he or she is *"Out to take advantage of me"; "Likely to treat me with disdain or disrespect"; "Unlikely to give me honest, full and timely disclosure"; "Likely to exacerbate any tension or ill will between me and my partner"; "Unlikely to encourage their own client to cooperate or to make reasonable concessions"; "Likely to approach the issues from a rigid legalistic framework"; "Likely to prolong the process unnecessarily or encourage conflict to increase their fees"*.

Mediators are more likely to begin the mediation process with more favourable expectations, as long as both clients are coming voluntarily and the mediator is careful to clarify that he or she is acting impartially to assist both clients. Lawyers, even CFL lawyers, are still in the role of advocate for their client and cannot offer the same assurance. They do need to overcome the initial fears clients have in order to conduct a productive, comfortable, and creative process.

Some tips for successful co-facilitation are:

- Meet face-to-face and spend some time getting to know each other as individuals to develop a feeling of comfort and a working relationship. This also provides information that each lawyer can use to reassure their client about the other lawyer.
- Discuss your understanding of the collaborative process, your values and goals for conducting such cases, the process you envision for this particular case.
- Share information about the clients' background, present circumstances, stage of grieving, personality, communication style, concerns about appropriateness, including abuse or power and control issues, addictions, mental health, and clients' goals and priorities.
- Create an agenda for the first four-way meeting in a consensus building manner.
- Discuss the location of the first (and possibly subsequent meetings), room set-up, seating arrangements, snacks, and how the meeting will be conducted, *i.e.*, who will lead off the introductions, how will the Collaborative Participation Agreement be dealt with, *etc.*, for all agenda items.

- Clarify the expectations for the way in which both counsel will address each other, their own and the other client. In collaborative cases, it is usual to adopt an informal, first name basis communication with an expectation that there will be a four-way conversation rather than a feeling of opposing "sides".
- Discuss who will keep notes and how progress reports will be created for clients.

2. What Is a Collaborative Divorce?

A Collaborative Divorce involves an integrated, cross-disciplinary team for delivering professional services to divorcing clients. It is the legal equivalent of a multi-disciplinary team in the mental health field. A range of expertise is utilized, for example, divorce coaches, mediators, business valuators, real estate agents, financial planners, or Certified Divorce Specialists. The coordinated efforts of several professionals, all acting in an impartial capacity, may be helpful to resolve the outstanding issues in a cost-effective and non-adversarial manner.

While other professionals may be involved in a Collaborative Family Law case, the Collaborative Divorce tends to be more of an ongoing working relationship between team members rather than an ad hoc arrangement. There may be a "case coordinator" who helps to allocate tasks to individuals according to professional training. For example, each parent may have a collaboratively trained Family Law lawyer as well as a divorce coach (usually a mental health professional) to assist with communication difficulties. The couple may retain a mediator to assist in developing a Parenting Plan and a Certified Divorce Specialist, accountant, or business valuator to help to resolve the property, support, and tax issues. The collaborative professionals hold team meetings from time to time to ensure that their roles are clear and they are working together constructively toward a common goal.

As with a Collaborative Family Law case, the lawyers, divorce coaches, and mediators must agree to withdraw if one or both parties choose to go to court. However, there can be an agreement that certain documents, particularly valuations of assets, will be available for the litigation and those financial experts can be called as witnesses to answer questions about their valuations.

(A) Steps in the Collaborative Divorce

The following steps would likely occur in a Collaborative Divorce, although the steps might vary with whom they see first. In some cases, parties would begin by hiring collaboratively trained lawyers, others might begin with a mediator or divorce coaches or an impartial financial expert. All of these professionals would likely be involved on a fairly regular basis with one of the professionals or the CFL lawyers managing the process.

1. If the couple first approach collaboratively trained lawyers, then the steps would likely be as follows:

- each client meets with a collaboratively trained lawyer and signs a *Collaborative Divorce Retainer*;
- the lawyers arrange a four-way meeting and the lawyers and clients sign a *Collaborative Divorce Participation Agreement*;
- the lawyers refer both clients to one or two divorce coaches;
- the lawyers or the divorce coaches refer the children of the clients to a children's counsellor (if needed);
- the lawyers refer the clients to a mediator to work out a Parenting Plan, or, in the alternative, the divorce coaches assist with this task;
- these professionals and the parents sign a *Collaborative Divorce Participation Agreement*;
- all participants meet to clarify roles, agree on information sharing, decide on the range of professionals to involve, agree on a process, set time lines and follow-up meetings, *etc.*;
- the lawyers follow the steps in a CFL process, as outlined above, to work out the financial issues;
- Collaborative Divorce professionals hold interdisciplinary meetings from time to time to ensure that they are aware of each other's progress and any obstacles to resolution.

2. If the clients first approach a mediator to resolve their issues, the steps would likely be as follows:

- clients meet with the mediator and sign a *Collaborative Divorce Mediation Retainer and Participation Agreement*;
- mediator refers both clients to one or two divorce coaches (if needed);
- mediator refers children of the clients to a children's counsellor (if meeting children is not an area of expertise and if needed);
- mediator refers clients to CFL lawyers to assist with property and financial issues;
- Collaborative Divorce professionals hold an interdisciplinary meeting to clarify their roles, exchange information, and set timelines for completing their tasks;
- mediator assists the couple to develop a Parenting Plan;
- each collaborative lawyer meets with his/her client to sign a *Collaborative Divorce Retainer* and then follows the steps in a CFL process as outlined above;
- Collaborative Divorce professionals hold interdisciplinary meetings from time to time to ensure that they are aware of each other's progress and any obstacles to resolution.

3. What Is Collaborative Mediation?

Collaborative Mediation begins with clients selecting mediation as their preferred method of dispute resolution. These clients frequently have not yet seen a lawyer or retained counsel. They are usually fearful that lawyers will escalate the conflict and frustrate their hopes for a cooperative, non-adversarial negotiation outcome. Also, they prefer a process that encourages them to design their own terms for separation, are worried about losing control of decision-making, incurring high costs, and ending up in court.

Collaborative Mediation can address these concerns. Mediators, who are obliged to send clients for independent legal advice, can now refer clients to collaboratively trained lawyers who will not take the case to court and who make a commitment to assist in reaching a non-adversarial outcome. Everyone, including the lawyers, mediator, and both clients can be included under the umbrella of a *Collaborative Mediation Participation Agreement*, such that there is an agreement to resolve matters cooperatively. In the event that one or both parties decide to litigate, both lawyers and the mediator must withdraw.

In Collaborative Mediation, the mediator may assist the parties to mediate all issues (comprehensive mediation) or the mediator may help the parties to develop a Parenting Plan and then transfer responsibility for negotiating financial issues to the collaborative lawyers. The steps are:

- the clients meet first with the mediator and sign a *Collaborative Mediation Retainer*;
- mediator assists the couple to work out a Parenting Plan and helps to improve communication;
- mediator refers clients to CFL lawyers for independent legal advice and to assist with the preparation of financial disclosure;
- mediator meets children to determine their views and preferences or refers children to a children's counsellor (if needed);
- mediator invites collaboratively trained lawyers to a meeting to
  - — sign a *Collaborative Mediation Participation Agreement*
  - — establish communication guidelines
  - — review and finalize the draft memorandum of understanding with respect to the Parenting Plan
  - — determine how property will be valued (for example, using impartial valuators), what financial disclosure is needed and expected time lines for sharing financial information
  - — discuss any legal questions that might create an impasse; and
  - — clarify roles, including next steps.

At this point the clients either continue to meet with the lawyers, following the CFL model set out above, or they return to mediation to resolve the outstanding financial issues. A Certified Divorce Specialist, financial planner, or other impartial valuators may be asked to contribute their specific expertise.

A second five-way meeting is held once a draft memorandum of understanding has been prepared with respect to property and financial issues (or if an issue is creating an impasse due to different legal positions). At this time the collaborative lawyers help with any unresolved issues and finalize the Separation Agreement in a cooperative and timely manner. This Separation Agreement may be signed in this meeting or separately in each lawyer's office.

B. ASSESSING COLLABORATIVE OPTIONS

1. What Are the Advantages for Clients, Lawyers, and Mediators of Collaborative Family Law, the Collaborative Divorce, and Collaborative Mediation?

(A) CLIENTS

Benefits to clients of Collaborative Family Law, Collaborative Divorce and Collaborative Mediation:

- builds or restores trust between the parties;
- creates a less adversarial atmosphere in cases where the parties need ongoing cooperation;
- allows parties to gain a greater understanding of each other's needs, and promote agreements that are fair and will last;
- allows more control by the parties themselves in creating their own creative resolutions;
- other professionals, such as a mediator, pension valuator, or business appraiser are mutually retained, thus saving the client money;
- professional expertise is used to maximize the contribution to problem solving and minimize hostility;
- enhances the chances that the settlement will last;
- provides the additional safeguard of the lawyers' presence in high conflict separations;
- encourages a more timely, complete and cost-effective exchange of financial information; and
- decreases the risk of litigation.

What clients who have NOT experienced a traditional divorce often cannot appreciate is that they will not have to pay for interim motions, cross-examinations, preparation of affidavits, service of document fees, opposing experts, court filing fees, and extensive correspondence, and they will not have to endure delays of up to several years to resolve their case.

The emphasis on constructive problem solving is highly effective, efficient and reassuring to clients who have chosen a cooperative approach.

(B) LAWYERS

Benefits of a collaborative process for lawyers:

- collaborative family law cases are far less stressful;
- the results are likely to be welcomed by the clients and protect children from the harm created by adversarial tensions;

- families who cannot afford legal representation for the many steps in a court battle, are more likely to afford the assistance of collaborative professionals; and
- lawyers are more likely to be paid for the services they provide.

Clients often commence a separation with the unrealistic belief that their situation can be resolved in a single meeting with a few hours of paperwork. They are suspicious, concerned, and confused about the need for ANY professional assistance and fearful about what lawyers will bring in terms of stirring up additional conflict. They often want to preserve their privacy and see the need to hold meetings or share information as an invasion of their private lives. Even if they arrive at the lawyer's door in a state of anger, they often feel that their claim is justified and a strong lawyer's letter will achieve their preferred result. They need to be listened to carefully and then given realistic feedback as to how their needs can be met with a minimum of unnecessary conflict and cost. Clients who understand that the lawyer is committed to preventing an adversarial litigious process will be more likely to accept the necessary steps in completing their separation.

Concerns raised by lawyers:

- That the requirement to withdraw if a matter reaches an impasse and is headed to court is unfair to clients, because the clients must then look for new lawyers. They say that considerable time was spent building rapport and it is stressful and expensive for clients to begin a relationship with someone else.
  - The response to this concern is that if lawyers and clients know that the lawyer must withdraw if the case goes to litigation, everyone has the same strong incentive to settle.
- That they might be sued at a future date by clients if the agreement does not reflect outcomes that conform closely to what might be obtained in a Family Law trial.
  - The response to this concern is that Family Law reflects a "one-size-fits-all" standard of fairness that often does not meet with clients' goals or their definition of fairness. Lawyers need to clarify their client's personal goals, educate the clients as to the responsibilities and options available to them in Family Law and indicate when the agreements being reached deviate substantially from current outcomes. A clarifying reporting letter is important to ensure the clients are well informed, but should not undermine the clients' ability to fashion an agreement that is tailored to their personal needs and standards of fairness.
  - Family Law is not static. What is an expected outcome of a case at one time is very different several years later. Therefore, Family Law is a helpful guide, but should not constrain the couple's creativity, as

long as the agreement reflects their wishes and is not reached under duress.

— Collaborative lawyers have an easier time receiving payment for their services because client satisfaction is higher than litigated cases. Litigation lawyers may achieve an outcome that fits the Family Law legislation, but not reflect the client's wishes.

- Not every client, and not every case, is suitable for a collaborative approach. That is, if a case is precedent setting, or if the clients are at risk of harm, or if one or both is not acting in good faith, a traditional process will likely be preferable.

  — The response to this concern is that no one process will suit all families. This issue should be discussed with clients in the initial meeting so that the clients can make the judgment as to the best process for their circumstances.

(C) MEDIATORS

Benefits of a collaborative approach for mediators:

- there will likely be greater buy-in by the clients and other professionals consulted by the clients, for agreements that are reached in a collaborative mediation process;
- virtually guarantees that the cases sent to collaboratively trained lawyers will not end up in court;
- lawyers provide legal information and advice, prepare the financial disclosure so that clients make informed decisions in mediation, offer helpful "reality testing" for clients, and assist in establishing safety measures when power imbalance or domestic violence render traditional mediation inappropriate.

Additional roles for mediators:

- *divorce coaches* — if clients are high conflict or in the early stages of a separation, mediators can work to improve communication and build trust between the clients *before* they begin the Collaborative process;
- *child specialists* or mediators who are mental health professionals can interview children as impartial professionals to determine their views, concerns and preferences;
- assist in obtaining an acknowledgement or apology, or reach agreement on communication guidelines, to increase the chance of reaching a successful result;
- if an impasse is reached and feelings are high, a mediator could try to resolve the impasse and restore sufficient confidence so that the settlement process can continue;
- if the relationship between counsel is stressful due to personality differences, misunderstandings, or disappointed expectations, the mediator

could assist by improving their working relationship and communication strategies.

All of these roles are consistent with the goal of cooperative, constructive problem solving and all assist the clients to reach agreement through the efforts of a highly skilled team.

2. Role of Children in Collaborative Family Law (also see Chapter 9)

Where children are involved, the goal is to work out a Parenting Plan that is in the best interest of the children. If children are younger than 16, there needs to be some way to represent the children's needs, concerns, and preferences in the CFL process. If the parents are in agreement and there are no concerns about the children's welfare, the parents are in a good position to present what they believe is in the interests of their children.

If the parents disagree about the Parenting Plan, or if there are concerns about the children's mental health, special health, or educational needs, safety, or the capacity to parent, due to allegations of abuse, alcohol, or drug abuse or neglect, the lawyers need to recommend that other professionals become involved. For example, they could suggest that the parents retain a mediator with mental health training or experience in child development or a child specialist. The mediator assists the parents in developing a Parenting Plan by

- meeting with both parents, separately and together;
- meeting with the children, with the parents' consent, to determine their needs, concerns, and preferences. Children should not be asked questions that put them in a conflict of loyalties; however, they often benefit from having their voice heard and have helpful ideas about
  - — the length of absence from a parent that they can tolerate
  - — the importance to them of remaining in the matrimonial home or their school or community
  - — how transitions are best handled
  - — how they would like their parents to communicate with one another, especially when they are present or can overhear (and NOT to use them to deliver messages)
  - — whether it would be helpful to have one-on-one visits or have a sibling present
  - — their readiness to welcome new partners in their lives
  - — the role they would like their extended family to play, including their treatment of the "other" parent; and
  - — the importance of having a structured, predictable schedule versus an open, flexible plan that may be different each week;
- if there is a suspicion of child abuse, reporting to the Children's Aid Society;
- collecting information from the children's school or day care provider about the children's academic, social, and emotional status, and from the family doctor about any health care issues, allergies, dietary needs, *etc.*

These issues can impact the child's school adjustment or health and therefore the parent's need to be informed and reach a reasonable consensus on such significant items;
- arranging to meet with one or more children and one or both parents to address specific issues that may be causing conflict related to the Parenting Plan;
- summarizing the areas of agreement in a memorandum of understanding, and once the parents have approved the draft, reviewing a copy with both lawyers and the parents to finalize the Agreement.

If lawyers try to prepare a Parenting Plan without expertise in child development or without the children's input, they risk creating a plan that may not be developmentally appropriate, or that the children refuse to follow. If they are not familiar with significant health, discipline, and academic issues, they may not identify important items for the parents to discuss and include in the Parenting Plan. A mediator with expertise in involving children would be of assistance in talking to the children and raising such issues.

3. Parenting Coordinators

In order to ensure that a Parenting Plan worked out with the assistance of a mediator or child specialist is actually implemented and that subsequent issues are resolved in a timely and reasonable way so as to ensure the best interests of the children, the couple can be referred to a parenting coordinator. This individual is retained for a period of time to act as an educator, mediator, and arbitrator for day-to-day conflicts or proposed adjustments to the Parenting Plan. If the couple cannot resolve, for example, a request to take the children on a vacation on specific dates, or a change of school program, or enrollment in a particular extracurricular activity or changes to the regular schedule, the parenting coordinator meets with both parents and attempts to reach a resolution, and failing that makes a decision. In high conflict couples, this approach can be the safety net needed to ensure that there is a timely option to prevent conflicts from escalating and undoing the good work of the collaborative process.

4. Certified Financial Planners, Certified Divorce Specialists, and Valuators

At the time of separation, many couples are faced with financial challenges. Often one (or both) parties do not have the experience or confidence to manage his or her own finances. They do not know how to budget, how to estimate their current or long-term financial needs, or the most tax efficient way to divide property. It is difficult to negotiate if the parties are so imbalanced and if one person is unable to make an informed decision in response to a proposal for a financial settlement. These are the cases that often take an extended time to resolve or where one party makes unreasonable demands (too high or too low) out of insecurity or lack of information.

In these cases a *Certified Financial Planner or a Certified Divorce Specialist* can assist the less sophisticated party, both clients together, and perhaps the mediator or Collaborative lawyers, to consider creative options and develop a realistic budget as a basis for negotiation. Such an individual would be hired as an impartial expert. The Certified Divorce Specialist would meet with one or both clients and would then attend a meeting with the mediator or Collaborative lawyers, on an as needed basis.

Valuators in Collaborative processes are hired on behalf of both parties and need to support fair, informed, and voluntary outcomes. Unlike traditional Family Law cases where each side hires its own valuator (for valuing the home, business, or pension, *etc.*), in collaborative processes the valuator would be hired in an impartial capacity. This person would usually send the Collaborative lawyers, and possibly the mediator, a copy of his or her report. Unless there were serious questions about the report, valuators would not need to participate in any of the Collaborative meetings. Using a single, impartial valuator saves the couple money and reduces animosity.

Note: it is very important that the parties and their Collaborative lawyers are comfortable with any impartial experts who are retained. The proposed names should be checked out in advance with both parties and the collaborative lawyers to avoid anyone rejecting the experts after they have been retained or their report completed.

5. Who May NOT Be Appropriate for a Collaborative Model

Collaborative approaches share certain values and require a certain standard of behaviour from both clients and lawyers. Clients must feel that they are participating voluntarily, have the capacity to make decisions, and are reaching decisions with adequate information and without duress. If clients are fearful for their safety, are being pressured into unwise decisions or ones they do not understand, or are not entering voluntarily, one or both of them may lack the capacity to participate. The following are behaviours that require screening in advance to determine appropriateness:

- domestic violence, including the use of threats, unreasonable control, psychological or physical abuse with the other partner or the children;
- significant untreated psychiatric illness;
- untreated alcohol or drug addiction;
- dishonest and unscrupulous conduct;
- inability to be trusted or to keep commitments;
- inability or unwillingness to make decisions or take responsibility for their behaviour.

In each case, there would need to be separate screening as described in Chapter 2. Collaborative Law may be able to extend the boundaries of inclusion due to the presence of the lawyers, but ONLY if:

- the lawyers can establish ground rules with the clients that are monitored and maintained, such as
  - — no further incidences of abusive behaviours
  - — verified attendance at a group for "anger management" or counselling
  - — attendance at a recommended treatment program or therapist
  - — full and frank, verified financial disclosure.

The dilemma is that for such clients, traditional litigation rarely achieves a better result, unless the law can establish boundaries that can be enforced and find ways to ensure everyone's safety. Too often the abusive partner can "win" by a form of litigation abuse, persisting until the other party has no further funds, continually harassing or threatening the other person, failing to keep commitments or abide by court orders. Collaborative processes cannot resolve all cases and rely for their integrity on the integrity of all of the participants.

SUMMARY

This chapter has introduced a number of new models for achieving the goal of a non-adversarial, reasonably cooperative separation. It is the wish of most people who are embarking on this difficult passage in their life to participate in a process that does not further diminish their self-esteem, and results in a fair, win-win agreement. Where children are involved, most participants also hope to maintain a respectful and possibly friendly relationship. Only collaborative approaches can support such objectives.

ANNOTATED BIBLIOGRAPHY

Boyan, S.M., and Termini, A.M. *The Psychotherapist as Parenting Coordinator in High Conflict Divorce: Strategies and Techniques*. New York: The Haworth Clinical Practice Press, 2005.

Cameron, N. *Collaborative Practice: Deepening the Dialogue.* The Continuing Legal Education, British Columbia, 2004. An excellent resource for the Collaborative Divorce Model, with a CD-ROM of precedents for the practitioner. This book describes the skills necessary for Collaborative Practice, the roles of various professionals who are part of the team and the choices available to clients who do NOT want an adversarial process.

Fagerstrom, K., Wilde, D., Thompson, P., Nurse, R., Kalish, M., Ross, N., and Wolfrum, T. *Divorce: A Problem to Be Solved, Not a Battle to Be Fought.* Brookwood Publishing, 1997. One of the earliest texts to introduce professionals and clients to the concept of Collaborative Divorce. A helpful, easy to read guide for a more amicable approach to divorce.

Landau, B. "What Role, if any, should Children have in Collaborative Law?" *Matrimonial Affairs* (OBA), January, 2005.

Landau, B. "Mediation and Collaborative Law: A Promising Partnership". *Family Mediation News* (ACR*)*, Summer, 2003 and *Legalworks* (CCH), August, 2004.

Landau, B. "Collaborative Law and Mediation: Expanding the Non-Adversarial Menu for Divorcing Couples". *Ontario Psychologist*, Summer, 2002.

Landau, B., and Landau, S. *Collaborative Family Law, Collaborative Divorce & Collaborative Mediation.* ADR Manual, CCH, Canada, 2002. This extensive article describes these non-adversarial models in detail, setting out the steps in each and includes precedents for those setting up a Collaborative Practice.

Macfarlane, J. *The New Lawyer: How Settlement is Transforming the Practice of Law*. Vancouver: UBC Press, 2008.

Saposnek, D. *Special Issue on Collaborative Family Law.* ACR's Family Mediation News, Summer, 2003, with contributions by Stu Webb, Pauline Tesler, Barbara Landau, Chip Rose, and Julie MacFarlane.

Sheilds, R., Ryan, J., and Smith, V. *Collaborative Family Law: Another Way to Resolve Family Disputes.* Thomson Canada Ltd., 2003. This is a thorough, clear and reader-friendly book that can be offered to clients to assist them, as well as other professionals who are engaging in a Collaborative Law process. It has theoretical, skills based and practical information, along with helpful precedents for the new practitioner.

Tesler, P. *Collaborative Law: Achieving Effective Resolution in Divorce without Litigation.* Section of Family Law, American Bar Association, 2001. Tesler's book is the first major book in describing in detail the Collaborative Family Law process and how it differs from an adversarial process. It has practical checklists and precedents, especially directed at an American audience, but easily adapted in other jurisdictions.

Tesler, P., and Jackson, J. (eds.). *The Collaborative Review, the Journal of the International Association of Collaborative Professionals (IACP).* This journal/newsletter has many very helpful short articles for the practitioner and is mailed to members of IACP.

Tesler, P., and Thompson, P. *Collaborative Divorce: The Revolutionary New Way to Restructure Your Family, Resolve Legal Issues, and Move On with Your Life.* Collins: 2006.

Webb, S., in collaboration with Ouskey, R.D. *The Collaborative Way to Divorce: The Revolutionary Method that Results in Less Stress, Lower Costs, and Happier Kids — Without Going to Court.* New York: Hudson Street Press (Penguin), 2006.

Chapter Six

Custody Assessments

A. ASSESSMENT PROCEDURE

1. Mediation — The First Step

A chapter on custody assessments has been included in this book because the authors take the position that the clients should be offered an opportunity to find a mediated solution to the issues in dispute. Except in cases of serious abuse, a mediative approach should be tried first for the following reasons:

- Parents should be encouraged to take responsibility for their children, and parents are in the best position to know their children and understand what parenting arrangement would be in the best interests of their children.
- If the assessor does not attempt mediation as a first step, then the parties are almost inevitably headed for an adversarial court battle. Such a battle is not in the children's best interests, nor in the parent's best interests.
- If the parties do succeed in reaching a settlement with the assistance of a mediator, they are more likely to accept the result and not to re-litigate in the future.
- A mediated settlement is likely to save the parties considerable emotional strain as well as considerable expense.

In a few cases, judges have disapproved of a mediative approach out of a concern that if a party was not willing to reach a resolution and an opinion was required from an assessor, there might be a perception of bias by the assessor. A party might feel pressured to reach an agreement out of fear that the assessor would favour the party who was willing to "settle". Also, some professional groups have discouraged professionals from playing more than one role with the same clients; that is, offering an opportunity to resolve issues in a mediative role within the context of an assessment. However, the same concern could be raised for mediation-arbitration or for Parenting Coordination. That is, the same professional assists in resolving matters cooperatively and if an impasse is reached, makes a binding decision. (Note: the assessor makes only recommendations that are not binding and therefore the PC or arbitrator has considerably more power.) This issue is still under discussion. Some custody assessors have resolved this issue by first completing their assessment with recommendations and then offering the parties an opportunity to "mediate" the implementation or fine tuning of the result.

In cases where the clients have chosen Collaborative Law, the Collaborative Participation Agreement precludes an assessment. An assessment is seen as a process that is chosen in contemplation of litigation, to assist a judge in arriving at what is best for children. It is contrary to the spirit of Collaborative Law which seeks to avoid courts as an option. If Collaborative Law or mediation is not successful, a referral might be made to an assessor by new lawyers who are retained when the collaborative counsel withdraw.

2. Purpose of Custody Assessment

In conducting a custody assessment, it is important to decide what is the purpose of the assessment. Is the purpose to determine who is the best parent? Or, is the purpose to develop a Parenting Plan that would be in the best interests of the children? There is a fundamental difference in attitude between these two initial starting points. If the assessor considers the purpose to be determining the best parent, then the following assumptions might apply:

- The assessor probably presumes that the result will be sole custody to one of the two parents (as opposed to a joint custody or a shared parenting arrangement).
- The assessor will attempt to determine which parent is better than the other (for example, with respect to financial status, educational achievement, job security, or personality strengths).
- The assessor probably emphasizes a clinically oriented assessment process. Information gathering is likely to be through psychological testing and individual interviews, as opposed to joint meetings of both parents.
- The assessor will probably spend very little time with the spouses together trying to mediate a cooperative Parenting Plan.
- The assessor will probably place more emphasis on the stated or perceived preference of the children for one parent over the other.
- It is highly likely that the assessor will prepare a full custody assessment report, which will be submitted to the parties and the court.
- The case is likely to proceed to trial with the assessor called as a witness by the parent who is "preferred" in the assessment report.

On the other hand, if the assessor starts from the premise that the purpose of an assessment is to develop a cooperative Parenting Plan that is in the best interests of the children, then the assumptions are somewhat different, namely:

- The assessor is likely to place considerable emphasis on attempting to reach a mutually agreeable settlement.
- In the absence of serious abuse issues, the assessor is likely to take the position that it is important for the children to have a warm and loving relationship with both parents and that a desired outcome is an arrangement that maximizes the children's opportunity to spend time with both parents in an atmosphere of reduced tension. This outcome presumes two competent and caring parents.
- The assessor is likely to spend considerable time with the children to observe the ways in which they relate to both parents, and then with both parents together to consider various alternatives for cooperating so as to meet the children's needs, interests, and wishes.

- The assessor is likely to focus more on the future of the parenting relationship than on the past or even the present. That is, the assessor will be interested in determining to what extent both parents are willing to share parental responsibilities and are competent to carry these out.
- The assessment will focus on the communication between the parents and their ability and willingness to cooperate in the interests of their children.
- The assessor is likely to explore the possibility of a joint custody or shared parenting arrangement, particularly in cases where there are two reasonably competent parents who have the ability to set aside their individual differences in the interests of the children. In some cases, the parents dislike each other intensely, live very different lifestyles, but respect each other's parenting ability, recognize that they both love the children and are loved by the children, and on this basis are prepared to cooperate in their parenting.
- The assessor is likely to focus on factors that might undermine the cooperation or make a shared parenting arrangement more difficult, such as considerable distance between the parents, unwillingness to share the transportation, the attitude of a new spouse that may obstruct cooperation, a poor parent-child relationship, distrust or fears of abuse between the spouses or directed at the children.
- The assessor will encourage the parties to reach their own settlement so that they can avoid an adversarial battle, and in many cases the assessor will not need to prepare a detailed assessment report. The more usual result would be a memorandum of understanding by the assessor followed by minutes of settlement prepared by the solicitor.

3. Differences Between Mediation and Assessment

In what way is an assessment different from mediation?

In an assessment, unlike closed mediation, the assessor is asked to prepare a report containing his or her observations, opinions, and recommendations. This may occur whether or not the parties reach an agreement. In closed mediation, the mediator prepares a report only with respect to those issues resolved in mediation. The mediator does not include his or her observations, opinions, or recommendations. In open mediation, the mediator may prepare a report that is similar to an assessment, although possibly not as detailed, and will only include recommendations if this is specifically requested by the parties. A report in open mediation could include the mediator's observations with respect to issues that were not resolved.

Mediation is a process that essentially emphasizes the private ordering of dispute resolution. That is, the parties are expected to resolve their own difficulties by arriving at a voluntary settlement. An assessment is a process whereby an impartial expert makes recommendations (where these are requested by the parties or the judge) which are then considered by a judge who makes a decision for the parties as to how their dispute will be resolved. There is no requirement that the parties accept the assessor's recommendations, and the final resolution is imposed by the court.

The assessment report will carry considerable weight with the court, and for this reason the assessor must spend additional time, which would not be needed in mediation, learning about the special needs, interests, wishes, and stages of development of the children, and about the capacity of the parents to parent and to cooperate with each other.

An assessment focuses on what information an assessor needs in order to arrive at a recommendation, whereas mediation focuses on what information the parties need in order to resolve their dispute on their own.

An assessor must do a complete and thorough investigation, including contacts with a number of collateral sources to ensure that the procedure followed meets acceptable professional standards and to ensure that his or her report is considered credible by the court. A mediator who is not being asked for recommendations does not need to carry out an extensive investigation.

4. Assessment Interviews

The following are basic guidelines for the types of interviews and data collection procedures that are usually carried out in an assessment.

(A) Meeting of Assessor and Both Counsel

The objectives of this meeting are the same as those set out in Chapter 4 with respect to mediation. However, there are some additional purposes.

It is important for the assessor to clarify with counsel that he or she will be attempting to arrive at a settlement as a part of the procedure. The assessor also needs to make clear with counsel what will be expected of him or her if the mediative approach is successful. Will the assessor still be expected to prepare a full custody assessment, or will a memorandum of understanding with a brief report be adequate?

It is recommended that an assessor not prepare a full assessment report unless it is required by the court for the following reasons:

- The assessment report is likely to be lengthy and more costly than the memorandum of understanding and a brief report.
- A full custody assessment often includes information that could be upsetting to one or both parties and will likely weaken rather than encourage cooperative parenting. Many parents feel defensive, somewhat humiliated, and often considerably distressed at having their weaknesses exposed.
- The information contained in a full assessment report may be used by one or both parties as further ammunition for their continued battle with each other.
- If a settlement is reached, it is best to emphasize the positive results and state what the parties did that was good, rather than expose their

weaknesses. The settlement itself may be undermined by disputes over details in an assessment report.

The assessor should clarify the fact that if an assessment report is prepared, the assessor would agree to be called as a witness by either party and would be willing to be cross-examined by both.

The assessor should clarify the payment of fees during the assessment process, and for the preparation of a report or agreement. It is desirable to have all fees shared throughout, so that there is no suggestion that the assessor has produced a favourable report for the party who is paying his or her fees. This is also in keeping with the assessor's position that he or she is concerned with the best interests of the children and is impartial as between the parties. However, it is likely that the parent who is favoured in the report will pay for the assessor to appear in court as an expert witness.

(B) MEETING OF ASSESSOR AND BOTH PARTIES TOGETHER

See Chapter 4 for a discussion of the objectives of this meeting. The following aims should also be considered.

- The assessor should explain to the parties that they will be encouraged to develop a cooperative Parenting Plan on their own rather than leave the decision with respect to their children to strangers such as the assessor or a judge.
- The assessor should clarify with the parents what will happen in the event that they do reach an agreement. That is, the assessor may prepare a memorandum of understanding and a brief report rather than an assessment report, unless the assessment report is required by the court.
- The assessor should explain the implications with respect to fees if the parties settle versus if the parties fail to settle and an assessment report and expert witness testimony are required. If at all possible, the assessor should ask the parties to share his or her fees for the entire process. If this is not possible, or if one party will pay the majority of the fees, the assessor should obtain an agreement in writing that the other party will not raise the issue of who paid the fees to allege bias by the assessor in favour of the spouse who paid.

(C) MEETING OF ASSESSOR WITH EACH PARTY SEPARATELY

Some assessors prefer to meet initially with the parties separately and then hold a joint meeting at some other time. This is a preferred approach in cases of domestic violence where one party feels intimidated or at risk.

This issue was discussed in Chapters 2 and 4 with respect to mediation, and the discussion is relevant to assessments.

(D) Home Visit

In a custody assessment, it is recommended that the assessor meet the children in their home environment. While some assessors prefer to see children in their offices, and in some cases this is necessary (for example, if the family lives a considerable distance away), nevertheless a home visit is important for the following reasons:

- Children are far more comfortable in a familiar setting, and communication with the assessor will be enhanced.
- It is more likely that a child will show normalized behaviour in a family setting than in the assessor's office. Also, the child is likely to be far less anxious and more communicative.
- A home visit provides the assessor with considerable information about the family's lifestyle and the extent to which the family is child-oriented. This information is more difficult to obtain in an office setting.
- The assessor is able to evaluate parenting ability more accurately in a home setting than in an office interview. For example, the assessor has an opportunity to observe the type of nutrition given the children, the adequacy of stimulation available, the appropriateness of the living arrangements, and the desirability of the neighbourhood. In addition, it is more likely that the assessor will observe typical family patterns and discipline techniques in a home setting.
- The assessor should visit with the children in each parent's home in order to observe differences in the home environment and parent-child relationships.

The assessor may choose to hold a number of meetings in the home on the day of each home visit, for example, with both parents and the children, with one parent and the children, with all children together, with each child separately, with each parent separately, with the children with one parent and a new partner, with the new partner alone, with a regular babysitter alone, or with extended family members who are directly involved in the care of the children alone. Meetings with the parent alone, the new partner, the babysitter, or extended-family caregivers could be held at the office on a different day, if preferred, or if necessary because of time constraints.

It is recommended that the first home visit be in the home where the children spend the majority of their time. The aim is to make the children feel as comfortable as possible when meeting the assessor and engaging in the assessment interviews. The same procedure should be followed during the second home visit with the non-custodial parent.

(E) Meeting with Parties Together on One or More Occasions

Additional meetings with both parties may be necessary, prior to reaching an agreement or preparing a report, for such reasons as the following:

- to offer the parents information as to the children's response to the separation;

- to improve the parents' ability to communicate about parenting issues; and
- to determine whether the parents can work out their own parenting plan for sharing responsibilities and time with the children.

Additional meetings may be needed with the children with one or both parents or with one child and a particular parent, with parents and their new partners, or with the entire family.

In difficult cases, a second evaluator could be used to provide independent observations of the children, parents, new partners, or other significant figures.

5. Comments with Respect to Home Visits

The assessor should discuss with both parents prior to a home visit how the visit will be explained to the children. The children should be told essentially that the assessor is a professional person whom the parents have asked to help them work out a Parenting Plan that will be in the best interests of the children. During the visit, the assessor will be spending time with both the parents and the children.

Prior to speaking to the children, it is important to ensure that the children have been told by both parents that they are free to say whatever they wish to the assessor, that the parents' feelings will not be hurt by what they may say, and that there will be no negative repercussions for them. The children should also be told that while their views will be considered, their parents or, in the alternative, a judge, will be making the final decision.

It is usually best to hold a meeting of both parents together with the children, or at least one parent with the children, prior to seeing the children individually. The children need some time to become comfortable in the presence of the assessor, and the assessor needs some context of family interaction before beginning the individual sessions with each child. The assessor should ensure that the meetings with each child are held in private and in a setting where the child is most comfortable.

During the home visit the assessor needs to be tuned into such things as:

- whether there is affection shown between the parents and each child;
- whether there are appropriate toys and educational stimulation;
- the standard of cleanliness in the home;
- whether nutritious meals and snacks are served;
- whether there are pictures of the children, trophies, or other items that indicate the value of the children to the parent;
- the daily routines for the children;
- whether the children are fearful, clinging to the parent, or independent and confident in meeting strangers;
- the parent-child interaction, that is, whether the parent gives each child praise, encourages independence, sets reasonable limits, values the child's suggestions and opinions, or is critical or controlling, uses lax or excessive discipline, and minimizes the child's contribution.

The assessor should observe the interaction between the siblings to determine whether the siblings are supportive of each other or vying for attention. Do they include or exclude each other? Do they bicker or get along reasonably well? Does the parent intervene in an appropriate way when necessary with the children?

The assessor should eat one meal with the family, if possible, and observe:

- how nutritious the meal is;
- the types of limits and expectations with respect to table manners;
- whether the children are comfortable and participate in the conversation, or are ignored and uncomfortable.

The assessor should observe the quality of interaction between the children and other significant figures who are to be interviewed, in terms of how they are greeted by the children, whether there is any display of affection, or whether they are largely ignored.

At the end of the day, before the assessor leaves, it is desirable to hold a brief meeting between the children and the parent(s) just to sum up the day and ensure that everyone is clear about the next step in the process. The next step may be a home visit at the other spouse's home, and the children should be informed about when this will occur and what the purpose of the meeting will be. This will make the children more relaxed for the second visit.

6. Collateral Sources

In addition to interview information, the assessor needs to collect information from external sources that have relevant and, it is hoped, reliable information with respect to the needs, interests, and stages of development of the children, as well as the parenting capacity of both parents. Such information can be collected through reports, telephone conversations, and, if necessary, direct visits with such sources as:

- the school;
- the family doctor;
- other mental health professionals;
- the Children's Aid Society;
- the public health nurse; or
- the employer.

7. Standards of Practice

As with mediation, it is important for the assessor to establish that he or she:

- has appropriate qualifications with respect to education, training, and experience;
- adheres to a professional code of conduct as set out by his or her professional discipline; and
- adheres to a code of conduct established by a recognized professional organization for mediators and/or assessors.

The credibility or weight given to an assessment report will be determined by its thoroughness and its conformity with ethical standards. The court will be particularly interested in the following types of information:

- the amount of time spent in the total assessment process;
- who was interviewed, what combination of persons, for how long, and on how many occasions;
- what collateral sources were contacted;
- whether significant allegations were followed up (for example, with respect to alcohol, drug, or physical abuse, emotional disturbance, or criminal behaviour);
- whether the assessor attempted to resolve the dispute through mediation prior to making recommendations;
- whether the assessor explained the nature of the recommendations to the parties and counsel prior to submitting the report to court (and possibly prior to preparing the report);
- whether the report was up to date (that is, did the assessor update his or her observations close to the time of the trial?);
- whether the report was thorough; and
- whether the assessor presented a fair and balanced account of the parties in the report and in the testimony given in court.

B. PREPARATION OF CUSTODY ASSESSMENT REPORTS

If the parties reach agreement or substantial agreement, the assessor should summarize the areas of agreement reached. Where the parties reached an impasse or where the plan was below a reasonable standard of care for a child, the assessor should set out his or her recommendations. For each recommendation, the assessor should provide a rationale focusing on why that recommendation was in the best interests of the child (see Chapter 9 and Appendix IV).

This report should also contain a brief outline of the topics described below. However, a lengthy family history or evaluation of the parties is usually not necessary and could provoke feelings of resentment which could undermine a cooperative parenting plan.

In the event that the parties fail to resolve their dispute and a full assessment report is required, the following types of information should be included:

Referral Sources

The report should state whether this is a court-ordered assessment or one that is being conducted on the consent of the parties. The report should indicate whether the parties jointly selected the assessor or whether the assessor was selected by one of the parties over the opposition of the other. If the recommendation for an assessment was made by an external agency, such as the Children's Aid Society, this should be indicated.

Reasons for Referral

The report should indicate whether the referral was made to help the parents develop a cooperative parenting plan, select one parent in preference to the other, investigate allegations of child abuse, alcoholism, or mental disorder, or for some other reason(s). The events leading to the referral should be stated clearly.

It should also be clear whether the report was prepared for a contested custody trial, a child welfare trial, or because one or both parents wished to review existing custody and access arrangements.

Objective(s) of Assessment

The report should set out the questions to be answered by the assessment. For example, is the primary concern the best parenting arrangements, or is the issue restricted to the most appropriate access schedule or the involvement of a new partner in the children's lives?

Qualifications of Assessor

The report should contain a brief summary of the assessor's qualifications and a full *curriculum vitae* should be attached to the report.

Assessment Process

The report should state who was seen or spoken to and for how long, and what materials, reports, or court documents were reviewed. This information can be included in paragraph or chart format.

Family History

The report should contain relevant family history, that is, information pertaining to the objectives of the assessment. This may include a history of the marriage, the early parenting of the child, the reasons for the marriage breakdown, if relevant, the present parenting plan, and any difficulties or positive features of the present plan.

History of the Child and Assessor's Observations

This section should include information with respect to the child's physical, psychological, social, emotional, and educational development. Included should be information with respect to the child's strengths and weaknesses, as well as special needs and abilities.

Summary of Observations of Family and of Information from Other Sources

The report should contain a summary of family dynamics in relation to possible parenting arrangements, and should summarize the relevant information from such sources as the school teacher, family doctor, and other involved professionals.

Discussion of Alternative Parenting Arrangements

The report should discuss viable parenting options in light of the objectives of the assessment. The relative strengths and weaknesses of the alternatives should be considered.

Recommendations

The assessor may then wish to set out in specific terms the final recommendations with respect to the involvement of each parent in the child's life. This can include such recommendations as:

- sole versus joint custody;
- the primary residence of the child (if any);
- the amount of time to be spent with each parent, including the specific days and times for access;
- the manner in which parental responsibilities and privileges should be shared, such as health care, educational planning, religious training, and access to information;
- what should occur if one parent moves out of the jurisdiction or far enough away such that the access arrangements are no longer feasible;
- the method of dispute resolution to be used if the parents have a further dispute with respect to custody of or access to the children.

It is important for the assessor to indicate to both the parties and counsel that he or she will be available to meet with one or both parties prior to the trial date for the following purposes:

- to discuss the recommendations;
- to make a further attempt at settlement;
- to refer one or both parties for professional assistance, such as counselling or treatment for alcohol abuse; and
- for additional information with respect to the needs of the children and how both parents can meet these needs.

The assessor should maintain a position of impartiality as between the parents and should remember throughout this process that the primary task is to devise a parenting plan that will be in the best interests of the children. A good assessment report is not one that helps one parent win and destroys the other parent, but rather one that makes constructive, reasonable recommendations that will eventually lead to a reduction of tension and an improvement in relationships between the children and both parents.

Rationale for Recommendations

The assessor should set out in this section the criteria that he or she is applying in making recommendations. Also, the assessor should summarize those key facts and observations with respect to each criterion that is relevant to a recommendation. For example, if the stability of the child's living arrangements is an important factor to the assessor, the report should make this clear. A summary should be given of the relevant facts and observations with respect to how each parent would affect the stability of the child's living arrangements. For example, one parent might be a professional musician and plan to take the child on extended world tours with nannies and tutors available. The other parent might be engaged in employment that does not require travelling and that would result in the child growing up in a familiar community, near friends and extended family members. The assessor should indicate how the different Parenting Plans would impact on the child's stability.

C. MEDIATION-ARBITRATION OR PARENTING COORDINATOR ROLE

An alternative role is that of a mediator-arbitrator, using a mental health professional. In this role, the parties try first to mediate the custody and access issues. If an impasse is reached, the mediator-arbitrator has the authority to make a binding award on any outstanding issues.

A similar role is played by a Parenting Coordinator. However, the Parenting Coordinator is employed to resolve disputes that arise following a custody assessment or a mediated or negotiated agreement or court order. For example, in the case of a dispute about the implementation or interpretation of terms or if there were a change of circumstances.

Usually the Parenting Coordinator is chosen voluntarily by the parties; however, recently there have been a few cases that suggest that judges may have the ability to order attendance at a Parenting Coordinator for appropriate, that is high conflict, couples. Whether chosen voluntarily or by court order, the Parenting Coordinator is jointly retained to resolve specific categories of dispute (*e.g.*, time sharing arrangements, contribution to special expenses) for a particular period of time. The Parenting Coordinator attempts to assist the couple to resolve their differences using mediation skills. However, these couples have difficulty reaching agreement, so their retainer states that if they reach an impasse, the Parenting Coordinator will make a decision which both will abide by for an agreed upon time or until a new arrangement is reached by mutual consent.

The parents enter a Parenting Coordinator retainer which spells out the issues to be dealt with, the process to be followed, who will participate in the process, the conditions under which the Parenting Coordinator decides the issue and the fee arrangements.

SUMMARY

If an assessment rather than mediation has been requested, either by the court or by the parties or their counsel, many assessors follow a process that is similar to the mediation process. That is, with the consent of the parties, many assessors offer the parties the opportunity to mediate the issues in dispute, or at least narrow their differences, in the hope that they can arrive at their own resolution, without the need for an adversarial court proceeding. This mediative approach may occur prior to the assessor's recommendations or following the recommendations in order to work out an implementation plan.

However, an assessment should be distinguished from mediation in that there is an onus on the assessor to form an objective, independent evaluation of the parties in the event that the parties fail to reach an agreement. This may also be true of open mediation, where the mediator is required to prepare a report with recommendations.

Whenever the assessor or mediator must make recommendations, a more thorough process of information gathering is generally followed. Additional meetings are usually arranged with persons other than the parties themselves, such as with children, nannies, or other consistent caretakers, new partners, and extended family members in the case of custody disputes, or accountants or property evaluators in the case of financial disputes.

ANNOTATED BIBLIOGRAPHY

"Association of Family and Conciliation Courts Model Standards of Practice for Child Custody Evaluation" (1994), 32: 4 *Family and Conciliation Courts Review*, 504-513.

Baris, M., Coates, C., Duvall, B., Garrity, C., Johnson, E., and LaCrosse, E. *Working with High Conflict Families of Divorce.* New Jersey, Jason Aronson, Inc., 2001.

Brown, C. "Custody Evaluations: Presenting the Data to Court" (1995), 33 *Family and Conciliation Courts Review* 446-461.

Chisholm, B., and MacNaughton, C. *Custody/Access Assessments: A Practical Guide for Lawyers and Assessors*. Toronto: Carswell, 1990. A comprehensive description of practical procedures and post-assessment issues from authors trained in social work and the law respectively.

Chodos, L. *Parenting Coordination: The Cutting Edge of Conflict Management with Separated/Divorced Families.* CLE Program, Special Lectures 2006, Family Law, Law Society of Upper Canada.

Custody/Access Assessment Guidelines: Report of the Interdisciplinary Committee for Custody/Access Assessments. Toronto: The Ontario Psychological Foundation, 1987. These guidelines were revised in 1996 by the Ontario Interdisciplinary Association of Custody and Access Assessors and reprinted by the Psychology Foundation of Canada. Toronto, 1996.

Gardner, R. *Family Evaluation in Child Custody Litigation.* New Jersey: Creative Therapeutics, 1982. This is a practical guide to performing custody assessments and includes a very useful discussion about the interview process, including who to interview, what information to collect, and also how to prepare a report.

Haynes-Seman, C., and Baumgarten, D. "Improvement of Clinical and Legal Determinations in Cases of Alleged Child Sexual Abuse" (1995), 33 *Family and Conciliation Courts Review* 472-483.

Hysjulien, C., Wood, B., and Benjamin, G. "Child Custody Evaluations: A Review of Methods Used in Litigation and Alternative Dispute Resolution" (1994), 32: 4 *Family and Conciliation Courts Review*, 466-489.

Keeney, B., ed. *Diagnosis and Assessment in Family Therapy*. Rockville: Aspen Publications, 1983. A collection of papers by some of the foremost family therapists and diagnosticians in the United States and Canada, describing how to make family assessments more comprehensive.

Parry, R., Broder, E., Schmitt, E., Saunders, E., and Hood, E. *Custody Disputes: Evaluation and Intervention.* Toronto: Lexington Books, 1985. This book contains a number of interesting chapters written by experienced professionals with respect to the theory and practice of custody assessments.

Skafte, D. *Child Custody Evaluations: A Practical Guide.* California: Sage Publications Inc., 1986. This book is an informative, highly readable guide for those preparing custody evaluations.

Stahl, P. *Performing Child Custody Evaluations: A Guide Book.* Thousand Oaks, California: Sage Publications, 1994. An in-depth integration of case history and procedures for custody evaluators. Other issues include professional liability and burnout, with appendices providing sample forms and ethical standards.

Taylor, A., and Bing, H. "Settlement by Evaluation and Arbitration: A New Approach for Custody and Visitation Disputes" (1994), 32: 4 *Family and Conciliation Courts Review*, 432-444.

Chapter Seven

Family Law Arbitration

A. ARBITRATION VS. MEDIATION-ARBITRATION

Arbitration involves appointing a neutral third party (the arbitrator) to review the evidence presented by the parties and to render a decision which is binding on the parties. By contrast, mediation-arbitration ("Med-Arb") is a process that commences as a mediation. If and when an impasse has been reached, the mediation terminates and an arbitration commences. Over the past 10 years, Med-Arb has become increasingly popular amongst the Family Law bar in Ontario, particularly in the Greater Toronto Area. Usually a senior member of the Family Law bar or a retired judge is chosen to fulfill the role of arbitrator or mediator-arbitrator for financial issues and a mental health professional for issues related to children.

Parenting Coordination (often referred to as "PC") is a form of Med-Arb that is often used with high-conflict couples to assist them by counselling, mediating and arbitrating issues related to their children.[1] PC is a "hybrid role" that is a blending of legal and mental health functions and requires specialized skills and knowledge. The skills required of a PC have been described as follows: "Parenting Coordinators generally are mental health professionals experienced in working with high-conflict families going through separation and divorce. In addition, they have particular expertise in the following areas: a range of conflict resolution techniques such as mediation and arbitration, an understanding of child development, family systems theory, case management, characteristics of high conflict families and how to assess the impasse, personality characteristics and how to develop effective strategies for helping these particular parents. Finally, they must have knowledge of the relevant legislation."[2]

Over 90 per cent of Med-Arb cases resolve in the mediation phase and never reach the arbitration phase. However, it's often the "stick" of the arbitration that assists the mediator-arbitrator in moving the parties to a negotiated resolution. In addition to being an effective way to assist parties in reaching agreements, there is evidence that negotiated agreements (such as those reached via mediation or Med-Arb) are respected by the parties to a greater extent than court-imposed judgments.[3]

---

1 See Linda Chodos, "Parenting Coordination: The Cutting Edge of Conflict Management with Separated/Divorced Families" (Paper presented to the Law Society of Upper Canada Continuing Legal Education Program, Special Lectures 2006, Family Law, 3 and 4 April 2006) for an excellent overview of Parenting Coordination.

2 *Ibid.*, at p. 14-4.

3 Marion Boyd, "Dispute Resolution in Family Law: Protecting Choice, Promoting Indecision" (December 2004) ("Boyd Report") at p. 74.

Notwithstanding Med-Arb's substantial benefits, the process is still controversial amongst some members of the Family Law bar. In their article "Mediation-Arbitration: a contentious but often effective compromise", Claude Thomson and Annie Finn point out that "many experienced and highly ethical neutrals remain convinced that mediation and arbitration by the same person are inherently incompatible."[4] The authors explain that a mediator "focuses on the interests of the parties and encourages a settlement according to the parties' best-interests, not necessarily in a manner that respects their legal rights and obligations. In contrast, an arbitrator is expected to fairly and impartially decide according to the law and the evidence by delivering an award that finally determines the legal rights of the parties".[5] Some critics contend that the traditional form of Med-Arb may provide parties with opportunities and even incentives to undermine the mediation process. Some fear that parties may attempt to persuade the mediator, with a view to influencing his or her final award when the mediation does not result in settlement. Med-Arb also gives rise to interesting questions about the nature and extent of disclosure during mediation, in light of some parties' fears that such disclosure will prejudice the arbitration process.

While earlier cases seemed to reflect a lack of judicial understanding of the practice of mediation-arbitration, the recent decision of the Ontario Court of Appeal in *Marchese v. Marchese*[6] suggests that the Med-Arb process is now well recognized by the courts. In *Marchese* the parties entered into a Consent Order which provided for the parties to "attend for mediation/arbitration with Mr. E. regarding all issues in the action". After his efforts to mediate were unsuccessful, Mr. E. issued a Notice to Arbitrate. At the arbitration, Mr. E. made an interim award and adjourned the balance of arbitration. The husband asked the court to stay the pending arbitration and the arbitrator's interim award. The husband argued that:

- no arbitration agreement was entered into by the parties;
- the Consent Order required the parties to submit to mediation or arbitration, but not both; and
- the arbitration was "invalid" because Mr. E. was precluded at law from acting both as mediator and arbitrator of the financial disputes between the parties.

The appeal was dismissed by the Ontario Court of Appeal. It held:

> We do not agree with the submission that there is any ambiguity in the words "mediation/arbitration" or that those words mean "mediation or arbitration." Mediation/arbitration is a well recognized legal term of art referring to a hybrid dispute resolution process in which the named individual acts first as a mediator and, failing agreement, then proceeds to conduct an arbitration. We note that it was appellant's solicitor who suggested this process, naming a well known practitioner

---

4 C. Thomson and A. Finn, "Mediation-Arbitration: A Contentious But Often Effective Compromise", *The Lawyers Weekly* (15 September, 2006) at p. 9.

5 *Ibid.*

6 [2007] O.J. No. 191, 35 R.F.L. (6th) 291 (Ont. C.A.).

who regularly conducts mediation/arbitrations and who has written papers on the topic explaining precisely what that process entails. The motion judge did not err in rejecting the contention that there was no agreement to arbitrate.

We do not agree that the provision permitting the parties to return to court undermined the agreement to arbitrate or permitted the appellant to resile from it. That provision was simply to provide for implementation of the results of the mediation/arbitration in a final court decree.

In our view, a mediation/arbitration agreement may be reconciled with the *Arbitration Act*, s. 35 which prevents an arbitrator from "conducting any part of the arbitration as a mediation." If s. 35 applies (a point we need not decide) it can be waived and the agreement to engage in "mediation/arbitration" in this case amounted to a waiver.[7]

B. ADVANTAGES AND DISADVANTAGES OF ARBITRATION[8]

1. Advantages

In considering Family Law arbitration (including Med-Arb) with their clients, family lawyers typically list the following advantages and disadvantages:

(A) ACCESSIBILITY AND ADAPTABILITY

In arbitration, the parties define the issues to be determined, the procedure to be followed, and the scope of appeal rights. Procedural issues (for example, financial disclosure) are typically resolved in a conference call with the arbitrator, rather than in a formal motion before a judge.

(B) COSTS

Because the parties can agree on the procedure to be followed, an arbitration is typically less formal, more efficient, and therefore less costly than a trial of the same issues. If the parties opt for Med-Arb and the case settles in the mediation phase, the cost will be even less.

(C) PREDICTABILITY

In the court system the litigants have no choice over the judge and little control over the timetable. In arbitration, the parties choose their arbitrator and the timetable for the case. Arbitrators are typically chosen because of their reputation for knowledge of the field, skills as a mediator, and fairness as an arbitrator.

---

7 *Ibid.*, at paras. 4-6.

8 Adapted from Stephen Grant, "Alternative Dispute Resolution in Family Law: What's Not to Like?" (Paper presented to the Law Society of Upper Canada Continuing Legal Education Program, Mediation and Arbitration for Family Law Lawyers, 13 November 2007) [unpublished].

(D) PRIVACY

For parties who seek a confidential forum for the resolution of their case, arbitration offers obvious advantages over the courts. However, there are limits on the guarantee of privacy (such as where there is an appeal or judicial review, the mandatory reporting of child protection concerns, *etc.*).

(E) ENFORCEABILITY

While the *Arbitration Act, 1991*[9] provides for rights of appeal and judicial review of arbitral awards, the courts are currently showing considerable deference to the decisions of arbitrators. Unless the arbitrator commits an obvious error of fact or law (depending on the grounds for appeal) or denies a party procedural fairness, the court will not substitute its opinion for that of the arbitrator. An arbitral award can be converted into a court order and enforced as such.

(F) SPEED

Unlike the court system (where first court dates can be three months down the road and trial dates many months later), arbitration often results in a final resolution of the case within 30 to 90 days of the initial call to the arbitrator.

(G) SOCIAL UTILITY

By removing cases from the court system, ADR alternatives such as arbitration free up judicial resources to deal with the cases that remain in the system. Med-Arb and arbitration give the parties more control over the choice of decision-maker, the design of the process and more direct participation in the outcome than a court process and therefore parties are more likely to accept/abide by the result.

2. Disadvantages

(A) COSTS

Initially, some parties are put off arbitration by the requirement that they pay the fees of the arbitrator (as opposed to the court system, where the judge is supplied by the state); however, even where the mediation is unsuccessful and the matter proceeds to arbitration, the total cost (including the arbitrator's fees) is usually much less than what it would have been in the courts.

(B) JURISPRUDENCE

Judges often decry the fact that cases which are resolved in arbitration do not help to advance the development of the law. While this is true, most parties to a Family Law case are more interested in the timely and cost-efficient resolution of their dispute, rather than in the development of the law. The law publishers

---

[9] S.O. 1991, c.17, as am.

are exploring ways of reporting to the profession significant decisions made in arbitrations.

(C) PROCESS

Because the majority of arbitration cases are in fact mediation-arbitrations, the concerns noted above regarding the "fairness" of the mediation-arbitration process continue to be of concern to many who participate in it. The procedural and ethical rules governing mediation-arbitrations will continue to evolve, as we have more experience with this process.

(D) "TWO-TIER" JUSTICE

Since arbitration tends to be chosen by more affluent parties, thereby leaving the court system to deal with less affluent people (including a higher percentage of unrepresented), it can be criticized as contributing to a two-tier justice system.

C. CASES THAT ARE NOT SUITABLE FOR ARBITRATION

Experience has taught us that certain types of cases are not suitable for arbitration or mediation-arbitration. They include the following:

- where there is or has been domestic violence or a significant power imbalance;
- where the parties cannot afford the fees of the arbitrator;
- where the parties will not submit to screening or obtain independent legal advice on the arbitration agreement;
- where the parties cannot agree on the terms of the arbitration agreement;
- where one or both of the parties refuse to apply Canadian law;
- where one or more of the parties will likely not comply with an arbitral award;
- where the court is required to compel financial disclosure;
- where the case requires the appointment of the Office of the Children's Lawyer; and
- where the case involves the rights or obligations of third parties.

D. THE FAMILY ARBITRATION AGREEMENT

1. Requirements for a Valid Family Arbitration Agreement

A "family arbitration agreement" is an agreement by which two or more persons agree to submit to arbitration a dispute that has arisen or may arise between them[10]. A "family arbitration" means an arbitration that deals with matters that could be dealt with in a marriage contract, separation agreement, cohabitation

---

[10] *Arbitration Act, 1991*, *ibid.*, s. 1.

agreement, or paternity agreement under Part IV of the *Family Law Act*[11]and is conducted exclusively in accordance with the law of Ontario or of another Canadian jurisdiction.[12] As a result of recent amendments to the *Arbitration Act, 1991*,[13] faith-based arbitrations in the Family Law context are of no legal effect.

2. Formalities

In order to be enforceable, a family arbitration agreement must be in writing and signed and witnessed.[14] Each party must receive independent legal advice before signing the agreement.[15] Each party must disclose to the other all significant assets, debts, or liabilities existing when the family arbitration agreement is made.[16] The family arbitration agreement must specify the grounds for appeal. While the statutory right to appeal an award on a question of law with leave cannot be waived, the parties can add additional grounds for appeal (a question of law without leave, a question of fact, or a question of mixed fact and law).[17] The right to seek judicial review of an award on the ground of procedural unfairness cannot be waived.[18]

3. Secondary Arbitration

Many of the rules that apply to formal Family Law arbitrations are impractical in the context of Parenting Coordination. As a result, a number of these rules have been relaxed for PC's. The *Family Law Act*[19] defines a "secondary arbitration" as a family arbitration that is conducted in accordance with a separation agreement, a court order, or a family arbitration award that provides for the arbitration of possible future disputes relating to the ongoing management or implementation of the agreement, order, or award.[20] In the case of a secondary arbitration, it is not necessary for the parties to receive independent legal advice before participating in the secondary arbitration and the formal requirements for awards (in writing, reasons, *etc.*) need not be met.[21]

4. Screening

As part of the family arbitration agreement, the arbitrator is required to confirm that the parties have been separately screened for domestic violence and power imbalances and that he or she has considered the results of the screening and

---

11 R.S.O. 1990, c. F.3.
12 *Arbitration Act, 1991*, S.O. 1991, c. 17, s. 1.
13 *Ibid.*
14 *Family Law Act*, R.S.O. 1990, c. F.3, s. 55(1).
15 *Ibid.*, s. 59.6(1)(*b*).
16 *Ibid.*, s. 56(4)(*a*).
17 *Arbitration Act, 1991*, S.O. 1991, c. 17, ss. 45(1), (2), and (3).
18 *Ibid.*, s. 3.2.
19 R.S.O. 1990, c. F.3.
20 *Ibid.*, s. 59.7(2).
21 *Ibid.*, s. 59.7(1).

will do so throughout the arbitration.[22] To date, there is no standard practice as to who conducts the screening and what the report on the results of the screening should contain. Those who specialize in screening for domestic violence agree that the same person, usually a mental health professional, should screen both parties as issues of power and control require that the screener consider not only external behaviour, but also the impact on the victim. (The first interview should be with the woman unless there is advance information suggesting that the woman may be the pretender of abusive or controlling behaviour.) Some Family Law arbitrators leave the screening requirement to be satisfied by the lawyers who provide the parties with independent legal advice before entering the family arbitration agreement. This presumes that those lawyers know their clients well, will be present at the arbitration, and are confident that there are no concerns about violence or control. In mediation and Med-Arb, the screening is often conducted by the mediator, especially if he/she is a mental health professional. Other Family Law arbitrators insist that the screening be conducted by one mental health professional who sees both parties. Others prefer to do the screening themselves, except in the case of a pure arbitration, where this option is prohibited.

5. Terms of the Family Arbitration Agreement

An arbitrator derives his/her authority from the terms of the arbitration agreement which the parties have executed. A typical family arbitration or Med-Arb agreement will contain the following provisions:

- Identification of the arbitrator and the substantive issues to be determined;
- A waiver of the parties' rights to litigate in the courts;
- The proceedings will be private and confidential, except as required by law;
- The law that shall govern the arbitration (law of Ontario or another Canadian jurisdiction);
- If the agreement provides for mediation, an express waiver of s. 35 of the *Arbitration Act, 1991*[23] (which otherwise prohibits an arbitrator from also acting as a mediator);
- The procedure for the arbitration, including any pre-arbitration conference;
- Whether the arbitrator may retain experts to assist him/her;
- The grounds for terminating the arbitration and the consequences of a termination;
- The arbitrator's obligation to deliver an award;
- The grounds for appeal;
- The rights to enforce the award;
- The arbitrator's fees and disbursements.

---

[22] *Family Arbitration Regulation*, O. Reg. 134/07, s. 2(4) 5.

[23] S.O. 1991, c. 17.

Parties to a family arbitration agreement may contract out of any of the provisions of the *Arbitration Act* except the following:

- the rules that the parties must be treated equally and fairly and each party must be given an opportunity to present a case and to respond to the other party's case;
- the court's power to set aside an award based on procedural irregularity or unfairness or to allow an appeal from an award as the basis of an error of law;
- the court's power to declare an arbitration to be invalid;
- the court's power to enforce an award;
- the arbitrator's obligation to apply the law of Ontario or another Canadian jurisdiction.

A sample Med-Arb agreement and family arbitration agreement can be found in Appendix V.

E. CONDUCT OF THE ARBITRATION

Subject to the provisions of the *Arbitration Act, 1991*[24] and the arbitration agreement pursuant to which he/she is appointed, the arbitrator determines the procedure to be followed in an arbitration. The arbitrator determines the time, date and place of the arbitration, taking into consideration the parties' convenience and the other circumstances of the case. The arbitrator will fix a date for the parties to deliver their statements setting out the facts supporting their positions, the points at issue, and the relief sought. The parties may submit with their statements the documents that they consider relevant or may refer to the documents or other evidence they intend to submit. The arbitrator may direct the parties to submit to oral examination under oath or to produce records or documents in their possession prior to the commencement of the arbitration.

The arbitrator may conduct the arbitration on the basis of documents or affidavits or may hold a hearing for the presentation of evidence and for oral argument; however, the arbitrator must hold a hearing if a party requests it. If a hearing is held, the arbitrator may make awards and give directions with respect to the taking of evidence as if it were a court proceeding. While hearsay evidence is admissible at an arbitration, too great a reliance on it in arriving at an arbitrator's decision has been held to constitute a denial of a party's right to natural justice and a reviewable error.

In some cases, the parties may prefer an alternate procedure. For example, in a "boardroom procedure", instead of hearing from one witness at a time, the arbitration hearing will deal with one issue at a time. The parties prepare an agenda listing all of the issues in dispute and then address them issue-by-issue so that all that is to be said by all parties on any issue is said at one session of the arbitration hearing. This helps the arbitrator to assimilate all of the evidence more easily and can result in a more efficient hearing.

---

[24] *Ibid.*

F. POWERS OF THE ARBITRATOR

Subject to the terms of the arbitration agreement, the powers of the arbitrator include the following:

- To decide questions of law or to refer such questions to the court;
- To rule on its own jurisdiction or on the validity of the arbitration agreement;
- To make an order for the detention, preservation or inspection of property;
- To determine the procedure to be followed during the actual hearing and to determine when and where the hearing will be conducted;
- To appoint an expert;
- To administer an oath or affirmation and to require a witness to testify;
- To order specific performance, injunctions and other equitable remedies;
- To make interim and final awards;
- To dismiss claims where a party fails to cooperate or to proceed without the party who is not cooperating and/or delaying;
- To award costs, including the arbitrator's fees.

After the arbitrator has heard each party's evidence and argument, the arbitrator must render an award in accordance with the evidence and the law. The award must be in writing and must state the reasons on which it is based. Within 30 days of receiving the decision, a party may request an explanation by the arbitrator. The making of the award terminates the arbitration.

G. ENFORCEMENT OF FAMILY ARBITRATION AWARDS

A family arbitration award is enforceable under the *Family Law Act*[25] only if:

(a) The family arbitration agreement under which the award is made is in writing and complies with the Regulation[26] under the *Arbitration Act, 1991*;[27]

(b) Each of the parties has received independent legal advice before signing the family arbitration agreement;

(c) The formalities regarding the award have been met; and

(d) The arbitrator has complied with the Regulation.

Upon application, a court may make an order in the same terms as the arbitral award.

H. TRAINING REQUIREMENTS

The Regulation[28] under the *Arbitration Act, 1991*[29] requires a family arbitrator to have the training set out on the Attorney General's website. All family

---

25 R.S.O. 1990, c. F.3.

26 *Family Arbitration Regulation*, O. Reg. 134/07.

27 S.O. 1991, c. 17.

28 *Family Arbitration Regulation*, O .Reg. 134/07.

29 S.O. 1991, c. 17.

arbitrators must receive a training program of at least 14 hours (taught within a 7-day period) in screening parties for domestic violence and power imbalance. An additional 5 hours of training on these topics is required every 2 years. All family arbitrators who are not members of the Ontario Bar or another Canadian Bar must complete 30 hours of training on Ontario Family Law. Family arbitrators are also encouraged to take courses on how to be an arbitrator, although there are no legal requirements that they do so. Completion of an approved 40-hour course in Family Law arbitration will qualify a family arbitrator to apply for the ADR Institute's Certified Family Arbitrator designation.

I. THE ROLE OF THE PARENTING COORDINATOR

A Parenting Coordinator (or "PC") is typically appointed jointly by the parties in a dispute resolution clause in their Separation Agreement or court order to assist the parties in resolving future disputes arising out of child-related issues. In Ontario, the courts have consistently held that they have no jurisdiction to appoint a PC unless both parties consent. The PC is usually a mental health professional (psychologist or social worker) who has received specialized training in dealing with these types of conflicts.

There is no legislation in Canada governing Parenting Coordination. As a result, each PC develops his or her own contract which determines the scope of the PC's jurisdiction, the procedure the PC follows, an agreement for fees and retainers, *etc*. The PC's role may include some or all of the following:

(a) Assist with the implementation, maintenance and monitoring of the Minutes of Settlement/Parenting Plan, court orders and/or arbitrated decisions;
(b) Address any anticipated conflicts in the child(ren)'s scheduling that occur;
(c) Develop any additional clauses to clarify any given situations and events that unfold that were not initially anticipated when the Parenting Plan was developed;
(d) Monitor the child(ren)'s adjustment;
(e) Assist in the maintenance of the child(ren)'s relationship with each parent;
(f) Assist the parents to communicate more effectively;
(g) Assist with the exchange of information about the child(ren) (*i.e.*, health, welfare, education, and religion) and his/her routines that may be otherwise impossible and/or ineffective in accordance with the methods provided for in the Parenting Plan;
(h) Make final decisions relating to "major" decisions (*i.e.*, relating to education, child(ren) welfare, medical, and/or religion) if the parents are unable to come to a mutual agreement *and* if this method of dispute resolution is consistent with the court order and/or Minutes of Settlement/ Parenting Plan;
(i) Make binding decisions, if necessary, pertaining to *temporary* changes to the regular and/or holiday parenting time schedule to accommodate special events or circumstances for the child(ren) and/or the parents;

(j) Resolve conflicts between the parents concerning the child(ren)'s participation in recreation, enrichment, or extra-curricular activities and programs;
(k) Address movement of clothing, equipment, toys, and personal possessions between households;
(l) Address child(ren)'s travel arrangements;
(m) Clarify and resolve different interpretations of the Parenting Plan;
(n) Resolve conflicts concerning health care, education, passports, activities, religious education, and events that are not otherwise provided for in the Minutes of Settlement/Parenting Plan.

J. THE PRE-ARBITRATION CONFERENCE

Once it has been determined that an arbitration will be held, most arbitrators will conduct a pre-arbitration or a preliminary conference with counsel (or with the parties, if they are unrepresented) to determine the procedure for the hearing. The conference can be conducted in person or by way of conference call. The issues to be determined and resolved include the following:

- Determining who is the applicant and who is the respondent. This will determine which party goes first in the presentation of evidence;
- Reviewing the terms of the arbitration agreement and confirming that it has been properly executed by the parties, the lawyers providing independent legal advice and the arbitrator as required by the Regulation;[30]
- Confirming the issues to be determined;
- Setting a timeline for delivery of position statements and whether or not pleadings from previous litigation are to be relied on;
- Setting a timeline for delivery of financial statements and net family property statements, if required;
- Determining the disclosure to be made by each party and a timeline for compliance;
- Arranging a conference call or motion to deal with a failure to comply or other interim proceedings;
- Determining the names of witnesses to be called, the anticipated time required for each witness' evidence, and a timeline for the exchange of witness statements;
- Arranging for the issuance of any summonses to witness that are required;
- Determining what expert evidence, if any, has been obtained or is going to be required and a timeline for the production of expert reports;
- Determining the exact time and place of the hearing and the number of days required for the hearing;
- Reviewing the results of the screening and addressing any issues that arise from the screening;

---

[30] *Family Arbitration Regulation*, O. Reg. 134/07.

- Dealing with any issues as to the attendance at the hearing by non-parties;
- Confirming arrangements for a court reporter, if required;
- Determining the procedure to be followed in the presentation of evidence;
- Confirming what rules of procedure and evidence will apply;
- Confirming the fees and retainer arrangements required by the arbitrator;
- Reminding the parties of the cost consequences of offers to settle and the failure to accept offers.

Attached as part of Appendix V is a suggested Pre-Arbitration Conference Form that both counsel (or the parties, if unrepresented) should complete prior to the pre-arbitration conference. The matters discussed and agreed upon during the pre-arbitration conference should be confirmed in writing by the arbitrator. Careful attention paid to these issues will increase the likelihood of the arbitration hearing proceeding in an equitable, fair, and effective manner.

K. KEEPING CONTROL OF THE HEARING

It is the arbitrator's responsibility to control the hearing. In this context, "control" means managing the hearing as efficiently as possible without disrespecting the principles of a fair hearing. The following tips for keeping control of the hearing may be useful:

- Understand the players and the background of the dispute.
- Earn respect of counsel and parties by treating them with respect.
- Develop sufficient competence and display appropriate judicial temperament.
- Do not pretend to understand something said if you do not.
- Arrive on time.
- Advise the parties of expected break times.
- Ensure that breaks are reasonable.
- Be fastidious about consulting with counsel about hearing logistics.
- Do not set a time limit for the hearing.
- Come prepared.
- Come to the hearing with an open mind, not an empty mind.
- Give your full and undivided attention to what is taking place in the hearing room.
- Take detailed notes.
- Be careful of ceasing to take notes.
- Use your note-taking to control the pace of the hearing.
- Questions for witnesses should be asked in a non-aggressive manner.
- Maintain an attitude of inquiry, rather than judgment.
- If necessary, permit parties to take a short break to allow time for things to calm down following a heated exchange.
- Think and speak respectfully at all times.
- Avoid excessively friendly or humorous behaviour.
- Never be seen to look at your watch.

- Avoid making remarks not germane to the hearing.
- Invite counsel to have their say (and right of reply) on any contentious issue before you make up your mind.
- Remember that how things are done is as important as the outcome.

L. DETERMINING THE FACTS

The arbitral award must indicate the reasoning used by the arbitrator to come to his or her decision. The first step in those reasons is determining the facts upon which the award is based. The following are suggestions as to how the arbitrator should deal with evidence in hearings, in deliberations, and in rendering awards.

1. Keeping Track of the Evidence

The arbitrator must listen carefully to the evidence and attempt to take detailed notes. These notes should reflect the name of the witness and what stage (direct examination, cross-examination, *etc.*) the evidence was elicited. Since it is impossible to take verbatim notes, the arbitrator should attempt to summarize the important evidence, except where the precise words used in evidence are important. The arbitrator should develop short-hand techniques for recording questions and answers. The arbitrator should take time to observe the demeanour of the witnesses and to note any impressions of the witnesses in his or her notes. References to exhibits should be highlighted and annotated in the arbitrator's copy of the exhibits brief. The arbitrator should review and edit his or her notes at the end of each day. Where the case involves a number of issues, the arbitrator should index his/her notes by issue. He/she should flag areas of the evidence where he/she wishes to ask questions. The arbitrator must take care not to prejudge the case and should pay particular attention to counsel's closing arguments. If there is any doubt as to what the issues to be decided are, the arbitrator should ask counsel to clarify them in their closing argument.

2. What Evidence Can and Should the Arbitrator Consider?

Opening statements and closing argument by counsel are not evidence. Evidence is information that is presented under oath or affirmation, in exhibits or by the parties' agreement to establish the facts on which the arbitrator is to make his/her decision.

3. What Is the Difference Between Facts and Evidence?

Factual determinations are based on the examination and evaluation of the information or "evidence" that has been presented. Evidence, therefore, is the data for factual decision-making. Evidence of a fact is information that tends to prove it.

Evidence must be admissible: that is, relevant to the proceeding and not otherwise excluded by some rule of law. Evidence can be direct (a witness testifies from personal observation) or circumstantial. An inference may be drawn from other proven facts. Hearsay evidence (a witness testifying as to a statement made by another person outside of the courtroom offered to prove the truth of the statement) is generally only admissible if it is necessary and reliable.

4. Expert Evidence

Only experts can give opinion evidence, as opposed to other witnesses who give factual evidence concerning direct observations and/or information known to the witness. A Family Law arbitrator will often be confronted by conflicting evidence from two or more experts (for example, mental health professionals testifying on custody and access issues or valuators testifying as to financial issues). The manner in which the expert evidence has been assessed should be dealt with in the arbitrator's decision and reasons. The basis for the arbitrator's decision to rely upon, discount, or reject an expert opinion must be fully set out and may include consideration of the following:

- Is the opinion relevant to the matter in issue?
- How do the assumptions relied upon by the expert in giving an opinion compare to the facts found by the arbitrator?
- How extensive are the expert's qualifications compared to other experts?
- How relevant are the expert's qualifications to the matter in issue?
- Was the expert's evidence credible?
- How objective did the expert appear to be? Did he or she appear to be partisan?

To the extent any of these factors are relied upon, the arbitrator's reasons should fully explain why one or more of these factors apply.

5. Arbitrator's Use of Own Expertise

An arbitrator will often be confronted with the situation where he/she is tempted to use his/her own expertise in order to determine the facts. The caselaw has held that an arbitrator can use his/her expertise in assessing the evidence, but the evidence has to be before the arbitrator before he or she can assess it. In other words, an arbitrator cannot substitute his/her experience for proper evidence in the arbitration.

6. Assessing Credibility

In many cases, an arbitrator will have to make decisions concerning the credibility of witnesses. When determining credibility, an arbitrator may wish to use some or all of the following criteria:

- the appearance and demeanour of the witness
- the witness' opportunity to observe
- the witness' capacity to remember

- the probability or reasonability of the evidence
- internal consistency of the evidence
- external consistency of the evidence
- the witness' interest in the outcome.

This list of factors is not exhaustive. To the extent that any of these factors are relied upon, the arbitrator's reasons should fully explain why one or more of these factors apply.

7. The Evidentiary Basis for the Decision

In order for an arbitral award to withstand judicial scrutiny, the decision must have a clear evidentiary foundation. The reasons should contain a review of the evidence. Where there are disputes over the facts, the arbitrator should make specific findings as to the facts, indicating which evidence has been accepted and which has been rejected. When the arbitrator makes a finding of credibility, he/she should state the reasons for that conclusion. The reasons should deal with the substantial points raised by the parties and must disclose the reasoning process used by the arbitrator to arrive at his/her decision.

M. CONFIDENTIALITY OF ARBITRATION PROCEEDINGS

One of the advantages of the arbitration process over the court system is the confidentiality of arbitration proceedings. However, the confidentiality of the process is subject to a number of significant limitations. Any application to the court to surprise, stay, appeal, review, or enforce an arbitral award is not subject to the umbrella of arbitral confidentiality. Secondly, the arbitrator is required to file a report about the award with the Attorney General in accordance with the Regulation[31] under the *Arbitration Act, 1991*.[32] Thirdly, an arbitrator is required to report a child in need of protection in accordance with s. 72 of the *Child and Family Services Act*.[33] Fourthly, the arbitrator may be required to disclose confidential information to prevent a person's death or serious harm. Finally, there have been circumstances in which courts have required that information produced in an arbitration be produced to the court in an unrelated proceeding. The family arbitration agreement should advise of these limitations so as to avoid surprises if and when they arise.

During the mediation phase of a Med-Arb, one party may disclose information to the mediator on the basis that the mediator not disclose this information to the other party. Such disclosures (such as the parties' bottom line in a negotiation) can be very useful for the mediator. If, however, the case proceeds to an arbitration, how does the arbitrator deal with that information in the arbitration? Because the arbitrator's role is to determine the dispute solely on

---

31 *Family Arbitration Regulation*, O. Reg. 134/07.

32 S.O. 1991, c. 17.

33 R.S.O. 1990, C.11.

the basis of the evidence led in the arbitration, the arbitrator must ignore the confidential information given to him/her in the mediation phase. If the arbitrator is uncomfortable with being placed in that situation, then he/she should decline to promise confidentiality when the issue first arises in the mediation.

N. RECORD OF FAMILY ARBITRATION

Every arbitrator who conducts a family arbitration must create a record of the arbitration containing:

(a) the evidence presented and considered;
(b) the arbitrator's notes taken during the hearing, if any;
(c) a copy of the signed arbitration agreement, and the certificates of independent legal advice;
(d) if the screening for power imbalances and domestic violence was conducted by someone other than the arbitrator, the report on the results of the screening; and
(e) the award and the arbitrator's written reasons for it.

An arbitrator who conducts one or more secondary arbitrations under a separation agreement, court order, or family arbitration award (including a parenting coordinator), must create a record containing:

(a) a copy of the separation agreement, court order, or family arbitration award; and
(b) for each secondary arbitration conducted by the arbitrator under the separation agreement, court order, or family arbitration award:

    (i) the evidence presented and considered;

    (ii) the arbitrator's notes taken during the hearing, if any; and

    (iii) the award and the arbitrator's written reasons for it.

An arbitrator shall keep the record of an arbitration for at least 10 years after the date of the award.

O. THE ARBITRATOR'S REPORT

Every arbitrator who conducts a family arbitration must report the following information about the award to the Attorney General in the form provided by the Attorney General:

(a) the date and length of the hearing, if any, leading to the award;
(b) the matters addressed in the arbitration and in the award;
(c) details of the following, to the extent relevant to the award:

    (i) the ages of the parties to whom the award relates, the length of their relationship, their approximate incomes and the approximate total value of each party's assets;

(ii) the ages and genders of any children of any party to whom the award relates, and custody and access arrangements and child support awarded in respect of them;

(iii) spousal support awarded;

(iv) equalization of property awarded;

(v) any provision in the award restraining contact or communication between the parties.

These reports shall be provided to the Attorney General:

(a) for family arbitrations completed during the period from April 1 to September 30, on or before November 30; and

(b) for family arbitrations completed during the period from October 1 to March 31 of the following year, on or before May 31.

P. CHALLENGING FAMILY ARBITRATION AWARDS

Where parties have contracted to arbitrate a dispute, courts are loath to intervene. Section 6 of the *Arbitration Act, 1991*[34] makes it very clear that court intervention in matters submitted to arbitration are limited to four situations:

1. To assist the conducting of arbitrations.
2. To ensure that arbitrations are conducted in accordance with arbitration agreements.
3. To prevent unequal or unfair treatment of parties to arbitration agreements.
4. To enforce awards.

The *Arbitration Act, 1991* sets out a comprehensive code for appeals and review by judges of arbitral awards.[35] There are a number of ways in which parties may challenge arbitration awards. Under the *Arbitration Act, 1991*, parties may appeal an arbitration award under s. 45, may attempt to set aside the award under s. 46, or may move to declare the arbitration invalid under s. 48.

1. Appealing an Arbitration Award

Under s. 45, a party may appeal an award to the court on a question of law with leave. The court shall only grant leave if it is satisfied that the importance to the parties of the matters at stake in the arbitration justifies the appeal and that determination of the question of law at issue will significantly affect the rights of the parties.[36] A party may appeal an award to the court on a question of law without the requirement of leave, if the arbitration agreement so provides.[37] A party may also appeal an award to the court on a question of fact or on a question of mixed fact and law, if the arbitration agreement so provides, without

---

[34] S.O. 1991, c. 17.

[35] *Kucyi v. Kucyi*, [2005] O.J. No. 5626, 206 O.A.C. 113 (Ont. Div. Ct.).

[36] *Arbitration Act, 1991*, S.O. 1991, c. 17, s. 45(1). According to s. 3(2)(*v*) of the Act, however, the parties can no longer contract out of their right to appeal on a question of law.

[37] *Arbitration Act, 1991*, *ibid.*, s. 45(2).

the requirement of leave.[38] While parties to a non-family arbitration agreement can contract out of all appeal rights, parties to a family arbitration agreement cannot contract out the right of appeal on a question of law. [39]

On any appeal, the court may confirm, vary, or set aside the award or may remit the award to the arbitral tribunal with the court's opinion on a question of law. The court may give directions about the conduct of the arbitration[40] or require the arbitral tribunal to explain any matter.[41]

There have not been many Ontario cases in which a party to a family law arbitration has sought appellate review of an award pursuant to s. 45 of the *Arbitration Act, 1991*. The cases that do exist generally demonstrate the court's reluctance to intervene where parties have elected to submit to Family Law arbitration and have clearly demonstrated that the arbitrators are entitled to a high standard of review. In *Robinson v. Robinson*[42] the court held that it should not interfere with the arbitrator's award unless it is satisfied that the arbitrator acted on the basis of a wrong principle, disregarded material evidence, or misapprehended the evidence.

An appeal of an award or application to set aside an award must be commenced within 30 days after the appellant or applicant receives the award, correction, explanation, change, or statement of reasons on which the appeal or application is based, unless the appellant or applicant alleges corruption or fraud.[43]

2. Setting Aside an Award

Section 46(1) of the *Arbitration Act, 1991*[44] preserves the right of a party to apply to the court to set aside an arbitral award under any of the following circumstances:

1. A party entered into the arbitration agreement while under a legal incapacity.
2. The arbitration agreement is invalid or has ceased to exist.
3. The award deals with a dispute that the arbitration agreement does not cover or contains a decision on a matter that is beyond the scope of the agreement.
4. The composition of the tribunal was not in accordance with the arbitration agreement or, if the agreement did not deal with that matter, was not in accordance with the Act.
5. The subject-matter of the dispute is not capable of being the subject of arbitration under Ontario law.
6. The applicant was not treated equally and fairly, was not given an opportunity to present a case or to respond to another party's case, or was not given proper notice of the arbitration or of the appointment of an arbitrator.
7. The procedures followed in the arbitration did not comply with the Act.

---

[38] *Ibid.*, s. 45(3).
[39] *Ibid.*, s. 3.2.
[40] *Ibid.*, s. 45(5).
[41] *Ibid.*, s. 45(4).
[42] *Robinson v. Robinson*, [2000] O.J. No. 3299 (Ont. S.C.J.).
[43] *Arbitration Act, 1991*, S.O. 1991, c. 17, s. 47(2).
[44] S.O. 1991, c. 17.

8. An arbitrator has committed a corrupt or fraudulent act or there is a reasonable apprehension of bias.
9. The award was obtained by fraud.
10. The award is a family arbitration award that is not enforceable under the *Family Law Act.*

A party must bring an application to set aside an award within 30 days of receiving the award, correction, change, or statement of reasons on which the application is based.[45] Parties cannot contract out of the right of review under s. 46(1).[46]

A party who participates in a family arbitration, despite being aware of non-compliance with a provision of the *Arbitration Act, 1991* or the arbitration agreement and does not object to the non-compliance within the appropriate time, is not deemed to have waived the right to object to such non-compliance. Accordingly, the court may set aside an award on any of the grounds described above, whether or not the party in question objected on a timely basis to the non-compliance.[47]

The courts have been hesitant to set aside arbitration awards under s. 46. Section 19(1) of the *Arbitration Act, 1991* requires arbitrators to treat the parties equally and fairly. Section 19(2) further requires each party "shall be given an opportunity to present a case and to respond to the parties' cases". In *Hercus v. Hercus,*[48] Templeton J. stated that the concept of treating a party "equally" infers an "even balance" and "uniform approach". Arbitrator Terrence W. Caskie, in his paper "ADR-Arbitration: Conduct of the Hearing",[49] states that the following rules of natural justice apply to the conduct of all arbitration hearings:

- Adequate notice of time and place of hearing is given.
- Each party is allowed to lead evidence and cross-examine.
- Each party is allowed to make submissions and respond to the other party's submissions.
- The hearing is conducted in the presence of both parties.
- The process ensures that each party knows clearly the case to be met.
- Each party is allowed to make submissions if the arbitrator desires to consider evidence that has not been put into the record by either party.
- Each party is treated equally and fairly.

In *Kainz v. Potter,*[50] the court considered the arbitrator's duty under s. 19 of the *Arbitration Act, 1991* in allowing an appeal from an award of supervised access. Dr. L., the parties' child assessor, was chosen by them as their arbitrator

45 *Ibid.*, s. 47(1).

46 *Ibid.*, s. 3.1. iv.

47 *Arbitration Act, 1991*, S.O. 1991, c. 17, s. 4(2).

48 [2001] O.J. No. 534 (Ont. S.C.J.).

49 Paper presented to the Law Society of Upper Canada Continuing Legal Education Program, Effective Use of ADR in Family Law Practice, 3 December 2001) [unpublished], at p. 3-2.

50 [2006] O.J. No. 2441, 33 R.F.L. (6th) 62 (Ont. S.C.J.); also see *Hercus v. Hercus*, [2001] O.J. No. 534 (Ont. S.C.J.); *Likins v. MacKenzie*, 2003 CarswellOnt 3007; *Webster v. Wendt*, [2001] O.J. No. 622, 3 C.P.C. (5th) 378 (Ont. S.C.J.).

for parenting issues under their separation agreement. The court held that although Dr. L. was not expected to conduct the arbitration proceedings as if he had legal expertise, he failed to meet the minimum standard of fairness to both parties by sometimes allowing P. and his counsel at the arbitration hearing to run the hearing. The court held that K., who chose to represent herself at the arbitration hearing, was entitled to receive some assistance from the adjudicator so that she could fairly present her case, including directions on procedure, the nature of the evidence that can be presented, the calling of witnesses, the form of questioning, requests for adjournments, and even the raising of substantive and evidentiary issues.[51] The court held that the arbitration hearing was "replete with numerous procedural and evidentiary flaws" that were unfair to K., including leading questions on some very contentious issues that were put to P. and his witnesses during their examination-in-chief; unchecked hearsay evidence presented by P. and his witnesses; frequently allowing P. to deviate from, and take liberties with, the questions put to him, and to give his opinion about past proceedings, awards, and evidence that were not before the tribunal; and frequent and unchecked reference to materials from previous court hearings, mediations, assessments, and arbitrations making it difficult to define the official record of this arbitration.

Successful attacks on Family Law arbitral rulings are fairly uncommon. However, there are a number of grounds on which arbitral awards can be challenged. If there is evidence of unfairness, or even an appearance of unfairness, particularly where there is an unrepresented party as there was in *Kainz v. Potter,* a court may find that the arbitrator breached his or her duty to act equally and fairly under s. 19 of the *Arbitration Act, 1991.*

3. Declaration of Invalidity

Section 48 of the *Arbitration Act, 1991*[52] empowers the court to declare an arbitration invalid prior to the issuance of the award under several circumstances. An arbitration may be declared invalid if a party entered into the arbitration while under legal incapacity,[53] if the arbitration agreement is invalid or has ceased to exist,[54] if the subject-matter of the dispute is not capable of being the subject of arbitration under Ontario law,[55] or if the arbitration agreement does not apply to the dispute.[56] If the arbitration is declared invalid, a party may seek an injunction against the commencement or continuation of the arbitration.

---

[51] *Kainz v. Potter, ibid.*, at para. 65.
[52] S.O. 1991, c. 17.
[53] *Ibid.*, s. 48(1)(*a*).
[54] *Ibid.*, s. 48(1)(*b*).
[55] *Ibid.*, s. 48(1)(*c*).
[56] *Ibid.*, s. 48(1)(*d*).

SUMMARY

This chapter considered the advantages and disadvantages of arbitration, outlined the terms of a family arbitration agreement and explained the role and power of the arbitrator. We reviewed how the arbitrator controls the hearing and determines the facts and the power of the court to challenge arbitrations and arbitral awards.

ANNOTATED BIBLIOGRAPHY

Caskie, T.W. "Conduct of the Hearing" (Paper presented to the Law Society of Upper Canada Continuing Legal Education Program, Effective Use of ADR in Family Law Practice, 3 December 2001) [unpublished].

Chodos, L. "Parenting Coordination: The Cutting Edge of Conflict Management with Separated/Divorced Families" (Paper presented to the Continuing Legal Education Program, Special Lectures 2006 Family Law, 3 and 4 April 2006) (Toronto: Law Society of Upper Canada, 2006).

Epstein, P. "Mediation/Arbitration: Some Thoughts on the Process" (Paper presented to the Law Society of Upper Canada Continuing Legal Education Program, Effective Use of ADR in Family Law Practice, 3 December 2001) [unpublished].

Epstein, P., and Gibb, S. "Family Law Arbitrations: Choice and Finality Under the Amended *Arbitration Act, 1991* and *Family Law Act*" (Paper presented to the Continuing Legal Education Program, Special Lectures 2006 Family Law, 3 and 4 April 2006) (Toronto: Law Society of Upper Canada, 2006).

Franks, A. "Mediation and Arbitration – Case Law Update" (Paper presented to the Law Society of Upper Canada Continuing Legal Education Program, Mediation and Arbitration for Family Law Lawyers, 13 November 2007) [unpublished].

Grant, S. "Alternate Dispute Resolution in Family Law: What's Not to Like?" (Paper presented to the Law Society of Upper Canada Continuing Legal Education Program, Mediation and Arbitration for Family Law Lawyers, 13 November 2007) [unpublished].

Gover, B.J., and Latimer, P. "Mastering the Fact-Finding Process" (Paper presented to the Law Society of Upper Canada Continuing Legal Education Program, Mediation and Arbitration for Family Law Lawyers, 13 November 2007) [unpublished].

Himmel, A. "Mediation/Arbitration Agreements: The Binding Comes Undone" (2002), 20 *Canadian Family Law Quarterly* 55.

Joseph, G., and Stangarone, M. "Challenging Arbitration Awards and/or Removing the Arbitrator under the *Arbitration Act, 1991*" (Paper presented to the Law Society of Upper Canada Continuing Legal Education Program, Mediation and Arbitration for Family Law Lawyers, 13 November 2007) [unpublished].

Mamo, A.A. "Conducting the Arbitration Hearing" (Paper presented to the Law Society of Upper Canada Continuing Legal Education Program, Mediation and Arbitration for Family Law Lawyers, 13 November 2007) [unpublished].

Thomson, C., and Finn A. "Mediation-Arbitration: A Contentious But Often Effective Compromise" *The Lawyers Weekly* (15 September 2006).

Wilson, J. "Family Law Mediation and Arbitration Challenging Mediation-Arbitration, Arbitration (and Secondary Arbitration) Awards" (Paper presented to the Law Society of Upper Canada Continuing Legal Education Program, Mediation and Arbitration for Family Law Lawyers, 13 November 2007) [unpublished].

Wolfson, L.H., and Kovitz, J.L. "The New Family Arbitration" (Paper presented to the Law Society of Upper Canada Continuing Legal Education Program, Mediation and Arbitration for Family Law Lawyers, 13 November 2007) [unpublished].

Chapter Eight

Dispute Resolution Outcomes

There are several possible outcomes for parties engaged in dispute resolution depending on the process they choose. In mediation, the outcome is a Memorandum of Understanding, in Collaborative Practice it is a Separation Agreement, in court it is an Order or Minutes of Settlement and in Arbitration, it is an Award. This chapter contains a number of helpful hints for drafting the various dispute resolution outcomes.

A. AGREEMENT BY PARTIES IN MEDIATION

If the parties reach an agreement on one or more issues, the mediator prepares a report containing the specific terms agreed to by the parties. The form of the mediator's report should be worked out in discussions with both counsel and the parties, preferably at the beginning of mediation, so that all parties are clear about what they will receive from the mediator. The report is usually called a *memorandum of understanding*.

If the clients have retained collaborative lawyers, the mediator should send a copy of the memorandum of understanding to both counsel and arrange a five-way meeting to discuss any proposed changes to the memorandum. It is usually helpful for the mediator to speak to counsel in advance of the meeting with clients:

- to identify any potential areas of conflict and begin to consider ways to resolve such differences constructively;
- to offer clarification about any parts of the agreement that are unclear or to suggest improvements to wording;
- to review creative alternatives reached by the clients that fall outside of the Family Law legislation; and
- to develop an agenda for the meeting with clients.

Often one such meeting can accomplish the equivalent of several individual meetings between each lawyer and his or her client. The end result is that the lawyers can incorporate the memorandum into a final Separation Agreement which can be signed and witnessed with both clients and their lawyers present.

If one or both parties have initiated court proceedings, then the issues resolved in mediation can be incorporated into *minutes of settlement* that would be filed with the court on consent in order to terminate the legal proceedings. These are not cases in which collaborative lawyers would be involved.

1. Memorandum of Understanding

This document should outline in clear, unambiguous language the specific agreement reached on those issues sent to mediation.

One of the factors that contributes to couples returning to court to re-litigate agreements is the lack of precision of the wording in the agreement. It is very important that the mediator state as clearly and specifically as possible what responsibilities or privileges each party will have. If the parties are to share responsibilities and privileges, it should be clear:

- what responsibilities each party will bear;
- what privileges each party will have;
- under what circumstances a party will have such responsibilities and privileges;
- what notice one party is required to give to the other party;
- whether the responsibility is something that a particular spouse is required to do or whether it is something that the spouse can be requested to do, if he or she is available; and
- what will happen if one party is unable or unwilling to fulfill a responsibility or accept a privilege.

In general, it is preferable to set out:

- specific times for access visits on weekends, during the week, on statutory holidays, during school breaks, and at other times;
- specific times and locations for pickup and delivery; and
- whether the parties intend to permit additional access time on request and whether this will trigger an expectation for compensatory time.

The mediator can explain to the parties that in the future, once they are more comfortable with each other's involvement, they can behave in a more flexible way with respect to access times. However, at the beginning, particularly with clients who do not trust each other, a schedule that clarifies their respective rights and obligations is usually helpful.

It is very important to include the parties' intentions with respect to changes in custody or access arrangements in the event that the parties move more than a certain distance apart. Families are very mobile, and one or both spouses may move due to a job, a new relationship, for economic or other reasons. An arrangement that has worked well for a number of years may suddenly grind to a stop because a party wishes to move out of the city or even out of the province or country. It is important to anticipate that this may happen and to include a provision to cover this possibility. Many cases end up in litigation when this situation is not anticipated.

In cases of financial mediation, it is important to consider material changes in the parties' circumstances, such as:

- the loss of a job;
- obtaining employment for a previously unemployed spouse;
- the effect of illness or long-term disability;
- the death of a spouse; or

- the remarriage of one or both spouses.

All of these factors could constitute a material change of circumstances that should trigger a re-examination of the original agreement. The process that the parties wish to follow when there is a material change in circumstances should be included in the agreement.

If the parties have agreed to mediate a new arrangement in the event that there is a material change in circumstances (such as remarriage or a move to a new province), the agreement should state how the mediator will be chosen and how the mediator's fees will be shared. That is, will one party pay the full cost, will the fees be shared 50-50, or will the fees be paid in proportion to gross income at the time?

It may be desirable to have an interim agreement, possibly for three to six months, before completing a final agreement. This would give the parties a chance to evaluate whatever plan they have chosen, both in terms of the best interests of the child and their own needs. An interim agreement would also give the parties an opportunity to adjust to the separation. At the time set for termination of the agreement, the parties could return to mediation to review the contents of the interim agreement and decide whether to continue with it indefinitely, for a further period of time, or whether to make appropriate changes. A time-limited agreement may be preferable in the following circumstances:

- if the child's needs, wishes, and/or stage of development change, and it is desirable to reconsider the previous parenting plan;
- if the parties' circumstances change such that a review is warranted;
- if the parties do not have independent legal advice, and a time-limited agreement would limit the effect of any adverse legal consequences.

If one or both parties refuse to obtain independent legal advice, the mediator should not witness the signature of the parties on the memorandum of understanding. If both parties have lawyers, it is recommended that the lawyers be invited to a five-way meeting as described above and the memorandum of understanding can be incorporated into a separation agreement by the lawyers and be signed in the presence of the lawyers. It the lawyers are not collaboratively trained, they may prefer to have the memorandum sent to them for signing in their respective offices.

Unless the mediator is a trained lawyer, the mediator should not attempt to draft a Separation Agreement for the parties. This is because:

- the mediator could be charged under provincial legislation with the unauthorized practice of law;
- the mediator may not appreciate the implications of certain clauses dealing with custody, financial matters, and releases in terms of their legal significance for the parties;
- the mediator could be sued if one or both parties are prejudiced as a result of clauses that are included in or omitted from the agreement; or
- the legal position of one or both clients could be adversely affected because of the mediator's lack of legal training.

Some lawyers hold the view that even if the mediator is a lawyer, he or she should not draft the complete separation agreement because:

- the mediator may only be dealing with some of the issues in dispute and therefore not have adequate information with respect to all of the issues and their implications for both parties that normally would be included in a complete agreement;
- drafting a separation agreement may create some role confusion in the client's mind about whether the mediator is acting as a mediator or a lawyer; and
- the solicitors for the clients may feel the mediator is usurping their role.

This issue should be fully discussed with both the clients and their solicitors in advance to clarify the expectations of all parties and avoid future confusion or problems. In fact, the lawyers and clients may wish to have the mediator draw up specific clauses of the separation agreement relating to mediation because:

- the mediator who is legally trained both understands the nature of the agreement reached and can express the client's wishes most clearly;
- the parties are saved the expense of having one or both lawyers who were not present during the discussions try to draft these particular clauses.

The authors recommend that even mediators who are lawyers draft a memorandum of understanding which could be changed into a separation agreement once the parties have received independent legal advice. The mediator should not witness the parties' signatures to the separation agreement.

In addition to the memorandum of understanding, the mediator should prepare a brief report. If the parties have initiated legal proceedings, then the brief report would be sent to the judge along with the minutes of settlement and a copy of the memorandum of understanding.

The memorandum of understanding should be sent to the parties and to their legal counsel, prior to signing, so that the clients can obtain independent legal advice. Both in the memorandum of understanding and in the brief report, the mediator should indicate that the parties have been strongly advised to obtain independent legal advice prior to signing any agreement.

This brief report should contain the following types of information:

- a statement of the issues that were sent to mediation;
- a statement of which issues were resolved and which issues are still in dispute;
- who was seen during the mediation, how often, in what combinations, and for what total period of time;
- a summary of the terms of the memorandum of understanding and some additional explanation or encouragement for the parties with respect to implementing the memorandum of understanding;
- the intention of the parties when arriving at an agreement;
- the basic responsibilities and privileges of each parent in the context of the best interests of the children;

- any significant concerns or possible obstacles that were identified during the mediation that may affect the ability of one or both parties to carry out the terms of the agreement, along with any suggestions for handling these difficulties if they should arise.

The mediator should indicate that he or she would be available to assist the parties should there be some initial difficulties in implementing the agreement or should difficulties arise in the future due to a material change in circumstance or developmental changes in the children. The covering report should also encourage the parties to overlook their own differences as spouses in order to cooperate in the best interests of their children. This is particularly important in situations where both parents want to maintain a close and loving relationship with the children.

2. Separation Agreement

The mediator should review the memorandum of understanding with the clients to be sure it accurately reflects their wishes and then should send counsel a copy of the memorandum of understanding, which can be incorporated into a full separation agreement. Unless the parties were engaged in comprehensive media-tion, a separation agreement usually takes into consideration a number of issues that were not discussed during the mediation process.

Once certain issues have been agreed upon during mediation, the clients and their counsel usually continue to negotiate other related issues. For example, if the mediation involved custody and access issues, the lawyers might deal with financial matters, and would then draft a separation agreement including clauses with respect to:

- child support;
- spousal support;
- cost-of-living increase in support;
- division of property;
- possession and ownership of the matrimonial home;
- division of debts;
- material change in circumstances;
- share of pension funds; and
- releases with respect to future claims and liabilities.

It is hoped that the mediation process will set the tone for cooperative and reasonable bargaining with respect to issues that are not covered by mediation. The mediator should communicate to the lawyers any approaches that might prove helpful in maintaining a cooperative atmosphere. If the remaining issues are dealt with in an adversarial manner, it may undermine the parties' trust in each other and their willingness to fulfill their agreement on the issues that were sent to mediation.

It is ideal if clients have retained collaborative lawyers to work through issues not dealt with in mediation. The mediator should invite the lawyers to participate in a meeting initially without clients in order to:

- brief the lawyers as to the emotional state of the clients at that time;
- discuss any urgent matters that impact the issues the lawyers will be addressing;
- discuss the communication skills, personality styles, and sensitivities of the clients;
- discuss helpful strategies for working successfully with the clients, so as to bring the case to a positive conclusion.

If the parties are in a collaborative process, they will be expected to disclose information to each other fully and at an early stage. This will help to minimize suspicion and distrust and encourage settlement. This approach should make the approach of Collaborative Family Law lawyers more compatible with the type of approach and objectives used by mediators.

The clients should be included in a five-way meeting to conclude the parenting issues so that these do not become entangled with any difficult financial matters. It is also an excellent time to build the clients' confidence in their capacity to negotiate, based on their success in resolving issues related to their children. It also offers an opportunity for the lawyers to see first hand how the clients communicate with the mediator's assistance.

3. Minutes of Settlement

If one or more parties have initiated litigation, then those issues that have been resolved in mediation can be finalized in minutes of settlement. This document is filed with the court, and in most cases, the judge will sign an order in keeping with the terms of the minutes of settlement.

In the event that there are still outstanding issues that have not been resolved, partial minutes of settlement can be filed with the court that deal with only those issues that have been settled.

B. PARTIAL AGREEMENT OR NO AGREEMENT BY PARTIES

In the event that the parties fail to agree on one or more of the issues in dispute, the mediator or one or both parties may terminate the mediation process. One or both lawyers may recommend that mediation terminate, but the decision is made by the clients or mediator.

1. Termination by Mediator

The mediator may decide to terminate the mediation process, prior to an agreement, for various reasons. For example:

- Unequal bargaining power can arise because of many factors, such as the following: one party has achieved an emotional divorce, while the other party is still longing for reconciliation; one party has a good grasp of relevant information with respect to the issues in dispute, but the other party has very little knowledge or information about the issues in dispute (this arises particularly with financial matters); one party uses duress on the other party (for example, physical violence, threats, harassment, refusal to pay support, threatened legal action for custody, or withholding of access); differences in education; differences in financial status; differences in emotional stability; differences in motivation for ending the marriage (for example, desire to remarry, or guilt regarding marriage breakdown).

- The mediator feels that one party is delaying the mediation in order to take advantage of a status quo situation (that is, one party may have *de facto* custody of the children and believe it is to his or her advantage to delay mediation).
- The parties may be so hostile to each other that the mediation is unlikely to be productive and may even be destructive of the emotional health of one of the parties.
- One party may be willing to enter an agreement that the mediator feels is detrimental to the well-being of the children. The mediator should exercise this discretion carefully. In mediation, the emphasis should be on private ordering, that is, allowing the parties to arrive at a bargain that they feel is reasonable and acceptable. However, if a mediator participates in what is really an unconscionable transaction, then the mediator, on ethical grounds, should withdraw. This is particularly true when there is a risk to children. In any event, if the mediator suspects abuse or neglect of children, the mediator has a statutory duty to report to the child welfare authorities. This duty should be explained to the parents.
- One party fails to make proper financial disclosure or in fact misleads the other party with respect to finances.
- One party refuses to pay the mediator's fees within a reasonable period of time.

In the event that the mediator plans to terminate mediation without agreement by the parties, the mediator should inform the parties of the decision to terminate and should then contact counsel. The mediator should explain to both the parties and counsel the basis for the termination.

If the mediation is open mediation, then the mediator could prepare a report with respect to the mediation process, at the request of one or both parties. If the mediator has been asked for recommendations, then the mediator should include recommendations with respect to the issues in dispute as was agreed upon. In preparing the report the mediator should indicate:

- the amount of time spent in mediation;
- who was seen and the reasons for termination;
- a statement as to whether it would be desirable for the mediation to continue at a future date and under what circumstances (for example, once one or both parties have participated in counselling); or
- constructive suggestions as to how to deal with the major obstacles to a mediated solution.

2. Termination by Party(ies)

One or both parties may decide to terminate the mediation process because of:

- perceived bias by the mediator, for example, with respect to the sex, age, ethnic or racial group, socio-economic status, or religious preference of a party;
- a lack of confidence or trust in the mediator or the other party;
- a personality conflict with the mediator;
- discomfort during the mediation process, particularly in meetings with the other party;
- threats, abuse, or a perceived inequality of bargaining power;
- a belief that the mediator is not acting in an impartial manner;
- a belief that the mediator does not have a sufficient understanding of the children's needs; or
- a belief that the other party is using the delay to his or her advantage.

If one or both parties decide to terminate, this should be discussed directly with the mediator to see whether the issue(s) can be resolved. If the party still has some concerns, the party should discuss the matter with his or her lawyer.

The mediator should be open to hearing comments and criticisms about his or her process, and where the concerns are justified, the mediator should endeavour to change his or her behaviour in order to meet the needs of the parties, but this should not be done so as to please one party over another. If the mediator believes that certain changes would be desirable, these changes should be discussed first with the other spouse, so that it will not appear that one spouse is manipulating the mediator.

If the party is still not satisfied, then he or she can terminate the mediation. The party or the party's lawyer should draft a letter to the mediator and the opposite lawyer indicating the reasons for the withdrawal. The letter should also contain an indication of circumstances, if any, under which mediation could be resumed.

3. Termination Suggested by Lawyer(s)

Mediation can only be terminated by a client or the mediator. The lawyer can advise his or her client to terminate and raise concerns with the mediator, but it is not the lawyer's prerogative to make that decision. Certainly, it would be responsible conduct for the lawyer to voice his or her concerns with the client and the mediator if:

- the lawyer believes that the mediator has a bias on an issue that is highly relevant to the mediation (for example, with respect to the sex of the custodial parent, the age of the custodial parent, religious preference, sexual orientation, racial or ethnic group, or socioeconomic status, *etc.*);
- the lawyer is concerned that the other party is taking advantage of the mediation process either for delay or for initiating legal proceedings that are in direct conflict with the mediation process. For example, one

lawyer might suspect that the other spouse is dissipating or transferring assets to prevent them being shared with the other spouse; or
- the lawyer loses confidence in the procedure followed by the mediator.

In the event that the lawyer wishes the mediation process to terminate, the lawyer should first discuss his or her concerns with the client. The lawyer should attempt to determine whether the concerns he or she has are in fact perceived by the client or perceived by other individuals who are involved in the mediation process. If the lawyer is not satisfied, the lawyer should discuss the concerns directly with the mediator. Prior to taking any action to terminate the mediation, the lawyer should obtain instructions from the client on the client's wishes.

4. Termination by Mediator-Arbitrator

For those issues that are resolved in mediation, the mediator should refer to the suggestions set out above for memoranda of understanding. For those issues that require an arbitrated outcome, reference should be made to the section on Arbitration Awards.

C. REPORTS

1. Closed Mediation

In closed mediation, the mediator only reports on the issues that were resolved during mediation. In this case, a memorandum of understanding is drawn up by the mediator specifying the issues that were agreed to.

For those issues where agreement was not reached, the mediator simply states, "agreement was not reached on the following issues", and lists the issues.

In closed mediation, the mediator does not report on the process and does not make any recommendations.

In closed mediation cases, the mediator usually has an agreement with the parties or a court order specifying that he or she would not be called to court as an expert witness to give evidence on behalf of either party.

2. Open Mediation

If requested by one or both parties or the court, the mediator can report on all issues sent to mediation, whether or not they were resolved.

The content of the report depends on the open mediation agreement. This report may contain one or more of the following:

- a report on issues that are resolved;
- for those issues that are not resolved, a statement by the mediator about the process followed, the parties' positions on these issues, and the obstacles to an agreement; and/or
- if requested by one or both parties, recommendations by the mediator about the resolution of the issues that are still in dispute.

The mediator should discuss the nature of the report requested with the parties prior to beginning the mediation. That is, is the mediator expected to prepare a report with recommendations in the event that mediation is not completely successful?

For those issues that were resolved by the parties, the mediator would usually not make a personal comment about the agreement reached. Exceptions to this would be if the court has ordered the mediator to provide an opinion on the adequacy of the settlement reached or if the mediator is concerned that the agreement creates some danger for the children. The report would usually focus on those issues where agreement was not reached. In these cases, if the mediator has been requested to make recommendations, the mediator should set out a fair, reasonable, and workable plan for the parties and the court to consider.

In the event that the clients and mediator entered a Collaborative Participation Agreement, the mediator would most likely be barred by this agreement from appearing in court on behalf of one of the parties. One option is that the clients and mediator might agree to the mediator preparing a non-binding summary of the agreements reached, a description of the issues still to be resolved and a suggestion, if requested, as to how these issues might be resolved. The spirit of such suggestions would be to stimulate further discussion and commitment by the parties to reach an acceptable, non-adversarial agreement.

3. Arbitration Award

Unlike the other dispute resolution outcomes described in this chapter, an arbitration award is not a record of the terms agreed to by the parties. An award is the finding and decision of an arbitrator made upon the submission in an arbitration. An award is final and binding on the parties, subject to any rights of appeal. The arbitrator will make findings of fact based on the evidence submitted during the arbitration. That evidence can consist of oral testimony, documents, physical evidence, or expert opinion. In assessing the evidence and finding the facts, an arbitrator should consider the following guidelines:

- An issue between parties is not to be resolved by reference to the number of witnesses appearing on behalf of each.
- An arbitrator may choose to believe all of what a witness said, or part of it, or may reject the evidence entirely.
- An arbitrator may find that there are discrepancies between the testimony of one witness and that of others requiring the arbitrator to determine which testimony is to be preferred.
- The arbitrator should carefully observe the witness' demeanour when giving evidence.
- The arbitrator should consider the extent of the witness' opportunity to observe the matter about which testimony is given.
- Does the witness have an interest in the outcome of the arbitration?
- How probable or improbable is the witness' story?
- Were there internal contradictions in the testimony of a witness?

The award must be in writing, signed by the arbitrator and dated. The award must include a clear resolution of the issues submitted to the arbitrator as well as what each party is to do or entitled to receive. The award must contain the arbitrator's reasons for the award. The reasons should inform the parties as to how the arbitrator arrived at his/her decision and what evidence was significant or not taken into account. The reasons must be clear and thorough enough to permit a court hearing an appeal or application for review to assess whether the arbitrator made a substantive or procedural error. Once the award has been made, it is final and cannot be amended by the arbitrator.

Justice John Laskin suggests the following seven strategies for writing persuasive decisions:[1]

1. Think and plan before you write.
2. Write a good introduction or overview (identify the key issue(s) that need to be decided).
3. Use an issue-driven structure (rather than chronological or in the order that the evidence was led).
4. Use the principle of proximity (keep facts and legislation near the issues to which they are relevant).
5. Write point first or always give the context before the details (in other words, state your conclusion followed by the reasons for that conclusion).
6. Make your reasoning transparent (explain the logic path you followed to reach your conclusions).
7. Edit your reasons (aim to be clear and concise).

ANNOTATED BIBLIOGRAPHY

Brownstone, Judge H. *Tug of War: A Judge's Verdict on Separation, Custody Battles, and the Bitter Realities of Family Court.* Toronto: ECW Press, 2009. This is a delightfully candid plea for parents to avoid adversarial battles. It paints a realistic picture of the outcomes litigants can expect should they embark on a court process to resolve their disputes.

Cameron, N. *Collaborative Practice: Deepening the Dialogue.* The Continuing Legal Education Society of British Columbia, 2004. An excellent resource for the Collaborative Divorce Model, with a CD-ROM of precedents for the practitioner.

Epstein, P., and Gibb, S. "Family Law Arbitrations: Choice and Finality Under the Amended *Arbitration Act, 1991* and *Family Law Act*" (Paper presented to the Continuing Legal Education Program, Special Lectures 2006 Family Law, 3 and 4 April 2006) (Toronto: Law Society of Upper Canada, 2006).

---

[1] J. Laskin, "Seven Strategies for Writing Persuasive Decisions", The Canadian Institute, February 2006.

Folberg, J., and Taylor, A. *Mediation: A Comprehensive Guide to Resolving Conflicts without Litigation.* San Francisco: Jossey-Bass Publishers, 1984. This book contains a discussion about preparing the settlement agreement. See particularly Part Two, "Mediation Stages, Concepts and Skills", Chapter 3, "Stages in the Mediation Process", at p. 38.

Joseph, G., and Stangarone, M. "Challenging Arbitration Awards and/or Removing the Arbitrator under the *Arbitration Act, 1991*" (Paper presented to the Law Society of Upper Canada Continuing Legal Education Program, Mediation and Arbitration for Family Law Lawyers, 13 November 2007).

Gold, L. *Between Love and Hate: A Guide to Civilized Divorce.* New York: Plenum Press, 1992. See *supra*, Chapter 4, Annotated Bibliography.

Lyster, M. *Child Custody – Building Parenting Agreements that Work.* Berkeley, California: Nolo Press Inc., 1997. This book contains extensive details about what to include in a Parenting Plan. This is a helpful guide, especially for those who are new to the field and are non-lawyers.

Ricci, I. *Mom's House, Dad's House: Making Two Homes for your Child. Second Edition.* New York: A Fireside Book, published by Simon & Schuster, 1997. This is a practical and systematic guide for parents who are considering a shared parenting arrangement after divorce. Ricci describes how to shift from a spousal relationship, which is ending, to a parenting relationship, which is continuing. She has a number of practical tips, checklists, guidelines, sample agreements, *etc.*, which parents can adapt to their own situation.

Saposnek, D. *Mediating Child Custody Disputes.* San Francisco: Jossey-Bass Publishers, 1998. This book has practical suggestions with respect to drafting a mediation agreement. See particularly Part Two, "Structuring the Mediation Process", Chapter 7, "Drafting the Mediation Agreement", at p. 135.

Sheilds, R., Ryan, J., and Smith, V. *Collaborative Family Law: Another Way to Resolve Family Disputes.* Toronto: Thomson Canada Ltd., 2003. This book has helpful precedents for the Canadian CFL practitioner, including a sample Separation Agreement.

Tesler, P., *Collaborative Law: Achieving Effective Resolution in Divorce without Litigation.* Section of Family Law, American Bar Association, 2001. Tesler's book is the first major book in describing in detail the Collaborative Family Law process and how it differs from an adversarial process. This book has several helpful precedents.

Chapter Nine

Protecting the Best Interests of Children

A. THE EFFECTS ON CHILDREN OF SEPARATION AND DIVORCE

In most cases, Parenting Plans will be worked out with the assistance of a mediator or child specialist. While it is helpful for collaborative lawyers to be familiar with the impact of separation and divorce on parents and on children at different developmental stages, such knowledge is critical for mediators and arbitrators if they are deciding custody and access issues. In the case of arbitrators, their role is different from the mediation role described below as they are making awards as to the Parenting Plan following a hearing.

At the time of separation, most parents are so caught up in their own pain, grief, and reduced self-esteem that it is difficult for them to focus on the needs of their children. In addition, most parents lack adequate information from which to predict their children's responses or to make decisions that would be in the best interests of their children. This information should be provided in an impartial, constructive manner that avoids laying blame on either parent for the children's responses to the separation.

In the initial meeting with the parents and in subsequent individual and joint meetings, it is important for the mediator to give the parents information about the likely impact of separation and divorce on the children and themselves.

As well, the mediator can assist the parents by discussing some helpful techniques for dealing with their children, so that the parents will feel more in control, less helpless in dealing with their children's reactions, and will behave in a more constructive manner than if their energies were spent on self-blame or blaming the other spouse.

The mediator should emphasize that it is important for the parents to share information about the children's responses and to cooperate in their reaction, because this is in the children's best interests. If the parents undermine each other's approaches to discipline and caretaking, the children will quickly learn to play one parent off against the other and are likely to lose respect for both parents.

By emphasizing a cooperative parenting approach, the mediator is helping to divert the parties from their own battle and beginning to model the way in which they must pool their efforts to assist their children, even at a time of high emotional stress. The parents need to learn to focus on the needs of the children, rather than on the fault of the other spouse.

The following information may be helpful:

- Children are often unaware of conflict in a marriage or that the conflict is out of the ordinary until one parent is packing his or her bags to leave. Even though parents may see the marriage as intolerable and believe that this has been obvious for some period of time, children tend to accept their family as a "normal family" and do not anticipate a marriage breakdown. Parents need to understand that many children may be shocked by a separation.
- Children are usually very attached to both parents and loyal to their family of origin. Most children are very upset and depressed at the loss of a parent and of their intact family unit.
- Children are sometimes fearful about the consequences of their parents' separation and/or divorce. If they have grown up in religious families, they may see divorce as contrary to moral or religious principles, and they may be ashamed and uncomfortable about telling their friends or teachers. This is particularly true for boys who are less likely to be aware that other children are living in separated families. Also, they may worry about abandonment or about not being able to see both parents often enough or in a comfortable environment.
- The basic fears of most children at the time of separation relate to their own security. For example, children may have the following concerns:
  — Who will take care of me?
  — Will I be able to see both of my parents?
  — Where will I live?
  — Who will take care of the parent who is not living with me?
- Children may feel responsible for the marriage breakdown and may feel equally responsible for returning the family to an intact unit. That is, children often worry about such things as:
  — What did I do that was so terrible that my parent is leaving?
  — Was it my fault that the marriage broke down?
  — What can I do to save the marriage?
  — If I am really good, will the parent who left come back?

There are a number of studies that have examined the characteristics displayed by children at different developmental stages after separation or divorce. Some have focused on the harm associated with divorce, and some have reached more optimistic conclusions about the long-term effects. As the research becomes more sophisticated and includes an increasing number of longitudinal studies, there is growing consensus that the outcomes depend on several factors. For example, Judith Wallerstein, Joan Kelly, Janet Johnson, Philip Stahl, and Peter Jaffe, highlight a number of risk factors, such as:

- Physical, psychological, verbal abuse, or witnessing of abuse (has an especially negative effect on boys). Boys who witness abuse are far more likely than the general population to become abusers.
- Level of conflict. In cases of high conflict, more frequent transitions and increased access may result in more emotional and behavioural disturbance (especially among girls). That is, research showed that children in

high-conflict situations were more likely to show signs of depression, withdrawal, aggression, physical symptoms such as stomach aches and headaches, and to have more problems getting along with their peers than those with fewer transitions.

- Psychological disturbance in parents, such as depression, anxiety, psychoses, personality disorder.
- Lack of economic support or unpredictable support leading to an economic decline.
- Poor or lack of relationship with non-custodial parent was a predictor of poor adjustment, especially for boys.

The work of Hetherington, Wallerstein, Emery, and Ahrons, summarize the factors that help children succeed. They refer to factors that support resilience in children of divorce, such as:

- Warm supportive relationships with both parents;
- Regular predictable access arrangements;
- Stable social support system, *i.e.*, school, social activities, contact with peers and extended family (the actual physical custody and visitation arrangements are less important than the quality of the ongoing family relationships);
- Predictable, adequate economic support;
- Involvement in and support for children's schoolwork, activities and other daily routines;
- Witnessing of constructive conflict resolution between parents;
- Developmentally appropriate Parenting Plans;
- Willing to accommodate to the other parent's important priorities, especially where this benefits the children or the family as a whole.

Children respond to separation and divorce in different ways at different developmental stages.

The following is based on the work of Dr. Judith Wallerstein and Dr. Joan Kelly, as well as Neil Kalter, Rhonda Freeman, and Robert Emery. This summary highlights their findings with respect to the reactions of children at different stages of development.

Infants and Toddlers — birth to 3 years

- *Disruption in sleeping or eating patterns.*
- *Increased irritability or distress with normal separations from primary caretaker*: Absences of several hours, even when left with a family caregiver are stressful.
- *Heightened fear of strangers.*
- *More intense and frequent temper tantrums*: Infants are sensitive to the increased emotional distress of their parents and demonstrate emotional ability as a result of disruptions to their daily routines.
- *Fear of abandonment and yearning for the absent parent*: Infants' thinking is concrete and they cannot imagine what is not within their immediate view or attention. An absent parent has "disappeared",

leaving children fearful and confused, especially by unpredictable and prolonged absences.

- *Increased aggressiveness toward primary caregiver*: The child's temperament is a key factor in their adjustment. Some children are easy-going and respond well to change — they enjoy novelty and show no distress at shifts in their routines. Others require far more structure, predictability and consistency and display evident distress when their routines are changed or when faced with unexpected events. Once the parents develop a stable plan with a primary residence for the child and frequent, short, predictable contacts between the child and the other parent, the child's level of stress will usually subside.

Unfortunately, fathers of infant children are more likely to withdraw from contact or feel frustrated and peripheral to their child's life. They may feel insecure about their ability to care for the child and often enlist a new girlfriend or older family member as an assistant. This usually causes resentment in the primary caregiver who may interpret this as "sloughing off their responsibilities" on someone else. The lack of confidence in parenting is especially true if the father had minimal involvement in solo care for the child prior to separation. It is important to help these fathers understand that had they stayed together until the child was pre-school age, the mother would likely have played the predominant care giving role and the child would still grow up knowing, and having a close relationship with, his/her father.

Pre-school children — 3 to 5 years

- *Fear of abandonment.*
- *Sleep disturbances and nightmares.*
- *Confusion, anxiety, and distress*: Children are confused and unsure about the changes in their family life, because they do not understand the reason for the separation and cannot explain to themselves many of the changes in the routines in their life.
- *Regression and diminished emotional independence*: Children may demonstrate their anxiety and insecurity by lapses in toilet training, increased clinging behaviour, increased fears, for example, of the dark.
- *Strong reconciliation fantasies.*
- *Feelings of guilt*: Children are egocentric and may blame themselves for the marriage breakdown.
- *Increased aggression and diminished social skills*: Children may display a greater irritability with siblings, parents, peers, or in school. They may withdraw from peer group activities or show an increase in controlling behaviours. This anger may stem from the child's feelings of loss or rejection. Many children witness explosions of rage between their parents or the parents may be so preoccupied with their own feelings of hurt and depression that they are emotionally unavailable to the child.

School age — 6 to 8 years

- *Pervasive sadness and grieving*: This is sometimes related to the intensity of turmoil in the home, but some children are intensely sad even when their parents are not demonstrating great distress.
- *Preoccupation with their own bitterness, humiliation, and plan for revenge.*
- *Yearning for the departed parent*: This is similar to grief for a dead parent.
- *Feelings of rejection, abandonment, and fear.*
- *Fantasy of responsibility for marriage breakdown.*
- *Reconciliation fantasies.*
- *Anger*: The child often directs anger at the custodial parent or whichever parent the child believes is responsible for the marriage breakdown. Anger is also directed at teachers, friends, and siblings in many cases.
- *Loyalty conflicts*: The child feels caught in a tug of war between both parents, that is, having to accept one parent and reject the other.
- *Unable to understand parent's needs separate from their own.*
- *Changes in academic and social behaviour.*

School age — 9 to 12 years

Children at this stage are more aware of parental conflict and the causes and consequences of divorce. They have some ability to explain to themselves what is happening.

- *Profound feelings of loss, rejection, helplessness, and loneliness.*
- *Feelings of shame, moral indignation, and outrage at the parents' behaviour.*
- *Extreme anger, temper tantrums, and demanding behaviour*: The child tends to take sides or align with one parent and to render judgments of parents' behaviour. Boys are more likely to act out aggressively.
- *Fears, phobias, and use of denial.*
- *Fears with respect to the absent parent*: Children often worry about the well-being of the absent parent.
- *Increased somatic complaints*: Children, especially girls, may experience more headaches, stomach aches, and sleep disorders.
- *Loyalty conflicts*: The child identifies one parent as the good parent and one as the bad parent.
- *Have difficulty accepting their parents' dating — especially girls.*
- *Low self-esteem*: The child may have increased problems in school and with peers and become involved in delinquent activities.
- *Believe if parents tried harder they could reconcile*: Children may believe they have the ability to influence the parents' decision.

Adolescence — 13 years and older

Adolescents often express anger at the parents because they experience the following feelings:

- *Overburdened*: They feel burdened by the increased responsibility for younger siblings and emotionally weak parents.
- *Anger and rejection*: They have to share visits with new partners and often hear the other parent criticized or discussed with disrespect.
- *Feelings of shame and insecurity*: They are ashamed of the parents' childish behaviour, particularly if the conflict continues over a considerable time period.
- *Confusion*: They feel torn between wanting to be with their friends and wanting to go on an access visit.
- *Anxiety*: They have fears about forming long-term relationships and they are anxious about their own future marriage.
- *Economic insecurity*: They worry about money, that is, whether the custodial parent will be able to provide for them.
- *Loyalty conflicts*: They are used to carry messages between parents in conflict.
- *Confusion re parental role*: They have a heightened awareness of their parents' sexual behaviour. As a result, adolescents often display increased promiscuous behaviour at an earlier age and tend to withdraw from parental contact and control.

Young Adults — over 18

Wallerstein found that adult children of divorce reported that the divorce experience forever changed their lives:

- Their childhood was more stressful, less carefree, more lonely, less nurturing, allowed less time for their own friendships and play.
- They felt more vulnerable, with less time and support from parents and extended family, and had more fragile or uncertain relationships with their parent's new partners.
- They were less trusting of their own relationships, had more difficulty with sexual and emotional intimacy and with long-term commitment.
- They had increased anxiety when adjusting to change, were more fearful about failing in their own relationships, and about exposing their children to divorce. Therefore, a greater number were fearful about entering relationships or having children.
- They had fewer models of how to work out conflicts in a cooperative manner, were insecure about their own conflict resolution skills, and therefore divorce was more readily considered as an option.
- They felt ongoing anger and resentment toward their parents, especially fathers, for their behaviour leading up to and following the separation.

The good news is that many of these children do overcome their fears of loss and betrayal and do learn how to build and sustain meaningful adult relationships. However, Judith Wallerstein sees this as happening as a result of considerable effort and some good role modelling or nurturing by a well-adjusted adult figure. The work of Mavis Hetherington, Connie Ahrons, Bob Emery, and Philip Stahl indicates that the majority of children of divorce are resilient and do lead healthy productive lives; however, many face increased obstacles, especially if the divorce was high conflict.

On a positive note, Ahrons, in her longitudinal study of 173 adult children, found some surprising results that support the resilience of most children:

- 76 per cent do not wish that their parents were still together;
- 79 per cent believe that their parents' decision to divorce was a good one;
- 79 per cent believe their parents are better off post-divorce;
- 78 per cent feel they are better off or not affected by the divorce.

Rhonda Freeman, Director of Families in Transition (Family Service Association of Toronto), has identified eight key factors that affect children's adjustment to their parents' divorce.[1] She notes that some children after a period of adjustment cope with the challenges of divorce but a sizeable minority experience long-term consequences. The factors that predict adjustment are listed below in order of importance. The hierarchy reflects contemporary research and clinical practice.

1. *Parental Conflict*: Research has consistently found that the level of conflict between parents is a critical factor influencing children's post-divorce emotional, social, and academic adjustment.
2. *Economic Resources for Raising Children*: There is considerable evidence documenting the significant rise in child poverty in female-headed single-parent families. Approximately 40 per cent of these families fall below the poverty line within a year of separation. For this group of children there may be an impact on nutrition, living conditions, and access to post-secondary education and recreational programs. In some families, adequate economic resources may not have been available prior to the parents' separation. The situation will not improve with separation. Or, despite the *Child Support Guidelines* implemented by the federal government in May 1997, payers may be inconsistent or negligent. Anecdotal evidence suggests that Parenting Plan decisions are increasingly influenced by a desire to minimize child support obligations.
3. *Parenting Capacity:* The research of Wallerstein and Kelly[2] and others has documented the reduced ability of parents to carry out the tasks of parenting. Higher conflict separations and ongoing litigation may result in a diminished capacity to parent that extends well beyond the first year of separation. Parents may be preoccupied with meeting their own needs and less available to deal with their children's needs.

---

[1] R. Freeman, "Parenting after divorce: Using research to inform decision-making about children" (1998), 15 *Canadian Journal of Family Law* 79-131.

[2] J.S. Wallerstein and J.B. Kelly, *Surviving the Breakup: How Children and Parents Cope with Divorce* (New York: Basic Books Inc., 1980).

4. *Divorce Environment*: It is not the divorce, *per se*, that is difficult for children. Rather it is the cumulative stress they live with. Therefore, to the extent possible, children adjust more easily if changes are implemented gradually. Remaining in the matrimonial home for a period of time, or at a minimum in the same neighbourhood and attending the same school, helps children cope with the myriad of changes in their lives. Children should have information, appropriate to their age and stage of development, about the changes and how their lives will be affected.

   If at all possible, the existing child-care arrangements should be maintained after separation. This enables the children to be with familiar babysitters, day-care providers, *etc.*, and eases the transition experience.
5. *Parent/Child Relationship*: Families benefit from learning and utilizing a language that respects all family members and their importance in the child's life. Language such as *parenting partnership* and *parenting plan* (rather than archaic terminology such as custody and access) is more inclusive and honours the contribution of both parents to the ongoing development of the children. Non-adversarial language shifts the focus to one of parenting responsibilities rather than rights. Children become the winners.

   The presence of familiar and predictable routines can reassure children, especially young children, that their relationship with both parents will continue. Children benefit from a predictable and consistent residential schedule that provides for time with each parent. Clear Parenting Plans help to minimize conflict and allow for children's usual activities.
6. *Roles and Boundaries in the Post-divorce Family*: After separation, parent-child boundaries may become blurred. It can be all too easy for a child to become the confidante or support system for a parent. Some parents have difficulty separating their needs from those of their children. They may project their issues and concerns on to the children. Unclear boundaries are a source of confusion and distress.
7. *Children's Questions, Concerns, and Fears*: Children need opportunities to talk about their questions and concerns. Younger children may be less able to formulate questions and benefit from parental assistance in this regard. Discussions about the changing family circumstances require sensitivity and tact as some children may feel disloyal to a parent.
8. *Valuing Cultural and Religious Heritage*: Canada's population is increasingly diverse. Religious and cultural affiliations can be an important source of support for families. At times, they may contribute to parental conflict. Parenting plans need to value the traditions and heritage of both parents.

1. Residential Schedules

Parents who enter mediation or Collaborative Law are concerned about determining the most appropriate residential schedule for their children. It is important to note that while scheduling is probably the most significant concern of parents, it is really only one aspect of a larger Parenting Plan (see discussion in Chapter 4). The recent literature recommends a more sophisticated view that takes into account a number of factors such as:

- the child's developmental stage;
- the level of conflict between the parents;
- the ability of the parents to communicate reasonably and put the children's needs first — ahead of their differences;
- the child's prior relationship with each parent;
- each parent's capacity to parent, including their experience, motivation, mental health, alcohol, or drug abuse;
- the child's temperament and maturity;
- each parent's availability, given their hours of work; and
- the geographic distance between parents.

All of these variables must be weighed in arriving at a particular plan. Also, within one family, individual differences between children need to be considered. Many researchers have suggested that it is often preferable for families to work out interim parenting arrangements at the time of separation, rather than create a permanent schedule. The period of separation can be chaotic with many decisions and changes happening in a context of high emotion. Letting things cool off, having some experience with the reality of decisions that must be made, observing the children's adjustment, and seeing how the post-separation relationship between parents develops, can be valuable input. Are the parents able to disengage and put the child's interests ahead of their personal hurt? Often providing some initial stability and then building a longer term schedule on the family's experience is often wise.

As children age, it is appropriate to expect changes in the schedule; therefore, it is ideal to have parents return to mediation to review their parenting arrangements as children transition to different developmental stages or as major changes occur in the separated family's circumstances.

The following principles can offer some general guidance for difficult situations. These principles need to be applied to the particular circumstances of each family. The most frequent circumstances that create difficulty are:

(A) High-conflict Families
(B) Overnight Schedules for Infants
(C) Presence of New Partners prior to or at Separation
(D) Mobility
(E) Abuse Issues

(A) HIGH-CONFLICT FAMILIES

The higher the conflict:

- the less contact there should be between parents at transitions or when a child might observe or overhear interactions between parents;
- the fewer the number of transitions between parents' homes. Where possible transitions should take place between a parent and a mutually acceptable third party, or at a daycare centre, school, religious institution, public restaurant, *etc.*;
- the more detailed and structured the parenting plan should be;
- the greater the need for consistency and predictability, to minimize the need for ongoing negotiations;
- the less likely it is that a joint or shared parenting arrangement will be in the best interests of the child, either for decision-making or shared residence;
- the more likely that communication will work best using e-mail, a parenting communication notebook, or the presence of a mutually trusted third party.

(B) OVERNIGHTS FOR INFANTS UNDER 3 YEARS OF AGE

In families with infant children, there is often tension about developing a plan that is reasonably comfortable for the child and at the same time fosters a bond with both parents. It is especially helpful for families with infants to create a plan for under 3 years of age and then review the plan once the child is over 3 years. If parents insist on a long-term plan, there should be stages established for under 3 years, 3 to 6 years, 6 to adolescence, and older. This will help to reduce the anxiety of the parent who spends less time initially with the child. Ideally there should be a review with the mediator or child specialist at each major transition.

The issue of infant overnights has sparked considerable controversy, with some researchers strongly advocating for or against overnight visits for children under 3. Usually this conflict appears with fathers arguing in favour of "equal time" and mothers being anxious about any overnights or more than one overnight at a time. In the opinion of many practitioners, there is no one right answer, but rather, it depends on many factors.

As a general rule, it is preferable for infants to have a primary residence, usually with the mother, with frequent, short, daytime contacts with the father. It is helpful to gradually move in increments toward overnights as the child approaches 3 years, starting with a daytime nap, followed by a meal, then an occasional overnight (*e.g.*, one overnight on alternate weekends), adding additional time in keeping with the child's comfort level. If the child is uncomfortable or resistant, the best advice is to go at the child's pace and assume there is no fixed rule as individual children's temperament varies as does the competence and experience of parents.

Most researchers suggest that the following factors need to be evaluated in deciding when a particular child is ready for an overnight:

- level of conflict between the parents and confidence in each other's parenting;
- child's special needs, *e.g.*, health care, sleep difficulties, nursing schedule, *etc.*;
- parent's ability to provide basic physical care-taking;
- attachment to each parent;
- capacity to parent: whether there are concerns about excessive use of drugs or alcohol, emotional problems or personality deficits;
- child's comfort level with each parent (when the other parent is not present);
- child's personality or temperament;
- length of time the child can endure separation from each parent, given the child's immature sense of time, without undue stress or disruption of each parent-child relationship;
- practical issues, *e.g.*, distance between parents, work schedule, support system, availability of caretakers, other (older) siblings, availability of adequate separate space for the child.

(c) Presence of New Partners Prior to or at Separation

This is an issue that impacts children quite differently from their parents. For parents, the presence of a new partner prior to or within the first year after separation usually elicits a response of moral outrage. An affair causes the injured parent to react as if the other parent was no longer trustworthy in any aspect of a parenting partnership. Almost inevitably negotiations occur in an atmosphere of bitterness and high conflict. For children, the reaction depends on their developmental stage, but in general the presence of a new partner within the first year or two means:

- they will have to share their limited parenting time — often experienced as a partial abandonment and a loss of intimacy with their parent;
- their parents are less likely to reconcile (what most children long for);
- they will be expected to welcome someone they probably resent or whose presence is not really welcome, especially if they are still adjusting to the reality of the separation;
- their familiar patterns and customs will change to accommodate the newcomer;
- they may need to become "friends" with the new partner's children, usually as a replacement for one-on-one time with their parent.

Children are usually not ready to accept new partners into their lives until a minimum of one year post-separation. Children go through a similar pattern of grieving to their parents, are usually far less prepared for the decision to separate, and feel that they have no choice in most of the changes in their lives that result from the separation. New partners add many layers of complexity to their lives and from the children's perspective add little value. This attitude usually changes if the parents can wait until the children have adapted to the separation. New partners should not be introduced until there has been a period of stability with a lessening of tension, and the children have accepted the fact that the parents will not reconcile and the children have developed a secure new lifestyle with each parent.

Also, parents should not introduce a series of short-term partners to children. Once children are ready to accept new people, they will not form multiple attachments. Parents should only introduce people when they believe the relationship will be permanent. At this point the new partner should be introduced gradually, and should respect the need for a continuing one-on-one relationship between a parent and a child.

(D) Mobility

This is a very important issue in the United States where many individuals end up living in different states. In Canada, families are somewhat less mobile; however, when a parent wishes to relocate, this issue usually triggers a high-conflict response. Parents, especially of children who are too young to travel on their own, feel they are losing the opportunity to build or maintain a close "living" relationship with their children. To some extent the level of conflict depends on the reason for the move; for example:

- to improve a career opportunity;
- to be close to family of origin;
- for health reasons;
- to provide better educational or lifestyle opportunities for the children.

These are usually seen as positive reasons to move and are less likely to cause an adversarial response, especially if there is a willingness to accommodate frequent or extended visits with the other parent. The parent who wishes to move needs to make an extra effort to keep the other parent involved, and to assume an additional financial burden for the visitation, in addition to encouraging such creative options as the regular use of e-mail and Internet connections.

When the move is intended to interfere with visitation or is to pursue a new relationship (particularly within a year of separation), and the moving parent refuses or cannot compensate for the other parent's increased costs and inconvenience, the situation can deteriorate quickly. It is important for the mediator or collaborative lawyer to discuss the reasons for the move with the client individually and to encourage a generous response to requests by the other parent for increased flexibility and a contribution to the additional expenses.

(E) Abuse Issues

This is a difficult issue because it raises concerns about the child's, and possibly the parent's, safety. In cases where alcohol, drugs, mental health problems, or physical or emotional abuse are an issue, it is important to involve professional resources. When working out Parenting Plans, care must be taken to consider safety measures, such as:

- no contact between parents at transition (transitions should be at a daycare, school or with a third party as intermediary);
- highly structured schedules, including the use of supervised access centres if such exist, or using mutually trusted adults as supervisors to ensure safety;
- no drugs or alcohol while with the child;
- a commitment to maintain doctor recommended doses of anti-psychotic or anti-depressive medication;
- an understanding that joint custody or shared decision-making is unlikely to work while these concerns continue.

If there are breaches of the agreed-upon or court-imposed ground rules, then visitation may need to be suspended until safety can be assured. A mediator is obligated to report abuse or safety concerns with respect to children to the Children's Aid Society and threats of harm involving a parent or other adult to police.

The decision about a residential schedule needs to consider all of the factors set out above and, in addition, needs to consider:

- individual differences in temperament, stage of development, and quality of relationships for different siblings;
- the physical accommodation and distance between parents;
- whether the parents fit the description of "high conflict", "distant or highly disengaged", or "cooperative and effective co-parents";
- the relationship between new partners and the children as well as with the former spouse.

One fairly consistent finding in the literature and recent case law is that joint custody is not advisable for high-conflict couples. If children are exposed to ongoing hostility, threats, and physical and verbal abuse between their parents, they are left confused and frightened for their own and their parent's safety. These children may feel more like hostages in a war zone than the focus of love and concerned attention. For a joint custody arrangement to be workable, the recent divorce literature suggests that parents need to respect each other as parents, communicate reasonably well, be able to put their conflicts aside, and make their children's needs a priority.

B. GATHERING RELEVANT INFORMATION

Depending on the issues being mediated or addressed in collaborative law, the following information should be collected from the parties and other relevant sources.

In the case of open mediation or an assessment, the mediator should collect more background information than would be necessary for closed mediation. This is because the mediator may be asked for recommendations and should have a good factual basis for the recommendations. In the case of closed mediation, the mediator should use his or her discretion about what information might be desirable in order to understand the nature of the conflict and to facilitate a settlement.

For custody and access issues, the mediator should collect information with respect to the following:

- childhood history of each parent;
- dating and marital history;
- involvement in child care during the marriage and following separation;
- employment history; and
- future plans (remarriage, residence, and employment).

If the mediation involves financial issues, then the mediator will need the following information:

- educational and employment history;
- past and present financial status; and
- future plans (education or retraining, employment, remarriage).

Similar financial information is likely needed in collaborative cases.

The following are examples of the type of information to be collected. Remember that detailed historical information may not be necessary for Collaborative Law or mediation, especially closed mediation. It is important to collect information that is relevant to the issues in dispute and that provides a context to understand the family members. What is relevant will vary with the circumstances of each case.

1. Childhood History of Each Parent

The childhood history of each parent gives valuable clues about the character development and personality of the parent. The type of care received by a parent significantly affects his or her approach to parenting.

Information could be collected with respect to such matters as:

- the relationship between the parent and each of his or her parents;
- the relationship of the parents to each other: Was there a marriage breakdown? If so, what were the circumstances and how did each family member react?
- the atmosphere in the home: Was it a happy home? Was there a great deal of conflict?
- the personality of each parent, particularly with respect to his or her parenting: Was each parent warm and able to show affection or undemonstrative, patient or impatient, easygoing or demanding, involved or preoccupied with matters outside the family?
- the type of discipline used? Was the punishment fair and reasonable or excessive?
- domestic violence: Were there incidents of domestic violence, either experienced directly or witnessed by the child?
- the siblings, including the relationship with each sibling and the occupation and marital status of each sibling;

- the parents' attitude to religion and the role of religion or other moral values in the household;
- the history of significant problems with respect to alcohol, drugs, mental illness, or criminal activities in the family of origin;
- the work history, including time spent at home parenting; and
- other significant events or perceptions in relation to the childhood history.

It is important to determine whether the parent had a loving, secure, stable, home environment or whether the parent grew up in an abusive, deprived, or neglectful environment. Of particular importance is the nature of discipline, the role that each parent played in the family, and the degree to which the child felt accepted and loved as opposed to unwanted and inadequate.

The type of family background and parenting experienced by the mother and father have a considerable influence on how each of them will parent and their expectations about how their partner should participate in parenting. The mediator should ask the parents how their own childhood history has affected their parenting and how they think the childhood history of their partner has affected their partner's parenting.

2. Marital History

It is important to determine the history of the relationship between the parents in order to find out:

- whether the relationship was satisfactory at any time;
- whether the parents loved and respected each other at any point during the relationship;
- at what point and for what reasons one or both parents changed their feelings about the relationship;
- whether both parties accept the need for a separation or whether one party is hoping for a reconciliation and is unable to separate emotionally from the relationship; and
- whether the parents were able to cooperate with each other in the past and the present level of trust and cooperation, particularly with respect to the children.

At this point there may be some consideration of the possibility of reconciliation. That is, in appropriate cases, the mediator should clarify with both parties whether either or both feel that there is some possibility of saving the marriage. The fact that the parties would like to consider reconciliation does not mean that mediation would necessarily terminate. The parties might find it helpful to have an interim agreement worked out through mediation, so that they can then consider reconciliation free of anxiety about an adversarial legal proceeding during this time period. In the event that the parties have separated or are considering a period of separation, such an agreement would help to preserve the parties' rights while they consider their future relationship.

If the parties have decided to separate permanently and if custody and access are issues, then the mediator should obtain a history of the relationship before and after marriage. This is particularly important for open mediation in the event that all of the issues in the dispute are not resolved in mediation or for situations where the mediator has been asked to prepare an assessment report. The following types of information should be gathered:

- a brief history of the relationship from the time of meeting until the time of the marriage, including what each parent found attractive and unattractive about the other, and whether the relationship was a stable relationship prior to marriage or living together;
- who initiated the decision to marry and how the other partner felt about the marriage;
- the attitude of the extended family to the marriage;
- any major religious or cultural differences between the families and how these affected their relationship;
- when they decided to have children, who decided, and how the other partner reacted;
- the involvement of both parties throughout the pregnancy and at the time of delivery; and
- how the marital relationship changed after the birth of each child.

If the parents had a strong marriage at one point and did love and respect each other, it is important for the mediator to help the parties recall the strengths of the marriage at a time when the parties may only be able to see the weaknesses and feel the disappointed expectations. If there was some evidence of parental cooperation during the lifetime of the children, the couple should reflect on how beneficial the cooperation was, not only for the parents, but particularly for the children. The mediator should emphasize that it is important for parents to continue to act cooperatively as parents, even though the spousal role may be at an end. By helping the couple to relive what is good in the relationship and bringing this to their attention, the mediator can sometimes begin to dissolve the present feelings of anger and hurt.

The review of the marital history is also useful for deterring the couple from blaming the marriage breakdown on one party or the other. The couple can be helped to reframe the reasons for the marriage breakdown so as to remove allegations of fault and feelings of guilt. For example, the couple may discover that the marriage broke down primarily because of differences in culture, values, personality, or interests, or because they had very different expectations about marriage and family life to begin with. Often marriages fail when couples are unable to support each other emotionally through a significant crisis, such as difficulties conceiving a child, a business failure, or a tragic loss such as the death of a child, a sibling or the premature death of a parent, especially following a lengthy illness.

By reducing blame, the mediator can often begin the process of developing a more cooperative relationship. In addition, if the parties no longer feel they are personally to blame for the marriage failure, they will be less likely to feel the need to justify their behaviour to the children. This could help to reduce loyalty conflicts, where each parent blames and criticizes the other and encourages the children to take sides. Loyalty conflicts and a lack of cooperation create a tremendous emotional strain on children and are significantly related to poor adjustment to the separation and divorce.

An important reason for collecting the marital history, particularly with the couple present together, is to test the emotional climate between the parties and to help the mediator predict the likelihood that the parties will be able to cooperate in the future.

3. Parental Involvement in Child Care

It is suggested that the mediator obtain information about each parent's involvement with the children and sharing of parental responsibilities within the context of the marital history. At this time, the mediator should deal with each parent's perception of his or her own attitudes and the other parent's with respect to the following:

- affection for the children and concern for their safety and welfare;
- method of discipline used by each parent and each parent's views on his or her own and the other parent's discipline techniques (do the parents approve of each other's methods? do they feel these methods are appropriate and effective for meeting the needs of the child?);
- sharing of parenting tasks and responsibilities from the birth of the child to the present time (did one parent take primary responsibility for the care of the child?) and attitude to each other's involvement and opinion of each other's competence to do parenting tasks, both in the past and in the future;
- competence in providing direct parenting, and interest and involvement in significant aspects of the child's life, for example, school, extra-curricular activities, medical and health care needs.

It is preferable to obtain this information when the discussion is not centred on the question of custody, but rather more informally during a discussion of the marital history. It is also recommended that this discussion occur with the parties together, so that each party can respond to the other party's perception of his or her parenting role.

If information emerges that suggests abuse or neglect with respect to the children, the mediator should pursue these topics in more depth with each parent individually and, in addition, should check any external sources, such as doctors, hospital records, the Children's Aid Society, police records, and other relevant sources, to determine the extent of any harm done.

The mediator should avoid any prolonged discussion of these allegations with both parties present for the following reasons:

- The parent who is making the allegations is likely to make them in a more dramatic, forceful, and hostile manner when the other parent is present.
- The accused parent is likely to feel defensive and demoralized, and is therefore likely to minimize the incidents and their effects. In addition,

the accused parent may feel the need to rebut any allegations, because of a desire not to lose face in front of the other parent, particularly with the mediator present.

- It may be easier for the mediator to get a more truthful, balanced account of any abusive incidents if the parties are seen individually.
- One parent may be afraid to make serious allegations in an open and honest manner in front of the other parent for fear of reprisal.
- A joint discussion of serious allegations is likely to make subsequent communication and cooperation between the parties more difficult.

For these reasons, the mediator should deal with serious allegations on an individual basis and in a constructive and supportive manner.

If there are allegations of abuse or neglect, the mediator has a statutory obligation to report the suspicion of abuse to the appropriate child welfare authorities. For example, in Ontario, the statutory duty is set out in s. 72 of the *Child and Family Services Act*.[3] The mediator should tell the parents that this is his or her legal duty, during the initial meeting. Once the mediator has reported, he or she should offer an explanation to each parent about what was reported and why, provided that the Children's Aid Society believes that this would not jeopardize the safety of the child or either parent.

If the mediator feels that one or both of the parents need some assistance in parenting skills or mental health counselling in relation to parenting ability, the mediator should make a referral to an appropriate professional or agency. The mediator should not become involved in an individual counselling relationship with one of the parents, as this would violate his or her impartial role.

4. Employment History

This information is necessary for both financial mediation and for the mediation of custody and access disputes, as well as for collaborative cases. The income of the parents is necessary to determine the level of spousal and child support. Also, the employment history gives some indication of the motivation of the parents, their stability, goals, lifestyle, and ability to relate to individuals outside the home.

If one spouse has not been employed outside the home for several years, it is important to determine when that spouse can become self-supporting and at what financial level. It may be helpful to refer this spouse, usually the woman, to career counselling to assist with career selection and job skills. In addition, women who have been out of the workforce for some time often feel inadequate, insecure, and frightened at the prospect of re-entering the workforce.

These concerns should be addressed, because they will have an impact on how quickly the individual will become self-supporting. If both parents will now be working outside the home, this usually necessitates a greater sharing of parenting responsibilities. This issue should be discussed with both parties to be

---

[3] R.S.O. 1990, c. C.11, as am.

sure the children's needs are met in a way that is fair and reasonable to both parents.

5. Future Plans

The mediator and collaborative lawyer should discuss the parents' work schedule, the likelihood that a parent will change jobs or move some distance away, any plans for remarriage, and other issues that may impact on the family's financial status or necessitate a change in the parenting arrangements. It would be important for the parents to take these factors into account in working out a plan for the present and in designing a procedure for changing the parenting arrangements, should the need arise in the future.

SUMMARY

This chapter has provided information about the impact of separation and divorce on children at different developmental stages, as well as factors that contribute to resiliency in children. This information is essential background for creating Parenting Plans that will help to minimize the negative consequences of divorce.

This chapter also discussed the types of information that mediators, as well as divorce coaches, and child specialists need to collect to help families create a Parenting Plan that meets the needs of children.

This background information is also important for arbitrators who are issuing Parenting Plan awards and collaborative lawyers who are working in an interdisciplinary team and who need to understand their client's needs and objectives.

ANNOTATED BIBLIOGRAPHY

Ahrons, C. *The Good Divorce: Keeping Your Family Together When Your Marriage Comes Apart*. New York: Harper-Collins Publishers, 1994. Ahrons defines the "good divorce" and challenges the myth that divorce inevitably turns adults into bitter enemies. Ahrons provides a number of specific suggestions to help families continue to meet the needs of their children.

Ahrons, C. *We Are Still Family: What Grown Children Have to Say About Their Parents' Divorce*. New York: HarperCollins, 2004. This book reflects the experiences and wisdom of 173 children of divorce. It dispels some of the current, negative myths about the impact of divorce, contains helpful guidance for parents currently struggling with the challenges of separation, highlights individual differences in resilience, and optimistically states that it is never too late to improve the lives of your children.

Ahrons, C., and Rogers, R. *Divorced Families: Meeting the Challenge of Divorce and Remarriage*. New York: W.W. Norton & Co., 1987. The primary focus of this book is how different families cope with the normal but complicated relationship changes that result from divorce and remarriage.

Bala, N., and Bailey, N. "Enforcement of Access & Alienation of Children: Conflict Reduction Strategies & Legal Responses", *Canadian Family Law Quarterly,* Vol. 23, No. 1, December 2004.

Baris, M., Coates, C., Duvall, B., Garrity, C., Johnson, E., and LaCrosse, E. *Working with High Conflict Families of Divorce: A Guide for Professionals.* New Jersey: Jason Aronson Inc., 2001. This is a valuable guide to several options for assisting "revolving door" clients; that is, those who continually return to court. It contains very helpful descriptions of each role along with potential ethical pitfalls. It also includes practical precedents for contracting with high-conflict couples.

Barrette, P. *Positive Parenting During Separation & Divorce*. Ancaster, Ontario: Reconcilable Differences, 1994. This booklet contains helpful information about the needs of children at different stages of development. It also highlights "games" parents play that triangulate their children and add considerable stress following separation.

Barsky, A. *Conflict Resolution for the Helping Professions*. Toronto: Nelson/ Thomson Learning, 2000. This book is a useful and practical resource for those in the helping professions.

Behrman, R., ed. *The Future of Children: Children and Divorce*. Vol. 4, No. 1. Los Altos, California: The David and Lucile Packard Foundation, Spring 1994. This issue contains a number of articles by leading lawyers and mental health professionals on a wide range of topics about the impact of divorce on children.

Emery, R. *The Truth About Children and Divorce.* New York: Penguin Books, 2004. This is an excellent, easy-to-read resource for all professionals involved with separating couples and should be recommended reading for their clients. This book deals with all the practical questions that clients ask and practitioners need to be able to answer, including how to tell children about a separation, developmentally appropriate Parenting Plans, and how these plans need to be modified for high-conflict couples.

Epstein, P., and Madsen, L. "Joint Custody with a Vengeance: The Emergence of Parallel Parenting Orders", (2004) 22 *Canadian Family Law Quarterly*, 1-35. This provocative article examines high-conflict cases in which "parallel parenting" was ordered to preserve a relatively equal role for each parent even when parental communication and cooperation was absent.

Farrell, W. *Father and Child Reunion: How to Bring the Dads We Need to the Children We Love.* New York: Jeremy P. Tarcher/Putnam, 2001. This book summarizes research with respect to the important role fathers play in both intact and separated families.

Francke, L.B. *Growing Up Divorced: How to Help Your Child Cope with Every Stage — From Infancy Through the Teens.* New York: Fawcett Crest Books, 1983. This book was written by a parent who experienced divorce. She has combined her own perceptions with a review of major research in the field.

Freeman, R. *Parenting Plans: Making Decisions in Children's Best Interests.* LSUC, Special Lectures, 2000, 78-135. This is an excellent paper summarizing the recent literature on parenting plans and includes helpful guidelines for working with parents, an extensive bibliography, and a series of charts setting out developmental considerations when creating Parenting Plans. These charts reflect the work of a number of well-known researchers in child development.

Freeman, R. *Successful Family Transitions: An Evaluation of Intervention Strategies.* Toronto: Family Service Association of Metropolitan Toronto, 1995.

Freeman, R., and Freeman, G. *Managing Contact Difficulties: A Child-Centred Approach.* Paper presented to Family, Children & Youth Section, Department of Justice Canada, 2003. This paper provides an excellent review of the literature on parent alienation and the results of a national consultation process on child-parent contact difficulties after divorce. It identifies the type of behaviours that contribute to contact difficulties, and contains suggestions for addressing these issues in the best interests of the child. This paper is grounded in research and contributes to better informed policies and strategies for dealing with the small, but challenging number of families that exhibit these problems.

Gardner, R. *The Boys and Girls Book About Divorce.* New York: Bantam Books, 1970.

Gardner, R. *The Parent's Book About Divorce.* New York: Bantam Books, 1979. These two books are written by an experienced clinician who offers many insights about the impact of divorce and separation on children and their parents. The children's book can be read with children or by an adolescent and can be used as the basis for their discussions during a counselling process.

Garrity, Carla B., and Baris, Mitchell A. *Caught in the Middle — Protecting the Children of High-Conflict Divorce*. San Francisco, California: Jossey-Bass, 1994. This is an excellent book for understanding the impact on children of high-conflict divorces. It has helpful charts that differentiate between high- and low-conflict families in terms of recommended Parenting Plans at different developmental stages.

Gold, L. *Between Love and Hate: A Guide to Civilized Divorce*. New York: Plenum Press, 1992. See *supra*, Chapter 4, Annotated Bibliography.

Gould, Jonathan W., and Stahl, Philip M. "Never Paint by the Numbers". *Family Court Review*, Vol. 39, No. 4, October, 2001.

Hetherington, E.M., Cox, M., and Cox, R. "Play and Social Interaction in Children Following Divorce". (1979), 35 *Journal of Social Issues* 26. This article presents the results of a longitudinal study on the effects of divorce on play and social interaction in 48 middle-class white pre-school children from divorced families. These children were compared to 48 children from non-divorced families and were studied at intervals of two months, one year, and two years after divorce. This study found that the adjustment to divorce appeared to be more difficult for boys than girls.

Hetherington, E.M., and Kelly, J. *For Better or Worse: Divorce Reconsidered*. New York: W.W. Norton and Co., 2002. This book is a review of the recent literature on divorce and debunks some of the traditional stereotypes about the negative impact of divorce on children.

Hickey, E., and Dalton, E. *Healing Hearts: Helping Children and Adults Recover from Divorce*. Carson City, Nevada: Gold Leaf Press, 1994. This is an excellent book to help parents to heal emotionally so that they can in turn help their children deal constructively with the challenges and changes brought by divorce.

Hodges, W. *Interventions for Children of Divorce: Custody, Access, and Psychotherapy, Second Edition*. New York: John Wiley and Sons, Inc., 1991. This book reviews the literature on different parenting arrangements and their impact on children at different ages. The author also discusses mediation and custody assessments as two interventions that may assist parents going through separation.

Ives, S.B., Fassler, B., and Lash, M. *The Divorce Workbook: A Guide for Kids and Families*. Vermont: Waterfront Books, 1985. This is a practical workbook for use by therapists to help children express their feelings about separation and divorce through art.

Jaffe, P., Wolfe, D., and Wilson, S. "Children of Battered Women". (1990) *Developmental Clinical Psychology and Psychiatry*. Newbury Park, California: Sage Publications. This publication summarizes the research on the impact of family violence on children, including gender differences.

Johnston, J., and Campbell, L. "A Clinical Typology of Interparental Violence in Disputed-Custody Divorces". (1993), 63 *American Journal of Orthopsychiatry* 1. Based on two studies of high-conflict divorcing families, four characteristic profiles of inter-parental violence were identified: ongoing or episodic battering by males, female-initiated violence, interactive violence controlled by males, and violence engendered by separation or post-divorce trauma. A fifth profile consisted of psychotic and paranoid reactions. These different profiles generate different issues to consider in mediation.

Johnston, J., and Campbell, L. *Impasses of Divorce: The Dynamics and Resolution of Family Conflict*. New York: The Free Press, 1988. This book makes an important contribution toward understanding the dynamics of high-conflict couples and offers innovative approaches to mediation.

Johnston, J., and Roesby, V. *In the Name of the Child: A Developmental Approach to Understanding and Helping Children of Conflicted and Violent Divorce*. New York: The Free Press, 1997. This is a thorough and well-written text on the needs of high-risk children who are exposed to parental violence. This book assists clinicians, mediators, and lawyers understand the special provisions needed to protect the safety of these children when a Parenting Plan is being designed.

Kalter, N. *Growing Up With Divorce*. New York: The Free Press, 1990. Kalter, a psychologist, describes how children experience divorce and makes recommendations for ways in which parents and professionals can reduce children's stress and enhance their adjustment. This is a valuable book for both parents and professionals.

Kelly, J. "The Best Interests of the Child — A Concept in Search of Meaning". (1997), 35 *Family and Conciliation Courts Review*, 377-387.

Kraft, M. "Rethinking Access for Children under Age 3". (2003), 22 *Canadian Family Law Quarterly*, 37-54. This article sets out the case for overnight access with very young children.

Kruk, E. *Divorce and Disengagement: Patterns of Fatherhood Within and Beyond Marriage*. Halifax: Fernwood Publishing, 1993.

Lamb, M., and Kelly, J. "Using the Empirical Literature to Guide the Development of Parenting Plans for Young Children", *Family Court Review*, Vol. 39, No. 4, October, 2001.

Lamb, M., Sternberg, K., and Thompson, R. "The Effects of Divorce and Custody Arrangements on Children's Behavior, Development, and Adjustment", *Family and Conciliation Courts Review*, Vol. 35, No. 4, October 1997.

Lansky, V. *Divorce Book for Parents: Helping Your Children Cope with Divorce and its Aftermath*. New York: Signet (a division of Penguin Books U.S.A., Inc.), 1989. Lansky is a divorced parent with many practical tips for preparing both adults and children for the experience of separation.

Lund, M. "A Therapist's View of Parental Alienation Syndrome". (1995), 33:3 *Family and Conciliation Courts Review*, 308-323. This article explores many possible reasons for Parent Alienation Syndrome and suggests possible interventions.

McDonough, H., and Bartha, C. *Putting Children First — A Guide for Parents Breaking Up*. Toronto: University of Toronto Press, 1999. This is a good resource book for parents and professionals and provides a step-by-step guide to the emotional work parents must do to make their divorce manageable for themselves and their children.

McKnight-Erickson, M., and Erickson, S. *The Children's Book — For the Sake of the Children: A Communication Workbook for Separate Parenting After Divorce*. West Concorde, Minn.: CPI Publishing, 1992. This is a useful workbook to assist parents to share information, especially about young children.

Ricci, I. *Mom's House, Dad's House: Making Two Homes for Your Child, Second Edition*. New York: A Fireside Book, Published by Simon & Schuster, 1997. This is a practical and systematic guide for parents who are considering a shared parenting arrangement after divorce. Ricci describes how to shift from a spousal relationship, which is ending, to a parenting relationship, which is continuing. She has a number of practical tips, checklists, guidelines, sample agreements, *etc.*, which parents can adapt to their own situation.

Ross, J., and Corcoran, J. *Joint Custody with a Jerk: Raising a Child with an Uncooperative Ex*. New York: St. Martin's Press, 1996. This is a helpful guide to constructive communication with an ex-spouse. Despite a provocative title, this book encourages self-reflection about steps each parent could take to create a less conflicted environment for children.

Santrock, J.W., and Warshak, R.A. "Father Custody and Social Development in Boys and Girls". (1979), 35 *Journal of Social Issues* 112. This study examined 33 boys and 27 girls from 60 white middle-class families ranging in age from 6 to 11 years. One-third of the children came from families in which the father was awarded custody, one-third from families in which the mother was awarded custody, and one-third from parentally intact families. Videotaped observations were used to evaluate the children's social development in the three research groups.

Saposnek, D. *Mediating Child Custody Disputes.* Revised Edition, San Francisco: Jossey-Bass Publishers, 1998. This book would be useful to the mediation practitioner and contains a number of concrete suggestions and case examples for creating Parenting Plans that focus on the best interest of the children.

Shaffer, M. "The Impact of Wife Abuse on Child Custody and Access Decisions" (2004), 22 *Canadian Family Law Quarterly*, 85-151.

Solomon, J., and Biringen, Z. "Another Look at Developmental Research", *Family Court Review*, Vol. 39, No. 4, October, 2001.

Solomon, J., and George, C. "The Effects on Attachment of Overnight Visitation in Divorced and Separated Families — A Longitudinal Follow-Up", in *Attachment Disorganization*, Chapter 9. New York: Guilford Press, 1997.

Stahl, P.M. *Parenting After Divorce: Resolving Conflicts and Meeting Your Children's Needs*. Atascadero, California: Impact Publishers, 2007.

Taylor, A. *The Handbook of Family Dispute Resolution Mediation Theory and Practice.* San Francisco, California: Jossey-Bass, 2002. This is an excellent text for mediators helping to create Parenting Plans. There is a very helpful developmental guide to parenting arrangements by age of child and nature of the parent-child relationship.

Wallerstein, J.S., and Blakeslee, S. *Second Chances: Men, Women, and Children a Decade After Divorce*. Revised Edition. New York: Ticknor & Fields, 1996. This book follows the same families as *Surviving the Breakup* (see below), 10 years after divorce. Wallerstein's conclusion is that divorce is not a short-term crisis, but a profoundly life-changing event for all concerned. The focus in this book is on adolescents and young adults a decade after divorce.

Wallerstein, J.S., and Kelly, J.B. *Surviving the Breakup: How Children and Parents Cope with Divorce*. Revised Edition. New York: Basic Books Inc., 1996. This is the best-known report of research on the effects of separation and divorce on children and parents. It is a longitudinal project, and at the time the book was published, children and parents were studied at various intervals up to 5 years following separation or divorce. This is an extremely readable, enlightening book that can be used to assist parents in understanding the consequences, and to help parents plan a strategy for dealing with the aftermath of separation and divorce.

Wallerstein, J.S., Lewis, J.M., and Blakeslee, S. *The Unexpected Legacy of Divorce: The 25 Year Landmark Study*. New York: Hyperion, 2000. This book completes the follow-up of families in *Surviving the Breakup* and is an excellent resource on the effects of separation on children once they reach adulthood. This book could be recommended to clients.

Ware, C. *Sharing Parenthood After Divorce: An Enlightened Custody Guide for Mothers, Fathers and Children*. Toronto: Bantam Books, 1984. This is a book written by a parent who attempted mediation as a method of resolving a contested custody dispute. She reports on her own experience and the experience of many other couples with respect to sharing parenthood after divorce. She is a strong advocate for both the mediation process and for a shared approach to parenting.

Warshak, R. "Overnight Contact Between Parents and Young Children", *Family and Conciliation Courts Review,* Vol. 38, No. 4, October 2000.

Chapter Ten

Legal Issues: Custody and Access

A. CUSTODY AND ACCESS

Often the most significant issue in dispute between parents is who will have custody of the children. On a psychological level, this is often a competition for control, affection, continuity of lifestyle, and acceptance as a parent. Feelings of anger, a desire for revenge, fear of loneliness, and guilt compete with feelings of genuine concern about the welfare of the children and the knowledge that children need both parents and usually show better psychological adjustment if the conflict between the parents is kept to a minimum.

Often the party who is successful in winning custody succeeds in other aspects of the dispute, such as obtaining exclusive possession of the matrimonial home, support, and familiar family possessions. The party who loses custody of the children faces the most radical change in lifestyle, and even if that parent chooses to leave the marriage, he or she often experiences strong feelings of loneliness, depression, a sense of failure, guilt, or rejection.

The more adversarial the process for determining custody and the more the law establishes one parent as a winner and the other as a loser in custody matters, the more devastating the psychological effect on both parents and children. Within this psychological context, the following is a discussion of the law of custody, at both provincial and federal levels, including alternative orders that can be made by the court.

1. What Is Custody?

In the context of parental disputes over children, custody refers to the totality of rights and duties in relation to the child. That is, it encompasses both control of the physical person of the child and the right to make decisions about the child's upbringing.

Custody essentially includes the following rights:

- the right to control the child;
- the right to make decisions regarding the child's education, religion, and lifestyle; and
- the right to grant or withhold consent to the marriage of an underage child.

Custody also includes such responsibilities as:

- providing for the child's physical, mental, and moral care and development; and

- providing for the child's basic needs, such as food, clothing, and housing.

Custody is often used interchangeably with guardianship; however, guardianship is really a broader term that applies in situations other than "legal custody" in the sense described above.

2. What Is Access?

Access is defined as the right of the non-custodial parent to visit with the child. An order for access does not include the legal right to make decisions with respect to the child's upbringing nor does it include the legal responsibility for the child's care and control. The purpose of access is to encourage the continuation of a parent-child relationship following a marriage breakdown. A non-custodial parent who has access rights no longer has a legal right to participate as a parent in many significant areas of the child's life, such as determining the child's residence, education, or religion.

The non-custodial parent has the same responsibilities for the care of the child as any adult acting in a caretaking capacity. That is, the non-custodial parent is responsible for emergency health care, informing the custodial parent of any delay in returning the child at the agreed-upon time, and requesting in advance any changes in the visitation schedule.

In some provinces, such as Ontario, and under the federal *Divorce Act*,[1] anyone who has access to the child has a legal right to make inquiries and receive information about the health, education, and welfare of the child.

3. Custody Disputes: The Historical Context

Under the English common law, children were considered to be the property of their fathers, and custody awards were routinely made to fathers.

During the 19th century, the industrial revolution resulted in many fathers working away from the home and mothers remaining in the home as the primary caretakers of children. In addition, society began to place a higher value on children as more children survived the high risk of infant mortality. Legally, the courts shifted from a preference for fathers as custodians to mothers as custodians. This was particularly true of young children. During the early 1900's, the "tender years" doctrine was applied as the principal rule for determining custody disputes. That is, custody was routinely awarded to mothers, particularly for children under the age of 7, unless the mother was found to be unfit.

In the mid-1970's a further cultural change took place that had an effect on the criteria for awarding custody. The child's needs and interests became a more important factor, and custody was awarded on the basis of "the best interests of the child". Custody awards were not supposed to be contingent on the sex of the parent, but rather were to reflect the best interests of the child. In fact, the courts still demonstrated a considerable preference for maternal custody, unless the

---

[1] R.S.C. 1985, c. 3 (2nd Supp.).

mother was demonstrated to be unfit.

In the 1980's, a number of social factors had an impact on custody awards; for example, such changes as:

- more women were in the workforce and out of the home;
- more men were participating in child rearing and household tasks; and
- there was a greater concern about discrimination on the basis of sex, as it applied both to women and to men.

In keeping with the movement toward greater sharing of parental rights and responsibilities during the marriage, the early 1990's saw an increased trend toward continued sharing of the parental role even after marriage breakdown. This trend was responsible for the movement away from a determination of sole custody to one parent (that is, exclusive parental rights to one parent) toward a concept of continued parental cooperation and sharing after the marriage has ended. This trend has led to a number of variations in the traditional award of custody to one parent and access to the other.

4. Custody Arrangements

(A) Sole Custody

Sole custody refers to an order whereby one custodial parent is awarded the totality of rights and duties in relation to the child. Custody can be determined by the courts, or it can be determined by the parties through their own agreement.

(B) Shared Custody

Shared custody is a term that has emerged from the *Child Support Guidelines* which will be discussed in Chapter 11. It was intended to address the situation where one or more children spend approximately equal time residing with each parent (at least 40 per cent of the time). In these cases, the parent who would ordinarily pay child support (usually the father) can argue that he should pay less support to the other parent because he has greater financial costs in his own home. The courts will take such an argument into account as well as the relative financial position of both parties and who in fact is paying most of the child care costs. As a general rule, the courts do not reduce child support if the mother is not working or is earning considerably less than the father. The goal appears to be to create a relatively equal standard of living in both homes. In recent years the term "shared custody" is appearing in more agreements to reflect the greater involvement by fathers in caretaking tasks, such as taking children to doctor and dentist appointments, extra-curricular activities, taking children to and from school, *etc.*

(C) SPLIT CUSTODY

There are two ways in which the term "split custody" is used today. First, split custody refers to an arrangement whereby one parent has the sole responsibility for making certain types of parenting decisions or has the sole responsibility for certain custodial rights (incidents of custody) and the other parent has the sole responsibility for other decisions or rights. For example, if one parent was Catholic and the other Protestant, they could decide, or a judge could order, that the Catholic parent had the right to decide the children's school placement and the other parent could decide the child's religion. This can be a recipe for ongoing conflict if the Catholic parent enrolls the child in a separate school and the other parent refuses to have the child baptized in the Catholic church and takes the child to a Protestant church.

If one parent is indifferent to a particular parental right and the other cares deeply, without opposition from the other parent, this can be a way of resolving a dispute. For example, one parent may not be religious, but is very involved in the children's extra-curricular activities, and the other parent may feel strongly about religion, but is not heavily invested in sports. Provided there is no serious disagreement about the children's involvement, the more interested parent may be given the right to make religious (and if necessary school placement) decisions, and the other parent may have primary responsibility for extra-curricular activities. They could decide that significant health care decisions would be made jointly. This is an example of split custody.

The term split custody has emerged from the *Child Support Guidelines*. It means that one parent has full custody of one or more children and the other parent has full custody of one or more of the other children. Usually each parent would have the right of access to the other child or children. This has implications for support payments as set out in Chapter 11, and it has psychological implications for the children's relationship with each other and with each parent. If this is the outcome of choosing sides in a parental war, it can result in a lifetime rift between siblings. If it reflects a stage of development (*e.g.*, a teenage boy wants more contact with his Dad), then, with some sensitivity and good planning by the parents, his relationship with other siblings can be preserved.

(D) ALTERNATING CUSTODY

Alternating custody means that one parent has full custody, including care and control of the child, for a specified time period, and then the other parent has full custody, including care and control, for a specified time period (not to be confused with alternating or rotating residence, which is described below in (E) "JOINT CUSTODY").

While the child is residing with one parent, that parent is entirely responsible for all decisions with respect to the child's upbringing, although the non-custodial parent usually has the right to access. This custody arrangement divides, rather than shares, the custodial responsibilities between the parents.

Such an arrangement may be used in cases where the parents live far apart, in different provinces, states, or countries and the children spend part of the year with each parent or spend alternating years with each parent. This is to be distinguished from joint custody, which will be discussed next.

(E) JOINT CUSTODY

In contrast to alternating custody, joint custody preserves, at all times, both parents' joint legal responsibility for the upbringing of the child. That is, even following separation, both parents maintain their legal rights and responsibilities for significant decisions affecting the child.

Joint legal custody does not necessarily mean that the child spends an equal amount of time physically living with each parent. There is no requirement that the child spend any particular amount of time with each parent, although both parents retain their legal status as parents.

In California and some other jurisdictions in the United States, courts distinguish between joint legal custody and joint physical custody:

- *Joint legal custody* means that both parents retain the right to make decisions with respect to the child.
- *Joint physical custody* means that the child spends a substantial amount of time living with each parent. In California, children who live at least 30 per cent of the time with each parent are considered to be in a joint physical custody arrangement.
- *Sole legal custody* means that one parent has the legal right to make all decisions with respect to the child's upbringing.
- *Sole physical custody* means that the child primarily resides with one parent and has access visits with the other parent.

In California, any combination of the above-mentioned aspects of custody is possible. That is, a family can have joint legal and joint physical custody, or joint legal but sole physical custody, or sole legal and sole physical custody, or sole legal but joint physical custody.

In Canada, couples who have joint custody of their children generally share decisions with respect to upbringing, but the children spend more time living with one parent. In recent years this type of joint custody has increased to about 40 per cent of Canadian custody orders and cases resolved in mediation probably have an even higher percentage. Also, there are a growing number of cases in which parents share both decision-making and physical care and control on an approximately equal-time basis. This most often occurs when parents have a cooperative and respectful relationship, live in the same school district and have school age children.

Under both provincial and federal legislation, it is possible for a court to order joint custody, particularly in cases where the parties consent to such an order. However, the Northwest Territories is the only jurisdiction in Canada to specifically include the term "joint custody" as an option available to the judge under its custody provisions. The legislation does not contain either a presumption or a preference for joint custody, but rather permits the judge, in appropriate cases, to make such an order.

In practice, Canadian courts usually do not make joint custody orders in cases where the parties do not request it, particularly if there is evidence that the parties cannot cooperate with each other in the interests of their children. There are some exceptions to this general rule, particularly at the stage of an interim custody order. At this point, the court may make a joint custody or alternating custody award to preserve the status quo as between the parties until the date of trial.

A number of couples who mediate rather than litigate the issues of custody and access decide on a shared parenting arrangement, that is, in effect, some form of joint custody. According to the research data collected by Howard Irving in the early 1980's on a sample of 201 Ontario couples, joint custody appears to have many benefits for both parents and children. Particularly where these arrangements were arrived at voluntarily, the parents reported a higher level of satisfaction; it was found that co-parental relationships were likely to be less litigious than sole custody arrangements: the children tended to be happier when they maintained frequent, reliable, and ongoing contact with both their parents, and this arrangement encouraged joint fiscal responsibility, with a far higher percentage of joint custodial fathers paying support.

Some studies have not found this relationship between joint custody and payment of support. For example, in jurisdictions such as California, where support obligations are reduced if a father agrees to spend a substantial amount of time with the children, research[2] shows that despite these agreements, children usually spend the majority of their time living with their mother. In Canada, the federal support guidelines could have the same effect; that is, support obligations may be reduced if couples agree on joint physical custody,[3] although most children will likely continue to spend the majority of their time living with their mother. In mediation, fathers frequently seek to have the children 40 per cent of the time and also request a reduction in child support. This can be a divisive issue particularly in cases in which the father earns substantially more than the mother. This issue is discussed in greater detail in Chapter 11.

Other studies[4] have found that the level of conflict between the parents is an important factor in parental satisfaction, as is the fact that they reached a joint

---

2 See E. Maccoby and R. Mnookin, *Dividing the Child: Social and Legal Dilemmas of Custody* (Cambridge, Mass.: Harvard University Press, 1992).

3 See Chapter 9. Section 3 of the *Federal Child Support Guidelines*, SOR/97-175, allows a judge some discretion to reduce child support if the children spend at least 40 per cent of their time with each parent.

4 See H.H. Irving and M. Benjamin, "Shared Parenting in Canada: Questions, Answers and Implications" (1986), 1 *Canadian Family Law Quarterly* 79; J. Kelly, "Current Research on Children's Post-Divorce Adjustment: No Simple Answers" (1993), 31 *Family and Conciliation Courts Review* 1; and E. Maccoby and R. Mnookin, *Dividing the Child: Social and Legal Dilemmas of Custody* (Cambridge; Mass.: Harvard University Press, 1992).

custody agreement voluntarily. Another factor is the proximity of the parents' residences to each other and to the children's schools. Arrangements need to be practical to maintain a high level of satisfaction and ongoing cooperation.

5. The Criteria for Awarding Custody as Determined by Provincial and Federal Statutes

Custody decisions are made under both provincial legislation and federal legislation. Usually, custody decisions reached prior to divorce are made pursuant to a provincial statute, although interim orders can be made under the federal *Divorce Act*.[5]

At the time of divorce, custody and access decisions are considered a part of corollary relief, that is, relief that the courts can grant in conjunction with their power to grant a divorce under the federal *Divorce Act*. It is also possible to apply for a custody order under a provincial statute at the time of divorce.

When an action for divorce is commenced under the *Divorce Act*, any application for custody under a provincial statute that has not as yet been determined by the court is stayed, except by leave of the court. This is because the decision under the federal Act would be constitutionally paramount to a decision under a provincial Act. Therefore, there would be no reason for competing claims under the two Acts to proceed at the same time.

Provincial statutes and the federal *Divorce Act* vary in the way in which they describe custody and in the criteria that are used in determining custody. Some statutes refer only to the best interests of children, whereas other statutes set out specific criteria for the judges to consider in making a custody award.

For example, the Ontario *Children's Law Reform Act*[6] sets out very specifically the criteria to be applied by a judge in making an order of custody. These criteria reflect the common law position on custody awards. As a result, even in those provinces that do not set out elaborate criteria for determining custody, most jurisdictions would apply the same or similar criteria on the basis of common law.

The Ontario *Children's Law Reform Act* deals with custody as follows:

> 24(1) The merits of an application under this Part in respect of custody of or access to a child shall be determined on the basis of the best interests of the child, in accordance with subsections (2), (3) and (4).
>
> (2) The court shall consider all the child's needs and circumstances, including,
>
> (*a*) the love, affection and emotional ties between the child and,
>
> (i) each person entitled to or claiming custody of or access to the child,
>
> (ii) other members of the child's family who reside with the child, and
>
> (iii) persons involved in the child's care and upbringing;
>
> (*b*) the child's views and preferences, if they can reasonably be ascertained;
>
> (*c*) the length of time the child has lived in a stable home environment;

---

5 R.S.C. 1985, c. 3 (2nd Supp.).

6 R.S.O. 1990, c. C.12.

(*d*) the ability and willingness of each person applying for custody of the child to provide the child with guidance and education, the necessaries of life and any special needs of the child;

(*e*) any plans proposed for the child's care and upbringing;

(*f*) the permanence and stability of the family unit with which it is proposed that the child will live;

(*g*) the ability of each person applying for custody of or access to the child to act as a parent; and

(*h*) the relationship by blood or through an adoption order between the child and each person who is a party to the application.

(3) A person's past conduct shall be considered only,

(*a*) in accordance with subsection (4); or

(*b*) if the court is satisfied that the conduct is otherwise relevant for the person's ability to act as a parent.

(4) In assessing a person's ability to act as a parent, the court shall consider whether the person has at any time committed violence or abuse against,

(*a*) his or her spouse;

(*b*) a parent of the child to whom the application relates;

(*c*) a member of the person's household; or

(*d*) any child.

(5) For the purposes of subsection (4), anything done in self-defence or to protect another person shall not be considered violence or abuse.

It is important to note that this statute apparently does not establish a preference for biological parents over psychological parents, and in addition it specifically excludes matrimonial fault or other aspects of past conduct if they are not relevant to parenting ability. It is often necessary for the mediator in discussions of custody, as well as in discussions of support, to point out to the parties that the court does not make awards of custody or support on the basis of matrimonial fault.

By way of contrast, the federal *Divorce Act* does not set out the criteria for evaluating the child's best interests, although it does adopt "best interests" as the sole test for determining custody awards. One unique feature of the federal Act is that it places a heavy emphasis on ensuring that the child has an opportunity to spend considerable time with both parents. In fact, to preserve the child's relationship with both parents, the Act directs the court to give consideration, when determining custody awards, to the parent who is most likely to encourage the involvement of the non-custodial parent. This Act is similar to the Ontario Act in that matrimonial fault is expressly excluded as a factor in awarding custody or access, unless the conduct is relevant to parenting. At the present time there is a proposal to substantially change the way that custody is viewed, from both a policy and a procedural perspective. Although this proposal is still a few years from becoming legislation, it is having a strong impact on the outcome of mediated, negotiated, and litigated cases. This is an exciting and a fairly revolutionary document which will be reviewed later in this chapter. First, it is important to understand the provisions of the *Divorce Act* that are currently in effect as set out below:

> 16(8) In making an order under this section, the court shall take into consideration only the best interests of the child of the marriage as determined by reference to the condition, means, needs and other circumstances of the child.
>
> (9) In making an order under this section, the court shall not take into consideration the past conduct of any person unless the conduct is relevant to the ability of that person to act as a parent of a child.
>
> (10) In making an order under this section, the court shall give effect to the principle that a child of the marriage should have as much contact with each spouse as is consistent with the best interests of the child and, for that purpose, shall take into consideration the willingness of the person for whom custody is sought to facilitate such contact.

The federal and provincial statutes also differ in their descriptions of entitlement to custody, and the rights and privileges of the custodial and the non-custodial parents. For example, the Ontario *Children's Law Reform Act* deals with these issues in the following way:

> 20(1) Except as otherwise provided in this Part, the father and the mother of a child are equally entitled to custody of the child.
>
> (2) A person entitled to custody of a child has the rights and responsibilities of a parent in respect of the person of the child and must exercise those rights and responsibilities in the best interests of the child.
>
> (3) Where more than one person is entitled to custody of a child, any one of them may exercise the rights and accept the responsibilities of a parent on behalf of them in respect of the child.
>
> (4) Where the parents of a child live separate and apart and the child lives with one of them with the consent, implied consent or acquiescence of the other of them, the right of the other to exercise the entitlement of custody and the incidents of custody, but not the entitlement to access, is suspended until a separation agreement or order otherwise provides.
>
> (5) The entitlement to access to a child includes the right to visit with and be visited by the child and the same right as a parent to make inquiries and to be given information as to the health, education and welfare of the child.

It is clear that this Act sets up an equal statutory entitlement on the part of fathers and mothers to custody of their children. In addition, while the Act does not prevent an order of joint custody, it is written from the perspective of a sole custody award. It does not at any time specifically mention joint custody or split or alternating custody.

This Act does give some of the rights of a parent to the non-custodial parent. That is, it does give the non-custodial parent a right to make inquiries and be given information with respect to the child's health, education, and welfare. However, it should be noted that this is a right to information and not a right to participate in decision-making.

Under the federal *Divorce Act* the entitlement to custody and the allocation of rights and privileges between the custodial and non-custodial parent are as follows:

> 16(1) A court of competent jurisdiction may, on application by either or both spouses or by any other person, make an order respecting the custody of or the access to, or the custody of and access to, any or all children of the marriage.
>
> (2) Where an application is made under subsection (1), the court may, on application by either or both spouses or by any other person, make an interim order respecting the custody of or the access to, or the custody of and access to, any or all children of the marriage pending determination of the application under subsection (1).
>
> (3) A person, other than a spouse, may not make an application under subsection (1) or (2) without leave of the court.
>
> (4) The court may make an order under this section granting custody of, or access to, any or all children of the marriage to any one or more persons.
>
> (5) Unless the court orders otherwise, a spouse who is granted access to a child of the marriage has the right to make inquiries, and to be given information, as to the health, education and welfare of the child.
>
> (6) The court may make an order under this section for a definite or indefinite period or until the happening of a specified event and may impose such other terms, conditions or restrictions in connection therewith as it thinks fit and just.
>
> (7) Without limiting the generality of subsection (6), the court may include in an order under this section a term requiring any person who has custody of a child of the marriage and who intends to change the place of residence of that child to notify, at least thirty days before the change or within such other period before the change as the court may specify, any person who is granted access to that child of the change, the time at which the change will be made and the new place of residence of the child.

This statute does not presume that the parents have an equal entitlement to custody. There is no reference to joint custody in the legislation (only in a marginal note, which has no statutory significance); however, the *Divorce Act* does establish a right to information by the non-custodial parent, including the right upon application to be notified of a change of address if the custodial parent decides to move to a new location.

6. Current Issues

(A) Custodial Designation

This chapter has used the traditional legal language of "custody" of and "access" to the child. However, over the past decade, in North America, Australia, and England, there has been an increasing awareness of the impact on parents of the language used to describe their ongoing role with their children. In the first place, "custody" is an ownership concept. We use it to describe who owns or has possession of an object, such as, "I have custody of the dining room chairs." In criminal law, it has connotations of detaining people against their will, such as,

"We took the prisoner into custody." Neither of these concepts is an attractive way to describe a parent-child relationship, nor does it address the fears, concerns, or needs of many parents. Also, the concept of custody is, "If I have it, you don't." It is a win/lose term which suggests that if a parent loses custody, he or she will lose the opportunity to have an important role or relationship with the child. It is this fear that propels most custody battles. Mediators and mental health professionals have criticized the language in the *Divorce Act* on the basis that it actually fuels unnecessary litigation between parents.

Fighting over the custodial label usually does not address the important responsibilities of parenting. In England, the *Children Act, 1989*[7] clearly illustrates the shift in language from "custody" of children to that of "parental responsibility", which is defined as "all the rights, duties, powers, responsibilities and authority which by law a parent of a child has in relation to the child and his property".

Most parents who fight over "custody" are not fighting over who will carry out the tasks or responsibilities of being a parent; they are usually fighting over their own rights as parents. This is not in the child's best interests because, especially after a separation, it is difficult for either parent to meet all of the needs of the child on his or her own. A better approach would be for both parents to arrive at a Parenting Plan that shares the responsibilities, regardless of the choice of custodial designation.

The trend, particularly by mediators, is to try to shift the focus to how the parents are going to carry out their responsibilities as parents, and as a last step, to decide on a custodial label where necessary. By helping parents to focus on how they will each contribute to a Parenting Plan (rather than on what to call it), there are usually several benefits, namely:

- Neither parent carries the entire burden of responsibilities, which is particularly important if both parents are in the workforce after separation.
- Children's needs are met more adequately. Single parents are often unable to offer their children the same opportunities that they could prior to separation. Parental cooperation helps to minimize any losses.
- Both parents continue to see themselves as having a significant parenting role.
- Both parents have some time to meet their own personal needs, which will likely enhance their ability to parent.
- Parenting responsibilities will change with the age of the child, the work schedule of each parent, their proximity to each other, *etc.* A plan that focuses on responsibilities rather than labels is more flexible and can adapt to changing circumstances.

The same concerns apply to the term "access". Access is a possessory term and has little to do with maintaining a relationship between a parent and child. Parents (usually fathers) often feel disenfranchised by the terminology of being

---

[7] (U.K.), c. 41, s. 3(1).

reduced to an "access" parent. They often feel they are being relegated to the stature of a visitor or distant relative. Access parents may feel no commitment to carry out responsibilities, particularly if their efforts are not recognized as contributing to parenting. Ironically, the access parent is often resented by the custodial parent as being the "Santa Claus" parent, while the custodial parent feels overburdened by the weight of trying to meet all of the practical, economic, and recreational needs of the children.

When parents fight over a custodial label, what they usually want is to have an important role or to maintain a significant relationship with the child. Even if the main issue is to have the child primarily reside with that parent, most parents would really appreciate the other parent's assistance in carrying out parenting tasks and would expect to consult the other parent on significant issues. Both parents are usually satisfied with this type of Parenting Plan, but the label is often the focus of a divisive battle that undermines any cooperation.

Today the trend is to avoid battles over custodial labels and, instead, to encourage mediation clients to work out a parenting plan that will define their roles and responsibilities in relation to the children. The emphasis is on the *responsibilities* of parenting rather than on the *parent's rights*.

The plan should clarify which parent will carry out specific parenting tasks and how each parent will participate in decision-making. Also, it should deal with what time the child will spend with each parent on a regular basis and during school breaks, statutory holidays, and other special days. It should also clarify the process to be followed if a material change in circumstances occurs, such as a move to another city, a remarriage, or a parent's illness, and how the parents will resolve significant conflicts in the future. To the extent that the parenting plan offers a clear road map, the number of future conflicts will be reduced. Mediation is a very effective process for designing Parenting Plans that are tailored to the special needs and circumstances of the entire family.

In December, 1998, the Federal Government released the Report of the Special Joint Committee of the House of Commons and the Senate on Child Custody and Access. This Report, entitled "For the Sake of the Children", addressed a number of important issues for mediators and collaborative lawyers, including the use of language, Parenting Plans, and the role of mediation. In December 2002, after much discussion, the Minister of Justice introduced Bill C-22 in an attempt to make significant changes in the approach to Family Law. These proposals never became law. They generated considerable conflict between father's rights groups (who wanted a presumption of joint custody) and women's rights groups (who wanted greater protection for abused women and children) and were dropped by the government. However, the proposals did represent an important shift in thinking about the goals of post-separation parenting and the process used to resolve disputes about children. Therefore, the key recommendations are summarized below:

- The Preamble stated that children are entitled to maintain a close and continuous relationship with both parents after separation (this principle is qualified in cases of abuse to children and/or the other parent).

- That children have an opportunity to be heard by a skilled professional where the decisions directly affect them.
- That all litigating parents be required to attend a parent education program designed to increase their awareness of the responses of parents and children to separation, the needs of children at various developmental stages, the benefits of cooperative parenting, parental rights and responsibilities, and the availability of mediation and other methods of dispute resolution.
- A requirement that both parents receive relevant information and records from appropriate professionals or the other parent, with respect to the child's medical, academic, and recreational records, unless the court makes an order to the contrary.
- That all parents be encouraged to develop a Parenting Plan, on their own, or with the help of a trained mediator or dispute resolver. This Parenting Plan should include details about each parent's responsibilities for the children's residence, decision-making, and financial security, as well as a process for resolving future disputes.
- That the relationships of children with grandparents, siblings and other extended family members be recognized as significant and incorporated into the Parenting Plan, where it is in the best interests of the children.
- That divorcing parents be encouraged to attend at least one mediation session to help them develop a Parenting Plan, unless concerns about domestic violence make this inappropriate. There should first be screening for abuse and where there is a history of abuse, mediation should not proceed unless the safety of the victim can be assured and the risk of violence has passed. In these cases, the parenting plan would focus on parenting responsibilities and contain measures to ensure the safety and security of the parents and children.
- That "shared parenting" and a detailed parenting plan replace the terms "custody" and "access". The specific arrangements should reflect the child's best interests.

In Bill C-22, "custody orders" were to be replaced with "parenting orders" and "access orders" with "contact orders". In addition, the vague criteria defining the "best interests" test under s. 16 of the *Divorce Act*[8] was to be replaced with a list of 12 specific criteria, many similar to but expanding on s. 24 of the *Children's Law Reform Act*,[9] These include:

> 16.2(1) In making an order under section 16 or 16.1 or paragraph 171(*b*) or (*c*), the court shall take into consideration only the best interests of the child of the marriage.
>
> (2) In determining what is in the best interests of the child, the court shall consider all the needs and circumstances of the child, including

---

8 R.S.C. 1985, c. 3 (2nd Supp.).

9 R.S.O. 1990, c. C.12.

(*a*) the child's physical, emotional and psychological needs, including the child's need for stability, taking into account the child's age and stage of development;

(*b*) the benefit to the child of developing and maintaining meaningful relationships with both spouses, and each spouse's willingness to support the development and maintenance of the child's relationship with the other spouse;

(*c*) the history of care for the child;

(*d*) any family violence, including its impact on

(i) the safety of the child and other family members,

(ii) the child's general well-being,

(iii) the ability of the person who engaged in the family violence to care for and meet the needs of the child, and

(iv) the appropriateness of making an order that would require the spouses to cooperate on issues affecting the child;

(*e*) the child's cultural, linguistic, religious and spiritual upbringing and heritage, including aboriginal upbringing or heritage;

(*f*) the child's views and preferences, to the extent that those can be reasonably ascertained;

(*g*) any plans proposed for the child's care and upbringing;

(*h*) the nature, strength and stability of the relationship between the child and each spouse;

(*i*) the nature, strength and stability of the relationship between the child and each sibling, grandparent and any other significant person in the child's life;

(*j*) the ability of each person in respect of whom the order would apply to care for and meet the needs of the child;

(*k*) the ability of each person in respect of whom the order would apply to communicate and cooperate on issues affecting the child;

(*l*) any court order or criminal conviction that is relevant to the safety or well-being of the child.

(3) In this section, "family violence" includes behaviour by a family member causing or attempting to cause physical harm to the child or another family member, or causing the child or another family member to reasonably fear for his or her safety or that of another person, but does not include acts of self-protection or protection of another person.

This legislation was never passed and there seems to be very little political interest in addressing, what in many cases, were progressive and constructive reforms. In practice, many more families have sought out non-adversarial options and it is now common for detailed parenting plans to be worked out that encourage a greater sharing of responsibilities and time with children, where appropriate.

(B) PARALLEL PARENTING VERSUS JOINT CUSTODY

At the same time as the proposals for amending the *Divorce Act*[10] were being discussed, a number of controversial high conflict custody cases emerged. When judges were faced with the dilemma of which parent to choose in these bitter battles, the courts decided on a compromise resolution. The compromise appears to have been influenced by some of the principles in the proposed legislation, but without the parental cooperation. "Parallel parenting" is the modern equivalent of Solomon's order to divide the child. The premise is that children need a relationship with both parents and if the parents cannot cooperate then, like children who are too young to play cooperatively, they need separate and parallel domains of authority. This is considered a form of joint custody, but without any of the cooperation or shared communication that is usually implied.

For example, in *Broder v. Broder*,[11] Trussler J. of the Alberta Court of Queen's Bench made an extremely detailed parallel parenting order in a case with what he described as an overly aggressive father and parties who should have as little contact as possible, except in extreme emergency situations. In this case, Justice Trussler described parallel parenting as follows:

1. A parent assumes responsibility for the children during the time they are with that parent.
2. A parent has no say or influence over the actions of the other parent while the children are in the other parent's care.
3. There is no expectation of flexibility or negotiation.
4. A parent does not plan activities for the children during the other parent's time.
5. Contact between the parents is minimized.
6. Children are not asked to deliver verbal messages.
7. Information about health, school, vacations is shared in writing usually in the form of an access book.

The cases in which parallel parenting is awarded have in common an inability to communicate or to make decisions together. Usually there is such interpersonal animosity that one or both spouses claim that if custody were awarded to one parent, the other would be marginalized or alienated from the children.

Contrary to the concept of two good parents continuing to share responsibilities and decision-making although living in separate homes, these cases reveal a reluctance on the part of judges to award sole custody to either parent despite the absence of respect, communication or cooperation.

In these cases, the judges delineate the residential times in great detail and try to create two separate and parallel universes for the children, by giving each parent sole authority over certain decisions. For example, the father can make religious decisions or health care decisions and the mother can make educational decisions. The result is often an ongoing power struggle. For example, the father

---

[10] R.S.C. 1985, c. 3 (2nd Supp.).

[11] [1998] A.J. No. 1046, 42 R.F.L. (4th) 143 (Alta. Q.B.).

may choose to raise the child Protestant and the mother may place the child in a Catholic school or the mother may decide, on the recommendation of the child's teacher, that the child needs medication for ADD, but the father may claim that is a medical decision and refuse.

In the opinion of many professionals, parallel parenting, as a form of joint custody, is creating a hostile minefield for children who will be exposed to ongoing conflict about multiple issues. There is no easy way to protect children caught in this type of warfare. At some point the children may decide that they cannot handle the tension, and they may reject one (or both) of their parents, possibly for many years. One option is to arrange for a parenting coordinator who can assist such high conflict couples on an ongoing basis.

(C) JOINT CUSTODY

An order of joint custody is usually intended for cases in which there is a history of shared care-taking during the marriage and parental cooperation and reasonable communication post-separation. In recent years the number of couples choosing joint custody or shared parenting has risen considerably. Nick Bala and Nicole Bailey reported that in 2002, joint *legal* custody was ordered in 42 per cent of divorces, with mothers receiving sole custody in 49 per cent of cases and fathers being awarded sole custody in 9 per cent of cases. Most of these orders were based on parental agreements.

There have been many cases addressing the issue of whether joint custody should be ordered against the wishes of one or both parents. Two recent cases decided by the Ontario Court of Appeal in January 2004 offer helpful guidance as to the criteria that will be applied. These cases are consistent with recent divorce literature on the advisability of joint custody arrangements when couples are in high conflict and unable to cooperate and also with the recommendations of many mental health professionals who focus on the child's best interests rather than parents' rights. In *Kaplanis v. Kaplanis*,[12] a case involving a 3-year-old child, Weiler J. speaking for a unanimous bench found that the key criteria for a joint custody award are:

- A history of cooperation between the parents;
- A history of appropriate communication, despite differences between them;
- The ability to set aside their differences to communicate and act cooperatively in the child's best interests;
- The nature of the bonds between the child and each parent;
- Each parent's capacity to parent, including their past experience in caring for the child individually;
- The practical plan of care put forward by each parent and how the child would benefit from such an arrangement;

---

[12] [2005] O.J. No. 275, 249 D.L.R. (4th) 620 (Ont. C.A.).

- The age and stage of development of the child, with a greater need to communicate effectively with infants and very young children who are unable to communicate their own needs effectively;
- The child's expressed wishes, where the child is old enough to express them. The older the child the more the child's cooperation is needed in carrying out the order. When a child is too young to communicate his/her wishes, expert evidence may be needed to assist the judge in determining how the child's psychological and emotional needs would be advanced by the proposed custody order or Parenting Plan.

In a case decided by the same bench the same day, *Ladisa v. Ladisa*,[13] Weiler J. *et al.* found that the oldest child, who was over 16 years of age, should be allowed to choose where she wished to live. A joint custody order was made with respect to her two younger siblings, ages 13 and 9, on the basis that:

- The "love, affection and emotional ties" between all three children and both parents were equally strong;
- Both parents were available and competent to care for the children, and had a history of sharing parenting responsibilities;
- The children expressed a wish to spend equal time with each parent or had in fact spent periods of time residing with each parent;
- The parents had a history of communicating reasonably when their children or third parties were present and had demonstrated the ability to make decisions together involving the children;
- The parents had a history of setting aside their differences and working together on issues of education, health care, meeting the children's financial needs, special projects, transferring items between homes, *etc.*

It is important to note that in *Ladisa*, the parents were *not* in agreement about the joint custody order and their communication was far from perfect. In fact, the mother had applied for sole custody and the trial judge had ordered that, apart from an emergency, all communication between them was to be indirect, *i.e.*, by e-mail or a communication book.

The two judgments set out above make it clear that custody decisions are fact-based. That is, they depend on the particular circumstances and capacity of the individuals involved. The guidance they provide is to focus on the best interests of the child, rather than on parents' entitlements or any *prima facie* preference for a parent based on gender.

One criticism raised by those who support a joint custody presumption is that the *Kaplanis* case will encourage a parent (usually a mother) to be uncooperative and escalate the level of conflict as a tactic to "win" sole custody of the child. However, both *Kaplanis* and *Ladisa* took a historical view of the parents' behaviour from *before* the time of separation. Also, if a parent did inflame conflict deliberately to "win" custody or if a lawyer advised a client to provoke hostility, this should be a factor to consider in weighing that parent's capacity to

---

[13] [2005] O.J. No. 276, 11 R.F.L. (6th) 50 (Ont. C.A.).

act in the child's best interests. With an increasing emphasis on mediation and Collaborative Law, such tactics should greatly diminish.

(D) DECLARATIONS OF PARENTING

A recent case expanded the definition of parents to include same-sex couples. Section 4 of Ontario's *Children's Law Reform Act* ("CLRA")[14] allows the court to issue a declaration as to who is a child's father and mother. In *A.A. v. B.B.*,[15] the Ontario Court of Appeal exercised its *parens patriae* jurisdiction to declare that both the child's biological mother and her same-sex partner were the child's "mothers" within the meaning of the CLRA.

(E) MOBILITY

For many years the courts have struggled with the issue of whether, or under what circumstances, a custodial parent can remove a child from the jurisdiction where he or she lived at the time of separation. Initially, the courts took the position that, unless the decision was unreasonable (for example, the move was only to prevent the non-custodial parent from exercising access) or there were special circumstances, the custodial parent had the right to move with the child. As in *Wright v. Wright*,[16] the focus was on the rights of the custodial parent, unless that was contrary to the terms of a Separation Agreement. Following passage of the *Divorce Act, 1985*[17] and the Ontario *Children's Law Reform Act, 1977*[18] (or similar statutes in other provinces), the courts adopted the "best interest of the child" test, as in *Carter v. Brooks*[19] *and Young v. Young.*[20]

In the *Carter v. Brooks* decision, Morden A.C.J.O. rejected the idea of developing a fixed list of criteria or a presumption in favour of the custodial parent in mobility cases. Instead he stated:

> I think that the preferable approach in the application of the standard [*i.e.*, the best interests test] is for the court to weigh and balance the factors which are relevant in the particular circumstances of the case at hand, without any rigid preconceived notion as to what weight each factor should have. ... At the end of the process the court should arrive at a determinate conclusion on the result which better accords with the best interests of the child.[21]

However, in the case of *MacGyver v. Richards*,[22] Abella J.A. took a different approach. She started from the observation that the custodial parent "must be

---

14 R.S.O. 1990, c. C.12.

15 [2007] O.J. No. 2, 83 O.R. (3d) 561 (Ont. C.A.).

16 [1973] O.J. No. 2170, 1 O.R. (2d) 337, 40 D.L.R. (3d) 321, 12 R.F.L. 200 (Ont. C.A.).

17 S.C. 1986, c. 4 [now R.S.C. 1985, c. 3 (2nd Supp.)].

18 S.O. 1977, c. 41 [now R.S.O. 1990, c. C.12].

19 [1990] O.J. No. 2182, 2 O.R. (3d) 321, 30 R.F.L. (3d) 53 (Ont. C.A.).

20 [1993] S.C.J. No. 112, [1993] 4 S.C.R. 3, 108 D.L.R. (4th) 193, 49 R.F.L. (3d) 117 (S.C.C.).

21 *Carter v. Brooks*, [1990] O.J. No. 2182, 2 O.R. (3d) 321, 30 R.F.L. (3d) 53 (Ont. C.A.) at p. 328 O.R.

22 [1995] O.J. No. 770, 22 O.R. (3d) 481, 11 R.F.L. (4th) 432 (Ont. C.A.).

understood as bearing a disproportionate amount of responsibility"[23] and therefore:

> In deciding what restrictions, if any, should be placed on a parent with custody, courts should be wary about interfering with that parent's capacity to decide, daily, what is best for the child. ... Those judgments may include whether to change neighbourhoods, or provinces, or partners, or jobs, or friends, or schools, or religions.[24]

She concluded that:

> When, therefore, a court has been asked to decide what is in a child's best interests, and a choice must be made between the responsible wishes and needs of the parent with custody and the parent with access, it seems to me manifestly unfair to treat these wishes and needs as being on an equal footing.[25]

This issue of mobility was decided by the Supreme Court of Canada in the case of *Gordon v. Goertz*.[26] The majority decision written by McLachlin J. held that the sole test was "the best interests of the child, having regard to all the relevant circumstances relating to the child's needs and the ability of the respective parents to satisfy them".[27] The focus of the inquiry is not the interests and rights of the parents. Each case turns on its own unique circumstances and the only issue is the best interests of the child in the particular circumstances of the case. "The inquiry does not begin with a legal presumption in favour of the custodial parent, although the custodial parent's views are entitled to great respect."[28] In assessing the best interests of the child, the judge should more particularly consider, *inter alia*:

(a) the existing custody arrangement and relationship between the child and the custodial parent;

(b) the existing access arrangement and the relationship between the child and the access parent;

(c) the desirability of maximizing contact between the child and both parents;

(d) the views of the child;

(e) the custodial parent's reason for moving, *only* in the exceptional case where it is relevant to that parent's ability to meet the needs of the child;

(f) disruption to the child of a change in custody;

(g) disruption to the child consequent on removal from family, schools, and the community he or she has come to know.[29]

In the end, the importance of the child's remaining with the parent to whose custody it has become accustomed in the new location must be weighed against the continuance of full contact with the child's access parent, its extended

---

23 *Ibid.*, at p. 490 O.R.

24 *Ibid.*, at p. 491 O.R.

25 *Ibid.*, at p. 492 O.R.

26 [1996] S.C.J. No. 52, [1996] 2 S.C.R. 27, 134 D.L.R. (4th) 321, 19 R.F.L. (4th) 177 (S.C.C.).

27 *Ibid.*, at p. 342 D.L.R.

28 *Ibid.*

29 *Ibid.*

family, and its community. The ultimate question in every case is this: what is in the best interests of the child in all the circumstances, old as well as new?

This decision will have a significant effect on the position taken by the parties in mediation.

Since the child's best interest in each case is the appropriate test, the mediator will need to help the parties consider the criteria set out by McLachlin J. in addition to such factors as:

- whether the move would improve the quality of life for the child and custodial parent;
- whether there is a new partner, and the child's relationship with that person;
- if there is a new partner, the stability of this family unit;
- the child's ties to extended family, friends, school, and the community in the current versus the proposed location;
- the distance proposed, and the willingness of the custodial parent to facilitate a meaningful access plan;
- the financial resources of both parents for carrying out a meaningful access plan; and
- the age of the child and any special needs or abilities.

In mediation, the question of mobility is often the most difficult issue on which to reach agreement, even if there is no move contemplated at the time of separation. It is important for the mediator to be familiar with the current statutes and case law on this subject because they will have an important impact on the negotiations. Also, it is a reality that today's families are more mobile than in the past, and therefore the issue of mobility should be discussed in every mediation involving custody and access. Any agreement reached will need to be described with great care to ensure that the parties' wishes are clearly and accurately reflected. Most often parties do not know what the future will hold, and it is often reasonable to set out some general principles about mobility and a method for resolving disputes should they arise. For example, parties might agree to

- first inform the other parent at least 30 days (or preferably more) in advance as to the location and reason for the proposed move;
- discuss the implications of a proposed move directly with the other parent in the hope of reaching a mutually acceptable plan; but if an impasse is reached, then
- return to mediation; and if this does not result in an agreement within a specified time, then
- request that the lawyers be involved in trying to negotiate a resolution; and if this is unsuccessful in a specified time period, then
- proceed to arbitration with an arbitrator selected on consent, or
- proceed to litigation with respect to any unresolved issues.

Note: In collaborative cases the collaborative lawyers would have to withdraw if litigation was chosen, and the clients would have to retain new counsel.

It may be appropriate for the parties to agree that during the time they are trying to resolve the conflict, the custodial parent may move, but the child remains in the jurisdiction. This provision would encourage parents to give as much notice as possible of a pending move and would also encourage them to set a reasonable time frame for reaching a resolution.

(F) CONTACT DIFFICULTIES

Ideally children maintain and/or develop a close and nurturing relationship with each parent after separation or divorce. This does not always happen and a detailed discussion paper by Rhonda and Gary Freeman summarizes the main reasons for contact difficulties or access problems. These include:

- The parent's emotional state at the time of separation; for example the level of hostility by a rejected or abused spouse;
- The nature of the parent-child relationship prior to separation;
- The mother's support for ongoing contact or for the level of contact desired by the father;
- The developmental stage of the child. A greater number of children experience a reduction in contact and even abandonment when they are infants — or when the father begins a new family. More fathers than mothers do not feel comfortable caring for an infant; the infant's schedule, and dependence on the mother, may discourage new fathers from maintaining contact;
- Infants benefit from short frequent contact and this may be disruptive to a parent's work schedule;
- The level of conflict between the parents over the residential schedule discourages regular contact by the father and creates a stressful atmosphere for the child;
- The child's temperament may make the child reluctant to leave the mother for periods of time to spend time with the father. This can feel hurtful to the father and leaves both parents suspicious as to why the child is unhappy at transitions. Often fathers blame mothers for "alienating" the child and mothers may suspect that the child's distress is caused by some form of abuse or neglect;
- Adversarial litigation exacerbates contact difficulties, at the same time as a schedule is being negotiated. Affidavits contain extremely hurtful accusations and fuel escalating tensions, just when cooperation and de-escalation is needed.

While the cases with such difficulties frequently have a tragic impact on children and draw considerable media attention, research suggests that these types of cases represent a small minority of divorcing families. While the estimates of high conflict couples ranges from 10 per cent to 20 per cent of all divorcing couples, those who display contact difficulties is estimated to be no more than 2 per cent of this high conflict subgroup. While one parent may exhibit more alienating behaviours than the other, both parents often contribute to the problem. Families are unique and the causes of contact difficulties vary with the particular circumstances, including the emotional maturity and temperament of the participants, the child's stage of development, and level of conflict involved. Set out below are some suggestions for intervening or reducing the incidence of contact difficulties in the interests of the child. For more detail, please refer to the paper by the Freemans cited in the bibliography.

- Provide ways for the child's voice to be heard;
- Use neutral assessors with clear authority from the court;
- Implement Family Law rules to minimize delay in litigation of custody and access disputes;
- Use the authority of the court to hold parents accountable for following schedules that are ordered;
- Provide trained professionals to assist parents in developing, implementing, and monitoring a contact plan, including the resolution of disagreements in a timely fashion.

In recent years the American Bar Association convened a meeting of researchers and clinicians with expertise in contact difficulties. They agreed on four key principles for working with these families, namely:

- Reduce parent conflict;
- Assure children's physical security;
- Provide adequate support services to reduce harm to children; and
- Assist families to manage their own affairs.

These principles underlie a number of recommended strategies for assisting parents to develop arrangements that reflect children's best interest. According to a thorough review by Nick Bala and Nicole Bailey, as well as the work of Freeman and Freeman, the most effective methods for addressing contact difficulties or enforcing access are conflict reduction strategies. These include:

- Parent and professional education about the criteria used by the courts in deciding residential schedules and contact arrangements;
- Ensuring that the parents understand the process that will be used to resolve contact difficulties;
- Encouraging the use of "extra legal responses" to resolve the source of contact difficulties where possible that is encouraging the use of mediation, counselling and access supervision or a parenting coordinator;
- Developing contact arrangements tailored to a particular child's and family's circumstances;
- Minimizing adversarial behaviours by lawyers that escalate tensions and hostility;
- Ensuring that there is a strategy for including the child's perspective;
- Taking abuse allegations seriously by investigating and intervening as needed;
- Judicial education about the source and effective management of contact difficulties;

- Ensuring that parents consistently appear before the same judge, that decisions are timely, the results monitored, and parents held accountable for following agreements reached or court decisions.

SUMMARY

This chapter has examined different types of custodial arrangements. It is important to understand the various options for custody, because the parties may be unaware of the alternatives, and this information could facilitate a settlement. In addition, a number of current issues in the field were explored in terms of their significance for mediation. Mediators need to continually update their knowledge about such issues as they will have an impact on the positions taken by the parents and will help to identify the underlying concerns that need to be addressed.

ANNOTATED BIBLIOGRAPHY

Bala, N., and Bailey, N. "Enforcement of Access & Alienation of Children: Conflict Reduction Strategies & Legal Responses" (2004), *Family Law Quarterly* 1. This is a comprehensive article outlining some of the reasons for access difficulties and a number of conflict reduction strategies and legal responses for addressing the problems.

Bowman, M.E., and Ahrons, C.R. "Impact of Legal Custody Status of Fathers' Parenting Post-Divorce" (1985), *Journal of Marriage and the Family* 481. This study examines 28 joint-custodial fathers and 54 non-custodial fathers with respect to (a) contact and activities with the children and (b) shared responsibility and decision-making. The results demonstrated that joint-custodial fathers were more involved with their children than non-custodial fathers one year after divorce.

Coulter, L. *Two Homes: A Parent's Guide to Joint Custody in Canada*. Toronto: Harper Collins Publishers, 1990. See *supra*, Chapter 4, Annotated Bibliography.

Dillon, P., and Emery, R. "Divorce Mediation and Resolution of Child Custody Disputes: Long-Term Effects" (1996), 66 *American Journal of Orthopsychiatry* 1.

Epstein, P., and Madsen, L. "Joint Custody with a Vengeance: The Emergence of Parallel Parenting Orders" (2004), 22 *Canadian Family Law Quarterly*, 1-35. This provocative article examines high-conflict cases in which "parallel parenting" was ordered to preserve a relatively equal role for each parent even when parental communication and cooperation was absent.

Fidler, B., Bala, N., Birnbaum, R., and Kavassalis, K. *Challenging Issues in Child Custody Disputes: A Guide for Legal and Mental Health Professionals*. Toronto: Thomson Carswell, 2008.

Freeman, R., and Freeman, G. *Managing Contact Difficulties: A Child-Centred Approach.* Paper presented to Family, Children & Youth Section, Department of Justice Canada, 2003. This paper provides an excellent review of the literature on parent alienation and the results of a national consultation process on child-parent contact difficulties after divorce. It identifies the type of behaviours that contribute to contact difficulties, and contains suggestions for addressing these issues in the best interests of the child. This paper is grounded in research and contributes to better informed policies and strategies for dealing with the small, but challenging number of families that exhibit these problems.

Irving, H., and Benjamin, M. "Mobility Rights and Children's Interests: Empirically-Based First Principles as a Guide to Effective Parenting Plans" (1996), 13:3 *Canadian Family Law Quarterly*, 249-260.

Joyal-Poupart, R. "Joint Custody". In E. Sloss, ed., *Family Law in Canada: New Directions*. Ottawa: Canadian Advisory Council on the Status of Women, 1985, p. 107. This author examines custody legislation and jurisprudence in a number of jurisdictions. Arguing from the feminist point of view, he takes the position that joint custody should only be granted in cases where parents expressly request it.

Kelly, J. "Current Research on Children's Post-Divorce Adjustment: No Simple Answers" (1993), 31 *Family and Conciliation Courts Review* 1. This is a sophisticated research summary on the current knowledge about factors affecting children's post-divorce adjustment.

Lyster, M. *Child Custody: Building Parenting Agreements That Work.* Berkeley: Nolo Press, 1997. This is a practical, self-help book for those who want suggestions as to what to include in a Parenting Plan for children at different stages of development.

Maccoby, E., and Mnookin, R. *Dividing the Child: Social and Legal Dilemmas of Custody*. Cambridge, Mass.: Harvard University Press, 1992. This is the report of an extensive longitudinal study of California families post-separation. It looks at the parenting arrangements as well as the economic consequences of divorce.

McWhinney, R. "The 'Winner-Loser Syndrome': Changing Fashions in the Determination of Child 'Custody'" (1995), 33:3 *Family and Conciliation Courts Review*, 298-307.

Pearson, L., and Galloway, R. (Joint Chairs). Report of the Special Joint Committee of the House of Commons and the Senate on Child Custody and Access, *For the Sake of the Children.* December, 1998.

Ricci, I. *Mom's House, Dad's House: Making Two Homes for Your Child,* Second Edition. New York: A Fireside Book, Published by Simon & Schuster, 1997. This is a practical and systematic guide for parents who are considering a shared parenting arrangement after divorce. Ricci describes how to shift from a spousal relationship, which is ending, to a parenting relationship, which is continuing. She has a number of practical tips, checklists, guidelines, sample agreements, *etc.*, which parents can adapt to their own situation.

Roman, M., and Haddad, W. *The Disposable Parent.* New York: Holt Rinehart & Winston, 1978. This book explores the impact on fathers, in particular, and on children of sole custody awards. The book makes a case for a shared parenting approach.

Ryan, J. "Joint Custody in Canada: Time for a Second Look" (1986), 49 R.F.L. (2d) 119, and published in B. Landau, ed. *Children's Rights in the Practice of Family Law.* Toronto: Carswell Publishing Co., 1986. This article reviews the literature on joint custody and reflects the optimism of the 1980's that joint custody would be a preferred approach to parenting following divorce.

Shaffer, M. "The Impact of Wife Abuse on Child Custody and Access Decisions". (2004) 22 *Canadian Family Law Quarterly*, 85-151.

Stahl, P.M. *Parenting After Divorce: Resolving Conflicts and Meeting Your Children's Needs.* Atascadero, California: Impact Publishers, 2007.

Tompkins, R. "Parenting Plans: A Concept Whose Time Has Come" (1995), 33:3 *Family and Conciliation Courts Review*, 286-297. This article encourages parents and those assisting them to develop detailed Parenting Plans to increase clarity and reduce conflict after separation.

Wilson, J. *Wilson on Children and the Law.* Markham, Ont.: LexisNexis Canada, 2004. This is a well-written and comprehensive text on children's law.

Chapter Eleven

Legal Issues: Support and Property

A. SPOUSAL SUPPORT

Spousal support is designed to provide financial assistance to a dependent spouse following the breakdown of a relationship. Provincial statutes have the jurisdiction to deal with spousal support prior to a divorce being granted. After a divorce and during divorce proceedings themselves, the federal government has jurisdiction to deal with support under the *Divorce Act*.[1] If the parties have never married, support is only available pursuant to provincial statutes.

1. Who Qualifies?

Only spouses who are or were married to each other can obtain support under the *Divorce Act*. As a result of court decisions finding that the former definition of "spouse" ("either a man or a woman who are or were married to each other") violated the *Canadian Charter of Rights and Freedoms*, the definition of "spouse" now reads "either of two persons who are married to each other".

In most provinces, legislation providing for spousal support applies not only to married spouses but to common-law partners as well. An example of such extension of support rights is found in the Ontario *Family Law Act*.[2] Part III of the *FLA* extends the definition of "spouse" for this purpose to include not only spouses who are married to one another, but also:

> 29. ... either of two persons who are not married to each other and have cohabited,
>
> (*a*) continuously for a period of not less than three years, or
>
> (*b*) in a relationship of some permanence, if they are the natural or adoptive parents of a child.

For spousal support purposes, such "common-law" spouses (including same-sex spouses) have the same rights and obligations as married spouses. Where spouses have cohabited prior to marriage, their entire period of cohabitation should be reviewed when determining both the entitlement and the quantum of support.

Many provincial statutes impose a time limit on when claims for spousal support can be made. Until recently, the *FLA* barred any application for support (without authorization from the court) after two years have elapsed from the date

---

1 R.S.C. 1985, c. 3 (2nd Supp.).

2 R.S.O. 1990, c. F.3, as amended ("*FLA*").

of separation. This limitation period has recently been repealed. There is no time limitation under the *Divorce Act*.

2. Legislative Criteria

The *Divorce Act* provides in s. 15.2(1) that a court may make whatever order it deems "reasonable" for the support of a spouse. The factors that a court is to consider are set out in s. 15.2(4):

> (4) In making an order under subsection (1) or an interim order under subsection (2), the court shall take into consideration the condition, means, needs and other circumstances of each spouse, including:
>
> (*a*) the length of time the spouses cohabited;
>
> (*b*) the functions performed by each spouse during cohabitation; and
>
> (*c*) any order, agreement or arrangement relating to support of either spouse.

In addition to these factors, the *Divorce Act* sets out in s. 15.2(6) the specific objectives of an order for support:

> (6) An order made under subsection (1) or an interim order under subsection (2) that provides for the support of a spouse should:
>
> (*a*) recognize any economic advantages or disadvantages to the spouses arising from the marriage or its breakdown;
>
> (*b*) apportion between the spouses any financial consequences arising from the care of any child of the marriage over and above any obligation for the support of any child of the marriage;
>
> (*c*) relieve any economic hardship of the spouses arising from the breakdown of the marriage; and
>
> (*d*) in so far as practicable, promote the economic self-sufficiency of each spouse within a reasonable period of time.

Similarly, s. 33(8) of the *FLA* provides that an order for spousal support should:

> (*a*) recognize the spouse's contribution to the relationship and the economic consequences of the relationship for the spouse;
>
> (*b*) share the economic burden of child support equitably;
>
> (*c*) make fair provision to assist the spouse to become able to contribute to his or her own support; and
>
> (*d*) relieve financial hardship, if this has not been done by orders under Parts I (Family Property) and II (Matrimonial Home).

Spousal support cases are usually fact-specific and involve a balancing of the recipient's need for support and the payor's ability to pay. The court will also consider how each spouse's ability to become self-supporting was affected by the roles adopted during the marriage. For example, the court will consider whether one spouse's career was interrupted while the other spouse's career developed, how the domestic and child care responsibilities were apportioned between the spouses, *etc.* Where one spouse has been out of the workforce to assume the role of a traditional homemaker, these facts may affect both the amount and duration of the support order.

In determining the amount and duration of support under the *FLA*, the court is required to consider all the circumstances of the parties, including the following criteria:

(*a*) the parties' current assets and means;
(*b*) the assets and means that the parties are likely to have in the future;
(*c*) the dependant's capacity to contribute to his or her own support;
(*d*) the respondent's capacity to provide support;
(*e*) the parties' ages and physical and mental health;
(*f*) the dependant's needs, in determining which the court shall have regard to the accustomed standard of living while the parties resided together;
(*g*) the measures available for the dependant to become able to provide for his or her own support and the length of time and cost involved to enable the dependant to take those measures;
(*h*) any legal obligation of either party to provide support for another person;
(*i*) the desirability of either party remaining at home to care for a child;
(*j*) a contribution by the dependant to the realization of the respondent's career potential;
(*k*) if the dependant is a spouse,
 (i) the length of time the parties cohabited,
 (ii) the effect on the spouse's earning capacity of the responsibilities assumed during cohabitation,
 (iii) whether the spouse has undertaken the care of a child who is of the age of 18 years or over and unable by reason of illness, disability or other cause to withdraw from the charge of his or her parents,
 (iv) whether the spouse has undertaken to assist in the continuation of a program of education for a child 18 years of age or over who is unable for that reason to withdraw from the charge of his or her child,
 (v) any housekeeping, child care or other domestic service performed by the spouse for the family, as if the spouse were devoting the time spent in performing that service in remunerative employment and were contributing the earnings to the family's support;
 (vi) the effect on the spouse's earnings and career development of the responsibility of caring for a child; and

(*l*) any other legal right of the dependant to support, other than out of public money.[3]

In the discussion that follows, we will assume that the husband is the payor and that the wife is the recipient, although that need not always be (and in many cases, is not) the case.

3. Entitlement

Much has been written over the years as to the changes in the attitude of the courts toward spousal support. At one time it was necessary to show that the recipient spouse's need was "causally connected" to the parties' relationship. Today, however, the courts are no longer insisting on this as a prerequisite for entitlement to support. In certain circumstances, the courts have recognized an obligation to pay spousal support even if the dependant spouse's need was caused by factors (*e.g.*, illness, loss of employment, *etc.*) totally unrelated to the marital relationship.[4]

4. Determining the Amount

An analysis of spousal support usually begins with a consideration of the dependant's needs and the payor's ability to pay support. After the financial disclosure is exchanged, the parties can review the recipient's budget to determine what amount of support is necessary in order to meet her reasonable expenses. Since spousal support is taxable to the recipient and deductible to the payor, care should be given to ensure that the recipient's after-tax income will enable her to meet her day-to-day expenses, in combination with any other sources of income that are available. The payor's income and budget must also be reviewed in order to ensure that a sufficient portion of his income is left to meet his reasonable needs. If there is not enough income available to provide each spouse with sufficient income to satisfy his or her budget, each spouse will likely have to forgo expenses which may have been reasonable prior to the separation, but are no longer affordable.

Recently, many courts have moved away from a budget-driven analysis in favour of a consideration of the effect of a proposed support award on each party's net disposable income. Many courts now approach these cases from the starting point that after both child and spousal support have been determined, each party should have approximately 50 per cent of the family's net disposable income. A 50/50 division may not, however, be appropriate in all circumstances. For example, where a recipient wife has several children in her home and the payor husband has none, some courts have ordered spousal and child support in amounts which leave the wife and children with approximately 60 per cent of the family's net disposable income. To date, most courts have resisted a formula

---

3 *FLA*, s. 33(9).

4 *Bracklow v. Bracklow*, [1999] S.C.J. No. 14, [1999] 1 S.C.R. 420, 44 R.F.L. (4th) 1 (S.C.C.).

approach to spousal support, preferring to retain the discretion to determine each case in accordance with its own unique facts.

5. Duration

Since the Supreme Court of Canada decision in *Moge v. Moge*,[5] time-limited support orders are used only in cases of either short marriages or where neither spouse has significantly compromised his or her income-earning potential as a result of the marriage. In other cases, spousal support is generally made open-ended (that is, without a time limit). In some cases the order is subject to review (a redetermination based upon each party's financial circumstances at the time of the review) at a pre-determined date. In most cases the order is subject to a variation in the event of a material change in circumstances (a change in the condition, means, needs or other circumstances of either spouse since the making of the original spousal support order). At one time, limited term support orders were the rule unless the dependent spouse could establish that he or she could not reasonably be expected to become self-supporting within the foreseeable future. Until recently, such time limits have been imposed in exceptional cases. As a result of the *Spousal Support Advisory Guidelines* ("*SSAG*") (see below), the duration of the support order is now geared to the length of the marriage.

There are significant differences between a review order and a time-limited order. With a review order, the review is a determination of support in the first instance, not a variation. Therefore, there is no requirement to show a material change in circumstances.[6]

6. The Spousal Support Advisory Guidelines

In recent years, the law of spousal support has been the target of increasing criticism by lawyers, judges, and the public as a result of the lack of certainty and predictability. In an effort to remedy this problem, the Federal Department of Justice has produced the *SSAG*. Unlike the *Federal Child Support Guidelines*,[7] the *SSAG* are intended to be informal, advisory, and to operate within the existing legislative framework. While many courts were slow to adopt the use of the *SSAG*, most will now consider them as a guide to the exercise of their discretion.

The *SSAG* do not address the issue of entitlement. Therefore, entitlement can be viewed as a "threshold issue" that must be met before the *SSAG* are applied in determining the amount and duration of support that is appropriate (discussed below). Generally, considerable income disparity between the parties following the marriage will meet the threshold for entitlement (however, income disparity will not "automatically" entitle a wife to support). The *SSAG* do not set out how

---

5 [1992] S.C.J. No. 107, [1992] 3 S.C.R. 813, 43 R.F.L. (3d) 345 (S.C.C.).

6 *Bergeron v. Bergeron*, [1999] O.J. No. 3167, 2 R.F.L. (5th) 57 (Ont. S.C.J.).

7 SOR/97-175 ("*Guidelines*"). See Appendix VII.e (CD-ROM).

much disparity will warrant entitlement to support. There are few cases where "no entitlement" to support have been found. However, these rare cases involve circumstances such as: "short marriages, second marriages, claims by men or claims by non-custodial parents".[8]

The *SSAG* contain two basic formulas: the "without child support" formula and the "with child support" formula. The dividing line between the two is the absence or presence of a dependent child or children of the marriage, and a concurrent child support obligation, at the time spousal support is determined. Both formulas use income-sharing, rather than budgets, as the method for determining the amount of spousal support. The formulas produce ranges, rather than a single number, for the amount and duration of support. The precise number chosen within that range will be a matter for negotiation or adjudication, depending upon the facts of a particular case.

The "without child support" formula is built around two crucial factors: the gross income difference between the spouses and the length of the marriage. Both the amount and the duration of support increase incrementally with the length of the marriage, as can be seen in the summary box below.

The Without Child Support Formula

Amount ranges from 1.5 to 2 per cent of the difference between the spouses' gross incomes (the gross income difference) for each year of marriage (or, more precisely, years of cohabitation), up to a maximum of 50 per cent. The range remains fixed for marriages 25 years or longer at 37.5 to 50 per cent of income difference.

Duration ranges from 0.50 to one year for each year of marriage. However, support will be indefinite if the marriage is 20 years or longer in duration or, if the marriage has lasted 5 years or longer, when the years of marriage and age of the support recipient (at separation) added together total 65 or more (the rule of 65).

Cases with dependent children and concurrent child support obligations require a different formula, the "with child support" formula.

There are three important differences between the "without child support" formula and the "with child support" formula. First, the "with child support" formula uses the net incomes of the spouses, not their gross incomes. Second, this formula divides the pool of combined net incomes between the two spouses, not the gross income difference. Third, the upper and lower percentage limits of net income division in the "with child support" formula do not change with the length of the marriage.

Set out below is a summary version of the basic "with child support" formula used to determine the amount of spousal support to be paid where the payor

---

8 *Spousal Support Advisory Guidelines* (July 2008), online: http://www.justice.gc.ca/eng/pi/pad-rpad/res/spag/ssag_eng.pdf at p. 39. See Appendix VII.h (CD-ROM).

spouse pays both child and spousal support to the lower income recipient spouse who is also the parent with custody or primary care of the children. Because this formula involves calculations as to each spouse's after-tax disposable income, sophisticated computer software is required to apply this formula.

The Basic With Child Support Formula
(1) Determine the individual net disposable income (INDI) of each spouse: • Guidelines Income minus Child Support minus Taxes and Deductions = Payor's INDI • Guidelines Income minus Notional Child Support minus Taxes and Deductions Plus Government Benefits and Credits = Recipient's INDI (2) Add together the individual net disposable incomes. Determine the range of spousal support amounts that would be required to leave the lower income recipient spouse with between 40 and 46 per cent of the combined INDI.

Duration under this basic "with child support" formula also reflects the underlying parental partnership rationale. Initial orders *are* indefinite in form, subject to the usual process of review or variation. There *are*, however, outside time limits on the cumulative duration of spousal support, which would structure the process of review and variation. There are two tests for duration and whichever produces the longer duration will apply:

- First is the longer-marriage test, which is modelled on the maximum duration under the "without child support" formula, *i.e.*, one year of support for every year of marriage, and which will likely govern for most marriages of 10 years or more.
- The second test is the shorter-marriage test, which sets the outside time limit for support at the time that the last or youngest child finishes high school and which will typically apply for marriages under 10 years. In these shorter-marriage cases, there will likely be review conditions attached. Relatively few cases will reach this outside time limit and those that do will likely involve reduced amounts of top-up support by that time.

As with the *Federal Child Support Guidelines*, there is a ceiling and a floor that sets the range of incomes to which the formulas apply. The ceiling is the income level for the payor spouse above which any formula gives way to discretion, set here at a gross annual income for the payor of $350,000. The floor is the income level for the payor below which no support is to be paid, here set at $20,000.

7. Variation and Review

Regardless of whether the support order is indefinite or time-limited, the court retains the jurisdiction to change either the quantum or the duration, or both, in instances that warrant such a change. In a variation application, the applicant has the onus of satisfying the threshold test of a material change in circumstances. The test for a material change is set out in s. 17(4.1) of the *Divorce Act*:

> 17(4.1) Before the court makes a variation order in respect of a spousal support order, the court shall satisfy itself that a change in the condition, means, needs or other circumstances of either former spouse has occurred since the making of the spousal support order or the last variation order made in respect of that order, and, in making the variation order, the court shall take that change into consideration.

In Ontario, s. 37(2) of the *FLA* provides a similar requirement for a material change in circumstances prior to any variation.

The Supreme Court of Canada has dealt with the meaning of the phrase "change in circumstances" in s. 17(4) of the *Divorce Act*.[9] In *Willick v. Willick*,[10] the court held that a material change of circumstances means a change that, if known at the time the order was made, would likely have resulted in different terms in the support order. If the facts relied on as constituting a change were known at the relevant time the original support order was made, these facts cannot be relied on as a basis for variation.[11]

The *Willick* decision poses an interesting problem for payor spouses who wish to vary their spousal support obligations because of retirement. Courts will have to determine if retirement was taken into account in the making of the prior support order. If so, reduced income due to retirement may not be enough to constitute a material change in circumstances.

Often separating spouses choose to deal with spousal support provisions in a Separation Agreement. The Supreme Court of Canada's decision in *Miglin v. Miglin*[12] dealt with an application to vary spousal support provisions contained in a domestic contract. The Court held that a court should only set aside a release of spousal support in a Separation Agreement when the Agreement has not been negotiated in unimpeachable fashion or where the Agreement fails to be in substantial compliance with the overall objectives of the *Divorce Act*. The *Miglin* decision is seen as limiting the court's discretion to vary spousal support provisions (including spousal support releases) contained in Separation Agreements.

Unlike a variation (in which one party must prove that there has been a material change in circumstances), a "review" is a redetermination of the amount and/or duration of a support order. While reviews have become increasingly popular in negotiated agreements, the courts have demonstrated a reluctance to impose them except in very limited circumstances.[13]

---

9 *Willick v. Willick*, [1994] S.C.J. No. 94, [1994] 3 S.C.R. 670 (S.C.C.) dealt with an application to vary child support. However, the court's analysis of material change in circumstances is relevant to a discussion regarding spousal support.

10 *Ibid.*

11 See also *B. (G.) v. G. (L.)*, [1995] S.C.J. No. 72, [1995] 3 S.C.R. 370, 15 R.F.L. (4th) 201 (S.C.C.).

12 [2003] S.C.J. No. 21, [2003] 1 S.C.R. 303 (S.C.C.).

13 *Fisher v. Fisher*, [2008] O.J. No. 38, 88 O.R. (3d) 241, 288 D.L.R. (4th) 513, 232 O.A.C. 213, 47 R.F.L. (6th) 235 (Ont. C.A.).

B. CHILD SUPPORT

1. Who Qualifies?

Under the *Divorce Act*,[14] only a spouse or a former spouse may apply for a determination of child support. A child of one or both of the spouses has no standing to bring a claim for child support under this legislation. By way of contrast, under most provincial legislation, a claim for child support can be made by a child, his or her parent, or a social welfare agency that is providing benefits for the child.

For child support purposes, a child is usually defined as someone under the age of majority or over the age of majority and unable to support himself or herself for certain prescribed reasons. For example, in Ontario, s. 31(1) of the *FLA* obliges each parent to pay child support for someone either under the age of 18 or over the age of 18 and in full-time attendance at an educational institution. Under the *Divorce Act*, a child is entitled to support if he or she is a "child of the marriage", which is defined as a child of two spouses or former spouses who:

> (*a*) is under the age of majority and has not withdrawn from their charge; or
>
> (*b*) is the age of majority or over and under their charge but unable, by reason of illness, disability or other cause, to obtain the necessaries of life.[15]

The courts have interpreted this definition to include a child who is in full-time attendance at a post-secondary educational institution and maintaining residence with either of the parents.

Both the federal and provincial legislation set out the objectives for an order for child support. The *Federal Child Support Guidelines* were intended to:

(a) establish a fair standard of support for children that ensures that they continue to benefit from the financial means of both spouses after separation;
(b) reduce conflict and tension between spouses by making the calculation of child support orders more objective;
(c) improve the efficiency of the legal process by giving courts and spouses guidance in setting the levels of child support orders and encouraging settlement; and,
(d) ensure consistent treatment of spouses and children who are in similar circumstances.[16]

Pursuant to the *FLA*, an order for the support of a child should: (a) recognize that each parent has an obligation to provide support for the child; and (b) apportion the obligation according to the child support guidelines.[17]

Although the *Guidelines* do not expressly address the issue of whether a child's need must be proven before support will be ordered, a review of their application over the past three years indicates that proof of need is no longer

---

[14] R.S.C. 1985, c. 3 (2nd Supp.).
[15] *Ibid.*, s. 2(1).
[16] SOR/97-175, s. 1.
[17] *FLA*, s. 33(7).

required, except in certain situations (*i.e.*, children over the age of majority, shared custody situations, and spouses standing in the place of a parent). In the usual case, the issue is not whether a child is entitled to support, but rather, how much support should be paid.

2. Determining the Amount

(A) The Table Amount

Pursuant to s. 3 of the *Federal Child Support Guidelines*, where a child is under the age of majority, the amount of support is presumptively determined by locating the amount indicated in the applicable table. The amount of support is determined by reference to the payor's income and the number of children for whom support is to be paid. Reference should be made to the table for the province in which the payor spouse ordinarily resides.

(B) Child Over the Age of Majority

Where a child is over the age of majority, s. 4 of the *Guidelines* provides that the amount of support is determined by applying the *Guidelines* as if the child was under the age of majority. However, if that amount is found to be inappropriate, the amount shall be the amount that a court considers appropriate having regard to the condition, means, needs and other circumstances of the child and the financial ability of each spouse to contribute to the child's support. The quantum of support should therefore reflect the child's needs, including his or her ability to contribute to his or her support.

It is unclear how courts should approach support for a child who attends post-secondary education away from home. To award support based on the tables and then apportion the additional living expenses (*i.e.*, residence, food, *etc.*) may unfairly duplicate the child's expenses for the bulk of the year. In some cases, courts have calculated the table amount of support to include the live-away student only for those months in which the student actually resides with the parent claiming child support for that child.

(C) Special or Extraordinary Expenses

Upon either spouse's request, an additional amount (often referred to as an "add-on") may be ordered to cover all or a portion of certain prescribed expenses. Pursuant to s. 7 of the *Guidelines*, a court may apportion between the spouses the net cost of the following special or extraordinary child-related expenses:

(a) child care expenses incurred as a result of the custodial parent's employment, illness, disability or education or training for employment;
(b) that portion of medical and dental insurance premiums attributable to the child;
(c) health-related expenses that exceed insurance reimbursement by at least $100 annually per illness or event, including orthodontic treatment,

professional counselling provided by a psychologist, social worker, psychiatrist or any other person, physiotherapy, occupational therapy, speech therapy and prescription drugs, hearing aids, glasses and contact lenses;

(d) extraordinary expenses for primary or secondary school education or for any educational programs that meet the child's particular needs;

(e) expenses for post-secondary education; and,

(f) extraordinary expenses for extra-curricular activities.[18]

While the last category initially caused a flurry of litigation, it is now clear that the table amount already includes an allowance for non-extraordinary extra-curricular activities. The court may only order the sharing of a listed expense where the expense is not subsumed in the table amount. In order to be shareable, expenses must also be both reasonable and necessary in light of the ability of the parents to pay, the ability of the child to contribute and the family's historical spending pattern prior to separation. Certain expenses (*e.g.*, private school, summer camp, hockey lessons, horseback riding, and the like) may therefore be shareable in one family but not in another.

If a court is satisfied that the special expenses should be shared, the allowable portion (after taking into consideration any tax benefits and the child's contribution to the expense) may be apportioned between the parents in proportion to their respective incomes at the time the expense is incurred. Because s. 7 is discretionary, the court has discretion to apportion the expense in some other fashion, where appropriate.

(D) Split Custody

Where one or more children reside with each parent, s. 8 of the *Guidelines* provides that the amount of support payable is the difference between the amount that each spouse would pay to the other if a child support order was granted against each spouse. For example, if the husband would otherwise be required to pay to the wife $1,000 per month for two children who reside primarily with her and the wife would otherwise be required to pay to the husband $500 per month for a child who resides primarily with him, the difference ($500) would be payable by the husband to the wife on a monthly basis. In such cases, there is no explicit discretion to depart from this formula, although the court does retain its discretion when dealing with add-ons.

(E) Shared Custody

The presumptive approach set out in s. 3 of the *Guidelines* assumes that the child resides primarily with the recipient parent and that such parent is primarily responsible for all of the child's expenses. If a non-custodial spouse exercises a right of access to or has physical custody of a child for not less than 40 per cent

---

[18] *Guidelines*, s. 7(1).

of the time over the course of a year, that parent will likely incur greater costs in relation to the child than a parent who has the child in his care for a lesser period. In these circumstances, s. 9 provides that the amount of child support is determined by taking into account the table amount that would be payable by each parent to the other if the child was residing with the other parent, the increased costs of shared custody arrangements, and the conditions, means, needs, and other circumstances of each spouse and of any child for whom the support order is sought.

The "40 per cent rule" has proved to be very problematic. There is no consensus amongst the courts as to how the 40 per cent is to be calculated. There is no unanimity as to how "time" is to be calculated, while most courts count overnights, rather than days, hours, or school-days. Most courts start from a presumption that the custodial parent has the child 100 per cent of the time and then reduce the total time by the time the child is with the other parent in order to determine if the 40 per cent threshold is met. It is quite common to find fathers who insist upon either shared residence or increased access to the children in order to reduce their child support obligations as well as mothers who adopt the opposite strategy. While attaining the 40 per cent level does not guarantee a payor a reduction in the level of child support payable, it does allow the court much more discretion to consider the payor's circumstances than would be the case if the 40 per cent barrier had not been met. The case law has been inconsistent as to how that discretion should be exercised. While the initial cases favoured various formula approaches, the later cases rejected formulas in favour of exercising discretion on a case-by-case basis.

In *Contino v. Leonelli-Contino*,[19] the Supreme Court of Canada held that once the 40 per cent threshold has been reached, the presumption that the table amount should be paid by one spouse to the other for the support of the child no longer applies. At that point, the table amount becomes only one factor to be taken into account under s. 9 when deciding on the appropriate amount of child support.

(F) INCOME OVER $150,000

Where the payor earns in excess of $150,000 per year, the amount of support is first determined by reference to the *Guidelines*. If, however, the court considers that amount to be inappropriate, the payment is determined first by reference to the table payment for the first $150,000 of income; with respect to the balance of the spouse's income, the support award will consist of any amount that the court considers appropriate, having regards to the conditions, means, needs, and other circumstances of the children and the financial ability of each spouse to contribute to the support of the children. To date, the courts have been reluctant to depart from the table amount, even where it is clearly in excess of the cost of maintaining the child in question. In determining if the table amount is

---

[19] [2005] S.C.J. No. 65, [2005] 3 S.C.R. 217 (S.C.C.).

appropriate in high-income cases, the courts consider the lifestyle that children in intact families with comparable family incomes would enjoy.

(G) SPOUSE IN PLACE OF A PARENT

Where the spouse against whom a child support order is sought is not a natural or adoptive parent but instead stands in the place of a parent (for example, a step-parent or a person who has treated the child as if he or she is the person's child), the amount of the child support order is the amount the court considers appropriate, having regard to the *Guidelines* and any other parent's legal duty to support the child. Such "other parent" includes both a parent against whom a child support order is in place and a parent who has the ability to pay child support but is not currently doing so. Where there are no other potential support payors, the table amount will likely apply.

(H) UNDUE HARDSHIP

Under s. 10 of the *Guidelines,* either parent may apply to the court to award an amount of support that is different from the amount prescribed by the *Guidelines* on the basis that the prescribed amount would cause that spouse undue hardship. In order to advance a claim of undue hardship, a parent must first prove that his household would have a lesser standard of living than the household of the other spouse if support was ordered in accordance with the *Guidelines* amount. Reference should be made to Schedule II of the *Guidelines* for the comparison of household standards of living test. If that threshold is met, the parent must also prove that the order would cause him or her undue hardship. Examples of circumstances which may amount to undue hardship include the following where the parent:

- has responsibility for an unusually high level of debts reasonably incurred to support the family;
- has unusually high access expenses;
- is legally obligated to support someone else;
- has a legal duty to support another child; or
- has a legal duty to support any person who is unable to obtain the necessaries of life due to an illness or disability.[20]

While the above list is not exhaustive, a review of the above items indicates the kinds of factors that may form the basis of a claim for undue hardship. In practice, the courts have been reluctant to vary a support award in the absence of clear evidence that the support order would cause significant hardship to the requesting spouse.

---

[20] *Guidelines*, s. 10(2).

(I) DETERMINATION OF INCOME

Because child support is now based largely, if not solely, on the payor spouse's level of income, determining his income becomes a crucial step in quantifying the payor's obligation to pay support. In most cases, it is not difficult to determine the payor's income. Where a payor is employed, his income can be determined by reference to his T-4 statement(s) and recent pay stubs. The payor spouse must report income from all sources, incurring income from investments, capital gains or dividends, rental income, RRSP or RRIF income, CPP/OAS payments, amongst others. The figure for total income shown on line 150 of the payor's T-1 general tax return should capture most, if not all, of this income. The *Guidelines* require that the most current income information be used to reflect the payor's current ability to pay support. If the payor's income has changed since his last tax return, support should be based on his new level of income.

If the above approach does not fairly represent the income available to the payor, s. 17 of the *Guidelines* allows a court to look at the payor's most recent three taxation years to determine the appropriate annual income. If the payor's income has consistently increased or decreased over the previous three years the court may determine annual income based on the most recent taxation year. If the income has not consistently increased or decreased, the court may utilize the average over the most recent three years or such other amount as the court considers appropriate. If the spouse has received a non-recurring amount, the court may include such portion of the amount as the court considers appropriate.

Business, professional, and other income are also included in the payor's annual income. A court may add back into the payor's income all or part of expenses that have been deducted from income for tax purposes but do not really reduce the payor's ability to pay support. Many expenses that are routinely deducted in determining net income for income tax purposes are not deductible for the purposes of the *Guidelines*. Schedule III of the *Guidelines* provides for a number of adjustments to income that are intended to convert total income for tax purposes into actual disposable income for purposes of the *Guidelines.* The payor's tax returns and business financial statements should be carefully scrutinized by an accountant or lawyer to ensure that all deductions taken are permitted by the *Guidelines*. Examples of questionable deductions include:

- capital cost allowance or depreciation;
- wages or other benefits paid to or on behalf of persons with whom the payor or his corporation does not deal at arm's length (unless they are proven to be reasonable);
- personal expenses (*i.e.*, vehicle, travel, or entertainment expenses); and,
- notional expenses (*i.e.*, home offices).

Pursuant to s. 18 of the *Guidelines*, where a spouse is a shareholder, director, or officer of a corporation and the annual income shown on his or her income tax return does not fairly reflect all of the money available to the spouse through his position, a court may determine the spouse's annual income for child support purposes to include:

- all or part of the pre-tax income of the corporation; or
- any amount commensurate with the services that the spouse provides to the corporation, provided that the amount does not exceed the corporation's pre-tax income.

Pursuant to s. 19, a court has broad discretion to impute income to a payor spouse for the purpose of determining his child support obligation where he is not properly utilizing his or her resources, including the circumstances where he:

- is intentionally under-employed or unemployed;
- is exempt from paying income taxes;
- lives in a country with lower income tax rates;
- has intentionally diverted income;
- has property that isn't utilized reasonably to generate income;
- has failed to provide income information;
- unreasonably deducts expenses from income;
- derives a significant component of income from sources that attract a preferential tax rate (*i.e.*, dividends or capital gains); and,
- is a beneficiary under a trust and is or will be in receipt of income or other benefits from the trust.

The above is meant to provide an outline of how income is determined under the *Guidelines*. A review of the post-*Guidelines* case law has shown that most judges are taking a broad approach to the disclosure requirements and that attempts to limit financial disclosure (for whatever reason) are rarely successful. Hopefully, this will encourage clients in mediation to exchange financial disclosure at an early stage, which should lead to a quicker resolution of the financial issues.

C. PROPERTY

1. Provincial Property Division Statutes

Unlike custody, access, spousal support, and child support (which are all subject to shared jurisdiction between the federal and provincial governments), property division is within the exclusive jurisdiction of the provinces. As a result, each province has enacted its own statute providing for the equitable division of property in the event of a marriage breakdown. While each is somewhat unique, most share many common features. Part I of the Ontario *Family Law Act*[21] is typical of most.

Under the *FLA*, the value of all "net family property" ("NFP") accumulated by spouses during the marriage is to be shared equally when a marriage ends. NFP is defined as the value of all property owned by a spouse on the "valuation date" (the earliest of the date of separation, the date of divorce, or the day before the death of one spouse) after deducting (1) the spouse's debts and other

---

21 R.S.O. 1990, c. F.3.

liabilities on the valuation date, and (2) the net value of property, other than a matrimonial home, owned by the spouse on the marriage date and calculated as of that date. NFP excludes the value of the following property owned by a spouse on the valuation date:

- property, other than a matrimonial home, that was acquired by gift or inheritance from a third person after the marriage date;
- income from such gifts or inheritances from third parties, if the donor or testator has expressly stated that such income is to be excluded from the recipient spouse's NFP;
- damages or a right to damages for personal injuries, nervous shock, mental distress, or loss of guidance, care and companionship, or the part of a settlement that represents those damages;
- proceeds or a right to proceeds of a life insurance policy that are payable on the death of the life insured;
- property, other than a matrimonial home, into which property referred to in the four preceding categories can be traced; and
- property that the spouses have agreed by a domestic contract is not to be included in the spouse's NFP.

Apart from property falling within one of these categories of deductions or exclusions, the value of all property acquired by a spouse during a marriage will be considered part of his or her NFP. The onus of proving that a specific deduction or exclusion applies rests on the person claiming its benefit. The importance of obtaining timely valuations and keeping complete records of all acquisitions is obvious.

The general rule under the *FLA* is that, in the event of marriage breakdown, the spouse with the lesser of the two NFPs is entitled to receive an amount equal to one-half of the difference between them. (For example, if the wife's NFP is $200,000 and the husband's is $400,000, the wife is entitled to an equalization payment of $100,000.) In the event of death, the surviving spouse has a similar right.

Under the *FLA*, a court may award a spouse an amount that is more or less than half the difference between the spouses' respective NFPs only if it is of the opinion that equalizing the NFPs would be "unconscionable" in light of one or more of eight factors specified in the Act. The use of the word "unconscionable" indicates that only in the most exceptional cases will the division of NFPs not be an equal one. This is consistent with the philosophy specifically articulated in the Act, which states:

> ... child care, household management and financial provision are the joint responsibilities of the spouses and ... inherent in the marital relationship there is equal contribution, whether financial or otherwise, by the spouses to the assumption of these responsibilities, entitling each spouse to the equalization of the net family properties, subject only to [the enumerated] equitable considerations.[22]

---

[22] *Ibid.*, s. 5(7).

2. The Matrimonial Home

Ontario's *FLA* is typical of most provincial property legislation in its special treatment of the matrimonial home. The *FLA* gives the matrimonial home special status by providing that it will always be considered part of the titled spouse's NFP, regardless of how or when it was acquired. A matrimonial home is defined as a property in which a person has an interest and that is, or if the spouses have separated, was at the time of separation, ordinarily occupied by the person and his or her spouse as their family residence. A family can have more than one matrimonial home. In addition to a house, condominium, cottage, or chalet, a matrimonial home could also consist of a mobile home, trailer, or boat.

According to Part II of the *FLA*, both spouses have an equal right to possession of a matrimonial home. Any provision in a marriage contract limiting the right of possession is unenforceable. Where the spouses are unable to continue living together, either spouse may apply to the court for an order for the exclusive possession of a matrimonial home. The court may order that one spouse be given exclusive possession of the home or part of it, or of some or all of its contents for such period as it sees fit regardless of the ownership of the property. In determining whether to make an order for exclusive possession, the court is directed by the Act to consider the following factors:

(*a*) the best interests of the children affected;

(*b*) any existing orders under Part I (Family Property) and any existing support orders;

(*c*) the financial position of both spouses;

(*d*) any written agreement between the parties;

(*e*) the availability of other suitable and affordable accommodation; and

(*f*) any violence committed by a spouse against the other spouse or the children.[23]

The statute requires that in considering the best interests of a child, the court must consider the possible disruptive effects on the child of a move to other accommodation and the child's views and preferences, if they can reasonably be ascertained.

Part II of the *FLA* also places restrictions on a spouse's ability to dispose of or encumber (that is, mortgage) his or her interest in a matrimonial home. The Act provides that a spouse's interest in a matrimonial home may not be disposed of or encumbered unless:

(*a*) the other spouse joins in the instrument [that is, signs the deed or mortgage] or consents to the transaction;

(*b*) the other spouse has released all rights under this Part by a separation agreement;

(*c*) a court order has authorized the transaction or has released the property from the application of this Part; or

---

23 *Ibid.*, s. 24(3).

(*d*) the property is not designated by both spouses as a matrimonial home and a designation of another property as a matrimonial home, made by both spouses, is registered and not cancelled.[24]

3. Rights of Common-law and Same-sex Spouses

Historically, individuals leaving common-law or same-sex relationships have had to turn to common-law trust remedies in order to obtain a share of property registered in the name of the other party, since provincial property division statutes did not apply to such relationships.

Under the common law, as a general rule, each spouse will retain the property to which he or she has title. This rule may be helpful with respect to real property, automobiles and bank accounts, but what about furniture and furnishings and similar assets where "title" to the asset is less clear? In such cases, title will usually rest with the spouse who paid for the article. What if both common-law spouses have contributed money or labour to the acquisition or improvement of property that is registered in the name of only one spouse? In that case, the non-titled common-law spouse may argue that there was, at all material times, a common intention between the parties that the beneficial ownership of the asset was to be jointly shared and that, as a result, the court should find that the titled common-law spouse holds some or all of the beneficial ownership *in trust* for the other party. Depending upon whether the common intention was stated expressly ("if we ever separate, we'll sell the home and split the proceeds equally" or "what's mine is yours") or is just implied from the conduct of the spouses (they both refered to it and treated it as "our home"), the court may find either an express or implied trust giving each spouse a one-half interest in the property. In the case where one spouse purchases property and places title in the name of the other common-law spouse, the court may achieve the same result by applying the doctrine of resulting trust.

What if the non-titled common-law spouse has contributed money or labour to the acquisition of property but there was no intention to own the property jointly so as to justify the finding of an express, implied, or resulting trust? In such a case, the non-titled party could ask the court to impose a constructive trust in his or her favour. In order to establish a constructive trust, the court must find an enrichment of one party, a corresponding deprivation of the other, and the absence of any legal reason for the enrichment (such as a contractual or employment relationship). Further, the retention of the benefit must be "unjust" in the circumstances of the case.

For many years, advocates for common-law and same-sex spouses have argued for an extension of the provincial property legislation to individuals in such relationships. This change is slowly beginning to occur. In 2000, the Nova Scotia Court of Appeal held that the traditional definition of "spouse" (that is, a married person) in that province's *Matrimonial Property Act*[25] violated the

---

[24] *Ibid.*, s. 21.

[25] R.S.N.S. 1989, c. 275.

Canadian Charter of Rights and Freedoms.[26] However, this decision was appealed to the Supreme Court of Canada. In 2002, the Supreme Court allowed the appeal and held that the application of the *Matrimonial Property Act* to married persons only was not discriminatory. The majority of the Supreme Court held that the decision not to marry was a personal one, and that many common-law couples made the choice to avoid marriage and therefore, the legal consequences flowing from it. The majority held that ignoring the differences between married and unmarried cohabiting couples removes the choice that individuals have to choose alternative family forms as respected by the State.[27]

With the Supreme Court of Canada's decision in *Walsh*, there is currently no requirement that provincial property statutes be amended to extend the property equalization rights to common-law and same-sex couples. However, in response to the Nova Scotia Court of Appeal's decision (and prior to the S.C.C. allowing the appeal), the Government of Nova Scotia passed a law providing for the Registration of a Domestic Partners' Declaration. The Declaration, registered in the Vital Statistics Office, is open to both common-law heterosexual and same-sex couples. It provides these couples with many of the same rights and obligations that married couples have under a number of Nova Scotia's statutes, including the *Matrimonial Property Act*. Filing a Declaration provides couples with these benefits and obligations immediately, in some instances eliminating the requirement to meet the definition of common-law spouse.[28]

Similarly, provincial statutes in several other provinces and territories have been amended to include common-law couples in their marital property regimes. These include Saskatchewan, Northwest Territories, and Nunavut. Manitoba has passed but not yet proclaimed such legislation.

As a result of the enactment by the federal government of the *Civil Marriage Act*,[29] in 2005, married same-sex spouses now enjoy the same property rights as married heterosexual spouses, while non-married common-law and same-sex spouses will have to continue to rely on common-law trust principles to support their property claims.[30]

---

26 *Walsh v. Bona* (21 April 2000), unreported (N.S.C.A.).

27 *Walsh v. Bona*, [2002] S.C.J. No. 84, [2002] 4 S.C.R. 325, 2002 SCC 83, 32 R.F.L. (5th) 81 (S.C.C.).

28 Service Nova Scotia, Government of Nova Scotia, Vital Statistics, online: www.gov.ns.ca/snsmr/access/vitalstats/domestic-partnership.asp.

29 S.C. 2005, c. 33.

30 The *Civil Marriage Act*, *ibid.*, came into force on July 20, 2005, legalizing same-sex marriage in Canada. British Columbia, Manitoba, Newfoundland and Labrador, New Brunswick, Nova Scotia, Ontario, Quebec, Saskatchewan, and Yukon had legalized same-sex marriage in their provinces before the *Civil Marriage Act* came into force.

D. FINANCIAL DISCLOSURE

1. Legal Obligation to Disclose

The first step in any mediation of financial issues is full financial disclosure. Financial disclosure is a necessary precondition for the proper resolution of property or support issues. There are both practical and legal reasons for this. Practically speaking, it is impossible for the parties to agree on a reasonable level of support without having a clear idea of each party's income and needs. Similarly, the parties cannot approach the question of property division without knowing what property there is to be divided and the value of that property.

Agreements can be set aside if the parties failed to disclose to each other their significant assets, income, and liabilities existing at the time an agreement was made. Section 56(4)(*a*) of the *FLA* provides that a court may set aside a domestic contract or a provision in it if a party failed to disclose to the other significant assets, debts, or other liabilities, in existence when the domestic contract was made. The policy reasons behind this rule are obvious. If a husband fails to disclose to his wife an asset worth $100,000 that yields annual income of $10,000, and the wife accepts a level of support that she believes is all the husband can afford, she has relied on misleading information to reach her decision about settlement. Similarly, if the asset hidden by the husband is one that should be equalized under provincial legislation, she has been unfairly deprived of $50,000 of the equalization payment. All decisions should be informed ones; if the wife in either case had known the true state of affairs, she might not have accepted either the level of support or the property settlement that she did. Because she did not have a complete picture, she would likely be able to attack the agreement in the future. Since the goal of mediation is to reach not only an agreement, but one that will be legally binding on the parties, there is no point in mediating financial issues without complete financial disclosure; to do so is to invite an attack on whatever agreement is reached.

To make full disclosure, particulars of all income, assets, and liabilities must be disclosed. Even though a party might object, he or she must still disclose the following assets:

- property acquired after separation;
- property and income the other party knows nothing about;
- property owned prior to the marriage;
- property acquired by inheritance or gift;
- property that provincial law exempts from sharing; and
- property that will be shared pursuant to provincial legislation.

2. Valuation Issues

Full financial disclosure requires the disclosure of both the existence of an asset and its value. Identifying the asset is usually quite simple. Valuing the asset may be extremely complicated. Valuators can differ widely in their estimates of the value of a particular asset, and certain types of valuation is more of an art than a science. Generally speaking, the value of any particular asset will be its fair market value — the price a willing buyer will pay to a willing seller on the open market. It is not book value, replacement value, or cost. It will often be necessary to obtain professional opinions on the valuation of various assets such as real estate, employment pensions, shares in private companies, family businesses, professional practices, and things of that nature. Certain types of assets (*e.g.*, a contingent interest in a discretionary trust) may have no fair market value, but still have considerable value to the owner of the asset. In such cases, the court will adopt what it finds to be the "fair value" of the asset in light of all of the circumstances.

Debts and liabilities must also be disclosed and valued. These may include contingent liabilities, such as notional costs of disposition that would be attracted on the sale of the asset. For example, when valuing the matrimonial home, it is customary to deduct from the estimated sale price of the matrimonial home any outstanding mortgages, liens, or encumbrances, as well as the real estate commission and legal fees and other costs of disposition that would likely be paid on a sale.

The issue of notional disposition costs or tax costs should be approached with care. If an asset is being sold as part of the overall property settlement, these costs will be incurred, and should be deducted as reasonable liabilities. If the asset is not being sold, the issue may arise as to whether or not there should be any deduction for what are truly "notional" costs. The party who owns the asset will want to reduce its value by arguing that he will incur the costs at some point in the future, at the very least on his death, when the *Income Tax Act*[31] will deem a disposition. The other party (who seeks to establish the highest value for the asset) will argue that such costs are speculative, at best, and should be ignored or significantly discounted. Courts will generally allow a deduction for notional dispostion costs if they are satisfied that the costs will likely be incurred.

Pensions give rise to many complex valuation problems. A report prepared from an actuary should always be obtained according to the specific guidelines mandated by the Canadian Institute of Actuaries. Even these reports must be scrutinized with care, and analyzed in accordance with the prevailing valuation principles established by the case law. The value of the pension will be significantly discounted to reflect the taxes that will be payable on the pension payments.

3. Supporting Documentation

Most jurisdictions have specific court forms that are used to make financial disclosure. These forms typically contain sections where the spouse is required to list income from all sources, monthly expenses, assets (often segregated into categories such as land, bank accounts, securities, and the like), and debts and liabilities. The financial statement that is used in certain courts of the Ontario

---

[31] R.S.C. 1985, c. 1 (5th Supp.).

Superior Court of Justice is an example of this type of financial form. It is reproduced below in section G, Example of Financial Disclosure Form. Although this form is designed for court use, it is also used in cases that are determined outside of the court (such as mediation). It is customary for the parties to exchange sworn financial statements and then to produce whatever additional documentation is required in order to substantiate the figures set out in their statements.

The information in each party's financial statement should be verified by supporting documentation. Examples might include some or all of the following:

- income tax returns to substantiate income;
- financial statements to substantiate the value of shares in corporations;
- bank statements to substantiate the total value of bank accounts and RRSPs;
- real estate appraisals to substantiate the value of real estate;
- pension statements and actuarial valuations to determine the value of pensions;
- benefits package statements to disclose the value of all benefits available to an employee (for example, stock options and employee loans, *etc.*);
- partnership or shareholders' agreements to show the rights and obligations the partners or shareholders may have *vis-à-vis* each other, and to indicate the value of the partner's or shareholder's interest;
- insurance policies to confirm the choice of beneficiary, the extent of the insurance, and benefits payable and the case surrender value (if any) of the policy; and
- copies of leases, utility and tax bills, credit card statements, *etc.*, to corroborate estimated personal living expenses.

This list is not meant to be exhaustive, but to illustrate some areas where supporting documentation and professional valuations could, and often should, be obtained.

E. INCOME TAX IMPLICATIONS: SUPPORT

The resolution of support and property matters are made more complicated by the application of many income tax issues. In many cases the tax issues are as significant and difficult as the Family Law issues themselves. Most separating spouses will not be aware of the legal questions or how they should be anwered. In this section we will address a number of the major income tax issues related to support; in the next section we will consider certain income tax issues related to property.

1. Who Is a "Spouse" for Tax Purposes?

The *Income Tax Act* defines "common-law partner" to include:

> a person who cohabits at that time in a conjugal relationship with the taxpayer and

(1) has so cohabited with the taxpayer for a continuous period of at least one year, or

(2) would be the parent of a child whom the taxpayer is a parent, if this Act were read without reference to paragraphs 252(1)(*c*) and (*e*) and subparagraph 252(2)(*a*)(iii),

and, for the purposes of this definition, where at any time the taxpayer and the person cohabit in a conjugal relationship, they are, at any particular time after that time, deemed to be cohabiting in a conjugal relationship unless they were not cohabiting at the particular time for a period of at least 90 days that includes the particular time because of a breakdown of their conjugal relationship.[32]

2. Child Support

As of May 1, 1997, the *Income Tax Act* was amended to change significantly the rules governing the tax-deductibility of child support payments. Prior to that date, child support payments were generally tax-deductible. Child support payments made pursuant to agreements or orders made on or after May 1, 1997, are neither deductible to the payor, nor taxable to the recipient. Payments made after May 1, 1997, pursuant to orders or agreements that were entered into prior to May 1, 1997, continue to be deductible and taxable until they are amended by either a further agreement or court order.

Where an order or agreement provides for the payment of support for both a spouse and one or more children, the payment will be deemed to be for the support of the children unless the order or agreement clearly indicates a contrary intention. It is therefore critical to address not only the allocation of support between a spouse and the children, but how best to maximize the tax benefits available to the family by way of that allocation.

3. Spousal Support

A support payment can be a single, once-and-for-all payment designed to sever all ties between the spouses or may be a series of payments that are to continue indefinitely or until a particular date or until an event occurs. Each type of payment has certain advantages and disadvantages.

Lump sums have the advantages of finality and of severing ongoing ties between the parties. Once paid, the recipient spouse need not worry about future default and difficulties in collection. Their disadvantages are that they are not tax-deductible to the payor, they may carry the risk of being varied in the future to provide for more money if they have been dissipated, and they cannot be retracted if the other spouse marries or lives in a common-law relationship (two situations that might result in the termination or variation of an ongoing periodic support obligation). In recent years some courts have permitted recipient spouses to obtain additional spousal support after they have dissipated their lump sums, notwithstanding explicit releases in which such rights were relinquished.

---

[32] *Ibid.*, s. 248(1).

Periodic payments have the advantages of being tax-deductible to the payor, and of being subject to termination if certain conditions are met (such as the recipient's remarriage, cohabitation, or employment). They are also variable if either spouse suffers or enjoys a material change in circumstances. Their disadvantages are that they continue an ongoing and often lengthy financial relationship between the spouses. They also carry the risk of default and the related cost and aggravation of attempts to collect, and therefore they provide a fertile ground for continued conflict and resentment between the spouses. Periodic payments are far more common than lump sums in spousal support agreements, usually because ongoing funds are required by a dependent spouse to meet day-to-day expenses, and the payor spouse does not have enough capital to fund an adequate lump sum payment.

In the typical separated family, the income which previously supported one household must now support two households. The deductibility of spousal support payments allows for the splitting of income between separated parties, thereby increasing the after-tax income available for the family as a whole. However, the *Income Tax Act* has very stringent requirements that must be met in order to make spousal support payments deductible. These requirements are as follows:

- the parties must be living separate and apart, and remain living separate and apart during the remainder of the taxation year;
- the payments must be made pursuant to a written separation agreement or a court order;
- the payments must be for the maintenance of the recipient;
- the payments must be a predetermined amount of money payable on a periodic basis (that is, at fixed, recurring intervals); and
- once paid, the funds must be at the sole discretion of the recipient.

Spousal support payments made prior to the signing of an agreement will only be deductible if:

- the payment is made in the year of or in the year immediately preceding the year in which the agreement or order was made;
- the agreement specifically refers to the prior payments and states that they are agreed to be deductible to the payor and included in the income of the recipient; and
- all of the other criteria regarding deductibility have been met.

If a payor wishes to claim a deduction for voluntary payments he has made, a negotiated agreement that allows this deduction will often require the payor to pay the tax payable by the recipient on account of these voluntary payments. Making prior payments deductible can confer a significant benefit on the payor, even if he pays the tax attracted by the payments in the hands of the other spouse. Where a payment is deductible to the payor, an equivalent amount will always be included in the income of the recipient.

4. Third Party Payments

Often a payor spouse may wish to make certain support payments directly to a third party for the benefit of the other spouse and children. These types of payments may include medical and dental expenses, private school or university fees, camp fees, or mortgage and utility payments. Spousal support payments made to a third party will be tax-deductible if the following criteria are met:

- the parties are living separate and apart both when the expense is incurred and when it is paid;
- there is a written separation agreement or court order that specifically describes the obligation to pay (for example, "the husband will pay all camp fees");
- both parties must agree that the payments are to be tax-deductible to the payor and taxable to the recipient;.
- the agreement or court order must refer specifically to the application of ss. 60.1(2)[33] and 56.1(2)[34] of the *Income Tax Act*; and
- the payments must be for the support of a spouse or former spouse.

Now that the tax rules have changed with regard to child support, only those third party payments that are clearly referable to the support of a spouse (rather than a child) will be eligible for the tax deduction.

5. Personal Income Tax Credits

Various credits can be claimed by taxpayers to reduce the amount of tax they pay. All taxpayers are entitled to a personal credit and, in some cases, a married or equivalent to married credit is available. For separated spouses, the spouse who has custody of the children can claim the equivalent to married credit for one child, and the dependant credit for other children as well as certain child-care expenses. There are various computer programs available which will calculate the respective tax positions of the parties, given various support scenarios. It is strongly suggested that any mediator whose practice includes financial mediation of any kind should invest in this type of computer program, and learn how to use it. Since tax rates and rules change frequently, it is important to keep up to date. As is the case with all tax matters, expert tax advice should always be obtained.

F. INCOME TAX IMPLICATIONS: PROPERTY

The *Income Tax Act*[35] contains a number of provisions designed to allow separating spouses to avoid many of the taxes that would usually apply to the

---

33 Am. S.C. 1994, c. 7, Sched. VIII, s. 22(1).

34 *Ibid.*, s. 18(1).

transfer of capital property between the spouses. These provisions generally permit the transfer of the tax liability to the spouse who ultimately disposes of the property to a third party.

1. Transfer of Capital Property Between Spouses

Capital property transfers between related or unrelated parties are generally considered to be taxable transactions. Where capital property (such as real estate, a business, securities, *etc.*) is transferred between spouses pursuant to a written agreement or court order in settlement of matrimonial property rights, the *Income Tax Act* provides for a tax-free "rollover" which puts the transferee into the same position as the transferor for tax purposes. The spouses may, however, if they choose to do so, elect to have the property transferred at its fair market value for tax purposes, thereby triggering a capital gain in the hands of the transferor.

2. Principal Residence Exemption

The family home is given special treatment, not only by provincial family law legislation, but also by the *Income Tax Act* in terms of its tax treatment. The *Income Tax Act* gives a taxpayer's "principal residence" special tax treatment; provided that certain conditions are met, any capital gain realized on the sale of the principal residence will be tax-free. A couple may have only one principal residence prior to separation, which may be designated as such if, and only if:

- the taxpayer, his or her spouse or former spouse, or dependent child ordinarily inhabits the property after 1981;
- no other property is designated in this way by the taxpayer or his or her spouse (except for a spouse who has been living separate and apart from his or her spouse throughout the year); and
- the taxpayer is a resident of Canada.

If the spouses separate and one of them owns the home and the other spouse lives in it, it will still remain the principal residence of the titled spouse. The spouses will continue to be viewed by the *Income Tax Act* as a single family unit until the end of the year in which they separate, and during that time they can have only one principal residence. If they remain living separate and apart, in the following years each can designate his or her own principal residence, in order to obtain this special tax treatment.

3. Registered Retirement Savings Plans

Registered Retirement Savings Plans provide a popular way to amass savings in a tax-efficient fashion. A yearly contribution to an RRSP to the statutory maximum is fully tax-deductible, creating an immediate tax saving to the owner. Interest earned on contributions to an RRSP are not subject to tax until funds are withdrawn from the plan at which time they are fully taxable in the hands of the

---

[35] R.S.C. 1985, c. 1 (5th Supp.).

recipient. Usually RRSP funds are accumulated until the taxpayer's retirement years, when he or she has minimal other income, at which time they are taxed at a lower rate than they would have been when they went into the plan. If it is necessary to use the funds in an RRSP to fund an equalization payment, a huge tax liability would result if the general rules were applied.

The *Income Tax Act* provides special rules for separated spouses that allow for a less onerous result. All or part of one spouse's RRSP can be transferred on a tax-free basis to the other spouse's RRSP if the following conditions are met:

- the transfer is made on or after marriage breakdown;
- the transfer is made pursuant to a written separation agreement or court order;
- the order or agreement requires the transfer in settlement of property issues that arise out of the marriage;
- the funds must go directly from one plan into another; and
- Revenue Canada must receive a copy of the order or agreement and a special form signed by the parties within 30 days of the transfer.

While it will be advantageous from a tax point of view for the original owner of the RRSP to make use of these special rules, it may not be to the advantage of the recipient spouse to receive the funds this way. If the recipient spouse needs the funds immediately to purchase a home or meet living expenses, the collapse of her RRSP or the withdrawal of funds from it will trigger an immediate income tax liability in her hands. If a lump sum payment is funded by an RRSP transfer, the recipient spouse will end up with less cash in hand than she would receive if a simple lump sum cash payment was made. These considerations should be taken into account when the division of property is negotiated.

4. Attribution of Income and Capital Gains

The *Income Tax Act* contains a number of rules (known as the "Attribution Rules") that must be considered when property is transferred between spouses. According to the Attribution Rules, income arising from the transfer of capital property between non-separated married parties will be included in the income of the transferor and not the transferee. However, where the property has been transferred pursuant to a written agreement or court order following a marriage breakdown, any income arising from the transferred property will be included in the taxable income of the transferee and not the transferor from the date the property is transferred as long as the parties remain separate and apart.

The tax treatment is different for any capital gain which arises when the transferred property is sold by the transferee to a third party. As between married parties, the capital gain arising on the sale will be included in the capital income of the transferor; however, separating spouses have an opportunity that is not available to other married parties. They may file a written joint election with Revenue Canada in which they agree that the capital gain attribution will not apply to any subsequent sale of the property. Pursuant to such an election, the transferee (rather than the transferor) will pay the taxes that will arise from the subsequent sale of the property to a third party.

There are many other tax issues that may arise or require consideration as part of the resolution of matrimonial property issues. As with all tax matters, the potential issues are complex and expert advice should always be obtained. While mediators must be aware of the issues and ensure that expert advice is obtained when required, mediators should refrain from providing tax advice, unless they are qualified to do so. Unless they are qualified to dispense income tax advice, mediators should refrain from doing so.

G. DOMESTIC CONTRACTS

There have been two recent Supreme Court cases that have important implications for couples negotiating agreements, namely, *Miglin v. Miglin*[36] and *Hartshorne v. Hartshorne*.[37] These decisions basically emphasize that the courts will enforce agreements made either before marriage or at the time of separation, with a few exceptions. This highlights the importance of ensuring that agreements are reached voluntarily, without duress, by informed parties, who have had independent legal advice. The following sets out the court's analysis in these cases. *Miglin* is a case involving a Separation Agreement. Both parties had independent legal advice at the time and five years later, after they divorced, Ms. Miglin applied to vary the terms of the previous agreement. The Supreme Court found that:

- The first stage of analysis is to consider "all the circumstances surrounding that agreement, first, at the time of its formation, and second, at the time of the application" (at para. 64). That is, was there any reason to discount it, including any circumstances of oppression, pressure, or other vulnerabilities (at paras. 80-81). While the courts would consider circumstances less than "unconscionability", it would not presume an imbalance of power (at para. 82) and it would take into account the nature of legal representation as this might overcome any systemic imbalances between the parties (at para. 83).
- The second stage is to consider whether the parties' prediction of their future circumstances was accurate; that is, whether it reasonably anticipated their situation at the time the application to vary was made. Also, were their intentions in substantial compliance with the relevant statute? That is, in order to overturn an agreement, the applicant would need "to show that these new circumstances were not reasonably anticipated by the parties, and have led to a situation that cannot be condoned" (at para. 88).
- Family contracts should be enforced, based on the following principle: "Parties must take responsibility for the contract they execute as well as for their lives. It is only where the current circumstances represent a

[36] [2003] S.C.J. No. 21, [2003] 1 S.C.R. 303 (S.C.C).

[37] [2004] S.C.J. No. 20, [2004] 1 S.C.R. 550 (S.C.C.).

significant departure from the range of reasonable outcomes anticipated by the parties, in a manner that puts them at odds with the objectives of the Act, that the court may be persuaded to give the agreement little weight" (at para. 91).

In *Hartshorne*, both parties were lawyers. The wife was presented with a marriage contract on the eve of the wedding and despite her feelings of being under duress, and the advice of her lawyer that the agreement was unfair, she signed it.

As with *Miglin*, the Supreme Court upheld the agreement and applied the following reasoning:

- It looked first at the current result of applying the agreement;
- It considered whether the clients had accurately predicted their future circumstances; and
- It looked at whether the result was in substantial compliance with the relevant statute.

The important message for mediation and Collaborative Law is that agreements that are negotiated will likely be upheld. Therefore, the parties need to create agreements with the expectation that it will be difficult to change unless they both consent.

H. FINANCIAL STATEMENT

The following is a Financial Statement that is used in the Ontario Superior Court of Justice for the purposes of both the *Family Law Act* and the *Divorce Act*.

ONTARIO

Court File Number

(Name of court)

at

Court office address

Form 13.1: Financial Statement (Property and Support Claims) sworn/affirmed

Applicant(s)

Full legal name & address for service — street & number, municipality, postal code, telephone & fax numbers and e-mail address (if any).	Lawyer's name & address — street & number, municipality, postal code, telephone & fax numbers and e-mail address (if any).

Respondent(s)

Full legal name & address for service — street & number, municipality, postal code, telephone & fax numbers and e-mail address (if any).	Lawyer's name & address — street & number, municipality, postal code, telephone & fax numbers and e-mail address (if any).

INSTRUCTIONS

1. USE THIS FORM IF:
   - you are making or responding to a claim for property or exclusive possession of the matrimonial home and its contents; or
   - you are making or responding to a claim for property or exclusive possession of the matrimonial home and its contents together with other claims for relief.
2. DO NOT USE THIS FORM AND INSTEAD USE FORM 13 IF:
   - you are making or responding to a claim for support but NOT making or responding to a claim for property or exclusive possession of the matrimonial home and its contents.

1. **My name** is *(full legal name)* ____________

   I live in *(municipality & province)* ____________

   and I swear/affirm that the following is true:

   My financial statement set out on the following *(specify number)* ________ pages is accurate to the best of my knowledge and belief and sets out the financial situation as of *(give date for which information is accurate)* ____________ for

   Check one or more boxes, as circumstances require.

   ☐ me
   ☐ the following person(s): *(Give name(s) and relationship to you.)*

FLR 13.1 (September 1, 2005)

Continued on next sheet →

(Français au verso)

Form 13.1: **Financial Statement (Property and Support Claims)** **(page 2)**

Court file number

NOTE: *When you show monthly income and expenses, give the current actual amount if you know it or can find out. To get a monthly figure you must multiply any weekly income by 4.33 or divide any yearly income by 12.*

PART 1: INCOME

for the 12 months from *(date)* ______________ to *(date)* ______________

Include all income and other money that you get from all sources, whether taxable or not. Show the gross amount here and show your deductions in Part 3.

	CATEGORY	Monthly
1.	Pay, wages, salary, including overtime (before deductions)	
2.	Bonuses, fees, commissions	
3.	Social assistance	
4.	Employment insurance	
5.	Workers' compensation	
6.	Pensions	
7.	Dividends	
8.	Interest	

	CATEGORY	Monthly
9.	Rent, board received	
10.	Canada Child Tax Benefit	
11.	Support payments actually received	
12.	Income received by children	
13.	G.S.T. refund	
14.	Payments from trust funds	
15.	Gifts received	
16.	Other *(Specify. If necessary, attach an extra sheet.)*	
17.	**INCOME FROM ALL SOURCES**	

PART 2: OTHER BENEFITS

Show your non-cash benefits — such as the use of a company car, a club membership or room and board that your employer or someone else provides for you or benefits that are charged through or written off by your business.

ITEM	DETAILS	Monthly Market Value
	18. TOTAL	

19. GROSS MONTHLY INCOME AND BENEFITS *(Add* **[17]** *plus* **[18]**.*)* **$** ______________

PART 3: AUTOMATIC DEDUCTIONS FROM INCOME

for the 12 months from *(date)* ______________ to *(date)* ______________

	TYPE OF EXPENSE	Monthly
20.	Income tax deducted from pay	
21.	*Canada Pension Plan*	
22.	Other pension plans	
23.	Employment insurance	
24.	Union or association dues	

	TYPE OF EXPENSE	Monthly
25.	Group insurance	
26.	Other *(Specify. If necessary, attach an extra sheet.)*	
27.	**TOTAL AUTOMATIC DEDUCTIONS**	

28. **NET MONTHLY INCOME** *(Do the subtraction:* **[19]** *minus* **[27]**.*)* **$** ______________

Continued on next sheet →

FLR 13.1 (September 1, 2005)

(Français au verso)

Form 13.1: Financial Statement (Property and Support Claims) **(page 3)**

Court file number

PART 4: TOTAL EXPENSES

for the 12 months from *(date)* ______________ to *(date)* ______________

NOTE: This part must be completed in all cases. You must set out your TOTAL living expenses, including those expenses involving any children now living in your home. This part may also be used for a proposed budget. To prepare a proposed budget, photocopy Part 4, complete as necessary, change the title to "Proposed Budget" and attach it to this form.

	TYPE OF EXPENSE	Monthly
Housing		
29.	Rent/mortgage	
30.	Property taxes & municipal levies	
31.	Condominium fees & common expenses	
32.	Water	
33.	Electricity & heating fuel	
34.	Telephone	
35.	Cable television & pay television	
36.	Home insurance	
37.	Home repairs, maintenance, gardening	
	Sub-total of items [29] to [37]	
Food, Clothing and Transportation etc.		
38.	Groceries	
39.	Meals outside home	
40.	General household supplies	
41.	Hairdresser, barber & toiletries	
42.	Laundry & dry cleaning	
43.	Clothing	
44.	Public transit	
45.	Taxis	
46.	Car insurance	
47.	Licence	
48.	Car loan payments	
49.	Car maintenance and repairs	
50.	Gasoline & oil	
51.	Parking	
	Sub-total of items [38] to [51]	
Health and Medical *(do not include child(ren)'s expenses)*		
52.	Regular dental care	
53.	Orthodontics or special dental care	
54.	Medicine & drugs	
55.	Eye glasses or contact lenses	
56.	Life or term insurance premiums	
	Sub-total of items [52] to [56]	

	TYPE OF EXPENSE	Monthly
Child(ren)		
57.	School activities (field trips, etc.)	
58.	School lunches	
59.	School fees, books, tuition, *etc.* (for children)	
60.	Summer camp	
61.	Activities (music lessons, clubs, sports)	
62.	Allowances	
63.	Baby sitting	
64.	Day care	
65.	Regular dental care	
66.	Orthodontics or special dental care	
67.	Medicine & drugs	
68.	Eye glasses or contact lenses	
	Sub-total of items [57] to [68]	
Miscellaneous and Other		
69.	Books for home use, newspapers, magazines, videos, compact discs	
70.	Gifts	
71.	Charities	
72.	Alcohol & tobacco	
73.	Pet expenses	
74.	School fees, books, tuition, *etc.*	
75.	Entertainment & recreation	
76.	Vacation	
77.	Credit cards *(but not for expenses mentioned elsewhere in the statement)*	
78.	R.R.S.P. or other savings plans	
79.	Support actually being paid in any other case	
80.	Income tax and *Canada Pension Plan* *(not deducted from pay)*	
81.	Other *(Specify. If necessary attach an extra sheet.)*	
	Sub-total of items [69] to [81]	
82.	**Total of items [29] to [81]**	

SUMMARY OF INCOME AND EXPENSES

Net monthly income *(item* **[28]** *above)* =$ ______________

Subtract actual monthly expenses *(item* **[82]** *above)* =$ ______________

ACTUAL MONTHLY SURPLUS/DEFICIT =$ ______________

Continued on next sheet →

(Français au verso)

FLR 13.1 (September 1, 2005)

Form 13.1: **Financial Statement (Property and Support Claims)** (page 4)

Court file number

PART 5: OTHER INCOME INFORMATION

1. I am ☐ employed by *(name and address of employer)*

☐ self-employed, carrying on business under the name of *(name and address of business)*

☐ unemployed since *(date when last employed)*

2. I attach the following required information *(if you are filing this statement to update or correct an earlier statement, then you do not need to attach income tax returns that have already been filed with the court)*:
   - ☐ a copy of my income tax returns that were filed with the Canada Revenue Agency for the past 3 taxation years, together with a copy of all material filed with the returns and a copy of any notices of assessment or re-assessment that I have received from the Canada Revenue Agency for those years; or
   - ☐ a statement from the Canada Revenue Agency that I have not filed any income tax returns from the past 3 years; or
   - ☐ a direction in Form 13A signed by me to the Taxation Branch of the Canada Revenue Agency for the disclosure of my tax returns and notices of assessment to the other part for the past 3 years.

   I attach proof of my current income, including my most recent
   ☐ pay cheque stub. ☐ employment insurance stub. ☐ worker's compensation stub.
   ☐ pension stub. ☐ other *(Specify.)*

3. ☐ *(check if applicable)* I am an Indian within the meaning of the *Indian Act* (Canada) and all my income is tax exempt and I am not required to file an income tax return. I have therefore not attached an income tax return for the past three years.

PART 6: OTHER INCOME EARNERS IN THE HOME

Complete this part only if you are making or responding to a claim for undue hardship or spousal support. Indicate at paragraph 1 or 2, whether you are living with another person (for example, spouse, roommate or tenant). If you complete paragraph 2, also complete paragraphs 3 to 6.

1. ☐ I live alone.
2. I am living with *(full legal name of person)* ____________
3. This person has *(give number)* ____________ child(ren) living in the home.
4. This person ☐ works at *(place of work or business)* ____________
   ☐ does not work outside the home.
5. This person ☐ earns *(give amount)* $ ____________ per ____________
   ☐ does not earn anything.
6. This person ☐ contributes about $ ____________ per ____________ towards the household expenses.
   ☐ contributes no money to the household expenses.

Continued on next sheet →

 (Français au verso)

Form 13.1: Financial Statement (Property and Support Claims) **(page 5)**

Court file number

PART 7: ASSETS IN AND OUT OF ONTARIO

If any sections of Parts 7 to 12 do not apply, do not leave blank, print "NONE" in the section.

The date of marriage is: *(give date)* ....

The valuation date is: *(give date)* ....

The date of commencement of cohabitation is (if different from date of marriage): *(give date)* ....

PART 7(a): LAND

*Include any interest in land **owned** on the dates in each of the columns below, including leasehold interests and mortgages. Show estimated market value of your interest, but do not deduct encumbrances or costs of disposition; these encumbrances and costs should be shown under Part 8, "Debts and Other Liabilities".*

Nature & Type of Ownership *(Give your percentage interest where relevant.)*	Address of Property	Estimated Market Value of YOUR Interest		
		on date of marriage	on valuation date	today
			83. TOTAL VALUE OF LAND	$

PART 7(b): GENERAL HOUSEHOLD ITEMS AND VEHICLES

Show estimated market value, not the cost of replacement for these items owned on the dates in each of the columns below. Do not deduct encumbrances or costs of disposition; these encumbrances and costs should be shown under Part 8, "Debts and Other Liabilities".

Item	Description	Indicate if NOT in your possession	Estimated Market Value of YOUR Interest		
			on date of marriage	on valuation date	today
Household goods & furniture					
Cars, boats, vehicles					
Jewellery, art, electronics, tools, sports & hobby equipment					
Other special items					
			84. TOTAL VALUE OF GENERAL HOUSEHOLD ITEMS AND VEHICLES	$	

Continued on next sheet →

(Français au verso)

Form 13.1: Financial Statement (Property and Support Claims) (page 6)

Court file number

PART 7(c): BANK ACCOUNTS, SAVINGS, SECURITIES AND PENSIONS

Show the items owned on the dates in each of the columns below by category, for example, cash, accounts in financial institutions, pensions, registered retirement or other savings plans, deposit receipts, any other savings, bonds, warrants, options, notes and other securities. Give your best estimate of the market value of the securities if the items were to be sold on the open market.

Category	**INSTITUTION** *(including location)*/ **DESCRIPTION** *(including issuer and date)*	Account number	Amount/Estimated Market Value		
			on date of marriage	on valuation date	today
85. TOTAL VALUE OF ACCOUNTS, SAVINGS, SECURITIES AND PENSIONS				$	

PART 7(d): LIFE AND DISABILITY INSURANCE

List all policies in existence on the dates in each of the columns below.

Company, Type & Policy No.	Owner	Beneficiary	Face Amount	Cash Surrender Value		
				on date of marriage	on valuation date	today
86. TOTAL CASH SURRENDER VALUE OF INSURANCE POLICIES					$	

PART 7(e): BUSINESS INTERESTS

Show any interest in an unincorporated business owned on the dates in each of the columns below. An interest in an incorporated business may be shown here or under "BANK ACCOUNTS, SAVINGS, SECURITIES, AND PENSIONS" in Part 7(c). Give your best estimate of the market value of your interest.

Name of Firm or Company	Interest	Estimated Market Value of YOUR Interest		
		on date of marriage	on valuation date	today
87. TOTAL VALUE OF BUSINESS INTERESTS			$	

Continued on next sheet →

Form 13.1: Financial Statement (Property and Support Claims) (page 7)

Court file number

PART 7(f): MONEY OWED TO YOU

Give details of all money that other persons owe to you on the dates in each of the columns below, whether because of business or from personal dealings. Include any court judgments in your favour, any estate money and any income tax refunds owed to you.

Details	Amount Owed to You		
	on date of marriage	on valuation date	today
88. TOTAL OF MONEY OWED TO YOU		$	

PART 7(g): OTHER PROPERTY

Show other property or assets owned on the dates in each of the columns below. Include property of any kind not listed above. Give your best estimate of market value.

Category	Details	Estimated Market Value of YOUR interest		
		on date of marriage	on valuation date	today
89. TOTAL VALUE OF OTHER PROPERTY			$	
90. VALUE OF ALL PROPERTY OWNED ON THE VALUATION DATE *(Add items [83] to [89].)*			$	

PART 8: DEBTS AND OTHER LIABILITIES

Show your debts and other liabilities on the dates in each of the columns below. List them by category such as mortgages, charges, liens, notes, credit cards, and accounts payable. Don't forget to include:

- *any money owed to the Canada Revenue Agency;*
- *contingent liabilities such as guarantees or warranties given by you (but indicate that they are contingent), and*
- *any unpaid legal or professional bills as a result of this case.*

Category	Details	Amount Owing		
		on date of marriage	on valuation date	today
91. TOTAL OF DEBTS AND OTHER LIABILITIES			$	

FLR 13.1 (September 1, 2005)

Continued on next sheet →

(Français au verso)

Form 13.1: **Financial Statement (Property and Support Claims)** **(page 8)**

Court file number

PART 9: PROPERTY, DEBTS AND OTHER LIABILITIES ON DATE OF MARRIAGE

Show by category the value of your property and your debts and other liabilities ***as of the date of your marriage.*** *DO NOT INCLUDE THE VALUE OF A MATRIMONIAL HOME THAT YOU OWNED ON THE DATE OF MARRIAGE IF THIS PROPERTY IS STILL A MATRIMONIAL HOME ON VALUATION DATE.*

Category and details	Value on date of marriage	
	Assets	**Liabilities**
Land		
General household items & vehicles		
Bank accounts, savings, securities & pensions		
Life & disability insurance		
Business interests		
Money owed to you		
Other property *(Specify.)*		
Debts and other liabilities *(Specify.)*		
TOTALS	$	$
92. NET VALUE OF PROPERTY OWNED ON DATE OF MARRIAGE *(From the total of the "Assets" column, subtract the total of the "Liabilities" column.)*	$	
93. VALUE OF ALL DEDUCTIONS *(Add items* **[91]** *and* **[92]**.)	$	

PART 10: EXCLUDED PROPERTY

Show by category the value of property owned on the valuation date that is excluded from the definition of "net family property" (such as gifts or inheritances received after marriage).

Category	Details	Value on valuation date
	94. TOTAL VALUE OF EXCLUDED PROPERTY	$

Continued on next sheet →

(Français au verso)

Form 13.1: **Financial Statement (Property and Support Claims)** **(page 9)**

Court file number

PART 11: DISPOSED-OF PROPERTY

Show by category the value of all property that you disposed of during the two years immediately preceding the making of this statement, or during the marriage, whichever period is shorter.

Category	Details	Value
	95. TOTAL VALUE OF DISPOSED-OF PROPERTY	$

PART 12: CALCULATION OF NET FAMILY PROPERTY

	Deductions	BALANCE
Value of all property owned on valuation date *(from item* **[90]** *above)*		$
Subtract value of all deductions *(from item* **[93]** *above)*	$	$
Subtract total value of excluded property *(from item* **[94]** *above)*	$	$
96. NET FAMILY PROPERTY		$

☐ I do not expect changes in my financial situation.

☐ I do expect changes in my financial situation as follows:

☐ I attach a proposed budget in the format of Part 4 of this form.

NOTE: ***As soon as you find out that the information in this financial statement is incorrect or incomplete, or there is a material change in your circumstances that affects or will affect the information in this financial statement, you MUST serve on every other party to this case and file with the court:***

- ***a new financial statement with updated information, or***
- ***if changes are minor, an affidavit in Form 14A setting out the details of these changes.***

Sworn/Affirmed before me at ______________________
municipality

in ______________________
province, state or country

on ____________ ______________________
date *Commissioner for taking affidavits*
(Type or print name below if signature is illegible.)

____
Signature
(This form is to be signed in front of a lawyer, justice of the peace, notary public or commissioner for taking affidavits.)

FLR 13.1 (September 1, 2005) (Français au verso)

SUMMARY

Chapter 11 has been expanded to include a detailed analysis of the *Federal Child Support Guidelines*, as well as a more extensive discussion of property rights under provincial property legislation. The section on spousal support has been updated to include a section on variation as well as the draft *Spousal Support Advisory Guidelines* that were released by the federal government in January 2005. The section dealing with the rights of common-law and same-sex spouses has been revised to reflect recent case law. Finally, the section dealing with the income tax implications of support and property transactions has been substantially expanded.

ANNOTATED BIBLIOGRAPHY

Abel, S., and Sussman, E. "Child Support Guidelines: A Comparison of New York, New Jersey, and Connecticut — A Synopsis" (1995), 33:4 *Family and Conciliation Courts Review*, 426-445.

Achten, S. "Living Life by Formula" (1996), 13:3 *Canadian Family Law Quarterly*, 205-217.

Cochrane, M. *Surviving Your Divorce: A Guide to Canadian Family Law, Fourth Edition.* Toronto: John Wiley and Sons Ltd., 2007.

Cochrane, M. *Family Law in Ontario: A Practical Guide for Lawyers and Law Clerks.* Aurora, Ont.: Canada Law Book, 2008 (looseleaf).

Cole & Partners, *The Tax Principles of Family Law*, 2009.

Davies, C. "The Emergence of Judicial Child Support Guidelines" (1995), 13:2 *Canadian Family Law Quarterly*, 89-110.

Finnie, R. "Child Support Guidelines: An analysis of Current Government Proposals" (1995), 13:2 *Canadian Family Law Quarterly*, 145-162.

Hewlett, S. *When the Bough Breaks: The Cost of Neglecting Our Children.* New York: Basic Books, a division of Harper-Collins Publishers, 1991.

Mamo, A. "Apportionment of Child-Care Costs: The Emergence of Judicial Guidelines" (1995), 13:2 *Canadian Family Law Quarterly*, 111-43.

Weitzman, L. *The Divorce Revolution: The Unexpected Social and Economic Consequences for Women and Children in America.* New York: The Free Press, 1985. This is an important book documenting the serious hardship faced by women and children after divorce.

Wolfson, L. *The New Family Law*, Toronto: Random House, 1987. This is an easy-to-read description of the *Family Law Act* of Ontario.

Chapter Twelve

The Mediator as Expert Witness

A. WHEN EXPERTS ARE REQUIRED TO TESTIFY

Prior to beginning the mediation, assessment, arbitration, or parenting coordinator process, it is important to consider the circumstances under which a mediator, an assessor, or a parenting coordinator might have to appear in court or at an arbitration. It should be clear to the clients and the mediator that the mediator could be subpoenaed to testify if he or she was involved in one of the following procedures:

- *Open mediation, an assessment, or a parenting coordination where these processes were court ordered.* Pursuant to ss. 30(7) and 31(5) of the Ontario *Children's Law Reform Act,*[1] the mediator/assessor is required to submit a report to court, he or she can be summonsed by one or both parties as a witness, and the other party or parties may cross-examine the mediator/assessor on the contents of the report. In this case, the mediator/assessor might be called to appear in court (or at an arbitration) even if the parties have come to an agreement on all issues. This would occur if the judge or arbitrator wanted additional information on how the agreement was arrived at, whether the clients appeared to have equal bargaining power, and, therefore, whether the agreement was reached voluntarily. The mediator/assessor might be asked to comment on the fairness of the agreement by counsel, the judge, or arbitrator. In the case of a parenting coordinator, the judge could request a report if the parties failed to agree on the issues referred to the parenting coordinator, if ground rules were breached (*e.g.*, no drug or alcohol use while caring for a child) or if the parties were bargaining in bad faith.
- *Open mediation, an assessment, or parenting coordination where the parties do not reach an agreement on one or more issues.* The mediator/assessor/parenting coordinator may be summonsed by one or more parties to appear in court or at an arbitration. The other party or parties may then cross-examine the mediator/assessor on the mediation process and the contents of any report that was written. This could occur whether or not the mediation or assessment was court ordered.
- *Closed mediation, where the mediation was court ordered pursuant to a statute that permitted closed mediation.* In this case, it is unlikely that the mediator would be summonsed to appear in court. For example, statutes such as the Ontario *Children's Law Reform Act*, ss. 31(4)(*b*) and 31(7), or

---

[1] R.S.O. 1990, c. C.12.

the Ontario *Family Law Act*,[2] ss. 3(4)(*b*) and 3(6), permit closed mediation and establish a statutory privilege for any communication made during the course of mediation. Section 31(7) of the *Children's Law Reform Act* (and s. 3(6) of the *Family Law Act*) state with respect to closed mediation that:

> 31(7) ... evidence of anything said or of any admission or communication made in the course of the mediation is not admissible in any proceeding except with the consent of all parties to the proceeding in which the order was made under subsection (1).

It is not clear whether the mediator could be summonsed to give evidence in a proceeding that was not under the statute that permitted closed mediation. For example, it is not clear whether the mediator could be required to testify in child welfare proceedings or in proceedings under the *Criminal Code*.[3] These statutes do not confer any special statutory privilege on the discussions held in mediation. Similarly, unless there is an order pursuant to s. 10(4) or (5) of the *Divorce Act*,[4] there is a remote possibility that the mediator could be called as a witness in divorce proceedings and compelled to reveal what would otherwise be confidential communications. Section 31(7) of the Ontario *Children's Law Reform Act* and s. 3(6) of the *Ontario Family Law Act* do say that any admission or communication made in the course of mediation is not admissible in any proceeding except with the consent of all parties to the proceeding, but to date there has been no case law to indicate whether that statutory privilege would be respected in proceedings under another statute. While the discussions in mediation might be protected at common law as settlement negotiations, this privilege might not apply to other proceedings, particularly a child welfare case, where the primary concern is the best interests of the child. It is important for mediators to understand and to communicate to clients any limitations on the confidentiality they can promise their clients.

- *Closed mediation arranged by agreement, that is, not pursuant to a court order for closed mediation.* The mediator may have an oral or written agreement with the parties and/or their counsel that the mediation is to be closed. This means that any admission or communication made during the course of the mediation is to be confidential and the mediator is not to be called as an expert witness in any proceeding. If this agreement is not made pursuant to an order under a statute such as the Ontario *Children's Law Reform Act*, which has provision for closed mediation, then the communications may not be kept confidential in subsequent litigation. In these circumstances, it is possible that the mediator could claim a privilege based on the common-law protection

---

[2] R.S.O. 1990, c. F.3.
[3] R.S.C. 1985, c. C-46.
[4] R.S.C. 1985, c. 3 (2nd Supp.).

extended to settlement negotiations that take place when litigation is pending or contemplated. However, the mediator could not guarantee clients that he or she would not be required to testify if subpoenaed. It is important for mediators to explain to clients that they cannot guarantee confidentiality, particularly if it is believed that the mediator has relevant information about the safety of children or threats of harm to the parties or their families.

1. Privilege

The term "privilege" is often confused with "confidentiality". It is very important that both the mediator/assessor and the clients and their counsel understand the difference between these terms and are clear about whether the relationship is a privileged relationship or a confidential one. For the relationship to be privileged, at least one of the following conditions must be met:

- There must be statutory protection, such as under the Ontario *Children's Law Reform Act*, the British Columbia *Family Relations Act*,[5] or the *Divorce Act*. For a statutory privilege to apply, there must be a court order pursuant to the relevant statute.
- There must be a relevant common-law privilege. For example, there is a common-law privilege that protects settlement negotiations when litigation is pending or contemplated. Several recent court decisions in Ontario and British Columbia, as well as in the United States and England, have ruled that mediation discussions entered into for the purpose of settling issues that were the subject of pending litigation were privileged. Recourse to the common-law privilege may be available in cases where no statutory privilege applies.
- The court may make a finding that it is in the public interest to protect certain communications. Wigmore has established four fundamental conditions that must be met before privilege will be extended to communications. These are:
  1. The communications must originate in a *confidence* that they will not be disclosed.
  2. This element of *confidentiality must be essential* to the full and satisfactory maintenance of the relation between the parties.
  3. The *relation* must be one which in the opinion of the community ought to be sedulously *fostered.*
  4. The *injury* which would inure to the relation by the disclosure of the communications must be *greater than the benefit* thereby gained for the correct disposal of the litigation.[6]

---

5 R.S.B.C. 1996, c. 128.

6 8 *Wigmore on Evidence* (McNaughton ed. 1961) § 2285, at 527.

If the relationship is privileged, then any communications or admissions made during the course of the mediation may only be disclosed if all of the parties to the communication consent to the disclosure.

The privilege belongs to the clients, rather than the mediator. Therefore, if both clients wish to waive the privilege, they may do so, and the mediator may disclose the contents of their communication.

2. Confidentiality

Confidentiality is a legal, moral, and ethical duty to keep certain matters secret or confidential. Most mental health professionals and other professionals have an ethical duty, often set out in professional codes of conduct, to maintain a confidential relationship with their clients. That is, they are bound not to disclose any communications made during professional contacts, with certain exceptions.

There may be a conflict between privilege and confidentiality in that professional communications may not be privileged, even though the professional has promised to keep information confidential. For example, a doctor, psychologist, or social worker may be compelled to testify, even though his or her professional relationship is based on confidentiality. Only the solicitor-client relationship is protected by privilege. However, the court has the discretionary power to exclude confidential communications if the court concludes that there are strong public policy reasons for doing so. It should be made clear to clients that there can be no protection for confidential communications if there is a concern about possible abuse to children.

It is very important for the mediator, the clients, and their counsel to consider the issues of confidentiality and privilege prior to the mediation beginning. The following issues should be clarified:

- whether the appointment of the mediator is pursuant to a statute that confers privilege or whether it is by agreement of the parties; and
- whether the mediation is open or closed. If it is closed mediation pursuant to a statute that confers privilege, then the communications will be privileged.

Once these issues are decided, then if the mediation is by agreement of the parties (not pursuant to a court order), the agreement should include a specific reference to a "without prejudice" relationship based on the common-law privilege afforded settlement negotiations. If the mediation is open or if an assessment is requested, the agreement should indicate that the communications will not be privileged. However, the relationship would still be confidential in the sense of most professional-client relationships.

The confidentiality belongs to *the clients*, rather than the mediator. Therefore, if both clients wish to waive the confidentiality, they may do so and the mediator may disclose the contents of their communication.

3. Subpoena

In an *open* process or if there is a risk to someone's safety, a mediator/assessor/parenting coordinator may appear in court or at an arbitration on consent; that is, if he or she has been called as a witness by one or more parties, the mediator/assessor/parenting coordinator may agree to appear without the need for a subpoena.

Regardless of whether he or she is prepared to appear without a subpoena, the party or parties wishing to call this person may issue a subpoena, which is a court document that requires the mediator/assessor/parenting coordinator to appear on a particular day, at a particular time, at a particular place, in order to give testimony with respect to particular proceedings. The subpoena must be served personally on this person.

The subpoena usually requires that the mediator/assessor/parenting coordinator bring all relevant notes and documents with him or her. With respect to any notes made on the file, it is not permissible for the mediator/assessor/parenting coordinator to keep a separate personal file and an official office file. Any notes made during the course of the mediation/assessment/parenting coordination process would have to be brought to court.

The party issuing the subpoena is usually under an obligation to provide conduct money to the mediator/assessor/parenting coordinator, and without the provision of conduct money, the subpoena is not valid.

If he or she is served with a subpoena, then it would be a contempt of court if the mediator/assessor/parenting coordinator failed to appear. The consequences of being found guilty of contempt of court may be a fine and/or a jail sentence, on the particular statute or jurisdiction.

Clearly, if there is a court action, the case cannot be a collaborative case and both collaborative lawyers would have to withdraw. Many mediators who are retained privately without a court order sign a Collaborative Participation Agreement with the clients and collaborative lawyers stating that in the event the matter goes to court, they will withdraw.

B. QUALIFICATIONS OF EXPERT WITNESS

The general rule in litigation is that the judge is the trier of fact. That is, the judge draws inferences from the evidence presented in court and reaches a decision on the issues in dispute.

In making decisions in cases involving custody of or access to children, the court often relies on opinion evidence given by expert witnesses. These expert witnesses are not bound by the same evidentiary restrictions as ordinary witnesses. That is, expert witnesses (those who establish special qualifications for dealing with the issues in dispute) are permitted to include hearsay in their evidence. In addition, the expert witness is permitted to draw inferences based on facts, hearsay, research findings, and other sources for arriving at an opinion. The process used by an expert in drawing inferences is very similar to the judicial role and is very much broader than the usual role of a witness. Because of the special latitude given the expert, it is important that the expert have the necessary qualifications for giving opinion evidence. The more qualified the mediator/assessor, the more likely the trier of fact (the judge) will permit the witness to give an expert opinion and will give weight or credibility to that expert opinion.

The expert has to establish his or her expertise in the following areas: education, training, experience, and methods of practice and code of conduct.

1. Education

To deal with parenting plans and issues related to children, the mediator/assessor should have:

- a post-graduate degree in a mental health field, such as psychology, social work, psychiatry, or counselling;
- ongoing attendance at relevant educational programs and conferences to upgrade skills and information with respect to mediation and assessments; and
- up-to-date knowledge of the mediation/assessment literature, as well as literature on child development, parenting skills, and the impact of separation and divorce on families.

2. Training

The mediator/assessor should have:

- completed a training program conducted by recognized authorities on mediation and assessments or taught such a program; and
- ongoing contact with a peer group of competent professionals for the purpose of case consultation, sharing of information, and supervision.

3. Experience

The mediator/assessor should:

- have an ongoing professional practice with mediation and/or assessment cases;
- belong to a recognized professional organization for mediators and/or assessors; and
- have published articles or research findings in professional newsletters, journals, or books for mediators and/or assessors or have spoken at conferences or seminars attended by other professionals.

4. Methods of Practice and Code of Conduct

The mediator/assessor should:

- conduct the mediations and/or custody assessments according to well-recognized standards of practice within the profession;

- be prepared to outline the methodology used and be able to justify this methodology on the basis of the generally accepted standards of practice in the field and the needs of the particular case; and
- subscribe to a code of conduct set out by his or her professional discipline (for example, psychology, psychiatry, or social work), and in addition adhere to a code of conduct for mediators and/or assessors as set out by a recognized professional organization for mediators and/or assessors.

The mediator/assessor should provide the clients, their counsel, and the court (if relevant) with an up-to-date *curriculum vitae* that outlines all of the qualifications as set out above that are relevant for conducting mediation or assessments.

In the event that the parties are unable to agree on an individual to conduct an assessment, the court should have sufficient information to determine which individual is most qualified for the task.

C. GUIDELINES FOR GIVING TESTIMONY IN COURT

In mediation/assessment cases, the expert is usually attempting to determine what is in the best interests of the children, and does not view himself or herself as acting for any of the parties. The expert performs something of an *amicus curiae* role, that is, a friend of the court. Given the impartial role of the mediator/assessor, he or she should be very careful to maintain that neutral stance and not be drawn into taking particular positions because they are of benefit to one of the parties.

Prior to trial, it is important that the mediator/assessor offer the parties and counsel an opportunity to meet with him or her in order to give the mediator/assessor any relevant, up-to-date information. This opportunity should be offered to both sides.

In a number of cases that go to court, a settlement can be reached during the course of the trial by one or both counsel or the judge asking for a brief recess for the parties to meet and discuss whether any of the issues can be resolved. The mediator/assessor should indicate to the judge and to the parties and their counsel that he or she will be available, during the course of the trial, if this might prove helpful in reaching a settlement. This again underlines the impartial role of the mediator/assessor.

If the expert is to testify, the first task is to determine whether the expert is qualified to give opinion evidence. Opposing counsel may argue that the court should not accept a witness's report or testimony as that of an expert. If counsel's argument is successful, then the mediator/assessor will not be able to give opinion evidence and will not be able to rely on any hearsay in his or her testimony. It is important that the mediator/assessor bring an up-to-date *curriculum vitae* to court and be prepared to respond to questions about why, in general and specifically in this case, he or she should be permitted to give expert testimony.

The judge will weigh the mediator/assessor's credibility and this credibility will depend on such factors as:

- the qualifications of the mediator/assessor;
- the methodology used in the case and how closely this methodology approximates the standards in the field;
- the code of ethics followed;
- the factual basis from which the mediator/assessor drew his or her conclusions;
- the mediator/assessor's appearance (the mediator/assessor should always appear in court well dressed and well groomed); and
- the impression of impartiality as opposed to partiality. Was the mediator/assessor paid exclusively by one side? If so, was this agreed to by the parties in advance? Did the mediator/assessor see both sides in the dispute, and did the mediator/assessor spend approximately equal amounts of time with each? Were the mediator/assessor's facts gathered from a variety of sources, including independent sources, or were the facts gathered primarily from those with a stake in the proceedings, that is, supporters of one party?

The mediator/assessor must be prepared to testify in court if a report has been submitted, and to be cross-examined on this report. Unless there is a statutory exception to being called, the mediator/ assessor should expect to be called as a witness and give *viva voce* evidence.

Following establishment of the credentials of the professional, the party who called the mediator/assessor will ask questions. This is known as the examination-in-chief. The counsel conducting the examination is not permitted to ask leading questions. That is, the counsel cannot ask questions suggesting a particular answer. The questions must be open ended, and it is wise for the mediator/assessor to meet with the counsel who will be doing the examination-in-chief in advance of court in order to determine those areas that will be covered.

The mediator/assessor will next be cross-examined by the opposing counsel. The purpose of cross-examination is to reduce the credibility of the expert's opinion. It is permissible when cross-examining for the counsel to suggest answers or to lead the witness, but it is not permissible to badger the witness.

When being cross-examined, it is important for the expert to remain professional and unemotional. He or she should not take the questions personally and should not respond with sarcasm or hostility. It is always permissible to ask for a question to be repeated. If the answer to a question is unknown, or if a question is outside of the area considered by the mediation or assessment, it is wise to state that directly. The mediator/assessor should not argue with the questioner and not interrupt while the questions are being asked. The expert's answers will probably be cut short. The cross-examiner will try to stop the expert from talking when he or she is saying things that are not helpful to the opposing party. The counsel who conducted the examination-in-chief will have an opportunity to ask certain questions at a later time during the re-examination.

When giving testimony, the expert should speak slowly and clearly so that it is easier for the court reporter and the judge to make notes about the testimony. It is very irritating to the judge to have to keep reminding the expert witness to speak up and slow down.

It is required that the mediator/assessor take his or her entire file to court, that is, the report, as well as any notes made during interviews or telephone conversations. In addition, he or she should take all reports, documents, or other materials that were relied on as a basis for the mediation/assessment report. The expert's file will likely be examined by both counsel prior to asking questions in court.

If there are no notes made from interview conversations, the expert's report will likely have greatly reduced credibility. If memory is relied on for details of conversations and interviews, the judge is likely to put far less weight on the expert's ultimate report and recommendations than if careful notes were made during sessions.

When asked about opinions or recommendations, it is very important for the mediator/assessor to remember to state the factual basis for his or her recommendations. If the basis for the expert's opinion is solely hearsay, and if that hearsay information comes from a biased source, then again his or her recommendations will have little weight.

If the expert is asked a question and cannot remember the answer or the facts on which an answer would be based, it is permissible to use notes to refresh his or her memory. If the expert wishes to look at notes, then it must be established that the notes were made contemporaneously with the event; that is, the notes were made at the time or very close to the time of interviews or conversations and therefore are likely to be accurate. In addition, it must be established that the notes were made personally by the mediator/assessor.

If the mediator/assessor asks to see notes to refresh his or her memory, then counsel are likely to ask to see those notes. The notes should be in the mediator/assessor's personal handwriting, not dictated notes that were subsequently typed, because these notes may not be acceptable.

Many mental health professionals have a considerable fear of testifying in court. They are afraid of being humiliated, badgered, and asked questions they perceive to be irrelevant to the best interests of children. In addition, appearances at court are often inconvenient and disrupt a busy practice. Professionals often have to wait hours, if not days, to be called, and this causes further inconvenience and discomfort.

Many mental health professionals are critical of the legal system, because it appears that an adversarial approach is harmful, rather than helpful, to the family as a whole. It often appears to the mediator/assessor that the purpose of counsel is to cause psychological damage to the other party, rather than to find a solution to the problem that would be the most satisfactory for the children and even for the family as a whole.

It is important for the mediator/assessor to understand that the purpose of the court procedure is not to arrive at a therapeutic outcome. The purpose of the court system is to arrive at the truth, and the premise of our court system is that the truth is best obtained by a battle of two strongly partisan adversaries, namely, counsel. There is a growing awareness that the adversarial process is not the most suitable for Family Law matters, and therefore, there is a gradual change in attitude and approach, both in the legislation and the actual court practice.

Both the legislation and courtroom procedure are moving away from matrimonial fault as a basis for deciding Family Law disputes. However, it is still the role of counsel for the party who is not satisfied with the mediator/assessor's report to try to reduce the report's weight in the eyes of the court as a means of promoting his or her client's position.

Because of the great weight and latitude normally given to experts' reports, it is important that the report and expert opinion be capable of withstanding a strong test as to their credibility. Instead of looking at this as a personal attack, the mediator/assessor should welcome the opportunity to have his or her facts and opinions tested thoroughly by the court process as a safety check. In the event that the report is based on poorly researched facts, on biased opinions, or on insufficient time with the parties, it is important for the family to have a weak report exposed. Similarly, if a report has been prepared on the basis of a thorough examination and the recommendations are carefully thought out, then the mediator/assessor and all of the parties concerned are likely to have more confidence in it. It is in the public interest to have these reports, which are given such great weight by the courts, thoroughly tested.

SUMMARY

The main forms of the book is on non-adversarial processes in which the parties reach their own agreement voluntarily, with the assistance of collaborative lawyers and mediators. This chapter outlines expectations and advice for those cases where a collaborative approach is not possible.

ANNOTATED BIBLIOGRAPHY

Bala, N., and Saunders, A. "Understanding the Family Context: Why the Law of Expert Evidence Is Different in Family Law cases" (2003), 20 *C.F.L.Q.* 277.

Brown, C. "Custody Evaluations: Presenting the Data to Court" (1995), 33 *Family and Conciliation Courts Review*, 446-461.

Grant, S. *An Evidence Refresher*. Toronto: CBAO Institute, 1997.

Kirkpatrick, G. "Should Mediators Have a Confidentiality Privilege?" in "Legal and Family Perspectives in Divorce Mediation" (1985), 9 *Mediation Quarterly* 85. This article examines the question of the limitations on the expert refusing to testify in court. It considers the balance between the right to privacy and the court's need to know.

Sopinka, J., and Lederman, S. *The Law of Evidence in Civil Cases*. Toronto: Butterworths, 1974. This is the leading text on the law of evidence in civil cases.

Thompson, R. "Are there *Any* Rules of Evidence in Family Law?" (2003), 21 *C.F.L.Q.* 245.

Weisman, N. "The Admissibility of Hearsay Evidence: Defining and Applying Necessity and Reliability Since R. v. Kahn" (1995), 13:2 *Canadian Family Law Quarterly*, 67-87.

Wigmore on Evidence (McNaughton ed. 1961).

Ziskin, J. *Coping with Psychiatric and Psychological Testimony*, Vols. 1 and 2. California: Law and Psychology Press, 1981 (Supplement, 1983). This book offers a strong critique of expert evidence in child custody cases, as well as in criminal and personal injury cases. The author is a psychologist and a lawyer, and uses both professional backgrounds to prepare the lawyer for cross-examination of the mental health expert. This book would be very valuable for both mental health professionals and lawyers dealing with contested custody cases.

Chapter Thirteen

Professional Conduct Issues

A. STANDARDS OF PRACTICE FOR MEDIATION, COLLABORATIVE LAW, AND ARBITRATION

Mediation, collaborative practice, and arbitration are relatively new ways to resolve divorce issues. Family mediation began in the 1960's in California, but really spread across North America and beyond in the 1980's. Collaborative Law started in the early 1990's, initially among lawyers but by the end of the decade was expanding to other professional groups. Family arbitration has been an option for Family Law lawyers since the passage of the *Arbitration Act*[1] in 1991, but before that rabbis and other clergy have acted as arbitrators for members of their faith communities.

As the use of mediation, collaborative practice, and arbitration becomes more widespread, there is considerable agreement among the professionals, as well as among legislators, judges, and potential clients, that the following issues require greater clarity and consistency, namely:

- What is mediation? What is arbitration?
- What are the standards of practice that define responsible, competent professional practice as a mediator or arbitrator?
- Is there a mechanism for supervision and discipline of mediators and arbitrators? That is, does a member of the public or another profession have a mechanism for complaining about conduct by a mediator or arbitrator that is inept, unprofessional, or unethical?
- If there is a governing body, what are its powers and procedures for decision-making?
- What are the qualifications, that is, the training and experience, necessary to be a mediator or arbitrator?
- Are there guidelines for appropriate procedures to follow, a fee structure, and other rules of practice that distinguish a good mediator or arbitrator from a poor one?
- Are there or should there be special rules of practice for lawyers acting as mediators or arbitrators?
- Are there potential conflicts between the lawyer's role as counsel and the lawyer's role as mediator or arbitrator?
- Similarly, are there possible conflicts between the role of the mental health professional as clinician and his or her role as mediator or arbitrator?

---

[1] *Arbitration Act, 1991*, S.O. 1991, c. 17.

These basic questions deal with the issues of standards of practice, ethical conduct, and the qualifications necessary to become a mediator or arbitrator. It is important to address these issues for the following reasons:

- Mediation and arbitration are practices that cross professional boundary lines; that is, at present there is no single profession that governs these practices and monitors the standards of practice within these professions.
- Mediators and arbitrators come from a variety of disciplines, namely, law, psychology, social work, psychiatry, counselling, and other disciplines whose standards of professional conduct may be in conflict with the standards that are considered desirable for mediators or arbitrators.
- The interests of the public need to be protected. One of the distinct advantages of mediation and arbitration is the fact that parties can arrange their own settlement of issues in dispute in an atmosphere of confidentiality. The key elements of mediation and arbitration are private ordering of dispute resolution and confidentiality. However, these elements also create a great risk if the parties are unequal in bargaining power, if the mediator or arbitrator is incompetent or unethical, or if the parties fail to disclose adequate information for reaching an appropriate solution. Because litigation tends to be conducted in public, while mediation and arbitration tend to be conducted in a private setting, protection of the public can only be achieved by the enforcement of standards of practice, codes of professional conduct, and, eventually, procedures for certification and licensing.

Each of these processes will be considered separately as there are different ethical considerations.

1. Definition of Mediation

Most definitions of mediation incorporate the following elements: Family mediation is a *non-adversarial* process, in which a qualified and *impartial third party* (the mediator) helps the family resolve their disputes *voluntarily* by agreement, which is based on *sufficient information*, and includes *independent legal advice* for each participant.[2]

Most definitions of mediation emphasize the fact that the mediator must act in an impartial role.

The mediator must:

- ensure that the parties reach a consensual agreement, that is, without duress;
- ensure that the parties are properly informed, that is, that all relevant information has been exchanged;
- ensure that the agreement reached is fair and reasonable, particularly where children are involved;

---

2 This definition is taken from the Code of Professional Conduct, in the Code of Ethics of the Ontario Association for Family Mediation, set out below in Appendix VIII.4, and the Code of Professional Conduct of Family Mediation Canada, set out below in Appendix VIII.c (CD-ROM).

- ensure that the parties are not under a disability (such as emotional disturbance, intellectual impairment, or fear of physical abuse) during the negotiations;
- clarify with the clients his or her professional role, that is, that the mediator is acting as a mediator and not as a lawyer, psychologist, or other professional. For example, the mediator (if a lawyer) should clarify with the clients that he or she cannot be the solicitor for either client if he or she has been their mediator. Similarly, the mediator should explain that he or she cannot be the individual clinician for either party after he or she has acted in the impartial role of mediator.

2. Codes of Professional Conduct

Codes of professional conduct contain both standards of practice and a code of ethical conduct. These terms can be described as follows:

- *Standards of practice* refer to the minimally acceptable, commonly understood practices of a profession. These standards are designed to protect the public and ensure a reasonable level of competence among practitioners. If followed, the standards of practice should protect a mediator from liability, because the standards establish the reasonable level of care to be exercised by a person practising mediation.
- A *code of ethical conduct* is usually thought of as the moral and social obligations of the professional that are imposed by the governing body on members of the profession. Adherence to an ethical code is usually required as a prerequisite to certification or licensing. Ethical codes have been described as the "do nots" of each profession. There are a number of conflicts still to be resolved between the ethical code of mediators and the ethical codes of some other disciplines, such as law or certain mental health professions. In addition, guidelines for the qualifications for mediators, and their certification, have recently been developed by Family Mediation Canada.
- *Codes of professional conduct* are intended to govern the behaviour of professionals when they are acting in their capacity as mediators. These codes are not intended to replace or in any way compete with the codes of conduct of the mediator's basic profession, that is, law, psychology, social work, or other. The major elements that are present in most codes of professional conduct for mediators are set out below.

(A) Competence

It is recognized that mediators may be trained in different professional disciplines; however, the following levels of competence are essential:

- The individual should have specific training in the skills, knowledge, and techniques necessary to be an effective mediator.
- The mediator should agree to mediate only those issues for which he or she has adequate training and experience. That is, lawyers should not

mediate custody and access issues unless they have specific training and knowledge with respect to such matters as child development, family dynamics, the effects on children and adults of separation and divorce, appropriate parenting techniques, and stages of physical, emotional, and social development of children. Similarly, a mental health professional should not agree to mediate such issues as property division, support, or complex financial arrangements unless he or she has adequate training in Family Law, income tax, and, in some cases, accounting.

- Mediators should cooperate with other professionals who are assisting the clients, such as lawyers, accountants, or business evaluators and, in fact, should suggest that relevant professionals be retained to assist with specific issues in the mediation. For example, if the mediation is dealing with the issue of division of property, specialists such as business evaluators, accountants, or real estate appraisers may be needed to provide the necessary background information for mediating the issues in dispute.
- The mediator should attend continuing education programs and read recent literature with respect to mediation to ensure that his or her mediation skills are up to date.

(B) Duty to Describe Mediation Process and Its Cost at Outset

The mediator should discuss the following information with the clients by telephone prior to the first session and/or during the first session:

- the process to be followed during mediation, including whether the meetings will be conjoint, individual, or a combination of conjoint and individual; also, who will be included in these meetings and the location of the meetings;
- a definition of mediation, and the difference between mediation and other forms of conflict resolution that would be available to the parties (such as litigation, arbitration, or marital counselling);
- the issues to be discussed in mediation;
- whether the mediation is to be open or closed, that is, the issues of privilege and confidentiality;
- the requirement to make full disclosure of all relevant information with respect to the issues being mediated;
- the advisability of both parties having independent legal advice throughout the mediation process and certainly prior to signing any mediated agreement;
- the process for terminating the mediation by either the clients, the mediators, the lawyers, or the court; and
- the mediator's fees and billing practices, including the hourly rate, the activities for which the clients will be charged, the method of billing, whether a retainer is required, cancellation policy, and expert witness fees if required in court.

During the process of explaining the mediation process to the clients, the mediator should also be assessing the suitability of the clients for mediation; that is, whether the clients show significant signs of emotional disturbance, or whether it appears that one party is under duress by the other party to the point where mediation would not be possible.

If for some other reason related to the client's personality, or the ability of the mediator to relate to the clients, the mediator believes that the mediation is unlikely to be successful, then the mediator should share this information with the clients and either terminate the mediation or refer the clients to some other mediator who might be more successful.

If the mediator does not have the special knowledge or expertise to deal with the particular issues in dispute in the case, then he or she should terminate the mediation and assist the clients in finding a mediator with the requisite background.

(C) IMPARTIALITY

One of the primary features of mediation is the private ordering of dispute resolution. The role of the mediator in this process is to facilitate communication, offer educational input, and ensure that the parties are fully informed. All of these roles must be fulfilled in an impartial manner. That is, the mediator must disclose to the clients any biases the mediator might hold that are relevant to the issues in dispute. For example, if the mediator has strong beliefs that the custodial spouse should not be employed outside the home, or that young children should be in the primary care of a mother, or that it is important for children to have a strong religious upbringing, or that it is important for children to be raised in a home setting with mother and father figures, then these biases or beliefs should be communicated to the parties if custody of and access to children is being discussed. The mediator should discuss these beliefs or biases during the orientation session, that is, before the mediation process is under way. If relevant biases or beliefs do not become apparent until later, then they should be raised at the first opportunity.

The mediator should not mediate those cases where he or she has had a significant prior involvement, that is, if the mediator or a partner or an associate of the mediator has conducted individual therapy or counselling with either of the parties previously, or if the mediator has acted as legal counsel for either of the parties. In some cases the mediator may have offered marital counselling to the couple, and this may create some problems with respect to ethical standards. This is less of a problem if the clients initially contracted with the mediator to provide marital counselling but, if the counselling should fail or the couple decide to separate, to mediate some or all of the terms of a Separation Agreement. That is, the contract contemplated from the beginning that mediation would be tried in the event that the couple decided to separate. In any event, it would be essential as a minimum for the mediator to discuss fully with the clients the nature of the prior involvement and would require the express consent of both participants prior to continuing with mediation. The mediator should clarify the differences between his or her prior involvement and the specific tasks to be performed in mediation. Some codes of conduct expressly prohibit mediators from acting when there has been any form of significant prior involvement, either as a mental health professional or as a lawyer. Other codes of conduct are more flexible, but in every case, it is essential that the mediator make full disclosure of prior involvement and obtain the consent of both parties in writing.

Another area that needs consideration is whether the mediator can change from the role of mediator into the role of counsellor for one or both parties following the mediation process. It is probably inappropriate for the mediator, once he or she has taken on an impartial role, subsequently to take on any form of partial role in dealing with the parties. There are several issues that should be considered. For example, it is important for the client and for the general public to maintain a distinction between the role of the mediator and the role of the therapist. By changing from one role to another, the mediator may create a confusion of roles and give the clients contradictory messages about the mediation process. In the event that the clients need the assistance of the mediator to deal with subsequent disputes, the mediator would be unable to assist if, following mediation, he or she had offered counselling services to one of the parties.

There are some circumstances where it may be appropriate for the mediator to continue assisting the couple in an impartial capacity following the mediation. For example, if the parties wish further assistance in developing communication skills so as to carry out effectively the mediation agreement, the mediator is probably in a very good position, given his or her knowledge of the parties and their communication problems, to assist in this matter. This is unlikely to be in the form of long-term therapy, but rather is directed at implementing effectively a mediation plan. This could also be seen as preventing a breakdown of the mediation agreement because the parties lack the essential skills to carry it out.

It may also be appropriate for the mediator to assist in monitoring how the parents are carrying out their agreement and its impact on the children from time to time. Again this is an impartial role, and if the mediator did not carry out this function, then the parties would have to go to a totally new professional at considerable expense and further emotional turmoil for them and the children. Also, it would take some time to develop a sufficient relationship with the new professional so that the individual could monitor their progress. The key test is whether the mediator is maintaining an impartial role and whether the purpose of the assistance is to implement and stabilize the plan developed in mediation.

It is not appropriate for the mediator to represent either party as a lawyer, either prior to or subsequent to the mediation process. Some codes of conduct permit the mediator to act as a lawyer for one or both parties in uncontested matters or in matters that are totally unrelated to the divorce proceedings. Other codes of conduct prohibit not only the mediator, but also any partners or associates in the law firm, from acting on behalf of either party, either in contested or possibly even in uncontested matters in the future. It is probable that all codes of conduct would prohibit, as a minimum, acting on behalf of either party in a contested legal matter arising out of any of the issues discussed during the mediation. This would prohibit any representation of a party in a matter related to the divorce or separation and would probably prohibit a lawyer who had mediated financial and property issues from acting as the lawyer in real estate matters arising out of the divorce, such as the sale of the matrimonial home.

It is important for lawyers who are mediators to check not only the code of conduct for mediators in their jurisdiction, but also the code of conduct for their law society. The broadest rule is a prohibition against representing either spouse on any matter at any point in the future. As a minimum, it is essential that the lawyer discloses any prior involvement to the clients, either legal involvement or as a mediator, and that both clients consent, preferably in writing, to any subsequent involvement. It would be unwise and probably unethical for a lawyer to act in any contested Family Law matter once the lawyer has acted as a mediator.

The mediator should take constructive steps to ensure that the agreement will be fair and reasonable to both parties and the children. It is important that the mediator encourage both parties to have independent legal representation, preferably from the outset of mediation, so that both parties are aware of their legal entitlements and are making an informed decision. The mediator should ensure that both parties have full disclosure of all relevant information prior to reaching an agreement on any issue in dispute. This may mean referring one or both clients to an accountant, real estate appraiser, or business evaluator for expert advice as to valuations of property or the tax consequences of certain options. Or, it may mean consulting a doctor, teacher, or mental health professional about the children's health, educational progress, or emotional adjustment. The mediator can raise concerns about the fairness of settlement proposals directly with both parties together, as well as in individual caucuses. The purpose would be to ensure that each individual understood his or her rights and was making an informed decision without duress.

On the one hand, mediation is a voluntary process whereby parties reach an agreement that they have engineered. Mediation encourages private ordering, but on the other hand there is an obligation on the part of the mediator to prevent a grossly unfair result, particularly where children are involved. While the mediator should not interfere with most settlements arrived at by the parties, nevertheless the mediator may need to intervene in the following types of circumstances:

- where the mediator realizes that there is a considerable inequality of bargaining power between the spouses, such that one spouse appears to be under duress by the other spouse to reach a particular agreement;
- where one party is seriously emotionally disturbed, or has an addiction to drugs or alcohol, and is therefore unable to negotiate as an equal;

- where one or both parties pose a risk of harm to the children or to each other;
- where one party is withholding significant relevant information from the other and refuses to disclose this;
- where one party is feeling so guilty about the marriage breakdown or is so anxious to reconcile that he or she is unable to protect his or her own interests; and
- where one party is being coerced to give up certain rights in return for other benefits. For example, one spouse may be pressured into giving up the right to support in exchange for custody of the children.

In all of these circumstances, it is important for the mediator to discuss these issues with the clients and, if necessary, with their solicitors. If the mediator feels that the issue can be resolved by referring one or both clients out for additional assistance, from a therapist or an accountant, for example, then this should be done, and the mediation may need to be delayed until this occurs. If the situation cannot be remedied, then the mediator may have to withdraw from the mediation and should write a letter to the clients and their lawyers confirming their withdrawal. It may not be advisable for the mediator to explain the reason for this action if the explanation would reveal information shared in confidence and if this could jeopardize the safety of either party.

(D) Duty of Confidentiality

In both open mediation and closed mediation, the mediator should clarify from the outset that he or she will not voluntarily disclose to any third party information that is obtained during the mediation process except under the following circumstances:

- if both parties consent to the release of information in writing to a particular individual or organization;
- if the mediator is ordered to disclose information by an appropriate judicial authority or is required to disclose information by law;
- if the mediator has reasonable cause to believe that there may be an actual or potential threat to human life or safety;
- if non-identifying information is needed for research or educational purposes. If the clients are the subject of research, they should each have given their consent to participate.

The mediator should explain to the clients that even though the mediator will not voluntarily disclose information, he or she may be obligated to do so, for example, if the mediator learns information that creates a concern about physical or sexual abuse of children. In this case, the mediator would be under a statutory or ethical duty to provide the child welfare authorities with this information. In addition, even if the parties agree in writing that the mediator will not be called as an expert witness to testify in court, the court may decide that the mediator's testimony is essential to the issues in dispute and may require that the mediator testify.

It is important for the mediator to determine whether there are individuals whom the mediator should speak to with respect to the issues in dispute. For example, in a child custody dispute, the mediator may consider it essential to speak to the schoolteacher and the family doctor. In financial mediation, the mediator may wish to speak to the accountant or a property appraiser. The mediator should ask the spouses to sign a consent form permitting the mediator to receive and, if necessary, exchange information with specific individuals or agencies. In addition, the mediator will want permission to speak to the lawyers, new spouses, and significant caretakers for the children. In each case, it is important that both parents consent to these discussions.

(E) INDEPENDENT LEGAL ADVICE

It is the duty of every mediator to advise clients to obtain independent legal advice prior to commencing mediation and certainly before signing any agreement. The purpose of independent legal advice is to ensure that both clients are fully informed about:

- their legal rights and entitlements;
- alternative proposals for resolving the issues in dispute; and
- the consequences of an agreement under the law. For example, the clients must understand that the agreement will be binding unless the agreement was made under duress or without full disclosure of relevant information.

Lawyers can assist the clients to prepare and then swear their financial information forms.

Today clients can select collaboratively trained lawyers, who, along with mediators, protect clients from an unwanted court battle. Lawyers along with their clients and a mediator sign a Collaborative Mediation Participation Agreement committing to resolve all issues as amicably as possible. Clients are reassured that the involvement of lawyers will support, rather than undermine their desire for a fair, well informed and durable agreement with a minimum of acrimony.

(F) DUTY TO ENSURE NO HARM OR PREJUDICE TO PARTICIPANTS

The mediator is under a duty to suspend or terminate mediation whenever he or she believes that the process may be harmful or prejudicial to one or more of the participants. That is, the mediator should suspend or terminate the mediation when the mediator suspects that one or both parties are either unwilling or unable to participate effectively in the mediation process. For example, one party may be suffering from a serious emotional disorder, have a substance abuse problem or be a victim of domestic violence and be unable to bargain in a reasonable manner. The mediator should also end mediation when he or she believes that the mediation is no longer useful, in order to avoid unnecessary expenses for the clients.

If the mediation process is suspended or terminated, the mediator should suggest additional professional services to the parties, if they are appropriate. For example, the mediator may recommend that one or both parties obtain individual counselling or that one or both parties have the assistance of an accountant or tax lawyer prior to resuming mediation.

The mediator has a duty to ensure that both clients are reaching agreement freely, voluntarily, and without duress. Despite the mediator's obligation to ensure that participants are not harmed or prejudiced by their participation in mediation, it is also a fundamental principle of mediation that the participants can design their own agreement, voluntarily, without being bound by statutes or common law. The mediator must walk a fine line between permitting the clients to design their own agreement and permitting an unreasonable agreement to occur. At a minimum, the mediator needs to draw the client's attention to possible areas of unfairness, and may need to discuss these with the client's counsel. The most helpful reference for the mediator to reflect on these issues is the Domestic Violence Policy adopted by OAFM as part of its Code of Conduct in 1994 and included in Appendix I.1.

These are the principal issues that are generally addressed in professional codes of conduct. Several examples of such Codes of Professional Conduct are included in the Appendices, such as the one adopted by the Ontario Association for Family Mediation.[3] This was the first code of conduct for family mediators in Canada. Family Mediation Canada has also adopted a federal code,[4] and several provinces have developed their own provincial codes. In addition, the ADR section of the Canadian Bar Association – Ontario has developed a model Code that can apply to a wide range of non-family mediation cases.

3. Role of the Lawyer

The role of the lawyer in the practice of Family Law has changed considerably during the past two decades. According to the traditional role, each spouse selected a lawyer who would represent his or her interests against the other spouse. That often precipitated the entry of spouses into a system that made them adversaries even when there may have been no particular issue in conflict.

Conversely, the expanding use of family mediation and Collaborative Law has created at least three possible role options for lawyers when couples have made a decision to separate or divorce.

(A) Independent Legal Advocate

As an independent legal advocate, the lawyer performs the following functions:

- is familiar with the practice of law and supportive of family mediation;
- represents one of the spouses in conflict;

---

[3] Set out below in Appendix VIII.4.

[4] Set out below in Appendix VIII.c (CD-ROM).

- where appropriate, recommends that clients try mediation and refers clients to a mediator;
- consults on the terms of mediation with the mediator and other lawyer; and
- maintains contact with the client and mediator, as necessary during the mediation process.

Specifically, Rule 2.02(3) of the Commentary in the Rules of Professional Conduct of the Law Society of Upper Canada, requires that:

> 2.02(3) The lawyer shall consider the use of alternative dispute resolution (ADR) for every dispute, and, if appropriate, the lawyer shall inform the client of ADR options and, if so instructed, take steps to pursue those options.

In the past few years collaborative Family Law has emerged as an excellent partner for mediation. When clients retain a mediator either before or after they retain collaborative lawyers, they will most very likely end up with an agreement that combines legal advice applied creatively to their personal circumstances, with a process that empowers them to take responsibility for the final outcome. The lawyer clearly reflects and protects his or her client's interests, but at the same time is mindful of the impact on the other spouse and the family unit as a whole. This usually enhances the likelihood of reaching agreement.

(B) IMPARTIAL LEGAL CONSULTANT

This option is not accepted at present in Canada but is accepted in some jurisdictions in the United States.

As an impartial legal consultant, the lawyer performs the following functions:

- contracts carefully with both spouses to ensure that his/her functions preclude representing either spouse in any capacity during or after mediation;
- functions as an impartial consultant on legal issues and points of law to the couple;
- provides neutral input to both spouses about their rights and responsibilities before the law; and
- consults with the mediator as required, to remain informed on the progress of the couple and the issues resolved.

(C) MEDIATOR

This is a non-traditional role because lawyers usually represent one of the sides in a dispute.

As a mediator, the lawyer performs the following functions:

- places herself/himself in a non-adversarial position impartially between the two spouses;
- contracts carefully with both spouses to ensure their understanding that she/he is not functioning as a legal advocate for either spouse;

- encourages each spouse to obtain separate legal counsel (some lawyers as mediators will refuse to mediate unless separate legal counsel is arranged);
- establishes collaboration with both lawyers consistent with the professional practice of family mediation; and
- submits a memorandum of understanding outlining agreements reached to both clients and their lawyers when mediation is concluded.

The roles and functions now possible for lawyers specializing in Family Law are expanding with the introduction of Collaborative Law. Lawyers who wish to practice either as mediators or as collaborative lawyers benefit considerably from attending family mediation training programs. Collaborative Law requires the ability to co-facilitate with another lawyer; this is a task that involves advanced mediation skills.

4. Areas of Conflict for Lawyers Acting as Mediators or as Collaborative Lawyers

There is some concern that there may be conflicts between the requirements for lawyers when they are acting in a legal capacity and when they are acting as mediators. The most important concern is whether lawyers are violating their code of professional legal conduct by acting on behalf of parties who are in a conflict of interest. Virtually all codes of conduct for lawyers require that they act in a partisan fashion and clearly advocate their client's position. There are usually strong rules prohibiting or limiting any situations in which lawyers may be acting for parties who are adverse in interests.

Those jurisdictions that have addressed the issue of the lawyer as mediator generally have set out special rules in order to protect the public and preserve the traditional role of the lawyer. That is, most codes of professional conduct require that the lawyer acting as mediator must make the clients aware of the following:

- whether the lawyer has acted previously in some capacity for one or both parties. This matter must be disclosed to the other party and fully discussed. If the lawyer has acted in a legal capacity for one or both parties, the lawyer probably should not act as a mediator in the case;
- that the mediator will strongly recommend that both parties obtain independent legal advice throughout the mediation process and certainly before signing any agreement;
- that the lawyer who is acting as a mediator will not give independent legal advice to either party;
- that the mediator can give legal information, but cannot explain the implications of the law with respect to each party's specific position;
- that the mediator will require full disclosure of all relevant information prior to negotiating a settlement on any issue;
- that the mediator will not act on behalf of either or both clients in a legal capacity following the mediation. This is particularly true of any contested

legal matters, especially if they arise out of issues referred to mediation; and

- that the mediator will not deal with issues that are beyond the mediator's special training as a lawyer. For example, if the lawyer who is acting as a mediator does not have special training in dealing with issues related to custody of and access to children, then these issues will not be included in the mediation process.

In Ontario, the Law Society of Upper Canada has a special rule governing lawyers acting as mediators.[5]

One amendment that the Law Society made to the existing Rules of Professional Conduct[6] for lawyers practising in Ontario is Rule 4.07, which now includes a specific reference to mediation.

The Law Society Rules provide the following guidelines to those lawyers who wish to practise family mediation. They suggested the following guidelines:[7]

- A lawyer acting as a family mediator should not provide legal advice, but rather should encourage the parties to obtain independent legal advice. The lawyer-mediator can give legal information.
- If the lawyer-mediator drafts an agreement for the parties' consideration, he or she should expressly advise and encourage the clients to get independent legal advice concerning the agreement.
- The lawyer acting as mediator and any member of his or her law firm should not accept legal work arising from the mediation. The purpose of this guideline is to avoid a possible conflict of interest.
- The Law Society should encourage mediators to obtain additional academic and professional training in mediation.
- The lawyer acting as mediator should be aware, and should make the parties aware, that the mediator may not be able to keep the contents of any communication from either of the parties confidential or privileged. In addition, the lawyer acting as mediator should explain to the parties that the communications he or she receives as a mediator are not protected by solicitor-client privilege and there is a possibility that the mediator could be forced to reveal all or part of a communication if ordered by a court of law to do so.
- The Law Society should inform lawyers acting as mediators that professional liability insurance through the Law Society will cover a lawyer acting as a mediator. Non-practising lawyers or those who restrict their practice to mediation should be encouraged to obtain separate insurance coverage as mediators.

---

5 See Appendix VIII.a (CD-ROM), Rules of Professional Conduct, Rule 4.07. This section sets out the specific behaviour required of lawyers who are acting as mediators in Ontario.

6 *Ibid.*

7 *Ibid.*, Rule 4.07, Rules of Professional Conduct.

For collaborative lawyers, perhaps the greatest area of conflict is the requirement to act as an advocate.[8]

While this appears to create a conflict for collaborative lawyers, being an advocate does not preclude collaboration and cooperative behaviour, especially if this is an informed choice made by the client. Not every client wants to pursue litigation or to "win" a legal battle at the expense of long-term goodwill, flexibility, emotional harm to their children, inordinate legal costs, and prolonged uncertainty. In family cases many clients see the benefit of preserving their relationships as primary, and while they want to be informed about their rights and responsibilities, they also want the ability to make decisions that provide the outcomes that they will have to live with.

Collaborative lawyers do need to maintain their role as advocates; however, they can do so by determining the client's intentions and personal goals and help them achieve those — not just a narrowly defined entitlement under a particular statute. In Collaborative Law, as in mediation, the clients have made a choice to proceed in a non-adversarial manner, to follow certain rules of conduct, and to consciously seek out a solution that is acceptable to all. The collaborative lawyer's task is to facilitate this overall goal.

Collaborative lawyers need to think about redefining their skills. Instead of advocating *against* the other side, on their client's instructions, they can advocate *on behalf of* the procedural, psychological, and substantive interests that will benefit and be accepted by everyone. In collaborative cases, the clients agree to take the family unit into consideration — not just the interests of one party. In this context the lawyer as advocate can fall within the Law Society's expectations and meet his or her client's needs.

5. Qualifications for Mediators

A number of provincial family mediation associations in Canada, the ADR Institute of Ontario, Family Mediation Canada ("FMC"), and the Association for Conflict Resolution ("ACR") in the U.S., have made considerable progress in developing standards for practising mediators. By way of example, the standards for "Accredited Family Mediators" of the Ontario Association for Family Mediation and for Certified Family Mediators of the ADR Institute of Ontario, include the following:[9]

---

8 *Ibid.*, Rule 4.01, Rules of Professional Conduct.

9 Adapted from the Ontario Association for Family Mediation, application form for "Accredited Mediator" status and from the Training Requirements of the ADR Institute of Ontario for "Certified Family Mediators". Reproduced with permission.

CRITERIA FOR ACCREDITED FAMILY MEDIATORS (OAFM) & CERTIFIED FAMILY MEDIATORS (ADR INSTITUTE OF ONTARIO)

AREAS OF COMPETENCE

In order to qualify for and maintain membership in the Ontario Association for Family Mediation as an "Accredited Family Mediator" (hereinafter referred to as Acc. FM (O.A.F.M.)), or in the ADR Institute as a "Certified Family Mediator" (hereinafter referred to as C. F. Med) an applicant/member must satisfy the Association that he or she possesses the qualifications set out below:

1. PROFESSIONAL EDUCATION:

Applicants must provide proof of a university degree or proof of having attained FMC certification or an equivalent.

2. KNOWLEDGE OF MEDIATION THEORY AND SKILLS

A basic knowledge of family mediation theory and skills is essential. For the purpose of application for membership, or continuing membership, an applicant/member must have completed:

A. Sixty (60) (or 66 for the ADR Institute of Ontario) hours of mediation education, including a 40 hour family mediation training course and 20 (26) hours of family mediation skills training. The 40 hour family mediation training course must be taught by an OAFM/ADR Institute accredited mediator or approved by the OAFM, FMC, ADR Institute of Ontario or equivalent.
The family mediation training course must include a minimum of five hours in each of the following categories:[10]
   (i) Conflict resolution theories;
   (ii) Psychological issues in separation, divorce, and family dynamics and power imbalances;
   (iii) Issues and needs of children in separation and divorce;
   (iv) Mediation process and techniques, including role playing;
   (v) Family Law including custody, support, asset evaluation and distribution, taxation as it relates to separation and divorce; and
   (vi) Family economics (not required if the basic training is limited to custody mediation).

The additional 20 hours can be achieved by attendance at one or more advanced trainings, relevant workshops and conferences.

---

[10] These categories are those suggested by the Academy of Family Mediators as requirements of basic mediation training for people applying for full membership in that organization.

AND

B. A minimum of 14 hours on domestic violence education.

OR

C. Taught such a course him/herself; and
D. Had an exceptional amount of applicable personal experience and in-service training.

NOTE: If the applicant lacks the minimum qualifications outlined in 1 or 2 above, he/she shall submit a résumé and contact the Accreditation Committee to discuss his/her acceptability for membership on an individual basis.

3. EXPERIENCE AND CONSULTATION/SUPERVISION IN THE ACTUAL PRACTICE OF MEDIATION

An Acc. FM (O.A.F.M.) or a C. F..Med. (ADR Institute of Ontario) must:

A. Applicants who possess a law degree or a graduate degree must provide proof (*i.e.*, letter from supervisor, peer references) of a minimum of six years of relevant work experience in human service; and
B. Submit a minimum of five family related cases mediated to the point of agreement. The mediator should consult with or be supervised by a practising O.A.F.M. Accredited Family Mediator for a minimum of one hundred hours including five cases mediated to the point of agreement. The consultation could include co-mediation; supervision; and peer consultation. The applicant must submit letter(s) from Acc.F.M. or C. F. Med. mediator(s) confirming co-mediation; supervision; and/or peer consultation of required one hundred (100) hours, including five (5) cases mediated to point of agreement for O.A.F.M. and ten (10) cases mediated to point of agreement for the ADR Institute of Ontario.
C. Submit the 5 (or 10) contracts to mediate which indicate the working relationship with the clients for the cases in (B) above.

4. STANDARDS OF PRACTICE

A. Code of Professional Conduct (Ethics) including the O.A.F.M. Abuse Policy :

An Acc. F. M. must commit himself/herself and adhere strictly to the O.A.F.M. and/or ADR Institute Code of Professional Conduct as a Standard of Practice. No mediator shall venture into an area of practice beyond his/her own area of expertise.

B. Continuing Education:

An Acc. F. M. and C.F. Med. must continue, and submit proof of his/her mediation education through attending courses and workshops and reading about new developments in the field. Continuing education must be a minimum of 10 hours of course-work relating to the practice of family mediation each year.

C. Liability Insurance:

All candidates at the time of application for the status of Acc. F. M. and C.F. Med. as well as at the time of annual renewal, must provide proof of current liability insurance covering the practice of mediation in an amount not less than $1,000,000.

It is important to note that anyone can become a member of the Ontario Association for Family Mediation or the ADR Institute; however, in order to qualify for the membership category entitled "Acc. F. M." or "C.F. Med.", an individual would have to meet the criteria set out above. There are similar or higher standards in other provinces. (See Appendix VIII re qualifications for mediators and arbitrators.)

B. RULES OF CONDUCT FOR COLLABORATIVE LAWYERS

Collaborative Family Law Lawyers have adopted fairly similar Codes of Conduct or Standards of Practice, across North America. A copy of the IACP Standards for Training and Ethics appears in Appendix III.m (CD-ROM). The following rules apply across North America; namely, it is expected that collaborative lawyers will:

- encourage their clients to make full disclosure of all relevant information. If their client refuses, the CFL lawyer should resign;
- work to minimize or mitigate power imbalances;
- resolve issues arising from the separation in a collaborative manner;
- use an interdisciplinary approach, that is, a referral to another professional (such as a divorce coach, mediator, counsellor, or financial advisor) when that is helpful to the client;
- respect, support, and work collaboratively with other non-adversarial dispute resolution processes, such as mediation;
- not use threats or intimidation;
- complete their work in a timely and efficient manner;
- remain respectful and model appropriate behaviour for their clients and the other lawyer;
- not deceive, mislead, or take unfair advantage of a mistake made by the other party or his/her lawyer;
- consider the welfare of children to be paramount;
- reduce emotional turmoil;
- not reserve the right to represent their client in court;

- commit to educating the public about non-adversarial approaches;
- sign a Collaborative Participation Agreement with both clients and the other lawyer; and
- not attempt to impair the neutrality of experts retained jointly.

1. Collaborative Membership and Training Requirements

Increasingly, Collaborative Law organizations have opened their membership on an equal basis to non-lawyer professionals, including psychologists, social workers, mediators, child specialists, divorce coaches, Certified Divorce Professionals, Financial Analysts, and Chartered Accountants. In most jurisdictions, members are required to attend a family mediation course (*e.g.*, a minimum of 40 hours) and several days of specialized Collaborative Law training (*e.g.*, a minimum of 21 hours). This training emphasizes the CFL model, including the involvement of an interdisciplinary team that will vary with the needs of each family. When there is no requirement to acquire mediation skills, the amount of CFL training is usually increased (*e.g.*, 40 hours). In a number of provinces attendance at an Interest-Based Negotiation course is encouraged (*e.g.*, 21-40 hours) in addition to the training described above.

There is a growing awareness that the issue of power imbalance and abuse require additional training to ensure that agreements are reached voluntarily, without duress or intimidation. The presence of lawyers and the requirement of prompt and full financial disclosure may reduce the concern about a lack of informed consent. Since lawyers are obligated to withdraw if their clients are behaving in a misleading or unethical manner, some of the concerns of women who are pressured or manipulated into unreasonable deals are addressed. What remains is the need to screen for appropriateness to ensure the parties are participating in good faith and are reaching agreements voluntarily.

C. FAMILY ARBITRATORS

1. Qualifications for Family Arbitrators

The ADR Institute of Ontario has taken the initiative in setting standards of professional training for Family Arbitrators in Ontario. They created the designation of Certified Family Arbitrator ("C.F.Arb.") with the following criteria:

- The candidates have completed an approved 40-hour Family Arbitration course;
- The candidates have arbitrated or co-arbitrated at least five family cases (broadly defined);
- The candidates have been observed and approved by a Qualifying Arbitrator through one or more of the following: co-arbitration, practicum, role-playing, videotaped arbitration (of a family related case), or other processes approved by ADR Canada; OR

- The candidates have successfully completed a competency assessment program approved by ADR Canada; and
- The candidates have $1M E&O liability insurance.

In addition, all family arbitrators must have attended a 2-day course in screening for domestic violence and power imbalances (completed within one week). Also, non-lawyer arbitrators must have completed a minimum of 30 hours of training in Family Law, that is, the law of custody, support, and property division.) See Appendix VIII.2.

2. Professional Conduct Issues for Family Arbitrators

The Rules of Professional Conduct require that a lawyer who acts as a mediator shall, at the outset of the mediation, ensure that the parties understand fully that the lawyer is not acting for either party but as an impartial professional attempting to assist the parties to resolve the matters in issue and, although communications within the mediation process may be covered by the other common law privilege for settlement negotiations, they will not be covered by solicitor/client privilege. In acting as a mediator or arbitrator, a lawyer must not give legal advice (as opposed to legal information, which is permissible during the mediation phase).

A mediator (and an arbitrator, when settlement discussions occur during an arbitration) should encourage the parties to seek the advice of separate counsel before and during the mediation and arbitration process. In the event of a settlement, the mediator/arbitrator should insist that the parties arrange for their lawyers to prepare or review a draft agreement and to obtain independent legal advice before executing that agreement. Where the parties reach an agreement during either phase of mediation/arbitration, the mediator/arbitrator may make a consent award at the request of either party. This ensures that any agreement reached is enforceable.

SUMMARY

This chapter has reviewed the ethical considerations and standards of conduct for both mediators and collaborative lawyers. As both fields mature as professions and services to the public, it is important that these matters be given serious consideration. In the past the presence of a judge in a public forum acted as a safeguard. Today, most of these cases are conducted in private, by individuals who may or may not be under the scrutiny of a professional body. To establish and maintain the credibility of the field, we need to continually reflect on our standards of practice and ethical boundaries.

ANNOTATED BIBLIOGRAPHY

Bernard, S.E., Folger, J., Weingarten, H., and Zumeta, Z. "The Neutral Mediator: Value Dilemmas in Divorce Mediation". In Lemmon J.A., ed. "Ethics,

Standards and Professional Challenges" (1984), 4 *Mediation Quarterly* 61. This chapter considers both a neutral and interventionist approach to mediation in the light of ethical considerations.

Cameron, N. *Collaborative Practice: Deepening the Dialogue.* The Continuing Legal Education Society of British Columbia, 2004. An excellent resource for the Collaborative Divorce Model, with a CD-ROM of precedents for the practitioner. This book describes the skills necessary for Collaborative Practice and raises some interesting ethical dilemmas for CFL practitioners.

Cooks, L., and Hale, C. "The Construction of Ethics in Mediation" (1994), 12:1 *Mediation Quarterly*, 55-75.

Dibble, C. "Bargaining in Family Mediation: Ethical Considerations". In Lemmon J.A., ed. "Ethics, Standards and Professional Challenges" (1984), 4 *Mediation Quarterly* 75. This article considers both the dangers and benefits of bargaining in family mediation and addresses the role of the mediator.

Engram, P., and Markowitz, J. "Ethical Issues in Mediation: Divorce and Labour Compared". In Lemmon J.A., ed. "Making Ethical Decisions" (1985), 8 *Mediation Quarterly* 19. This article examines the ethical procedures for divorce mediators by comparing divorce mediation to labour mediation.

Folberg, J., and Taylor, A. *Mediation: A Comprehensive Guide to Resolving Conflicts without Litigation.* San Francisco: Jossey-Bass Publishers, 1984. See particularly Part Four, "Mediation As a Profession — Educational, Ethical and Practical Dimensions", p. 233. See also Chapter 10, "Ethical, Professional and Legal Issues", p. 244. This chapter contains a comprehensive exploration of ethics, standards of practice, confidentiality, and mediator liability.

Folberg, J., Taylor, A., and Salem, P. *Divorce and Family Mediation: Models, Techniques, and Applications*. Guilford Press, 2004. This thorough text covers the theory and practice of mediation with articles by many leaders in the family mediation field.

Gentry, D. "Mediator Attitudes and Preferences Concerning Mediator Certification" (1994), 11:4 *Mediation Quarterly*, 353-359.

Goldberg, S., Green, E., and Sander, F. "A Dialogue on Legal Representation in Divorce Mediation". In Lemmon, J.A. ed. "Making Ethical Decisions" (1985), 8 *Mediation Quarterly* 5.

Landau, B. "Identity Crisis: Mediation, Lawyers and Mental Health Professionals" (1985), 11 *Therapy Now* 9. This article explores the role conflicts experienced by lawyers and mental health professionals in relation to mediation and custody assessments.

Lande, J. "Mediation Paradigms and Professional Identities". In Lemmon J.A., ed. "Ethics, Standards and Professional Challenges" (1984), 4 *Mediation Quarterly* 19. This article considers how mediation principles derived from general theories of dispute resolution may conflict with the American Bar Association's Standards of Practice for Family Mediators.

Macfarlane, J. *The New Lawyer: How Settlement is Transforming The Practice of Law.* Vancouver: UBC Press, 2008. An important text that reflects on the shift in the role of lawyers and the skills needed to be effective. Interviews with both clients and lawyers highlight how lawyers need to adapt to the client's desire for a less adversarial approach to dispute resolution.

Mamo, A. *Conducting the Arbitration Hearing.* (Paper presented to the Law Socirty of Upper Canada Continuing Legal Education Program, Mediation and Arbitration for Family Law Lawyers, 13 November 2007) [unpublished].

Milne, A. "The Development of Parameters of Practice for Divorce Mediation". In Lemmon J.A., ed. "Ethics, Standards and Professional Challenges" (1984), 4 *Mediation Quarterly* 49. This article considers various practice principles that would best serve the client, the mediator, and the practice of mediation.

Milne, A. "Model Standards of Practice for Family and Divorce Mediation". In Lemmon J.A., ed. "Making Ethical Decisions" (1985), 8 *Mediation Quarterly* 73. This chapter contains guidelines for practice for both court-connected and private family mediators. These are included in a draft code prepared by the Association of Family and Conciliation Courts in 1983-84.

Morris, C., and Pirie, A., ed. *Qualifications for Dispute Resolution: Perspectives on the Debate.* Victoria, B.C.: U Vic Institute for Dispute Resolution, 1994. This is an excellent collection of articles on mediator qualifications and other important practice issues. Of particular interest are the introduction by Catherine Morris, and Part Three: Critical Perspectives, including the articles by Michelle Lebaron Duryea, Cheryl Picard, and Andrew Pirie.

Perlmutter, F. "Ethical Issues in Family Mediation: A Social Perspective". In Lemmon J.A., ed. "Making Ethical Decisions" (1985), 8 *Mediation Quarterly* 99. This article focuses in particular on mediation services for low-income families.

Pirie, A. "The Lawyer as Mediator: Professional Responsibility Problems or Profession Problems?" (1985), 63 *Canadian Bar Review* 279. This author outlines the important ethical issues for lawyers who are acting as mediators to consider and makes recommendations that the bar associations not overly regulate mediation by lawyers at this point in time.

Saposnek, D. *Mediating Child Custody Disputes*. San Francisco: Jossey-Bass Publishers, 1998. See Part Five, "Challenges and Professional Issues", particularly Chapter 15, "Ethics, Values and Morals in Mediation", p. 303.

Saposnek, D. "What Is Fair in Child Custody Mediation". In Lemmon J.A., ed. "Making Ethical Decisions" (1985), 8 *Mediation Quarterly* 9. This article examines the concept of fairness from different perspectives — individual, family, sociopolitical, cultural, and moral — and considers whether this would result in different recommendations.

Schepard, A. "Model Standards of Practice for Divorce and Family Mediators", *Family and Conciliation Courts Review,* Vol. 38, No. 1, January 2000.

Sheilds, R., Ryan, J.P., and Smith, V. *Collaborative Family Law: Another Way to Resolve Family Disputes.* Thomson Canada Ltd., 2003. This book has helpful precedents for the Canadian CFL practitioner.

Silberman, L. "Professional Responsibility Problems of Divorce Mediation" (1982), 16 *Family Law Quarterly* 107. This article outlines the response of the various bar associations in the United States to lawyers acting as mediators.

Taylor, A. "The Four Foundations of Family Mediation: Implications for Training and Certification" (1994), 12:1 *Mediation Quarterly*, 77-88.

Tesler, P. *Collaborative Law: Achieving Effective Resolution in Divorce without Litigation.* Section of Family Law, American Bar Association, 2001. Tesler's book is the first major book in describing in detail the Collaborative Family Law process and how it differs from an adversarial process. It has a copy of the Code of Conduct for CFL Lawyers in the United States.

Wilson, J. *Family Law Mediation and Arbitration Challenging Mediation-Arbitration, Arbitration (and Secondary Arbitration) Awards.* (Paper presented to the Law Society of Upper Canada Continuing Legal Education Program, Mediation and Arbitration for Family Law Lawyers, 13 November 2007) [unpublished].

Wolfson, L., and Kovitz, J. *The New Family Arbitration.* (Paper presented to the Law Society of Upper Canada Continuing Legal Education Program, Mediation and Arbitration for Family Law Lawyers, 13 November 2007) [unpublished].

Appendix I Contents

Screening for Domestic Violence

Appendix I.1

OAFM Policy on Abuse

Reproduced with the permission of the Ontario Association for Family Mediation

MEDIATION OF DISPUTES INVOLVING DOMESTIC VIOLENCE

Adopted at the OAFM Annual General Meeting, June 1994. Many of the concepts and recommendations come from the "Report from the Toronto Forum on Woman Abuse and Mediation, June, 1993".

INTRODUCTION (FROM TORONTO REPORT)

1. History:

In June of 1991, the Ontario Association for Family Mediation launched an effort to involve North American professional dispute resolution associations in the development of joint policy statements regarding women abuse and mediation. This effort was a direct response to the concerns raised by women's and children's advocates. In May of 1992, 14 mediators representing officially and unofficially the Academy of Family Mediators, Family Mediation Canada, the Ontario Association for Family Mediation and the Society of Professionals in Dispute Resolution met with approximately 50 women's and children's advocates for the purpose of hearing their serious concerns about mediation in cases of abuse. Representatives of the black, native, immigrant and handicapped women's communities were invited to address the additional concerns of these groups. In March of 1993, representatives of most major family mediation associations met with several leaders and front line workers who assist abused women and children, including women of colour, immigrant woman and men who batter. Together they prepared joint recommendations for presentation at the 1993 meetings of the mediation associations.

It was agreed that these recommendations would address primarily:

- the education and training of mediators,
- the skilful screening of candidates for mediation,
- safety issues in mediation,
- alternatives to mediation for abused women.

The concern behind these recommendations was the alarming police statistics that show that more than 95% of complaints to police about abuse are made by women against male perpetrators. A recent survey by Statistics Canada revealed that approximately half of all women have experienced at least one incident of violence since the age of sixteen and 25% of all women have experienced violence at the hands of a current or past marital partner. This incidence is higher in separated or divorced women. The Toronto Forum concluded that "violence against women and its impact on children continue to pose serious questions for dispute resolution professionals and the practice of mediation. Women's advocates, mediators, mental health workers, lawyers and the judiciary are increasingly working together to understand the complex consequences of women abuse. In recent years, efforts at dialogue and collaboration have increased among mediators and women's advocates. They are starting, albeit cautiously, to address co-operatively and constructively the benefits and risks associated with mediation and the unique needs of abused women".

A Word about Language:

The Toronto Forum chose to use the phrase "Woman Abuse" to highlight the fact that complaints about physical abuse, stalking and endangerment in intimate relationships are made primarily by women against men. Where abuse is directed at men by women or where abuse occurs in same sex relationships, the same principles and safeguards should apply. Throughout the rest of this document the term domestic violence or abuse will refer to any woman, man or child who experiences the use or threat of physical, psychological, emotional or economic intimidation, coercion or force in an intimate relationship. The concern in mediation is the impact that abuse has on its victim. Abuse functions to secure power and control for the abuser and to undermine the safety, security, self esteem and autonomy of the abused person.

Abuse is defined broadly to include, but not be limited to:

- physical violence, including assault (pushing, shoving, slapping, choking, hitting, biting, kicking, etc.);
- sexual assault;
- kidnapping, confining;
- use of or threat with a weapon;
- threats against children;
- unlawful entry;
- destruction or theft of personal property;
- violence against pets;
- stalking, harassment;
- psychological and verbal abuse including sarcastic, degrading and humiliating comments and name calling;
- controlling and/or manipulative behavior;
- withholding of economic and other resources;
- penalizing the abused person for asserting his/her independence or autonomy, etc.

The following standards of practice acknowledge that "parties to mediation must be able to negotiate safely, voluntarily, and competently in order to reach a fair agreement. Mediation cannot be fair if one of the parties is unable to mediate effectively and competently. "Abuse in intimate relationships poses serious safety risks and may significantly diminish a person's ability to mediate". For this reason, mediators need to identify "which cases are inappropriate for mediation, which are appropriate for specialized mediation and which may proceed in the usual way".

OAFM SAFETY STANDARDS

Assumption: Mediation in cases of Domestic Violence is probably inappropriate.

Family mediation cases in which there is or has been domestic violence are complicated and can be dangerous to the participants and the mediator. Therefore, beginning mediators and mediators not trained or experienced in domestic violence should not accept referrals of these cases, but rather should refer them for screening to a more appropriate resource (such as a lawyer or woman's advocate) or to an experienced mediator who has considerable professional experience in dealing with cases involving domestic violence. Another choice would be for an inexperienced mediator to co-mediate with someone who has considerable professional experience dealing with domestic violence in order to screen for appropriateness.

- Parties to mediation must be able to negotiate safely, voluntarily, and competently in order to reach a fair agreement. If the level of domestic violence is sufficient to jeopardize a party's ability to negotiate without fear or duress, the case should not be mediated. The criterion should be the victim's ability to participate effectively.
- There should be no mediation concerning the violence, itself. For instance, an offer to stop the abuse in exchange for something else should not be allowed in the mediation process.
- When safety is an issue, the mediator's obligation is to provide a safe environment for cooperative problem-solving or, when this does not seem workable, to help the clients consider more appropriate alternatives.
- Above all, the mediator must promote the safety of all participants in the mediation process and its outcome.

OAFM STANDARDS FOR ASSESSING WHETHER MEDIATION MAY BE APPROPRIATE

A. Prior to commencing mediation, all clients should be screened for any occurrences of abuse to determine which cases are inappropriate for mediation, which require additional safeguards, in addition to, or instead of mediation, and which should be referred to other resources.
   1. Conduct initial screening separately with the parties. This could be done a variety of ways. For example, preliminary screening could take place within a brief telephone contact. This should be supplemented by a face-to-face interview or a written questionnaire.

Using a structured questionnaire, basic information can be gathered which includes details about any history of abuse. If screening is not done separately, a victim may be unwilling to reveal the presence of abuse and/or may be placed at risk for revealing the abuse.

2. Screening should continue throughout the mediation process.

B. The issue of voluntariness is critical when it comes to creating a safe place for couples to meet and negotiate.

OAFM recommends that mediation be voluntary on the part of the participants. It would be acceptable to mandate couples to orientation sessions at separate times during which information could be given about available options for resolving family law disputes (litigation, mediation, arbitration, custody assessments, lawyer assisted negotiation, etc. and about the impact of separation and divorce on parents and children). Inquiries about abuse should be made during the separate orientation sessions, before mediation is offered as an option.

C. Clients should be strongly encouraged to consult with attorneys prior to mediation and certainly before an agreement is finalized.

D. Mediators must be knowledgeable about abuse:

Training for mediators should include the following:

1. Issues related to physical and psychological abuse and its effect on family members;
2. The impact that abuse (including witnessing abuse) has on children;
3. Effective techniques for screening, implementing safety measures, and safe termination;
4. Referral to appropriate resources, in addition to, or instead of mediation;
5. Sensitivity to cultural, racial and ethnic differences that can impact the mediation process that may be relevant to domestic violence.

E. Where a decision is made that mediation may proceed, mediators need to meet standards of safety, voluntariness, and fairness. When mediators have concerns, they should inform their clients that they are *not* neutral about violence or safety. Mediators should inform clients that they have a positive obligation to report past or present child abuse and threats of future abuse to any of the participants.

Procedural guidelines:

1. Obtain training about abuse and become familiar with the literature.
2. Never mediate the fact of the abuse.
3. Never support a couple's trading non-violent behaviour for obedience.
4. Set ground rules to optimize the protection of all parties.
5. When appropriate and possible, arrange separate waiting areas and separate arrival and leaving times, permitting the victim to arrive last and leave first with a reasonable lag in time for safety purposes.

6. Use separate meetings throughout the mediation process when appropriate, necessary, and/or helpful.
7. Consider co-mediation with a male/female mediation team, as an option.
8. Allow a support person to be present in the waiting room during screening, and/or during the mediation session.
9. Maintain a balance of power between the couple, and, if this is not possible, terminate the mediation process and refer the couple to an appropriate alternative. Such alternatives might include shelters, therapists, abuse prevention groups, and attorneys.
10. Where fairness of outcome may be an issue, the mediator should refer the clients to their counsel, financial advisor, support person, or other relevant resource for information and advice.
11. Terminate the mediation if either of the participants is unable to mediate safely, competently, and without fear or coercion. Precautions should be taken in terminating to assure the safety of the parties. For example, the mediator should not reveal information to one party or to the court that could create a risk for the other party.
12. Consider offering a follow up session to assess the need for a modification of the agreement.

THE OAFM BOARD AFFIRMED THE FOLLOWING GUIDELINES:

1. OAFM encourages its members to work with the diverse cultural and ethnic groups serving adults and children to improve public awareness and the development of a wider range of options and services for victims of abuse.
2. OAFM agrees to incorporate this policy within their standards of practice outlining the conduct expected of mediators in cases of abuse and clarifying that mediators must *not* be neutral with regard to violence or safety. The Standards of Practice should reflect that safety must take priority over neutrality.
3. OAFM agrees to work with government to develop standards to govern the practice of mediation.
4. OAFM requires all Practicing Members to participate in a minimum of five hours training on domestic violence including screening, safety measures, safe termination, and alternatives to mediation, when mediation is not appropriate.

Approved June 11, 1994

Appendix I.2

Intake Form with DV Screening Questions

INTAKE FORM (With DV Screening Questions)

CONTACT INFORMATION

Date:	Who Called? Husband Wife
Service:	Referred By:
Husband	***Wife***
Address:	Address:
E-mail:	E-mail:
Phone: Res. ( )	Phone: Res. ( )
Bus. ( )	Bus. ( )
Cell: ( )	Cell: ( )

Children: No Yes # ______	Ages:
Living Arrangements: Together Separate Children residing with?	

LEGAL COUNSEL

Husband's Lawyer:	Wife's Lawyer:
Address:	Address:
Phone: ( )	Phone: ( )
Fax: ( )	Fax: ( )
E-mail:	E-mail:
Assistant:	Assistant:

INTERN

Approval for Intern? Husband: Yes No Wife: Yes No	
Intern:	Fax: ( )
Phone: Res. ( )	E-Mail:
Bus: ( )	Fee collected? Yes No
Cell: ( )	

Sample Intake Domestic Violence Screening Questions

I'm going to go through a list of questions now that I ask everyone who calls for an appointment:

- *Have there ever been any incidences of PHYSICAL ABUSE between you and your spouse?*
  Any hitting, kicking, pushing, or choking? What about throwing things or destroying property? Have either of you ever used threats or intimidation?

  ____

  ____

  ____

- *What about VERBAL or EMOTIONAL ABUSE?*
  Any name-calling or put-downs? Any suicide threats or severe jealousy?

  ____

  ____

  ____

- *And what about ALCOHOL AND DRUG ABUSE?*
  Have you or your spouse ever had a drinking problem? Do either of you use illegal drugs?

  ____

  ____

  ____

- *Who chose to come to Mediation/Arbitration/Collaborative Law? Can you express your opinions openly without fear of reprisals when in the same room as your spouse?*

  ____

  ____

  ____

** It is best to go through the list as casually or matter-of-factly as possible. Leave time for responses.* ***Be on the alert for pauses or vague answers*** *– they often mean that the person is carefully considering their reply and may be hiding some information. If there is acknowledgement of abuse, probe for frequency and severity, and if any counseling has been sought.*

*** The purpose of this list is to provide the professional with more information before he/she begins Mediation, Arbitration, or Collaborative Law. If there is disclosure of abuse, and such that the victim is not able to negotiate with the other spouse safely, voluntarily and without duress, the mediator or collaborative lawyer will likely decide not to go ahead and to safety plan with the victim over the phone*

Administrative Follow up:

Information provided: Website address Brochure C.V. Thanks for booking letter

Client Questionnaire Date sent: _______ Sent via: Fax Mail E-mail
Counsel Mtg. Required?: Yes No If Yes, Date Booked: ___________
Initial Appointment Booked on: _______________ Time: ____________

Information:

Appendix I.3

The Landau Domestic Violence Screening Interview

The following is a breakdown of areas to explore when screening for domestic violence and control issues. In both Mediation and Arbitration, if there is any concern about domestic violence or control issues that has surfaced in the phone intake and/or the client questionnaire, then it is important to meet individually with the parties *before* meeting jointly and signing the Retainer Contract. In Arbitration, screening must occur before Arbitration commences.

The screener meets first with the abused party, or the party who is most at risk, and second with the alleged abuser, preferably on different days, in order to gather the information necessary to either proceed with Mediation or Arbitration or to safely terminate. Also, at the beginning of the individual meetings, it is important to make it clear to each party that the purpose of the meeting is *to determine whether or not Mediation or Arbitration are appropriate for them.* If domestic violence is discovered in the individual meeting with Party A, and Mediation or Arbitration is deemed inappropriate, then the screener should safety plan with Party A and safely terminate in the meeting with Party B.

FAMILY MEDIATION and ARBITRATION SCREENING QUESTIONS

Dr. Barbara Landau

NOTE:

Fam Arb* – Arbitrator cannot screen. Parties must be screened separately. Preferably both parties are screened by the same screener.

Med-Arb* PC, or Med – Mediator can screen. Parties must be screened separately and by the same screener.

* Screening Report goes to Arbitrator & AG

PURPOSE: Screen for **VOLUNTARY PARTICIPATION** (choice of process without fear or intimidation or pressure from a spouse, extended family or community), **INFORMED CONSENT** (understanding of Canadian Family Law) & for **CAPACITY** to state their views **WITHOUT DURESS.**

1. **Building Rapport:** I want to thank you (NAME of CLIENT) for coming today. As I mentioned to you this is required preparation for those who are considering Family Mediation, Arbitration or Med-Arb.

2. **Goal:** The purpose of this meeting is to ensure that you have an opportunity to review the various options so you can make an informed and voluntary decision as to what process best fits your circumstances. The reason this meeting is required is because separation and divorce are emotionally stressful events for most people. This is a time when tensions run very high and it is important to ensure that the needs and safety of parents, children and others are taken into account.

   I will be asking you some questions about the decision to separate, your family, and your relationship with your spouse. Then we will discuss the choice of options for addressing future parenting plans, as well as support and property issues. The focus will be on HOW these issues might be resolved, NOT on specific legal advice.

3. **Confidentiality:** What we discuss today will not be shared with your partner (or counsel).

   - If you are planning to use Family Arbitration, I do have a duty to report to the Arbitrator whether you and your partner seem appropriate for that process and whether any changes to the usual procedure would be needed e.g. separate arrival and leaving times, or the involvement of counsel.

- I also have a duty to let someone know if there are safety concerns or a risk of harm for you or your children (e.g. police or Child Welfare). I will discuss this with you.

4. **Decision to Separate:**
   - How did the decision to separate come about? Who decided?
   - Can you tell me something about the circumstances?
   - How do you feel about the decision to separate? How does your spouse feel?

5. **Current living arrangements:**
   - Are you still living under one roof?
   - Are you working?
   - What is your immigration status?

6. **Family History:**
   - Can you tell me something about your family – Who is in your family?
   - Relationship between your parents?
   - Abuse, alcoholism, drugs in parents, siblings, or extended family?
   - Current support system – siblings, extended family?

7. **Marital History:**
   - Quality of relationship from beginning to present: How did you meet?
   - Can you tell me how decisions are made in your family – for example about the children (education, health care, religion, etc.?)
   - What about financial issues (e.g. purchase of a car? Where to live? Whether to work outside the home?)
   - Have there been in the past 6 months or at any time in the relationship, instances of:
     - Physical or sexual abuse;
     - Psychological or verbal abuse;
     - Concerns about drugs, alcohol or mental health?
   - Do you have any concerns about the safety or wellbeing of the children with your spouse? with you?
     with new partners? or extended family?

8. **Dispute Resolution Options:**
   - How was the decision made to try Family Mediation or Arbitration?
   - Who suggested this option?
   - Why do you think this option is a good choice?
   - Do you have any questions or concerns about this process?
   - What might be the disadvantages? Challenges?
   - What other options did you consider?

- How does your partner feel about this (or other) option(s)?
- What would happen if you told your partner/family members that you preferred to have your separation issues negotiated by lawyers or decided by a judge?

9. Capacity to Participate in the Process:

In Family Mediation or Arbitration you need to be able to express your views about what you would like and why, with your partner in the same room.

- Can you state your views safely with your partner present?
- What would you be concerned about if your views were quite different from your partner?
- Would there be a conflict/fight after you left the Mediator's/ Arbitrator's office?
- What is the worst thing that might happen? (esp. a concern if still living together.)
- What would you do if you feared such conflict?

10. ILA: (Note: the screener may be the lawyer although this is <u>not</u> recommended.)

For a valid arbitration, it is important that you understand your basic rights and obligations under the FLA & Divorce Act.

- Are you aware that for you to have an enforceable agreement, Canadian Law must be followed?
- Do you plan to have your lawyer present at the arbitration? Why? Why not? Is the Arbitrator trained in Canadian Law?
- If you deal with financial issues are you aware that both of you need to make full financial disclosure?
- Does your spouse understand these requirements and are you both prepared to accept them? What would happen if one of you did not agree with these requirements?

11. Decision & Report: Options

a) If client wants to proceed & Screener concurs

<u>Report:</u>

- Participating voluntarily, no DV or serious power imbalance that will affect decision making or ability to participate
- no changes to the usual process are required.

b) If client wants to proceed & Screener does <u>not</u> concur

<u>Report:</u>

- Screener feels Mediation or Arbitration are **not** appropriate (i.e. safety concerns, not voluntary, etc.), **<u>OR</u>**
- Screener feels there need to be changes in the process to ensure safety or basic legal requirements/fairness (e.g. if party wants to

waive requirement for financial disclosure or right to support out of fear or 'tradition').

- Screener sets out recommended changes in the process or necessary safeguards without details or assigning blame.

c) If one spouse decides NOT to proceed (& other wants to proceed)

Report:

- Screener feels Mediation or Arbitration are **not** appropriate (don't reveal information that could create a safety concern)

d) If both spouses decide NOT to proceed (e.g. The parties decided that Mediation or Arbitration will not meet their needs)

Report:

- Both parties have decided that these are not appropriate options.

Appendix I.4

Landau Screening Categories

In determining whether mediation, arbitration or collaborative law are appropriate in a particular case, these categories may prove useful:

CATEGORY A. Appropriate: Both parties are entering mediation, arbitration or collaborative law VOLUNTARILY, both have CAPACITY, and SAFETY is not a concern.

[No Violence or Fear of Violence and No Abusive or Controlling Behaviours]

OUTCOME A. Mediation/Arbitration/Collaborative Law can proceed without specialized conditions. Screening for violence, controlling and coercive tactics continues throughout the process.

CATEGORY B. Possibly Appropriate: Both parties are entering mediation, arbitration or collaborative law VOLUNTARILY and both would have capacity and safety would not be a concern IF certain CONDITIONS were met and/or there was a SPECIALIZED PROCESS. In order for mediation or arbitration to go ahead, both parties have to agree to the conditions/changes.

[No Violence or Fear of Violence, but other Abusive or Controlling Behaviours]

OUTCOME B. Victim DOES want to mediate, arbitrate or select collaborative law. Both parties may have capacity if SPECIALIZED PROCESS and under certain CONDITIONS. If both agree to conditions as prerequisite, then mediation or collaborative law continue with ongoing screening and enforcement of conditions. If one or both do not agree to conditions, NO MEDIATION, ARBITRATION OR COLLABORATIVE LAW and, if necessary, safety planning and referral.

CATEGORY C. Not Appropriate: The victim does NOT want to mediate, arbitrate or participate in collaborative law and/or or both parties LACK CAPACITY, and/or SAFETY IS A CONCERN, and a specialized process would not satisfy these issues.

[Violence or Fear of Violence]

OUTCOME C. No Mediation/Arbitration/Collaborative Law. Safety planning and referral.

Appendix I.5

Characteristics of "A", "B", & "C" Couples

A) APPROPRIATE FOR MEDIATION, ARBITRATION & COLLABORATIVE LAW CONDUCTED IN THE USUAL MANNER

- History of consultation or joint decision making
- Respect for each person's point of view (including differences)
- Absence of fear or intimidation
- Confidence in each other's parenting
- Trust i.e.: belief that the other is participating in good faith
- Control is not a significant part of the relationship
- No pattern of abusive behaviour, physical, sexual, or economic, by one party toward the other

B) POSSIBLY APPROPRIATE WITH CONDITIONS & SPECIALIZED PROCESS

- Set ground rules for communication in sessions and between sessions (e.g. no calls or attempts to influence the other spouse outside the mediation, arbitration or collaborative law, 4 way meetings)
- In Mediation, hold primarily individual sessions
- Have abuser arrive first and leave last or sit in separate waiting areas

- Agree to a support person if requested (either in the waiting room or session)
- Consider co-mediation (possibly with a male/female co-mediation team or conduct the mediation with the (collaborative) lawyers present to assist with co-facilitation
- Set preconditions: eg both obtain independent legal advice, financial advice, full financial disclosure and valuations (if money or property issues discussed)
- Require attendance at counselling, anger management, set rules re no alcohol or drugs
- Continue to screen & monitor compliance with preconditions and safety plan – if no compliance NO MEDIATION, ARBITRATION or COLLABORATIVE LAW
- If preconditions not followed, e.g. if abuser continues to need to control abused spouse or is easily frustrated by the idea of not getting all that he wants – NO MEDIATION, ARBITRATION or COLLABORATIVE LAW

C) NOT APPROPRIATE – NO MEDIATION, ARBITRATION OR COLLABORATIVE LAW

- If victim does not wish to Mediate, Arbitrate or participate in Collaborative Law and is not choosing the process voluntarily
- If one or both parties are unable to negotiate or there are indicators that the abuser is capable of seriously injuring or killing his spouse &/or children (e.g.: recently obtained a weapon, expressing suicidal thoughts or threats to wife and/or children)
- If victim is unable to promote her own needs i.e. she tries to meet the abuser's needs instead of her own
- If abuser does not recognize that she has separate interests and the right to assert these interests
- If victim is afraid to have abuse revealed i.e.: if abuse is not out in the open, then ground rules can't be implemented
- Safety Plan and refer to alternatives

Note: Arbitration and Collaborative Law may expand the boundaries somewhat because of the presence of lawyers who can assist in protecting the victim's interests. However in cases where the victim does not choose Arbitration or Collaborative Law or is in danger or the agreement is being reached under duress, Arbitration or Collaborative Law are INAPPROPRIATE.

* "She" is used for victims of abuse and "he" is used for abuser. The same policy would apply if the man was the victim of abuse and the woman was the abuser.

** Mediators have an ethical obligation to assist both parties excluded from mediation by providing appropriate referrals and safety planning. Lawyers have a duty to assist their own clients to obtain appropriate assistance and to put in place safety measures for themselves and their children.

Appendix I.6

Conflict Assessment Protocol

SCREENING CLIENTS FOR ABUSE IN DIVORCE MEDIATION CASES*

Linda Girdner, Ph.D.

Conflict Assessment Protocol (CAP)

This screening protocol is designed to be used by mediators in court, community, or private practice settings. Separate screening sessions are conducted by the mediator or intake person with each party subsequent to an initial introduction to mediation. This introduction can be a description of mediation from the judge or commissioner who ordered/referred the case to mediation, an introductory videotape or written materials about mediation supplied by the service provider, or a face-to-face orientation with the same or a different mediator or intake person.

The screening session has four parts:

- the introduction;
- questions about decisions, conflict, and anger;
- questions about specific abusive behaviours; and
- closure to the separate screening session.

The same basic set of questions is asked of both parties. The following is a suggested text:

I Introduction to Separate Screening Sessions

The reason why I am meeting with you individually is to give you and your spouse the opportunity to tell me about concerns you might have about mediation and your situation. I also will be asking you specific questions about how you and your spouse get along, so that I can assess whether mediation is appropriate for you and how I might help you.

I will not share any of the information you tell me with your spouse unless I have your permission.

Is there anything you would like to ask me or tell me before we continue?

(If not, reassure the client that there will be other opportunities to ask questions. If so, allow the client to speak briefly. In responding, restate his/her question or comment as a concern, if appropriate. Then reassure the client that there will be additional opportunities to ask questions. By opening with this question, the mediator enables the client to express something which might otherwise interfere with the client's ability to be attentive and responsive during the rest of the session.)

Could you tell me a little about how the decision to divorce was reached? (I generally ask this in the orientation session and open the topic in the individual session with a statement based on the client's earlier response, such as: "It sounds like you don't want the divorce. Could you tell me about that?")

II Decisions, Conflict, and Anger

Now I am going to ask you some specific questions about how you and your spouse got along over the course of your relationship.

How were decisions made in your marriage?
Given me an example.
How did you react/feel about that?
How did your spouse react/feel about that?

Tell me about other ways in which decisions were made?
Give me an example.
How did you react/feel about that?
How did your spouse react/feel about that?

How would you like for decisions to be made in mediation?
What would the two of you need to do for that to happen?

What happens when the two of you fight (have a conflict) about something?
Tell me about a time when the two of you had a fight (conflict).
What happened then?
What did you do?
Tell me about other ways in which you both fought.
What things do you fight about?

What do you think you both might fight about in mediation?
How would you like to work things out in mediation?
What would need to change for that to be possible?

How about anger? How do you and your spouse act when angry?
Describe an occasion when you were angry.
What did you do?
What did your spouse do?
What types of things make you angry?
Describe an occasion when your spouse was angry.
What did s/he do?
What did you do?

How will I know that your spouse is feeling angry in mediation?
How will I know that you are feeling angry?

Have you ever been afraid of your spouse? Or s/he of you?
If yes, what is it that you are afraid of exactly?
Do you think s/he would ever physically harm you? Has s/he ever?
What happened?
Were there other times?

III Specific Abusive Behaviours

Now, I'm going to describe things that some people do when they are angry or try to get their way. I want you to think back over the entire time that you and your spouse have been together and tell me if any of these things have ever happened. Please take your time.

Have either of you ever used threats? In other words, saying something bad would happen if the other person didn't do what s/he was told?

Has there ever been any shoving or pushing?
Choking, biting, hitting, or kicking?
Did either of you ever prevent the other from leaving a situation?
Did either of you ever threaten to or actually destroy the other person's property or harm pets?
Did either of you ever force the other to do anything against his or her will? (e.g. sexual acts)

Were there other ways (physically or psychologically) in which you and your spouse showed anger or tried to get your way in your marriage, that we haven't mentioned yet today? (If the woman acknowledges that there has been abuse, probe for frequency and severity)

Let me continue some more questions.

Does your spouse control most of your daily activities?
Do you control most aspects of your spouse's life?

Have you or your spouse ever been violently or constantly jealous of the other?

Have either of you ever used or threatened to use a knife, gun, or other weapon to harm the other or anyone else?
Do either of you own, or have either of you recently considered purchasing a weapon?
Has your spouse ever contemplated or attempted suicide?
Have you?

Now I have a few questions about alcohol and drug use.

Have you or your spouse ever had a drinking problem?
Has anyone ever complained about your drinking or your spouse's drinking? (Probe further, if necessary, for the extent of the problem and its consequences)
Do you or your spouse use illegal drugs? (probe further, if necessary, for type of drug, frequency, and consequences of use)
Tell me about it.
Has treatment been sought?
How do you think this problem will impact your/your spouse's ability to mediate or ability to follow through on any agreements your reach?

How about the children: have any of the children ever been abused by an adult physically, sexually, or psychologically? (If it is not a clear no — explore. Clarify whether the harm constitutes child abuse and whether the child is in danger.)

IV Closing the Separate Screening Session

I've been asking you a lot of specific questions about you and your spouse and how you have handled things in the past. Next I would like to ask you some questions about concerns you might have right now and your expectations for the future.

First, do you have any questions for me about mediation?

What is it that concerns you the most about mediating with your spouse?

What are you afraid your spouse might do to undermine mediation?
What could s/he do to assure you that won't happen?

What might your spouse think you would do to undermine mediation?
What could you do to assure him/her that won't happen?

What would you like to see as an outcome of mediation?
What do you think your spouse would like to see as an outcome?
What would need to happen for it to be a workable and livable outcome for each of you and be in the interests of your children?

Is there anything else you would like to ask or tell me?

If you remember something later that you did not bring up in this session, don't hesitate to let me know.

Is there anything that you have told me in our time together that you would not want me to tell your spouse?

Assessing Responses

The mediator needs to remain constantly alert for cues that there has been abuse. The abusers are likely to minimize or rationalize their actions. The abuser might be quite controlling and abrasive with the mediator or might be accommodating and charming. The abused are likely to deny or diminish any abusive behaviour and blame themselves. They are likely to fear that revealing the abuse will put them in danger. The mediator needs to use follow-up questions to clarify responses and to more clearly understand the situation.

If a client reveals that s/he has been abused, and the mediator has asked questions to better understand the situation, the mediator needs to suspend the remainder of the interview and address the client's needs. These needs include **acknowledgement, safety, and access to information.** The text will vary considerably depending on the immediate needs of the client.

Suggested text with woman who has been abused:

I know it is difficult to talk about this. I am glad you were able to tell me, because now I am better able to help you.
First, I want to say that this should not have happened to you and it is not your fault.

There are resources in the community to help you.
Do you have an attorney for your divorce?
Have you told your attorney about this? (If not, encourage her)
Where are you living now?
Do you feel safe there?

Do you know what a protective order is? (explain protective orders and peace bonds)
Do you know about shelters for women who have had similar experiences?
I'd like to take a moment now and tell you about them.
There are also other victim assistance programs.
(Provide hand-outs with information and phone numbers. Have her call right then or have her practice making the call.)

In mediation, both parties need to be able to speak up for themselves.

It sounds like you are afraid of your husband sometimes. How might that affect your ability to speak up for yourself?

Also, in mediation each needs to be able to accept the other person might disagree with them.

How do you think your husband would react if you disagreed with him about money or the kids in mediation?

Mediation is not appropriate for everyone. I think from what we have been talking about it does <u>not</u> sound like it would work well for you.

I suggest that you follow through on the other things that we have discussed and talk with your/an attorney.

* *Reproduced with permission from Linda Girdner, Ph.D.*

Appendix I.7

DOVE Screening Instrument by Desmond Ellis

***Family Court Review* 2006, 44, 658-671**

Domestic Violence, DOVE and Divorce Mediation*

Desmond Ellis Ph.D
La Marsh Centre
on Violence &
Conflict Resolution,
York University
Ontario, Canada
desellis@yorku.ca

Noreen Stuckless Ph.D
Department of Psychology
York University
Ontario, Canada

* We wish to thank The Patricia Allen Memorial Fund for funding the research that produced DOVE.

Abstract

The primary objective of this paper is to describe DOVE, a 19-item instrument designed to assess and manage the risk of domestic violence between partners during and following their participation in divorce mediation. Assessing risk, more specifically how DOVE can be used to assess risk, is described first. The resulting risk scores (TOTDOVE) are used to assign individuals to risk categories. Problems associated with using categorical, frequency and probability risk assessment formats in interpreting and communicating risk are discussed in the second segment of the paper. A dual, categorical/probability format is advocated. Managing risk using Safety Plan interventions that are linked with risk category and predictor sub scores on control, conflict, dysphoric/borderline personality, substance abuse and anger.

DOMESTIC VIOLENCE, DOVE AND DIVORCE MEDIATION

Introduction

Some critics of divorce mediation claim that it is "unsafe for women" (American Bar Association, 2000; Fund for Dispute Resolution, 1993; Fischer, Vidmar & Ellis, 1993; Ontario Association of Interval and Transition Houses, 1989; Transition House Association of Nova Scotia, 2000). An investigation of this claim yields the following two conclusions. First, it is not supported by research findings. Specifically, we found no evidence indicating that: (a) abused women are more likely than non-abused women to be the victims of physical violence and/or emotional abuse during and following their participation in divorce mediation; (b) abused women participating in divorce mediation are more likely to be victims of male ex-partner violence than abused women participating in adjudication or lawyer-negotiated separations/divorces (Ellis & Stuckless, 1992; Ellis & Stuckless, 1996; Ellis, 2000; Ellis & Anderson, 2005; Ellis, Stuckless & Wight, 2006).

Second, critics fall into two groups. Group one includes those who flatly reject divorce mediation and implicitly or explicitly recommend adjudication or lawyer negotiations as alternatives (e.g., Fischer, Vidmar & Ellis, 1993; Ontario Association of Interval and Transition Houses, 1989; Transition House Association of Nova Scotia, 2000).

Group two includes those whose criticisms include suggestions for more effectively assessing and managing the risk of domestic violence during and following mediation (e.g., American Bar Association, 2000; Fund for Dispute Resolution 1993). DOVE (Domestic Violence Evaluation) is a research-based response to their suggestions.

A review of the literature and mediation practice reveals that DOVE is not the only response to the challenge of domestic violence between separating/ divorcing partners participating in divorce mediation. Violence screening instruments have been created by Erickson and McKnight (1990), Girdner (1990) and the Woman Abuse Council of Toronto (2000), implemented by 17 court-connected mediation services in Ontario, and 149 US court-based mediation programs surveyed by Pearson (1996). Collectively, these responses provided a foundation for the creation of DOVE. At the same time, they present three problems that a more effective instrument would have to solve.

First, findings from a number of studies indicate that there are, minimally, two major types of male partner violence, control motivated and conflict instigated (Ellis & Stuckless, 1996; Ellis, Stuckless & Wight, 2006, Johnson, 1979; Johnson & Leone, 2005). Yet, questions measuring both types of violence are either not included in assessment instruments (e.g., Erickson and McKnight,

1993; Woman Abuse Council of Toronto, 2000), or male partner violence is defined as control motivated and measured using an instrument (Conflict Assessment Protocol) designed to measure conflict instigated violence (e.g., Girdner, 1990).

Second, Safety Plan interventions were either not integrated or not fully integrated with assessment data. For example, the assessment instrument used by mediators in one of Ontario's Family Courts does not include a Safety Plan. Girdner's triage instrument includes a Safety Plan but interventions other than exclusion from mediation are not identified for males in the highest risk category, "those most likely to experience harm" (p.374).

Third, none of the instruments we reviewed had been actually tested and validated by research findings. As a result, "males who have threatened suicide in relation to marital separation/divorce" or who have be "convicted of assaulting anyone" are excluded from mediation in the absence of any evidence indicating that these factors are statistically significant predictors of violence when the parties were living together and after they lived apart (Girdner, 1960: 374)

Creators of DOVE deal with these problems in the following ways. First, questions measuring control motivated and conflict instigated violence are included in the assessment segment (Part 1). Second, a Safety Plan with interventions focusing on safety during and following participation in mediation are fully integrated with assessment risk scores. Third, DOVE has been empirically validated by the results of a two-year field study of couples participating in divorce mediation in two family courts (Ellis, Stuckless & Wight, 2006).

The primary objective of this paper is to describe DOVE in sufficient detail for it to be used by divorce mediators, family lawyers and family court judges to reduce or prevent violence between partners who are separating or are separated.

Rationale for Using DOVE

Using a violence screening instrument such as DOVE to achieve this objective is warranted by the relatively high level of risk associated with separating (high base rates). Findings reported by Ellis, Stuckless and Wight (2006) indicate that a relatively high proportion of separated women experienced male partner violence and abuse after they separated. Specifically, 71 per cent (n=80) of them reported being assaulted, seriously harmed physically, emotionally abused and/or seriously harmed emotionally. Post-separation rates for each type and level of violence and abuse are presented in Ellis, Stuckless & Wight (2006).

The use of DOVE is also warranted by its demonstrated ability to identify 19 statistically significant predictors of male partner violence and abuse against female partners after they separated (Table 1).

Table 1 Statistically significant predictors of post-separation violence and abuse against female partners by male ex-partners

Predictors
Past violence
1. assaulted
2. seriously hurt physically
3. sexually assaulted
4. left home because of partner's violence
5. called police because of partner's violence
Past abuse
6. emotionally abused
7. seriously hurt emotionally
Emotional dependency
8. threats to harm kill self if partner left
9. threats to harm/kill partner if partner left
10. possessive/jealous
Relationship problems
11. hard to get along with
12. communication deficits
13. blame
14. anger
Mental health problems
15. taking medication
Control
16. tried to control partner
17. used violence/abuse to control partner.
Substance abuse
18. drinking
19. drugs

A third reason for using DOVE is that it links violence prevention interventions with (a) level of risk (b) the presence of specific types of predictors and (c) types and levels of violence and abuse.

DOVE – Part 1

DOVE is a two-part, 19 item instrument designed to assess (Part 1) and manage (Part 2) the risk of domestic violence during and following participation in divorce mediation. The earliest version of DOVE included 33 items. The results of a pilot project indicated that the number of items (hypothesized predictors) should be reduced to 19. These items were validated by data collected from three independent sources – surveys of women in four shelters for battered women, a review of the literature and the authors' own theory and research on linkages between separation and violence.

The 19 items are statistically significant predictors of assaults, assaults that result in serious physical injury, sexual assaults, emotional abuse and emotional abuse that results in serious emotional harm. More specifically, the significant predictors refer to conduct, events and experiences that occurred or were present when the partners were living together. For example, male partner assaults against female partners when the couples lived together predicts male partners assaults against female partners after they separated (n =72, r. 386 p<.001). Another example. Male partner control (item 18) predicts female partner reports of being seriously hurt physically following separation (n=56, r. 297 p<. 026) (Ellis, Wight & Stuckless, 2006). In addition to different types of assault and levels of physical and emotional abuse the items identified in Table 1 refer to seven different sub-sets of predictors. They are, past violence, past abuse, emotional dependency, relationship problems, mental health problems, control and substance abuse.

Assessing Risk

Part 1 of DOVE is administered by the mediator to each partner privately at intake. Both partners are asked to respond to them as victims, observers or knowledgeable persons. As a result, Part 1 completed by female partners provide information about male partners and *vice versa.*

Risk assessment items included in Table 1 are measured using answers to the questions and responses to the statements described in the Appendix. The questions and statements refer to two time periods, when the partners lived together and after they separated. Answers and responses relevant to the first time period are used to predict answers and responses to the same questions and statements relevant to the second time period.

An examination of the Appendix will reveal that DOVE items were measured in terms of their frequency when they referred to the conjugal period and dichotomously when they refer to the period following separation. This was done because, in pre-testing DOVE, we found that partners were reluctant to take the time to answer all questions when they had to provide frequency answers for all items covering both time periods. A number of them responded by skipping questions. The number of skipped questions was markedly reduced when the time taken to complete Dove was reduced to about 12 minutes by replacing frequency answers by categorical yes/no answers for items relevant to the period following separation. In those cases where questions were not answered, the "80% rule" was invoked in calculating the risk scores used to locate individuals in risk categories.

The "80% rule" was used to (a) eliminate cases where individuals did not respond to 80% or more of the questions and statements identified in table 1, and (b) calculate risk scores for individuals who responded to 80% or more but not all (100%) of the of the questions and statements.

A noteworthy feature of the procedure used in placing individuals in risk categories is the use of four different measures in calculating risk scores. These are, different types of violence and abuse reported by victims (PRESENCE); how frequently they experienced violent and/or abusive acts (TOTFREQ); experiencing violent and/or abusive acts since separation (SINSEP); and the seriousness of physical and emotional injuries (ELEVATED).

Risk scores vary in the weight attached to them. Pilot project findings suggested that risk scores should be weighted as follows: More recent (SINSEP) scores are weighted more heavily than pre-separation (conjugal) scores. Predictors of serious physical injury (ELEVATED) are weighted more heavily than predictors that are not significantly associated with this outcome. Elevated predictors present since separation (ELSINSEP) are weighted most heavily (Appendix).

Four risk categories are identified in the Appendix. These are Low, Moderately High, High and Very High. Placement of individuals in one of these four risk categories is dependent upon their risk scores. Risk category cut-off points were empirically generated so as to produce roughly equal numbers in each category. Findings from an on-going study of domestic violence during the high risk four-month period following the closing of the mediation file will provide a more valid empirical basis for maintaining or changing cut-off points.

Two methods of calculating TOTDOVE scores and using them to place individuals in risk categories are described in detail in the Appendix. Method A, the simplest and quickest, can be used where partners answer all 19 questions and statements. We found that mediators can ensure that all 19 questions/statements are responded to by administering DOVE themselves instead of handing DOVE to partners and asking them to complete it. Partner responses to DOVE questions and statements can be directly entered into a computer and an EXCEL-based software package is available for immediately calculating total DOVE scores (TOTDOVE) and assigning individuals to risk categories.

How do we know that partners' answers to DOVE questions and statements are accurate? Criterion related validity is usually used to answer this question, but we could not use it because medical, police and child welfare data that would corroborate answers are treated as confidential. In other cases corroborative data could not be used because they were incomplete. For example, family court files could not be used because assault charges laid by the police were not included in them. One step we did take was to compare male and female partner responses to specific questions such as, "Called police because partner physically assaulted me". Comparisons yielded consistent answers. In addition, we looked for consistency in the answers provided by each partner to different questions. Thus, all female partners who reported calling the police because they were physically assaulted by their male partners (Item 7 in DOVE) also reported being assaulted by them (Item 1).

Procedures for calculating risk scores and placing individuals in risk categories are described in the last segment entitled *Administering DOVE: Instructions.*

Communicating Risk

Using DOVE to assess risk may yield accurate predictions of relatively frequently occurring, specific types and levels of male partner violence and abuse over a relatively short, high-risk period of time, yet the way in which risk is interpreted and communicated to others "can render risk assessment ... completely useless or even worse than useless, if it gives [assessors themselves and others] the wrong impression" (Heilbrun, Dvoskin, Hart & McNeil, 1999:94). Impressions created by risk assessment formats influence decision-making, and wrong impressions or interpretations can lead to bad or improper decisions about Safety Plan interventions that may adversely affect the quality of life of both partners.

The impressions and interpretations of mediators and other assessors are strongly influenced by the amount and kind of information produced by the risk assessment format they are using. Violence risk assessment formats that produce more information without inflating or deflating the risk posed by individuals being assessed yield more accurate impressions and interpretations than those that provide relatively little information and exaggerate the risk posed by individuals being assessed. Of the three risk assessment formats most frequently cited in the literature, categorical formats (high, medium, low) yield less information than frequency (20 out of 100) and probability (20%) formats. Moreover, for organizational, policy or fund-raising purposes, categorical formats can be used to inflate or deflate risk by creating cut-off points that increase the number of individuals in different risk categories (Slovic, Monahan & MacGregor, 200: 293).

DOVE assesses risk by using a categorical format (Low, Moderately High, High and Very High – Appendix) but it provides more information by providing an empirically generated range of risk scores for each risk category. Moreover, DOVE risk categories are linked with Safety Plan interventions aimed at managing risk. Still, this format suffers from its inability to provide quantitative assessments of risk for individuals in each of the four categories. Frequency and probabilistic formats provide this information. Findings on "serious physical injury since separation" for partners in the family court sample reported by Ellis, Stuckless and Wight (2000) can be used to illustrate the point.

Serious physical injuries

Risk category	*Dove scores*	*N*	*no*	*yes*	*% yes*
Low	0 to 19	42	37	5	12
Moderately high	19.1 to 2.7	23	18	5	23
High	27.1 to 37	37	23	14	38
Very high	37.1 to 100	24	11	13	54

The risk category format provides four risk category names and the range of DOVE scores linked with them. The following additional information is provided by the frequency format or scale: 5 out of 42 partners in the low risk category, 5 out of 23 partners in the moderately high risk category, 14 out of 37 partners in the high risk category and 13 out of 24 partners in the very high risk category for seriously injuring an ex-partner. The probabilistic format/scale provides the following additional information: 12% of the partners in the low, 23% of partners in the moderately high, 38% of partners in the high and 54% of the partners in the very high risk category for seriously injuring an ex-partner.

> **In interpreting the categories/figures presented above it is important to note that they refer to a median of three years since separation. Assuming that the serious injuries reported by separated women are equally distributed across the three years, the percentages must be divided by three to yield a "past 12 months" rate. Thus, the yearly rates reported by women in the low and very high risk categories would be 4% and 18% respectively.**

Frequency and probability formats provide additional information but the latter are less likely than the former to exaggerate the risk posed by partners (Slovic, Monahan and MacGregor, 2000). These researchers found that "at any given level of likelihood, a patient [partner] was judged as posing a higher risk if that likelihood was derived from a frequency scale (e.g. 10 out of 100) than if it was derived from a probability scale (e.g., 10%) (p.271). Why? Because assessors, and the people to whom they communicate risk using a frequency scale tend to focus on the numerator, the number of individuals likely to behave violently and not on the denominator, "out of how many" individuals. Focusing on the numerator elicits "frightening images" (p.292) and fear leads to higher perceptions of risk.

For this reason, we suggest a dual categorical/probability format approach. To this end, we included risk estimates for assaults, assaults resulting in serious injuries, emotional abuse and emotional abuse resulting in serious emotional harm against female ex-partners on the last page of the Appendix. As data from the second, post-mediation phase of this study are collected and analyzed the percentages reported will become more stable and will include data on male partner victims because the sample size will be much greater.

Guidelines for communicating risk are described in *Administering DOVE: Instructions.*

Managing Risk

Risk is managed by invoking interventions suggested by the Safety Plan. The DOVE Safety Plan is grounded in two assumptions. The first one is that partners who do not interact with each other in person, or who only interact with each other in the presence of third parties who can act as guardians or serve as credible witnesses are unlikely to physically harm each other. Separating and separated partners who do not communicate with each other, or who only communicate with each other through third parties who are trusted by recipients are unlikely to abuse each other emotionally.

The second assumption is that individuals who are highly motivated to harm their ex-partners are more likely to do so than individuals whose motivation is low. The relation between the first (opportunity) and second (motivation) assumption is *additive.* That is, violence and abuse can occur when the motivation to harm is low or absent, but the situation in which both partners are present instigates violence and/or abuse, and also when the opportunity for violence/abuse is low or absent, but the motivation to harm is high.

An example of the first kind of additive relation is provided by the case of a divorced mother who comes to her ex-husband's home to pick up their seven-year old child after his week-end stay. The exchange had always been cordial, but she is verbally attacked when she asks him for the child-support money he had promised to pay when she arrived, and she is slapped by him when she threatens to report him the government agency responsible for enforcing child support orders.

An example of the second additive relation is provided by the case of an ex-wife who has gone into hiding with her two young children because she is afraid the husband will harm her. She is found with a serious stab wound administered by the ex-husband who spent a lot of time and money tracking her down.

The Safety Plan interventions invoked by mediators, family lawyers or judges using DOVE are dependent upon the individual's risk category placement and scores on five treatment modalities. Risk category placement should elicit interventions aimed at making participation in divorce mediation safer and fairer. Interventions focusing on mediation procedures are cumulative. That is, interventions invoked for individuals in a higher risk category include those invoked for individuals in a lower risk category plus additional interventions appropriate for the higher risk category. Interventions invoked for individuals placed in the four risk categories are presented in the DOVE Administration: Instructions segment at the end of the article.

Within each risk category DOVE scores may vary with respect to one or more of five treatment modalities to which the parties can be referred. Three of them refer to the frequency and seriousness of violence and abuse - *Coercive Control Motivated, Conflict Instigated, Anger Instigated. Substance Abuse* is the fourth and *Dysphoric-Borderline Personality* is the fifth modality (Appendix). Appropriate treatment interventions are those that are explicitly designed to treat individuals with high scores on one or more of these modalities. (Adams, 1988; O'Leary, Neidig & Heymann, 1995; Ptacek, 1998). Although it was not identified as a statistically significant predictor of post-separation violence, conflict is included because it predicts emotional abuse and also because children are harmed by high levels of conflict between separating and separated parents (Ellis & Anderson, 2006; Special Joint Committee on Custody and Access, 1998).

Procedures for managing risk are described in *Administering DOVE: Instructions.*

Caveats

We conclude this article by repeating two points made in the conclusion of an earlier article (Ellis, Stuckless & Wight, 2000). First, DOVE is not a substitute for but a supplement to the professional judgment and intuition of divorce mediators and any other relevant information they may have access to.

Second, safety interventions should be requested from female victims of male partner violence, and their recommended interventions should be taken seriously. They know their partners very well and are highly motivated to promote their own safety as well as the safety of their children.

References

Adams, D. (1988) Treatment models of men who batter: A pro-feminist analysis. In K. Yllo & M. Bograd (Eds.) *Feminist perspectives on wife abuse*. Pp. 90-113. Newbury Park, CA: Sage.

American Bar Association (2000) *Report to the House of Delegates.* Commission on Domestic Violence section of Dispute Resolution.

Ellis, D. (2000) Safety, equity and human agency: Contributions of divorce mediation. *Violence Against Women,* 6, 1012-1027.

Ellis, D., & Anderson, D. (2005) *Conflict resolution: An introductory text.* Toronto: Emond-Montgomery.

Ellis, D., Stuckless, N., & Wight, L. (2006) Separation, domestic violence and divorce mediation. *Conflict Resolution Quarterly* (Winter, Forthcoming)

Ellis, D., & Stuckless, N. (1996) *Mediating and negotiating marital conflicts.* Thousand Oaks, CA: Sage.

Ellis, D., & Stuckless, N. (1992) Pre-separation abuse, marital conflict mediation and post-separation abuse. *Mediation Quarterly,* 9, 205-225.

Erickson, S., & McKnight, M. (1990) Mediating spousal abuse divorces. *Mediation Quarterly*, 7, 377-388.

Fischer, K., Vidmar, N., & Ellis, r. (1993) The culture of battering and the role of mediation in domestic violence cases. *SMU Law Review*, 46, 2117-2174.

Fund for Dispute Resolution (1993) Report for the Toronto Forum on Woman Abuse and Divorce mediation. Waterloo, Ontario.

Girdner, L. (1990) Mediation triage: Screening for spouse abuse in divorce mediation. *Mediation Quarterly,* 7, 365-376.

Heilbrun, K., Dvoskin, J., Hart, S., & McNeil, D. (1999) Violence risk communication: Implications for research, policy and practice. *Health, Risk and Society,* 1, 91-106.

Johnson, M.P. (1995) Patriarchal terrorism and common couple violence: two forms of violence against women. *Journal of Marriage and the Family,* 57, 283-294.

Johnson, M.P., & Leone, P.M. (2005) The differential effects of intimate terrorism and situational couple violence: findings from the National Violence Against Women Survey. *Journal of Family Issues,* 26, 322-349.

O'Leary, K.D., Neidig, P.H., & Heymann, R.E. (1995) Assessment and treatment of partner abuse: A synopsis for the legal profession. *Albany Law Review,* 58, 1215-1234.

Ontario Association of Interval and Transition Houses (1989) *Stop the violence against women.* Background report. Toronto.

Pearson, J. (1996) *Divorce mediation & domestic violence.* Center for Policy Research, Denver, Colorado.

Ptacek, J. (1998) Why do men batter? In K.Yllo & M. Bograd (Eds.) *Feminist perspectives on wife abuse.* Pp. 133-157. Newbury Park, CA: Sage.

Slovic, P., Monahan, J., & MacGregor, D.G. (2000) Violence risk assessment and risk communication; The effects of using actual cases, providing information and employing probability versus frequency formats. *Law and Human Behavior,* 24, 271- 296.

Special Joint Committee on Custody and Access (1988) *For the Sake of the Children.* Parliament of Canada, Ottawa.

Transition House Association of Nova Scotia (2000) *Abused women in family mediation: A Nova Scotia Snapshot.* Halifax, Nova Scotia.

Woman Abuse Council of Toronto (2000) A Tool for risk assessment in woman abuse situations. Toronto.

DOVE SCREENING TOOL & ADMINISTRATION: by Desmond Ellis

INSTRUCTIONS

INTAKE

Prior to the start of mediation, mediator personally administers DOVE to each party separately.

SUGGESTED LANGUAGE

Divorce mediation is best able to help parties solve important problems they want to have solved when both parties feel safe in fully expressing their thoughts and feelings. If only one party feels safe, then he/she may feel that any agreement they may reach will not be fair. In order to provide a safe and fair divorce mediation process, we ask all separating/divorcing ex-partners a few questions about different kinds of events that may have occurred *when they were living together* and *after they separated* (began living in separate homes). If you find a question upsetting, please let me know so we can talk about it.

ASSESSING RISK

Procedure

1. [a] Count the total number of risk markers circled/ checked [0, 1, 2, 3, 4 or 5] **excluding** d/k and n/a. Enter total number of MARKERS line.	MARKERS Sub-total scores
[b] Assign **1** point for each risk marker present [1, 2, 3, 4, or 5 circled/checked]. **Add** them to calculate *total present score* [PRESENT].	1. PRESENT
2. **Add** the numbers circled/checked for each risk marker. Thus, if 3, 4 and 5 are circled for questions 16, 17 and 18, add 3, 4 and 5. Add the numbers circled for all 19 questions to obtain a *total frequency score* [TOTFREQ].	2. TOTFREQ
3. Assign **2** points for each risk marker present since separation. **Add** points to calculate total *since separation score* [SINSEP]	3. SINSEP
4. Assign **3** points for each ELEVATED RISK MARKER present. These are identified on the next page. **Add** points to calculate *total elevated risk marker total Score* [ELEVATED]	4. ELEVATED
5. Assign **5** points for each ELEVATED risk marker present SINCE SEPARATION. **Add** points to calculate total *elevated risk marker since separation score* [ELSINSEP]	5. ELSINSEP

6. There are two methods [a] and [b] of calculating TOTSCORE depending upon the MARKERS score.
   [a] If MARKERS score is 19, add five sub-total scores to calculate total risk score [TOTSCORE] TOTSCORE
   [b] If MARKERS score is less than 19 then:
   Add five sub-total scores Enter total on
   Line ________

Divide total by MARKERS score
   Multiply by 19 to calculate [TOTSCORE] TOTSCORE

Example- Method [b]
   MARKERS = 16
   5 sub-total scores (PRESENT to ELSINSAP) = 124
   Divide 124 by 16 = 7.8
   Multiply 7.8 by 19 = 148 = TOTSCORE

7. **Divide** TOTSCORE by 2.25 to calculate *total DOVE Score* [TOTDOVE] TOTDOVE
8. Use TOTDOVE scores to assign clients to RISK CATEGORIES by placing a check mark on the appropriate line. The TOTDOVE score ranges for different risk categories are:

Scores	Risk Category
0 to 19	LOW __
19.1 to 27	MODERATE__
27.1 to 37	HIGH __
37.1 to 100	VERY HIGH __

Elevated Risk Markers
1. Physically assaulted
4. Seriously hurt physically
6. Medications for mental health problems
7. Called police
9. Complained about drinking
11.Outbursts of anger
13. Poor communication/social skills
18. Possessive/jealous
19. Control

COMMUNICATING RISK

Use a categorical/probability format. For example, an ex-partner who, on the basis of his/her DOVE score is placed in the HIGH risk category (p.10) is a member of a risk category in which 38% of ex-partners located in the same risk category were reported to have inflicted serious injuries on his/her ex-partner and 62% were not reported to have done so. If the ex-partner's DOVE score places him/her in the VERY HIGH risk category (p.10), then he is a member of a risk category in which 54% of ex-partners in the same category were reported to have inflicted serious injuries on his/her ex-partner and 46% were not reported to have done so.

NOTE: These risk estimates are for ex-partners who were reported to have inflicted serious injuries "since separation". You are primarily interested in "abuse or physical violence occurring during or following participation in divorce mediation". These data are in the process of being collected from a court-connected divorce mediation service in Kingston, Ontario. Results will be published in an updated website in Spring 2008. In order to collect the same data for your own clients, administer DOVE 2 (see DOVE website) by telephone to them 4 months after their mediations ended. Stable results require information from at least 50 male and 50 female clients. If this information is sent to us, we shall integrate it with ours as well as information sent to us from other divorce mediation services in the US and Canada. Divorce mediators can then make much more reliable risk estimates using a categorical/probabilistic format.

Categorical/probability risk assessments for violence and abuse reported by female ex-partners to have been perpetrated by male ex-partners since separation are presented below. These data were obtained from clients of two family court connected divorce mediation services.

ASSAULTS		
Risk category	n	% yes
Low	18	0
Moderately high	15	7
High	20	13
Very high	19	16
ASSAULTS RESULTING IN SERIOUS INJURY		
Low	18	28
Moderately high	14	36
High	21	62
Very high	16	63
EMOTIONAL ABUSE		
Low	19	37
Moderately high	17	71
High	20	85
Very high	17	88
SERIOUSLY HURT EMOTIONALLY		
Low	18	28
Moderately high	14	36
High	21	62
Very high	16	63

MANAGING RISK

Managing risk requires the mediator to make decisions of two kinds. The first involves procedural interventions. The second involves referrals for appropriate treatment by community-based agents and agencies.

Procedural Interventions

Low risk

1. Clearly stated written "rules of civility" that encourage respectful communications and specifically exclude coercive conduct during and between mediation sessions
2. Parties agree in writing to terminate mediation if the mediator obtains credible evidence of threatened or actual violence and/or abuse
3. Face-to-face mediation
4. Referrals to appropriate treatment interventions

Moderate risk

5. Mediator carefully monitors compliance with violence/abuse prevention rules during private interviews with partners, and/or by communicating with third parties identified as trusted contact persons by partners
6. Partners arrive and leave at different times or routes and do not wait in the same room
7. Mediators provide both partners with a list of community resources such as shelters, men's programs, health services, male and female support groups and legal information
8. Face-to-face mediation with advocate or supporter present, or shuttle mediation
9. Referrals to appropriate treatment interventions

High risk

10. Partners given safety warnings in writing
11. Interpersonal contact only takes place in public places or with trusted third parties present
12. Arrange for third party to be present during exchanges of children, or third party transports children
13. Communication only through trusted third parties or through journals exchanged with children and subject to monitoring by mediator
14. Partners escorted to and from premises where mediation is being conducted
15. Shuttle, telephone or online mediation
16. Referral to appropriate treatment interventions

Very high risk

17. Referral to appropriate treatment interventions
18. Telephone or online mediation if referrals produce credible evidence of positive personal and/or situational change

Question/Statement	When: At any time while you were living together How Often?						How Often? Since you separated- start living in separate residences Check one for each Question/Statement			
	Never	Once	A Few Times	Often	Very Often	All the Time	Yes	No	N/A	D/K
18. Partner was extremely possessive and jealous	0	1	2	3	4	5				
19. Partner tried to control you	0	1	2	3	4	5				

Is there anything you wish to add? If yes, please write in the space below.

Thank You

REFERRAL INSTRUCTIONS

Control Motivated & Conflict Instigated

a. Enter the number checked for each item (from 1 to 5)

b. Add them to derive a reading score

c. Add 3 to total score if item 3*, another 3 if item 4* and another 3 if item 5* is checked "1 or more times". Add 9 if all three items are checked "1 or more times"

d. Add 3 to total score for each item checked"since separation"

e. If the total score is 33 or more **AND** the combined score for items 17 and 19 is 5 or more label this **Control Motivated**

f. If the total score is 33 or more **AND** the combined score for items 17 and 19 is less than 5 label this **Conflict Instigated**

DOVE ITEMS

1 2 3* 4* 5* 7 8 17 19

Dysphoric/Borderline

a. Enter the number checked for each item (1 to 5)

b. Add them to derive a total score

c. Add 3 to total score if item 15 is checked and another 3 if item16 is checked "1 or more times". Add 6 if both items are checked "one or more times".

DOVE ITEMS

6 12 13 14 15 16 18 9 10

d. Add 3 to total score for each item checked "since separation"
e. If the total score is 33 or more **OR** Items 15 or 16 are checked one or more times "since separation" label this **Dysphoric/Borderline**

Substance Abuse

a. Enter the number checked for each item (1 to 5) 9 10
b. Add them to derive a total score
c. Add 3 for each item checked "since separation"
d. If the total score is 8 or more and the item 9 score is higher label this **Substance Abuse/a** if the item 10 score is higher label it **Substance Abuse/d**; if both scores are equally high label it **Substance abuse/ad.**

Anger

a. Enter the number checked for Item 11 (1 to 5) 11
b. Add 3 if it was checked "since separation"
c. If the total score is 6 or more label this **Anger instigated**

DOVE SUB-SCORES & TREATMENT MODALITIES

Treatment Modality A : Control Motivated

Group programs that directly confront and challenge the male partner's attempts to control his female partner through the use of violence and abuse. Usually in a group context, attempts are made to change values and ways of thinking that legitimate the male partner's sense of entitlement and his firm belief that his violence and abuse are justifiable (Lundy Bancroft, *Why Does He Do That?: Inside the Minds of Angry and Controlling Men* (2002)).

Examples: EMERGE (Connecticut); Duluth Abuse Intervention Project MN. Feminist – Cognitive-Behavioral treatment group groups

Treatment Modality B : Conflict Instigated

Violence and abuse are ways of settling conflicts that are used by partners who do not possess the skills needed to settle conflicts in ways that do not inflict physical of emotional harm on each other. Group programs aimed at teaching these skills and motivating partners to use them in settling conflicts are grounded in this assumption.

Examples: Cognitive-behavioral group programs and conflict resolution programs

Treatment Modality C: Dysphoric/Borderline

Group programs aimed specifically at helping patients manage depression and the severe emotional trauma, rage and despair associated with perceiving separation/divorce as utter abandonment.

Example: Dialectical Behavioral Therapy

Treatment Modality D: Substance Abuse

Violence and abuse are used by partners when they have consumed or are consuming alcohol, have or are using drugs with violence/abuse eliciting characteristics or are in a stressed/agitated state because they cannot get the drugs they want or are addicted to, and further violence/abuse can be prevented by eliminating the use of alcohol and drugs. Group programs aimed at preventing partner violence and abuse by eliminating the use of alcohol and drugs are grounded in this assumption.

Examples: Alcoholics Anonymous; Feminist-Cognitive-Behavioral treatment groups

Treatment Modality E: Anger Instigated

Group programs aimed undermining the legitimacy of using anger as a justification for violence and abuse, and teaching and motivating partners to control their anger and/or express their angry feelings non-violently.

Examples: Anger management treatment groups; Cognitive-behavioral treatment groups

* *Reproduced with permission from Prof. Desmond Ellis.*

Appendix I.8

Modifying Mediation or Collaborative Law

Helpful Hints for B Couples, and Possibly C Couples

1. Check the level of comfort being in the same room, and discussing issues when the other person is present.
2. What would happen if there was a disagreement?
3. Check with respect to safety during mediation or collaborative law:
   a. What are their living arrangements — do they live together? Check possible risk to children.
   b. Check safety pre, during and post mediation or collaborative law sessions.
   c. Create guidelines for communication between sessions and in the sessions.
   d. Determine whether support people are needed, either in the waiting room or in the session.
4. Check to be sure they have independent legal advice.
5. Determine their financial status — is the woman receiving interim support, can they afford to pay your fees, or the fees of independent lawyers?

Appendix I.9

Safe Termination of Mediation or Arbitration

For "C" and Possibly "B" Couples

Do's — Meeting With Victim (Statistics suggest that the victim will be a woman. Where this is not the case, substitute the appropriare gender.)

After screening and deciding NOT to go ahead. …

- Find out about their current situation.
- Ask how they arrived at the decision to come to Mediation or Arbitration.

- Discuss why Mediation or Arbitration are not appropriate and alternatives that might better protect her and the children.
- Ask victim what would be a helpful approach for terminating safely i.e. ask the victim for advice as to how to approach termination of Mediation or Arbitration with the abuser (rely on her wisdom).

Safety Planning:

With Victim

- Form a plan with the victim about next steps (suggest resources, discuss details of a plan).
- Tell victim what you will tell abuser and make a safety plan for her and the children in case abuser blames victim.
    - Ask: Are you worried about your safety now? How will abuser react to Mediation or Arbitration not going ahead?
    - Especially if they are still living together, ask: Do you feel safe in your present living arrangement? If not, have you talked to a woman's advocate or lawyer? Encourage her to do so — give names, addresses, and phone numbers. Help her make contact.
    - Do you know of any emergency shelters in case you need to find a place of safety for you and the children? Give names and phone numbers.
    - Do you have any other safe place to go? Do you have any money? Have you ever contacted the police?

Do's — Meeting With Abuser

- Clarify the purpose of the confidential initial meeting, i.e. to determine the best option for approaching their marital issues (Mediation or Arbitration is one option).
- Find out how the separation decision was made, and how the abuser feels about the decision (his "hopes" with respect to the decision).
- Find out why he chose mediation and what his understanding of mediation is.
- Find out how he and the partner made decisions in the marriage. Was the decision-making satisfactory? Were there any obstacles to good decision-making?
- Return to purpose of meeting and clarify "any misunderstandings".
    - Assist abuser to see that mediation is unlikely to be suitable or productive or meet his needs (i.e., it is not likely to succeed and therefore there will be added delay and cost).
    - Utilize abuser's language, information, and rationale if appropriate.
    - State that mediator has a "gut feeling", based on his or her experience, that mediation is unlikely to succeed in this case, i.e., take personal responsibility for termination.
    - For "B couples", if guidelines are set and not adhered to, focus on this as the basis for termination.

- Tell abuser that they are not ready for mediation. Suggest what needs to happen first (e.g., counselling re effect of separation). They may be ready in the future.

Safety Planning

With Abuser

- Ask: Do you have a lawyer? Encourage him to get one. Give names, addresses, and phone numbers.
- Ask: Do you have a counsellor? Encourage him to get one and to enter a Batterer's Treatment Program if appropriate.

Do Not's

- If abuse has not already been disclosed, don't reveal abuse to abuser's solicitor or to court because this could endanger victim.
- Don't blame or put down victim.

Appendix I.10

Landau Domestic Violence Screening Report for Arbitration

Dr. Barbara Landau

Note: Screener circle "YES" or "NO" for all of the following statements

SCREENING FOR VOLUNTARINESS, DOMESTIC VIOLENCE, SIGNIFICANT POWER IMBALANCE ISSUES, CAPACITY FOR PARTICIPATION

1. Both parties are entering Family Arbitration voluntarily YES NO

IF YES: Continue Screening IF NO: Recommend No Family Arbitration

---

2. The screener has concerns about:
   - domestic violence or the safety of one or both parties YES NO
   - drug or alcohol abuse YES NO
   - mental illness YES NO
3. The screener has safety concerns affecting the children YES NO

NOTE: IF ANSWER TO QUESTION 2. OR 3. IS "YES" THE SCREENER MAY HAVE A REPORTING OBLIGATION

4. The screener has concerns about the parties participating and giving evidence in the presence of the other due to fear, intimidation or duress
YES NO

5. The screener recommends
   - the presence of counsel in the Arbitration YES NO
   - other procedural measures to ensure safety YES NO

OUTCOME: If questions 2-5 are answered "NO" recommend arbitration with no special procedures or preconditions.

IF ANSWERS to QUESTIONS 2-5 ARE "YES"
RECOMMENDED OUTCOME: The arbitration should proceed only if one or more of the following relevant conditions are in place: SCREENER CHECKS ALL THAT ARE APPROPRIATE:

Modifying the Process:
- The alleged abuser arrives first and leaves last and is seated in a separate waiting area
- The parties are represented and counsel are present at all times
- Evidence is given by sworn affidavit and the lawyers argue the case without the parties
- The parties remain in separate rooms and the arbitrator and counsel move between the rooms to address the issues so both sides have an opportunity to respond to evidence

Preconditions:
- Ground Rules are established to limit and/or structure communication and contact between parties outside of the arbitration e.g. no communication re: issues submitted to med-arb between sessions
- The parties are living separate and apart in different residences
- An interim parenting plan is in place with considerations for the safety of the children e.g. detailed structured plan, minimize parental contact at transitions, etc. (allows parents to separate)
- Participation in Anger Management and/or drug or alcohol treatment and/or counseling

ALTERNATIVES TO FAMILY ARBITRATION: Court, custody assessment, or negotiations between lawyers for the parties.

WHO RECEIVES THE REPORT?
- The arbitrator Note: Obligation to continue to screen throughout.

The arbitrator makes a statement to counsel or the parties if NOT represented that either the parties ARE or ARE NOT appropriate or MAY BE appropriate for Arbitration under certain conditions. If the conditions are accepted, the Arbitration proceeds with the arbitrator monitoring the conditions. If the conditions are not accepted or are breached the arbitration may not proceed.

NOTES:

1. The regulations create a need to balance the safety of participants with the requirement of arbitrator impartiality.
2. If lawyers are present, evidence should be led on any issue noted in Q's 2-5 especially evidence affecting safety of the children or the parents.
3. A safety plan should be in place in advance of presenting this evidence e.g. the parties should be living in separate residences, to avoid safety concerns triggered by presenting such evidence

---

Appendix I.11

Clarke & Murphy Confidential Screening Report for Family Arbitration

Antoinette Clarke and Darlene Murphy

Name of Screener
Address
Contact numbers

Re: ____

This report confirms that the parties' ____________________________ and ____________________________ have each completed an individual screening session with ______________________. The purpose of the screening is to identify domestic violence and power imbalances that exist between the parties as these relate to the arbitration process.

Screening recommendations are based on responses to a questionnaire, specific questions asked by the screener and the screener's assessment of the information given by each party.

O YES FAMILY ARBITRATION IS RECOMMENDED

Based on the results of the individual screening sessions with each of the parties it is determined that the parties may proceed with Family Arbitration.

O FAMILY ARBITRATION IS NOT RECOMMENDED AT THIS TIME

Based on the results of the individual screening sessions with each of the parties it is determined that at this time the parties should not proceed with Family Arbitration at this time.

FOLLOW UP

O Yes

The parties have been provided with referrals to community resources and/or alternative options for resolving their issue(s).

O No

The parties have not been provided with referrals to community resources and/or alternative options for resolving their issue(s).

NOTE

This report may be used only to determine suitability for arbitration and safety issues. The report is not to be used to decide any issue in arbitration, including credibility of the parties.

______________________________	______________________
Name of Screener	**Date report completed**

Confidential Screening Report for Family Arbitration #2

Name of Screener
Address
Contact numbers

Re: ____

This report confirms that the parties ________________________ and ________________________ have each completed an individual screening session with ____________________. The purpose of the screening was to identify domestic violence and power imbalances that exist between the parties as these relate to the arbitration process.

Screening recommendations are based on responses to a questionnaire, specific questions asked by the screener and the screener's assessment of the information given by each party.

O YES FAMILY ARBITRATION IS RECOMMENDED

Based on the results of the individual screening sessions with each of the parties it is determined that the parties may proceed with Family Arbitration.

O ONLY WITH THE FOLLOWING PROTECTION(S) IS FAMILY ARBITRATION RECOMMENDED

Based on the results of the individual screening sessions with each of the parties it is recommended that the parties may proceed with Family Arbitration only with the following measures in place:

____

____

____

____

____

____

____

____

O FAMILY ARBITRATION IS NOT RECOMMENDED AT THIS TIME

Based on the results of the individual screening sessions with each of the parties it is recommended that the parties should not proceed with Family Arbitration at this time.

FOLLOW UP

O Yes

The parties have been provided with referrals to community resources and/or alternative options for resolving their issue(s).

O No

The parties have not been provided with referrals to community resources and/or alternative options for resolving their issue(s).

NOTE

This report may be used only to determine suitability for arbitration and safety issues. The report is not to be used to decide any issue in arbitration, including credibility of the parties.

______________________________ ____________________

Name **Date**

Appendix II Contents

Mediation

Appendix II.1

Outline of Mediation Procedure

As a general outline, the procedure in mediation is as follows:

(a) *Intake call(s) and pre-mediation screening:*

- clarify how clients were referred and why;
- collect basic background information, including whether clients are living together or separately (addresses and phone numbers), ages of children, and issues to be mediated;
- conduct preliminary screening for abuse;
- explain the mediation process, fees, *etc.*;
- obtain names, addresses, and phone numbers of solicitors;
- ask if lawyers have been collaboratively trained and retained as CFL lawyers; and
- send out an information package regarding mediation and client questionnaire (include questions about abuse, control, comfort level negotiating with the other party, demographic information, and preferred outcome on issues)

(b) *Meet with counsel for the parties in order to:*

- establish whether mediation will be open, partially open, or closed;
- determine whether a Collaborative Mediation can be used;
- clarify what issues are to be mediated;
- clarify payment of fees;
- review and sign retainer contract and Collaborative Mediation Participation Agreement;
- permit counsel, in each other's presence, to summarize the significant issues in the case and any legal steps taken;
- screen for abuse and control; and
- explain the mediation or Collaborative Mediation process.

(c) *Meet with the parties together*[*] *in order to:*

- explain the mediator's role as an objective, impartial professional as between the parents;
- encourage the parents to consider the best interests of the child(ren) in reaching a resolution to the issues in dispute;
- if one or both do not have a lawyer, discuss importance of independent legal advice and recommend both retain a Collaborative Family Law Lawyer.

---

[*] If there is any concern about abuse or control, an individual screening meeting should take place at separate times before a joint meeting and before a decision is made to mediate. The victim of abuse (usually the woman) should be interviewed first.

- discuss the differences between open, partially open, and closed mediation in order to determine each party's preference;
- review and sign retainer contract;
- observe and try to improve the communication between the parents; and
- assist the parents to identify the issues and encourage them to work towards their own resolution of the issues in dispute, particularly where children are involved.

(d) *Meet with each parent individually in order to:*

- obtain relevant personal and relationship history;
- explore each parent's needs, interests, concerns and goals for the mediation; and
- screen for abuse and control.

(e) *Meet with the child(ren) individually, with siblings (if any), and possibly with each parent* (this step is necessary for custody and access mediation only) in order to:

- screen for abuse, fear, intimidation or witnessing abuse;
- identify concerns and special needs and interests; and
- obtain constructive suggestions, preferences and priorities from the child's perspective (without asking the child to take sides).
- assess each child's temperament, maturity and ability to adapt to change; and
- assess child's comfort level with extended family and readiness to accept new partners.

(f) *Meet with other significant adults* who are influential in decision-making or who will be playing a caretaking role, such as new and common-law spouses, grandparents, and other caretakers (this step is usually only necessary in custody and access mediation).

(g) *Request information from sources relevant to the issues in dispute*, such as lawyers, schools, family doctors, mental health professionals, (and if property or financial issues are involved) Certified Divorce Specialist, accountants, property appraisers, business valuators, *etc.*

(h) *Prepare a Memorandum of Understanding and/or report:*

- If parents reach agreement, set out the agreement reached.
- If parents do not reach agreement, any report depends on whether it is "*open*" or "*partially open*" or "*closed*" mediation.

In my experience, mediation takes approximately twelve to twenty hours of interviews. It is difficult to judge the exact number of hours because this depends on the number of issues to be mediated, the type of issues, the complexity of the situation, the number of parties involved, the level of conflict between the parties, and their willingness to reach a voluntary agreement. Preparation of a Memorandum of Understanding and/or a report (in open mediation) requires additional time.

Appendix II.2

Best Practices Tips

NOTE: Mediators are advised to follow the best practices tips set out below:

1. *Do strongly encourage clients to get independent legal advice* preferably before mediation and certainly before any agreement is finalized.
2. *Suggest that the clients consider retaining collaboratively trained lawyers* as this will ensure that everyone shares a commitment to the goal of a non-adversarial resolution.
3. *Do strongly encourage clients to get the emotional* counselling that they or their children need in order to negotiate reasonably and in good faith.
4. *Do require clients to make full financial disclosure* if discussing support or property issues in mediation.
5. *Encourage the clients and their lawyers, to agree to a single, mutually agreeable valuator* for all valuations of real estate, pensions, businesses, *etc.*, to minimize costs and the possibility of a battle between experts.
6. *Do not permit clients to sign an agreement in your office.* If a mediator drafts an agreement and witnesses it (that is, creates a contract or legally binding agreement), he or she is carrying out the unauthorized practice of law and is liable to being charged by the Law Society in his or her jurisdiction.
7. *Do send the Memorandum of Understanding* to the parties' lawyers for review, redrafting and signing.

Appendix II.3

Confidential Client Questionnaire

PLEASE COMPLETE ALL PHONE NUMBERS & ADDRESS INFORMATION IN FULL

DATE: ______________REFERRED BY: ______________________

I, HUSBAND/WIFE/ /COMMON-LAW PARTNER (circle one)

NAME: ____

(Please include middle name)

DATE OF BIRTH:_____/_____/_____ PLACE OF BIRTH: ______

MO. DAY YEAR

CURRENT CITIZENSHIP? _____________ S.I.N.: _____________

LENGTH OF RESIDENCE IN ONTARIO:___

LENGTH OF RESIDENCE IN CANADA:___

HOME ADDRESS:____________ BUS. ADDRESS: ______________

____________ ______________

(incl. postal code) ____________ ______________

HOME TELEPHONE:(____)____ BUS. TELEPHONE: (____)____

CELLULAR: ( )____________E-MAIL: ______________________

MAIL CORRESPONDENCE TO? HOME: BUSINESS:

EDUCATION:

____

NAME OF EMPLOYER: _____________________________

ARE YOU SELF EMPLOYED? YES NO

OCCUPATION:________________ FULL TIME: PART TIME:

LENGTH OF EMPLOYMENT WITH PRESENT EMPLOYER:
________ YEARS ________ MONTHS

GROSS INCOME FROM EMPLOYMENT(before deductions): $_____

INCOME FROM OTHER SOURCES: $___________________

HAVE YOU RETAINED COUNSEL? YES: NO:

ARE THEY COLLABORATIVE LAW TRAINED? YES: NO:

DOES YOUR SPOUSE/PARTNER KNOW? YES: NO:

NAME OF COUNSEL______________________________
TELEPHONE: ( ) ___________________
ADDRESS: (include postal code):

____

EMAIL ADDRESS:____

RELATIONSHIP INFORMATION

DATE OF COHABITATION______________________
DATE OF MARRIAGE ___________________

AGE AT TIME OF MARRIAGE: _____________
CITY OF MARRIAGE: ________________________

CURRENTLY RESIDING TOGETHER? YES NO

(ANTICIPATED) DATE OF SEPARATION? ______________
DO YOUR CHILDREN KNOW ABOUT THE SEPARATION? YES NO

PRESENT MARITAL STATUS: MARRIED COMMON-LAW

SEPARATED WIDOWED SINGLE DIVORCED

WHO INITIATED THE SEPARATION? HUSBAND WIFE

ARE/DID YOU PREVIOUSLY ATTEND **MARITAL/FAMILY** COUNSELLING? YES NO

COUNSELLOR:________________SPECIALTY: ______________
TELEPHONE: ( ) ___________
<u>FULL</u> ADDRESS (include postal code):

____

____

DATES ATTENDED COUNSELLING: FROM: ________ TO: ______

TOTAL NUMBER OF SESSIONS: ____________

ARE YOU INTERESTED IN FURTHER MARITAL COUNSELLING?

YES NO

ARE YOU INTERESTED IN RECONCILIATION? YES NO
ARE/DID YOU ATTEND **INDIVIDUAL** COUNSELLING?

YES NO

COUNSELLOR:_________________SPECIALTY: ______________
TELEPHONE: ( ) ___________
<u>FULL</u> ADDRESS (include postal code):

____

DATES ATTENDED COUNSELLING: FROM: ______ TO: ______

TOTAL NUMBER OF SESSIONS: ____________

*****COMPLETE PAGE 5 FOR ANY ADDITIONAL THERAPIST/COUNSELLOR INFORMATION*****

PREVIOUS RELATIONSHIPS

HAVE YOU COHABITATED WITH A PARTNER PRIOR TO CURRENT RELATIONSHIP? YES NO

WERE YOU : COMMON-LAW OR/ MARRIED

NAME OF PREVIOUS PARTNER: ____________________________

TIME PERIOD OF RELATIONSHIP: FROM: ______ TO: ________

CHILDREN FROM PREVIOUS MARRIAGE/ RELATIONSHIP

NAME	AGE	BIRTHDATE (mo./day/yr.)	RESIDING WITH
HUSBAND: __________	______	____/____/____	____________________
____________________	______	____/____/____	____________________
____________________	______	____/____/____	____________________
WIFE:			
____________________	______	____/____/____	____________________
____________________	______	____/____/____	____________________
____________________	______	____/____/____	____________________

PLACE AN * BESIDE ANY OF THE CHILDREN LISTED ABOVE INVOLVED IN THE PRESENT DISPUTE.

ARE YOU PAYING **CHILD** SUPPORT? YES NO
AMOUNT: $__________ PER: ________ (mo./yr.)

ARE YOU PAYING/RECEIVING (circle) **SPOUSAL** SUPPORT?

YES NO
IF YES, FOR/FROM (NAME):

____

AMOUNT: $_______________PER:________________ (month or year)

PAYING/RECEIVING (circle)

TOTAL AMOUNT OF SUPPORT $_______PER:____ (month or year)

CHILDREN OF PRESENT MARRIAGE/RELATIONSHIP

(BEGINNING WITH THE ELDEST CHILD)

Child #1

NAME:_______________ BIRTHDATE:___/___/___ AGE:______
mo. /day / yr.

RESIDING WITH: ______(mother/father/guardian) GRADE: _____

SCHOOL NAME: ____

TEACHER'S NAME: __________PRINCIPAL'S NAME:________

TELEPHONE: ( )____________

SCHOOL ADDRESS (include postal code):______________________

____

Child #2

NAME:_________ BIRTHDATE:___/___/___ AGE:______
mo. /day / yr.

RESIDING WITH: __________(mother/father/guardian) GRADE: __

SCHOOL NAME: ____

TEACHER'S NAME: __________PRINCIPAL'S NAME:________

TELEPHONE: ( )____________

SCHOOL ADDRESS (include postal code):______________________

____

Child #3

NAME:_________ BIRTHDATE:___/___/___ AGE:______
mo. /day / yr.

RESIDING WITH: __________(mother/father/guardian) GRADE: __

SCHOOL NAME: ____

TEACHER'S NAME: ___________PRINCIPAL'S NAME:_________

TELEPHONE: (   )_____________

SCHOOL ADDRESS (include postal code):________________________

____

Child #4

NAME:__________ BIRTHDATE:___/___/___ AGE:_______
mo. /day / yr.

RESIDING WITH: ___________(mother/father/guardian) GRADE: __

SCHOOL NAME: ____

TEACHER'S NAME: ___________PRINCIPAL'S NAME:_________

TELEPHONE: (   )_____________

SCHOOL ADDRESS (include postal code):________________________

____

DOCTORS

Note: Fill in once if all family members have the same doctor.

DOCTOR TO: (please circle patient) HUSBAND WIFE
CHILD #1, 2, 3, 4

NAME:_______________________ TELEPHONE: (   )___________
SPECIALTY:_________________LAST SEEN: ___________________
FULL ADDRESS (include postal code):

____

____

NAME:______________________ TELEPHONE: ( )__________
SPECIALTY:_________________LAST SEEN: __________________
FULL ADDRESS (include postal code):

____

____

NAME:______________________ TELEPHONE: ( )__________
SPECIALTY:_________________LAST SEEN: __________________
FULL ADDRESS (include postal code):

____

____

NAME:______________________ TELEPHONE: ( )__________
SPECIALTY:_________________LAST SEEN: __________________
FULL ADDRESS (include postal code):

____

____

ADDITIONAL THERAPISTS/ COUNSELLORS/ SOCIAL WORKERS

FOR: (please circle patient) HUSBAND WIFE CHILD #1, 2, 3, 4

COUNSELLOR:_________________ SPECIALTY: ______________

FULL ADDRESS (include postal code):___________________________

____

TELEPHONE: ( )_______________ FAX: ( )_________________

DATES ATTENDED COUNSELLING: FROM: _______ TO: _____

TOTAL NUMBER OF SESSIONS: ____________

FOR: (please circle patient) HUSBAND WIFE CHILD #1, 2, 3, 4

COUNSELLOR:_________________ SPECIALTY: ______________

FULL ADDRESS (include postal code):___________________________

____

TELEPHONE: (   )______________ FAX: (   )_______________

DATES ATTENDED COUNSELLING: FROM: _______ TO: _____

TOTAL NUMBER OF SESSIONS: ___________

FOR: (please circle patient) HUSBAND WIFE CHILD #1, 2, 3, 4

COUNSELLOR:________________ SPECIALTY: _____________

FULL ADDRESS (include postal code):_________________________

____

TELEPHONE: (   )______________ FAX: (   )_______________

DATES ATTENDED COUNSELLING: FROM: _______ TO: _____

TOTAL NUMBER OF SESSIONS: ___________

FOR: (please circle patient) HUSBAND WIFE CHILD #1, 2, 3, 4

COUNSELLOR:________________ SPECIALTY: _____________

FULL ADDRESS (include postal code):_________________________

____

TELEPHONE: (   )______________ FAX: (   )_______________

DATES ATTENDED COUNSELLING: FROM: _______ TO: _____

TOTAL NUMBER OF SESSIONS: ___________

BABYSITTER/DAYCARE CENTRE

NAME:__________________ TELEPHONE: (   ) _____________

FOR (child's name): ____________________

FULL ADDRESS (include postal code):

____

____

NAME:__________________ TELEPHONE: (   ) _____________

FOR (child's name): ____________________

FULL ADDRESS (include postal code):

____

____

CHILDREN'S GRANDPARENTS

NAME:________________ TELEPHONE: (   )______________

MATERNAL PATERNAL

FULL ADDRESS (include postal code):

____

____

NAME:________________ TELEPHONE: (   )______________

MATERNAL PATERNAL

FULL ADDRESS (include postal code):

____

____

FAMILY BACKGROUND

1. WHAT WE DO BEST AS PARENTS

IS:____

____

____

____

____

____

2. MY SIGNIFICANT CONCERNS ABOUT PARENTING ARE:

____
____
____
____
____

3. MY HOPES/GOALS FOR PARENTING IN THE FUTURE ARE:

____
____
____
____
____

4. MY REASONS FOR SEPARATING ARE:

____
____
____
____
____

5. MY SIGNIFICANT CONCERNS ABOUT MY RELATIONSHIP WITH MY SPOUSE ARE:

____
____
____
____

6. MY SIGNIFICANT HOPES/GOALS FOR MY RELATIONSHIP WITH MY SPOUSE ARE:

____
____

____

____

7. DURING THE RELATIONSHIP IMPORTANT DECISIONS HAVE BEEN MADE ABOUT:

(checkmark (✓) the appropriate responses for each)

	BY MY SPOUSE	BY ME	JOINTLY
a) Household finances	________	________	______
b) Purchases of family property	________	________	______
c) Children's Education	________	________	______
d) Children's Health Care	________	________	______
e) Children's Religious Training	________	________	______
f) Children's extra curricular activities	________	________	______

COMMENTS: (whether you are able to make decisions with regards to the children co-operatively)

____

____

8. PLEASE **CIRCLE** ANY RESPONSES IF THEY APPLY TO YOUR RELATIONSHIP WITH YOUR SPOUSE (OR PARTNER)

Have there been any incidents of:	**In the past 6 months?**		**At any time in the relationship?**	
Verbal/Psychological Abuse	YES	NO	YES	NO
Physical Abuse	YES	NO	YES	NO
Alcohol Abuse	YES	NO	YES	NO
Drug Abuse	YES	NO	YES	NO

PLEASE EXPLAIN:

____

____

____

____

9. A) ARE YOU ABLE TO DISCUSS IMPORTANT ISSUES AFFECTING YOUR FAMILY WITH YOUR SPOUSE? YES NO

   B) CAN YOU MAKE DECISIONS ABOUT THE CHILDREN COOPERATIVELY? YES NO

EXPLAIN:

____

____

____

____

PARENTING ARRANGEMENTS

DO YOU SPEND (plse. circle answer):

TOO MUCH TIME / TOO LITTLE TIME / THE RIGHT AMOUNT OF TIME WITH EACH CHILD?

COMMENTS:

____

____

____

____

IF YOU ARE LIVING SEPARATELY, DESCRIBE PRESENT PARENTING ARRANGEMENTS ON A MONTHLY CYCLE: (please circle the time YOU are scheduled to spend with the child(ren), it will be assumed the remaining time will be spent with the other parent)

WEEKEND # 1 / 2 / 3 / 4 WITH MOTHER/FATHER
TIME: FROM ______ TO: _________

WEEKDAYS (Week 1) M / T / W / T / F WITH MOTHER/FATHER
TIME: FROM ________ TO: _________

WEEKDAYS (Week 2) M / T / W / T / F WITH MOTHER/FATHER
TIME: FROM ________ TO: _________

WEEKDAYS (Week 3) M / T / W / T / F WITH MOTHER/FATHER
TIME: FROM ________ TO: _________

WEEKDAYS (Week 4) M / T / W / T / F WITH MOTHER/FATHER
TIME: FROM ________ TO: _________

POSSIBLE ISSUES IN DISPUTE

DO YOU ANTICIPATE A DISPUTE REGARDING (circle area of dispute):

CUSTODY / ACCESS / CHILD SUPPORT / SPOUSAL SUPPORT /

POSSESSION OF THE MATRIMONIAL HOME / DIVISION OF PROPERTY

/ DEBTS / OTHER:

____

DESIRED CUSTODY ARRANGEMENT:
SOLE CUSTODY TO: ______________________ JOINT CUSTODY

LIVING EXPENSES

SPOUSAL SUPPORT

ARE YOU PRESENTLY PAYING /OR RECEIVING SPOUSAL SUPPORT?

IF YES, HOW MUCH PER MONTH: $ ___________________

CHILD SUPPORT

ARE YOU PRESENTLY PAYING OR/ RECEIVING CHILD SUPPORT?

IF YES, TOTAL AMOUNT PER MONTH: $______ (FOR ALL CHILDREN)

PAYMENTS ARE MADE: REGULARLY IRREGULARLY

IS THE FAMILY RESPONSIBILITY OFFICE (FRO) INVOLVED?
YES NO

COMMENTS:

____

____

I WOULD LIKE:

THE CHILDREN TO REMAIN IN THE MATRIMONIAL HOME WITH ME WITH MY SPOUSE OR/ SALE OF THE MATRIMONIAL HOME
OTHER (please explain):

____

____

____

____

OTHER ASSETS: HAVE THEY BEEN DIVIDED? YES NO

COMMENTS:

____

____

DEBTS

SIGNIFICANT DEBTS OF WIFE (explain):

____

____

SIGNIFICANT DEBTS OF HUSBAND (explain):

____

____

JOINT SIGNIFICANT DEBTS (explain):

____

____

NEW RELATIONSHIPS

DO YOU HAVE A NEW PARTNER? YES NO
IF YES, DOES YOUR WIFE/PARTNER KNOW? YES NO

IF YES, RESIDING TOGETHER? YES NO
DO THE CHILDREN KNOW? YES NO

NAME OF NEW PARTNER:____________ TELEPHONE: ( )________
DOES YOUR NEW PARTNER HAVE CHILDREN? YES NO

NAME OF CHILD:________________________ AGE: ___________
NAME OF CHILD:________________________ AGE: ___________
NAME OF CHILD:________________________ AGE: ___________

IS THE PARTNER PAYING OR/RECEIVING FINANCIAL ASSISTANCE WHILE IN YOUR NEW RELATIONSHIP? NO
AMOUNT PAYING/RECEIVING $ _________ PER (month/year)_________

DO YOU HAVE ANY ADDITIONAL CONCERNS OR COMMENTS? (attach page if necessary)

____
____
____
____
____
____
____
____
____
____
____
____
____

Appendix II.4

Closed Mediation Retainer Contract

RE: <client and client>

1. It is hereby agreed that Mediator, Registered Psychologist, is retained to act as the Mediator with respect to the following issues:

   (i) parenting arrangements for the <children>;
   (ii) child support and spousal support;
   (iii) possession of the matrimonial home;
   (iv) division of financial assets; and
   (v) other financial issues.

2. It is acknowledged that the Mediator is an impartial third party whose role is to assist the parties to negotiate an agreement with respect to the outstanding issues.

3. In attempting to bring about an Agreement, the Mediator will meet with the parties for joint sessions and on occasion for individual sessions. The Mediator may include in the mediation process any other significant third party, such as the <children>, legal counsel or other significantly involved persons, following consultation with the parties.

4. Information shared with the Mediator during individual sessions may be shared with the other party, at the Mediator's discretion, unless the individual interviewed requests that specific information be kept confidential. The Mediator may disclose any relevant information if there is a threat to anyone's safety.

5. With the exception of the Client Questionnaire (which is confidential), Mediator will make copies of all correspondence received from the parties including legal documents, faxes, emails or tapes for the other party prior to reviewing such correspondence. The purpose is to ensure that both parties have an opportunity to review and respond to any information given to Mediator. It is also to maintain Mediator's impartiality. If, the correspondence raises concerns about a party's safety, the person providing the information should discuss this with Mediator before submitting the information.

6. It is acknowledged that Mediator will be acting as a Mediator and will not be giving either party legal advice. The parties are strongly advised to obtain independent legal advice, preferably before mediation commences, but in any event, before a final Agreement is reached, to

ensure that they are fully informed of their legal rights and obligations and the legal implications of such an Agreement. In the event that the parties do not have independent legal advice prior to signing an Agreement, it is recognized that:

(i) the parties may not be making fully informed choices in light of their respective legal rights; and
(ii) the Agreement they reach is less likely to be enforced by a court.

7. The Mediator may obtain information from relevant sources and may consult such persons and read such reports, records or documents as she deems necessary for arriving at an Agreement following consultation with the parties. It is agreed that the parties will:

(i) make full disclosure of all relevant information reasonably required for the Mediator to understand the issues being mediated; and
(ii) execute any Releases of Information necessary for the Mediator to obtain relevant information.

8. If issues related to property or support are discussed during the mediation process, then the parties will:

(i) make full financial disclosure to each other, the Mediator, and both counsel;
(ii) undertake not to hide or dispose of any assets; or
(iii) not cancel or change any beneficiaries of life insurance policies and health care policies while the mediation is in process.

9. The parties understand that interim agreements with respect to parenting arrangements, and child and/or spousal support will be factors to be considered by the courts, in the event that an agreement is not reached in mediation.

10. In the event that information obtained during the mediation discloses an actual or potential threat to the safety of any of the participants or a breach of the *Child and Family Services Act* or *Criminal Code*, the Mediator is obligated to report such information.

11. Neither party nor anyone acting on their behalf will take any fresh steps in the legal proceedings between the parties with respect to those issues that are being mediated, without prior notice to the Mediator and the other party.

12. If the parties reach agreement on some or all of the issues, the Mediator will prepare a Memorandum of Understanding with respect to those issues which will be sent to both counsel to review with the parties.

13. If the parties fail to agree on one or more issues it is understood that:

    (i) the Mediator will not prepare a report or make recommendations with respect to any issues that are not resolved in mediation;

    (ii) in the case of financial issues, any documents prepared for the purpose of financial disclosure may be used by the parties in future proceedings, with their consent;

    (iii) if the parties do not reach an agreement through mediation on any specified issue, that will be so reported by the Mediator;

    (iv) anything said or any admission or communication in the course of the mediation is <u>not</u> admissible in any legal proceeding;

    (v) anything said or any admission or communication made in the course of the mediation by the parties, the Mediator and/or the Mediation Intern is confidential and may not be communicated to outside parties without the express permission of all parties and the Mediator. This does not apply to any circumstances or communication as outlined in paragraph 10 above;

    (vi) both parties agree <u>not</u> to subpoena Mediator or the Mediation Intern's notes or records; and

    (vii) neither the Mediator nor the Mediation Intern will be called as a witness by or on behalf of either party in any legal proceeding.

14. It is agreed that:

    (i) <client and client> will each pay a retainer of $xxxx ($xxxx total) and share the cost of mediation equally/in proportion to income;

    (ii) In addition to the mediator's fees, the parties will pay the costs of all disbursements relating to the mediation, including the costs of long distance telephone calls, courier, photocopies, neutral experts engaged in the mediation process (e.g., accountants, psychologists), travel expenses, parking and any other disbursements incurred by the Mediator in relation to the mediation. Interim accounts shall be sent out to the parties and payment shall be due when rendered;

    (iii) the hourly rate will be $xxx per hour during regular office hours and is subject to change upon notice by the Mediator;

    (iv) <client and client> are jointly responsible for the total time spent by the Mediator. The costs of mediation will not be broken down or allocated, based upon the amount of individual time spent by the Mediator with or on behalf of each individual party unless specifically agreed to in advance between the parties and the Mediator; and

(v) from time to time the Mediator may request an additional retainer to cover anticipated future steps in the mediation. The mediation will not continue until the retainer is paid.

15. Any report or Memorandum of Understanding will not be released until all outstanding professional fees and disbursements related to the mediation have been paid in full.

16. Interest will be charged at the Prime Rate on all accounts outstanding after 30 (thirty) days at the time the account is rendered.

17. Cancellation Policy

The notice must be provided during regular business hours Monday through Thursdays, between 9:00 am and 4:30 pm.

(a) The clients will be billed for an appointment in which there is less than 48 hours (2 full business days) notice prior to cancellation. In the event that the meeting is scheduled for more than 2 hours then 4 full business days (Monday through Thursday) notice must be provided. The clients will each be responsible for bills arising from his/her own cancellation.

(b) Once a date has been agreed upon for a 5 (or 6) way Counsel Meeting, the following charges will apply to either the client for re-scheduling or cancellation of the meeting:

(i) if 7 or more business days notice a $100 fee will be charged;

(ii) if between 5 and 7 business days notice a $150 fee will be charged; or

(iii) if 4 business days or less the entire session will be billed.

If a cancellation is due to the illness of a child or a circumstance beyond their control, the clients will share the cancellation fee equally. These charges are regardless of the reason for the cancellation, except at the Mediator's discretion.

18. It is understood that either of the parties may terminate the mediation process at any time. If a party wishes to terminate, he or she will first discuss the concerns with Mediator to see if they can be addressed satisfactorily. The Mediator may suspend or terminate mediation whenever:

(i) The process is likely to harm or prejudice one or more of the participants; or

(ii) The usefulness of the mediation process is exhausted; or

(iii) The Agreement being reached is unreasonable.

The Mediator will first advise the parties of the reason why she believes the mediation should be terminated.

19. Each of the undersigned acknowledges that he/she has read this Retainer and agrees to be bound by the terms herein.

DATED at ________, this <u><day></u> day of <u><month></u>______, 20--.

______________________________	______________________________
WITNESS	<husband>
______________________________	______________________________
WITNESS	<wife>
______________________________	______________________________
WITNESS	Mediator, Mediator

NOTE: Also have a version of this Retainer signed by the lawyers indicating they have read and are in agreement with the terms of the Retainer.

Appendix II.5

Partially Open Mediation Retainer Contract

RE: <client and client>

1. It is hereby agreed that Mediator is retained to act as the Mediator with respect to the following issues:

   (i) parenting arrangements for the <children>;
   (ii) child support and spousal support;
   (iii) possession of the matrimonial home;
   (iv) division of assets; and
   (v) other financial issues.

2. It is acknowledged that the Mediator is an impartial third party whose role is to assist the parties to negotiate an agreement with respect to the outstanding issues.

3. In attempting to bring about an Agreement, the Mediator will meet with the parties jointly and on occasion in an individual caucus. The Mediator may include in the mediation process any other significant persons, such as their lawyers, <children>, or other significantly involved persons or professionals, following consultation with the parties.

4. Information shared with the Mediator during individual sessions may be shared with the other party, at the Mediator's discretion, unless the individual interviewed requests that specific information be kept confidential. The Mediator may disclose any relevant information if there is a threat to anyone's safety.

5. With the exception of the Client Questionnaire (which is confidential), Mediator will make copies of all correspondence received from the parties including legal documents, faxes, emails or tapes for the other party prior to reviewing such correspondence. The purpose is to ensure that both parties have an opportunity to review and respond to any information given to Mediator. It is also to maintain Mediator's impartiality. If, the correspondence raises concerns about a party's safety, the person providing the information should discuss this with Mediator before submitting the information.

6. It is acknowledged that Mediator will be acting as a Mediator and will not be giving either party legal advice. The parties are strongly advised to obtain independent legal advice, preferably before mediation commences, but in any event, before a final Agreement is reached, to ensure that they are fully informed of their legal rights and obligations and the legal implications of such an Agreement. In the event that the parties do not have independent legal advice prior to signing an Agreement, it is recognised that:

   (i) the parties may not be making fully informed choices in light of their respective legal rights; and
   (ii) the Agreement they reach is less likely to be enforced by a court.

7. The Mediator may obtain information from relevant sources and may consult such persons and read such reports, records or documents as she deems necessary for arriving at an Agreement following consultation with the parties. It is agreed that the parties will:

   (i) make full disclosure of all relevant information reasonably required for the Mediator to understand the issues being mediated; and
   (ii) execute any Releases of Information necessary for the Mediator to obtain relevant information.

8. If issues related to property or support are discussed during the mediation process, then the parties will:

   (i) make full financial disclosure to each other and the Mediator;
   (ii) undertake not to hide or dispose of any assets; or
   (iii) not cancel or change any beneficiaries of life insurance policies and health care policies while the mediation is in process.

9. The parties understand that interim agreements with respect to parenting arrangements, and child and/or spousal support will be factors to be considered by the courts, in the event that an agreement is not reached in mediation.

10. In the event that information obtained during the mediation discloses an actual or potential threat to the safety of any of the participants or a breach of the *Child and Family Services Act* or *Criminal Code*, the Mediator is obligated to report such information.

11. Neither party nor anyone acting on their behalf will take any fresh steps in the legal proceedings between the parties with respect to those issues that are being mediated, without prior notice to the Mediator and the other party. In the event that a party chooses to litigate, the mediation process will end.

12. If the parties reach agreement on some or all of the issues, the Mediator will prepare a Memorandum of Understanding with respect to those issues, which will be sent to both counsel to review with the parties.

13. If the parties fail to agree on one or more issues it is understood that:

    (i) if requested, by either party, the Mediator may prepare a report outlining the mediation process, the parties' positions on those issues, and the Mediator's non-binding suggestions with respect to any outstanding parenting issues; but not with respect to financial issues. This report will be distributed only to both parties and their counsel, only for the purpose of assisting in further negotiations;
    (ii) in the case of financial issues, any documents prepared for the purpose of financial disclosure may be used by the parties in future proceedings, with their consent;
    (iii) in the event that one party requests the report, that party will be responsible for paying the Mediator's fees in advance of the preparation or release of the report;
    (iv) anything said or any admission or communication made in the course of the mediation may be used in the report;
    (v) both parties agree not to subpoena Mediator and/or <mediation intern>'s notes or records; and
    (vi) neither the mediator nor the intern will be called as a witness by either party in any legal proceeding with respect to any of the issues being mediated.

14. It is agreed that:

    (i) <client and client> will each pay a retainer of $xxxx ($xxxx total) and share the cost of mediation equally/in proportion to income;
    (ii) In addition to the mediator's fees, the parties will pay the costs of all disbursements relating to the mediation, including the

costs of long distance telephone calls, courier, photocopies, neutral experts engaged in the mediation process (e.g., accountants, psychologists), travel expenses, parking and any other disbursements incurred by the Mediator in relation to the mediation. Interim accounts shall be sent out to the parties and payment shall be due when rendered;

(iii) the hourly rate will be $xxx per hour during regular office hours and is subject to change upon notice by the Mediator;

(iv) <client and client> are jointly responsible for the total time spent by the Mediator. The costs of mediation will not be broken down or allocated, based upon the amount of individual time spent by the Mediator with or on behalf of each individual party unless specifically agreed to in advance between the parties and the Mediator; and

(iii) from time to time the Mediator may request an additional retainer to cover anticipated future steps in the mediation. The mediation will not continue until the retainer is paid.

15. The parties will be jointly and severally liable for any unpaid mediation accounts. Interest will be charged at Prime Rate on all accounts outstanding after 30 (thirty) days at the time the account is rendered.

16. Cancellation Policy

The notice must be provided during regular business hours Monday through Thursdays, between 9:00 am and 4:30 pm.

(i) The clients will be billed for an appointment in which there is less than 48 hours (2 full business days) notice prior to cancellation. In the event that the meeting is scheduled for more than 2 hours then 4 full business days (Monday through Thursday) notice must be provided. The clients will each be responsible for bills arising from his/her own cancellation.

(ii) Once a date has been agreed upon for a 5 (or 6) way Counsel Meeting, the following charges will apply to either the client for re-scheduling or cancellation of the meeting:

(a) if 7 or more business days notice a $100 fee will be charged;

(b) if between 5 and 7 business days notice a $150 fee will be charged; or

(c) if 4 business days or less the entire session will be billed.

(iii) If a cancellation is due to the illness of a child or a circumstance beyond their control, the clients will share the cancellation fee equally. These charges are regardless of the reason for the cancellation, except at the Mediator's discretion.

17. Any report or Memorandum of Understanding will not be released until all outstanding professional fees and disbursements related to the mediation have been paid in full.

18. It is understood that either of the parties may terminate the mediation process at any time. If a party wishes to terminate, he or she will first discuss the concerns with Mediator to see if they can be addressed satisfactorily. The Mediator may suspend or terminate mediation whenever:

    (i) the process is likely to harm or prejudice one or more of the participants; or
    (ii) the usefulness of the mediation process is exhausted; or
    (iii) the Agreement being reached is unreasonable.

    The Mediator will first advise the parties of the reason why she believes the mediation should be terminated.

19. Each of the undersigned acknowledges that he/she has read this Retainer and agrees to be bound by the terms herein.

DATED at _____, this <day> day of <month>, 20--.

______________________	______________________
WITNESS	<husband>
______________________	______________________
WITNESS	<wife>
______________________	______________________
WITNESS	Mediator, Mediator

NOTE: Also have a version of this Retainer signed by the lawyers indicating they have read and are in agreement with the terms of the Retainer.

Appendix II.6

Open Mediation Retainer Contract

RE: <client and client>

1. It is hereby agreed that Dr. Collaborate, is retained to act as the Mediator with respect to the following issues:

(i) parenting arrangements for the <children>;
(ii) child support and spousal support;
(iii) possession of the matrimonial home;
(iv) division of assets; and
(v) other financial issues.

2. It is acknowledged that the Mediator is an impartial third party whose role is to assist the parties to negotiate an agreement with respect to the outstanding issues.

3. In attempting to bring about an Agreement, the Mediator will meet with the parties jointly and on occasion in an individual caucus. The Mediator may include in the mediation process any other significant persons, such as their lawyers, their <children>, or other significantly involved persons or professionals following consultation with the parties.

4. Information shared with the Mediator during individual sessions may be shared with the other party, at the Mediator's discretion, unless the individual interviewed requests that specific information be kept confidential. The Mediator may disclose any relevant information if there is a threat to anyone's safety.

OR

Information shared with the mediator during individual sessions will be kept confidential except with permission of the speaker. The Mediator may disclose any relevant information if there is a threat to anyone's safety.

5. With the exception of the Client Questionnaire, Dr. Collaborate will make copies of all correspondence received from the parties including legal documents, faxes, emails or tapes for the other party prior to reviewing such correspondence. The purpose is to ensure that both parties have an opportunity to review and respond to any information given to Dr. Collaborate. It is also to maintain Dr. Collaborate's impartiality. If, the correspondence raises concerns about a party's safety, the person providing the information should discuss this with Dr. Collaborate before submitting the information.

6. It is acknowledged that Dr. Collaborate will be acting as a Mediator and will not be giving either party legal advice. The parties are strongly advised to obtain independent legal advice, preferably before mediation commences, but in any event, before a final Agreement is reached, to ensure that they are fully informed of their legal rights and obligations and the legal implications of such an Agreement. In the event that the parties do not have independent legal advice prior to signing an Agreement, it is recognised that:

(i) the parties may not be making fully informed choices in light of their respective legal rights; and
(ii) the Agreement they reach is less likely to be enforced by a court.

7. The Mediator may obtain information from relevant sources and may consult such persons and read such reports, records or documents as she deems necessary for arriving at an Agreement following consultation with the parties. It is agreed that the parties will:

   (i) make full disclosure of all relevant information reasonably required for the Mediator to understand the issues being mediated; and
   (ii) execute any Releases of Information necessary for the Mediator to obtain relevant information.

8. If issues related to property or support are discussed during the mediation process, then the parties will:

   (i) make full financial disclosure to each other and the Mediator;
   (ii) undertake not to hide or dispose of any assets; or
   (iii) not cancel or change any beneficiaries of life insurance policies and health care policies while the mediation is in process.

9. The parties understand that interim agreements with respect to parenting arrangements, and child and/or spousal support will be factors to be considered by the courts, in the event that an agreement is not reached in mediation.

10. In the event that information obtained during the mediation discloses an actual or potential threat to the safety of any of the participants or a breach of the *Child and Family Services Act* or *Criminal Code*, the Mediator is obligated to report such information.

11. Neither party nor anyone acting on their behalf will take any fresh steps in the legal proceedings between the parties with respect to those issues that are being mediated, without prior notice to the Mediator and the other party.

12. If the parties reach agreement on some or all of the issues, the Mediator will prepare a Memorandum of Understanding with respect to those issues, which will be sent to both counsel to review with the parties.

13. If the parties fail to agree on one or more issues it is understood that:

   (i) if requested, by either party, the Mediator may prepare a report outlining the mediation process, the parties' positions on those issues, and the Mediator's recommendations with respect to any outstanding parenting issues; but <u>not</u> with respect to financial issues. This report will be distributed to both parties and their counsel, for the purpose of assisting in further negotiations;

(ii) in the case of financial issues, any documents prepared for the purpose of financial disclosure may be used by the parties in future proceedings, with their consent;
(iii) in the event that one party requests a report and calls the mediator as a witness, that party will be responsible for paying the Mediator's fees in advance of the preparation or release of the report or the appearance in court;
(iv) anything said or any admission or communication made in the course of the mediation may be used in the report; and
(v) the mediator may be called as a witness by either party in the legal proceedings with respect to parenting issues, but not with respect to financial or property issues.

14. It is agreed that:

(i) <client and client> will each pay a retainer of $______ ($_____ total) and share the cost of mediation equally.
(ii) interim accounts shall be sent out to the parties and payment shall be due when rendered;
(iii) the hourly rate will be $___ per hour during regular office hours and is subject to change upon notice by the Mediator; and
(iv) from time to time the Mediator may request an additional retainer to cover anticipated future steps in the mediation. The mediation will not continue until the retainer is paid.

15. Interest will be charged at Prime Rate on all accounts outstanding after 30 (thirty) days at the time the account is rendered.

16. <u>Cancellation Policy</u>
The notice must be provided during regular business hours <u>Monday through Thursdays</u>, between 9:00 am and 4:30 pm.
(a) The clients will be billed for an appointment in which there is less than 48 hours (2 full business days) notice prior to cancellation. In the event that the meeting is scheduled for more than 2 hours then 4 full business days (Monday through Thursday) notice must be provided. The clients will each be responsible for bills arising from his/her own cancellation.
(b) Once a date has been agreed upon for a 5 (or 6) way Counsel Meeting, the following charges will apply to either client for re-scheduling or cancellation of the meeting:
(i) if 7 or more business days notice a $____ fee will be charged;
(ii) if between 5 and 7 business days notice a $____ fee will be charged; or
(iii) if 4 business days or less the entire session will be billed.
If a cancellation is due to the illness of a child or a circumstance beyond their control, the clients will share the cancellation fee equally. These charges are regardless of the reason for the cancellation, except at the Mediator's discretion.

17. Any report or Memorandum of Understanding will not be released until all outstanding professional fees and disbursements related to the mediation have been paid in full.

18. It is understood that either of the parties may terminate the mediation process at any time. If a party wishes to terminate, he or she will first discuss the concerns with Dr. Collaborate to see if they can be addressed satisfactorily. The Mediator may suspend or terminate mediation whenever:

    (i) the process is likely to harm or prejudice one or more of the participants; or
    (ii) the usefulness of the mediation process is exhausted; or
    (iii) the Agreement being reached is unreasonable.

    The Mediator will first advise the parties of the reason why she believes the mediation should be terminated.

19. Each of the undersigned acknowledges that he/she has read this Retainer and agrees to be bound by the terms herein.

DATED at ____________, this <day> day of <month>, 20--.

______________________	______________________
WITNESS	Father
______________________	______________________
WITNESS	Mother
______________________	______________________
WITNESS	Dr. Collaborate, Mediator

OR

18. Counsel for the parties agree that they will assist the Mediator to obtain payment of his/her account in the same proportion as the parties are required to pay according to this Retainer. The Mediator agrees that he/she will notify the lawyers and the parties before the retainer is depleted and ask for a further retainer. The Mediation will not continue until a further retainer is received.

19. Counsel acknowledges receipt of this document and agrees, subject to approval by their client, that the terms herein describe the nature of the Mediation retainer.

DATED at __________, this _________ day of __________, 20 __.

___________	________________________
WITNESS	COUNSEL FOR THE FATHER
___________	________________________
WITNESS	COUNSEL FOR THE MOTHER
___________	________________________
WITNESS	MEDIATOR, DR. COLLABORATE

Appendix II.7

Sample Parenting Plan

PARENTING PLAN (Short Form)

Parenting Responsibilities that need to be decided upon are:

(1) Health Care:

- (a) Doctor appointments
- (b) Dentist appointments
- (c) Other appointments, i.e. Naturopath, Orthodontist, allergist, therapist, *etc.*
- (d) "Emergency" appointments
  - Medical care
  - Child care

(2) Transportation to and from:

- Extra-curricular activities
- Remedial programs
- Children's extended family (grandparents, cousins, aunts, and uncles)
- Friends (Birthday parties, *etc.*)

(3) Transportation to and from visits with parent

(4) Attendance at extra-curricular activities and school events:

- Parents
- Extended family
- New partners

(5) Involvement of new partners or extended family guidelines to minimize conflict and stress for children

(6) Shopping:

- For clothes
- For sporting or other equipment
- For gifts (for child's friends or family)

NOTE: **clarify payment for these items and whether the children can transfer items.**

(7) Access to information and how information will be shared for:

- Medical
- Dental
- Mental health
- Educational

(8) Parental decision-making:

- Education
- Health care (medical, dental, mental health, including counselling for child)
- Religion
- Extra-curricular activities, summer programs, remedial programs
- Other

(9) Child's name (*Change of Name Act*)

(10) Parental Communication:

- How
- When
- For what reasons

(11) Out-of-Province Travel:

- Passports
- (Notarized) Letter of approval

(12) Material Change of Circumstances – A review of parenting arrangements required if:

- Move by parent (notice re: when and where) so that present arrangements not feasible
- Children get older
- New partner
- Illness/disability of a child

- Death or disability of a parent
- Other

(13) Resolution of Future Disputes:

- Clarify process to be followed
- Clarify payment of fees

Appendix III Contents

Collaborative Practice

DOCUMENTS ON CD-ROM

Appendix III.1(a)

Collaborative Practice Legal Retainer (1)

COLLABORATIVE RETAINER AGREEMENT

BETWEEN: Client name
AND: Lawyer Name, Barrister and Solicitor

INTRODUCTION:

You have retained me to work with you to attempt to arrive at a fair and equitable settlement of your family law matter, using the process of Collaborative Practice.

Your spouse has also retained, or will be retaining, a lawyer to represent him or her in the same process, in order to avoid litigation while resolving your family matter. We will work together to take steps that are most appropriate to advance settlement of your case. This will include meetings with your spouse and his or her Collaborative lawyer. I will explain the legal issues involved, and you will let me know if you have any questions or do not understand any matter in connection with your case. You understand that I do not provide tax advice. We will work together to clarify your needs and interests, but you will make the final decisions and will authorize any settlement. I will prepare and/or review and discuss any Agreement (or other documentation effecting the settlement) with you before you will sign it. Although I will do my best when acting for you, and will provide you with my best legal advice, you understand that I cannot guarantee a successful outcome. You also understand that neither lawyer will represent either you or your spouse in any family law litigation between you and your spouse, should the collaborative process break down before settlement.

SCOPE AND DUTIES:

I agree to be your lawyer in the Collaborative Process once I receive a signed and dated copy of this Agreement. If your spouse declines to proceed with the Collaborative Process, this Retainer Agreement will be of no effect, and you and I will need to enter into a new Retainer Agreement for conventional representation before I can represent you.

My representation of you as a collaborative lawyer differs in some important respects from conventional representation. I will be retained only to assist you in reaching a comprehensive agreement with your spouse or partner, and for no other purpose. You also agree that while you participate in the Collaborative process, you give up your access to the Court system, your right to formally object to producing any documents or to provide any relevant information to the other participants, and the right to retain your own expert(s). To this end, you agree to make full disclosure of the nature, extent, and value of your income, assets and liabilities, and you will keep me informed of any changes affecting such disclosure. You authorize me to fully disclose all information, which in my discretion must be provided to your spouse and his or her lawyer.

The other difference in my representation of you is that by signing this "Retainer Agreement", you are agreeing that you may seek and/or receive my legal advice in the presence of your spouse and/or partner and not always in the privacy of a meeting between just the two of us.

TERMINATION AND RIGHT TO WITHDRAW:

Termination of the Collaborative Process

You retain the right at any time to terminate the collaborative process and to go to court, but this will end my representation of you. In fact, should settlement efforts break down to the extent that, in the opinion of either of us, the matter needs to move to court, either of us may terminate our relationship on notice to the other. If your spouse elects to go to court, that will also terminate my involvement in the process, and you and your spouse will need to retain alternate counsel to represent you. I will assist you to obtain a litigation lawyer and help you to make a smooth transition into the litigation process.

Right to Withdraw

If you have misrepresented or failed to disclose material facts to me and continue to withhold and misrepresent such information or refuse to give me instructions to make full disclosure to the other side, I am obliged to withdraw from the collaborative process and as your lawyer. I am also obliged to withdraw from your case if you have acted so as to undermine or take unfair advantage of the Collaborative Process.

I shall have the right to withdraw from your case if you do not make the payments required, or if our professional relationship is no longer productive.

Your Termination of My Retainer

You are free to terminate my retainer at any time. If you wish to continue with the collaborative process you will need to retain a new collaborative lawyer.

COMMUNICATION WITH EACH OTHER:

I will try to return your telephone calls or respond to your letters or e-mails as quickly as possible, but I will not always be able to do so on the same day that you have left a message. If the matter is urgent, please indicate so when leaving a message.

Copies of all correspondence that I receive or send on your behalf will be forwarded to you. These letters will be sent to your address on file, and they do not require your response unless otherwise indicated. You will advise me immediately of any changes in your address or telephone number.

CONFIDENTIALITY:

As your lawyer, I have to share relevant information about your case with your spouse's lawyer. However, unless I need to share this information as part of the Collaborative process, all information you give to me will be kept confidential between us. Please note that communication by e-mail or cell phone can be intercepted by unauthorized third parties. However, you agree that communications with you may be made by e-mail or cell phone unless you specifically advise me against it, in writing.

MY FEES:

Payment Arrangement

You have promised to pay me $ X per hour plus 5% GST, for any time I spend working on your case, billed in 6 minute intervals. Billable legal services include drafting, reviewing and responding to correspondence and e-mails, all telephone calls, office attendances, preparing and reviewing documents, preparing for and attending at meetings, travel time to meetings, reviewing your file, preparing and sending accounts and reporting letters to you, research, consultation with other lawyers and experts and generally all time spent in providing legal services to you in this matter. You will be notified in advance of any increase in fees.

Legal Assistants

There are many services, such as gathering information and preparing routine documents, that my assistants are well qualified to perform at a lower cost. My assistants work under my supervision, but may not give legal advice. I will charge you for work my legal assistants do at $X per hour. I will not charge you when the work is of a general secretarial nature.

Fees to Reflect the Value of our Services

Although the fees billed to you by my firm will generally be based on the actual time spent, the total fees charged may reflect the value of our service to you. For example, if I obtain an exceptionally good result for you, our total fees may be higher than a simple calculation of the total hours spent. When determining whether your final account will be adjusted up or down to a fair and reasonable amount, I will consider whether: I obtained an exceptionally good result for you; I had to put aside work on other files because yours was urgent; I had to spend time outside normal business hours, or whether the matter was particularly difficult or complex.

Disbursements

This Agreement will authorize payment for all necessary disbursements, which may include such items as courier charges, photocopying, faxes and long distance telephone calls. Photocopies and faxes are charged at X cents per copy. Disbursements may also include the costs to retain experts, since it may be necessary to retain the services of an accountant, appraiser, actuary or other expert to value certain assets. If we deem it advisable to retain an expert, your spouse's collaborative lawyer and I will help you to choose an expert and we will obtain the consent of all parties prior to the engagement of the expert's services.

Retainer

This Agreement will confirm our financial arrangement. You will provide me with a retainer of $X, which will be held in trust and applied to accounts rendered to you on a periodic basis. Please provide a cheque payable to Lawyer's Name, in trust. It may become necessary to ask you for a further retainer. At the conclusion of your case, any money remaining in trust will be returned to you.

Billing

Bills are due and payable when rendered. Any accounts which are 30 days overdue shall be charged interest at the current rate pursuant to the Solicitors Act calculated from the date the account is rendered. If you have any questions about your account, please contact my office. Please keep my office advised of any changes to your address or telephone number.

CLOSING YOUR FILE:

We will provide you with copies of documents and any correspondence in your file on an on-going basis. These belong to you and you should keep them together in a safe place. When our retainer is completed we will make any documents not previously provided available to you for pick-up, including any of your original documents left with us. You will be responsible to keep these for your future use. We retain the right to destroy documents remaining in our closed file when we decide it is appropriate.

If you need access to your file after it has been closed, there will be a file retrieval fee charged to you to retrieve the file from storage.

______________________________	______________________________
Date	**LAWYER'S NAME**

I have read this Retainer Agreement carefully and have received a copy. I understand this Agreement and I agree to be bound by its terms.

______________________________	______________________________
Date	**CLIENT NAME**

Appendix III.1(b)

Collaborative Practice Legal Retainer (2)

I, Tom/Linda McGee, retain Ricky Reasonable/Paul(a) Polite, to advise me with respect to the family law issues in my separation. At my request, you will be working collaboratively with my spouse's lawyer to resolve our family law issues in a manner satisfactory to both of us, through negotiation rather than going to court.

You have provided me with information, explained the Collaborative Law process and given me a copy of the Collaborative Family Law Participation Agreement to review. You also pointed out the advantages and disadvantages of this and other choices, including litigation, and I wish to retain you as a Collaborative Lawyer.

I understand that as part of the Collaborative Law process, you and my spouse's lawyer will not go to court. I have an obligation to provide full disclosure of all relevant information in an efficient manner and this information will be shared with my spouse. The success of the collaborative process depends on all participants behaving in good faith.

I agree to pay your fees and disbursements, including a retainer in the amount of $----- and I understand that your hourly rate is currently $----- per hour and is subject to change upon advance notice. I also agree to pay my share of the fees of any other professionals retained to assist me and my spouse in reaching a resolution of our outstanding issues. I understand that such experts will be retained to act in an impartial fashion and will not be called as expert witnesses in any future legal proceeding.

If my case cannot be settled on terms that are acceptable to me and my spouse, both lawyers must withdraw. If that happens, you will assist me to find a new lawyer (not associated with your firm) to represent me in court. In this case I agree to sign a consent and any necessary documents to allow you to withdraw and my new lawyer to receive my file.

Dated the --------- day of ------------------, 20---, at --------------------------------

________________________ ________________________

Tom/Linda McGee Ricky Reasonable/Paul(a) Polite

____

Appendix III.2

Collaborative Practice Participation Agreement

A. THE COLLABORATIVE LAW PROCESS

We, as participants acknowledge the following shared principles and understanding:

1. That the essence of "Collaborative Law" is the shared belief that it is in the best interests of Tom and Linda McGee, their son, Andy, and their families to resolve their family law issues through interest-based negotiations rather than litigation.

2. That the Collaborative Law process relies on negotiations carried out in an atmosphere of honesty, co-operation, integrity and professionalism, rather than on a Court-imposed resolution.

3. That the goal is to arrive at a fair and equitable agreement which will minimize, if not eliminate, the negative economic, social and emotional consequences of protracted litigation to Tom, Linda, Andy and their families.

B. NEGOTIATION IN GOOD FAITH: WITHOUT COURT OR OTHER ADVERSARIAL INTERVENTION

We, as participants agree to the following process:

4. To give full, honest and open disclosure of all relevant information, whether requested or not. Any request for disclosure of information will be made informally and such information will be supplied forthwith.

5. To engage in informal discussions and conferences to settle all issues. We will use our best efforts to create proposals which meet the fundamental needs of all Tom and Linda McGee and if necessary, to compromise to reach a settlement of all issues.

6. To settle this case without Court, or other adversarial intervention.

C. PARTICIPATION WITH INTEGRITY

We, as participants agree to the following code of behaviour:

7. To work to protect the privacy, respect and dignity of all involved, including Tom and Linda McGee and their families, their lawyers and any experts or consultants that may be offering assistance in this process.

8. To maintain a high standard of integrity and specifically not to take advantage of each other or of the miscalculations or inadvertent mistakes of others, but instead to identify and correct such errors.

D. CAUTIONS

We, as participants have received and understood the following cautions:

9. That while the Lawyers, Ricky Reasonable and Paul(a) Polite, share a commitment to the process described in this document, each of them has a professional duty to represent his or her own client diligently and is not the lawyer for the other party.

10. That Tom and Linda are still expected to assert their respective interests and their lawyers will help them do so, through vigorous good faith negotiation.

11. That there is no guarantee that the process will be successful in resolving the matters in dispute. We will attempt to build trust through our participation with integrity, but this may not overcome the distrust and irreconcilable differences which have led to the current breakdown of the marriage or relationship.

E. LAWYERS' FEES AND COSTS

12. Tom and Linda agree that our lawyers are entitled to be paid for their services. Each of us will be responsible for the payment of our own lawyer, and we agree to make funds available for this purpose.

F. EXPERTS AND CONSULTANTS

13. Tom and Linda and their lawyers agree that if experts or consultants are needed, we will retain them jointly, unless we agree otherwise in writing, and we will direct them to work in a neutral and cooperative effort to resolve issues.

G. CHILD'S ISSUES (IF APPLICABLE)

We have a shared commitment to arriving at a Parenting Plan that is in the best interests of Andy, and therefore agree to the following principles:

14. That in resolving issues about sharing the enjoyment of and

responsibility for our child, we will make every effort to reach amicable solutions, that are appropriate for Andy's stage of development, temperament and our availability to care for him.

15. We agree to act quickly to resolve differences related to our child. We may decide to engage the services of a Mediator to assist us in developing an appropriate Parenting Plan.

16. We agree not to seek a custody evaluation so long as the matters are being addressed through the Collaborative Law process.

17. We agree to minimize Andy's exposure to any conflict between us, and to promote a caring, loving and involved relationship between our child, both of us and our extended families.

18. If recommended by a professional, we agree to attend a parenting after separation seminar and to improve our communication as parents and to increase our understanding of the likely impact of separation on us and Andy, where such a program is available. Similarly, if a professional feels it would be in Andy's best interests, we will enrol him in a Children of Divorce program and support him in it.

H. ABUSE OF THE COLLABORATIVE PROCESS

19. Tom and Linda understand that their Collaborative Law Lawyers will withdraw from this case as soon as possible upon learning that either of us has withheld or misrepresented information or otherwise acted so as to undermine or take unfair advantage of the Collaborative Law process. Examples of such violations of the process are:

    - the secret disposing of property;
    - failing to disclose the existence or the true nature of assets and/or obligations;
    - failing to participate in the spirit of the collaborative process;
    - threatening litigation;
    - abusing our child;
    - using physical abuse or threats or intimidation against each other; or
    - planning to flee the jurisdiction of the Court with the child.

I. DISQUALIFICATION BY COURT INTERVENTION

We, as participants understand and agree with the following:

20. That the lawyers' representation is limited to the Collaborative Law process and that neither of our lawyers can ever represent us in Court in a proceeding against the other Party.

21. That in the event either of us chooses to abandon the Collaborative Law process, both lawyers will be disqualified from representing either of us.

22. That in the event that the Collaborative Law process terminates, Tom and Linda, as well as any experts, consultants or mediators, will be disqualified as witnesses, and their work product will be inadmissible as evidence unless we agree otherwise in writing.

23. If an agreement is reached, the lawyers may file such further divorce documents or other documents in accordance with the terms of the agreement and by consent of both lawyers.

24. That we will not disclose any statement, comment or disclosure made by either Tom or Linda, an expert, consultant, mediator or lawyer during the Collaborative Law process to any Court for any purpose unless a final settlement agreement is reached and Tom and Linda and their lawyers have agreed to such disclosure.

J. AGREEMENT AND PLEDGE

25. Tom and Linda and our lawyers have read this Participation Agreement, understand its terms and agree to comply with and carry out the spirit of this document.

Dated on the ____day of _______________, 20___ in ___________________.

Tom McGee
Husband (Father)

Linda McGee
Wife (Mother)

Ricky Reasonable
Lawyer for Husband (Father)

Paul(a) Polite
Lawyer for Wife (Mother)

Appendix III.3

Collaborative Mediation Retainer

The following is a Retainer that can be used when the clients begin dealing with their separation in mediation, rather than in an adversarial process, or when they begin a Collaborative Law process and then decide to resolve their parenting issues in mediation. The common objective is that the parties wish to avoid an adversarial approach and wish all professionals to share their commitment to this goal.

In the example below, the clients have chosen Comprehensive Collaborative Mediation (that is, they entered mediation to deal with both parenting and financial issues) and have agreed to retain Collaborative Lawyers when referred for independent legal advice.

Collaborative Mediation Retainer
Linda and Tom McGee

Linda and Tom McGee wish to resolve the issues in their separation in a non-adversarial manner, and as such they have agreed to the following terms:

1. Dr. Collaborator is retained to act as the Mediator with respect to the following issues:

   (i) parenting arrangements including custody of and access to the child;
   (ii) child support and spousal support;
   (iii) possession of the matrimonial home;
   (iv) division of financial assets; and
   (v) other financial issues.

2. The Mediator, Dr. Collaborator, is an impartial third party whose role is to assist Tom and Linda McGee to negotiate an agreement that meets the needs of both parties and their child.

3. In attempting to bring about an Agreement, the Mediator will meet with Tom and Linda McGee for joint sessions and on occasion for individual sessions. The Mediator may include in the mediation process any other significant third party, such as the child, legal counsel or other significantly involved persons, following consultation with Tom and Linda McGee.

4. Information shared with the Mediator during individual sessions may be shared with the other party, at the Mediator's discretion, unless the

individual interviewed requests that specific information be kept confidential. The Mediator may disclose any relevant information if there is a threat to anyone's safety.

5. Dr. Collaborator will be acting as a Mediator and will not be giving either party legal advice. Tom and Linda McGee have agreed to retain the services of Collaborative Family Law Lawyers as soon as possible to ensure that they are fully informed of their legal rights and obligations and the legal implications of any Agreement reached in mediation.

   As soon as the lawyers are retained, a Collaborative Mediation meeting will be held to introduce all the participants to each other, review and sign the Collaborative Mediation Participation Agreement, clarify roles and decide whether other professionals will be needed (such as accountants, valuators, etc.)

6. Tom and Linda McGee will make full disclosure and execute Releases of Information necessary for the Mediator to understand the issues being mediated with respect to parenting the child.

   When a tentative agreement is reached with respect to a Parenting Plan, a second Collaborative Mediation meeting will be held to review the Memorandum of Understanding with Tom and Linda McGee and their counsel, so that closure can be achieved on this issue. Once there is final agreement on the Parenting Plan, the Memorandum will be signed and witnessed with the lawyers.

   At this meeting any questions or concerns with respect to financial issues can be discussed so that the next part of the mediation process can proceed smoothly.

7. Prior to discussing issues related to property or support Tom and Linda McGee, with the assistance of their lawyers, will:

   (i) make full financial disclosure to each other and the Mediator;

   (ii) undertake not to hide or dispose of any assets; or

   (iii) not cancel or change any beneficiaries of life insurance policies while the mediation is in process.

8. In the event that information obtained during the mediation discloses an actual or potential threat to the safety of any of the participants or a breach of the *Child and Family Services Act* or *Criminal Code*, the Mediator is obligated to report such information.

9. If Tom and Linda McGee fail to agree on one or more issues it is understood that:

(i) the Mediator may prepare a report at the request of either party outlining the mediation process and Tom and Linda McGee's positions on those issues. She will not make recommendations with respect to any issues that are not resolved in mediation;

(ii) in the case of financial issues, any documents prepared for the purpose of financial disclosure may be used by Tom and Linda McGee in future proceedings, with their consent;

(iii) anything said or any admission or communication in the course of the mediation is <u>not</u> admissible in any legal proceeding;

(iv) In the event that Tom and Linda McGee are unable to resolve their issues in the Collaborative Mediation Process, the Mediator must withdraw and she will **<u>not</u>** be called as a witness, nor will her notes or other file documents be subpoenaed by, or on behalf of, either party in any legal proceeding; and

(v) the Mediator may be required by the court to testify despite this agreement to the contrary.

10. It is agreed that:

(i) client and client will each pay a retainer of $----- and share the cost of mediation equally; and

(ii) the hourly rate will be $---- per hour. The fees are subject to change upon notice by the Mediator.

11. <u>Cancellation Policy</u>
The notice must be provided during regular business hours <u>Monday through Thursdays</u>, between 9:00 a.m and 4:30 p.m.

(a) Tom and Linda will be billed for an appointment in which there is less than 48 hours (2 full business days) notice prior to cancellation. In the event that the meeting is scheduled for more than 2 hours then 4 full business days (Monday through Thursday) notice must be provided. Tom and Linda will each be responsible for bills arising from his/her own cancellation.

(b) Once a date has been agreed upon for a 5 (or 6) way Counsel Meeting, the following charges will apply to either client for re-scheduling or cancellation of the meeting:
(i) if 7 or more business days notice a $____ fee will be charged;
(ii) if between 5 and 7 business days notice a $____ fee will be charged; or
(iii) if 4 business days or less the entire session will be billed.

If a cancellation is due to the illness of a child or a circumstance beyond their control, Tom and Linda will share the cancellation fee equally. These charges are regardless of the reason for the cancellation, except at the Mediator's discretion.

12. It is understood that either of Tom and Linda McGee may terminate the mediation process at any time. If a party wishes to terminate, he or she will first discuss any concerns with the Mediator to see if these concerns can be resolved satisfactorily.

    The Mediator may suspend or terminate mediation whenever:

    (i) the process is likely to harm or prejudice one or more of the participants; or

    (ii) the usefulness of the mediation process is exhausted; or

    (iii) the Agreement being reached is unreasonable.

    The Mediator will first advise Tom and Linda McGee of the reason why she believes the mediation should be terminated.

13. Each of the undersigned acknowledges that he/she has read this Retainer and agrees to be bound by its terms.

DATED at ________, this _____ day of ____________, 20__.

____________________	____________________
WITNESS	Linda McGee
____________________	____________________
WITNESS	Tom McGee
____________________	____________________
WITNESS	Dr. Collaborator, Mediator

Appendix III.4

Collaborative Mediation Participation Agreement

Re: Jane and John Smith

A. THE COLLABORATIVE MEDIATION PROCESS

1. We acknowledge that the essence of "**COLLABORATIVE MEDIATION**" is the shared belief by the participants that it is in the best interests of Jane and John Smith and their children to (commit themselves to) resolve their family law issues through a non-adversarial, interest-based process rather than litigation.
2. Jane and John chose mediation supported by collaborative lawyers as their dispute resolution process for creating a Parenting Plan to promote the best interests of their children; and to reach an agreement with respect to a fair and equitable resolution of their property and support issues.
3. This process does not rely on a Court-imposed resolution, but does rely on all participants working together in an atmosphere of honesty, co-operation, integrity and professionalism geared toward the future well-being of the family.
4. The goal is to minimize, if not eliminate, the negative economic, social and emotional consequences of protracted litigation for Jane and John and their families.
5. Jane and John commit themselves to the Collaborative Mediation process and agree to seek a better way to resolve their differences justly and equitably.

B. NO COURT OR OTHER INTERVENTION

1. We commit ourselves to settling this case without Court intervention.
2. We agree to give full, honest and open disclosure of all relevant information, whether requested or not. Any request for disclosure of information will be made informally and such information will be supplied without delay.

3. We agree to engage in mediation meetings, informal discussions and, on an as needed basis, conferences including our lawyers or impartial experts, with a view to settlement of all issues.

C. NON-ADVERSARIAL PARTICIPATION

1. If experts or consultants are needed, Jane and John will retain them jointly, unless Jane and John and their lawyers agree otherwise in writing, and they will ask them to work in a neutral and cooperative manner to resolve issues.
2. We will work to protect the privacy, respect and dignity of all involved, including Jane and John Smith, the mediator, their lawyers, Sally Sure and Drew Certain, and any experts or consultants that may be offering assistance in this process.
3. We will maintain a high standard of integrity and specifically will not take advantage of each other or of the miscalculations or inadvertent mistakes of others, but will identify and correct them.

D. CAUTIONS

1. We understand that there is no guarantee that the process will be successful in resolving the matters in dispute.
2. We understand that the process cannot eliminate concerns about the differences which have led to the current breakdown of the marriage.
3. We understand that it is important that Jane and John understand how to protect their legal obligations and rights, and their lawyers will help them do so.
4. We understand that while the lawyers share a commitment to the process described in this document, each of them has a professional duty to represent his or her own client diligently and is not the lawyer for the other party.

E. PROFESSIONAL FEES AND COSTS

1. Jane and John Smith agree that Mediator and their lawyers Sally Sure and Drew Certain are entitled to be paid for their services. Jane and John are responsible for the payment of his or her own lawyer, and they will share the cost of other professionals in an equitable manner as agreed upon by them. Jane and John agree to make funds available for these services.

F. CHILDREN'S ISSUES

1. Jane and John Smith have engaged the services of a Mediator to assist them in developing an appropriate Parenting Plan that shares the responsibilities of parenting in a way that promotes their children's best interests.

2. We agree that in mediating the terms of a Parenting Plan we will make every effort to reach amicable solutions that share the responsibilities and enjoyment of parenting in a way that promotes the children's best interests.

3. We agree to act quickly to resolve differences related to Jane and John's children.

4. Jane and John agree not to seek a custody evaluation so long as the matters are being addressed through the Collaborative Mediation Process.

5. Jane and John agree to insulate their children from involvement in their disputes, and to promote a caring, loving and involved relationship between their children and both parents.

6. If recommended by a professional, Jane and John agree to attend a "parenting after separation program", involve the children in a similar program and participate in their own counselling to address the impact of the separation and their own personal issues.

G. NEGOTIATION IN GOOD FAITH

1. In Collaborative Mediation, each of us will be expected to take a reasoned approach in all disputes. Where our interests differ, each of us will use our best efforts to create proposals which meet the fundamental needs of Jane and John and their children, and if necessary, to compromise to reach a settlement of all issues.

2. Although each of us may discuss the likely outcome of a litigated result, neither of us will use threats of abandoning the Collaborative Mediation Process or of resorting to litigation as a way of forcing settlement.

H. ABUSE OF THE COLLABORATIVE PROCESS

1. Jane and John Smith understand that their Mediator and Collaborative Lawyers will withdraw from this case as soon as possible upon learning that his or her client has withheld or misrepresented information or otherwise acted so as to undermine or take unfair advantage of the Collaborative Mediation process.

Examples of violations of the process are:

- the secret disposing of property;
- failing to disclose the existence or the true nature of assets and/or obligations;
- unreasonably delaying financial disclosure or the valuation of assets;
- failing to participate in the spirit of the collaborative process;
- abusing the children of the parties;
- withholding the children contrary to the spirit of this Agreement and without the consent of the other parent; or
- planning to flee the jurisdiction of the Court with the children.

I. DISQUALIFICATION BY COURT INTERVENTION

1. Jane and John understand that their lawyers' representation is limited to the Collaborative Mediation process and that neither of their lawyers can ever represent them in Court in a proceeding against the other party.

2. In the event that the Collaborative Mediation process terminates, all experts and consultants and any documents prepared for the purpose of the Collaborative Mediation process may be used in future proceedings with the consent of both parties in writing.

3. We agree that subject to paragraph 2, we will not disclose any statement, comment or disclosure made by any party, mediator, expert, consultant or lawyer during the Collaborative Mediation process to any Court for any purpose unless a final settlement agreement is reached and both parties and their lawyers have agreed to such disclosure.

4. As part of the Collaborative Mediation process, one or both parties may ask the mediator for a non-binding opinion with respect to parenting issues only, but neither party will subpoena the Mediator to testify in any court proceeding.

5. If an agreement is reached, the lawyers may file such further divorce documents or other documents in accordance with the terms of the Agreement.

J. AGREEMENT AND PLEDGE

1. Jane and John Smith, Mediator, Sally Sure and Drew Certain hereby agree to the above and pledge to comply with and to promote the spirit and written word of this document.

Dated at ---------- on the <day> day of <month>, 20--.

______________________	______________________
WITNESS	wife
______________________	______________________
WITNESS	husband
______________________	______________________
WITNESS	Sally Sure (Counsel for husband)
______________________	______________________
WITNESS	Drew Certain (Counsel for wife)
______________________	______________________
WITNESS	Mediator

Appendix III.5

Steps in a Collaborative Practice Case

TOM AND LINDA McGEE

1. Linda calls Paul/a Polite, who is listed as a full member of the Collaborative Family Law Association, and is sent an information package explaining Collaborative Family Law.

2. Paul/a sends a similar package to Tom with a note saying that Linda had suggested he/she send it and offering the names of other Collaborative Family Lawyers.

3. First Meeting: Linda meets with Paul/a for an initial consultation which includes:
   - An overview of issues to be resolved and Linda's immediate and longer term needs
   - Discussion of dispute resolution options available
   - Consensus that a Collaborative approach would be preferred if Tom agrees
   - Linda signs a Collaborative Law Retainer retaining Paul/a

4. Tom agrees and retains Ricky Reasonable from the list.

   - Tom signs a Collaborative Law Retainer retaining Ricky.

5. Paul/a and Ricky have a preliminary "meeting" in person if they have not worked together previously, or by telephone if they have a good working relationship, in order to:
   - Schedule first 4 way meeting
   - Share observations of clients
   - Agree on agenda, prioritize issues, and identify sensitive areas
   - Agree on initial conflict management strategies

   (Note: in this case assume that Paul/a and Ricky know each other and have a good working relationship. If this were NOT the case what other steps would be necessary?)

6. Second Meeting: Each client meets with his/her own lawyer to:
   - Prepare for first 4 way meeting. Review basic principles in Collaborative Law Participation Agreement
   - Clarify issues to be discussed
   - Clarify role of lawyer and role of clients (i.e., clients take the lead and lawyers play a supportive and advisory role)
   - Coach client in effective, interest based presentation of issues. Ask open ended questions, explain "why" something is important, use "I" messages, avoid making assumptions or attacking the other person
   - Make appropriate referrals for supportive counseling, parent coaching and/or mediation, certified divorce specialist for financial advice, etc.

7. Third Meeting: First 4-way Collaborative Meeting to:
   - Explain Collaborative Family Law to be sure all have a similar understanding
   - Discuss and sign Collaborative Law Participation Agreement and review relevant Rules of Conduct

- Discuss how conflicts will be addressed and process for dealing with apparent impasses — clarify what will and what will NOT happen
- Identify issues to be addressed and the order of priority
- Allow clients to talk about marriage breakdown — why it happened and how each feels
- If appropriate, suggest relevant counselling resources to deal with emotional response to separation
- Determine how parenting arrangements for Andy will be worked out — i.e. likely involve an impartial professional with expertise in children's issues such as a mediator, parenting coach or child specialist. Consider Andy's needs and concerns. What will be each party's responsibility re arranging and paying for this person? Should this person attend for part of the next 4-way meeting?
- If there is time and clients are "ready", clarify information /documents to be exchanged (e.g., financial information forms, income tax returns, business statements, etc.)
- Discuss any temporary arrangements that need to be addressed (e.g., interim parenting arrangements, interim spousal and child support, and interim possession of the matrimonial home)
- Set time and location for next few meetings
- Agree on agenda for next meeting
- Determine who will summarize discussion in a Progress Note to be shared at next meeting

8. Fourth Meeting: Post-Meeting conference (Linda and Paul/a; Tom and Ricky) to:
    - Review satisfaction with 4-way Collaborative Meeting
    - Set up relationship with person dealing with Parenting Plans — ensure they understand and will abide by CFL principles (sign Collaborative Retainer?)
    - Collect or Prepare documents to be exchanged
    - Consider preliminary goals for settlement — yours and theirs (i.e., strategic brainstorming)

9. Fifth Meeting: Post-Meeting telephone conference between Paul/a and Ricky to:

    - Review progress made in first 4-way meeting and determine what worked well or did not work and how subsequent meetings could be improved
    - Discuss agenda for next 4-way meeting

10. Sixth Meeting: Second (or additional) 4-way Collaborative Meeting:

- Invite person assisting with Parenting Plans to attend part of 4-way meeting and to set up a subsequent meeting with the parents as soon as possible to discuss Andy's needs and the mobility issue
- Clarify WHAT information needs to be collected (e.g., house appraisal, business valuation, value of professional licence, and value of some household contents), HOW it will be collected, WHO will collect it and by WHEN
- Identify what each party hopes to achieve and/or is concerned about with respect to each issue. Spend time clarifying substantive, procedural and psychological interests
- Consider involvement of a Certified Divorce Specialist to assist with financial issues
- Determine who will summarize discussion in a Progress Note to be shared at next meeting (usually alternate)

11. Continue with pre- and post-meeting conferences between each client and his/her lawyer and/or between the 2 lawyers.

12. Seventh Meeting

    - Review draft Memorandum of Understanding re Parenting Plan and invite person assisting with Parenting Plan to participate
    - Finalize parenting plan
    - Review Progress Note from previous meeting
    - Review information collected by both parties
    - Generate options that meet each party's needs and interests
    - Determine who will summarize discussion in a Progress Note to be shared at next meeting (usually alternate)

13. Eighth Meeting

    - Invite Certified Divorce Specialist to attend
    - Arrive at agreements re property division and support (Note: nothing is final until all issues are resolved)
    - Determine who will prepare and serve the Divorce Petition and when and where it will be served

14. Prepare Draft Agreement

    - Decide who will draft comprehensive Agreement (based on Progress Notes and MOU re Parenting Plan)
    - Draft in language the parties' understand and will feel committed to follow
    - Review draft with each party separately and exchange suggestions for changes. If both parties agree, incorporate changes

15. Ninth Meeting: 4-way Collaborative Meeting to review Draft, discuss any proposed changes. Make corrections and sign.

16. Tom serves Response to Petition by mail and divorce papers filed for uncontested divorce.

Appendix III.6

Steps for Clients in the Collaborative Mediation Process

Outline of Steps for Clients in a Collaborative Mediation Case

1. Complete Intake Form

2. Initial meeting between Mediator and both Lawyers (only if lawyers are already retained, otherwise see step 6 for first involvement of lawyers)

3. Initial Mediation meeting (clients and Mediator)
   - Retainer contract
   - Overview of objectives
   - Determine process

4. Client Individual meetings with Mediator
   - Background
   - Goals

5. Clients retain Collaborative Family Law Lawyers and sign Collaborative Family Law Retainer to retain their own CFL Lawyers

6. Mediation meetings with both clients regarding Parenting Plan

7. 3-way meeting or conference call with Collaborative CFL Lawyers to plan 5-way meeting with clients, CFL Lawyers and Mediator

8. Create Memorandum of Understanding regarding Parenting Issues
   - Review with clients
   - Send to CFL Lawyers to review with their clients (if changes desired, discuss in 5-way meeting with Mediator)

9. 5-way Collaborative Mediation Meeting with CFL Lawyers, Mediator, and clients*
   - Signing of Collaborative Mediation Participation Agreement

- Finalize Parenting Plan
- Clarify financial issues

10. Mediation meetings regarding financial issues, for example:

    Property Division:
    - Matrimonial home(s) and contents
    - Pension
    - RRSP's
    - Value of business (if applicable)
    - Stock options
    - Life insurance
    - Other (debts, line of credit, and mortgage)
    - Pre-marital assets

    Support:
    - Spousal support
    - Child support
    - Medical/dental benefits
    - Private school
    - Special and/or extraordinary expenses and summer camp
    - Daycare and other special expenses

11. Create Memorandum of Understanding regarding Property and Financial Issues
    - Review with clients
    - Send to CFL Lawyers to review with their clients (if changes desired, discuss in 5-way meeting with Mediator)

12. 5-way Collaborative Meeting with CFL Lawyers, Mediator, and Clients to finalize Agreement*

***NOTE:**

- If Lawyers are involved before the mediation begins, schedule an initial meeting with them before the initial meeting with clients
- Mediator and CFL Lawyers debrief via a teleconference call, after each 5-way meeting

Appendix IV Contents

Custody Assessments

Appendix IV.1

Outline of Custody Assessment Procedure

As a general outline, the procedure in custody assessments is as follows:

(a) *Meet with counsel for the parties in order to:*

- clarify what the assessor's role will be;
- establish whether a "mediative" approach is to be attempted at some point in the assessment; that is, encouraging the parents to contribute to the development of their parenting plan;
- permit counsel, in each other's presence, to explain which factors they feel are particularly significant in the case;
- ask counsel to provide affidavits, notices of motion, transcripts of evidence, professional reports, and other documents relevant to the assessment issues; and
- clarify the payment of fees, including fees for the preparation of a report, court preparation, and attendance as an expert witness.

(b) *Meet with the parties together in order to:*

- explain the assessor's role as an objective, impartial professional as between the parents;
- clarify whether a "mediative" approach is to be attempted at some point in the assessment; that is, encourage the parents to contribute to a parenting plan whereby they share parental responsibilities and visitation with the child(ren) that is in the best interests of the child(ren);
- clarify the assessor's role, that is, to represent the best interests of the child(ren) in the event that the parents are not able to agree on a shared parenting plan;
- clarify the procedure to be followed in the assessment, including who is to be interviewed, in what location, and on how many occasions; and
- obtain the names of persons and agencies who have reliable and relevant information with respect to parenting capacity and the needs and interests of the child(ren).

(c) *Meet with each parent individually.*

- determine each parent's plan of care;
- obtain relevant personal and relationship history;
- explore each parent's needs, interests, concerns and goals with respect to a parenting plan; and
- screen for abuse and control.

(d) *Meet with the child(ren) individually, with siblings* (if any), and together *with each parent*.

- screen for abuse, fear, intimidation or witnessing abuse;
- identify concerns and special needs and interests;
- obtain constructive suggestions, and priorities from the child's perspective (without asking the child to take sides);
- assess each child's temperament, maturity and ability to adapt to change; and
- assess child's comfort level with extended family and readiness to accept new partners.

(e) *Meet with other significant adults* who will be playing a caretaking role, such as new and common-law spouses, grandparents, and other caretakers.

(f) *Request information from relevant sources* such as schools, family doctors, mental health professionals, *etc.*

(g) *Conduct home visits* to observe:

- the child(ren) interacting with each parent and step-parents, siblings, and step siblings;
- the neighbourhood setting of each home;
- the household routines as they pertain to the child(ren); and
- the standards of cleanliness, nutrition and disciplinary limits set.

(h) *Arrange for psychological testing* of the child(ren) and adults if necessary.

(i) *Prepare a Memorandum of Understanding and/or an assessment report.*
Custody assessments usually take approximately 20 to 30 hours of interviews and data collection. It is difficult to judge the exact number of hours because this depends on the complexity of the case, the seriousness of the concerns with respect to parenting capacity, the number of individuals involved, and the willingness of the parties to resolve the issues by agreement. Preparation of a Memorandum of Understanding and/or an assessment report requires additional time.

Appendix IV.2

Assessment Retainer Contract

Re: (*Client's Names*)

1. It is hereby agreed that (*Assessor's name*), Mental Health Professional, is retained to act as the Assessor with respect to:

(i) a parenting plan, including, custody of and access to the children of the marriage.

2. It is acknowledged that the Assessor is an impartial third party whose role is to assist the parties to negotiate an agreement to the extent that it is feasible in the circumstances, and where agreement is not possible, to prepare a report with recommendations as to a parenting plan that is in the children's best interests.

3. In conducting the Assessment, the Assessor will meet with the parties for joint sessions and on occasion for individual sessions. The Assessor will have the right at any time to include in the assessment process any other significant third party, such as the children, a new partner, grandparents, other relatives, legal counsel or other significantly involved persons as he/she deems necessary.

4. Information shared with the Assessor during individual sessions may be shared with the other party, at the Assessor's discretion, unless the individual interviewed requests that specific information be kept confidential. The Assessor may disclose any relevant information if there is a threat to anyone's safety.

OR

Information shared with the Assessor during individual sessions will be kept confidential except with permission of the speaker. The Assessor may disclose any relevant information if there is a threat to anyone's safety.

5. The Assessor may obtain information from relevant sources and may consult such persons and read such reports, records or documents as he/she deems necessary for arriving at an Agreement.

It is agreed that the parties will:

(i) make full disclosure of all relevant information reasonably required for the Assessor to understand the issues being assessed;
(ii) execute any Releases of Information necessary for the Assessor to obtain relevant information.

6. In the event that information obtained during the Assessment disclosed reasonable grounds to suspect that a child was or may be in need of protection or raised a threat to the safety of any of the participants, the Assessor is obligated to report such information to the appropriate authorities.

7. The parties understand that any interim agreement with respect to custody of or access to the children will be a factor to be considered by the courts, in the event that an agreement is not reached in the Assessment.

8. Neither party nor anyone acting on their behalf will take any fresh steps in the legal proceedings without prior notice to the Assessor and the other party with respect to those issues that are being assessed.

9. If the parties reach agreement on some or all of the issues, the Assessor shall prepare a Memorandum of Understanding with respect to those issues for consideration by the parties and their respective counsel. The parties are strongly advised to obtain independent legal advice, preferably before the Assessment commences, but in any event, before a final agreement is reached, to ensure that they are fully informed of their legal rights and obligations and the legal implications of such an agreement.

10. If the parties fail to agree on one or more issues it is understood that:

(i) the Assessor will prepare a report outlining the Assessor's recommendations;
(ii) anything said or any admission or communication made in the course of the Assessment may be used in the report; and
(iii) the Assessor may be called as a witness by either party in a legal proceeding and would be open to cross-examination by either counsel.

11. Copies of the report will be distributed to both counsel, both parties and the court prior to the court date.

12. It is agreed that;

(i) each party will pay a retainer of $ _________ each and will share the costs of the assessment equally;
(ii) interim accounts shall be sent out to the parties and payment shall be due when rendered;
(iii) the hourly rate will be $ _________ per hour and is subject to a change upon notice by the Assessor;
(iv) from time to time an additional retainer will be requested to cover the anticipated next steps in the assessment. The Assessment will not continue until the retainer is paid.

13. Interest will be charged at the Prime Rate on all accounts outstanding after 30 (thirty) days from the date the account is rendered.

14. Cancellation Policy

Notice of Cancellation must be provided during regular business hours Monday through Friday, between 9:00 am and 4:30 pm.

The clients will be billed for an appointment in which there is less than 48 hours (2 full business days) notice prior to cancellation. In the event that the meeting is scheduled for more than 2 hours then 4 full business days (Monday through Friday) notice must be provided. The clients will each be responsible for bills arising from his/her own cancellation.

If a cancellation is due to the illness of a child or a circumstance beyond their control, the clients will share the cancellation fee equally. These charges are regardless of the reason for the cancellation, except at the Assessor's discretion.

15. Any report or Memorandum of Understanding will not be released until all outstanding professional fees and disbursements related to the Assessment have been paid in full.

16. In the event that the Assessor is called to court, a separate fee shall be required for preparation and attendance as an expert witness. This fee shall be paid in advance by the party who is calling the Assessor as an expert witness.

17. Each of the undersigned acknowledges that he/she has read this Retainer and agrees to be bound by the terms herein.

DATED at ______, this ______day of _________, 20___.

WITNESS	FATHER'S NAME
WITNESS	MOTHER'S NAME
WITNESS	ASSESSOR

OR

18. Counsel for the parties agree that they will assist the Assessor to obtain payment of his/her account in the same proportion as the parties are required to pay according to this Retainer. The Assessor agrees that he/she will notify the lawyers and the parties before the retainer is depleted and ask for a further retainer. The Assessment will not continue until a further retainer is received.

19. Counsel acknowledges receipt of this document and agrees, subject to approval by their client, that the terms herein describe the nature of the Assessment retainer.

DATED at ______, this ______day of _________, 20___.

______________	______________________
WITNESS	COUNSEL FOR THE FATHER
______________	______________________
WITNESS	COUNSEL FOR THE MOTHER
______________	______________________
WITNESS	ASSESSOR

Appendix IV.3

Custody/Access Assessment Guidelines*

Ontario Interdisciplinary
Association of Custody/Access Assessors

PREFACE

The original *Custody/Access Assessment Guidelines* (1988) provided assessors with a detailed outline of the essential steps involved in conducting assessments in this challenging area. The authors ensured that consultation came from diverse professional perspectives resulting in a generic set of "commonly understood norms . . . [which] could then serve as the basis for future professional standards." Eight years later, this document still is the basic standard for providing parents, their lawyers and the court with important information and guidance in planning the care of children in separated families. It also has been employed by the various professional Colleges in making judgements about their members' performance in this emotionally charged area.

As assessors incorporated the *Guidelines* into their own practices, it became clear that aspects of the procedures could be clarified, expanded and rated for importance. The new *Guidelines* updates procedures with current practice, and

* **Authors:** Gary Austin Ph.D., C.Psych; Mario Bartoletti, Ed.D.; Barbara Chisholm, M.S.W.; Linda Chodos, M.S.W., C.S.W.; Barbara Landau, Ph.D., LL.B., LL.M.; Andrea Litvack, M.S.W., C.S.W.; and Howard Waiser, Ph.D., C.Psych. These Guidelines represent a revision of the original Custody/Access Guildelines which were published by the Ontario Psychological Foundation (now known as the Psychology Foundation of Canada) in 1988. Endorsed by the Psychology Foundation of Canada. Reproduced with the permission of the Ontario Interdisciplinary Committee on Custody/Access Assessment.

includes two new sections, one on Court Testimony and another on the Maintenance and Release of File Information.

Most important, the new *Guidelines* classifies all of the procedures as either "mandatory" or "discretionary" to define a primary base of necessary activities and some areas of flexibility. The meaning of these terms is as follows:

Mandatory: Procedures which must be done to provide an adequate custody and access assessment for the parents or the court. If a procedure is not done, then a comparable one should be done or a rationale should be provided.

Discretionary: Procedures which are recommended but which are subject to the clinical judgement of the assessor depending on such factors as variations in professional practice, case requirements, financial limits, time limits and so forth.

The Committee would like to emphasize that the *Guidelines* is not a manual that details all the clinical techniques, assessment criteria, ethical dilemmas *etc*., that this information can be found in a number of textbooks or training programs on custody and access assessments. Furthermore, the *Guidelines* do not set out the specific qualifications of an assessor, although the Committee recognizes the broad set of skills this area of forensic practice requires.

The Committee hopes that these guidelines assist assessors to offer parents, lawyers and the court, a quality service that leads to sound parenting plans for children experiencing separation and divorce.

(June 10, 1996)

I. PURPOSE AND PRESUMPTIONS

A. PURPOSE

The purpose of a custody/access assessment[1] is to advise parents, their lawyers and the court about those parenting arrangements which would be in the best interest[2] of the children[3] and within the capabilities of the family.

B. PRESUMPTIONS

1^{M}. that an assessment will only be undertaken by a mental health professional who is qualified to conduct custody and access assessment;[4]

2^{M}. that the parent[5] be strongly advised to have independent legal advice;

---

1 These guidelines do not address specific issues in relation to child welfare assessments or cases in which there is physical or sexual abuse.

2 The term "best interests" is defined, for example, in the Ontario *Children's Law Reform Act*, R.S.O., 1990, c. C.12, s. 24(2).

3 Throughout this report, the term "children" will be used to refer to either "child" or "children".

4 "Qualified" means that the assessor meets the standards set out in s. 30(1) of the *Children's Law Reform Act*, R.S.O., 1990, c. C. 12, or the relevant family law legislation in the jurisdiction where the assessment is being conducted.

3[M]. that a complete and impartial custody/access assessment cannot be conducted on a one-sided basis (*i.e.*, not on behalf of one parent alone, but only on behalf of the family as a whole;[6]

4[M]. that an assessor must disclose any prior relationship between the assessor and any member of the family and, in most cases, should not perform an assessment if there is a prior relationship of any kind unless with written consent.

5[M]. that the parties to the assessment be informed that the assessment process is not confidential, and that any information received by the assessor is subject to subpoena;

6[M]. that evidence of child abuse or imminent harm to an adult or child will be reported to the appropriate authorities;[7]

7[M]. that, in cases where issues arise that are beyond the scope of the assessor's expertise, the assessor will seek consultation with a professional in the area of concern.

8[D]. that joint sessions should be considered cautiously in cases of domestic violence and always with safeguards and on a voluntary basis;

9[D]. that the assessor explore the possibility of a settlement by encouraging the active participation and mutual cooperation of the parents.

10[D]. that parents contribute, whenever possible, to the development of the parenting plan that is in the best interests of their children;

11[M]. that, if ordered by the court, the assessor is obliged to prepare a report which may contain recommendations, to be submitted to the parents and lawyers, and to be filed with the court;

12[M]. that, after the completion of the assessment, the assessor and the parents should avoid switching the role of an assessor to a role that would render any possible future testimony and/or re-assessment invalid (c.f. closed mediation, therapy for one party).

II. PROCEDURE

A. Referral and Contracting

Although most referrals are made by lawyers, they may be made by other people such as parents, social service or court personnel and other professionals. The

---

5 The term "parents" in these guidelines includes foster parents, guardians, adoptive parents or any other people who may function as parents to the child.

6 One-sided assessments are partial, by definition, and therefore inadequate for determining the most appropriate parenting arrangements. In addition, when conducted on behalf of one parent, instead of both parents, they tend to exacerbate conflict within the family. Clinical contact with only one parent and the children in a treatment context may provide some limited understanding of the family, but does not constitute a complete custody/access assessment and therefore no recommendations with respect to custody and access issues should be made.

M Mandatory — those activities that ought to occur (see Preface)

D Discretionary — those activities that may occur (see Preface)

7 If disclosure of abuse occurs during the assessment, the assessor should consider suspending the assessment until the matter has been addressed.

assessor should first contract with the lawyers, if they have been retained, and then with the parents.

1M. Contracting with the Lawyers:

The assessor should communicate (meeting, letter or telephone) with all the lawyers prior to commencing the assessment, in order to accomplish the following:

a. to review the assumptions stated above;
b. to affirm that the assessor will act in an impartial and unbiased manner;
c. to identify the specific issues and questions to be addressed in the assessment;
d. to discuss the assessment procedure and rationale;
e. to determine the reporting procedure:
   (1) when the report is due,
   (2) the scope and distribution of the report, and
   (3) whether specific recommendations are required;
f. to agree on the fees, including an estimate of the total anticipated cost, the hourly rate, the proportion to be paid by each party and the method of payment (for example, by way of retainer or on account with the lawyers;[8]
g. to receive materials such as affidavits, court documents, reports and other relevant documents;
h. to clarify the nature of the communication process with the lawyers throughout the assessment process;
i. to clarify that the assessor will request of all referring lawyers that all pertinent written materials are copied to the other lawyer; and
j. to clarify that all written material from the assessor will be copied to all lawyers.

2M. Contracting with the Parents:

The assessor shall arrive at a contractual agreement with the parents. This process can be accomplished in individual or joint meetings at the discretion of the assessor. In cases involving domestic violence, a joint meeting may not be advisable.

The objectives of the contractual process are:

a. to review and confirm all of the contracting issues agreed to by the lawyers;
b. to discuss the assessment procedure, including:
   (i) who may be seen or contacted;

---

8 It may be advisable to obtain a retainer which should be held in a trust account pending provision of services.

(ii) what may take place during the sessions;
(iii) whether home visits will be conducted;
(iv) the lack of confidentiality of the assessment process; namely, that any information obtained or opinions formed, during the assessment may be included in the assessment report, which in turn may be filed with the court to become part of the public record;
(v) how long the process is likely to take.

c. to determine other relevant professional sources of information regarding the children's needs (for example, school teachers, the family doctor, mental health professionals, *etc.*); and to obtain signed consent forms to gather information from these sources.[9]

d. to clarify that all materials submitted to the assessor will be reviewed with both parents at the discretion of the assessor.

3[D]. Confirming letter or retainer contract:

The assessor may choose to summarize in writing the terms of reference and any contractual issues which have been agreed upon with the lawyers and the parents.

B. ASSESSMENT PROCESS

In the assessment process itself, the following contacts may be made. The type of contact, the order in which they are made and the amount of time spent on any one of them, will vary according to the individual case and the judgment of the particular assessor.

1[D]. In meeting with the parents together the following objectives should be considered:

a. to provide education regarding the effects of separation and divorce on children and parents, and regarding alternative parenting arrangements;
b. to observe the interaction between the parents and to attempt to improve the parents' communication;
c. to assess the parents' ability and willingness to cooperate with each other.

2[M]. Meeting with each parent individually:

a. to explore any issues such as: individual, marital and family history, spousal or child abuse, mental health, addictions, parenting ability, special concerns about the children, personal future plans, *etc.*;

---

[9] As a fee may be required to obtain such information from a professional, it should be explained that such fees will be treated as disbursements on the assessor's account.

b. to learn about their children, including any special needs they may have;
c. to discuss each parent's proposal with respect to parenting arrangements;
d. to consider each parent's willingness to cooperate with the other parent in sharing parental responsibilities;
e. to determine areas of agreement with respect to parenting arrangements.

3[M] Meeting with each parent and the children together:

a. to observe the interaction between each parent and the children with respect to emotional responses, discipline and the overall quality of their family relationships, including sibling interaction.
b. this meeting can be contraindicated in some exceptional cases, for example, in cases of abuse.

4[M]. Interviewing the children:

a. to ascertain each child's level of maturity, particular interests, aptitudes, abilities, special needs, daily routines *etc.*;
b. to assess the relationship among the children and each child's perception of his or her relationship and involvement with family members;
c. to assess each child's views regarding possible parenting arrangements where they can be reasonably ascertained;
d. to explore issues of safety among family member;[10]
e. to assess how each child is coping in all respects (for example, emotionally, socially and academically).

5[D]. Meeting with the family as a whole:

a. to familiarize oneself with the family as a whole and to form an impression of them as a group.

6[M]. Interviewing significant other caregivers\collaterals:

(Such as partners, grandparents, nannies, extended family members, step-siblings or others at the discretion of the assessor.)

a. to ascertain the nature of their relationships with the children and/or parents;
b. to determine their perspectives on the family and their views on possible parenting arrangements; and

---

10 If there are reasonable grounds to suspect that a child is or may be suffering, or may have suffered abuse, the assessor must report the suspicion and the information on which it is based to the local child protection agency (cf. the Ontario *Child and Family Services Act*, R.S.O., s. 68, 1990).

c. to see how they might contribute to and\or participate in any new parenting plan.

7[D]. Home visits:

The assessor may choose to visit each parent's home so as to enable the assessor:

a. to assess the family's behaviour in their own natural setting and
b. to observe the environment of each proposed home.

8[M]. Communication with relevant professionals (for example, mental health, physicians, educators, police, *etc.*):

a. to acquire from relevant professionals (usually by telephone or report) specific information about, as well as their general impression of, family members.

9[D]. Psychological testing:

Where the assessor has been trained and is qualified in this area, psychological testing may be used.

C. Analysis and Formulation

At this stage in the assessment, the assessor reviews all of the data collected and impressions formed in light of the nature and the objectives of the particular assessment.

1[M]. In those cases where the parents have reached agreement, the purpose of the analysis and formulation is:

a. to clarify and elaborate the parenting plan;
b. to evaluate the soundness of the plan especially with respect to the children;
c. to approve those aspects of the plan that are appropriate; and
d. to make any recommendations that may be necessary.

2[M]. In those cases where the parents have not reached agreement, the purpose is:

a. to formulate recommendations for a parenting plan (incorporating the parents' plan, where appropriate) based on a review of the entire assessment process.

D. Verbal Presentation of Findings

1[D]. Verbal presentation to the Lawyers:

a. to inform the lawyers as to the outcome of the assessment;
b. to explain the process of the assessment and the rationale for the findings;

c. to allow the lawyers to ask questions, offer comments or make factual corrections;
d. to give the lawyers an opportunity to achieve a settlement regarding a parenting plan;
e. to facilitate the acceptance and implementation of the plan; and
f. to advise the lawyers, should the matter be proceeding to trial, of the assessor's availability to meet with them, preferably together, to prepare for trial and of the assessor's willingness to be cross-examined by the lawyers.

2[D]. Presentation to the Parents (separately or together):

a. to inform the parents as to the outcome of the assessment;
b. to explain the rationale for any recommendations;
c. to allow the parents to ask questions or to offer any comments as well as to make any factual corrections;
d. to invite the parents to cooperate in an agreement, based on the assessment findings; and
e. to discuss implementation of the plan.

III. WRITTEN REPORT

A. Report of Parental Agreement

1[D]. When the parents have been able to develop a complete parenting plan that the assessor thinks is not contrary to the best interests of the children, the assessor may:

a. prepare a report describing the parenting plan;
b. provide a limited commentary on the plan;
c. recommend that it be implemented; and
d. assist the lawyers in preparing Minutes of Settlement.

B. Report in the Event of Parental Disagreement

If parental agreement has not been reached, the assessor should:

1[M]. prepare a report containing relevant information and the assessor's recommendations;

2[M]. include in the report sufficient information and rationale for the recommendations so as to assist the court in arriving at a judgment; and

3[M]. ensure that any potentially damaging material is presented in such a manner as to take into account its impact on family members and their relationships (bearing in mind who might read the report both now and in the future).

C. Comprehensive Assessment Report

The following headings identify the important information to be contained in a report; however, there may be individual differences in style and format depending on the assessor's judgement and the circumstances of the case.

1[M]. Referral Sources:

The report should state whether it is a court-ordered assessment or one that is being conducted on the consent of the parties, and the referral source.

2[M]. Reasons for Referral:

The report should set out the circumstances leading to the referral and the reasons given by the referral sources.

3[M]. Objectives of the Assessment:

The report should set out the issues to be addressed by the assessment; for example whether the primary concern is the best parenting arrangement or whether the issue is restricted to the most appropriate access schedule or the involvement of a new partner in the children's lives.

4[D]. Qualifications of the Assessor:

The report could contain a brief summary of the assessor's qualifications and a *curriculum vitae* should be attached to the report or provided prior to a trial.

5[M]. Assessment Process and Sources of Information:

The report should state who was seen or spoken to and the relevant reports and materials reviewed.

6[D]. Family History:

The report could contain relevant family history; that is, information that pertains to the objectives of the assessment.

7[M]. The Children:

The report should summarize the assessor's understanding of the children, including information and observations that are relevant to the objectives of the assessment.

8[M]. The Parents:

The report should identify the parents' issues and summarize the assessor's understanding of the parents, including information and observations that are relevant to the objectives of the assessment.

9[M]. Summary:

The report should contain a summary of the relevant information including the assessor's clinical opinions.

10[M]. Discussion of Alternative Parenting Arrangements:

The report may discuss viable parenting options in light of the objectives of the assessment. The relative strengths and weaknesses of the alternatives may be presented.

11[M]. Rationale for Recommendations:

The assessor should set out the criteria, which may include legislated criteria, used in making any recommendations and should summarize the key factors, with respect to each criterion, that are relevant to a recommendation.

12[D]. Recommendations:

The report may contain the assessor's specific recommendations about parenting arrangements and their implementation including the involvement of professionals or agencies.

IV. COURT TESTIMONY

Usually one parent's lawyer subpoenas the assessor to a trial, often the parent who is most supported by the report's recommendations. Usually this parent or the lawyer pays the assessor for the trial preparation and appearance. If the assessor is asked to testify, the following events may occur:

1[D]. Communication with Lawyers before court to provide:

a. an acknowledgement of the trial appearance notice;
b. an estimate of the costs for preparation, travel, and court testimony;
c. the conditions for consultation before the trial;
d. a *curriculum vitae*, if not provided earlier.

2[D]. Submission of the Clinical File:

a. if a lawyer wants to subpoena the clinical file, the assessor should receive a notice of motion and may wish to argue in motions court that parts of the file should not be open to the parents.

3[D]. Materials to bring to Court:

a. the entire clinical file and supporting documents.

V. MAINTENANCE AND RELEASE OF FILE INFORMATION

Custody and access files are a special case in that they contain information on conflicting parties whose interests likely differ and yet whose rights need to be protected. While it is indicated that some information should be released to parents, clinical judgment must be employed to determine if harm may result.

Policies for the release of file information may vary across disciplines and individual assessors should consult with their regulatory organization if they are uncertain how to proceed.

VI. COMMENTS ON THE *GUIDELINES* INVITED

A. COMMENTS

The Committee would be pleased to receive any comments on the *Guidelines* and any suggestions as to possible improvements. Also, should you wish to receive notification of any future work of the Committee, kindly send your name and address.

Persons wishing to receive further information about the association may write to:

Ontario Interdisciplinary Association of Custody/access Assessors
c/o LITVACK & CHODOS ASSOCIATES
40 Sheppard Avenue West
Suite 610
Toronto, Ontario
M2N 6K9
(June 10, 1996)

Appendix IV.4

Outline of Custody Assessment Report

1. Referral Sources
2. Reasons for Referral
3. Objectives of the Assessment
4. Qualifications of the Assessor
5. Assessment Process
6. Family History, Including Relevant Marital History, Child Development, and Family Dynamics

7. Summary of Observations of the Family and of Information from Other Sources
8. Summary of Important Issues
9. Alternative Parenting Arrangements
10. Rationale for the Recommendations
11. Recommendations of Assessor

Appendix V Contents

Family Arbitration

Appendix V.1

Family Arbitration Agreement

IN THE MATTER OF THE *ARBITRATION ACT, 1991*, S.O. 1991, c. 17, as amended, and the *FAMILY LAW ACT*, R.S.O. 1990, c. F.3, as amended

B E T W E E N:

Party-1

("Party-1 First Name")

- and -

Party-2

("Party-2 First Name")

FAMILY ARBITRATION AGREEMENT

1. SUBMISSION

1.1 This Agreement is a Family Arbitration Agreement made under the *Arbitration Act* and the *Family Law Act*. It is effective when:

(a) It has been signed by both parties and witnessed;

(b) Each Party's Certificate of Independent Legal Advice and each Lawyer's Certificate of Independent Legal Advice has been signed, in the forms attached; and

(c) The Arbitrator has signed the Certificate of Arbitrator, in the form attached.

1.2 The Arbitrator for this Arbitration is Mr./Ms. Arbitrator.

1.3 The Certificates of Independent Legal Advice and the Certificate of Arbitrator appended to this Agreement are part of this Agreement.

1.4 This Agreement may be signed in counterparts.

2. WAIVER OF RIGHTS TO LITIGATE IN COURTS

2.1 The parties waive any right to further litigate the issues listed in paragraph 4.1 below in court, pursuant to the *Family Law Act*, the *Divorce Act*, or any other statute or law, subject to the right of appeal and rights under the *Arbitration Act* and the *Family Law Act* as set out below.

2.2 Nothing in this Agreement impairs any enforcement rights that a party may have through the courts or otherwise.

2.3 On application by either party and subject to the court's discretion, the operative terms of this Agreement may be incorporated into a consent court order.

3. DEFINITIONS

3.1 In this agreement:

(a) "Party-1" means Party-1 who is one of the parties to this agreement;

(b) "Party-2" means Party-2 who is one of the parties to this agreement;

(c) "party" or "parties" means Party-1 or Party-2 or Party-1 and Party-2 collectively;

(d) "property" has the same meaning as used in the *Family Law Act*;

(e) "*Arbitration Act*" means the *Arbitration Act, 1991*, S.O. 1991, c. 17, as am. S.O. 2006, c. 1, s. 1; 2006, c. 19, Sched. C, s. 1(1);

(f) "*Child and Family Services Act*" means *Child and Family Services Act*, R.S.O. 1990, c. C.11;

(g) "*Children's Law Reform Act*" means the *Children's Law Reform Act*, R.S.O. 1990, c. C.12;

(h) "*Divorce Act*" means the *Divorce Act*, R.S.C. 1985 (2nd Supp.), c. 3, as amended;

(i) "*Family Law Act*" means the *Family Law Act*, R.S.O. 1990, c. F.3, as am. S.O. 2006, c. 1, s. 5; 2006, c. 19, Sched. B, s. 9, Sched. C, s. 1(1), (2), (4);

3.2 To the extent permitted by law, an Act of the legislature or parliament referred to by name, whether or not it is defined in paragraph 3.1 above, will mean that Act in force as of the date of the signing of this

Agreement. In the event that this provision invalidates the operation of any of the other provisions of this Agreement at the time they are sought to be enforced, then the Act referred to will be the one in force at the material time and will include any amendment or successor Act.

4. SUBSTANTIVE ISSUES

4.1 The following issues are being submitted for the determination of temporary relief, if appropriate, and for final determination:

- ☐ Custody of child(ren)
- ☐ Access to child(ren)
- ☐ Spousal Support
- ☐ Child Support — other than table amount
- ☐ Child Support — Section 7 expenses
- ☐ Equalization of Net Family Property
- ☐ Unequal division of Net Family Property
- ☐ Exclusive Possession of Matrimonial Home
- ☐ Indexing spousal support
- ☐ Child Support — table amount
- ☐ Exclusive Possession of Contents of Matrimonial Home
- ☐ Sale of Property
- ☐ Interim Fees and Disbursements
- ☐ Preservation/Non-Dissipation of Assets
- ☐ Non-harassment
- ☐ Costs
- ☐ Other (Attach Schedule)

5. CONFIDENTIALITY

5.1 The proceedings under this Agreement and the record thereof shall be private and confidential, except as may be necessary to implement or to enforce the Arbitrator's award, and subject to their being produced in proceedings for judicial review or appeal or as required by law. The parties, their counsel and the Arbitrator shall not disclose any information about the parties, the arbitration or the screening for power imbalances or domestic violence to anyone, except as required by law.

5.2 The parties acknowledge and agree that the Arbitrator's legal obligations to disclose may include:

(a) Filing a report about the award with the Attorney General in accordance with the Regulation under the *Arbitration Act, 1991*;

(b) Reporting a child in need of protection in accordance with section 72 of the *Child and Family Services Act*;

(c) Where he believes upon reasonable grounds that there is an imminent risk to an identifiable person or group of death or serious bodily or psychological harm, disclosing such confidential information that is required in the circumstances to prevent such death or harm.

6. APPLICABLE LAW

6.1 The arbitration shall be conducted in accordance with: *(choose either (i) or (ii))*

☐ (i) the law of Ontario, and the law of Canada as it applies in Ontario, or

☐ (ii) the law of ________________ (name other Canadian jurisdiction) and the law of Canada as it applies in that jurisdiction

7. MEDIATION

7.1 At the request of the parties, Mr/Ms. Arbitrator may act as a Mediator in this matter. The parties agree that the Arbitrator is not disqualified from adjudicating any or all issues because he/she has acted as a Mediator in an attempt to resolve the issues before him. The parties specifically waive section 35 of the *Arbitration Act.*

7.2 The parties agree that any mediation decisions are settlement negotiations and that disclosures made during the mediation discussions are inadmissible in the arbitration and in any future litigation or arbitration. The parties agree not to subpoena or otherwise require Mr/Ms. Arbitrator to testify regarding the mediation discussions or to produce records or notes of the mediation discussions in any future proceedings. No transcripts shall be kept of the mediation discussions.

8. PROCEDURE FOR ARBITRATION

8.1 The arbitration shall take place at the dates and times to be set by Mr/Ms. Arbitrator in consultation with the parties (and their counsel, if applicable)

8.2 The procedure for the arbitration shall be determined by Mr/Ms. Arbitrator in consultation with the parties (and their counsel, if applicable).

8.3 If a hearing is conducted, it may be conducted in person, electronically, by telephone, by teleconference, by written submissions or by any other procedure which shall be determined by Mr/Ms. Arbitrator in consultation with the parties (and their counsel, if applicable).

8.4 Mr/Ms. Arbitrator may determine a timetable for the delivery of briefs, financial disclosure and other documents.

8.5 Mr/Ms. Arbitrator may deliver notices, awards or other communications to the parties via ordinary mail, fax or e-mail.

8.6 If a hearing is held and unless the parties agree otherwise:

(a) All witnesses shall be sworn under oath or affirmed and shall be subject to cross-examination and re-examination, except that Mr. Wolfson may direct that some or all of the evidence be given by affidavit in such manner as he may direct; and

(b) All usual rules for the admissibility of evidence in court proceedings shall apply as amended by the *Arbitration Act,* the *Family Law Rules* and the *Rules of Civil Procedure,* where applicable.

8.7 The parties agree: *(Select one)*

☐ (a) There shall be a reporter, the cost of which shall be initially shared equally between the parties; or

☐ (b) There shall not be a reporter; or

☐ (c) There shall be a reporter appointed as required for all or part of any arbitration as determined by Mr/Ms. Arbitrator in consultation with the parties (and counsel, if applicable).

9. PRE-ARBITRATION CONFERENCE

9.1 Mr/Ms. Arbitrator may convene a pre-arbitration conference to determine:

(a) The issues for arbitration;

(b) The documents to be provided prior to the commencement of the arbitration;

(c) The order of presentation of evidence;

(d) The names, addresses and telephone numbers of witnesses to be called and a synopsis of their evidence;

(e) A timetable for pre-arbitration events, including the exchange of expert reports, the delivery of opening statements, the exchange of document briefs and questioning, if required;

(f) Estimates of the time required for the arbitration;

(g) Any physical arrangements necessary for the attendance of parties or witnesses; and

(h) Any issues arising out of the results of the screening.

10. EXPERT EVIDENCE FOR ARBITRATION HEARING

10.1 The parties specifically authorize Mr/Ms. Arbitrator to determine the necessity of retaining professional(s) to provide expert opinion(s) respecting any outstanding issues(s) and to retain such professional(s) as he deems appropriate.

10.2 The parties agree to contribute to the fees of the expert(s) in the amounts or proportions determined by Mr. Wolfson and authorize Mr/Ms. Arbitrator to include these fees as a disbursement on his account to the parties.

11. WITHDRAWAL FROM ARBITRATION

11.1 Neither party may unilaterally withdraw from this Agreement. However, the parties may jointly terminate this Agreement by their written agreement. Subject to paragraph 11.2, the Arbitrator shall proceed with an arbitration as provided for in this Agreement notwithstanding that one of the parties no longer wants to participate in the arbitration.

11.2 Mr/Ms. Arbitrator may at any time resign from his appointment as arbitrator by providing written notice of his resignation to the parties.

11.3 In the event that Mr/Ms. Arbitrator's appointment is terminated, and the parties are unable to agree on a replacement, a court of competent jurisdiction shall appoint a replacement arbitrator on either party's application to the court.

11.4 In the event that Mr/Ms. Arbitrator's appointment is terminated, the parties agree that any interim or interlocutory award(s) made by Mr/Ms. Arbitrator will continue to bind the parties and will continue in full force and effect as the basis for the continuation of the arbitration with the replacement arbitrator.

12. THE ARBITRATOR'S AWARD

12.1 After the evidence has been received and submissions on the law have been made, Mr/Ms. Arbitrator shall deliver an award on all issues submitted for determination.

13. APPEAL

13.1 Any Award may be appealed as follows: *(choose either (a) or (b))*

☐ (a) A party may appeal the Award in accordance with subsection 45(1) of the *Arbitration Act, 1991*; or

☐ (b) A party may appeal the Award on: *(choose one or more of the following)*

☐ A question of law,

☐ A question of fact,

☐ A question of mixed fact and law.

14. ENFORCEMENT

14.1 Subject to the appeal remedies and rights to apply to set aside Mr. Wolfson's Award under sections 45 and 46, respectively, of the *Arbitration Act* and subject to the other applicable provisions of the *Arbitration Act,* and the *Family Law Act,* all awards of the Arbitrator shall be binding upon the parties. Any temporary, interim or final award may be incorporated into a consent order of the Ontario Superior Court of Justice. Either party may apply for the enforcement of any award under section 59.8(5)(a) of the *Family Law Act.*

14.2 Upon the request of either party, Mr. Wolfson shall issue an arbitral award incorporating the terms of any agreement reached by the parties.

15. MR/MS. ARBITRATOR'S FEES AND DISBURSEMENTS

15.1 Mr/Ms. Arbitrator's fees shall be $XXX.XX per hour for the arbitration hearing, any pre-arbitration conference, interim arbitration, preliminary meetings, mediation, arrangements, preparation for the hearing, preparation of an award and any other services pursuant to this Agreement.

15.2 Each party shall provide Mr/Ms. Arbitrator with a retainer of $XXXX.XX, with this retainer to be refreshed from time to time as he shall direct.

15.3 In the event that one of the parties fails or refuses to pay to Mr/Ms. Arbitrator his/her share of Mr/Ms. Arbitrator's fees, disbursement or retainer accounts, Mr/Ms. Arbitrator may accept payment of the defaulting party's share from the other party and exercise his discretion re costs to require the defaulting party to reimburse the other party the amount of such payment.

15.4 Mr/Ms. Arbitrator is empowered to order interim fees and disbursements of the arbitration, including his retainer, fees and/or disbursements, on notice to the parties following receipt of submissions if either party wishes.

15.5 Mr/Ms. Arbitrator may withhold his award until all outstanding fees, disbursements, or retainers have been paid.

16. WAIVER OF LIABILITY

16.1 The parties hereby waive any claim or right of action against Mr/Ms. Arbitrator arising out of these proceedings.

17. SEVERABILITY OF TERMS

17.1 Each of the terms of this agreement are severable from the others and will survive the invalidity or unenforceability of any other term of this agreement.

Dated this _______ of _____________, 20__.

______________________________	______________________________
Witness	Party - 1
______________________________	______________________________
Witness	Party - 2

LAWYER'S CERTIFICATE OF INDEPENDENT LEGAL ADVICE

I, ______________________________, have explained to my client ______________________________ the meaning of the attached Agreement and have given to him/her independent legal advice prior to the signing of the Agreement. I have also explained to my client that the Agreement is a "domestic contract" within the meaning of the *Family Law Act*, and as such a court may set aside the Agreement under various circumstances about which I have informed him/her. In my opinion, my client is aware of the need for disclosure of significant income, assets, debts and liabilities existing when this Agreement is made and understands the nature and consequences of this Agreement. I am satisfied that my client is not signing this Agreement as a result of any duress or undue influence. My client has been separately screened for power imbalances and domestic violence and I am satisfied that my client is fully able to participate in this arbitration and is doing so voluntarily.

______________________________	______________________________
Date	Signature of Lawyer

PARTY'S CERTIFICATE OF INDEPENDENT LEGAL ADVICE

I, ____________________, confirm that I have received independent legal advice and have attached to this Agreement a copy of the Certificate of Independent Legal Advice that was provided to me under subsection 59.6(2) of the *Family Law Act*.

______________________________	______________________________
Date	Signature of Party

LAWYER'S CERTIFICATE OF INDEPENDENT LEGAL ADVICE

I, ____________________, have explained to my client ____________________________ the meaning of the attached Agreement and have given to him/her independent legal advice prior to the signing of the Agreement. I have also explained to my client that the Agreement is a "domestic contract" within the meaning of the *Family Law Act*, and as such a court may set aside the Agreement under various circumstances about which I have informed him/her. In my opinion, my client is aware of the need for disclosure of significant income, assets, debts and liabilities existing when this Agreement is made and understands the nature and consequences of this Agreement. I am satisfied that my client is not signing this Agreement as a result of any duress or undue influence. My client has been separately screened for power imbalances and domestic violence and I am satisfied that my client is fully able to participate in this arbitration and is doing so voluntarily.

______________________________ ______________________________

Date Signature of Lawyer

PARTY'S CERTIFICATE OF INDEPENDENT LEGAL ADVICE

I, ____________________, confirm that I have received independent legal advice and have attached to this Agreement a copy of the Certificate of Independent Legal Advice that was provided to me under subsection 59.6(2) of the *Family Law Act*.

______________________________ ______________________________

Date Signature of Party

CERTIFICATE OF ARBITRATOR

I, **Arbitrator**, confirm the following matters:

1. I will treat the parties equally and fairly in the arbitration, as subsection 19(1) of the *Arbitration Act, 1991* requires.

2. I have received the appropriate training approved by the Attorney General.

3. The parties were separately screened for power imbalances and domestic violence by someone other than me and I have considered his

or her report on the results of the screening and will do so throughout the arbitration.

Date ______________________ Signature of Arbitrator ______________________

Appendix V.2

Mediation Arbitration Agreement (1)

IN THE MATTER OF THE *ARBITRATION ACT, 1991*, S.O. 1991, c. 17, as amended, and the *FAMILY LAW ACT*, R.S.O. 1990, c. F.3, as amended

B E T W E E N:

Party-1

("Party-1 First Name")

- and -

Party-2

("Party-2 First Name")

MEDIATION-ARBITRATION AGREEMENT

1. SUBMISSION

1.1 This Agreement is a Submission to Arbitration made under the *Arbitration Act* and the *Family Law Act*. It is effective when:

(a) It has been signed by both parties;

(b) Each Party's Certificate of Independent Legal Advice has been signed, in the forms attached; and

(c) The Arbitrator has signed the Certificate of Arbitrator, in the form attached.

1.2 The Arbitrator for this Arbitration is _______________. As set out in this Agreement the Arbitrator may act as Mediator or Arbitrator, but throughout he/she shall be termed Mr./Ms. ___________.

1.3 The Certificates of Independent Legal Advice and the Certificate of Arbitrator appended to this Agreement are part of this Agreement.

2. WAIVER OF RIGHTS TO LITIGATE IN COURTS

2.1 The parties waive any right to further litigate the issues listed in paragraph 5.1 below in court, pursuant to the *Family Law Act*, the *Divorce Act*, or any other statute or law, subject to the right of appeal and rights under the *Arbitration Act* and the *Family Law Act* as set out below.

2.2 Nothing in this Agreement impairs any enforcement rights that a party may have through the courts or otherwise.

2.3 On application by either party and subject to the court's discretion, the operative terms of this Agreement may be incorporated into a consent court order. (*Optional*)

3. DEFINITIONS

3.1 In this agreement:

(a) "Party-1" means Party-1 who is one of the parties to this agreement;

(b) "Party-2" means Party-2 who is one of the parties to this agreement;

(c) "party" or "parties" means Party-1 or Party-2 or Party-1 and Party-2 collectively;

(d) "property" has the same meaning as used in the *Family Law Act*;

(e) "*Arbitration Act*" means the *Arbitration Act, 1991*, S.O. 1991, c. 17, as am. S.O. 2006, c. 1, s. 1; 2006, c. 19, Sched. C, s. 1(1);

(f) "*Child and Family Services Act*" means *Child and Family Services Act*, R.S.O. 1990, c. C.11;

(g) "*Children's Law Reform Act*" means the *Children's Law Reform Act*, R.S.O. 1990, c. C.12;

(h) "*Divorce Act*" means the *Divorce Act*, R.S.C. 1985 (2nd Supp.), c. 3, as amended;

(i) "*Family Law Act*" means the *Family Law Act*, R.S.O. 1990, c. F.3, as am. S.O. 2006, c. 1, s. 5; 2006, c. 19, Sched. B, s. 9, Sched. C, s. 1(1), (2), (4);

3.2 To the extent permitted by law, an Act of the legislature or parliament referred to by name, whether or not it is defined in paragraph 3.1 above, will mean that Act in force as of the date of the signing of this Agreement. In the event that this provision invalidates the operation of any of the other provisions of this Agreement at the time they are sought to be enforced, then the Act referred to will be the one in force at the material time and will include any amendment or successor Act. (*Optional*)

4. BACKGROUND

4.1 Details regarding cohabitation, marriage, date of separation (if dates not disputed) and names and dates of birth of children. (*Optional*)

5. SUBSTANTIVE ISSUES

<u>OPTION A</u>

5.1 The following issues are being submitted for the determination of temporary relief, if appropriate, and for final determination:

☐ Custody of child(ren)

☐ Access to child(ren)

☐ Spousal Support

☐ Indexing spousal support

☐ Child Support – table amount

☐ Child Support – other than table amount

☐ Child Support – Section 7 expenses

☐ Equalization of Net Family Property

☐ Unequal division of Net Family Property

☐ Exclusive Possession of Matrimonial Home

☐ Exclusive Possession of Contents of Matrimonial Home

☐ Sale of Property

☐ Interim Fees and Disbursements

- ☐ Preservation/Non-Dissipation of Assets
- ☐ Non-harassment
- ☐ Costs
- ☐ Other (Attach Schedule)

OPTION B

5.1 The issues submitted for arbitration shall be those defined in the previous court proceedings between the parties as amended in writing by the parties.

6. CONFIDENTIALITY

6.1 The proceedings under this Agreement and the record thereof shall be private and confidential, except as may be necessary to implement or to enforce the Arbitrator's award, and subject to their being produced in proceedings for judicial review or appeal or as required by law. The parties, their counsel and Mr./Ms. ________ shall not disclose any information about the parties, the mediation, the arbitration or the screening for power imbalances or domestic violence to anyone, except as required by law.

6.2 The parties acknowledge and agree that Mr./Ms. ________'s legal obligations to disclose may include:

(a) Filing a report about the award with the Attorney General in accordance with the Regulation under the *Arbitration Act, 1991*;

(b) Reporting a child in need of protection in accordance with section 72 of the *Child and Family Services Act*;

(c) Where he/she believes upon reasonable grounds that there is an imminent risk to an identifiable person or group of death or serious bodily or psychological harm, disclosing such confidential information that is required in the circumstances to prevent such death or harm.

7. APPLICABLE LAW

7.1 The arbitration shall be conducted in accordance with: *(choose either (i) or (ii))*

☐ (i) the law of Ontario, and the law of Canada as it applies in Ontario, or

☐ (ii) the law of ______________________________ (name other Canadian jurisdiction) and the law of Canada as it applies in that jurisdiction

8. MEDIATION

8.1 Mr./Ms. ________ shall conduct a mediation in respect of the issues in dispute. The procedure for the mediation (including the date, time and place) shall be determined by Mr./Ms. ________ in consultation with the parties, their counsel or both.

8.2 The parties specifically waive section 35 of the *Arbitration Act.* They agree that Mr./Ms. ________ may act as Mediator in this matter and that Mr./Ms. ________ is not disqualified from adjudicating any or all issues because he/she has acted as Mediator in an attempt to resolve the issues before him/her.

8.3 The parties agree that the mediation sessions are settlement negotiations and that disclosures made during the mediation sessions are inadmissible in the arbitration phase of this mediation-arbitration and in any future litigation or arbitration. The parties agree not to subpoena or otherwise require Mr./Ms. ________ to testify regarding the mediation or to produce records or notes of the mediation in any future proceedings. No transcripts shall be kept of the mediation proceeding.

8.4 Mr./Ms. ________ may meet with the parties together or separately with or without counsel present and with whomever Mr./Ms. ________ deems relevant to a resolution of the issues between the parties. Any meeting between Mr./Ms. ________ and any person who is not a party, shall be held only with the consent of the parties.

8.5 The parties acknowledge and agree that in assisting them in resolving the issues set out in paragraph 5.1 above, Mr./Ms. ________ will bc acting in his/her capacity as a mediator and that he/she will not provide legal advice to the parties individually or collectively. If, during the course of the mediation, the mediator expresses an opinion or comments on an issue, the parties acknowledge that the opinion or comment is not to be construed as constituting a statement of the law or legal advice in any respect.

8.6 The mediation shall continue until Mr./Ms. ________ determines that continued mediation is unlikely to result in a settlement, at which point he/she may terminate the mediation and set a date for an arbitration.

9. DOCUMENTS FOR MEDIATION (*Pick one of the following*)

OPTION A

9.1 Unless otherwise agreed between Mr./Ms. ________ and both of the parties, each party shall submit to Mr./Ms. ________ and the other party at least seven clear days prior to the commencement of the Mediation: *(Delete the items that are not applicable)*

(a) a brief written statement indicating the facts supporting his/her position in reference to the issues and to the relief sought;

(b) any relevant factual information about the relationship between the parties;

(c) what issues have been resolved, and the terms of any agreement;

(d) copies of any relevant reports, assessments or appraisals and any other documents upon which he/she wishes to rely;

(e) the party's current sworn Financial Statement;

(f) a comparative Net Family Property Statement;

(g) copies of any relevant court orders or agreements;

(h) any other information or documentation that he/she considers is important for the resolution of the issues; and

(i) such other documents that Mr./Ms. ________ directs.

OPTION B

9.1 Unless otherwise agreed between Mr./Ms. ________ and both of the parties, each party shall submit to Mr./Ms. ________ and the other party at least ____ clear days prior to the commencement of the Mediation: *(please check)*

☐ a Statement of Facts and Issues (to be prepared jointly, if possible);

☐ a Position Statement of no more than five typewritten double-spaced pages, setting out his/her position regarding the issues referred to in paragraph 5.1;

☐ a current sworn Financial Statement;

☐ his/her income tax returns and notices of assessment for the most recent three years;

- ☐ a comparative Net Family Property Statement;
- ☐ the reports of any experts being relied on by him or her;
- ☐ copies of relevant court proceedings;
- ☐ all other relevant documents;
- ☐ all relevant jurisprudence; and
- ☐ other (attach a schedule, if applicable).

OPTION C

9.1 The parties and Mr./Ms. ________ will determine what documentation is appropriate and necessary as the mediation progresses. If Mr./Ms. ________ concludes that there is insufficient documentation to enable the parties to participate in an informed negotiation, Mr./Ms. ________ may terminate the mediation and set a date for the arbitration.

10. PROCEDURE FOR ARBITRATION

10.1 The arbitration shall take place at the dates and times to be set by Mr./Ms. ________ in consultation with the parties (and their counsel, if applicable).

10.2 The procedure for the arbitration shall be determined by Mr./Ms. ________ in consultation with the parties (and their counsel, if applicable).

10.3 If a hearing is conducted, it may be conducted in person, electronically, by telephone, by teleconference, by written submissions or by any other procedure which shall be determined by Mr./Ms. ________ in consultation with the parties (and their counsel, if applicable).

10.4 Mr./Ms. ________ may determine a timetable for the delivery of briefs, financial disclosure and other documents.

10.5 Mr./Ms. ________ may deliver notices, awards or other communications to the parties via ordinary mail, fax or e-mail. *(Optional)*

10.6 Notwithstanding paragraph 8.3, Mr./Ms. ________ may, with the consent of the parties, admit into evidence documents or other information received by him/her during the mediation phase.

10.7 If a hearing is held and unless the parties agree otherwise:

(a) All witnesses shall be sworn under oath or affirmed and shall be subject to cross-examination and re-examination, except that Mr./Ms. ________ may direct that some or all of the evidence be given by affidavit in such manner as he/she may direct; and

(b) All usual rules for the admissibility of evidence in court proceedings shall apply as amended by the *Arbitration Act*, the *Family Law Rules* and the *Rules of Civil Procedure*, where applicable. *(Optional)*

10.8 The parties agree: *(Select one)*

☐ (a) There shall be a reporter, the cost of which shall be initially shared equally between the parties; or

☐ (b) There shall not be a reporter; or

☐ (c) There shall be a reporter appointed as required for all or part of any arbitration as determined by Mr./Ms. ________ in consultation with the parties (and counsel, if applicable).

11. PRE-ARBITRATION CONFERENCE

11.1 Mr./Ms. ________ may convene a pre-arbitration conference to determine:

(a) The issues for arbitration;

(b) The documents to be provided prior to the commencement of the arbitration;

(c) The order of presentation of evidence;

(d) The names, addresses and telephone numbers of witnesses to be called and a synopsis of their evidence;

(e) A timetable for pre-arbitration events, including the exchange of expert reports, the delivery of opening statements, the exchange of document briefs and questioning, if required;

(f) Estimates of the time required for the arbitration;

(g) Any physical arrangements necessary for the attendance of parties or witnesses; and

(h) Any issues arising out of the results of the screening.

12. EXPERT EVIDENCE FOR ARBITRATION HEARING

12.1 The parties specifically authorize Mr./Ms. ________ to determine the necessity of retaining professional(s) to provide expert opinion(s) respecting any outstanding issues(s) and to retain such professional(s) as he/she deems appropriate.

12.2 The parties agree to contribute to the fees of the expert(s) in the amounts or proportions determined by Mr./Ms. ________ and authorize Mr./Ms. ________ to include these fees as a disbursement on his/her account to the parties.

13. WITHDRAWAL FROM MEDIATION OR ARBITRATION

13.1 Neither party may unilaterally withdraw from this Agreement at either the mediation or arbitration stage. However, the parties may jointly terminate this Agreement by their written agreement. Subject to paragraph 13.2, the Arbitrator shall proceed with an arbitration as provided for in this Agreement notwithstanding that the mediation has been unsuccessful or that one of the parties no longer wants to participate in the arbitration.

13.2 Mr./Ms. ________ may at any time resign from his/her appointment as arbitrator by providing written notice of his/her resignation to the parties.

13.3 In the event that Mr./Ms. ________'s appointment is terminated, and the parties are unable to agree on a replacement, a court of competent jurisdiction shall appoint a replacement arbitrator on either party's application to the court. *(Optional)*

13.4 In the event that Mr./Ms. ________'s appointment is terminated, the parties agree that any interim or interlocutory award(s) made by Mr./Ms. ________ will continue to bind the parties and will continue in full force and effect as the basis for the continuation of the arbitration with the replacement arbitrator.

14. THE ARBITRATOR'S AWARD

14.1 After the evidence has been received and submissions on the law have been made, Mr./Ms. ________ shall deliver an award on all issues submitted for determination (within 30 days *(Optional)*).

15. APPEAL

15.1 Any Award may be appealed as follows: *(choose either (a) or (b))*

☐ (a) A party may appeal the Award in accordance with subsection 45(1) of the *Arbitration Act, 1991*; or

☐ (b) A party may appeal the Award on: *(choose one or more of the following)*

☐ A question of law,

☐ A question of fact,

☐ A question of mixed fact and law.

16. ENFORCEMENT

16.1 Subject to the appeal remedies and rights to apply to set aside Mr./Ms. ________'s Award under sections 45 and 46, respectively, of the *Arbitration Act* and subject to the other applicable provisions of the *Arbitration Act,* and the *Family Law Act*, all awards of the Arbitrator shall be binding upon the parties. Any temporary, interim or final award may be incorporated into a consent order of the Ontario Superior Court of Justice. Either party may apply for the enforcement of any award under section 59.8(5)(a) of the *Family Law Act.*

16.2 Upon the request of either party, Mr./Ms. ________ shall issue an arbitral award incorporating the terms of any agreement reached by the parties during the course of the mediation or arbitration.

17. Mr./Ms. ________'S FEES AND DISBURSEMENTS

17.1 Mr./Ms. ________'s fees shall be $• per hour for the arbitration hearing, any pre-arbitration conference, interim arbitration, preliminary meetings, mediation, arrangements, preparation for the hearing, preparation of an award and any other services pursuant to this Agreement. [**Alternative:** Mr./Ms. ________'s fees and disbursements shall be in accordance with the fee schedule attached to this Agreement.]

17.2 Each party shall provide Mr./Ms. ________ with a retainer of $•, with this retainer to be refreshed from time to time as he/she shall direct.

17.3 In the event that one of the parties fails or refuses to pay to Mr./Ms. ________ his/her share of Mr./Ms. ________'s fees, disbursement or retainer accounts, Mr./Ms. ________ may accept payment of the defaulting party's share from the other party and exercise his/her discretion re costs to require the defaulting party to reimburse the other party the amount of such payment.

17.4 Mr./Ms. ________ is empowered to order interim fees and disbursements of the arbitration, including his/her retaining fees and disbursements, on notice to the parties following receipt of submissions if either party wishes. *(Optional)*

17.5 Mr./Ms. ________ may withhold his award until all outstanding fees, disbursements, or retainers have been paid. *(Optional)*

18. WAIVER OF LIABILITY

18.1 The parties hereby waive any claim or right of action against Mr./Ms. ________ arising out of these proceedings.

19. SEVERABILITY OF TERMS

19.1 Each of the terms of this agreement are severable from the others and will survive the invalidity or unenforceability of any other term of this agreement.

20. INDEPENDENT LEGAL ADVICE

20.1 Each party confirms that he/she has received independent legal advice and has attached to this Agreement a copy of the Certificate of Independent Legal Advice that was provided to him/her under subsection 59.6(2) of the *Family Law Act*. Each party confirms the accuracy of the contents of that Certificate of Independent Legal Advice.

Dated this _______ of ______________ 20--.

________________________________ ________________________________

Witness Party - 1

____________________________ ____________________________

Witness Party - 2

CERTIFICATE OF INDEPENDENT LEGAL ADVICE

I, ____________________, Barrister & Solicitor, have explained to my client ____________________________ the meaning of the attached Agreement and have given to him/her independent legal advice prior to the signing of the Agreement. I have also explained to my client that the Agreement is a "domestic contract" within the meaning of the *Family Law Act,* and as such a court may set aside the Agreement under various circumstances about which I have informed him/her. In my opinion, my client is aware of the need for disclosure of significant income, assets, debts and liabilities existing when this Agreement is made and understands the nature and consequences of this Agreement. I am satisfied that my client is not signing this Agreement as a result of any duress or undue influence. My client has been separately screened for power imbalances and domestic violence and I am satisfied that my client is fully able to participate in this mediation-arbitration and is doing so voluntarily.

____________________________ ____________________________

Date Lawyer

CERTIFICATE OF INDEPENDENT LEGAL ADVICE

I, ____________________, Barrister & Solicitor, have explained to my client ____________________________ the meaning of the attached Agreement and have given to him/her independent legal advice prior to the signing of the Agreement. I have also explained to my client that the Agreement is a "domestic contract" within the meaning of the *Family Law Act,* and as such a court may set aside the Agreement under various circumstances about which I have informed him/her. In my opinion, my client is aware of the need for disclosure of significant income, assets, debts and liabilities existing when this Agreement is made and understands the nature and consequences of this Agreement. I am satisfied that my client is not signing this Agreement as a result of any duress or undue influence. My client has been separately screened for power imbalances and domestic violence and I am satisfied that my client is fully able to participate in this mediation-arbitration and is doing so voluntarily.

____________________________ ____________________________

Date Lawyer

CERTIFICATE OF ARBITRATOR

I, ____________, confirm the following matters:

1. I will treat the parties equally and fairly in the arbitration, as subsection 19(1) of the *Arbitration Act, 1991* requires.

2. I have received the appropriate training approved by the Attorney General.

3. The parties were separately screened for power imbalances and domestic violence and I have considered the results of the screening and will do so throughout the arbitration, if I conduct one.

_______________	_______________
Date	Signature of Arbitrator

Appendix V.3

Mediation Arbitration Agreement (2)

MEDIATION-ARBITRATION AGREEMENT (Parenting Coordination)

RE: Mother and Father

MEDIATION:

Mediation Issues and Process

1. We hereby appoint NAME… to act as the Mediator-Arbitrator with respect to the following issues:
   (i) xxxxxx;
   (ii) yyyyyy; and
   (ii) such other issues as both parties agree to submit to the mediation-arbitration process from time to time.

2. It is understood that Mediation-Arbitration (Med-Arb) is a process of dispute resolution which begins as assisted mediation and only becomes arbitration in which a binding decision is made by the

Mediator-Arbitrator if the parties are unable to resolve their dispute in the mediation process.

3. The following principles will apply to the mediation conducted by the Mediator-Arbitrator:

(i) In attempting to bring about an agreement, the Mediator-Arbitrator will meet with the parties for joint sessions and on occasion for individual sessions. The Mediator-Arbitrator may include in the mediation process, any other significant third party, such as the children, legal counsel or other significantly involved persons who are relevant to the issue in dispute, in consultation with the parties;

(ii) Both parents agree that if the issues are not resolved in mediation neither will argue in future that the Arbitrators Award should be set aside on the basis that the mediator held separate meetings with each parent. Both parties acknowledge that they have been advised that this may not satisfy the requirements of the *Arbitration Act*.

(iii) The parties will make full disclosure of all relevant information reasonably required to understand the issues being mediated and will execute any Releases of Information necessary for the Mediator-Arbitrator to obtain relevant information.

(iv) The Mediator-Arbitrator will be acting as a Mediator-Arbitrator and will not be giving either party legal advice. The parties are required to obtain independent legal advice, before mediation-arbitration commences, to ensure they understand the choice of process and their legal rights and obligations.

(v) The Mediator-Arbitrator is required to screen both parties separately and to report an actual or potential threat to the safety of any of the participants or a breach of the *Child and Family Services Act* or the *Criminal Code*.

(vi) Neither party nor anyone acting on their behalf will take any fresh steps in the legal proceedings between the parties with respect to those issues that are being mediated or arbitrated;

(vii) If the parties reach agreement on some or all of the issues, the Mediator shall prepare a Memorandum of Understanding with respect to those issues for consideration by the parties and their respective counsel.

ARBITRATION:

4. The parties intend to make their best efforts in good faith to resolve their outstanding issues through mediation. In the event that they are unable to agree on one or more issues as determined by the Mediator-Arbitrator or upon the delivery of written notice by either party to the other party and to the Mediator-Arbitrator, it is understood that Dr. Barbara Landau, acting as Arbitrator, will make a decision based upon the information presented during the arbitration.

Arbitration Process and Legal Requirements

5. At the outset of the Arbitration process, Dr. Barbara Landau will notify both parties that the process is now an Arbitration process. The following principles will apply to the arbitration:

   (i) It is acknowledged that the Arbitrator is an impartial third party who will render a decision (Award) on any outstanding issues as set out in paragraph 1 above. This decision shall bind the parties as if the decision was made by a trial judge of the Ontario Superior Court of Justice. The Arbitrator's decision in this matter shall be enforced under the *Family Law Act*, upon application or motion by either party, and shall be incorporated into a judgment in an action to vary their divorce settlement or any Separation Agreement or amended Separation Agreement that may be in effect from time to time;

   (ii) The procedures of the Arbitration, will be in a form prescribed by Dr. Barbara Landau and will reflect the parties' wish for the Arbitration to be conducted in an informal and cost-efficient manner. If the Arbitrator decides or at the request of a party, a hearing will be held. One week prior to the Arbitration, or at such other time as may be designated by the Arbitrator, both parties or their lawyers shall submit a statement to the Arbitrator which shall summarize the matters in dispute, the legal issues pending and any legal authority supporting his or her position on the issues submitted to Arbitration;

   (iii) If significant issues such as, but not limited to, a change in residence of the child are raised, the Arbitrator will offer a hearing;

(iv) The principles outlined in s. 20 and s. 24 of the *Children's Law Reform Act* and s. 16 of the *Divorce Act* will be considered in rendering a decision with respect to parenting arrangements for the children;

(v) The arbitration shall be conducted at the office of Dr. Barbara Landau (or at such other place as she designates) at a time and date to be determined by the Arbitrator in consultation with the parties;

(vi) The parties may attend the Arbitration with or without counsel. If they choose to attend without counsel, they are waiving their right to do so;

(vii) The Arbitrator may consult or retain such experts or witnesses as she wishes to assist her in the determination of legal issues. Dr. Barbara Landau will inform the parties as to whom she plans to consult or retain in advance and will inform the parties as to the reason for involving such individual(s);

(viii) The parties agree to pay the expert(s)' fees equally initially, subject to reapportionment as determined by the Arbitrator;

(ix) The Arbitrator will interview the children privately as to their views and preferences and may consider such information in a decision with respect to parenting arrangements. The parties will respect the children's confidentiality and will not ask the children to disclose any information given in private to the Mediator-Arbitrator. Each parent, by signing this agreement, acknowledges that he or she has been advised that this may not satisfy the requirements of the *Arbitration Act*, but each agrees that this is in the children's best interests and is intended to protect the children from the conflict. Each waives his or her right, at any time in the future, to argue that the Award with respect to parenting arrangements should be set aside on this basis.

(x) At least seven days prior to the commencement of the Arbitration, the parties will deliver to each other, the Arbitrator and the opposing counsel the following documents (unless the Arbitrator decides that one or more of these documents are not relevant to the issues being arbitrated):

(a) the reports of any experts being relied upon by him or her; such as, school report cards, therapists reports, medical reports, or other documents, where relevant;

(b) copies of court pleadings;

(c) all other relevant documents, to be prepared jointly if possible;

(d) a Statement of Facts and Issues, to be prepared jointly if possible, including:

(i) a Position Statement of no more than five typewritten, double-spaced pages setting out his or her position regarding the issues to be arbitrated;

(ii) a list of witnesses to be called; and

(iii) all relevant legal cases

(xi) Neither party may unilaterally withdraw from this Agreement at the Arbitration stage. However, with their joint consent in writing, both parties may terminate this Agreement during the Mediation stage. The Mediator/Arbitrator may, at her discretion, proceed with an Arbitration as provided for in this Agreement even though the Mediation has been unsuccessful or one of the parties no longer wants to participate in the Arbitration.

6. The mediator will not be called as a witness by either party in any legal proceeding with respect to any of the issues being mediated or arbitrated. Mediator-Arbitrator's notes and files from the mediation and arbitration are private and confidential, unless there is a judicial review, appeal or as required by law.

7. The parties acknowledge that the arbitrator is required by law to file a summary report about the award with the Attorney General, without information identifying the parties, in accordance with the regulations to the *Family Statute Law Amendment Act*.

8. The arbitration will be conducted in accordance with the law of Ontario, and the law of Canada as it applies in Ontario.

9. The provisions of the *Arbitration Act, 1991*, S.O. 1991, c. 17 as amended by the *Family Statute Law Amendment Act, 2006* apply to this Arbitration except where a provision of this agreement states otherwise. The parties specifically waive section 35 of the *Arbitration Act*. They agree that the Arbitrator may act as the Mediator and attempt to resolve the issues prior to arbitrating. The parties explicitly recognize the Mediator-Arbitrator has acted as their mediator prior to arbitrating the issue(s) in dispute, and agree not to challenge the fairness of the arbitration hearing on this ground.

10. Subject to the other provisions of this Agreement, the Arbitrator shall have the same powers as a judge of the Ontario Superior Court of Justice to make directions, which may be incorporated into orders, and impose sanctions. The Arbitrator may make findings of fact which will be binding on both parties.

11. The parties agree that the mediation sessions are settlement negotiations and without prejudice to the Arbitration stage. Documents provided during the Mediation stage are not admissible in the Arbitration stage or in any future litigation unless there is the consent of both parties.

12. Upon completion of the Arbitration, the Arbitrator shall issue an Award in writing no later than ---- days after the conclusion of the Arbitration or at such other date as the Arbitrator determines. A copy of the Award will be sent to each party and their respective counsel.

Fees

13. It is agreed that:

    (i) each party will pay a retainer of $xxxx ($xxxx total) and share all other costs of the Mediation-Arbitration equally, unless the Arbitrator orders otherwise;
    (ii) interim accounts shall be sent out to the parties and payment shall be due when services are rendered;
    (iii) the hourly rate of $xxx per hour is subject to change upon notice by the Mediator-Arbitrator; and
    (iv) from time to time an additional retainer will be requested to cover the anticipated next steps in the Mediation-Arbitration. The Mediation-Arbitration will not continue until the retainer is paid.

14. The Mediator-Arbitrator will bill for time spent in the mediation, telephone calls, reviewing emails, correspondence or other documents,

travel, preparation of progress notes, any pre-arbitration conference, preliminary meetings, hearing, preparation for the hearing, preparation of an award and any subsequent matters. The parties shall be jointly and severally liable for the fees and disbursements of the Mediator-Arbitrator.

15. In the event that one of the parties fails or refuses to pay to the Mediator/Arbitrator his or her share of the Mediator/Arbitrator's fees, disbursement or retainer accounts, the Mediator/Arbitrator may accept payment of the defaulting party's share from the other party and exercise her discretion re costs to require the defaulting party to reimburse the other party the amount of such payment.

16. Interest will be charged at the Prime Rate on all accounts outstanding after thirty (30) days from the date the account is rendered.

Cancellation Policy

17. The notice must be provided during regular business hours Monday through Thursdays, between 9:00 a.m. and 4:30 p.m.
    (i) The clients will be billed for a mediation appointment in which there is less than 48 hours (2 full business days between Monday and Thursday)) prior notice to cancellation. In the event that the meeting is scheduled for more than 2 hours then 4 full business days (Monday through Thursday) notice must be provided. The clients will each be responsible for bills arising from his/her own cancellation.
    (ii) Once a date has been agreed upon for an Arbitration Hearing or a Mediation meeting involving Counsel, the following charges will apply to the client responsible for the re-scheduling or cancellation:
        (a) if 7 or more business days notice a $100 fee will be charged;
        (b) if between 5 and 7 business days notice a $150 fee will be charged; or
        (b) if 4 business days or less the entire session will be billed.
    (iii) If a cancellation is due to the illness of the child or a circumstance beyond their control, the clients will share the cancellation fee equally. These charges are regardless of the reason for the cancellation, except at the Mediator/Arbitrator's discretion.

18. Any Memorandum of Understanding or Award will not be released until all outstanding professional fees and disbursements related to the Mediation-Arbitration have been paid in full.

Appeal Rights and Complaint Process

19. The parties shall have the right to review the Arbitrator's Award in accordance with s. 46 of the *Arbitration Act* and the right to appeal the Award only on a question of law, with leave, as provided in s. 45(1) of the *Arbitration Act* and the *Family Statute Law Amendment Act*.

20. If either party has a complaint about the way the Mediator-Arbitrator is dealing with him/her or any issue, he/she shall discuss it in person with the Mediator-Arbitrator before pursuing it in any other manner. If, after discussion, the party is not satisfied that the complaint has been dealt with to his/her satisfaction, then he/she must submit a written letter detailing the complaint to the Mediator-Arbitrator, to the other party and to any lawyers representing the parties and/or the children. The Mediator-Arbitrator shall provide a written response to the parties and lawyers within twenty (20) days.

21. The Mediator-Arbitrator will then meet with the complaining party and his/her lawyer to further discuss the matter.

22. If the complaint is not resolved after this meeting, the complaining party may file a motion on notice to the other party with the Court to remove the Mediator-Arbitrator as per the *Arbitration Act*. The motion shall proceed on the written documents submitted by both parties and the Mediator-Arbitrator, unless the Court Orders a hearing.

23. The Court shall determine if the Mediator-Arbitrator should be replaced and shall determine who shall be responsible for any portions of the Mediator-Arbitrator's time and costs spent in responding to the complaint and the Mediator-Arbitrator's lawyer's fees, if any.

24. The binding arbitrated decision shall be implemented and adhered to during the time the complaint process is in effect.

25. Neither party shall complain about the Mediator-Arbitrator to the Mediator-Arbitrator's licensing board without also complying with the above-noted complaint procedure.

26. The parties waive any claim or right of action against the Mediator-Arbitrator for any matters arising out of this Agreement with respect to actions performed by her in good faith.

27. Counsel acknowledges receipt of this document and agree, subject to approval by their client, that the terms of this document describe the nature of the Mediation-Arbitration agreement.

Or

28. Each of the parties acknowledges that he or she has read this agreement and agrees to be bound by its terms.

Dated at ______, this ________ day of _______month_______, 20--.

______________________	______________________
WITNESS	Counsel for Father
______________________	______________________
WITNESS	Counsel for Mother
______________________	______________________
WITNESS	Mediator-Arbitrator

CERTIFICATE OF INDEPENDENT LEGAL ADVICE

I, _________________, Barrister & Solicitor, of the City of _______________, in the Regional Municipality of _________________, have reviewed the attached Mediation-Arbitration Agreement (the "Agreement") and have fully explained to my client _____________________ the meaning and intent of the Agreement and have given to him/her independent legal advice prior to the Agreement being signed. I have also explained to my client that the Agreement is a "domestic contract" within the meaning of the *Family Law Act*, and as such a court may set aside the Agreement under various circumstances about which I have informed him/her. In my opinion, my client is aware of the need for financial disclosure existing when this Agreement is made, understands the nature or consequences of this Agreement, and is not signing this Agreement as a result of any undue influence placed upon him/her by any person.

______________________________	________________________
counsel name (signature above)	Date

ACKNOWLEDGEMENT OF CLIENT

I, ____________________, confirm that I have received independent legal advice. And have attached to this Agreement a copy of the Certificate of Independent legal advice (above) that was provided to me under subsection 59.6(2) of the *Family Law Act*. I have read the above Certificate, and I understand and agree with the statements set out in it.

______________________________ ______________________________

(Client name – signature above) Date

Statement of Arbitrator

I, Name of Arbitrator, confirm the following matters:

i. I will treat the parties equally and fairly in the arbitration, as subsection 19 (1) of the *Arbitration Act, 1991* requires;

ii. I have received the appropriate training approved by the Attorney General;

iii. The parties were separately screened for power imbalances and domestic violence and I have considered the results of the screening and will do so throughout the arbitration, if I conduct one.

______________________________ ______________

(Signature of Arbitrator) Date

Appendix V.4

Parenting Coordination Agreement

THIS IS AN AGREEMENT FOR PARENTING COORDINATION SERVICES AND ARBITRATION IN ACCORDANCE WITH THE

ARBITRATION ACT, S.O. 1991, c. 17 and the FAMILY LAW ACT, R.S.O. 1990, c. F.3.

BETWEEN:

[ ]

- and -

[ ]

PRINCIPLES

1. The parents acknowledge that their child(ren) will benefit from a meaningful relationship with both parents, that parental conflict will impact negatively on their child(ren)'s adjustment, and that every effort should be made to keep the child(ren) out of the parents' disputes.

2. The parents wish to retain the services of ________ as Parenting Coordinator (may subsequently be referred to as PC), to assist them in implementing, maintaining and monitoring the terms of the existing Minutes of Settlement ("Minutes" or also referred to as the Parenting Plan), dated ______________, and any subsequent Court Orders and previously arbitrated decisions as well as any other parenting matter as agreed upon by the parents.

3. The parents agree to voluntarily enter into this Agreement because of a desire to:

    a. de-escalate parental conflict
    b. prioritize the child(ren)'s best interests
    c. promote the child(ren)'s optimum adjustment
    d. resolve issues/disputes in a time and cost efficient manner
    e. benefit from the direction of a qualified professional

ROLE AND OBJECTIVES OF THE PARENTING COORDINATOR

4. The parents agree to retain ________ in her role as Parenting Coordinator to act as a neutral third party to expeditiously resolve issues that arise from the implementation of the Minutes (Parenting Plan) in a manner consistent with the child(ren)'s best interests and in a manner that attempts to minimize parental conflict. The Parenting

Coordinator may provide consultation to the parents and may coach and educate them about ways to better communicate about the child(ren) and about ways to better communicate with each other, with the ultimate goal of helping the parents resolve issues amicably and efficiently on their own, without having to involve the Parenting Coordinator.

5. Parenting Coordination involves two components: (1) The Parenting Coordinator attempting to resolve issues arising out of the Minutes/Parenting Plan through facilitation, consultation, coaching and education, all being non-decision making functions; (2) If it is apparent to the Parenting Coordinator that continued similar efforts are unlikely to resolve the issue, then to resolve the dispute the Parenting Coordinator may arbitrate (defined as a "secondary arbitration" by the *Family Law Act*, 59.7(2) in accordance with the Minutes/Parenting Plan and as set out in the decision-making process of this Agreement.

PARENTING COORDINATION SERVICES

6. The Parenting Coordinator is not entitled to override the Minutes and/or any subsequent Court Orders but upon agreement of the parents, may address any parenting issues mutually brought forth by the parents.

7. The scope of the Parenting Coordinator's role may include the following (*circle those that apply*):

   a. assist with the implementation, maintenance and monitoring of the Minutes/Parenting Plan, Court Orders and/or arbitrated decisions;
   b. address any conflicts in the child(ren)'s scheduling that occur;
   c. address any difficulties related to the children's transitions between the parents, including codes of conduct and transportation;
   d. develop any additional clarifying clauses that may be required given situations and events that unfold that were not initially anticipated when the Parenting Plan was developed;
   e. monitor the child(ren)'s adjustment;
   f. assist in the maintenance of the child(ren)'s relationship with each parent;
   g. assist the parents to communicate more effectively where possible and where not possible assist to disengage the parents;
   h. assist the parents with the exchange of information about the child(ren) (i.e., health, welfare, education, religion, routines, day-to-day matters, etc.) that may be otherwise impossible

and/or ineffective, in accordance with the methods provided for in the Parenting Plan;

i. where parents have joint custody and on consent and/or by delegation of the court, to make final decisions relating to "major" decisions (i.e., relating to education, health and welfare, and religion) if the parents are unable to come to a mutual agreement;

j. if necessary, make binding decisions pertaining to <u>temporary</u> changes to the usual and/or holiday parenting time schedule, to accommodate special events and circumstances for the child(ren) and/or the parents;

k. where not addressed by the Court Order and/or existing Parenting Plan, resolve conflicts concerning the child(ren)'s participation in recreation, enrichment or extra-curricular activities, lessons, and programmes;

l. address movement of the child(ren)'s clothing, equipment, toys and personal possessions between households;

m. address matters relating to the children's travel with one parent (i.e., protocol relating to passport exchange, itinerary, notarized permission letter, telephone calls with the non-resident parent, etc.);

n. clarify and resolve different interpretations of the Parenting Plan;

o. resolve conflicts concerning day to day health care, day to day education matters, passports, risky activities, and events that are not otherwise allocated for in the Minutes/Parenting Plan;

p. any other parenting function, issue or decision, not otherwise noted, as delegated by the courts or by mutual parental consent.

<u>EXCLUDED FROM PARENTING COORDINATOR'S DECISION MAKING ROLE</u>

8. The following specific issues are excluded from the scope of the Parenting Coordinator's decision-making authority:

   a. changes in the <u>usual</u> parenting time (residential) schedule that substantially reduce or substantially expand the child(ren)'s time with one or both parents or impact the quantum of child support;

   b. a change in the geographic residence of the child(ren);

   c. a change in legal custody (i.e., final decision-making authority).

WAIVER OF RIGHT TO LITIGATE IN COURTS

9. By submitting to arbitration of the issues designated in paragraphs 2 and 7 above, the parents hereby waive any right to further litigate those issues in Court, whether pursuant to the *Family Law Act*, R.S.O. 1990, c. F.3, as amended; the *Divorce Act*, R.S.C. 1985, c. 3 (2nd Supp.), as amended, or any other statute or law.

TERMS AND AGREEMENT TO COOPERATE

10. ________ is a registered psychologist and has relevant knowledge, including that in the areas of child development, family systems theory and dynamics, the effects of separation/divorce on children, adolescents, and adults, high conflict families, and psychological functioning, from which the parents wish to benefit. Notwithstanding, she is not functioning as a psychotherapist for either of us, our family, or our child(ren). The parents have stipulated to this appointment and the decision-making granted herein to the Parenting Coordinator. They further stipulate that ________ has the requisite professional qualifications and professionals skills to provide the service of Parenting Coordination.

11. The parents will cooperate with the Parenting Coordinator and agree to be bound by this Agreement.

12. The parties agree that this Agreement shall continue for a term of ________ months from the date of this agreement. Should the parents sign the agreement on different dates, the contract shall be valid from the latter of the two dates. To avoid a hiatus in services, the parents will advise the Parenting Coordinator and the other parent in writing no less than 2 months in advance of the expiry date of services whether or not they wish to renew the Agreement.

13. The Parenting Coordinator and the parents shall set a time and place for meeting within ______ days of signing this Agreement.

14. At the request of Dr. Fidler, the parents shall sign all releases of information required to implement the process. The parents shall provide all records, documentation and information requested by the Parenting Coordinator as soon as possible upon the request of the Parenting Coordinator from time to time.

15. The parents agree that the Parenting Coordinator can perform the function of parenting coordination, including both the decision-making and non-decision-making components described herein. They further agree that the fact that the Parenting Coordinator performs the non-

decision making component involving mediation, facilitation and conflict resolution does not disqualify her from arbitrating the same issues. In this regard, the parents waive s. 35 of *The Arbitration Act*, S.O. 1991, c. 17. The agreed to term of service stated below will be upheld notwithstanding that facilitated negotiation is part of the process and with the understanding that in other contexts, like mediation, for example and if there is no court order, a parent may withdraw from the process at any time.

16. The Parenting Coordinator is not a lawyer and will not be providing legal advice.

17. The parents will provide copies to the other parent of all written reports and letters from third parties that they provide to the PC, unless otherwise directed by the PC.

CONFIDENTIALITY

18. The Parenting Coordinator will meet separately with each party for the purpose of, among other things, screening the parties for the suitability of the process, including but not limited to, violence and power imbalances. The parties agree that any notes and intake material from the screening procedures will remain confidential to the Parenting Coordinator and will not be disclosed to the parties.

19. Subject to #18, the PC process is not confidential and the Parenting Coordinator may provide information and/or a report to the court, the parties, and their lawyers. Upon request of either one or both parents, ________ shall issue a report to the parents, their lawyers and the court. The party requesting the report shall pay fees for any such report. Any such report may be submitted as evidence in legal proceedings between us. Either parent may call ________ to provide evidence in Court, this evidence limited to that relating to disputes about parenting.

20. The parties acknowledge that in her function as an arbitrator, the Parenting Coordinator is required to provide certain information about the outcome of the arbitration to the office of the Attorney General pursuant to regulations made under the Family Statute Law Amendment Act (2006). All identifying information is removed in this report to the Ministry.

NON DECISION-MAKING COMPONENT (PROCESS PRIOR TO ARBITRATION)

21. If either parent has an issue relating to the child(ren) and/or the Parenting Plan falling within paragraphs 2 and 7 of this agreement that cannot be resolved with the other parent and after reasonable efforts to do so, he/she may contact the PC. The Parenting Coordinator in consultation with the parties shall have the authority to determine the protocol of all contacts and interviews, including who shall be required to attend such meetings/contacts.

22. During this non-decision making phase prior to arbitration, the Parenting Coordinator may communicate with one parent without the other being present. The Parenting Coordinator may communicate with the lawyers jointly and/or separately, unless determined otherwise at the start of the process. The Parenting Coordinator shall be entitled to pursue matters submitted by meeting with the parents jointly and/or individually, reviewing written materials, and considering any other information the PC determines is relevant. In addition the Parenting Coordinator may consult with professionals, family members and others such as therapists, custody assessors, educators, and health care professionals if the Parenting Coordinator believes the information may be relevant.

23. The Parenting Coordinator may interview/observe the child(ren) privately and/or with the parents together or individually. The Parenting Coordinator shall disclose information obtained from the children only with the children's consent and/or at the Parenting Coordinator's discretion.

24. There shall be no confidentiality concerning communications between the parents and the Parenting Coordinator and any third parties with whom the Parenting Coordinator may consult. The Parenting Coordinator may disclose to the parents all or part of any information she may have received from third parties, the other parent, and the children, subject to #23.

25. Agreements reached by the parents during the non-decision making phase shall be drafted by the PC and provided to the parents in draft form for their approval and final agreement, ultimately taken out as a consent Award. Any disparity in wording shall be resolved by the PC.

DECISION-MAKING COMPONENT (ARBITRATION PROCESS)

The Law

26. The arbitration shall be conducted in accordance with the law of Ontario, and the law of Canada as it applies in Ontario.

27. Issues related to the custody and access of the children (on an interim and permanent basis) shall be determined in accordance with the provisions of the *Children's Law Reform Act*, R.S.O. 1990, c. C.12 or, if a divorce has been granted or the parties are involved in divorce proceedings, then under the *Divorce Act*, R.S.C. 1985, c. 3 (2nd Supp.), as amended.

The Process

28. The parties appoint ________ to perform the arbitration function of the Parenting Coordination.

29. If the issue remains unresolved after a reasonable effort, or if one party chooses not to participate, and the Parenting Coordinator believes that further similar efforts are unlikely to be productive, or that the time constraints of the issue presented do not allow for further similar efforts, the PC shall proceed to arbitrate the issue in accordance with the arbitration provisions of this Agreement.

30. In the event one party maintains that issue is outside of the mandate and/or scope of the PC's authority as stipulated in paragraphs 2 and 7 of this agreement, the PC shall determine the matter taking into account the submissions of each parent.

31. The Parenting Coordinator shall advise the parents in writing that they are now engaged in Arbitration. Prior to the Arbitration, a meeting or conference call may occur to discuss procedural matters. An arbitration may be conducted in a hearing, a telephone conference call and/or by way of written documents. The parties specifically waive their rights under 26(1) of the Arbitration Act for this purpose. Subsequent to the meeting/call to discuss procedures, the time and place of the arbitration hearing, or in the case the arbitration is conducted by way of written submissions and documents, the timeline for written submissions and reply submissions, shall be provided in writing by the Arbitrator to the parents. In the case of an arbitration conducted in writing and by way of documents, submissions and reply submissions shall be made available directly to the PC (who then provides same to the parents) in the time-line determined by the PC, previously indicated to the parents in writing. Time-sensitive issues shall require a shorter time-line as determined by the Parenting Coordinator.

32. All communication during the arbitration shall be 3-way, be it by conference call, e-mail, fax or in meetings. All communications with the Arbitrator shall occur in the presence of the other party (telephone or meeting) and/or be copied to the other party. The same shall occur for all communications from the Arbitrator to the parties.

33. Should the parents decide that they wish to involve their lawyers in an arbitration, it may be by way of conference call, written submissions and/or hearing, depending on the circumstances. If they choose not to involve their lawyers they are waiving their right to do so.

34. The arbitration may proceed as notified, even if one parent fails to appear at the previously designated time and place, if one parent fails to provide his/her submissions in the time-line provided, and/or if one parent does not provide the sufficient retainer.

35. In her decision-making role as Arbitrator, the PC may rely on any information received including the PC's written records during attempts to resolve the issues up to that point. Notwithstanding, the parents shall provide full submissions, either verbal or in writing, and not assume any prior information provided shall be taken into account in the decision-making process.

36. To the extent that information relied upon by the PC is information that the PC has received from the children, the parties agree that they may not be privy to that information and disclosure of same to them by the PC shall be with the consent of the children, or at the PC's discretion. The parties specifically waive their rights under 26(3) of the Act for this purpose. Each parent, by signing this agreement, acknowledges that he or she has been advised that such may not satisfy the requirements of the Arbitration Act but that each agrees that such is in the child(ren)'s best interests. Each waives his or her right, at any time in the future, to rely on this discretionary disclosure by the PC to set aside the PC's decision on any issue and release his or her right to make such argument.

37. Subject to #23, #24 and #26 prior to rendering a decision and in time for the parties to respond, the PC shall summarize for the parents the information received from third parties.

38. From time to time, given the exigencies of the situation and time constraints, it may be necessary to have a summary disposition of a parental issue in order to accommodate the parents and the best interest of the children and avoid a further escalation of the parental conflict, which in turn poses a risk to children. Clause #32 shall be satisfied. Accordingly, in those circumstances, the parties accept and acknowledge

that the Parenting Coordinator has the authority to make a summary disposition of the issue within the parameters of the agreement hearing briefly from both parties in such a manner that the Parenting Coordinator deems appropriate.

Expert Evidence

39. The parties specifically give the PC the authority to determine the necessity of retaining professional(s) to provide expert opinions respecting any outstanding issue(s) and to direct the parties accordingly.

40. The parties agree that if arbitration is sought by either party or takes place and issues of law arise, then, in her sole discretion, ________ may obtain independent legal advice to assist her in the determination of those issues. The parties shall have access to any representations or opinions provided by such counsel. The cost of such counsel shall initially be borne by the parties equally subject to reapportionment by the Parenting Coordinator.

Reporter

41. The parties do not wish to have a reporter present at the arbitration of any issue and waive their right to have a transcript of the proceedings. If, however, in the absolute discretion of the Arbitrator, the Arbitrator decides that a Reporter should be present, then the Arbitrator may direct the parties to share the costs of the Reporter in such a fashion as the Arbitrator deems appropriate in all the circumstances.

The Award

42. The PC will, as soon as possible after the arbitration, render an award in writing that shall be delivered to the parents and counsel by fax or e-mail transmission. The PC may provide an oral decision to both parents in a meeting or conference call prior to releasing the written decision.

43. The PC's Award shall be final and binding upon the parents and shall be incorporated in a Consent Order of the Ontario Superior court of Justice (or the Superior Court of Justice, Family Court or Ontario Court of Justice).

REVIEWS AND APPEAL

44. The parties have the right to review the Arbitrator's Award in accordance with s. 46 of the *Arbitration Act*.

45. The parties have the right to appeal the Award on a question of law, with leave from the court as provided in s. 45(1) of the *Arbitration Act* and the *Family Law Act*, R.S.O. 1990, c. F.3.

46. In addition, the parties may appeal the Award on (check where appropriate):

[ ] a question of law (without leave);
[ ] a question of fact;
[ ] a question of mixed fact and law; or
[ ] none of the above.

TERMINATION OR WITHDRAWAL FROM THE PARENTING COORDINATION

47. (a) Neither parent may unilaterally withdraw from this Agreement prior to the issues being resolved. With their joint consent in writing, both parents may terminate this Agreement. Should one parent choose not to participate in the resolution of any issue, the Parenting Coordinator may proceed and fulfill her decision-making role.

(b) The Parenting Coordinator may resign any time she determines the resignation to be in the best interests of the child(ren), or if she is unable to serve out her term, upon thirty (30) days notice.

48. The PC's mandate terminates when:

a. the term of service in this Agreement expires;
b. the PC resigns or dies;
c. the parties agree to terminate it in accordance with paragraph 12, or
d. the court removes the PC.

49. The PC's resignation or the parties' agreement to terminate the PC's mandate does not imply acceptance of the validity of any reason advanced for challenging or removing her.

CHILD ABUSE REPORTING AND RISK OF HARM

50. The Parenting Coordinator is required to report to the appropriate child welfare authority (i.e., Children's Aid Society, Catholic Children's Aid Society, Jewish Child & Family Service, or Native Child & Family Services) and/or other relevant authorities if she has a reasonable suspicion that a child(ren) may be in danger of harm and/or abuse.

51. The PC is obliged to notify the proper authorities if she has a "reasonable suspicion" that a client may harm himself or herself or the other parent.

FEES

52. The fee for Parenting Coordination is at a rate of $_______ per hour. Fees are applied to all time expended in any/all professional activities, including administrative matters, associated with the PC process and/or arising from the PC process. This includes time spent in reviewing documents and correspondence, voice-mail, e-mail, travel, meetings, and telephone calls with the parents, their counsel and other professionals involved. Also included are any unpaid fees charged retroactively from the time that services are initially requested and the file is opened. This also includes disbursements paid to collateral sources for verbal and/or written reports and agency/hospital reports. Fees shall be applied to time required for deliberation and writing of memos and arbitrated decisions. Fees for testifying in court, preparation time for testifying and related travel time shall be paid for by the party that calls the PC to testify. Court-related fees (i.e., preparation time, attendance and travel) shall be obtained by way of retainer in advance of any services rendered.

53. There is considerable cost to opening the file and continuing scheduling issues with both the parents and collateral sources as required. A non-refundable administrative fee of $____ payable by each parent, or in accordance with the proportions that they have agreed to, shall be applied once the referral has been accepted. Accordingly there shall be no further charges for the PC and administrative assistant's time in connection with setting up the process and ongoing scheduling.

54. Record keeping requirements make it necessary to log and make a record of each and every e-mail, telephone call and/or message. For this reason a minimum fee (.1 or 6 minutes) may be charged for each telephone and e-mail contact. These charges shall not apply to brief contacts about scheduling.

55. Subject to the terms of paragraph 36 and 54, the parents shall share fees equally, unless indicated otherwise. Each parent shall provide an initial retainer of $________. Parties shall be advised in advance when further retainer is required. A minimum retainer (security deposit) of $__________ (2 hours) per parent shall be maintained in the account at all times, to be returned to the parents at the end of the PC's tenure, less any balance owing by either party. If the above terms are not satisfied, ________ shall postpone all services until the retainer terms are met. Non-payment of fees shall be grounds for the resignation of PC,

although ________ shall first give notice of her intention to resign and then allow either party a reasonable period of time to obtain a court order requiring this payment before resigning. In the period after the notice is given, ________ need not provide any services to the parents until her retainer is fully maintained.

56. If one of the parties fails to provide his or her fees as set out above, the Parenting Coordination may proceed and the fees for same may be paid by the other party. Such shall not be deemed to affect the ability of the PC to perform her arbitration function for the duration of her tenure. Any such payment may be enforced by the party who overpaid his or her share, in Court. An Award of costs may be made. This award shall take into account the retainer that has been paid and make the necessary adjustments.

57. Regular statements of the account detailing the date, service, time and hourly rate shall be provided. Your insurance company may not cover all of the services, although insurance company policies vary. If you require an additional statement for insurance purposes an administrative fee shall be charged for the provision of an additional statement.

58. A party shall be billed for an appointment in which there is less than 24 (twenty-four) business hours' notice prior to cancellation by that party, except for an appointment scheduled for 8:00 a.m. and/or after 4:00 p.m., in which case 48 (forty-eight) business hours notice is required prior to cancellation. A party shall be responsible for bills arising from his or her own cancellation with insufficient notice and/or failure to attend a scheduled appointment.

59. Notwithstanding this Agreement with respect to payment for services as stated above, the PC may modify this allocation if she finds that one parent is using her services disproportionately and, as a result, is causing the other parent greater expense. In addition, either parent may request that the fees be reallocated at any time during the Parenting Coordinator's term of appointment. Any decision shall follow the same process as required for the arbitration function of the Parenting Coordination.

60. In addition to reallocating fees, the Parenting Coordinator shall have the authority to impose an award of costs if the PC is required to arbitrate any issue. In addition to an award of costs, the PC shall have the authority to require one party to reimburse the other for any costs related to an Award, any expenses he/she may have suffered as a result of any breach of the Parenting Plan, and/or any breach of an arbitral award of the Parenting Coordinator.

For example, if one parent incurs additional day care expenses as a result of the other parent failure to pick up the child(ren) on time, then the Parenting Coordinator shall have the authority to require that parent to compensate the parent who incurred the expense. Or, for example, if one parent has to cancel a scheduled trip for the child(ren) that was pre-paid, as a result of the other parent's default of any terms of the Agreement or the breach of an arbitral award (e.g., delivery of the notarized permission letter), then the defaulting parent shall reimburse the other parent for any loss/expenses occasioned by the default or breach.

GRIEVANCES

61. If either parent has a grievance about the way the Parenting Coordinator is dealing with him/her or any issue, he/she (and with their lawyer if they prefer) shall discuss their concern in person with the Parenting Coordinator before pursuing it in any other manner. If, after discussion, the parent is not satisfied that the grievance has been dealt with satisfactorily, then he/she shall submit a written letter detailing the grievance to the Parenting Coordinator, to the other parent and to any lawyers representing the parents and/or child(ren). The Parenting Coordinator shall provide a written response to the parents and lawyers within twenty (20) days.

62. The Parenting Coordinator shall then meet with the complaining parent and his/her lawyer to further discuss the matter.

63. If the grievance is not resolved after this meeting, the complaining party may file a motion on notice to the other parent with the Court to remove the Parenting Coordinator as per the Arbitration Act. The motion shall proceed on the written documents submitted by both parents and the Parenting Coordinator, unless the Court Orders a hearing.

64. The Court shall determine if the Parenting Coordinator should be replaced and shall determine who shall be responsible for any portions of the Parenting Coordinator's time and costs spent in responding to the grievance and the Parenting Coordinator's lawyer's fees, if any.

65. An award shall be implemented and adhered to during the time the grievance process is in effect. Either party may apply to the Court to obtain a consent Court order implementing or interpreting the terms of the Parenting Coordinator's Awards (via Form 14C).

66. Neither party shall complain about the Parenting Coordinator to the Parenting Coordinator's licensing board without also complying with the above-noted grievance procedure.

WAIVER OF PARENTING COORDINATOR'S LIABILITY

67. The parties waive any claim or right of action against the Parenting Coordinator for any matters arising out of the in good faith functions performed by her under this Agreement.

INDEPENDENT LEGAL ADVICE

68. Each of the parties confirms that he/she has received independent advice. Attached to this Agreement is the certificate of independent legal advice that was provided to each party under subsection 59.6(2) of the *Family Law Act*.

69. Both parties:

a. understand their rights and obligations under this Agreement and the nature and consequences of this Agreement;
b. acknowledge that they are not under any undue influence or duress; and
c. acknowledge that they are both signing this Agreement voluntarily.

Dated:____________	________________________	____________
	Solicitor for Mother	Mother
Dated:____________	________________________	____________
	Solicitor for Father	Father

Certificate Of Independent Legal Advice

I, __________________, Barrister & Solicitor, have reviewed the attached Parenting Coordination Retainer Agreement (the "Agreement") and have fully explained to my client ________________ the meaning and intent of the Agreement and have given the client independent legal advice prior to the Agreement being signed. I have also explained to my client that the Agreement is a "domestic contract" within the meaning of the Family Law Act, and as such a court may set aside the Agreement under various circumstances about which I have informed my client. In my opinion, my client, understands the nature and consequences of this Agreement, and is not signing this Agreement as a result of any undue influence placed upon the client by any person. I hereby confirm that

I am satisfied that my client is fully able to participate in the Parenting Coordination and is signing the Agreement voluntarily.

________________________ ________________________

Date Lawyer

Declarations Of The Parenting Coordinator/Arbitrator

I, _______ confirm the following matters:

(a) I shall treat the parties equally and fairly in the arbitration, as subsection 19(1) of the Act requires.

(b) I have received the appropriate training approved by the Attorney General.

Check either (c) or (d):

(c) The parties were separately screened by me for power imbalances and domestic violence and I have considered the results of the screening and shall do so throughout the arbitration, if I conduct one.

(d) The parties were separately screened for power imbalances and domestic violence by someone other than me and I have considered his or her report on the results of the screening and shall do so throughout the arbitration.

____

Date

________________________ ________________________

Witness *Parenting Coordinator/Arbitrator*

The original Parenting Coordination template appeared in the Journal of Child Custody, Fidler, B. & Epstein, P. “Parenting Coordination in Canada: An Overview of Legal and Practice Issues”, Vol. 5 (1/2). It was updated in May 2009. See <www.familysolutionstoronto.ca> for further updates.

Appendix V.5

Pre-Hearing Conference Form

PRE-ARBITRATION CONFERENCE FORM

Name of party filing this form: ______________________________

Who is the Applicant? ______________________________

Date of execution of Family Arbitration or Mediation/Arbitration Agreement (attach copy) ______________________________

Substantive issues for this Arbitration

- □ **Custody**
- □ **Access**
- □ **Child Support**
- □ **Spousal Support**
- □ **Division of Property**
- □ **Exclusive possession of matrimonial home**
- □ **Ownership of property**
- □ **Preservation /Non-dissipation**
- □ **Non-harassment**
- □ **Sale of property**
- □ **Costs**
- □ **Other (attach schedule)**

....

Grounds for Appeal: □ **Question of Law with leave** □ **Question of fact**
□ Question of Law □ Question of mixed fact and law

Is a reporter required? □ **Yes** □ **No**

Are the court pleadings to be used as pleadings for the Arbitration? □ **Yes** □ **No**

Date for completion of questioning (if required) ______________________________

Names of witnesses I intend to call and estimated time required for his/her testimony (including cross-examination):

Name	**Time**	**Name**	**Time**
___________	___________	___________	___________
___________	___________	___________	___________
___________	___________	___________	___________
___________	___________	___________	___________

Date for delivery of:

Position Statements: ______________________________

Updated Financial Statements: ______________________________

Updated NFP Statements: ______________________________

Answers to disclosure requests: ______________________________

Witness Statements: ______________________________

Expert Reports: ______________________________

Requests to Admit: ______________________________

Exhibit Briefs: ______________________________

Agreed Statement of Facts: ______________________________

Briefs of Authorities: ______________________________

Other documents (specify): ______________________________

Arbitrator's Retainer ($__________/party): ____________________

Are any summonses to witness required? ______________________________

Estimated time required for my case (including argument): ________________

Date(s) scheduled for arbitration hearing: ______________________________

Names of any non-parties who I wish to attend hearing: __________________

____

Procedure for hearing:

All evidence under oath/affirmation:	☐ **Yes**	☐ **No**
Presentation of evidence as per court procedure:	☐ **Yes**	☐ **No**
Hearsay evidence may be admissible in Arbitrator's discretion	☐ **Yes**	☐ **No**
Except for (c), usual rules of admissibility of evidence:	☐ **Yes**	☐ **No**

Other issues: ______________________________

Any preliminary or procedural issues to be dealt with at/before the arbitration?

____

____

Other issues to be dealt with at the pre-arbitration conference: ______________

____

____

DATE THIS FORM COMPLETED:______________________, 20____
Counsel are requested to complete and return this form to the Arbitrator (with copies to all other counsel) prior to the pre-arbitration conference.

Appendix VI Contents

Dispute Resolution Outcomes

Appendix VI.1

Sample Letter to Counsel re Memorandum of Understanding

Dear Collaborative Family Law Solicitors,

RE: PAUL IAM PERFECT AND SHEILA NORYA NOTTE (PERFECT)

I am pleased to report that Sheila and Paul have reached an agreement with respect to a Parenting Plan that outlines how they plan to share parental rights, responsibilities and time with their children, Jordy and Kathy. In addition, as we discussed in our first five-way meeting, Sheila and Paul asked to continue in mediation to deal with the issues of the matrimonial home, support, and other property and financial issues. Again I am pleased to report that they succeeded in reaching agreement on all issues.

By way of summary, Paul and Sheila participated in the following process: They were seen in a combination of individual and joint sessions. In addition, each parent was seen with the children, and the children were seen both individually and in a sibling group. New partners were interviewed and the school, family doctor, and relevant mental health professionals were contacted with respect to information related to the needs and interests of the children.

During the mediation process, I held two Collaborative Mediation meetings with counsel and Paul and Sheila, in addition to conference calls, to finalize the parenting arrangements and the financial issues. All documents and reports provided by the solicitors with respect to financial disclosure were shared with both clients and reviewed by the mediator. Counsel were particularly helpful in preparing the client's sworn financial statements and an impartial accountant was jointly retained to value Paul's business. In addition, with the consent of Paul and Sheila and your approval, I arranged for an impartial actuary to value Paul's pension.

I have enclosed a copy of the Memorandum of Understanding drafted with respect to those issues sent to mediation. Since I am trained as a lawyer, I drafted the Memorandum so that it could be changed into a Separation Agreement quite easily once the parties have had independent legal advice.

We have arranged a five-way meeting next week to finalize Paul and Sheila's Agreement and I invite you to bring any proposed changes to the meeting for discussion. I will make any amendments that both parties agree on. I would appreciate receiving a copy of the final Agreement for my files, once the parties have had independent legal advice and have signed the Agreement.

I have enjoyed working with both the parties and counsel and would be more than willing to offer assistance in the future should there be a change in circumstances or should some difficulty arise that might be best dealt with through mediation.

Thank you for your cooperation in this matter.

Yours sincerely,

____

MEDIATOR

Appendix VI.2

Sample Memorandum of Understanding

This document is not intended to be a legally binding contract, but merely a statement of intention by the parties.

BETWEEN :

Paul Iam Perfect

(the "Father/Husband")

- and -

Sheila Norya Notte (Perfect)

(the "Mother/Wife")

MEMORANDUM OF UNDERSTANDING

1. BACKGROUND

(a) Paul and Sheila were married to each other in the City of _____, in the Province of ______ , on the ______ day of _______, ____.

(b) Paul and Sheila have two children of the marriage, namely Jordy, born on the _______ of ________________ (12 years of age) and Kathy born on the _______ of ________________ (9 years of age).

(c) Paul and Sheila have in fact lived separate and apart in the same home since the 1st of April, 20__ and plan to live separate and apart in different residences as of the 29th day of August, 20__. There is no reasonable prospect of reconciliation.

(d) Paul and Sheila have reached agreement, subject to advice from their lawyers, with respect to the following issues: a parenting plan for their children, Jordy and Kathy, child and spousal support, possession, ownership and division of their property, and equalization of their net family properties. This document sets out the agreements reached in Mediation.

2. FREEDOM FROM THE OTHER

(a) Both Paul and Sheila accept the fact of their separation and agree to respect each other's privacy and right to live separately.

3. STATEMENT OF PARENTING PRINCIPLES

(a) As the parents of Jordy and Kathy, we acknowledge that we are both devoted and loving parents and it is in the best interests of Jordy and Kathy to have a close relationship with both of us.

(b) This Agreement sets out our commitment to provide Jordy and Kathy with the best parenting we are capable of from our separate homes. We will carry out our responsibilities and conduct ourselves as parents so as to enhance our children's growth and development within the spirit of this parenting plan.

(c) We recognize that the level of tension between us during the past year has created an emotionally stressful situation for Jordy and Kathy. We both agree that in the future we will adhere to the following guidelines in order to reduce the level of conflict for our children and work toward an improved level of cooperation as parents:

(i) We will encourage Jordy and Kathy to love both parents and their extended family.
(ii) We will ensure that Jordy and Kathy participate in a Children of Divorce program and we will participate in counselling to deal with our own emotional issues related to the separation.
(iii) We will discuss parenting issues directly with each other, without using Jordy and Kathy as messengers and these discussions will take place when Jordy and Kathy are not present. When Jordy and Kathy are present we will speak to each other in a respectful manner.
(iv) We recognize that our parenting styles are different and agree to respect these differences. If a child complains about some aspect of parenting in the other parent's home, we will encourage that

child to discuss the issue directly with the other parent. If the child is uncomfortable, we will help the child to communicate with the other parent. We will listen to such complaints without making judgments or interfering.

(v) If we have concerns about the children's safety or well being while in the other parent's home, we will discuss that directly with the other parent and if the situation is not resolved satisfactorily, we will seek the assistance of an appropriate professional for dealing with the children or return to mediation.

(vi) We will hold weekly parenting telephone meetings at noon on Fridays and each of us will prepare an agenda of parenting issues to discuss. If we decide to change our present Agreement or to add new items, we will do so in writing and make sure we both have a signed copy.

(vii) We would both prefer to have the children continue attending the same church and therefore we agree to make all reasonable efforts to assist each other and the children to feel comfortable at this church.

(viii) We both agree that, if it is financially possible, we would like the children to continue to attend the Toronto French School. We both recognize that this means some financial sacrifices. If it is no longer possible or preferable for either child to attend, we will discuss this with each other before speaking either to the child or the school. We will try to work out a mutually acceptable alternative before enrolling the children in a different school and will return to mediation or speak to appropriate professionals at the school if we have difficulty resolving this issue.

4. PARENTING PLAN (RESIDENTIAL SCHEDULE)

Sheila and Paul agree that they have a shared parenting plan and the children will reside in each parent's home as set out below.

PARENTING SCHEDULE

Regular Times

(a) Jordy and Kathy will reside with their father at the following times:

(i) Each alternate weekend, a weekend to be defined as extending from Thursday after school until Monday morning. Paul will pick the children up after school and will return them to school. On the other week Paul will pick the children up after school on Thursday and return them to school on Friday morning.

(ii) Paul will take the children to church on the Sundays when the children are with him and Sheila will take them to church on the alternate Sundays.

(iii) Each month Paul can arrange to spend one mid-week evening with each child individually. He will give Sheila at least 48 hours' notice and, unless the children already have alternative plans, they will spend from after school until 7:30 p.m. with their father.

(b) The children will reside with their mother at all other times, except as otherwise stated in this Parenting Plan.

Telephone Contact

Kathy and Jordy will be permitted to have telephone contact with each parent and vice versa at all reasonable times prior to their bedtime.

School Breaks

Christmas School Break

Unless the parents agree otherwise, the children will spend the first part of the Christmas School Break with their mother in odd-numbered years and from Boxing Day in the morning until New Year's Day at 4 p.m. with their father. In even-numbered years the schedule will be reversed. The parents agree to meet by no later than November 15th of each year to finalize the specific dates. If one parent wants to take the children on a vacation for more than the time provided by this schedule, then they will discuss that prior to November the 1st. If one parent takes the children for a vacation during one Christmas Break, then the other parent will have the right of first refusal the following Christmas.

March School Break

(a) If the March Break is one week, the children will spend it with their father if he is able to take this time off work. He will let Sheila know his plans no later than February 1st. Paul will return the children on the Sunday before school begins by 4 p.m. (unless both parents agree to a different return date).

(b) If the March Break is two weeks, the children will spend one week with each parent, with the specific dates to be worked out between the parents by no later than February 1st.

Summer School Break

The children will spend up to three weeks with their father during the summer. Both Sheila and Paul agree that the children should not be away from contact with the other parent for more than two weeks at a time until the youngest child is ten years of age. Both parents agree that they will decide no later than March 1st of each year about the children's summer activities, day camp, and vacation plans with each parent.

Special Times

Statutory Holidays

Kathy and Jordy will spend the statutory holidays with the parent with whom they are residing on that weekend according to the regular schedule. That is, an additional day will be added to the regular schedule.

Professional Development Days

The children will spend professional development days with whichever parent is able to take the day off work. This will be arranged two weeks before the P.D. Day. If neither parent is available, the parent who is scheduled to be with them according to the regular schedule will take the responsibility of arranging alternative care for that day.

Birthdays

Each parent will plan a celebration for each child's birthday at a time when that child is with that parent. Both parents can contact or see the child on his or her birthday if that is convenient.

Parents' Birthdays

The children will celebrate each parent's birthday when they are with that parent. The children can contact the parent on the actual birthday, if that is convenient.

Mother's Day/Father's Day

The children will spend time with their mother on Mother's Day and their father on Father's Day, with specific times to be arranged by mutual consent of the parents.

Additional Access

Paul and Sheila will consult with each other with respect to additional time the children can spend one-on-one with each parent. Such arrangements will be made by mutual consent of the parents, taking into account the needs and interests of each child.

VARIATION OF PARENTING SCHEDULE

(a) Paul and Sheila agree that the terms of the parenting schedule may be varied upon at least 48 (forty-eight) hours notice to the other parent where it is shown that it would be in the best interests of the children to vary such parenting schedule. Such request for alteration of the parenting schedule will not be unreasonably withheld by either parent, unless it is in the best interests of the children not to accede to such a request.

(b) In the event that a parent cannot be with the children during the time that the children are scheduled to be with that parent, then the other parent will be offered an opportunity to be with the children before an alternative childcare arrangement is made.

5. PARENTING RESPONSIBILITIES, PARENTING RIGHTS AND MATERIAL CHANGES

PARENTING RESPONSIBILITIES

(a) Sheila and Paul will consult with each other in advance with respect to significant decisions about the children's education, medical care, dental care, mental health care and religion and with respect to significant expenditures for the children where both parents will be contributing to such expenditures.

(b) Both parents agree that Sheila will arrange the doctor and dentist appointments and will consult in advance with Paul if she wishes assistance in taking the children to these appointments. Sheila will continue to shop for the children's clothes. Paul will buy the sports items and equipment and will shop for clothing if Sheila or the children request this.

(c) Both parents agree to give their phone numbers and addresses to the children's school so that either can be contacted in the case of an emergency.

(d) Both parents agree that they will take responsibility for the children if they are ill or injured while in that parent's care. Sheila and Paul agree to notify the other parent if a child is ill or injured and either parent can ask the other parent for assistance, but if the other parent is unable or it is inconvenient, then the primary responsibility will remain with the parent with whom the children are residing at that time. This responsibility will include making alternative arrangements if neither parent is able to care for the children. Both parents agree that it is acceptable to call either Sheila or Paul's extended family for assistance if neither parent can stay home with the children.

(e) Both parents agree not to register the children for extracurricular activities during the time the children are scheduled to be with the other parent. Sheila and Paul agree to consult with each other at the beginning of each school semester before enrolling Jordy or Kathy in activities, particularly if they wish the assistance of the other parent in transporting the children or sharing the cost of the activity.

(f) Both parents agree to share the transportation of the children to and from extracurricular activities, including birthday parties, with specific times and arrangements to be determined by mutual consent of the parents. The parents will inform each other as soon as possible about invitations to birthday parties that take place when the children are with the other parent. The parent who will be taking the children will buy the birthday gift, unless the parents agree otherwise.

PARENTING RIGHTS

(a) Both parents have a right to receive significant information with respect to the children's education, medical care, dental care, and mental health care, including the right to receive school report cards and to hold interviews with the children's teachers and school principals. Each parent will make arrangements directly with the school, doctor, or dentist for the information he or she wishes to receive.

(b) Sheila and Paul both have a right to attend any extra-curricular activities involving the children. Extended family members may attend the children's extracurricular activities.

COMMUNICATION BETWEEN PARENTS

Sheila and Paul agree to set aside a regular time for a "parenting meeting" by telephone (probably Friday at noon). Sheila and Paul agree to establish an agenda of parenting issues to discuss at these times. Both parents agree that they will not use the children to carry messages between them, but rather will discuss parenting issues directly with each other. Sheila and Paul also agree to exchange information by email, *e.g.*, with respect to extracurricular activities, medical care, special events, *etc.* where this would be helpful and in the best interests of the children.

TRAVEL

Neither Paul nor Sheila will remove the children from the Province of Ontario without the consent of the other parent, except for a brief vacation, and such consent will not be unreasonably withheld. Paul and Sheila agree to give the other parent notice if the children are removed from the Province of Ontario for a brief vacation and such notice shall include the location and duration of the vacation [and/or the phone number of a contact person in case of an emergency]. Each parent shall give the other parent a notarized letter of consent if the children are to be removed from Canada for a brief vacation, for the purpose of satisfying the immigration authorities.

MOBILITY

Paul and Sheila agree to give each other a minimum of ninety days' notice if this is possible, prior to moving his or her residence, and such notice shall include the address and phone number of the new residence. If either parent changes his or her residence such that the aforementioned parenting schedule cannot be followed, then they agree that any new parenting schedule will be based on the principle of maintaining a close relationship between the children and both parents. If this occurs, Paul and Sheila agree to meet and discuss a revised parenting schedule. In the event that they cannot agree upon a revised schedule, they will attend mediation to discuss any changes prior to litigating such matters. Paul and Sheila agree that neither of them will move the children until the revised schedule has either been agreed upon or ninety days have elapsed from the date notice was given of the impending move.

CHANGE OF NAME OF CHILDREN

Paul and Sheila agree that neither parent will change the name of the children without the written consent of the other parent. This provision shall be deemed to be a bar to any such application.

DISPUTE RESOLUTION

(a) In the event that Sheila or Paul cannot agree on one or more significant issues in relation to the parenting arrangements or support:

(i) they agree to first give each other written notice of the nature of the disagreement;

(ii) if no agreement has been reached within 30 (thirty) days after notice has been given, the parties agree to participate in mediation with (*name of Mediator*) or another mediator chosen on consent of the parties to resolve any dispute. They may also consult with their respective solicitors to resolve any outstanding issues;

(iii) Paul and Sheila agree to share the cost of mediation in proportion to their gross income;

(iv) if no agreement has been reached through mediation or their respective solicitors within 90 (ninety) clear days after notice has been given, either parent may refer any dispute with respect to parenting arrangements or support to be determined by an Arbitrator selected by mutual consent; and

(v) If no agreement has been reached through mediation sixty (60) days after hiring a mediator, then Paul and Sheila can hire an Arbitrator chosen by mutual consent to resolve the issue. In the event that either party commences an application at court, both solicitors and the mediator must withdraw as set out in the Collaborative Mediation Participation Agreement, attached as Appendix "A".

6. FINANCIAL PROVISION

SPOUSAL SUPPORT

Retroactive/Income Tax Payments

(a) Paul made periodic payments of support to Sheila for the benefit of her and the children in this calendar year totalling $5,000 ($2,500 per month). These payments shall be considered as having been made pursuant to this Agreement. They may be deducted by Paul and included by Sheila in the calculation of their respective income taxes pursuant to the *Income Tax Act*, ss. 56.1(3)* and 60.1(3).

(b) Sheila will provide Paul with a copy of her 20__ tax return by the 30th of June 20__ (same year), and Paul will pay Sheila's taxes that are attracted by the support payments, such tax to be calculated as if the support was in addition to all other income so that Sheila will suffer no income tax consequence from such support payments.

CHILD SUPPORT

Regular Support

(a) Commencing on the first day of June 20__, and on the first day of each subsequent month, Paul will pay to Sheila for the support and maintenance of Jordy and Kathy the table amount in accordance with the Federal Child Support Guidelines. From June 1st, 20__ until May 1st, 20__ (following year) the table amount shall be $1,500 based on Paul's annual income of $125,000. These child support payments shall continue until one of the following occur:

(i) The child ceases to reside "full time" with Sheila;
(ii) Reside "full time" includes the child living away from the home to attend an educational institution, pursue summer employment, or take a vacation while otherwise maintaining his or her principal residence with Sheila;
(iii) The child becomes 18 years of age and ceases to be in full-time attendance at an educational institution. This would

* Section 56.1 was re-enacted S.C. 1994, c. 7, Sched VIII, s. 18.

include a period of up to one year while the child was working and/or travelling;

(iv) The child becomes 24 years of age;

(v) The child dies;

(vi) The child is no longer a child of the marriage;

(vii) Paul dies.

(b) The quantum of child support was based on the fact that Paul agreed to pay all the costs associated with the children's schooling as set out in "Additional Child Expenses", paragraph (a).

(c) Paul and Sheila agree that there will be an annual review of child support in May of each year and new annual payments will commence on June 1st. Both parents agree that the new amount of child support will be based on Paul's annual income for the previous year in accordance with the Child Support Guidelines.

SPOUSAL SUPPORT

Regular Support

(a) Commencing on the 1st day of June 20__, Paul will pay to Sheila, for her support, the sum of $2,000 per month until she:

(i) remarries;

(ii) cohabits with another man and becomes a spouse pursuant to s. 29 of the *Family Law Act*. If this occurs it will be deemed a material change in circumstances, and Paul and Sheila will return to mediation to discuss a reduction in her portion of support;

(iii) dies.

(b) If one of the conditions set out above occurs such that Sheila is no longer entitled to support, the parties agree to review the quantum of child support according to the procedure set out in paragraph 7.

Cost of Living Adjustment

(a) The amount of the monthly maintenance and support payments which Paul is required to make to Sheila for her support will be increased with each unit of increase in the Consumer Price Index, provided that:

(i) The amount of increase in such payments will be directly proportionate to the increase in the Consumer Price Index published by Statistics Canada under the heading "All Items", Ontario Area (not seasonally adjusted), with base year 1981 equal to 100.

(ii) Any increase will be made once a year only and becomes effective on the first day of June of each year, commencing on the first day of June 20__, and will be based upon the Consumer Price Index published immediately prior to the effective date of adjustment.

(iii) Any increase will be the lesser of:

(a) The percentage increase in the Consumer Price Index as calculated above;

(b) Paul's percentage increase in his total gross income from all sources. If Paul chooses to rely on this subsection he will, no later than May 1st in each year, produce to Sheila a copy of his tax returns for the two immediately preceding years, which will form the basis of the calculation of the percentage increase in his gross income from all sources. If in the end Paul fails to provide the income tax returns for Sheila, then the increase on June 1st of that year will be in accordance with the Consumer Price Index.

Post-dated Cheques

Paul shall forthwith deliver to Sheila twelve post-dated cheques, dated for the first of the month from June 1st, 20__ to May 1st, 20__, inclusive, for the amounts payable to Sheila pursuant to sections "Child Support" and "Spousal Support". Thereafter in each year on or before June 1st, Paul shall provide to Sheila a further twelve post-dated cheques for the next ensuing twelve-month period, and so on from time to time so long as he is obliged to make payments to Sheila pursuant to the "Child Support" and "Spousal Support" sections.

Post-Secondary Education

Paul and Sheila will contribute in proportion to their gross income toward the costs of the post-secondary education for Jordy and Kathy, which costs include tuition, residence, supplies, equipment, and other incidental expenses. The parents shall provide each other with proof of their incomes.

Additional Child Expenses

(a) Paul will pay the children's tuition at Toronto French School for so long as one or both of the children attends. If one or both children transfer to the public schools, then Paul and Sheila agree to review the quantum of child support according to the procedure set out in paragraph 7.

(b) Paul will pay for the children's extracurricular activities, camp fees, or other summer programs and remedial education. If Sheila wishes Paul's contribution, she will consult with Paul before enrolling the children in activities and will obtain his consent, and this consent will not be unreasonably withheld. When Sheila is earning more than $40,000, she will contribute in proportion to her gross income to these expenses.

Medical/Dental Benefits

(a) Paul is covered by Group Dental, Extended Health, and Drug Plans through his employment at ABC Creative Crafts Ltd. He will continue this coverage:

  (i) In the case of Sheila, until one of the following occurs:
    (a) the marriage is terminated; or
    (b) the benefit is no longer available to Paul through his employment.
  (ii) In the case of each child, so long as Paul is obligated to support each child and the benefit is available to Paul through his employment.

(b) Where Sheila is obligated to pay a fee directly to a dentist, hospital, health facility, or druggist in relation to any services which are covered in all or in part by Paul's plan, Paul will immediately endorse over to Sheila any cheque he receives from the plan or plans in reimbursement for all or part of the services for which Sheila has paid directly.

(c) Paul and Sheila will share in proportion to their gross income the cost of any medical, dental, and orthodontal expenses incurred by either parent for the children that are not covered by an insurance plan held by either parent. Paul and Sheila shall provide each other proof of their incomes. If Sheila wishes Paul's contribution, she will consult Paul in advance on any major dental or orthodontia treatment and obtain his consent, which consent will not be unreasonably withheld, before the commencement of the treatment.

7. MATERIAL CHANGE IN CIRCUMSTANCE

(a) Paul and Sheila intend paragraphs 4 and 5 and sections "Regular Support", "Cost of Living Adjustment", "Post-Secondary Education", "Additional Child Expenses", and "Medical/Dental Benefits" of this agreement to be final except for a variation because of a material change in circumstances, which shall include but not be limited to:

(i) a change in primary residence of the children;
(ii) a change in Sheila's marital status as set out in section "Regular Support" (a) and (b);
(iii) the parents' inability to work due to illness or disability;
(iv) a material change in income for either parent.

(b) In the event that the parents cannot agree on issues related to the parenting arrangements or support, they agree to follow the Dispute Resolution clause set out above.

8. MATRIMONIAL HOME

(a) Paul and Sheila purchased the "matrimonial home" located at __________, and took title in Sheila's name. Sheila and Paul agree that title to the matrimonial home will continue to be held in Sheila's name alone.

(b) Paul hereby releases to Sheila any and all interest he may now have or may afterwards acquire in the "matrimonial home", whether possessory or proprietary.

(c) Sheila will have exclusive possession of the "matrimonial home" hereafter.

(d) Sheila will pay all insurance premiums, monthly mortgage instalments, taxes and other expenses relating to the "matrimonial home", and will indemnify Paul from all such liability relating to the "matrimonial home".

(e) Paul and Sheila acknowledge that they have divided the contents of the "matrimonial home", in a manner satisfactory to both of them.

9. EQUALIZATION PAYMENT

Paul and Sheila acknowledge that the value of Paul's interest in his company, ABC Creative Crafts Ltd., and the value of her interest in the "matrimonial home" are approximately equal. Paul and Sheila acknowledge that the division of assets and liabilities as provided in this Agreement fully satisfies any and all entitlements each party has or may have to an equalization of their Net Family Properties.

10. LIFE INSURANCE

DOUBLE POLICY

(a) Paul carries two policies of insurance on his life with Good News Life Insurance Co., namely $350,000 (Policy Number 12345) and $50,000 (Policy Number 67890). Sheila also carries two policies of insurance on her life with Good News Life Insurance Co., namely $175,000 (Policy Number 24680) and $50,000 (Policy Number 13579). Both Paul and Sheila agree to maintain these policies with each other as sole, irrevocable beneficiary (in trust for the children) for so long as Jordy and Kathy are entitled to support under the provisions of this Agreement. Neither parent can change the beneficiary without the express written consent of the other parent. Both parents have filed a designation pursuant to the provisions of the *Insurance Act.* The surviving parent will act as a trustee for the benefit of Jordy and Kathy.

(b) Paul and Sheila will each give the other a true copy of this designation within 14 days from the execution of this Agreement. Paul and Sheila will maintain the policies in force, whether they do so through renewal from time to time or otherwise, and will pay or cause to be paid the premiums required on the policies as the premiums fall due. Paul and Sheila agree that if they are no longer covered by the policies in force, they will immediately obtain replacement coverage for the plan or policies (ensuring that there is no gap in coverage beyond their control) to the extent available at similar cost, and will maintain the replacement coverage and will pay the required premiums as they fall due and so on for each succeeding policy. Paul and Sheila agree that they will maintain the other parent as sole beneficiary (in trust for the children) of the policies for as long as either parent is required to support the children pursuant to the provisions of this Agreement.

(c) In the event that one parent dies, Paul and Sheila agree that the insurance proceeds are intended to fund Jordy and Kathy's child support needs and may be used *inter alia* to provide for Jordy and Kathy's educational, shelter, clothing, recreational, health care, dental care and mental health needs. The surviving parent will invest the insurance proceeds in prudent and safe investments. The surviving parent will encroach on interest first and the capital or principal as necessary for the benefit of Jordy and Kathy. Any remaining principal from the insurance, after the support obligation ends, will be paid out to the children in two equal installments with the first installment commencing 60 days after the support obligation ends. If Jordy or Kathy are not yet 25 years of age, then the first payment of principal will occur as soon as possible after that child's 25th birthday and the second and final installment will occur five years later as soon as possible after that child's 30th birthday. If both parents die before the capital and any accrued interest is fully paid out, Honest Guardians Inc. will act as trustee and will be bound by the same requirements as a parent as set out above.

(d) Paul and Sheila agree that when neither party is required to support the children pursuant to the provisions of this Agreement, then both parties may deal with their respective policies as they wish free from any claim by the other or by their estate, and both parties or their personal representatives will give and execute any consent or other document then required to enable either party to deal with the policies.

(e) Within 14 days of one party demanding it, that party will deliver proof to the other that the policies are in good standing. If Paul or Sheila defaults in payment of the premiums and the policies are no longer in good standing, the other party may pay any premiums and may recover them from the other together with all of their costs and expenses including their solicitor/client costs.

(f) If Paul dies without this insurance in effect, his obligation to pay support or maintenance pursuant to this Agreement will survive his death (notwithstanding section 6, "Child Support" of this Agreement) and will be a first charge on his estate.

11. PENSION FUNDS

CANADA PENSION PLAN

Both Paul and Sheila may apply under the Canada Pension Plan for a division of pension credits earned from the date of marriage up to the date of separation.

DEBTS AND OBLIGATIONS

(a) There is an outstanding line of credit with the CIBC bank in the amount of $50,000 in the name of both parties, which line of credit is collaterally secured by the matrimonial home. On April 1, 20__, the balance owing on the line of credit is approximately $15,000.00. Paul agrees to assume sole responsibility for repayment of this indebtedness and shall indemnify and save Sheila harmless with respect thereto. It is agreed that Paul will not utilize the line of credit for any further advances of funds, without Sheila's knowledge and consent in writing. Should Sheila utilize the line of credit after April 1, 20__, then she shall assume responsibility for such indebtedness.

(b) Neither party will contract in the name of the other or bind the other in any way for any debts or obligations.

(c) Except as provided in this Agreement, if debts or obligations are incurred by either party on behalf of the other, before or after the date of this Agreement, he or she will completely indemnify the other for all such debts or obligations or any related damages or costs.

12. Paul and Sheila agree that:

(a) they have had or have been advised to obtain independent legal advice;

(b) they have made and received full financial disclosure;

(c) they understand the terms of this Agreement; and

(d) are signing voluntarily, without duress.

13. COSTS

Paul and Sheila will each pay his or her own legal fees and disbursements incurred by him or her and will share equally the Mediator's fees and disbursements.

[**Note:** The clients should *not* sign the Memorandum of Understanding in the Mediator's office with the Mediator as witness. The Memorandum of Understanding should be sent to the lawyer for each party so that the clients can receive independent legal advice and then the parties can sign a Separation Agreement in their lawyers' offices. If this is a Collaborative Mediation or Collaborative Family Law case, the Separation Agreement can be signed in a four- or five-way meeting at the conclusion of the process, with the lawyers acting as witnesses to the Agreement. In these cases, the lawyers will include any necessary Releases or other legally necessary paragraphs to ensure a binding and complete Agreement.]

Appendix VI.3

Sample Arbitration Award

IN THE MATTER OF THE ARBITRATION ACT, 1991, S.O. 1991, c. 17

B E T W E E N:

Steve Jones (Father)

- and -

Lily Jones (Mother)

August 29, 20--

In an Arbitration Agreement entered into on August 28, 20-- (attached as Schedule 1), the parties and their counsel agreed as follows:

1. We hereby appoint Dr. Barbara Landau, Registered Psychologist, to act as the Mediator-Arbitrator with respect to the following issues:
   (a) For the academic year 20-- and 20-- should Sally and Bill reside primarily with their mother or with their father, according to the parenting schedule attached as Appendix 1. The parties agree that Dr. Landau shall include in her award that there shall be a de novo determination of this issue for the academic year 20--/20-- if either party so desires, and that she may be appointed to mediate/arbitrate the issue if the parties are unable to resolve it as between them. Dr. Landau shall incorporate the process to deal with any review in her award; and
   (b) such other issues as both parties agree to submit to the mediation-arbitration process from time to time.

Background

Steve and Lily Jones were married on June 5, 1997 and separated on January 10, 2005. Steve and Lily have two children of the marriage, twins named Sally and Bill, born on October 4, 1998. Lily and Steve lived separate and apart in the same home in Mississauga until April 10, 2006. After April 10, 2006, Steve moved to a 3-bedroom home in Mississauga close to the matrimonial home and Lily moved to a 2-bedroom townhouse (with a finished basement) in Etobicoke (Toronto).

Prior to moving out of the matrimonial home, Lily and Steve participated in mediation with the Peel Family Mediation Service and entered into an interim joint custody and shared residency agreement (as well as other issues) whereby the children spent alternate weeks with each parent from Friday to Friday. This interim agreement extended until August 30, 20-- with Steve and Lily agreeing to review the Parenting Plan before this date.

Both parties entered into mediation with me on July 4, 20-- to review the parenting arrangements for Sally and Bill, as well as reach an agreement on support and other financial issues. Steve and Lily were successful in mediating a detailed Parenting Plan, including a Regular Schedule setting out how the children would spend time with each of them (attached as Schedule 2). Despite considerable goodwill and respectful discussion they were not able to resolve the key issue of "should the children reside primarily with their mother or their father"? They agreed, in consultation with their counsel, to submit this issue to arbitration with me as arbitrator.

Before setting out each party's position, I wish to emphasize the important areas of agreement and the commendable efforts of both Lily and Steve. First they agree, as do their counsel that both are loving and competent parents. They agree that both are actively involved in their children's care and genuinely concerned about their welfare. Both have demonstrated their ability to meet the children's needs over the four months they have lived apart.

Also, Steve and Lily agree that the children love both parents and have adjusted very well to the separation. Both parents credit the children's good adjustment to the fact that they eased the children into the separation, living together for about eight months separate and apart in the matrimonial home after the decision to separate. They provided the children with the stability of a familiar neighbourhood and friends in Mississauga at the time when Lily moved to Etobicoke, and ensured regular and frequent contact with each parent. The children, who are 8 years of age, are pleased with the efforts their parents have made. Bill and Sally were aware of the tension between their parents when they lived together and in fact are relieved that they have separated.

When I met with the children, they had accepted the separation and adjusted well to the shared parenting arrangements. They enjoy their time with both parents and have made friends in both communities. Bill and Sally are polite, friendly, cooperative and very bonded to each other. They are healthy looking, happy and attractive children. Sally was more verbal and outgoing, Bill was more introverted and had difficulty expressing feelings. They both reported that the tension and conflict between their parents has decreased considerably since the separation.

On the issue of school placement, both children want their parents to decide. One child expressed a slight preference for the school that was familiar, but said that once new friends were made, it would be fine to go to the new school. Both accept the idea of spending much of the school week with one parent and most weekends with the other parent. They also thought it would be possible to go to one of the schools for the 20--/20-- academic year and then shift schools — if that was what their parents decided.

During the arbitration, both parents listened respectfully to each other's and the counsel's submissions. Even when difficult topics were addressed, each listened carefully and responded appropriately when it was that parent's turn. Both cooperated fully with the process and expressed their differences with clear and genuine feelings that remained focused on the needs of their children and at no time did their communication become hostile or denigrating. Lily's and Steve's conduct during the hearing is a testament to why their children are handling the separation so well.

Relevant Family Law

Both parties and their counsel made reference to the following statutory provisions in their arguments and I have relied on these provisions in my award.

According to the Ontario *Children's Law Reform Act* R.S.O. 1990, the following factors must be considered in determining what custodial arrangements are in the best interests of children:

> 24(1) The merits of an application under this Part in respect of custody of or access to a child shall be determined on the basis of the best interests of the child.
>
> (2) In determining the best interests of the child for the purposes of application under this Part in respect of custody of or access to a child, a court shall consider all the needs and circumstances of the child including,
>
> (*a*) (i) the love, affection and emotional ties between the child; each person entitled to or claiming custody of or access to the child,
>
> (ii) other members of the child's family who reside with the child, and
>
> (iii) persons involved in the care and upbringing of the child;
>
> (*b*) the views and preferences of the child, where such views and preferences can reasonably be ascertained;
>
> (*c*) the length of time the child has lived in a stable home environment;

(*d*) the ability and willingness of each person applying for custody of the child to provide the child with guidance and education, the necessaries of life and any special needs of the child;

(*e*) any plans proposed for the care and upbringing of the child;

(*f*) the permanence and stability of the family unit with which it is proposed that the child will live; and

(*g*) the relationship by blood or through an adoption order between the child and each person who is a party to the application.

(3) The past conduct of a person is not relevant to a determination of an application under this Part in respect of custody of or access to a child unless the conduct is relevant to the ability of the person to act as a parent of a child.

According to the *Divorce Act*, R.S.C. 1985, c. 3 (2nd Supp.), the following factors must be considered in deciding what is in the best interests of children:

(8) In making an order under this section, the court shall take into consideration only the best interests of the child of the marriage as determined by reference to the condition, means, needs and other circumstances of the child.

(9) In making an order under this section, the court shall not take into consideration the past conduct of any person unless the conduct is relevant to the ability of that person to act as a parent of a child.

PARTIES' POSITIONS

Lily's Position

Lily believes that the children have already adjusted well to their home with her in Etobicoke. She states that the fact that for the past four months they have spent equal time in Mississauga with their father and in Etobicoke with her, has helped to ease them into the transition. Lily believes that the change of school will have positive benefits, particularly for Bill, and will not be unduly stressful for the children.

Lily and her counsel stated that it was in the children's best interests to reside with her as P1 for the following reasons:

(a) The love, affection and emotional ties between the child and:

(i) each person entitled to or claiming custody of or access to the child,

(ii) other members of the child's family who reside with the child,

(iii) persons involved in the care and upbringing of the child;

Both parents acknowledge that the children love both of them. Lily claims that she can better meet the children's emotional needs, is able to demonstrate affection more easily, and she is better able to provide the psychological support and guidance they need. She gave examples of occasions when the children, Bill in particular, confided in her about difficult social situations and asked that Steve not be informed.

She further states that the children are not happy with their babysitter in Mississauga and prefer the sitter she has arranged as this is the mother of their friends. According to Lily, the Mississauga babysitter loses patience and yells at the children, does not provide adequate stimulation, cares generally for younger children and the children are bored in her care.

(b) the views and preferences of the child, where such views and preferences can reasonably be ascertained;

Both parents stated that at different times the children have expressed a preference for residing primarily with that parent. Lily maintains that recently one of the children stated that he or she hopes to go to Orchard Park Public School from her home.

(c) the length of time the child has lived in a stable home environment;

Lily moved to Etobicoke four months ago to reduce the commute to and from her job in Toronto. She maintains that she has provided a stable home environment during that period and that the children have adjusted well to this change. Her evidence was that the children are happy in her environment and have made new friends. Bill in particular has made and maintained three new friends and this has given him renewed confidence. Sally, who is very sociable, has had no difficulty adjusting. Lily states that the only change the children now face is attending a new school.

(d) the ability and willingness of each person applying for custody of the child to provide the child with guidance and education, the necessaries of life and any special needs of the child;

Lily indicates that while Steve is a loving parent and good at providing structure and routine, she believes she is better able to meet this criterion. Lily states that she is the parent who has fostered a closer relationship with the children's teachers and has consulted mental health professionals about the children's adjustment to the separation and in particular, Bill's special needs. According to Bill's Report Cards which were entered as an exhibit (attached as Schedule 3), Bill began to display difficulties paying attention in class and with social behaviour from an early age (in JK), and these difficulties have persisted, being most acute in the past year. Lily admits that she was unsure whether the increased difficulty was due to the added tension of the separation. Over a period of time, she consulted several psychologists and psychiatrists and the school about what steps to take. Lily expressed frustration that Steve did not take these concerns as seriously as she did and seemed to be reluctant to acknowledge that Bill potentially has some serious social problems that are impacting on his self-esteem. She was advised by the psychologist "to let the dust settle on the separation" before having Bill assessed and she followed this advice.

Lily believes that Orchard Park Public School provides a better school environment for both children in that it is a smaller school (230 pupils vs. 550 at Glenholme), has more supportive resources to meet Bill's special needs (*e.g.*, a social worker, a Rainbows program for Children of Divorce), and has a considerably higher academic ranking on EQAO standardized tests.

Lily also claims that she initiates discussions with the children on significant issues such as social relationships, how to make and keep friends, and the use of drugs. She also indicated that she really enjoys helping the children with their homework and taking them to midweek extra-curricular activities. Lily states that Steve becomes impatient and does not take as active a role in assisting the children with homework and is less motivated to take the children to midweek activities. According to her observations, Steve prefers to have the children work out their homework issues on their own, while he relaxes and plays videogames.

(e) any plans proposed for the care and upbringing of the child;

Lily indicated that she plans to have a friend living in her housing complex (also named "Lily" (whose children are friends of Sally and Bill) care for the children for ½ hour prior to school and after school until she can arrive home. This person offered daycare during the summer and the children indicated that they enjoyed this arrangement. Lily has arranged for a back-up person, who is also a friend living nearby, to care for them if the first daycare provider is not available. Lily described many nearby recreational areas and school playgrounds where the children could play after school. She claims the children are delighted with this arrangement.

Lily states that her work hours are flexible and she can do some work from home if necessary to care for the children. She can usually be contacted in cases of emergency.

(f) the permanence and stability of the family unit with which it is proposed that the child will live;

Neither parent mentioned this as a factor that distinguished their care.

Divorce Act:

> 16(8) In making an order under this section, the court shall take into consideration only the best interests of the child of the marriage as determined by reference to the condition, means, needs and other circumstances of the child.
>
> (9) In making an order under this section, the court shall not take into consideration the past conduct of any person unless the conduct is relevant to the ability of that person to act as a parent of a child.

Lily raised a sensitive issue with respect to Steve's past conduct. She claims, and Steve did not deny, that he uses marijuana, drinks beer, watches pornography and has a supply of pornographic magazines in his home. Her concern is that on occasion she has seen him high while the children were in his care or at times when they might return home and observe him. Her concerns are about both his ability to supervise the children while high and the role model he is providing. She is also concerned about the values he will offer to the children with respect to having and using illegal substances. She does not feel he shares her concerns or is sufficiently mindful about the possibility that the children could come across the pornography or his drugs and paraphernalia.

For all of these reasons she believes she should be P1.

Steve's Position

Steve cannot fathom why the children should change schools because in his view, stability means minimizing changes and therefore exposing the children to less stress. He believes that Bill and Sally are more likely to continue on their path of good adjustment if they remain in their familiar neighbourhood. Steve made every effort to purchase a home close to the matrimonial home, the Glenholme School, the children's friends, and longstanding daycare provider. He feels that to add a change of schools to the many adjustments separated children have to endure, is risking the children's well-being, especially Bill's.

Steve and his counsel stated that it was in the children's best interests to reside primarily with him as for the following reasons:

(a) the love, affection and emotional ties between the child and,

> *(i) each person entitled to or claiming custody of or access to the child,*
>
> *(ii) other members of the child's family who reside with the child, and*
>
> *(iii) persons involved in the care and upbringing of the child;*

Steve states that both he and Lily are competent parents. He indicated that he bonded with the children as a caretaker from their infancy as he was working out of the home at the time Lily returned to work after her maternity leave. Over the years Steve did everything he could to be a 50-50 caretaker, he cooked dinners, supervised the children, took them to the park and for bike rides and when he worked the evening shift, he was the caretaker while Lily was at work.

Now that they are living in different areas Steve arranged to be on a day shift on compassionate grounds so that he could be the primary caretaker for the children during the week. This meant a small drop in salary and is not a permanent placement, but he feels quite confident that he will remain on days. His day shift has made him more accessible than in the past when he could not be reached during work hours.

Steve also pointed out that Lily has several extended family members in the Orangeville area and her parents have a family cottage. By residing with Lily on weekends, the children could maintain a relationship with her extended family more easily. His extended family lives farther away in the Kingston area or in the Maritimes or in California.

(b) the views and preferences of the child, where such views and preferences can reasonably be ascertained;

Steve accepts that the children have expressed a desire to reside in both parents' area. However he states they have said to him that they would rather be in a school where they are comfortable, where they know the teachers and the other children.

(c) the length of time the child has lived in a stable home environment;

Steve feels the children have already had a number of adjustments: the sale of the matrimonial home, a new home with their mother, and a new home with him. He feels they would benefit from spending the 20--/20-- school year with him and then consider any further changes.

Steve pointed out that if the children attend Orchard Park Public School, they will need to change schools again in grade 6 (for a Junior High School) and again when they enter High School. In Mississauga they can remain in Glenholme until High School, necessitating only one future change.

(d) the ability and willingness of each person applying for custody of the child to provide the child with guidance and education, the necessaries of life and any special needs of the child;

Steve argues that the fact that the standardized EQAO scores for Orchard Park are considerably higher than the scores for Glengrove should not be taken at face value. There are a number of factors, such as socio-economic level, education level of parents, number of single parents, immigration status, *etc.* that need to be considered in assessing why the scores are so different. Steve did not dispute the fact that the scores are considerably higher at Orchard Park, but in his view these differences should be taken with a grain of salt and should not be the basis for making a move.

Steve acknowledges that Bill does have social problems and states that he has been helping him use his "I" statements rather than fight. He also contacted the teacher last spring to discuss Bill's behaviour, has regularly attended P-T meetings unless he was working shifts, and is capable of taking a more active role in contact with the school in the future if the children are with him.

Steve states that he does supervise the children doing homework, but after working all day, making dinner and cleaning up he feels entitled to relax, have a beer and play video games. He says he tries to have the children work more independently. When they ask for his help he asks "Have you read the question? Have you tried yourself?" Lily who may be coming in the door from work hears him "yelling" at the children, but he feels it is out of context and does not show an adequate appreciation of his efforts prior to her arrival. He resents her telling him what he should be doing.

> *(e) any plans proposed for the care and upbringing of the child;*

Steve plans to continue using the same daycare provider that he has used for the past 6 years. He trusts Laura and stated that both parents continued to use her even though both acknowledge that the children have stated that they are not having much fun at Laura's and she yells at them. He attributes their unhappiness to the fact that the children are expected to do their homework after having a snack and this isn't a lot of fun. However he appreciated Laura's assistance with homework as he could then spend more time bike riding or playing with the children.

Apparently at some point Laura stopped doing homework and didn't tell the parents and neither was aware of this until the school complained. Steve suggested he speak to Laura about the children's concerns and if they are not resolved, he would consider an alternative person who has cared for the children when Laura was on summer vacation.

Steve is particularly concerned about the midweek "commutes" the children will experience under their agreed-upon Regular Schedule. He notes that it will take longer for him to drive into Etobicoke than for Lily to drive to Mississauga as she will be going against traffic (likely 25 mins.). He is concerned that the children will resent the time in the car, although he acknowledged that so far they have not complained. He counted 77 commutes over the academic year and felt this would be a burden for the children.

> *(f) the permanence and stability of the family unit with which it is proposed that the child will live;*

This is the key issue for Steve. He does not feel that additional changes are in the children's best interest. He stated eloquently that Lily had the opportunity of growing up in the same school for all of public school and then all of high school — always in the same community. She has friends from grade one. On the other hand he changed schools frequently and feels this was a detriment to him as his oldest friends date from grade 11. He cannot believe that Lily is choosing to deny the children the opportunity she had growing up. For Steve this is an emotional issue and he wants to protect the children from the many moves he experienced, with the resulting social challenges.

Steve is concerned that Bill in particular will be adversely affected by additional changes as this will be more stressful for him. He has made his decisions with the goal of reducing the numbers of changes the children need to face, given that the parents' separation has already necessitated changes. Steve's strength is in establishing routines and reducing the number of new circumstances the children are exposed to.

> 16(8) In making an order under this section, the court shall take into consideration only the best interests of the child of the marriage as determined by reference to the condition, means, needs and other circumstances of the child.
>
> (9) In making an order under this section, the court shall not take into consideration the past conduct of any person unless the conduct is relevant to the ability of that person to act as a parent of a child.

Steve's counsel argued that this material should not be admitted as it was not relevant to parenting and had not been included in the original 2-page Position Statement. They were given an adjournment to consider these allegations. Steve stated clearly that his use of drugs and alcohol have greatly reduced since the separation, as has his contact with his friend who is a drug dealer. He claims the reduction in stress as a result of the separation has meant he feels less need for such substances. He made a commitment to put his drugs, paraphernalia, and pornography in places where they will not likely be found by the children. He stated that he has not been high while the children have been in his care since the separation, apart from a few beers at a friend's barbeque. He does not feel this use has impaired his parenting and is willing to consider taking this issue more seriously in the future.

For all of these reasons Steve believes he should be the primary parent.

DECISION

In my opinion, both Steve and Lily are making a very considerable effort to care for their children and provide a good level of parenting. I do not doubt the sincerity of their feelings for their children or the strength of their belief that they are making decisions in the best interests of Bill and Sally. In my opinion both parents have raised issues that are important and worthy of serious consideration. I believe that Bill and Sally will continue to have few long-term difficulties related to the separation, provided the parents continue to cooperate and work as a respectful parenting team.

The parents have already decided that the children will spend approximately equal time with each parent in each geographic area. Therefore the children will be living in **both** communities and with **both** parents. Given that they are now living in two different school districts, a decision is needed as to where the children will primarily reside during the school week for the school year 20--/20--. This is not an easy decision as these are two good parents and they have raised excellent points to consider.

I am persuaded by the evidence presented at the hearing that it is in the children's best interests to reside with Lily primarily during the school week and Steve primarily during the weekends.

My reasons, based on the criteria for best interests are set out in the *CLRA*, s. 24(2) and the *Divorce Act*, s. 16(8) and (9), are set out as follows:

1. Lily is better able to provide for the children's emotional needs. In the past she has more closely monitored Bill's social adjustment and academic challenges. During the marriage she participated more actively in the children's schooling, was more engaged in planning their extra-curricular activities and appears to be more responsive and flexible in addressing concerns that the children present, for example with respect to their daycare provider or their choice of extra-curricular activities. It is likely that Steve is capable of handling these responsibilities, but Lily has taken a leadership role in these areas. I was concerned that Steve minimized the long history of Bill's school difficulties and while neither parent has taken decisive action, I do feel that Lily is more aware of the concerns, and likely to take steps to further investigate and assist Bill. Her detailed explanation of how she was teaching him social skills this summer, and the resulting success — which I observed when friends came to call on both children — was persuasive.

2. I was impressed that Steve was also encouraging the children to use appropriate communication skills, such as "Use your 'I' statements", rather than responding physically. This will be helpful to build on Bill's recent social successes. It would be most helpful if both parents attended a similar program (at a different time and possibly at a different location) on teaching communication skills to children, so that there would be greater consistency in their approach and greater support for Bill. I mention this as a helpful suggestion.

3. It would be helpful for the children to participate in the Rainbows program as it will assist Bill in particular, to articulate his feelings. It would also assist Sally and Bill to express any feelings or concerns about the adjustments to the separation and the moves. It would be helpful if both parents supported this program and participated as requested by the school. Again this is offered as a helpful suggestion.

4. I believe that Orchard Park Public School offers certain advantages over Glenholme. It is a smaller school, it has greater professional supports and resources, Bill has a chance to make new friends and make a fresh start. Sally is a very capable and socially at ease child who will likely do well at either school. However I believe she would benefit from her mother's guidance and greater emotional responsiveness. These advantages outweigh the risks of a change of schools, given that both children have had time to adjust and make some friends prior to the shift.

5. At the same time the children will have the benefit of the stability of their familiar environment and friends in Mississauga on weekends and during school breaks. Steve's emphasis on structure and predictability is a nice balance to Lily's greater willingness to explore new patterns. Both parents have different strengths to offer the children and as they separate their marital lives, my hope is that they will be more open to learning from the suggestions and helpful contributions that each provides.

6. Steve raised the difficulty posed by midweek commutes. One option is for the parent who has a midweek visit to remain in the community where the children are going to school until the other parent returns on Wednesday night, especially if the weather is bad. This would require a discussion between the parents to work out an acceptable arrangement as this is a "night off" for Lily. If the benefits of a midweek overnight are offset by the difficulty of a Thursday morning or Monday morning commute and the parents cannot resolve this, they should return to med/arb to work out a resolution.

7. Counsel for Steve argued that s. 16(9) "the court shall not take into consideration the past conduct of any person unless the conduct is relevant to the ability of that person to act as a parent of a child", precludes the raising of past conduct. In my opinion, I am satisfied that the conduct was not raised to make a moral statement about the behaviours, but rather their implications for parenting. I am concerned about Steve's use of marijuana, pornography and possibly excess alcohol on occasion when the children are in his care. Specifically, I am concerned about the ability to ensure the safety of the children and I am concerned about having these items in the home in a place where they can be seen by the children. As the children get older, they are more likely to come across items that may be illegal or potentially harmful. This will raise issues of parental role modelling and guidance. During the marriage Steve admitted he was not responsive to Lily's requests to alter these behaviours or seek help. However since the separation, I am favourably impressed with Steve's commitment to reduce his use of marijuana, his understanding that he needs to be alert and drive safely when he is the responsible parent, and his willingness to take greater care to ensure the children are not exposed to his drugs or pornography. Perhaps the separation has reduced the stress of the marriage, and the fact that each parent is now a sole caretaker, has given Steve a chance to reflect on the implications for parenting the children.

8. **Review:** I understand and support Steve's wisdom in taking small steps and assessing the outcome. I think both parents are wise to reassess the children after one year to see how they well they adjust. The children seemed open to this idea as well. I suggest that the review include a report from the school social worker and that both parents take an active role in communicating with Orchard Park staff on a regular basis to monitor the children's progress. If the parents reach agreement on their own, they do not need to proceed with the Review. However if either parent feels a Review would be helpful, the Review will take place and the parents will share the cost equally, unless otherwise ordered in med/arb.

In the event that either parent wishes a Review, I suggest the parents contact me, Dr. Barbara Landau, once the Spring 20-- report card is sent out, and we set up a meeting in April 20-- to determine their views and establish the details of a process. This will likely include my speaking to the children's teachers, receiving a report from the school social worker and meeting with the children. My preference is that the issue of which parent will be the primary parent after the academic year 20--/20-- will be mediated and an arbitrated decision occur only if agreement cannot be reached. I recommend that Lily and Steve think in advance about the factors they will be considering in evaluating the children's situation and share their views, in the interest of maintaining a cooperative approach to parenting.

9. **Costs:** Both parties agreed that they would be responsible for their own costs for counsel and the arbitrator. This is fair as both parents worked out most of their Parenting Plan in mediation and the children will continue to spend approximately equal time with each of them.

I am willing to make any changes with respect to factual errors that are submitted to my office by September 7, 20--.

I wish Steve, Lily, Sally and Bill well in the academic year 20--/20--.

Signed at Toronto, this 29th day of August, 20--.

Dr. Barbara Landau (computer signature)

Barbara Landau, Ph.D., LL.M., C.Med.

Attachments: (these will be mailed out)

1. Arbitration Agreement entered into on August 28, 20-- by the parties and by counsel (attached as Schedule 1).
2. Regular Schedule setting out how the children will spend time with each parent in the academic year 20--/20-- (attached as Schedule 2).
3. Bill's Report Cards which were entered as an exhibit (attached as Schedule 3).

Appendix VII Contents

Legal Documents

DOCUMENTS ON CD-ROM

Appendix VIII Contents

Professional Conduct and Qualifications

Appendix VIII.1

Certified Family Mediator: ADR Institute of Ontario

ADR INSTITUTE of Ontario: CERTIFIED FAMILY MEDIATOR (Cert. F. Med.):

I. BACKGROUND AND EDUCATION REQUIREMENTS

1. Professional Education: A university degree or FMC Designation
2. Family Mediation Training:
   a) 26 hours family mediation theory and skills,
   b) 40 hours intact training in family mediation, and
   c) 14 hours training in domestic violence
3. 3 letters of reference from family mediators, source of referrals or clients

II. PRACTICAL EXPERIENCE REQUIREMENTS

1. Practice of Family Mediation:
   a) Mediate 5 family cases to a point of agreement under supervision (100 hours) by an experienced family mediator; and
   b) Mediate 5 family cases to point of agreement on one's own.

III. SKILLS ASSESSMENT

1. Complete a family mediation role-play before a committee of 2 experienced family mediators.

IV. PLEDGE

1. Commit to the ADR Institute's Code of Ethics and Code of Conduct

V. CONTINUING EDUCATION

1. Undertake 10 hours of continuing education each year relevant to family mediation

VI. INSURANCE

1. Maintain liability insurance for a minimum of $1,000,000 for the practice of mediation. (Not required for C. Med)

V. MEMBERSHIP

1. Must be a member of good standing of ADR Institute of Ontario and

ADR Institute of Canada, Inc.

VI. FEES PAYABLE TO ADRIO

- Application for certification: $300
- Membership in ADRIO — fee: $255
- $50 annual renewal fee

Appendix VIII.2

Certified Family Arbitrator: ADR Institute Of Ontario

ALL CANDIDATES MUST BE MEMBERS IN GOOD STANDING OF THE ADR INSTITUTE OF ONTARIO AND THE ADR INSTITUTE OF CANADA.

CRITERIA:

I. TRAINING

- Completion of an approved 40 hour Family Arbitration course;
- Completion of a 2 Day course in Screening for Domestic Violence in Mediation & Arbitration;
- Non-lawyer candidates: Completion of 30 hours of training in Family Law (i.e., Custody & Access, Property and Support); and
- Completion of all elements required by legislation and regulation.

OR

Acknowledged Expertise: Long experience as a family arbitrator and recognition of peers, as confirmed by a least 3 satisfactory letters of reference. (Please attach.)

AND

II. EXPERIENCE

- The candidate has arbitrated or co-arbitrated at least 5 family cases (broadly defined);
- The candidate has been observed and approved by a Qualifying Arbitrator through one or more of the following: co-arbitration, practicum, role playing,

video taped arbitration (of a family related case) or other processes approved by ADR Canada.

OR

The candidates have successfully completed a competency assessment program approved by ADR Canada; and

AND

III. INSURANCE

- The candidate has $1Million E&O liability insurance

AND

IV. CONTINUING EDUCATION

- The candidate acknowledges the requirement to obtain 10 hours of additional relevant training every two years from the date of this application in order to maintain the Certified Family Arbitrator Designation.

V. ANNUAL RENEWAL FEE

- Application Fee $300
- Renewal Fee $50

Appendix VIII.3

Ontario Association for Family Mediation Accredited Family Mediators Requirements

In order to qualify for and maintain membership in the Ontario Association for Family Mediation (hereinafter referred to as O.A.F.M.) as an "Accredited Family Mediator", an applicant/ member must satisfy the Association that he or she possesses the qualifications set out below:

1. PROFESSIONAL EDUCATION:

Applicants must provide proof of a university degree or proof of having attained FMC certification.

2. KNOWLEDGE OF MEDIATION THEORY AND SKILLS

A basic knowledge of family mediation theory and skills is essential. For the purpose of application for membership, or continuing membership, an applicant/member must have completed:

A. Sixty (60) hours of mediation education, including a 40 hour family mediation training course and 20 hours of family mediation skills training. The 40 hour family mediation training course must be taught by an OAFM accredited mediator or approved by the OAFM, FMC, or equivalent.

   The family mediation training course must include a minimum of five hours in each of the following categories:[1]

   (i) Conflict resolution theories;
   (ii) Psychological issues in separation, divorce, and family dynamics and power imbalances;
   (iii) Issues and needs of children in separation and divorce;
   (iv) Mediation process and techniques, including role playing;
   (v) Family Law including custody, support, asset evaluation and distribution, taxation as it relates to separation and divorce; and
   (vi) Family economics (not required if the basic training is limited to custody mediation).

   The additional 20 hours can be achieved by attendance at one or more advanced trainings, relevant workshops and conferences.

AND

B. A minimum of 14 hours on domestic violence education.

OR

C. Taught such a course him/herself; and

D. Had an exceptional amount of applicable personal experience and in-service training.

NOTE: If the applicant lacks the minimum qualifications outlined in 1, 2 above, he/she shall submit a résumé and contact the Accreditation Committee to discuss his/her acceptability for membership on an individual basis.

---

[1] These categories are those suggested by the Academy of Family Mediators as requirements of basic mediation training for people applying for full membership in that organization.

Appendix VIII.4

Code of Ethics: Ontario Association for Family Mediation Code of Professional Conduct

1. Foreword

The following rules are intended to govern the relations of family mediators with their clients, their professional colleagues, and the general public so that all will benefit from high standards of practice in family mediation. The rules are to be observed in spirit as well as in practice.

2. Definition of Terms

For the purposes of this Code, family mediation is defined as a non-adversarial process in which a qualified and impartial third party (the mediator) helps family members resolve their disputes. The resolution is voluntary and is based on sufficient information and advice for each participant.

In open mediation, if the parties fail to agree voluntarily on one or more issues, the mediator may prepare a report on the mediation and/or make recommendations. In open mediation, such a report may be used in subsequent court proceedings.

In closed mediation, there is no such report or recommendations and the process is entirely confidential.

3. Competence

It is the obligation of anyone acting as a family mediator to ensure that he or she is fully qualified to deal with the specific issues involved.

(a) It is acknowledged that family mediators will have a diversity of education and training, but the obligation to refrain from rendering services outside the limits of the family mediator's qualifications and capabilities remains.

(b) Family mediators shall co-operate with and endeavor to involve other competent professionals where the situation requires it.
(c) Family mediators shall engage in continuing education to ensure that their mediation skills are current and effective.
(d) Family mediators shall perform their service in a conscientious, diligent, and efficient manner in accordance with this Code of Conduct.

4. Duty of Confidentiality

The mediator shall not voluntarily disclose to anyone not a party to the mediation any information obtained through the mediation process except:

(a) non-identifying information for research or educational purposes; or
(b) with the written consent of the parties to the mediation contract; or
(c) where ordered to do so by an appropriate judicial authority or required to do so by law; or
(d) where the information discloses an actual or potential threat to human life or safety or a proposed breach of the Criminal Code of Canada.

If mediation is open, communications made in the course of the mediation and the mediator's report and recommendations may be disclosed to a third party only for the purposes of resolving the dispute whether by litigation or otherwise.

While closed mediation imposes the intention and the duty of confidentiality on the mediator, it cannot confer privilege, and the mediator should advise the parties that the intended confidentiality cannot be guaranteed.

5. Impartiality

The mediator has a duty to be impartial in relation to the participants. Impartiality requires that the mediator shall not have preconceived opinions in favour of or against one person or the other.

(a) The mediator shall disclose to the participants any biases he or she may have relating to the issues to be mediated.
(b) The mediator will refrain from mediating in cases where the mediator knows there has been any significant prior involvement by the mediator or any partner or associate of the mediator with one of the participants except after full disclosure of the involvement to, and express consent by, the other participant(s). The role of the mediator should be distinguished from the earlier relationship.
(c) A lawyer-mediator, or any partner or associate of such lawyer-mediator, should decline to represent either or both spouses in any subsequent legal matter related to the issues mediated. Rather, the mediator should keep him or herself available as a neutral to assist the parties in future in the event that any modifications are required to the mediated settlement.

(d) The perception of partiality on the part of the mediator by one or both participants does not in itself require the mediator to withdraw. In these circumstances, it is only the duty of the mediator to advise the participants of their right to terminate the mediation.

6. Agreement to Mediate

The mediator has a duty to explain the mediation process clearly to the participants before reaching an agreement to mediate. In particular, the mediator shall do the following:

(a) define mediation, distinguishing it from other methods of dispute resolution and from therapy and marriage counselling;
(b) determine the appropriateness of mediation for the participants in light of their particular circumstances;
(c) discuss the differences between closed mediation, open mediation and assessment, and the implications of each, and require the parties to choose open or closed mediation;
(d) advise participants that either of them or the mediator has the right to suspend or terminate the process at any time;
(e) explain the cost of mediation and reach an agreement with the participants regarding payment. It is inappropriate for the mediator to charge a contingency fee or to base the fee on the outcome of the mediation process;
(f) advise the participants of the role of independent legal advice in accordance with paragraph 9 of this Code. In the event the mediator is a lawyer, the lawyer-mediator shall inform the participants that he or she cannot represent either or both of them in any subsequent legal matter related to the issues mediated;
(g) discuss with the participants the mediator's specific procedures and practices;
(h) recommend that the agreement to mediate be written and signed by the parties and the mediator.

7. Potential Problems in Mediation

It is the duty of the mediator to advise the participants of potential problems that may arise during mediation. Some of these problems include:

(a) the possibility that one or both spouses may use the time during the mediation to dissipate or conceal assets;
(b) the fact that a status quo may be developing with respect to the custody of the children so that the non-custodial parent may be prejudiced in any future custody claim in the courts, notwithstanding any agreement to the contrary;

(c) the fact that information disclosed during the mediation may be used against a participant in the event of subsequent legal proceedings.
   (i) Even if the information disclosed directly in the mediation is confidential, it may open up lines of inquiry and/or reveal other information which might not otherwise have come to light in any subsequent litigation.
   (ii) A judicial authority may require disclosure of information revealed during mediation.

8. Information, Disclosure and Advice

It is the duty of a mediator to actively encourage the participants to make decisions based upon sufficient information, knowledge and advice:

(a) Every family mediator has an ongoing obligation to advise participants of the desirability and availability of independent legal advice. While neutral legal information may be made available to the parties, each should be encouraged to obtain legal advice.
(b) Where financial or property issues are involved, the mediator shall obtain an undertaking from the parties to make frank and full disclosure of their financial and related circumstances at the appropriate time in the mediation process. The mediator will assist the parties and their advisors to achieve such disclosure. A mediator has an ongoing obligation to advise both parties to obtain legal and other professional advice and assistance in this respect.

9. Independent Legal Advice

It is the obligation of every family mediator to advise clients:

(a) of the availability of independent legal advice for each spouse;
(b) of the advisability of obtaining it from the outset of the mediation;
(c) to obtain independent legal advice prior to signing the mediated agreement.

10. Duty to Minimize Harm or Prejudice to Participants

It is the duty of the mediator to suspend or terminate mediation whenever continuation of the process would harm or prejudice one or more of the participants.

(a) The mediator shall suspend or terminate mediation where the ability or the willingness of either of the participants to effectively participate in the process is lacking.
(b) The mediator shall suspend or terminate mediation when its usefulness is exhausted so that there is no unnecessary expense to the participants from unproductive mediation.
(c) If the mediator has suspended or terminated the process, he or she may suggest that the participants obtain appropriate professional services.
(d) When the mediator believes the agreement being reached is unreasonable, he or she shall so advise the participants.
(e) Notwithstanding impartiality, the mediator has the duty to promote the best interests of the children and to assist the parents to examine the separate and individual needs of each child.
(f) While the mediator has an obligation to minimize the harm or prejudice to participants in the process, it is a fundamental principle of mediation that competent and informed participants can reach an agreement which may not correspond to legal guidelines contained in the relevant statutes or case law or that does not correspond to general community expectations and standards.
(g) The mediator shall see that the participants are reaching agreement freely, voluntarily and without undue influence.

11. Public Communications

(a) The purpose of public statements concerning family mediation should be:
    (i) to educate the public generally about the process; and
    (ii) to present the process of mediation objectively as one of several methods of dispute resolution in order to help the public make informed judgments and choices.
(b) When advertising professional services, mediators should restrict themselves to matters which educate and inform the public. These could include the following to describe the mediator and the services offered: name, address, telephone number, office hours of the particular mediation service, highest relevant academic degree, relevant training and experience in mediation, appropriate professional affiliations and membership status, and any additional relevant or important consumer information.
(c) Public Communications should not imply that membership in the Ontario Association for Family Mediation constitutes certification as a mediator.

12. Duty to Encourage Reporting of Breaches of Code

It is the obligation of family mediators to encourage clients to report in writing real or apparent breaches of this Code forthwith to the Chairman of the

Standards and Ethics Committee and/or to the President of the Ontario Association for Family Mediation.

[**Note:** In 1994 OAFM added the Abuse Policy to the Code of Conduct]

Appendix VIII.5

Model Code of Conduct for Mediators: ADR Institute of Canada

ADR Institute of Canada, Inc. Model Code of Conduct For Mediators

---

The Model Code of Conduct for Mediators ("the Code)" applies in its entirety to every Mediator who is a member of the ADR Institute of Canada, Inc. ("the Institute"), or who accepts appointments from the Institute. While Mediators come from varied professional backgrounds and disciplines, every Mediator must adhere to the Code as a minimum. Being appointed as a Mediator confers no permanent rights to the individual, but is a conditional privilege that may be revoked for breaches of the Code.

The Institute, or any of its Regional Affiliates, is empowered to investigate alleged breaches, including temporarily suspending any Mediator from any of its rosters or membership in the Institute, pending the outcome of an investigation. The Institute is empowered to cancel membership in the Institute or remove any Mediator from its rosters if the Mediator is determined by the Institute either on its own behalf or upon the recommendation of any of its Regional Affiliates to be in breach of the Code. It will be the objective of the Institute to ensure that complaints are investigated fairly, and that no Mediator is arbitrarily suspended or removed.

I. OBJECTIVES FOR MODEL CODE OF CONDUCT FOR MEDIATORS

The main objectives of the Code for Mediators are as follows:

(a) to provide guiding principles for the Mediator's conduct;
(b) to provide a means of protection for the public; and
(c) to promote confidence in Mediation as a process for resolving disputes.

II. DEFINITIONS

In the Code:

"Mediation" means the use of an impartial third Party to assist the parties to resolve a dispute, but does not include an arbitration.

"Mediator" means the impartial person or persons, engaged to assist the parties to resolve a dispute, but does not include an arbitrator unless the arbitrator is acting as a mediator by consent of the parties.

"impartial" means being and being seen as unbiased toward parties to a dispute, toward their interests and toward the options they present for settlement.

III. PRINCIPLE OF SELF-DETERMINATION

1. Self-determination is the right of parties in a Mediation to make their own voluntary and non-coerced decisions regarding the possible resolution of any issue in dispute. It is a fundamental principle of Mediation which every Mediator shall respect and encourage.

2. The Mediator shall provide information about his or her role in the Mediation before Mediation commences, including the fact that authority for decision-making rests with the parties, not the Mediator.

3. The Mediator shall not provide legal or professional advice to the parties.

4. The Mediator has the responsibility to advise unrepresented parties to obtain independent legal advice, where appropriate. The Mediator also has the responsibility where appropriate to advise parties of the need to consult other professionals to help parties make informed decisions.

IV. INDEPENDENCE AND IMPARTIALITY

1. Unless otherwise agreed by the parties, a Mediator shall be and remain, at all times, wholly independent.

2. The Mediator shall be and remain wholly impartial and shall not act as an advocate to any party to the Mediation.

3. The Mediator shall not establish a professional relationship with or act for any of the parties individually in relation to the particular dispute that is the subject matter of the Mediation in any capacity, unless all parties consent after full disclosure.

4. If the Mediator becomes aware of his or her lack of impartiality, he or she shall immediately disclose to the parties that he or she can no longer remain impartial and shall withdraw from the Mediation.

V. CONFLICT OF INTEREST

1. The Mediator has a responsibility to disclose as soon as possible to the parties in dispute any personal interest, conflict of interest, bias, or circumstances likely to give rise to a reasonable apprehension or presumption of bias that are known to the Mediator, or which becomes known after his or her appointment.

2. Any Mediator who has made a disclosure pursuant to V.1 shall withdraw as Mediator, unless the parties consent to retain the Mediator.

3. The Mediator's commitment is to the parties and the process and he or she shall not allow pressure or influence from third parties (including, without limitation, persons, service providers, Mediation facilities, organizations, or agencies) to compromise the independence of the Mediator.

VI. CONFIDENTIALITY

1. The Mediator shall inform the parties of the confidential nature of Mediation.

2. The Mediator shall not disclose to anyone who is not a party to the Mediation any information or documents that are exchanged for or during the Mediation process except:

   (a) with the mediating parties' written consent;

   (b) when ordered to do so by a court or otherwise required to do so by law;

   (c) when the information/documentation discloses an actual or potential threat to human life;

   (d) any report or summary that is required to be prepared by the Mediator; or

   (e) where the data about the Mediation is for research and education purposes, and where the parties and the dispute are not, nor may reasonably be anticipated to be, identified by such disclosure.

3. If the Mediator holds private sessions (breakout meetings, caucuses) with a party, he or she shall discuss the nature of such sessions with all parties prior to commencing such sessions. In particular, the Mediator shall inform parties of any limits to confidentiality applicable to information disclosed during private sessions.

4. The Mediator shall maintain confidentiality in the storage and disposal of Mediation notes, records and files.

VII. QUALITY OF THE PROCESS

1. The Mediator shall make reasonable efforts to ensure the parties understand the Mediation process before Mediation commences.

2. The Mediator has a duty to ensure that he or she conducts a process which provides parties with the opportunity to participate in the Mediation and which encourages respect among the parties.

3. All Mediators have an obligation to acquire and maintain professional skills and abilities required to uphold the quality of the Mediation process.

4. The Mediator shall conduct himself or herself professionally at all times, and shall not engage in behaviour that will bring disrepute on the Mediator or the Institute.

VIII. ADVERTISING

In advertising or offering services to clients or potential clients:

1. The Mediator shall refrain from guaranteeing settlement or promising specific results.

2. The Mediator shall provide accurate information about his or her education, background, Mediation training and experience, in any representation, biographical or promotional material and in any oral explanation of same.

IX. FEES

1. The Mediator shall provide parties with the fee structure, likely expenses and any payment retainer requirements before Mediation commences.
2. The Mediator shall not base his or her fees on the outcome of Mediation, whether there is a settlement, what the settlement is, or the amount of the settlement.
3. The Mediator may charge a cancellation or a late/delay fee within the Mediator's discretion, provided the Mediator advises the parties in advance of this practice and the amount of the fee.

X. AGREEMENT TO MEDIATE

The Mediator, together with the parties, shall prepare and execute a Mediation Agreement setting out:

(a) the terms and conditions under which the parties are engaging the Mediator;

(b) any of the National Mediation Rules of the Institute which the parties agree shall not apply to the Mediation; and

(c) any additional rules which the parties agree shall apply to the Mediation.

Should the parties be unable to agree on a Mediation Agreement, the Institute's Standard Form Agreement to Mediate shall be used.

XI. TERMINATION OR SUSPENSION OF MEDIATION

1. The Mediator shall withdraw from the Mediation for the reason referred to in paragraph IV.4.
2. The Mediator may suspend or terminate the Mediation if requested, in writing, by one or more of the parties.
3. The Mediator may suspend or terminate the Mediation with a written declaration by the Mediator that further efforts at mediation would not be useful.

XII. OTHER CONDUCT OBLIGATIONS

Nothing in the Code replaces or supersedes ethical standards and codes which may be additionally imposed upon any Mediator by virtue of the Mediator's professional calling. Where there are conflicting codes of conduct, the Mediator shall be bound by the stricter of the codes.

Index

Note: *Material on CD-ROM is indicated by the designation "CD-ROM" and the Appendix number. All other references are to page numbers.*